THE LAW OF TORTS

Examples and Explanations

THE LAW OF TORTS

Examples and Explanations

Third Edition

Joseph W. Glannon

Professor of Law
Suffolk University Law School

ASPEN

PUBLISHERS

111 Eighth Avenue, New York, NY 10011
www.aspenpublishers.com

Aspen Publishers
Permissions Department
111 Eighth Avenue, 7th Floor
New York, NY 10011-5201

Printed in the United States of America.

ISBN 0-7355-4024-1

4 5 6 7 8 9 0

Library of Congress Cataloging-in-Publication Data

Glannon, Joseph W.
   The law of torts: examples and explanations/Joseph W. Glannon. — 3rd ed.
      p. cm.
   Includes index.
   ISBN 0-7355-4024-1
   1. Torts—United States. 2. Torts—United States—Problems, exercises, etc. I. Title.

KF1250.Z9 G58 2005
346.7303—dc22

                                                            2004063120

About Aspen Publishers

Aspen Publishers, headquartered in New York City, is a leading information provider for attorneys, business professionals, and law students. Written by preeminent authorities, our products consist of analytical and practical information covering both U.S. and international topics. We publish in the full range of formats, including updated manuals, books, periodicals, CDs, and online products.

Our proprietary content is complemented by 2,500 legal databases, containing over 11 million documents, available through our Loislaw division. Aspen Publishers also offers a wide range of topical legal and business databases linked to Loislaw's primary material. Our mission is to provide accurate, timely, and authoritative content in easily accessible formats, supported by unmatched customer care.

To order any Aspen Publishers title, go to *www.aspenpublishers.com* or call 1-800-638-8437.

To reinstate your manual update service, call 1-800-638-8437.

For more information on Loislaw products, go to *www.loislaw.com* or call 1-800-364-2512.

For Customer Care issues, e-mail *CustomerCare@aspenpublihsers.com*; call 1-800-234-1660; or fax 1-800-901-9075.

Aspen Publishers
A Wolters Kluwer Company

I dedicate this book to my wife, Annie

Contents

Preface to Students

This book is based on the common sense premise that students encountering complex legal issues for the first time will appreciate a book that provides clear, straightforward introductions to these issues, together with examples that illustrate how these principles apply in typical cases.

I have good reason to believe that the premise is valid. Some years ago I wrote a book on civil procedure, entitled *Civil Procedure: Examples and Explanations*, which uses the same approach. The book has been widely used in law schools across the country. Not only do many faculty members assign or recommend it, but many students have found their way to the book on their own or on the recommendation of other students who have found the approach helpful.

Each chapter of this book includes a brief introduction to the topic, followed by a set of examples that apply the concepts to particular fact situations. After the examples, I have included my analysis of each example. Unlike the typical questions found in the casebooks, which are often either too hard to answer or downright unanswerable, the examples here tend to start with the basics and move on to more sophisticated variations. If you study the readings for your Torts class and the introductions in this book, you should be able to respond effectively to most of the examples. Trying your hand at them and comparing your analysis to mine should help to deepen your understanding of the concepts and your ability to think critically about legal issues in general. It may also help to convince you that you are *capable* of learning the law, a type of feedback that law school seldom seems to provide.

You will also want to use the book to review the course toward the end of the year. Most casebooks contain representative cases and provocative questions and notes, but they do not explain the state of the law, or provide much context for the issues raised. Reading these chapters and reviewing the examples should help you to test your understanding of the topics covered and fill in the gaps left by your casebook.

This edition also includes three chapters that will be particularly helpful in preparing for exams. The first chapter explains the type of analysis law professors are looking for on a Torts essay exam (or any other first-year exam, for that matter). The second analyzes common mistakes students make in taking essay exams. The third includes several exam questions with sample answers and some comments on strategy. Law exams are quite different from others you've taken. These chapters will help you to understand the analytical approach most law professors want to see in the merry month of May.

Like every author, I hope that this book will go through many editions. If you have comments or suggestions for improvement, drop me a note at Suffolk University Law School, 120 Tremont Street, Boston, MA 02108-4977. Or, send me an e-mail at jglannon@suffolk.edu.

January 2005   *Joseph W. Glannon*

Acknowledgments

I wish to thank Dean Robert Smith and Suffolk University Law School for their support for this project. A special thanks goes to Professor Jeffrey Wittenberg, of the Suffolk Law faculty, for his kind help in reviewing several new chapters. I also wish to thank Miranda Hooker, Suffolk University Law School Class of 2004, and Matthew Dunn, Suffolk University Law School Class of 2006, for their able research assistance and comments on various chapters of the manuscript.

I appreciate the permission granted by the American Law Institute to reproduce sections, comments, and illustrations from the First and Second Restatements of Torts and the Third Restatement of Torts (Tentative Drafts), as well as the Second Restatement of Agency.

Finally, I appreciate the contributions of the many students who have sent me comments, corrections, and suggestions for improvement.

Special Notice

For several frequently cited treatises I have used shortened forms after the initial citation to the work. These are as follows: Harper, James & Gray, The Law of Torts (2d ed. 1986), cited as Harper, James & Gray; Prosser and Keeton, The Law of Torts (5th ed. 1984), cited as Prosser & Keeton; Minzer, Nates, eds., Damages in Tort Actions, cited as Minzer, Nates; Schwartz, Comparative Negligence (4th ed. 2002), cited as Schwartz; and Speiser, Recovery for Wrongful Death and Injury (3d ed. 1992), cited as Speiser.

THE LAW OF TORTS

Examples and Explanations

PART ONE

Intentional Torts

1

Fundamental Protections: The Tort of Battery

Introduction

The primitive world must have been a fairly scary place. Our ancestors had to cope not only with the awesome forces of nature, impossible to predict or control, but also with another unpredictable danger — other human beings. Doubtless, one of the primary reasons they decided to become "civilized" was to ensure physical security from each other.

Medieval England, from which our tort law evolved, sought to deter physical aggression through a criminal remedy, the "appeal of felony," for physical assaults and other invasions of personal interests. Harper, James & Gray, The Law of Torts §3.1 (3d ed. 1996). If the defendant was found guilty, she would be fined, that is, she would have to pay a sum of money or forfeit her goods to the crown. The appeal of felony helped to enforce the King's peace, but it did nothing to compensate the injured victim for her injury.

Over time, the English courts also developed civil tort remedies to compensate victims of physical aggression. This tort remedy differed according to the nature of the defendant's invasion. For example, the tort of battery authorized damages for deliberate, unwanted touchings of the plaintiff's person. Assault allowed recovery for placing the plaintiff in fear of an unwanted touching. False imprisonment was the remedy for unwarranted restraints on the plaintiff's freedom of movement. This chapter examines the action of battery, that most basic of tort remedies for invasion of the most basic of personal rights, the right to freedom from unwanted bodily contact.

It seems as though this ought to be a very short chapter. Even the law, with its tendency to overanalyze, can only complicate a seemingly simple matter so much. And battery seems like a simple matter. Jones hits Smith: She has invaded Smith's right to freedom from physical aggression and should be liable for any resulting injuries. All that is left to decide is how much Jones should pay.

Sometimes it is that simple, but often it is not. Jones may have bumped into Smith because Lopez pushed her, or she may have collided with Smith while jumping out of the way of an oncoming car. Perhaps she pushed Smith in order to prevent the car from hitting *her*, or while thrashing around in an epileptic seizure. Each of these cases involves an unauthorized touching of Smith, but Jones should not be required to compensate Smith for such blameless — or even helpful — invasions of Smith's physical autonomy.

Since the courts have refused to condemn all unwanted touchings, they have struggled to craft a definition of battery that limits recovery to those types of touchings the law seeks to prevent. Most courts define battery as the intentional infliction of a harmful or offensive contact with the person of the plaintiff. See Restatement (Second) of Torts §13. Under this definition the defendant must act, her act must be intentional (in the restricted sense peculiar to tort law), the act must cause a contact with the victim, and the intended contact must be either harmful or offensive to the victim. These requirements are discussed in detail below.

The Intent Requirement

As this definition indicates, battery protects against *intentional* invasions of the plaintiff's physical integrity. No contact is intentional if it is not the result of a voluntary act. If Lopez faints and falls on Jones, Lopez is not liable for battery, because she has not acted. It hardly seems fair to require her to pay damages to Jones for something she didn't "do" in any meaningful sense, that is, something that was not the result of her voluntary conduct. Similarly, if Smith pushes Lopez into Jones, Lopez has not acted, and would not be liable for battering Jones. See Restatement (Second) of Torts §2 (defining an act as an "external manifestation of the actor's will").

Even if the defendant has acted, however, in the sense of making a voluntary movement, that act may not be intentional as that term is used in the context of intentional torts. Suppose, for example, that Chu fails to look carefully in stepping off a bus, does not see Munoz coming along the street, and bumps into her. Chu's act of stepping off the bus is intentional in the sense that it was deliberate: She certainly intended to put her foot down and move off the bus, but she did not intend to cause the resulting contact with Munoz. To commit a battery, the defendant must not only intend to act; she must act *for the purpose of* inflicting a harmful or offensive contact on the plaintiff, or realize that such a contact is *substantially certain* to result.

> The word "intent" is used . . . to denote that the actor desires
> to cause consequences of his act, or that he believes that the
> consequences are substantially certain to result from it.

Restatement (Second) of Torts §8A. This definition lets Chu off the hook in the bus case, since her act was not intentional in the intentional tort sense. She did not act for the purpose of hitting Munoz, nor was she substantially certain that she would. The contact resulted instead from her failure to take proper precautions (such as looking where she was going) to avoid hitting Munoz. Chu may be liable for negligence, but she has not committed a battery.

Indeed, the purpose of the intent requirement is to confine intentional tort liability to cases in which the defendant acts with a higher level of culpability than mere carelessness: where she acts with a purpose, or with knowledge that the act will cause harmful or offensive contact to the victim. If Chu pushed Munoz to get her out of the way, she would meet this intent requirement, since she would be substantially certain that Munoz would find such a contact offensive. She would also meet the intent requirement if she pushed her to embarrass her in front of a friend — an offensive contact — or to cause her to fall in front of a car, an obviously harmful one.

The intent requirement in the Restatement is disjunctive, that is, it is met *either* by a purpose to cause the tortious contact *or* substantial certainty that such a contact will result. Suppose, for example, that Smith heaves a stone at her enemy Jones, though she thinks Jones is probably beyond her range. She is not substantially certain that she will hit Jones, but she acts with the desire to do so. This satisfies the intent requirement; if the stone hits Jones, Smith has committed battery.

Under this definition, an actor can possess tortious intent even though she bears the victim no ill will whatsoever. If Chu sees Jones walking along the street below and deliberately throws a bucket of water on her from a second story window, it is no defense that she was simply emptying the scrub bucket and did not mean to offend Jones. In intentional tort terms, she intends those contacts that she is substantially certain will occur, as well as those she desires to see happen. Indeed, a battery can be committed with the best of motives. In *Clayton v. New Dreamland Roller Skating Rink, Inc.*, 82 A.2d 458 (1951), for example, the defendant's employee attempted to set the plaintiff's broken arm, against her protests. While the employee was only trying to help, he knew (because the victim told him so) that she found the contact unwelcome, and consequently met the intent requirement for battery.

Transferred Intent

Although intentional tort law requires a very specific type of intent, that standard may be met if the actor intends to commit a battery on one person and actually inflicts one on somebody else. Suppose, for example, that Chu throws a rock at Smith, hoping to hit her, but her aim is bad and she hits Lopez instead. Chu would argue that she cannot be held liable to Lopez, since she had no intent to hit her — she was aiming at Smith.

Although Chu had no tortious intent toward Lopez in this example, she *did* have tortious intent toward Smith. In such cases, courts hold that the tortious intent to hit Smith *transfers* to Lopez. Restatement (Second) of Torts §16(2). Thus, where the actor tries to batter one person and actually causes a harmful or offensive contact to another, she will be liable to the actual victim.

Obviously, transferred intent is a legal fiction created to achieve a sensible result despite lack of intent toward the person actually contacted. The rationale for the doctrine is that the tortfeasor's act is just as *culpable* when her aim is bad as when it is good; it would be unconscionable if she were exonerated just because she hit the wrong person. Under transferred intent, she will be liable whether she hits her intended victim or someone else.

The transferred intent fiction also allows recovery where the actor attempts one intentional tort but causes another. If, for example, Chu tries to hit Smith with a hammer but misses, placing Smith in fear of a harmful contact but not actually causing one, her intent to commit a battery suffices to hold her liable for assault. Conversely, if she tries to frighten Lopez by shooting near her, but the bullet hits her instead, she will be liable for battery even though she intended to commit an assault instead.

Harmful or Offensive Contact

Not all intentional contacts will support a claim for battery. It would make little sense to allow Jones to bring a battery suit against every subway passenger who jostled her during rush hour. This kind of contact is an accepted fact of city life. Similarly, if Smith taps Jones on the shoulder to tell her that she dropped a glove, it is reasonable for Smith to expect that this touching is acceptable to Jones, as it would be to most of us.

To distinguish between such common, socially accepted contacts and actionable batteries, courts require that the defendant intend to cause either a harmful or an offensive contact. *Harmful* suggests broken arms, black eyes, and the like, but a great deal less will do. Section 15 of the Restatement (Second) of Torts defines *bodily harm* as "any physical impairment of the condition of another's body, or physical pain or illness." Of course, if the harm is minor, the plaintiff will recover very little, or be limited to nominal damages, but the courts will still have vindicated her right to physical autonomy.

Even if the contact is not harmful, it is tortious if it is offensive. If Smith chucks Jones under the chin in a demeaning manner, or spits on her, she has caused an offensive contact. Allowing a battery suit for such offensive contacts not only deters such personal invasions, it also provides Jones with a civilized alternative to retaliation. Since offensive acts are particularly likely to provoke retaliation, it is appropriate to provide a battery remedy for such contacts instead.

Of course, people don't all react the same way to every contact. If Smith goes around slapping folks on the back at the office party, Jones may find it obnoxious, but Cimino may be flattered by the attention. If the definition of offensive contact depended on the subjective reaction of each plaintiff, Smith would not know whether her conduct was tortious until she saw the reaction to it. Smith should have some way of determining whether a contact is permissible *before* she acts. To allow such advance judgments, courts use an objective definition of offensive contact. The Second Restatement, for example, defines a contact as offensive if it "offends a reasonable sense of personal dignity." Id. at §19.

Under this test, a contact is offensive if a reasonable person in the circumstances of the victim would find the particular contact offensive. An actor is not liable under this definition for a contact that is considered socially acceptable (i.e., that would not offend a "reasonable sense of personal dignity"), even though the victim turns out to be hypersensitive and is truly offended. On the other hand, if she makes a contact that the reasonable person *would* find offensive, it is not a defense that she did not mean to give offense, or that she did not realize that the victim would be offended.

What the reasonable person would find offensive varies greatly with the circumstances. Often a prior course of conduct between the parties indicates that they accept contacts that would ordinarily be considered offensive. Suppose that Burgess and Munoz routinely engage in horseplay at work, including backslapping, arm locks, bear hugs and the like. A stranger would undoubtedly find such contacts offensive, but Burgess and Munoz expect these contacts from each other. Burgess would be justified, given their previous interactions, in inferring that Munoz will not find such contacts offensive, though they would offend the "reasonable sense of personal dignity" of a new employee.

The Difference Between Contacts and Consequences

It is crucial to distinguish the intent to cause a harmful or offensive contact from the intent to cause a particular consequence which results from that contact. Suppose, for example, that Brutus decides to humiliate

Cassius by tripping him as he leaves the Senate building. Unfortunately, Cassius suffers a freak fall sideways over a railing and down a flight of stairs, causing a severe concussion. While Brutus intended to trip Cassius, he certainly did not intend the resulting freak injury. He did not act with a purpose to cause this unusual train of circumstances, nor was he substantially certain that tripping Cassius would result in serious injury.

However, Brutus did commit a battery on Cassius, and is therefore liable for all of Cassius's injuries. Brutus acted with the purpose to trip Cassius, which is surely an offensive contact. He succeeded in causing that contact when Cassius tripped. At that point, the battery was complete, and the law holds Brutus liable for all the consequences of the battery. Cassius may suffer no injury at all, or more injury than Brutus expects, or less, but if the touching itself is a battery, Brutus is liable for the resulting harm, whatever its extent may be.

The language of §8A of the Restatement is a bit confusing on this point: It states that the actor must intend "the consequences" of the act. However, the consequence to which §8A refers is the harmful or offensive contact itself, not the injuries that result from it. In our example, Brutus intended to trip Cassius; because he intended that "consequence," he is liable for the unintended fall down the stairs as well.

Perhaps another example will help to make this important distinction clear. In *Lambertson v. United States,* 528 F.2d 441 (2d Cir. 1976), an inspector ran up behind a worker in a meat packing plant, jumped on his back, and pulled a bag over his head. The worker stumbled forward, struck his face on some meat hooks, and sustained serious injuries. Evidently, the inspector in *Lambertson* acted in the spirit of horseplay; there was no suggestion that he intended the worker to hit the meat hooks or suffer serious injuries. Yet the court concluded that the inspector had battered the worker when he intentionally jumped on his back, since the reasonable person in the victim's circumstances would find that contact offensive. Since he battered the worker when he jumped on him, the inspector could be held liable for the consequences of that battery — the facial injuries — though he did not intend to cause them.

It is not hard to see the reason for this seemingly draconian rule: Batteries are intentional invasions of others' right of personal security. One purpose of intentional tort law is to deter such unauthorized contacts from the outset. Imposing the cost of all resulting injuries on the actor should serve this deterrent purpose. After all, intentional torts are eminently avoidable: Because they require a *deliberate choice* to invade another's rights, the actor need only restrain herself to avoid the invasion. Where she fails to do so, it seems appropriate to impose all resulting damages — even unintended damages — on her rather than the innocent victim.

The Contact Requirement

Even the seemingly self-evident requirement of a contact requires some explanation. Suppose Smith doesn't touch Jones at all, but pokes her with a ten foot pole or stretches a wire across the sidewalk as Jones approaches, causing her to fall. Surely the underlying policy of protecting physical autonomy supports liability in these cases. In each, Smith invades Jones's physical integrity in one way or another and intends to do so under the definition discussed above.

Although no part of her body has touched Jones in these examples, Smith has imposed an unauthorized *contact* on Jones. The defendant need not actually touch the plaintiff at all, or even be present at the time of the contact, to commit a battery. For example, setting the wire out for Jones, knowing that she will trip over it later, will satisfy the contact requirement. See Harper, James & Gray, §3.3, at 3:8-3:16 (3d ed. 1986). An actor is liable, regardless of whether she uses her fist, a nightstick, or a city bus to cause the contact, if it is intended to cause a harmful or offensive contact to the victim.

The contact requirement has also been extended to include objects intimately associated with the victim's body. Chu's sense of personal space can be breached as effectively if Lopez pulls her coat lapels or knocks off her hat as by a direct touching to the skin. Extending the sphere of personal autonomy to include such items protects against intrusive contacts that are very likely to be offensive, thus raising the ante in physical confrontations. Obviously, however, there are limits; if Lopez kicks the fender of Chu's vintage Ford Mustang, the contact requirement is probably not met, even if Chu is sitting in the back seat.

The following examples illustrate the elements of battery. In analyzing them, assume that the Restatement definitions apply.

EXAMPLES

The Bard, Updated

1.   Romeo likes to drive his souped up Trans Am around the high school parking lot, racing the motor, accelerating rapidly, and stopping on a dime. He arrives at school one winter morning, speeds across the parking lot, and screeches to a halt in a parking space, hoping to impress the ladies with his hot shot driving. Unfortunately, the parking lot is icy; the rear end of the car skids out of control, jumps the curb sideways, and knocks Thibault to the ground. Has Romeo battered him?

2.   When Romeo gets out of the car to apologize, Thibault yells, "What's the idea?" and gives him a push. Romeo slips on a patch of ice, hits his head on one of the mag wheels of his Trans Am, and suffers a serious concussion. Is Thibault liable for Romeo's injuries?

3.   Romeo and Juliet are an item, "going steady" as they said when I was in high school. Romeo comes up to Juliet in the school parking lot on Monday morning and gives her a hug, as he is accustomed to doing each morning. Unfortunately, Juliet is standing on a patch of ice and Romeo's embrace causes her to fall and fracture her arm. Is Romeo liable for battery?

4.   In an effort to make amends, Romeo starts to help Juliet up. Thoroughly annoyed, Juliet growls, "Don't touch me." Romeo, determined to be gallant, helps her up anyway, despite her efforts to pull away. Is this a battery?

Introducing Judge Fudd

5.   Romeo and Thibault are bitter rivals for Juliet's favor. After gym class, Romeo leaves a bar of soap on the floor of the shower Thibault usually uses, hoping that Thibault will slip and fall. He does, suffers injury and sues Romeo for battery. At trial, Judge Fudd, a well-meaning but sometimes inartful jurist, instructs the jury as follows:

> If you find that, when the defendant acted, he did not know that his act was substantially certain to cause a harmful or offensive contact to the plaintiff, you must find for the defendant.

Which party will object to Judge Fudd's instruction, and what is wrong with it?

6.   Romeo is sitting on a wall in front of the school. He sees Thibault wandering across the lawn, with his nose in a book, toward a trench recently excavated for some utility work. Cheering silently, he watches as Thibault ambles absent-mindedly toward disaster. To his delight, Thibault walks right into the trench, suffering minor injuries and considerable humiliation. Thibault sues Romeo for battery. What result?

No Offense Intended?

7.   Romeo considers himself irresistible. He is accustomed to flirting with the girls at will. He comes up to Ophelia, a new student, on her first day in the school and, by way of introduction, gives her a hug. She sues him for battery. Is he liable?

8.   Romeo is a sprinter on the track team. At the first meet of the season, he is nosed out by Mercutio, the star of the visiting team. In a burst of good sportsmanship, he goes over to Mercutio, slaps him heartily on the back, and says "great run, Mercutio!" Mercutio, who, it turns out, is very sensitive about being touched by strangers, reacts with rage at the contact. Is Romeo liable for battery?

9.   Romeo and Mercutio meet again at the regional finals. This time Romeo ends up the victor. After the race, he turns to Mercutio on the

track, punches his shoulder playfully and says, "Well, Mercutio, turnabout is fair play!" The humorless Mercutio sues him for battery. Is he liable this time?

10. Romeo races Mercutio again in the state finals, and loses. Infuriated, he takes his track shoes and hurls them into the crowded stands. They hit Polonius, causing facial lacerations. Can Polonius sue Romeo for battery?

Star-Crossed Lovers

11. Alas, poor Romeo. He still holds a candle for Juliet, and she won't even talk to him anymore. He finds her asleep at one of the carrels in the school library. A confirmed romantic, he slips up to her and kisses her on the cheek. Malvolio, the school sneak, later tells Juliet.
    a. Upset, she heads for court. Battery?
    b. You have recently passed the bar and hung out your own shingle. Juliet brings her sneaky kiss case to you and asks you to sue Romeo for her. Would you take the case?
    c. Assume Romeo had kissed the sleeping Juliet while they were still going together. However, Juliet does not find out about it until after they have broken up. Can she sue him for battery?

Some Touching Cases

12. Romeo gets the idea that Juliet is seeing Thibault. He decides to get even. Which of the following vengeful acts makes Romeo liable for battery?
    a. He confronts Thibault in the cafeteria and makes some very offensive allusions to his moral character.
    b. At the prom, he laces Thibault's lemonade with 100 proof vodka. Thibault drinks it.
    c. He laces Thibault's lemonade with vodka, but the gallant Thibault gives his drink to Juliet, who drinks it.
    d. He throws his own drink at Thibault. Unfortunately, Mr. Merola, the Vice Principal for Discipline, steps through the door at that moment and is hit instead.
    e. Just before the science fair, Romeo deliberately sits on Thibault's latest science project, an elaborate geodesic representation of an international space station, built from 5,000 toothpicks and Elmer's glue. Thibault is watching at the time.
    f. He blows cigarette smoke in Thibault's face.
    g. He shocks Juliet by offering to show her a photo of her favorite rock group but shows her some pornographic pictures instead.
    h. A motel manager rents a room to Thibault, even though he knows that the bed is infested with bedbugs.

13. Regan and GonEril, two teenagers, decide to wile away the afternoon standing on a bridge over the interstate, watching the traffic. Regan takes a mirror from her pocket and starts to shine it in the eyes of on-coming drivers. Cordelia, driving under the bridge, is temporarily blinded, swerves out of control and hits the bridge. Is Regan liable for battery?

EXPLANATIONS

The Bard, Updated

1.   Romeo has done a dumb thing, a clearly negligent thing, but he has not committed a battery. A battery requires an intent to cause a harmful or offensive touching. While Romeo certainly *did* cause a harmful contact, he didn't intend to under the Restatement definition. He did act intentionally in the sense that he deliberately drove his car across the lot. However, while this act was voluntary, he did not act with the purpose of hitting Thibault or with knowledge that he was substantially certain to do so; he was headed in another direction entirely. Nor, the facts suggest, was he trying to frighten Thibault or another student, which might support an argument for transferred intent. He was just showing off. Thus, his act was not intentional in the limited sense in which courts use that term for defining intentional torts.

In analyzing battery cases, always distinguish the intent to act from the intent to cause a harmful or offensive contact. Battery requires more than a deliberate act. It requires a deliberate act done for the purpose of causing a harmful or offensive contact, or which the actor knows to a substantial certainty will cause such a contact. If only a deliberate act were required, battery would encompass many cases where the actor intended no harmful or offensive contact. For example, a driver would commit a battery if she looked away from the road and got in an accident, even though she did not intend to hit the plaintiff. Or, a joker would be liable for battery for throwing a snowball at a tree, if a pedestrian unexpectedly stepped into the snowball's path. In both of these cases, the actor did a voluntary act. But these acts — like Romeo's in the example — were *not* done with the state of mind necessary to commit an intentional tort: either purpose or substantial certainty that a harmful or offensive contact would result. They may be negligent acts, if the actor failed to exercise due care, but they are not intentional torts.

2.   Although Thibault is justly angry with Romeo, that does not give him a license to retaliate against him. He has intentionally inflicted a contact that Romeo will find offensive, and perhaps harmful as well, and he is liable to him for battery.

But is he liable for the unanticipated and unintended concussion? As in the Brutus example in the introduction, Thibault is fully liable for all harm resulting from the battery. Although he had no intent—as that term is used in either the Restatement or everyday life—to cause Romeo's concussion, he did intend to push him. Since he committed a battery by doing so, he is liable for all the resulting injuries, even unexpected ones.

This rule, that a defendant who commits an intentional tort is liable for all the resulting harm, does not apply in negligence cases. Under negligence law, liability is limited to the foreseeable consequences of the defendant's act. See Chapter 9. However, because intentional torts are deemed more culpable, the courts generally hold the defendant liable for all the ensuing consequences, foreseeable or otherwise. This rule imposes very severe damages on Thibault for what seems like a relatively innocuous act—but it didn't turn out to be innocuous, did it? The Solomons of tort law have concluded that the loss in such cases should fall on the actor rather than the victim.

For an extreme example of this, see *Baker v. Shymkiv*, 491 N.E.2d 811 (Ohio 1983), in which a defendant's trespass to land led to an argument with the owner. During the argument, the owner had a fatal heart attack. The trespasser was held liable for it as a consequence of the intentional tort.

3.   Given their relationship and Juliet's past acceptance of Romeo's embraces, Romeo is justified in inferring that Juliet will not find his customary hug offensive. The reasonable person in Juliet's circumstances would not be offended by a hug from her boyfriend. But surely she finds falling down and breaking her arm harmful or offensive. Even if Romeo's hug isn't a battery, isn't causing her to fall on the ice one? (Remember that the contact need not be with the defendant; it can be with the ground or anything else.)

In this case, Romeo did not act with the intent of causing a harmful or offensive contact to Juliet. He had no reason to believe she would find the contact he intended—the hug—offensive, due to their relationship. And the contact she found harmful—the fall—he had no intent to cause: He did not act with a purpose to cause Juliet to fall or with substantial certainty that she would. While Romeo may be liable for negligence, for hugging her where the footing is slippery, he is not liable for battery.

Distinguish this case from Example 2. In that case, Thibault intended a harmful contact—the push. Thus, he committed a battery and was held liable for all the resulting harm, even though it was greater than he reasonably would have anticipated. Here, since Romeo did not intend a harmful or offensive contact, he did not commit a battery and consequently is not liable for battery even though the contact itself turned out to have harmful consequences.

4.   Poor Romeo; he was only trying to help. Maybe he even *was* helpful. But he still committed a battery.

In analyzing battery cases, it is important to distinguish between intent and motive. The motive for Romeo's act was honorable, but he still intended to cause a contact to Juliet that he knew she would find offensive, because she told him so. The elements of battery do not include acting from a malicious motive, nor will a virtuous motive prevent liability if those elements are present. The plaintiff has the right to decide for herself which contacts are beneficial; she need not submit to the prodding of any Romeo who wishes to be gallant. Juliet may prefer the higher risk of slipping to the touch of the klutzy and out-of-favor Romeo. That decision is hers, not his. Where Romeo substitutes his judgment for hers, he is liable for battery.

Because of the fundamental value placed on physical self-determination, courts have held defendants liable for battery, even though their motives were pure and their contacts beneficial. The classic example is *Mohr v. Williams*, 104 N.W. 12 (Minn. 1905), in which a doctor was held liable for battery when he operated on the plaintiff's left ear after the plaintiff had consented to surgery only on the right. Although the left ear was diseased, and the surgery was successful, the court concluded that the doctor had violated the patient's "right to complete immunity of his person from physical interference of others. . . ." Id. at 16.

Introducing Judge Fudd

5.   Thibault will object to the instruction, and rightly so. If Judge Fudd's instruction were correct, Romeo would not be liable. Although he hoped that Thibault would slip and fall, and put the soap there for that purpose, he could hardly be substantially certain that he would cause Thibault to fall, since he did not know that Thibault would use that shower or that if he did, he would slip on the soap. However, the intent requirement is satisfied either by an act done with substantial certainty that the contact will result *or* by an act done with the purpose to cause the contact. Restatement (Second) of Torts §8A, p. 5, supra.

In the practice of law, a word can make a world of difference. Here, the word *or* indicates that either substantial certainty or a desire to cause the result will suffice to establish intent. Since Romeo acted with the purpose to cause the contact, he cannot defend by arguing that it was a long shot that his plot would succeed. Judge Fudd's instruction is wrong. Thibault's lawyer should object to it and have it corrected before it leads the jury to return an erroneous verdict.

6.   If desire can make a battery, Romeo has surely committed one, since he fervently hoped Thibault would fall in, and was delighted when he did. And we know that Romeo need not directly touch Thibault to batter him: Contact with the trench suffices to meet the contact requirement. And certainly Thibault found the contact both harmful and offensive.

But Romeo is still not liable to Thibault. He has not done anything to cause the contact. To incur liability, he must *act*; he must inflict the contact, not simply hope for it. This contact results from the acts of others, not Romeo.

No Offense Intended?

7.   Obviously, Romeo is of the opinion that no woman in her right mind would object to his attentions. However, the question is not whether Romeo finds his conduct offensive. It is not even whether Romeo thinks that Ophelia will. As the introduction points out, the question Romeo must ponder before his dalliance with Ophelia is whether the reasonable person in Ophelia's circumstances would find it offensive. The answer to that question is almost certainly "yes." Most teenagers don't like being hugged by strangers, even attractive strangers.

So, offensiveness is determined by an objective test — whether the contact would be offensive to the reasonable person in the victim's circumstances. But isn't it true, even if Romeo's hug is "offensive" under this definition, that Romeo must *intend* an offensive contact, not just cause one? And, if Romeo genuinely believed that the new girl in school would welcome his attention, how can he be said to have intended an offensive contact? very likely Romeo will be held liable, even if he is too conceited to realize that this contact is offensive under the Restatement definition. Otherwise, he could avoid liability based on his testimony that he didn't think it would be offensive. Such a test would allow social boors to escape liability simply because they have poor judgment — or lie about what they understood — even though they inflict unwanted contacts on others.

8.   Romeo has again acted with good intentions, but we saw in Example 4 that good intentions will not negate a battery if the elements of the tort are established. However, those elements are not met here, since Romeo has no reason to believe that his slap will be offensive to a reasonable person under these circumstances: Congratulatory hugs and slaps are common among athletes on such occasions.

The requirement that the contact "offen[d] a reasonable sense of personal dignity" (Restatement (Second) of Torts §19) allows actors to make contacts with others that the ordinary person will not find offensive, without fear of a suit for battery. This requirement places the burden on the party with unusual sensibilities, such as Mercutio, to inform people of his susceptibility. Until he does, those who interact with Mercutio are protected if they conform to generally accepted standards of behavior.

If actors were liable to hypersensitive plaintiffs for generally accepted contacts like this, many everyday interactions would entail the risk of liability. Under that rule, Romeo could be sued for tapping a stranger on the shoulder to tell her she had dropped her umbrella, or brushing past a fellow passenger on the subway. To avoid liability, he would have to avoid all contact. The world might be a marginally safer place for the hypersensitive, but a great deal of spontaneity would be sacrificed.

9.   This example is like the last, except that here Romeo is aware before he acts that Mercutio is sensitive to physical contacts, even those generally accepted by others. The issue is whether the actor is liable for contacts that are not offensive under the Restatement's "reasonable-sense-of-personal-dignity" standard, but which the actor knows *will be* offensive to a particular hypersensitive individual.

The Restatement refuses to take a stand on this variation.

> The Institute[1] expresses no opinion as to whether the actor is liable if he inflicts upon another a contact which he knows will be offensive to another's known but abnormally acute sense of personal dignity.

Restatement (Second) of Torts §19, caveat. Despite the Restatement's caution, doesn't it seem clear that the values underlying battery support liability in this case? The purpose of battery is to protect individuals from unwanted intrusions on physical security. Where an actor knows that another *accepts* contacts that others would find offensive (for example, friends who routinely engage in rough horseplay), his actual knowledge protects him, despite the objective standard usually applied. Conversely, where he knows that another rejects contacts others would tolerate, that knowledge, not the objective standard, should govern his liability. Here Romeo knows this intrusion will be offensive to Mercutio, and he ought to avoid it, even if others would accept the contact.

10.   Romeo will doubtless argue that he had no intent, in the battery sense of the term, to hit Polonius. He did not desire to hit him, nor did he know to a substantial certainty that he would hit him — the shoes could have hit anyone.

Clearly, this is an anemic defense. As long as Romeo knew to a substantial certainty that the shoes would hit *someone*, he knew his act would cause a harmful or offensive contact to the person of another. It should not negate the tort that his act had a large number of potential victims. If that were the case, a terrorist who threw a bomb onto the mezzanine at O'Hare Airport would not be liable to the strangers he injured, since he couldn't be sure which ones would be hurt, and wished no ill will to any one of them in particular.

---

1. The Restatement is a summary of the accepted principles of tort law, published by the American Law Institute. It is not "the law" of any state unless expressly adopted by court or legislature, but it often reflects widely accepted principles. This is certainly true of the intentional tort sections of the Restatement, which are frequently followed in intentional tort cases from many states.

This is not really a case of transferred intent. It is not a situation in which he threw at a specific victim and hit another instead. Rather, it is a case in which the actor knows at the outset that he will cause a harmful or offensive touching to someone, but does not know who the victim will be. However, as in transferred intent cases, the intent requirement should be considered met, since Romeo's culpability is just as great here as if he threw at a particular victim.

Star-Crossed Lovers

11a.   Romeo's romantic gesture would be tortious if Juliet were awake, because it is an intentional contact that he knows she would find offensive. But can it be a battery if she doesn't even know about it?

One need only contemplate examples like the lecherous dentist and the anesthetized patient to confirm that battery must lie in this case. The underlying purpose of battery, to prevent invasions of physical security, will not be fully served if such conduct escapes liability. Juliet's right to be free of unpermitted touchings is infringed just as clearly when she is asleep as it would be if she were awake.

Romeo will probably argue that she did not find it offensive, since she was not even aware of the contact at the time. The argument will not fly. The requirement of offensive contact is met if it is a contact that the reasonable person in Juliet's circumstances would reject if given the choice. If immediate awareness of the contact were essential, a surgical patient could not be battered, even if the doctor gave her a nose job instead of the contemplated appendectomy. *Mohr v. Williams*, the case in which the doctor operated on the wrong ear, clearly indicates that the unconscious patient can be battered.

b.   There is no requirement to prove damages in order to establish liability for battery. Proving that Romeo intentionally caused an offensive contact establishes Juliet's right to a judgment in her favor. Getting a jury to say that Romeo battered her may even meet Juliet's purpose for bringing the action, to assuage her sense of the invasion of her person.

However, while a plaintiff has a theoretical right to sue for even a trivial invasion of her person, the majesty of the law is tarnished somewhat by practical realities. While damages are theoretically unnecessary in an intentional tort case, they are crucial as a practical matter. Most lawyers take tort cases on a contingent fee basis, under which they receive a percentage of the damages recovered as their fee. When there is little prospect of recovering substantial damages, the plaintiff will have a hard time finding a lawyer to take her case. Consequently, victims seldom recover for minor batteries, even if they are clearly actionable.

c.   Although Juliet may now be offended at the thought that Romeo had kissed her, she presumably would not have been at the time of the contact. The offensiveness of the contact must be judged at that time, not in retrospect. Romeo must act on his understanding of what Juliet considers offensive *when he acts*; he cannot be expected to assess his conduct against the possibility that they may have a falling out in the future. This is not a battery.

Some Touching Cases

12a.   This is not a battery. It is offensive contact, not offensive conduct, that is required.

b.   This is a case of indirect contact. Romeo did not touch Thibault but has intentionally caused him to come into contact with the alcohol because he acted with the purpose that Thibault would pick it up and drink it after he laced it. This is no different from lacing his drink with poison, although the effect is less drastic. So long as the reasonable teenager at the prom would find this offensive (a debatable issue, perhaps) this is a battery.

c.   Romeo's intent was for Thibault, not Juliet, to drink the vodka. He did not desire nor was he substantially certain that he would cause a contact with Juliet. However, under the doctrine of transferred intent, a party who attempts a battery on one person but mistakenly contacts another is liable for battery. Since Romeo intended to batter Thibault, he is liable if he causes a harmful or offensive contact to Juliet instead.

This fiction furthers the underlying purpose of battery law, to protect victims of acts intended to cause unwelcome or harmful touchings. Romeo is just as culpable when his plot goes awry as if it hits his intended target. Under the transferred intent doctrine, liability follows in either case.

d.   In this example, Romeo does not even know that Mr. Merola is around when he acts — presumably he would have restrained himself if he had. However, he acted with tortious intent toward Thibault. That intent will transfer to the unintended victim, even if the actor did not know that the unintended victim was there. Romeo tried to cause an offensive touching, and he did; he is liable for it under transferred intent.

e.   This is doubtless pretty upsetting to Thibault, but it is not a battery. Battery requires an intentional harmful or offensive contact to the person, not to one's property. No matter how proud Thibault is of his construction, this doesn't fit the elements. It would, however, constitute trespass to chattels, a distinct intentional tort involving interference with another's personal property.

f.   There is no doubt that Romeo's act here was intentional and meant to offend. The issue is whether Romeo has caused a contact with Thibault. Clearly, if he spat on Thibault, or took pebbles in his mouth and shot them at him, this would be a battery. But smoke? Why not? Smoke is a substance, the particulate products of burning. Why should it matter if the contact is with small particles propelled through the air, instead of a large rock propelled through the air? Although smoke is (arguably) less harmful, it is equally likely to offend, and was clearly meant to in this case. And isn't it equally likely to provoke a breach of the peace?

Advocates for the rights of nonsmokers have long argued that there should be a battery remedy for smoking. See A. Brody & B. Brody, The Legal Rights of Non-Smokers, 75-80 (1977); O. Reynolds Jr., Extinguishing Brushfires: Legal Limits on the Smoking of Tobacco, 53 U. Cin. L. Rev. 435, 456-458 (1984). However, the case law on the point is contradictory, and fails to apply battery analysis consistently. For example, *McCracken v. Sloan*, 252 S.E.2d 250 (N.C. App. 1979), found no battery where the defendant smoked in his office during a meeting with the plaintiff:

> Consent is assumed to all those ordinary contacts which are customary and reasonably necessary to the common intercourse of life. Smelling smoke from a cigar being smoked by a person in his own office would ordinarily be considered such an innocuous and generally permitted contact.

252 N.E.2d at 252. The reasoning in *McCracken* is probably outdated, but a more recent case finds no battery from second-hand smoke on even more dubious reasoning. In *Pechan v. Dynapro, Inc.*, 622 N.E.2d 108 (Ill. App. 1993), the plaintiff was continuously exposed to the defendant's smoke, had protested repeatedly, and allegedly was made ill by it. However, the court dismissed her battery claim with the following anemic reasoning:

> [T]he act of smoking generally is not done with the intent of touching others with emitted smoke. [The plaintiff] has not alleged that any of the office's smokers intended that she be exposed to their smoke, or that reasonable persons should have known that their smoke would have contacted [her] in sufficient quantity to reasonably cause the damages claimed.

622 N.E.2d at 119. This analysis blatantly ignores the substantial certainty prong of intent, as well as the maxim that damages are not an essential element of the battery tort.

In *Leichtman v. WLW Jacor Communications, Inc.*, 634 N.E.2d 697 (Ohio App. 1994), the court held that smoke can constitute contact for purposes of battery, where the defendant purposely blew smoke in the face of an antismoking advocate. "Furthermore, tobacco smoke, as 'particulate matter,' has the physical properties capable of making contact." 634 N.E.2d at 699. However, the court inconsistently distinguished the second-hand-smoke situation:

> We do not, however, adopt or lend credence to the theory of 'smoker's battery,' which imposes liability if there is substantial certainty that exhaled smoke will predictably contact a nonsmoker.

Id. Compare *Golesorkhi v. Lufthansa German Airlines*, 1997 WL 560013 (4th Cir. 1997) (dismissing claim under Virginia law for lack of a "physical touching").

The dubious reasoning in these cases reflects the discomfort courts encounter in extending a traditional tort like battery to new situations. If smoke is held a contact, how about obnoxious horn honkers, the odor of greasy french fries, or loud football spectators? Or, as one student nicely pointed out in my class, how about air pollution from Midwestern power plants? Taking matters further, if courts accept that smoke is contact, and that substantial certainty of that contact constitutes intent, will it recognize a right of second-hand-smoke victims to use self-defense? These problems make courts reluctant to follow the seemingly inevitable logic of smoke as battery. "The life of the law has not been logic: it has been experience." O. W. Holmes, The Common Law, Little, Brown and Company, 1881, 1.

g. The battery action is not a general remedy for obnoxious behavior, but a limit on physical invasions of the person. Here again there is no contact, unless the court were to stretch the contact requirement to include light waves. If it did, battery would lie in every case in which an unpleasant scene was foisted on the unwilling eye. The courts will leave the plaintiff to other remedies on these facts, such as infliction of emotional distress.

h. Here, the motel manager presumably had nothing against Thibault; he simply wanted the benefit of his patronage. But he rented Thibault a room with substantial certainty that Thibault would suffer an offensive contact — with the bedbugs. In a recent case, *Mathias v. Accor Economy Lodging Inc.*, 347 F.3d 672 (7th Cir. 2003), Judge Posner (a former Torts professor) suggested that such contact would constitute battery. Judge Posner cited "the famous case of *Garratt v. Dailey* . . . which held that the defendant would be guilty of battery if he knew with substantial certainty that when he moved a chair the plaintiff would try to sit down where the chair had been and would land on the floor instead." 347 F.3d at 675.

For another interesting case involving the "substantial certainty" prong of intent and an unusual contacts argument, see *Swope v. Columbian Chemicals Co.*, 281 F.3d 185 (5th Cir. 2002). In *Swope*, the plaintiff was an employee of a chemical company. He alleged that he was exposed at work on a daily basis to excessive levels of ozone, and that the company knew of the exposure and that it caused various health problems. The court held that these allegations stated a battery claim against the company. It noted that the victim need not be aware of the contact at the time it happens. Id. at 196.

In many states, employees cannot bring negligence suits for injuries suffered during their employment — they are limited instead to workers' compensation benefits. However, many workers' compensation statutes do allow suits against employers for *intentional* torts in the course of employment. Students often wonder why we should fuss over the distinction between intentional tort and negligence. *Swope*, in which the plaintiff's lawyer asserted an intentional tort claim to recover a significantly larger award, illustrates one reason that the distinction matters.

13. On first glance, this seems to be a battery because the plaintiff crashed into the bridge abutment. That's a contact if there ever was one.

However, Regan did not have the necessary intent to cause that contact. She did not either desire or know to a substantial certainty that Cordelia would crash into the wall. Presumably, she merely meant to annoy drivers, not to cause a crash, and it is far from substantially certain — though clearly possible — that this brief distraction would cause Cordelia to crash.

Regan did, on the other hand, intend to flash the mirror in Cordelia's eyes: She desired to cause that result, even if she was not substantially certain that her aim would be good enough to hit such a small moving target. But, of course, for battery, there has to be a *contact,* and that means the court would have to conclude that the light rays constitute "contact."

One reader sent me the following e-mail, arguing that the light here satisfies the contact requirement.

> The physics of light is divided into particle theory and wave theory. Although it is certain that light behaves as a wave, physicists more often describe it using particle theory. A particle of light is a photon imparting energy to a surface that it strikes. Under this theory, light is analogous to the smoke of example [12f]. Lasers are highly focused beams of photons having extremely high energy. The difference in a laser and reflected sunlight is a matter of degree, not nature.

This may be good science, but I'm not sure that it would persuade a court that calling light a contact would be good law. Accepting the argument opens the door to slippery slope arguments in the horn honking and other cases. If Regan had used a high-powered laser that burns through steel, the court would doubtless find a contact. On these facts, however, the court might conclude that there was no contact, and therefore no intentional tort. If not, there surely was recklessness or gross negligence, which, of course, gives rise to tort liability as well.

2

The Action for Assault: A Tort Ahead of Its Time

Introduction

Historically, tort law has been reluctant to protect mental tranquility alone. For example, courts have not allowed recovery for insult, or for disturbing the plaintiff's peace of mind through distasteful behavior or voicing unpopular opinions. True, some courts have recently begun to redress limited forms of psychic injury, such as infliction of emotional distress and invasion of privacy. But these have gained currency only in the last few decades. If the duration of the common law were an hour, this would represent only the past few minutes.

Assault, however, is an exception to this general principle. The action for assault, which has been with us virtually since the inception of the common law, does allow recovery for interference with peace of mind, even where there is no physical invasion of the victim's person or property. Unlike battery, which requires a tangible, physical invasion, assault protects one form of mental tranquility, the right to be free from fear or apprehension of unwanted contact. In this sense, assault has truly been a tort ahead of its time.

> One of the most important objects to be attained by the enactment of laws and the institutions of civilized society is, each of us shall feel secure against unlawful assaults. Without such security society loses most of its value. Peace and order and domestic happiness, inexpressibly more precious than mere forms of government, cannot be

enjoyed without the sense of perfect security. We have a right to live in society without being put in fear of personal harm.

Beach v. Hancock, 27 N.H. 223, 229 (1853). Assault, like battery, protects this right of personal security by authorizing damages for threatened invasion of the person. However, assault is definitely not a general remedy for interference with mental tranquility: It only protects against one narrow type of mental distress, the apprehension of immediate physical aggression.

The Restatement Definition

Because assault is an ancient remedy applied in many jurisdictions, the cases vary somewhat in describing its elements. In *Cucinotti v. Ortmann*, 159 A.2d 216, 217 (Pa. 1960), for example, the court held that "an assault may be described as *an act* intended to put another person in reasonable apprehension of an immediate battery, and which succeeds in causing an apprehension of such battery." Compare *Western Union Tel. Co. v. Hill*, 150 So. 709, 710 (Ala. App. 1933): "To constitute an assault there must be an intentional, unlawful, offer to touch the person of another in a rude or angry manner under such circumstances as to create in the mind of the party alleging the assault a well-founded fear of an imminent battery, coupled with the apparent present ability to effectuate the attempt. . . ." Despite such differences, the essence of these definitions is quite similar. The elements of the tort are distilled in the Second Restatement definition of assault:

> (1) An actor is subject to liability to another for assault if
> (a) he acts intending to cause a harmful or offensive contact with the person of the other or a third person, or an imminent apprehension of such a contact, and
> (b) the other is thereby put in such imminent apprehension.

Restatement (Second) of Torts §21. Under this definition, the defendant must (1) act with intent (2) to place the victim in apprehension of a harmful or offensive contact or to make such a contact, and (3) the victim must reasonably be placed in apprehension of such a contact. These requirements are discussed in detail below.

The Intent Requirement

Assault, like battery, requires intentional conduct, and in the same restrictive sense. The defendant must act with the *purpose* to cause apprehension of a contact or *substantial certainty* that the apprehension will result. Restatement (Second) of Torts §8A. Thus, as in a battery case, the defendant may not avoid liability by claiming that he did not mean to place the plaintiff in fear of an unwanted touching, if he knew to a substantial certainty that fear of a touching would result. Suppose that Owens throws a shot put across the infield while Jackson is standing in the landing area. Owens cannot avoid liability for assault by arguing that he was just warming up for the decathlon. If Jackson was looking at him, Owens must have known that Jackson would reasonably fear being hit. Thus his act is intentional under the Restatement definition, even though he did not do it for the purpose of placing Jackson in fear.

On the other hand, many cases in which plaintiffs are placed in fear of a touching are not intentional as that term is used in intentional tort law. If Jackson loses control of her car on Main Street, and careens over the curb in Owens's direction, Owens will doubtless be placed in fear of being run down. However, Jackson has not acted with a purpose to frighten Owens, or with substantial certainty that the act will frighten him. Jackson may be liable to Owens for negligence, but she has not assaulted him.

Even if Jackson acts intentionally in the sense that she *deliberately* swerves toward the curb, she lacks intent in the intentional tort sense if she does not desire or know to a substantial certainty that she will hit Owens (or place him in apprehension that she will hit him). For example, if Jackson suddenly realizes that her brakes have failed, and steers for the curb to stop the car, her act is intentional in the sense that it was a voluntary, deliberate act, but it would not be an assault if she did not know that Owens was there and would be placed in fear of being hit.

The Restatement definition also provides that one who attempts to batter the plaintiff but misses is liable for assault if the plaintiff is placed in apprehension of a blow. Restatement (Second) of Torts §21(1). Suppose, for example, that Rose, infuriated by Owens's bragging that he won more Olympic medals than she did, throws a shot put at him but misses. Even though Rose tried to commit a battery rather than an assault, she is liable to Owens for assault if he sees the shot put coming and is placed in fear of being hit. (On the other hand, if Owens is looking the other way and doesn't know of her act, he is not placed in fear of a harmful touching and has no tort claim for assault.)

This principle, that the intent to batter can also suffice for assault, is obviously akin to the transferred intent doctrine illustrated in Chapter 1. See Example 12c from that chapter, in which Romeo tried to batter Thibault by lacing his drink, but Juliet drank it instead. In that example, Romeo was liable for battery, even though he had no intent to cause a harmful or offensive contact to Juliet. He intended to batter someone, and did, though by mischance he ended up battering someone other than the intended victim. Somewhat analogously, Rose is liable to Owens for assault, even though she tried to batter him instead. She had the intent necessary to commit an intentional tort, and she did commit one, though by mischance she accomplished assault rather than battery.

Because assault only protects against fear of a harmful or offensive contact, the plaintiff must prove that she feared the type of contact that would support a battery claim if it actually occurred. Thus, the analysis in Chapter 1 of the meaning of *harmful or offensive* is also necessary in assault cases. If a contact would not have been harmful or offensive had it been made, the threat of that contact is not an assault either. If Leonard and Spinks often slap each other on the shoulder in jest before sparring, their contacts are not offensive and do not constitute battery. Thus, if Spinks moves to slap Leonard, he does not commit an assault, since Leonard anticipates a touching, but not a harmful or offensive one.

Nothing to Fear but Apprehension Itself

Actually, the word *fear*, though it is often loosely used in the cases, is not quite accurate. The Restatement definition requires that the defendant cause "apprehension" of a harmful or offensive contact. *Apprehension* as used here means the perception or anticipation of a blow, rather than fright. Assault protects not only against the fear of an unwelcome contact, but also against the mere expectation or anticipation of one. If Dillard threatens to spit on Baxter's shoes, Baxter will anticipate, or apprehend, an unwelcome and demeaning contact, which would be a battery if it actually took place. This anticipation is sufficient for an assault claim, even though Baxter is not frightened in the usual sense of that term.

The Restatement definition also requires that the apprehended contact be *imminent*, that is, the defendant's act must cause the victim to expect that he is about to be touched. This imminence requirement obviously raises slippery-slope problems. Since the dawn of the socratic method, Torts professors have tortured (no pun intended) students with barely distinguishable assault hypotheticals: Dillard swings an axe at Oda from a foot away, from four feet away, through a window, from across the room, from the end of the street but he's a faster runner than Oda, and so on. The Restatement suggests that "imminent"

> does not mean immediate, in the sense of instantaneous contact, as where the other sees the actor's fist about to strike his nose. It means rather that there will be no significant delay. It is not necessary that one shall be within striking distance of the other, or that a weapon pointed at the other shall be in a condition for instant discharge. It is enough that one is so close to striking distance that he can reach the other almost at once, or that he can make the weapon ready for discharge in a very short interval of time.

Restatement (Second) of Torts §29 cmt. b.

This explanation still leaves line-drawing problems in applying the imminence requirement. However, the fact that there will be close cases (again, no pun intended!) is hardly a fatal criticism of the requirement. Close factual issues of this sort will be decided by the jury, under careful instructions as to the meaning of assault. The jurors' practical intuition about what actions are likely to cause reasonable apprehension will lead to a just decision in most cases. On the other hand, it is clear that fear of a *future* contact will not support liability for assault. "If you try out for the Olympic team next month, I'm going to bust your nose" is not an assault, since the threat is not of an imminent contact.

Perhaps such threats for the future *should* be assaults. They are reprehensible, and may be very unsettling indeed to aspiring athletes. Realistically, however, the law can't protect everyone from everything; it has to pick its targets. Such general, future threats suggest possible, vaguely formed (and hence, changeable) intention, perhaps even mere braggadocio. Consequently, they are likely to be less intimidating than the raised fist of an incensed assailant. In addition, future threats leave the victim time to take other steps to prevent the harm, such as going to the police or avoiding the assailant. Thus, they are less likely to provoke immediate retaliation by the victim.

Sometimes a defendant may place the reasonable person in apprehension of an unwanted contact even though he could not actually batter her. Suppose, for example, that Landy brandishes a realistic looking toy pistol at Oda. It may reasonably appear to Oda that the pistol is real, and that Landy intends to shoot her. Even though Landy could not actually accomplish a battery with the toy pistol, this is assault, since she had the "apparent present ability" to cause an unwanted contact. Put another way, assault turns on whether the defendant's act would place a reasonable person in apprehension of an unwanted contact, not whether the aggressor is in fact able to make the threatened contact. Assault protects the victim's right to be free of meaningful threats of unwanted touchings. Landy's threat obviously could be mighty disturbing even if she could not actually shoot Oda. (On the other hand, if Oda knows the pistol is a toy, she will not apprehend such a touching, and Landy will not be liable for assault.)

The "Mere Words" Problem

The requirement that the victim anticipate an imminent battery has led many courts to hold that *mere words* alone cannot constitute an assault, because they do not sufficiently show the defendant's purpose to immediately batter the victim. For example, a defendant who growls at the victim "I'm going to wring your neck!" might be held not to commit an assault, but if he extracts a rope from his pocket and proceeds to wind it around his hands, his act provides the necessary evidence of an imminent intent to batter the plaintiff.

This problem of assault by words alone is intractable. The requirement that the defendant go beyond mere words to commit a threatening act is meant to distinguish between bluster and real aggression. Some cases have been quite strict in requiring such an act. In *Cucinotti v. Ortmann*, 159 A.2d 216 (Pa. 1960), for example, the plaintiffs alleged that the defendants confronted them and threatened that they would commit "immediate bodily harm upon the plaintiffs, and would strike the plaintiffs with blackjacks and would otherwise hit them with great force and violence." Id. at 218. The court held that the complaint did not state a claim for assault since no threatening act was alleged. The *Cucinotti* court even held that an allegation that the defendants produced the blackjacks and showed them to the plaintiffs would not state a claim for assault. Id. at 218-219.

The Second Restatement of Torts, however, suggests a more flexible approach to this problem:

> Words do not make the actor liable for assault *unless together with other acts or circumstances* they put the other in reasonable apprehension of an imminent harmful or offensive contact with his person.

Restatement (Second) of Torts §31 (emphasis added). The italicized clause suggests that circumstances may suffice to make words actionable as an assault, if they reasonably cause the victim to fear an imminent contact. Courts are likely to be realistic in assessing the defendant's intent; where the circumstances clearly indicate that he is about to strike, very little more than words — such as a step, a rolling up of sleeves, or a drawing back of fists — will suffice to take the case to the jury. Even without that, courts may allow recovery based on the words and surrounding circumstances alone, if those circumstances are compelling enough. For example, some courts, relying on §31 of the Second Restatement, would probably allow recovery on the facts of *Cucinotti*.

Conditional Threats

Other factors may also undermine the imminence element of assault. Suppose that Oda snarls at Rudolph, "If you hadn't fouled out of the hundred-meter competition, I'd beat you to a pulp." Here, Oda's own threat defeats the assault, since her words indicate that she does not plan to carry it out. Her comment is still unpleasant and unwelcome, but it is not likely to make Rudolph anticipate immediate invasion of her physical security. Similarly, the defendant who states, "If you were not an old man, I would knock you senseless," does not assault the plaintiff, since his own words negate the intent to cause a harmful contact.

Some threats, however, will constitute assault even though they are conditional. Suppose that Oda snarls at Rudolph, "If you don't get off this track, I'll kick your tail into next week." This folksy threat is conditional, in the sense that Rudolph can avoid the threatened battery by leaving. At least in theory, she need not fear a blow, because she holds the means of avoiding it. Obviously, however, this should still be an assault. Otherwise, Rudolph could be forced to abandon her right to walk the streets (or run the track) in order to avoid battery. Bullies would be able to impose their will on others by the threat of force, yet incur no liability. One need only pose a slightly more extreme hypothetical ("If you don't go to bed with me, I'll throw you out this window") to make clear that the imposition of a condition that the assailant has no right to impose will not defeat an assault, even though the plaintiff can avoid being struck by complying with the unlawful demand.[1] See Harper, James & Gray (3d ed. 1986), §3.5, at 3:21-3:22.

Criminal Assault Distinguished

Since the early days of the common law, assault has been recognized not only as a tort, but as a crime as well. However, the crime of assault has not always been equated with the tort of assault. Historically, criminal assault was usually defined as an attempt to commit a battery. *Pope v. State*, 79 N.Y.S.2d 466, 471 (1948), *aff'd*, 99 N.Y.S.2d 1019 (1950) (defining assault as "an unlawful offer or attempt with force or violence to do corporal hurt to another"); W. LaFave, Criminal Law §16.3 (4th ed. 2003). This definition does not specify that the victim must anticipate the blow; the mere attempt to batter suffices. Under this criminal law definition, if Haines throws a javelin at Mathias, intending to injure him, he commits a criminal assault, whether or not Mathias sees it coming. However, this would not constitute the civil tort of assault if Mathias were unaware of the oncoming javelin, since he would not be placed in apprehension of a blow.

By contrast, if Owens pretended to throw the javelin at Mathias simply to frighten him, without intending to release it, this would be an assault in the tort sense of the term (if Mathias saw him do so), since it would doubtless place Mathias in fear of being skewered. But it would not be criminal assault under the traditional approach if Owens had no intent to throw, since he had not in fact attempted a battery. Similarly, if an assailant has no ability to cause the battery, as where Mathias threatens Owens

---

1. On the other hand, if the defendant *does* have a right to make a conditional threat, he is not liable for doing so. "If you don't get off my land, I will put you off," threatens physical force, but the owner has a right to use reasonable force to eject a trespasser. Restatement (Second) of Torts §77. Even if this frightens the trespasser, it is not an assault, since the statement is privileged.

from a distance with an empty gun, he does not commit a criminal assault under the traditional definition, but would commit the tort of assault.

In recent years, many states have amended their criminal statutes to make conduct that constitutes assault in the tort sense punishable as a criminal assault as well. A majority of states now make either act—attempted battery or placing in fear of a battery—a criminal offense. W. LaFave, Criminal Law, 4th ed. §16.3. But the historical distinction lingers in the form of confusing statements in the cases, such as the oft-repeated statement that "every battery includes an assault." *Western Union Tel. Co. v. Hill*, 150 So. 709, 710 (Ala. App. 1933). That is clearly untrue in the tort context: If the defendant kicks a sleeping plaintiff, he commits the tort of battery, but not the tort of assault, since he has not placed the defendant in fear of the contact.

The following examples probe the various elements of assault. In considering them, assume that the Restatement definition applies. After the examples, there is a brief discussion of how to plead the elements of assault and battery, together with an illustrative complaint.

EXAMPLES

Fear and Trembling

1.   Hennie, an Olympic figure skater, is about to perform her final routine in the women's individual skating event. She brings her music tape, meticulously edited and carefully guarded over four years of preparation, into the arena and puts it on the table by the tape player. Wilson, a sports cartoonist with a sick sense of humor, puts the tape on the floor and pretends to jump up and down on it while Hennie looks on from across the ice. Hennie is terrified that it will be broken. Can she sue Wilson for assault?

2.   The malicious Wilson crawls into the grid above the rink and loosens a heavy Olympic banner. He drops the banner as Hennie skates under him, but it sails a bit and lands ten feet behind her. She then turns and sees the banner lying on the ice and is shocked to think how close she came to being injured.

   a. Does she have an assault claim against Wilson?

   b. Is Wilson guilty of the *crime* of assault?

3.   Wilson lets the banner go, aiming for the unsuspecting Hennie, who is concentrating on her routine. As the banner falls, she looks up, sees it coming, and skates to safety. Is this an assault?

4.   Assume that Hennie sees the banner coming, but she can't get out of the way in time. Hennie is hit, though not injured. Can she sue for assault?

5.   Wilson crawls up into the grid, sees a skater below, thinks it's Hennie, and drops the banner. However, the skater is actually Thomas, who looks

up, sees the banner falling, and barely escapes being hit. Can Thomas sue Wilson for assault?

Some Variations

6.   Button, Hennie's partner in the doubles competition, is sitting in the stands and sees the banner fall. He is terrified that she will be hit. He sues Wilson for assault. What result?

7.   Suppose that Button was warming up at the same time as Hennie. Wilson, while climbing across the grid to loosen the banner, knocks an iron clamp off a beam. Button, alerted by a spectator, looks up in alarm and sees it coming at him, but manages to duck out of the way. Is Wilson liable to him for assault?

8.   Wilson, a fan of the Russian sprinters, approaches the U.S. track coach. He shakes his fist and snarls, "If you run Ashford on the anchor leg of the women's four-hundred-meter relay tomorrow, I'll see that you never walk again." Is this an assault?

Judge Fudd at the Olympics

9.   Hennie is practicing for her routine while the Zamboni (that big machine that grooms the ice) circles the rink. As she gracefully executes a backward glide, Wilson yells to her, "Watch it! You're going to hit the Zamboni!" Although Hennie is startled, the Zamboni is actually on the other end of the rink. Hennie sues Wilson for assault.

  a. Whether Wilson is liable for this conduct will depend on how the jury is instructed on the definition of assault. Consider the Restatement definition and the definition in the *Cucinotti* case, both quoted at p. 22. If you represented Hennie, which would you ask Judge Fudd to use in instructing the jury, and why?

  b. If you represented Wilson, what other argument would you raise that Hennie could not meet the prima facie elements of an assault claim?

  c. Gibson, the driver of the Zamboni, realizes that Hennie is still somewhere on the ice, but starts grooming the ice anyway. Coming around the end of the rink, she suddenly reverses direction, turning quickly back the way she had come, and nearly hits Hennie, skating behind the Zamboni. Is this an assault?

The Impossible Dream

10. Corbett, a four-foot-nine-inch gymnast, approaches Press, a two-hundred-fifty-pound shot putter who has just beaten out the American favorite in the shot put competition. Shaking her fist at her, she growls,

"Press, wipe that smile off your face or I'll wipe it off for you!" Press sues Corbett for assault. Is she liable?

11. Press, as it turns out, is a sensitive type. She is so upset by Corbett's threat that she develops a phobia about competition and goes into therapy to overcome it. She sues Corbett for a substantial sum for these consequences. Is Corbett liable for them?

Outrageous Fortune

12. Mathias, a rival of Weismuller, decides to upset him before the finals. While Weismuller is warming up, Mathias runs at him suddenly, startling Weismuller, who turns to run and sprains an ankle. Weismuller is taken to the hospital. While he is being treated, there is a fire in the hospital and Weismuller is burned. Is Mathias liable for his burns?

EXPLANATIONS

Fear and Trembling

1.   In this example, Hennie clearly would be traumatized by Wilson's conduct, but would not succeed in an action for assault. Assault addresses only one narrow form of emotional distress, apprehension of a contact with the person of the plaintiff. That is not what Wilson has threatened in this case. Wilson did not intend to touch Hennie, nor did she fear that he would. Since assault only protects against threatened contacts with the plaintiff herself, this is not an assault.

It surely is obnoxious behavior, though. Hennie ought to have a remedy for such conduct, even if it can't be shoe-horned into the elements of assault. If it isn't assault, it must be *something*, or else the law ought to make it something and give it a name so Hennie can recover. Traditionally, the common law did not provide a remedy for such antisocial acts — the courts did not attempt to redress all grievances, but confined themselves to the most venal. Only recently have the cases begun to develop the tort of infliction of emotional distress, which allows recovery for acts that cause severe distress, regardless of whether a physical threat was made. See also Restatement (Second) of Torts §870 (supporting liability for intentional infliction of harm that does not fit the elements of traditional intentional torts). But the assault tort, too hoary with age to learn new tricks, only applies to threats to the plaintiff herself.

2a.   When Hennie turns and sees the banner, she realizes that she might have been hit and is justifiably upset, but this is still not an assault. There is a difference between apprehending an imminent injury and realizing, after the fact, that you have narrowly escaped one. The elements of assault require that the plaintiff be placed in fear of an imminent contact. Hennie's post hoc awareness that the banner almost hit her may be equally disturbing, but it isn't an assault.

As in the last case, our instincts tell us there should be a remedy for this kind of behavior. If there is, however, it will have to be under the rubric of intentional infliction of emotional distress or some other cause of action such as "prima facie tort" (see Restatement (Second) of Torts §870), not assault. The assault cause of action is too arthritic to be stretched this far.

b.   Under the traditional criminal law approach, an attempted battery is an assault. Wilson's act would constitute criminal assault if, as the example suggests, he acted with a purpose to hit Hennie when he dropped the banner. But the *tort* of assault is not synonymous with attempted battery; it requires that the actor place the plaintiff in fear of an impending, not a past, touching.

3.   In this case, Wilson tried to hit Hennie, not frighten her. Indeed, the success of his scheme probably turned on her ignorance of the peril, since she could skate away if she knew it was on the way. Thus, Wilson may try to argue that he did not intend to cause Hennie to apprehend an imminent contact, only to make the contact itself.

The argument fails under the Restatement definition of assault. Although Wilson only tried to commit the battery itself, he is liable for assault since he acted with tortious intent and placed Hennie in apprehension of a harmful touching. Under Restatement (Second) of Torts §21, the intent requirement is met if Wilson was trying *either* to cause the contact (as he was in this case) or to cause Hennie to apprehend it, and she actually suffers such apprehension.

4.   Since the banner actually hit Hennie, this is a battery, even though she suffered no injury. Only an unwelcome touching, not resulting harm, is necessary to complete the battery. But Hennie suffered an assault as well, since she saw the banner coming and was placed in apprehension that she would be hit by it. The torts of battery and assault often occur together, though of course the elements of each must be separately satisfied.

If Hennie had not seen it coming, she would have suffered a battery but not an assault, since she would not have experienced fear of the impending contact, but only the contact itself.

5.   The twist in this example is that Wilson made a mistake about who the skater was. Clearly, his act should be an assault. Wilson had the necessary intent to cause an assault (or a battery, which would also suffice) and he actually did place the skater in apprehension of a harmful touching. Yet, he had no intent to assault *Thomas*.

While this example looks a little like a transferred intent case, transferred intent does not apply. Wilson did not aim at one person and hit another: He aimed at Thomas and she is the one who suffered the apprehension. The problem is that he made a mistake about her identity.

In the law of intentional torts, this is analyzed under the aptly named doctrine of mistake. Generally, a tortfeasor will be liable to a victim even if mistaken about her identity. After all, Wilson saw Thomas, aimed at her, and meant to hit her. He's a bad actor; he *ought* to be liable! Imagine that he had shot Thomas, thinking she was Hennie. It would be outrageous if he could defend on the ground that he thought she was someone else. He can't. As the aggressor, Wilson is liable for his tortious act whether the victim is the person he thought she was or not.

There's a lovely old case on mistake, *Ranson v. Kitner*, 31 Ill. App. 241 (1888), in which the defendant shot and killed the plaintiff's dog, thinking it was a wolf. In *Ranson*, the court held the defendant liable, throwing the risk of the mistake on the defendant. It seems appropriate, where the actor acts for the antisocial purpose of causing a harmful or offensive touching, to place the risk of mistake on him. Another example is the intentional tort of trespass to land: Tort law holds an actor liable for trespass if she enters land of another, even if she mistakenly believes it to be her own. See D. Dobbs, The Law of Torts 99. The intent requirement is met, since the actor intended to enter the land; the law places the risk of mistake as to ownership on the actor.

Some Variations

6.   In this example, Button has been placed in fear that Hennie will suffer a harmful or offensive contact. This is not assault, however, because assault protects only the intended victim from threats of bodily contact, not bystanders who fear for the victim's welfare. Restatement (Second) of Torts §26 cmt. a.

Since threats to physical security are considered so antisocial, and are so easily avoided by a little self-restraint, why not allow Button to recover on facts like these? Broadening the right to recover would further deter assaultive conduct, and remedy real infringements of Button's mental tranquility.

Perhaps so, but if we allow Button to recover, why not Hennie's manager — or her boyfriend, or anyone in the audience, or anyone who sees it on TV? Naturally, Button has more at stake than some of these bystanders, but each may suffer real distress from the fear that Hennie will be injured. Opening up the tort to third persons may not be worth the candle, since in most cases the truly distressed person will be the intended victim.

7.   Wilson has placed Button in fear of a harmful or offensive contact with the clamp, but he has not acted intentionally in the restricted intentional tort sense. He may have carelessly knocked the clamp down, but he did not do it for the purpose of hitting or frightening Button, nor was be substantially certain at the time that it would do so.

At the time of the act, however, Wilson was on his way to commit an intentional tort on Hennie by dropping the banner on her. Can Button's counsel make a transferred intent argument based on this? It seems not; transferred intent applies where a specific act is done with tortious intent and misfires. Here, the act of knocking down the clamp was not done with intent to hit or frighten anyone. Button cannot prove intent by showing that Wilson was planning to commit a tort later on someone else. He must focus on the act that placed him in apprehension of a harmful touching. That act may have been negligent, but was not done for the purpose, or with substantial certainty, that it would cause such apprehension.

8.   In this example Wilson has threatened the coach with physical violence if he does not comply with Wilson's demands. Naturally, Wilson has no right to tell the U.S. track coach who to run in the relays, so the fact that the coach can avoid the threat by doing as he is told does not prevent this from being an assault. However, it isn't an assault anyway, since Wilson has not threatened the coach with an imminent contact. A threat to do something tomorrow almost certainly is not imminent; a future threat, while reprehensible, does not satisfy the imminence requirement.

Judge Fudd at the Olympics

9a.   It would be crucial for Hennie to convince the judge to instruct the jury in terms of the Restatement definition instead of that given in the *Cucinotti* case. *Cucinotti*, if you read the definition carefully, requires that the defendant place the plaintiff in apprehension of a *battery.* Here, presumably Hennie anticipated an accidental collision with the Zamboni, not a deliberate battery by the driver. If apprehension of a battery is necessary, Wilson would not be liable.

Under the Restatement definition, however, the defendant need only cause the victim to apprehend a harmful or offensive contact, not necessarily a contact by the defendant, or one which meets the elements of battery. See Restatement (Second) of Torts §25 (victim need not be placed in fear of a touching from the actor in order to constitute assault). Under the Restatement definition, Wilson could be liable, since he caused Hennie to fear a harmful contact, though not a contact with Wilson or one which would constitute a battery at all.

There are many ways an actor can place a victim in fear of harmful or offensive touchings without threatening a battery. Consider the following:

- When passing a construction site: "Watch out, a plank is falling on your head!"
- While camping in the desert: "Don't move; there's a rattler next to your foot!"
- While riding up in a ski lift: "Jump! the cable's about to snap!"

Such obnoxious tricks can be mighty disturbing to one's mental tranquility. The drafters of the Restatement evidently concluded that inflicting such apprehension should be actionable. See Restatement (Second) of Torts §25 illus. 1 (actor liable for sounding a buzzer behind the victim in the desert, placing him in fear of a snake bite). However, there apparently are no cases either imposing or denying liability in such circumstances.

b. Wilson's counsel will doubtless argue that this is a case of mere words, without any act. Yet, as the introduction suggests, words together with circumstances can create reasonable apprehension of unwanted contact. The Second Restatement (§31, cmt. d) gives the example of a thief who stands in the dark road, holding a gun but without moving, and says "stand and deliver!" These mere words, in context, certainly incite a fear of an imminent harmful touching; the discussion in the Restatement comment clearly suggests that the thief could be sued for assault.

Similarly, here, it seems likely that Wilson's words and excited tone of voice, together with the circumstance that Hennie is skating backwards while the Zamboni is grooming the ice, would reasonably cause her to fear hitting the machine, even if Wilson does not move a muscle. Under the Restatement's approach, a court would likely uphold a finding of assault on these facts.

c. Although Gibson has acted "intentionally" in the sense that she meant to turn the Zamboni, the example suggests that she did not know that Hennie was behind her. Thus, she did not act for the purpose of placing Hennie in apprehension, nor did she know to a substantial certainty that she would do so. Her act may have been negligent, but was not an assault.

The Impossible Dream

10. Perhaps your first response here is that Press would have to be dreaming to be at all intimidated by Corbett's threat. Given the disparity in their size, the reasonable shot putter would not have feared a threat from Corbett, so arguably no assault occurred.

However, while Press doubtless was not *frightened* by Corbett's threat, her conduct does cause Press to *apprehend* an unwelcome contact from her — surely Corbett has the present ability to attack Press, even if she was unlikely to cause her any substantial harm. The action for assault protects victims from the anticipation of unwelcome contacts, even where they are confident that they can adequately defend themselves. Put another way, assault turns on the acts and intent of the defendant, not on how good the victim is at self defense. The strong have a right to physical autonomy as well as the weak, and should not be placed in the position of having to defend themselves from such invasions. Corbett is liable for assault.

11. In this example, the plaintiff reacts to the assault in an unexpected manner. Corbett's threat would be a minor annoyance to the average shot

putter, but Press is a hypersensitive soul who is really upset and permanently affected by it. The example is reminiscent of Example 8 in Chapter 1, in which Mercutio is upset by a good-natured slap on the back that other athletes would casually accept.

Although it may be reminiscent of the Mercutio example, this case is different. In that example, Romeo did not commit a battery, since the reasonable person under the circumstances would not be offended by the contact Romeo made. Consequently, he was not a tortfeasor at all, and was not liable even though Mercutio was actually distressed. Here, however, Corbett did commit an assault, since she threatened a contact that would be offensive to the reasonable person. Consequently, she *is* a tortfeasor, and is liable for the damages Press suffers as a result of the tort — *all* the damages she suffers, even though they exceed the damage one would anticipate from the conduct.

The difference between these two examples is important to understand. In the Mercutio example, the fact that the reasonable person would not be offended by the contact goes to the existence of liability in the first place. In the Press example, because a reasonable person would find the impending contact offensive, the threat is tortious. Since Corbett has committed a tort, she "takes the plaintiff as she finds her"; she is liable for the actual damages Press suffers, even if they are greater than the average shot putter would experience from the tortious conduct.

Outrageous Fortune

12. In this example, Mathias clearly assaulted Weismuller. He will certainly be liable to him for the ankle sprain. But would a court go so far as to hold Mathias liable for the freak burn injury Weismuller suffered while at the hospital?

It is often broadly stated that intentional tortfeasors are liable for all the consequences of their torts, even unintended consequences. For example, where Brutus tripped Cassius in Chapter 1, and Cassius unexpectedly fell down the stairs, I suggested that Brutus would be liable for all of Cassius's injuries, even though they are greater than Brutus intended. See pp. 7-8.

However, the result may be different where the subsequent injury is unforeseeable, as the burn injury is here. If Mathias had caused Weismuller's ankle sprain through negligence, the concept of proximate cause would probably bar Weismuller from recovering for the unforeseeable burn injury. See Chapter 9. While courts often impose liability for unexpected consequences on intentional tortfeasors, there is probably some foreseeability limit in intentional tort cases as well. See Restatement (Second) of Torts, §435B (suggesting that the court, in deciding whether to impose liability for unforeseeable consequences of an intentional tort, should consider the actor's intention to cause harm, the degree of his moral wrong and the seriousness of the harm that he intended when he acted). Here, Mathias's spur-of-the-moment act seems relatively mild compared to the severe consequences that ensued and the unexpected manner in which they occurred. Despite the occasional language in the cases suggesting that there is no, proximate cause limit on intentional tort liability, the court might well refuse to make him pay for that harm, even though he committed an intentional tort.

Pleading Claims for Assault and Battery

These two chapters have analyzed the substantive elements of assault and battery, that is, the basic facts the plaintiff must show to establish that the defendant is liable. It may be useful to see how these elements are presented to a court in a complaint for assault and battery.

The first step in seeking recovery for a tort claim is to file a complaint alleging that the defendant has committed a tort and demanding damages. A well-crafted complaint should allege a *prima facie* case, that is, the basic facts establishing that defendant's conduct fits the elements of the tort for which the plaintiff seeks damages. In an assault complaint, the plaintiff must allege facts that show that the defendant intentionally placed her in fear of a harmful or offensive touching. A battery complaint must allege facts that show that the defendant intentionally caused such a harmful or offensive touching. In addition, the plaintiff should allege the harm that resulted from the assault, and the relief (usually money damages) that she seeks as compensation.

Often, a single incident will support claims for both assault and battery. Figure 2–1 is an example of such a complaint. Like most court papers, it is basically straightforward. It begins by identifying the parties (paragraphs 1 and 2) and then briefly setting forth the events that gave rise to the claim. See paragraphs 3-5. The complaint then recasts the facts in terms of legal causes of action, in individual *counts* or *claims for relief.* Paragraph 7 of Juliet's First Claim for Relief specifically alleges that Romeo's conduct satisfies the elements of an assault: an act ("threatened to strike her and shook his first"), intent ("intentionally"), and resulting fear of a touching ("placing her in fear that he was about to strike her"). Paragraph 8 does the same for the second assault alleged. Paragraph 11 similarly alleges the elements of battery. Thus, the complaint demonstrates that the plaintiff claims she can establish the facts necessary to recover for each tort. In addition, it alleges the injuries suffered as a result of the defendant's tortious acts (paragraphs 9 and 13).

Finally, Juliet's counsel includes a demand for damages (the "wherefore" clause following paragraph 13). The damage demand here far exceeds the actual out-of-pocket costs Juliet incurred; a large part of the injury in intentional tort cases is intangible emotional harm, such as distress, pain and suffering, and humiliation resulting from the invasion. Such damages are genuine but hard to quantify; hence, plaintiffs often demand a good deal more than their out-of-pocket damages in cases involving such intangible elements as pain and suffering, emotional distress, interference with reputation, or other psychic injuries. Similarly, punitive damages, which may be awarded for intentional torts in some states to punish and deter tortious conduct, also may lead to an award of damages which far exceeds the plaintiff's economic damages from the tort.

STATE OF WEST DAKOTA

CONKLIN COUNTY, SS.   CIVIL ACTION NO. 03-7192

JANE JULIET,

    Plaintiff,

    v.   COMPLAINT FOR ASSAULT
                                       AND BATTERY

RONALD ROMEO,

    Defendant

----

1. The plaintiff is an individual residing at 332 Ruiz Circle, Arlington, West Dakota.

2. The defendant is an individual residing at 11 Rolvag Way, Arlington, West Dakota.

3. On February 6, 2003, the defendant approached the plaintiff in the main hall of Arlington High School, in Arlington, West Dakota, raised his right arm with the fist clenched, and threatened to punch her if she did not stop seeing a classmate, Michael Mercutio.

4. When the plaintiff refused to agree, the defendant deliberately grabbed her by the arm, squeezed it hard, and knocked her to the ground.

5. As a result of the defendant's acts, the plaintiff suffered a bruised arm, and abrasions on both knees requiring medical treatment. She also suffered severe pain, fear, and emotional distress.

FIRST CLAIM FOR RELIEF — ASSAULT

6. The plaintiff repeats and realleges the allegations in paragraphs one to five of the complaint.

7. The defendant committed an assault on the plaintiff when he intentionally and without her consent threatened to strike her and shook his fist, placing her in fear that he was about to strike her.

Figure 2–1

8. The defendant committed a further assault when he intentionally and without her consent reached out to grab the plaintiff's arm, placing her in fear that he was about to strike her.

9. As a result of these assaults, the plaintiff suffered fear, humiliation, and emotional distress, and was unable to attend school or engage in other usual activities for two weeks.

SECOND CLAIM FOR RELIEF — BATTERY

10. The plaintiff repeats and realleges the allegations in paragraphs one to five of the complaint.

11. The defendant committed a battery upon the plaintiff when he intentionally and without her consent grabbed her arm and threw her to the ground.

12. As a result of the defendant's acts, the plaintiff suffered bruises and abrasions on both knees, extensive pain and suffering, fear, humiliation, and emotional distress.

13. As a further result of the defendant's acts, the plaintiff incurred $400 in medical expenses for treatment, and was unable to return to school or engage in other usual activities for a period of two weeks.

WHEREFORE, the plaintiff seeks the following relief:

1. Compensatory damages in the amount of $8,000.

2. Punitive damages in the amount of $10,000.

3. Interest from the date of judgment as allowed by W.D. Rev. Code §14:103.

4. Her costs of suit.

The plaintiff claims trial by jury in this action.

By her attorney

Luis Mendez
84 Main Street, Suite 4
Arlington, WD 58102
(901) 225-1093

Figure 2–1 *(continued)*

3

The Far Side of the Coin: Classic Defenses to Intentional Torts

Introduction

The preceding chapters describe the formal elements a plaintiff must prove in order to recover for battery and assault. These elements, it is said, are necessary to establish a "prima facie case," that is, a showing sufficient to allow a jury to conclude that the tort has been committed. However, the case is not over once the plaintiff has presented evidence to establish these prima facie elements. The defendant must be heard from, and very likely, she will offer another side to the story.

The defendant may defend by simply negating one or more of the prima facie elements of the tort. For example, she may present evidence in a battery case that she never touched the plaintiff, that she did so unintentionally, or that the touching was not one that the reasonable person would find offensive under the circumstances. In other cases, however, the defendant takes the position that, *even if* the prima facie elements of the tort are shown, she is not liable anyway, because of additional facts that allow her to avoid liability. Such additional facts are often referred to as *affirmative defenses*.

Some affirmative defenses have nothing to do with the underlying incident itself. For example, if Jones sues Smith for battery, Smith might defend on the ground that the claim is barred by the statute of limitations, the statutory period within which suit must be brought on a claim. This defense asserts that, even if Jones can prove that Smith intentionally inflicted a harmful or offensive touching on her, she is not liable, because the suit was brought too late. Or, Smith might plead that Jones had signed a release from liability (a contractual agreement not to sue on the claim, usually given for a sum of money paid in settlement). Again, this defense does not rely on a showing that no battery occurred, but rather on additional facts that demonstrate that there is no longer a right to sue for the claim.

Other affirmative defenses, however, relate more directly to the events that give rise to the claim. The classic example is self-defense. In Jones's action for battery, for example, Smith might plead that she hit Jones because she was warding off a blow from Jones. If she acted in self-defense, she was privileged to inflict the harmful or offensive touching on Jones, and will not be held liable for doing so.

Another common affirmative defense to intentional tort is consent. Courts generally hold that the victim's consent bars recovery for touchings that would otherwise constitute batteries. If Jones proves that Smith slapped her in the face, Smith might plead that she and Jones were rehearsing for a play, and that Jones consented to the slap as part of the script. If this is true, Smith's act was privileged; she will not be liable even if the slap was offensive and intentional.

A number of other privileges may also constitute defenses to battery and assault claims. Police officers enjoy a privilege to use reasonable force in the course of arrest. An actor who causes an intentional invasion of another's property interests may sometimes assert the defense of *necessity,* that an otherwise tortious act was privileged because it was done to prevent a greater harm. Teachers and parents enjoy a limited privilege to use force in disciplining children. And there are others. This chapter, however, focuses on self-defense and consent as examples of the effect of privileges on tort liability.

The Privilege to Use Force in Self-Defense

Self-preservation, they say, is the first law of nature. It is not surprising, then, that the law of torts has long recognized the privilege to use force to protect oneself from an aggressor. An actor who is privileged to use force in self-defense incurs no liability for doing so, in some cases even if she inflicts serious bodily injury or death upon her assailant.

However, self-defense is a limited privilege. It is not a general license to attack an aggressor, or to respond to unwarranted provocation, or to give blow for blow; it only authorizes the use of force to prevent an impending battery or to stop one which is in progress. Suppose, for example, that Jones slaps Smith on the face and announces, "There, now we are even." Smith has no privilege of self-defense on these facts. She does not need to use force in her own defense, because she is no longer threatened with a battery. True, she has been the *victim* of one, and may sue for it, but self-defense does not authorize a tort victim to respond to force with force. It is a privilege to forestall an impending battery, not to retaliate for prior ones.

Similarly, there is no right to attack another simply because the other may deserve it. Smith may not strike Jones because she makes derogatory statements about Smith's lineage or her politics. Nor may she invoke self-defense against threats of future harm, such as a threat to attack her at a later time. In such cases, Smith has peaceful legal remedies, and is required to resort to them rather than "taking the law into her own hands" by immediate physical force.

Even where the privilege arises, it is limited: the victim of an aggressor may only use reasonable force in self-defense. The victim is not licensed to extract an "eye for an eye," but only to use the force that she reasonably believes is necessary to avert the threatened harm. Smith may not knife Jones in the ribs to avoid a slap in the face, though she would certainly be privileged to block the blow or push Jones away. Smith may not even be privileged to use the same level of force used by the initial aggressor, if less will do to prevent the contact. Remember that the purpose of self-defense is not to remedy the wrong already inflicted; such redress should be sought through criminal prosecution or intentional tort damages. Self-defense is authorized solely to prevent a further intrusion that cannot be avoided by waiting for legal redress.

On the other hand, the victim will sometimes be privileged to use *more* force than was necessary to avert a threatened battery. The privilege to use force in self-defense turns on the victim's *reasonable belief* that force is necessary, even if, in fact, it is not. If Enemy Jones raises a knife before her, Smith has no time to conduct an investigation of Jones's motives before forestalling the blow. Smith would be privileged to strike Jones if she reasonably concluded that Jones was about to stab her, even if Jones actually intended to scratch his back with the knife. Restatement (Second) of Torts §63 cmt. i.

The limits on the privilege of self-defense reflect a policy of minimizing the use of force as a means of self-protection. Arguably, this goal would be furthered by always requiring victims to retreat — that is, to run away — before using self-defense. However, courts have refused to create a duty to retreat (even if it can be done with perfect safety) before using *nondeadly* force in self-defense. Such a duty would require the victim of threatened violence to relinquish her right to walk the streets. Our culture places a high premium on personal choice and independence; consequently, a "duty to run" has not met with public or judicial acceptance.

Thus, at least where nondeadly force is threatened, the victim is privileged to stand her ground and use nondeadly force in self-defense, even if retreat is feasible. Restatement (Second) of Torts §63 cmt. m.

Deadly Force in Self-Defense

While all courts recognize a limited right to self-defense, most impose additional restrictions on the right to use deadly force, that is, force that is "intended or likely to cause death or serious bodily harm." Restatement (Second) of Torts §65(1). The Second Restatement, for example, takes the position that an actor may use deadly force in self-defense only if she reasonably believes that she is threatened with deadly force "which can be prevented only by the immediate use of such [deadly] force." Id. Under this widely accepted approach, there is no right to use deadly force in response to the lesser threat of nondeadly force. If Smith raises her hand to slap Jones, Jones may not shoot her dead, or swing at her head with a hammer. Jones may use nondeadly force, or retreat, or suffer the slap and sue for battery, but she is not privileged to escalate the conflict by using deadly force.

Jones may not even be privileged to use deadly force if she is attacked with deadly force. Some jurisdictions, and the Second Restatement, require a victim of deadly force to retreat if it is safe to do so before using deadly force against the assailant. The Restatement offers this rationale for imposing a duty to retreat:

> the interest of society in the life and efficiency of its members and in the prevention of the serious breaches of the peace involved in bloody affrays requires one attacked with a deadly weapon, except within his own dwelling place, to retreat before using force intended or likely to inflict death or serious bodily harm upon his assailant, unless he reasonably believes that there is any chance that retreat cannot be safely made.

Restatement (Second) of Torts §65 cmt. g. The Restatement recognizes, however, that the victim need not retreat unless it is clearly safe to do so. If the victim has any doubt of that (as most will), she may use deadly force in self-defense.

A majority of jurisdictions reject the Restatement approach. Instead, they hold that the victim of an assault with deadly force is privileged to stand her ground and use deadly force in self-defense, even if retreat is feasible. V. Schwartz, K. Kelly & D. Partlett, Torts: Cases and Materials (10th ed. 2000) 104. Even the Restatement recognizes that one threatened with deadly force in her home need not retreat. This obviously reflects the widely shared view that one's home, if not quite a castle, ought at least to be an inviolable place of refuge.

Defense of Others

Interesting problems arise when an actor defends others rather than himself. Suppose, for example, that Sir Galahad comes around the corner and sees Goliath taking a swing at David. Inferring that Goliath is about to batter David, he punches Goliath. Is he protected from liability by a privilege of "defense of another"?

The basic premise in the cases has been that an intervenor such as Galahad has the right to use the same force to defend David that David could use to defend himself. Thus, if Goliath is about to batter David with nondeadly force, Galahad (like David) could use reasonable nondeadly force to prevent that battery. If Goliath was using deadly force, Galahad could use deadly force in defense of David, if necessary to forestall the battery.

But suppose that Galahad, when he comes around that corner, misconstrues the situation. Suppose that David had just reached into his pocket for a knife, and Goliath's impending blow was a privileged act of self-defense against an assault by David? Galahad may reasonably interpret the scene as an assault by Goliath, but suppose he is wrong?

The cases have taken two approaches to this "mistaken defense of other" problem. Some take the position that Galahad has a privilege to act upon his reasonable perception. Thus, if it reasonably appears to Galahad that Goliath is the aggressor, he may defend David from Goliath's blow, even if he is wrong. After all, we give *David* that privilege — to act upon his reasonable perception that he is being attacked, even if he is not. So why not give the same slack to Galahad, the virtuous intervenor? Under this approach, Galahad may use reasonable force to protect David so long as he reasonably believes that David is about to be the victim of a battery by Goliath.

Other courts have taken what is sometimes called the "shoe-stepping" approach to defense of others. Under this view (evidently a minority position), Galahad only has a privilege to defend David if David *actually* was privileged to defend himself. So, when Goliath swings at David in self-defense against the knife threat, but Galahad, arriving on the instant, perceives Goliath as the aggressor, Galahad would not be privileged to defend David, because David, as the initial aggressor, would not be privileged to defend himself. In a jurisdiction that takes this approach, Galahad acts at his own risk. If he is wrong about who the aggressor is, and defends the actual aggressor, he "steps into the shoes" of the aggressor (David in our example). He would not have a privilege to defend David, because David would not be privileged to defend himself from a blow by Goliath in self-defense. This approach suggests that intervenors should "look before they leap," while the reasonable mistake approach places a higher priority on Galahadism. See generally D. Dobbs, The Law of Torts 168-169.

The "Defense" of Consent

A second common affirmative defense to intentional torts is *consent*. Tort law generally accepts the maxim, *volenti non fit injuria* ("to one who is willing, no wrong is done"). Prosser & Keeton, The Law of Torts §18 at 112 (5th ed. 1984). If the victim of a harmful or offensive touching manifests consent to the contact, the defendant is usually not liable for causing it. This is an example of the premium our society places on the individual's right to craft her own fate, to choose for herself, even to make choices most of us would consider stupid or self-destructive.[1]

Although consent avoids liability, it may not be entirely accurate to call it a defense. If an element of battery is the unwelcome nature of the contact, arguably the plaintiff's consent negates a basic element of her prima facie case. See Restatement (Second) of Torts §892(1) (consent is "willingness in fact for conduct to occur"). On this reasoning, *lack of consent* should be an element of the plaintiff's prima facie case of battery, and the plaintiff should include an allegation of lack of consent in her complaint.[2] There is considerable authority that this is so. See Dobbs, 218; see also Restatement (Second) of Torts §10 cmt. c (plaintiff must plead lack of consent in cases involving personal interests, such as assault and battery). But some cases treat consent, like most privileges, as an affirmative defense that must be raised and proved by the defendant if she claims that the plaintiff consented to the contact. See, e.g., *Sims v. Alford*, 118 So. 395 (Ala. 1928).

This somewhat scholastic pleading question is less important than understanding what constitutes consent, and when it is effective to protect the actor from liability. Largely, common sense dictates the scope of consent. Common sense tells us that a person may consent to one touching but not another. Smith's acceptance of a "kiss in the moonlight" does not authorize Torres to have intercourse with her, nor does Vega's agreement to a fist fight with Jones authorize Jones to use a shotgun if he fares poorly in the battle. Common sense also tells us that one can manifest consent to a touching without signing a contract, or even uttering a word. Smith may agree to Torres's kiss with a look or a blush — and may similarly refuse without speaking.

Naturally, difficult factual issues will often arise as to whether the victim consented to the contact. However, paradoxically, the privilege does not turn on *actual* consent. Most courts hold that the defendant is privileged to make a contact where the plaintiff's words, gestures, or conduct

---

1. Another example is the negligence doctrine known as "assumption of the risk," discussed in Chapter 22.

2. Note that Juliet did include this allegation in her complaint for assault and battery. See Figure 2–1, p. 41, paragraph 11.

reasonably manifest consent to it, even if she was not actually willing to be touched. Restatement (Second) of Torts §892(2). The classic case for this proposition is *O'Brien v. Cunard S.S. Co.*, 28 N.E. 266 (Mass. 1891), in which the plaintiff received a shipboard vaccination prior to entering the United States. Although she later testified that she was unwilling to be vaccinated, she had stood in a line of two hundred women waiting to be vaccinated, had watched those in front of her receive their vaccinations, and had held up her arm to receive the shot. On these facts, the court held that the doctor was "justified in his act, whatever her unexpressed feelings may have been. In determining whether she consented, he could be guided only by her overt acts and the manifestations of her feelings." Id. at 266.

Common sense also suggests that consent that is based on a fundamental misunderstanding of the facts does not evidence true acceptance of a contact. This is illustrated by two recurring scenarios. In one, a doctor obtains a patient's consent to an examination by representing that it is for treatment purposes, but actually is seeking sexual gratification. In another, the defendant obtains the plaintiff's consent to sexual intercourse without revealing that she has a communicable venereal disease. In both cases, the plaintiff's consent is invalid, since, due to the defendant's misrepresentation (or, in the second case, failure to reveal crucial facts relevant to the plaintiff's choice), she did not appreciate the true nature of the intended contact and thus did not meaningfully consent to it.

Where the legislature has barred conduct to protect a disadvantaged class, even the plaintiff's *actual* consent may not create a privilege. For example, it has been held that consent to intercourse by a minor under the legal age of consent does not bar the minor from suing for battery. Statutory age-of-consent laws are intended "to protect a definite class of persons from their own immaturity." Harper, James & Gray §3.10, at 3:49-3:50. They prohibit the defendant's conduct *regardless of the minor's consent*, since the minor is deemed incapable of making a proper judgment about whether to engage in the conduct. Consequently, the defendant (the party who induces the minor to engage in the conduct) is subject to criminal prosecution even if the minor consented. To reinforce this legislative policy, courts hold that the defendant should also be barred from raising the minor's consent as an affirmative defense in a tort action based on the same conduct. See Restatement (Second) of Torts §892C(2).

Consent to Medical Treatment

Consent issues often arise in the context of medical treatment, since even therapeutic touchings have been viewed as batteries if the patient has not consented to them. Thus, the medical cases illustrate in one frequently recurring context the consent issues discussed more generally above.

For example, the treatment cases mirror the common sense principle that consent may include one touching but not another. In *Mohr v. Williams*, 104 N.W. 12 (Minn. 1905), *overruled on other grounds by Genzel v. Halvorson*, 80 N.W.2d 854 (Minn. 1957), a physician obtained a patient's consent to operate on her right ear, but, finding the left more seriously diseased, operated on it instead. Although the surgery was carefully done, it was held a battery, since the doctor's touching went beyond the scope of contact to which the patient had consented.

Mohr was a pretty clear case of exceeding consent, but many medical consent situations are more ambiguous. A recurring scenario is the surgeon who, after commencing surgery with the consent of the patient, encounters unexpected conditions which require extension of the procedure beyond that approved by the patient. For example, the surgeon might find it necessary, in an operation on the intestine, to remove part of it, or, in an operation for ovarian cysts, to remove the ovary. In a heart by-pass operation, the surgeon might find it necessary to make extensive, unanticipated incisions in the legs to locate suitable arteries for the by-pass procedure.

It would be nice if surgeons could satisfy the law's sense of propriety by waking the patient in such cases to obtain consent to the extension of surgery, but that would usually be impracticable or even dangerous to the patient. Ideally, such complications should be anticipated and addressed in advance, by obtaining the patient's consent (or refusal) to various predictable scenarios the surgeon may encounter. However, this is often not possible, because there is no reason to anticipate the extension. It is common practice for physicians to seek consent from a relative of the patient in such situations. Such "substituted consent" or "proxy decision-making" is "a practice so common in medicine over the last century that it has been impliedly accepted by law" and has been endorsed by many state statutes as well. B. Furrow et al., Health Law (2d ed. 2000) 840. Although there are few cases expressly holding that such substituted consent is valid, patients are much less likely to challenge a decision in which their family members have concurred. Thus, this practice greatly reduces the likelihood that suit will be brought based on lack of consent.

If no relative is available, the cases support a limited privilege to extend the surgery within the area of the initial incision, unless the extension involves the destruction of a bodily function, such as the amputation of a limb or loss of reproductive function.[3] See Prosser & Keeton at 118. While it is sometimes said that there is implied consent to such extensions (see Harper, James & Gray, §3.10, at 3:48), this privilege is not really

---

3. Even here, the surgeon may be privileged if delay would itself lead to death or loss of a bodily function.

based upon consent—which, by definition, has not been given. It arises from the exigencies of the situation, which allow the surgeon to choose for the patient based upon what the reasonable patient would consent to if she could be consulted.

A related issue is the emergency privilege to treat an unconscious patient, for example, the victim of an auto accident who requires immediate treatment, but is unconscious due to her injuries. If no relative is able to consent, the cases recognize a privilege to render such treatment if the reasonable person would consent to it, there is no reason to believe that the particular patient would not, and delay would involve a risk of death or serious bodily harm to the patient. See Prosser & Keeton at 117.[4]

The advance of medical science has also spawned a host of difficult consent issues now analyzed under the rubric of the "right to refuse treatment" or the "right to die." Such cutting edge issues take us far afield from traditional battery law, but they do reiterate, in an extreme context, the fundamental value our society places on personal autonomy. Most courts recognize the right of a competent adult to refuse treatment, even life-saving treatment, based on common law battery principles or the constitutional right of privacy or liberty. See *Cruzan v. Director, Missouri Dept. of Health*, 497 U.S. 261, 269-279 (1990) (reviewing cases based on consent and other theories); B. Furrow et al., Health Law (2d ed. 2000) 827-828. These cases reflect the same right to autonomy in making choices concerning one's body that underlies the traditional consent privilege in battery cases. Most of the current issues in this area involve not *whether* the individual has the right to refuse treatment, but *how* one must manifest that decision (for example, by advance health care directives or "living wills") and under what circumstances others, such as family members, may exercise a "substituted judgment" for a patient who is unable to make the decision herself.

The examples that follow explore the application of self-defense and consent to some fairly straightforward cases—and a few be-Fuddling ones as well.

EXAMPLES

Self-Defense Basics

1. In which of the following cases was the assailant's blow a privileged act of self-defense?

    a. Rollins makes a disparaging comment about Okina's husband. She slaps him in the face.

---

4. Here again, there may be a stricter standard if the treatment involves destruction of a major bodily function, as, for example, an amputation. In such cases, the privilege may only attach if delaying treatment would risk death or very serious consequences to the health of the patient. Prosser & Keeton, §18, at 117-118.

     b. Rollins goes to knock off Okina's hat. She pushes him back hard.

     c. Rollins punches Okina in the stomach and turns to go. Okina hits him with the umbrella she is carrying.

     d. Rollins, on the facts of the last example, sees Okina coming at him with the umbrella and pushes her away as she swings it.

     e. Rollins pushes Okina. She stabs the sharp point of her umbrella at his face.

     f. Zilla sees Enemy Kong running toward her excitedly. Fearful of an attack, she punches him in the chest. As it turns out, Kong had had a religious conversion and was rushing up to Zilla to apologize for past transgressions.

     g. Zilla sees Enemy Kong rushing at her with a bat. She throws a brick at him and hits Cusack, a bystander.

2.   Zilla is standing on a street corner when Kong, an old enemy, spies her. Kong advances toward her, shaking her fists and threatening to knock her down. Zilla, who is bigger, pushes at Kong with both hands as she is about to be hit, knocking Kong down. Unexpectedly, Kong falls on the stub of a metal post that had been cut off several inches above the sidewalk, and is gouged in the back. The wound requires 18 stitches and lands Kong in the hospital for three weeks. Is Zilla liable to him?

Never Sound Retreat

3.   Zilla is sitting in the front seat of her car with the door open. Kong, an old enemy, sees her from 100 yards down the street and charges at her with a knife. Zilla steps out of the car with a baseball bat, swings hard at Kong with the bat, and hits her.

     a. Assume that the principles of the Second Restatement §65, requiring retreat in certain deadly force cases, apply. Who is liable, and for what?

     b. Assume that the incident takes place in a state that does not require retreat before the use of deadly force. Is Zilla liable to Kong?

4.   Goliath meets David, who is considerably smaller than he is, on the street. Goliath objects to David's coat, which has a picture of the American flag covered over with a peace sign. He threatens to tear the flag right off the coat while it is on David's back, and moves toward him in obvious anger. David, convinced that it is his only means of self-defense, stabs Goliath with a pitchfork he is carrying.

     a. Is either party liable to the other, and if so, for what?

     b. On the same facts, assume that Goliath sees the pitchfork coming. To prevent being impaled, he picks up a two-by-four and hits David on the head with it. David suffers a concussion. Is Goliath liable for the injury to David?

c. Assume that David defended himself by pushing at Goliath with his arms outstretched, in an effort to knock Goliath down. Goliath, surprised by David's aggressive response, swings at him, knocking him down. Who is liable to whom?

Into the Fray

5.   Assume, on the basic facts of the last example, that Lancelot comes on the scene and sees David rushing at Goliath with the pitchfork after Goliath rushes him to grab the flag. To protect Goliath, he swings at David with a crowbar, hitting him on the head and injuring him. Is Lancelot liable to David?

6.   Suppose that Lancelot happens on the scene, and sees David about to push Goliath to prevent him from grabbing the flag on his jacket. Lancelot hits David in the stomach. Is Lancelot liable to David for battery?

Judge Fudd on the Cutting Edge of the Law

7.   Zilla is sitting on the bench at a softball game when she sees Kong bearing down on her with a knife. Unable to retreat, Zilla wards off the blow by hitting Kong with a baseball bat. On later examination, it turns out that the knife Kong was carrying was a child's toy, made of soft rubber.

Kong sues Zilla for battery. The case arises in a jurisdiction that does not require retreat before the use of deadly force. At trial, Judge Fudd instructs the jury as follows:

> You are instructed that the defendant was privileged to use that level of force reasonably necessary to defend herself from a threat of bodily harm.
> If you find that the defendant was attacked with nondeadly force, then the defendant was only privileged to use nondeadly force in self-defense. If you find that the defendant was attacked with nondeadly force, and that the defendant used deadly force in self-defense, then you must find for the plaintiff.
> If you find that the defendant was attacked with deadly force, then the defendant was only privileged to use that level of force reasonably necessary for her self-defense, which may include deadly force. If you find that the defendant used more force than was reasonably necessary, you must find for the plaintiff.

Who will object to the instruction, and why?

Macho Consent

8.   Franken approaches Stein in the street and threatens him: "If you don't hightail it out of here I will give you two black eyes." Stein refuses to budge, and Franken socks him in the eye. Has Stein consented to the touching?

9.   Hulk, a wrestler, brags to his friends at a bar about how strong he is. He braces himself and invites them to "just try to push me over." Brower, with a mighty shove, pushes at Hulk with both hands. Hulk loses his balance, stumbles backwards, and falls against the footrest in front of the bar. He suffers a separated shoulder, which ends his wrestling career. He sues Brower for battery. Is Brower liable?

What You Don't Know ...

10.   Rodriguez meets Alvord in a bar. They chat. One thing leads to another. They end up back at Rodriguez's apartment, and go to bed together. A month later, Rodriguez discovers that she has contracted a sexually transmitted disease from Alvord, and sues him for battery. If the evidence shows that Alvord did not know at the time of their tryst that he had the disease, will he be liable to her?

What You Do Know ...

11.   Carella is brought to the emergency room unconscious after an accident, in need of immediate surgery. In examining Carella, Dr. Langone finds that he is wearing a medical alert bracelet stating that, for religious reasons, he does not wish to be given blood transfusions. However, the surgery poses a much greater risk of death to Carella if he does not receive transfusions. In the absence of an objection from the patient, such transfusions would be required by good medical practice, and would be accepted by "the reasonable patient." Carella cannot be awakened to seek consent.

Dr. Langone performs the surgery and gives Carella six pints of blood. Is she liable for battery?

12.   Dr. Langone performs a hip replacement operation on Lew. She obtains consent from Lew for the operation, but does not inform him that in a small percentage of such operations one of the screws that secures the artificial hip may back off, requiring a follow-up operation to resecure it. Six months after the operation, Lew experiences problems with the hip, and x-rays reveal that the screw has backed off. He sues Dr. Langone for battery, arguing that he did not give a meaningful consent to the operation because he was not fully informed of the risks it entailed. How is the court likely to rule on the battery claim?

Shooting from the Hip

13.   Seaman is about to undergo surgery to remove a bony growth on his hip. As he is being prepped for the operation, Dr. Langone, the surgeon, comes in to see him. She presents Seaman with the following consent form, which Seaman signs:

1. I, <u>Walter Seaman</u>, hereby give my authorization and consent to an operation to be performed on me on

<u>September 1</u>,2004, by

Dr. <u>Paula Langone</u> for the purpose of correcting the following condition:

<u>remove bony growth from right hip</u>

2. I also consent to any further procedures, during, preceding, and after the operation, which Dr.

<u>Langone</u> deems necessary or desirable in order to correct the above-specified conditions or to remedy any other unhealthy condition she may encounter during the operation.[5]

Langone proceeds with the surgery. During the surgery, she discovers — as is commonly the case — that the hip joint is badly deteriorated, and performs a total hip replacement instead.

Seaman never regains full use of the hip. Upset that Langone had decided to do the replacement operation, he sues for battery. Which of the following arguments for the defendant do you find persuasive?

a. "This procedure was authorized even without the consent form. Virtually all patients would consent in this circumstance, since there was hardly any chance of improvement in function without the hip replacement. Thus, since the reasonable person would consent, I was justified in inferring that Seaman would as well."

b. "Even if the consent form is not valid, it would be unreasonable to interrupt this complex, invasive surgery to wake the patient and ask for consent. Frankly, as an experienced surgeon, I would never do it: There is a substantial risk in the surgery itself, and the incision would have to be opened a second time, which would multiply the chances of infection and retard the patient's recovery."

c. "The patient signed the consent form, which very clearly authorizes me to go beyond the procedure contemplated. Since the hip replacement was 'necessary or desirable to correct' the patient's problem, it was authorized by the consent."

You're the Doc

14. Seaman is about to have his hip surgery. Dr. Langone, fully aware of the need (both legal and ethical) to inform Seaman of the risks and possible extensions involved in the surgery, comes in to discuss these with Seaman. As she

---

5. Adapted, with changes, from a similar form in 15 Am. Jur. 2d Legal Forms, §202:161 (1993 revision).

begins her spiel about possible side effects and unexpected problems that may arise, Seaman stops her. "Doctor," he says, "I'm a businessman; I know stocks and bonds. You're a doctor; you know surgery. I'm sure there are risks involved, but I trust you. Do what has to be done for me and that'll be fine with me."

    a. During the operation, Langone determines that Seaman's hip has deteriorated to the point where a full hip replacement is necessary. She proceeds to do it. Seaman, upset with the result, sues her for battery. Is his claim barred by consent?

    b. During the surgery, Langone discovers that a major artery in Seaman's thigh has deteriorated, and should be excised. She does so. Later, Seaman has pain in the leg and sues Langone for excising the artery without consent. Is the claim barred by consent?

Damned If You Do ...

15. Willis is in an auto accident and is brought to the hospital unconscious. Because he has sustained internal injuries, Dr. Langone concludes that good medical practice requires immediate surgery. However, Willis is unconscious. Langone therefore talks with Willis's wife, but she refuses to agree to the surgery, on the ground that she is not sure that it is necessary and that surgery "gives her the creeps." What should Langone do?

EXPLANATIONS

Self-Defense Basics ...

1a.   Okina's blow is not in response to a threat of an unwanted physical contact; rather, it is in retribution for an insult. The privilege of self-defense authorizes physical force to forestall an invasion of the victim's person, not to respond to insults or to "get even." Okina's blow is a battery.

    b.   Here, Rollins has threatened an offensive contact to Okina's hat, not a physically harmful contact. However, his act, if completed, would be a battery—the unconsented contact with objects intimately associated with the body satisfies the contact requirement. So Okina is privileged to use reasonable nondeadly force to prevent the intrusion. Since her push probably constitutes reasonable force, the privilege of self-defense applies.

    c.   This is clearly retaliation rather than self-defense. Rollins's battery is over, he's leaving, and Okina therefore has no need to protect herself from an impending battery. Since she is not privileged, her blow is a battery. (Of course, Rollins's blow was as well.)

    d.   Even though Rollins committed a battery himself when he punched Okina, her later effort to strike him with the umbrella is an independent battery, as explained in the prior example. Because Okina's threatened blow with the umbrella is not privileged, it is an assault, and Rollins has a right to use reasonable force to defend himself against it. His push is therefore privileged.

e.   Rollins commits battery when he pushes Okina, which gives rise to a right on her part to use self-defense. However, she only has the right to use reasonable, nondeadly force in response to a nondeadly assault. Stabbing a sharp point into Rollins's face may well be excessive force, because it is "likely to cause death or serious bodily harm," such as putting out Rollins's eye. Her stab is likely an assault, and if it lands, battery.

f.   Here, Zilla thought that Kong was going to attack her, and therefore punched him in self-defense. However, she was wrong about the need to use self-defense, since Kong actually had no intent to attack her.

Zilla's act was privileged, even though she was mistaken about the need to use self-defense. Where she must act immediately, and reasonably believes that she is about to be battered, the privilege will apply. After all, what would *you* do? Right, you'd defend yourself, just as she did. Zilla is not "at fault" for acting on her reasonable understanding of the facts, rather than waiting meekly for Kong's blow to fall. Thus, most courts allow the privilege of self-defense, so long as the victim reasonably believed that she was about to be battered. D. Dobbs, The Law of Torts 164-165.

g.   Here, Zilla is threatened with deadly force, and responds with deadly force. Her act would be privileged in most jurisdictions, which allow a victim to use deadly force in self-defense against deadly force without any duty to retreat. (In a jurisdiction that followed the Restatement (Second) of Torts S. 65(3), Zilla would not be privileged to use deadly force against Kong if she could safely retreat from Kong's attack.) Assuming her throw would have been privileged if the brick hit Kong, is it privileged when it hits Cusack, an innocent bystander? Who should this unfortunate loss fall upon—the innocent Zilla or the innocent Cusack?

Analytically, Zilla has not committed battery on Cusack; she did not intend to cause a harmful or offensive touching to him. But, she *did* intend to cause one to Kong, so shouldn't the intent transfer to Cusack? No; to hold someone liable under the doctrine of transferred intent, you must first show that the actor's original intent in striking the blow was tortious. Here, if Zilla had a right to hit Kong in self-defense, her blow was not tortious toward Kong and therefore cannot be if it hits Cusack.

On a policy level, there may be stronger arguments for holding Zilla liable for Cusack's injury. If she invited Kong's attack, for example, it seems fairer to place the loss on her than Cusack. On appropriate facts, a court could reach that result by finding Zilla negligent for inviting a dangerous brawl in a crowded place. See Restatement (Second) of Torts, §75.[6]

2.   This example is reminiscent of several from the first two chapters, in which the actor intends a blow, but it causes more injury than she

---

6. *Kong* very likely would be liable to Cusack on a negligence theory, since it is foreseeable that his attack on Zilla would cause injury to bystanders. Harper, James & Gray, 3d ed., §3.11, 3:62.

expected it would. Here, Zilla intended the push, but she did not intend to impale Kong on the metal post. As in the earlier examples, Zilla's liability turns on whether she committed a tort in the first place. If she did, she is liable for the resulting harm, though greater than anticipated. If her act was not tortious, she is not liable, although serious injury resulted.

Here, of course, whether Zilla's act is tortious turns on whether she was privileged to push Kong down in self-defense. It certainly appears that she was. She was threatened with nondeadly force, a push, and responded with appropriate nondeadly force to ward off the blow. Since she was privileged to push Kong, the touching is not a battery, and Zilla is not liable, even though serious injury resulted.

Never Sound Retreat

3a.   Section 65 of the Second Restatement requires a person attacked with deadly force to retreat, if she may safely do so, before responding with deadly force in self-defense. The facts here suggest that Zilla could have retreated by closing the car door and driving away. If this is true, she would not have a privilege to defend herself with a baseball bat. If her blow is not privileged, it is a battery, so Zilla would be liable to Kong for the injury she inflicts.

Kong would also be liable to Zilla. Her charge down the street with the knife is clearly an assault—Zilla's overreaction doesn't change that fact, though it makes Zilla liable as well.

b.   As the introduction indicates, many states do not require retreat before the use of deadly force. Yet Zilla might be liable even in a jurisdiction that takes this view. A threat of deadly force does not automatically authorize the use of similar force in self-defense. Rather, it gives the victim a privilege to use force she reasonably believes necessary to prevent the threatened battery. That may include deadly force if such force appears necessary, but here Zilla could presumably have prevented the battery by simply closing and locking the car door. If so, she is not authorized to do more simply because Kong's attack threatens more serious harm.[7]

4a.   Goliath is liable to David for assault. He has no right to redesign David's jacket, and his move toward David reasonably puts David in fear that he is about to do so by force. But Goliath's assault does not justify David's use of deadly force in self-defense. The threat to David was of nondeadly force. Such a threat does not authorize him to use deadly force in self-defense. Thus, David is also liable to Goliath since he exceeded the scope of his privilege of self-defense.

---

7. Might a court hold that Zilla need not close the door because that would constitute "retreat"? Probably not; by closing the door, Zilla is not running away (a loss of face that many jurisdictions refuse to compel), but simply blocking the battery without directly exerting force against the aggressor.

The facts suggest that David, a smaller man than Goliath, used the only means at his disposal — his pitchfork — that would avoid the invasion of his person. However, this does not change the result. David is not authorized to use deadly force to prevent the threat of nondeadly force, even if his only alternatives are to run or submit to the battery. See Restatement (Second) of Torts, §63, cmt. j. While this may be humiliating to David, the policy reason for this conclusion appears sound: It is better that David suffer temporary humiliation and be vindicated later in court, than cause a serious injury or death to Goliath to prevent a fairly minor intrusion on David's rights.

This presupposes, of course, that David does not fear anything beyond having his coat ripped. If Goliath's conduct leads David to reasonably fear serious bodily injury himself, he would be entitled to use similar force in self-defense.[8] In order to determine the scope of David's privilege, it is necessary to characterize the type of force *Goliath* has threatened — or, more accurately, the type of force David reasonably anticipates. It is often difficult to say after the fact that the victim was unreasonable in perceiving a threat of deadly force, even if the assailant really intended something less — which is a forceful argument for aggressors to think twice before striking.

b. Here, Goliath is the initial, nondeadly aggressor, and David overreacts by using deadly force to protect himself from nondeadly force. By overreacting, he becomes a batterer himself, and would be liable to Goliath for any injuries resulting from his excessive force.

If Goliath is now the victim of a battery, it follows, doesn't it, that Goliath has a privilege to use self-defense against David's battery? Frankly, I'm not sure that it *should* follow: Goliath is the original aggressor here. Had he not provoked the fight, he would have had no need for self-defense. If Goliath is privileged to respond to the pitchfork with deadly force, he might provoke a quarrel fully expecting David to overreact, and then use his privilege to injure or kill him. It seems like poor policy to authorize Goliath to do that. On the other hand, it hardly seems sensible to require Goliath to meekly accept his fate at the tines of a pitchfork, either.

A middle ground would require Goliath, as the original aggressor, to retreat if possible before using deadly force against the victim-turned-aggressor. Apparently, some criminal cases have taken this approach. See Dressler, Understanding Criminal Law (3d ed.), §18.03; see also Model Penal Code, §3.04 and accompanying commentary. The Second Restatement of Torts takes the position that Goliath is privileged to use deadly force in self-defense once David converts the nondeadly quarrel into a deadly one. "One who intentionally invades or attempts to invade any of another's interests of personality, does not by his wrongdoing forfeit his privilege to defend himself by any means which would be privileged were he innocent of wrongdoing against any excess of force

---

8. Unless he has a duty to retreat, as he might in jurisdictions following the Restatement (Second) of Torts, §65.

which the other uses in self-defense." Restatement (Second) of Torts, §71(c) cmt. d.[9]

c.   This example is like the last, in that Goliath, the original aggressor, responds to David's self-defensive efforts by defensive efforts of his own. Here, however, David has not exceeded his privilege. He is using a reasonable method to ward off Goliath's initial attack. Thus, David is not a batterer; consequently, Goliath is not privileged to act in self-defense; he must either retreat or suffer David's blow. If he does more, he is liable, while David is not.

Into the Fray

5.   Here Lancelot, an interloper, comes on the scene, concludes that David is the aggressor, and intervenes to protect Goliath. If his interpretation were correct, there would be no doubt of his right to come to Goliath's aid. Tort law provides a privilege to defend others threatened with battery as well as to defend oneself. Restatement (Second) of Torts, §76.

However, here Lancelot is wrong; David is not the initial aggressor, he is acting in self-defense (but exceeding his privilege by using deadly force). Courts have taken two approaches to the situation in which an intervenor acts to protect an apparent victim of a tort (here Goliath) who was actually the initial aggressor. Some courts say that the intervenor may act on her reasonable belief that a battery is about to be committed. Under that rule, Lancelot's act would be privileged, since it reasonably appeared to Lancelot that David's attack was a battery. Other courts say that the intervenor steps into the shoes of the apparent victim, in this case, Goliath. Under this approach, Lancelot would only be privileged to use deadly force to defend Goliath if Goliath were privileged to do so himself. If Goliath had no privilege of self-defense, Lancelot's intervention would be battery.

Even under this second, shoe-stepping rule, Lancelot's act may have been privileged. If Goliath had no chance to retreat, he was privileged to respond to David's pitchfork with deadly force, even though he was the initial aggressor. See Example 4b. If so, then Lancelot shares Goliath's privilege.

6.   The outcome of this case will depend on the approach the jurisdiction takes to defense of a third person. If, under the relevant law, the intervenor is authorized to act on his reasonable perception, Lancelot would be privileged, since David appeared to be the aggressor. If the law of the jurisdiction only gives Lancelot a privilege to defend Goliath if Goliath himself would have a privilege of self-defense (the "shoe-stepping" approach), Lancelot would not be privileged and would be liable for battery.

---

9. Since no privilege arises under the Second Restatement to use deadly force if retreat is feasible, the Restatement position appears to echo the criminal cases. If this is true, Goliath would only be liable if he could have retreated safely before invoking the two-by-four.

Judge Fudd on the Cutting Edge of the Law

7. Judge Fudd's instruction is incorrect for several related reasons that would seriously prejudice Zilla's case. First, the instruction suggests she must have *actually* been attacked with deadly force in order to have a privilege to use deadly force in self-defense. This is not always true: Zilla would have the right to use deadly force if she *reasonably believed* that she was threatened with deadly force. See Restatement (Second) of Torts, §65 (premising right to use deadly force on reasonable belief that assailant threatens deadly force).

Second, Judge Fudd's instruction makes her privilege turn on whether the force she used was *actually* necessary to repel Kong's attack. Because Kong's knife was harmless, Zilla did not actually have to use deadly force to avoid it. However, she may have *reasonably believed* that such force was necessary for her self-defense, if she thought the knife was real. Because an assault victim has no time to verify her perceptions of the force with which she is threatened, the law allows her to act on her reasonable belief that deadly force is necessary. Because Judge Fudd's instruction does not allow the jury to consider Zilla's state of mind in determining whether she was privileged, it is improper.

Such distinctions may appear hypertechnical, but many verdicts in tort cases are reversed for such subtle mistakes in instructing the jury. The be-Fuddled instructions throughout this book should give you useful practice in reading jury instructions critically. If you acquire this skill, sometime down the road you will be glad that you did.

Macho Consent

8. This example is reminiscent of the conditional threat example (Example 8) in Chapter 2. As in that example, the aggressor here threatens to hit the victim if she does not comply with a condition. The condition ("hightail it out of here") is one that the aggressor has no right to impose. In Chapter 2 we concluded that such threats are assaults. By the same logic, the aggressor commits a battery if she follows through on the threat.

Obviously, this analysis of conditional threats compels the conclusion that Stein does not consent to Franken's punch by standing his ground. Franken has no right to force Stein to choose between his freedom of movement and a punch in the eye. His refusal to comply with this impermissible condition does not constitute consent to the ensuing blow, which is an obvious battery. Nor would the reasonable person construe his act of standing his ground as a manifestation of consent. The more logical inference is that Stein simply refuses to be bullied.

9. Forgive me for belaboring once again the distinction between *contacts* and *consequences*. Here, Hulk, for his own macho reasons, has invited his friends to try to knock him over. He is willing that they should try, though he does not expect any of them to succeed. He has consented to

the exact contact that Brower has imposed, though he did not anticipate the harmful consequence (the separated shoulder) of the contact. Since he consented to the contact, it is not tortious, and Brower is not liable despite the ensuing injury.

What You Don't Know ...

10. The Introduction explains that sometimes the mistaken understanding of a consenting party will render her consent ineffective, because she acts without understanding the true nature of the contact she is accepting. For example, if Alvord knew that he had a sexually transmittable disease, and had sexual relations without telling Rodriguez, her acceptance of the contact would be based on a misunderstanding facilitated by his failure to reveal a fact central to her decision. His act would smack of misrepresentation by omission, and vitiate the "meeting of the minds" upon which true consent is based.

Where Alvord does *not* know about his condition, however, there is no disparity in the understanding of the parties at the time of consent, and no misrepresentation by Alvord. True, Rodriguez didn't know all the facts when she consented to the contact, but neither did Alvord. They both consented to a contact that entailed some risks, as most do. The court would very likely find Rodriguez's consent effective and deny recovery on the battery claim.

What You Do Know ...

11. Generally, health professionals have a privilege to render emergency treatment to unconscious patients who cannot consent, if the reasonable patient in the same circumstances would accept the treatment. In effect, the law presumes that the actual patient would accept what the reasonable patient would. However, this presumption would clearly be overcome if Carella sat up and said "Hey, no transfusions." The autonomy principle underlying battery law allows each person to make his own choices about his bodily integrity, including choices that differ from majoritarian choices or those generally viewed as reasonable. Battery law supports that autonomy, by requiring consent to physical invasions, even therapeutic invasions.

In this case, Carella's bracelet informs Dr. Langone of Carella's choice just as clearly as she could in person. Dr. Langone must honor this choice, despite her disagreement with Carella's judgment, or even her knowledge that it may prove fatal to Carella. If she fails to honor it, she can be held liable for battery.

If you were Dr. Langone, would you give the transfusions anyway? Perhaps you would choose to save Carella's life even if you might get sued. After all, how much would a jury award Carella under these circumstances? Probably not much. But it is clear that ignoring Carella's clear choice disregards a solemn, considered value choice by the patient about contacts with her person. If Dr. Langone called hospital counsel before giving the transfusions, counsel would doubtless advise her that doing so could lead to liability for battery.

12. Lew's argument in this case is not that he never consented to the surgery, but that he *would not have* consented to it if he had understood the full risks it entailed. Arguably, such cases could be thought of as intentional tort claims, on the theory that Lew's consent without all the facts was not true consent, and that Dr. Langone's failure to adequately inform him of those risks constitutes a kind of deceit by omission. But courts today generally treat such "lack of informed consent" claims as negligence cases. The thinking is that the patient did consent to the operation, so performing it is not battery. But the failure to explain to the patient all of the material risks of a medical procedure, while it does not void the consent, is a breach of the surgeon's duty of care to fully inform the patient, so that he can make a meaningful choice about his treatment. Thus, the court will likely dismiss the battery claim, but allow Lew to replead a negligence claim against Dr. Langone for breach of the duty to provide adequate information about the operation so that Lew could give "informed consent" to it.

Shooting from the Hip

13a. This argument appears to be based on the premise that Langone need not ask for Seaman's consent where it is obvious that the reasonable person would consent. The argument is unimpressive. The privilege of consent is based on the *individual patient's* acceptance of the contact, not on the fact that most patients would agree to it. As the previous example illustrates, the value our society places on personal autonomy supports the individual's right to make a choice that is different from that of the hypothetical reasonable person.

Langone's argument would change the question from whether the patient *did* consent to whether the reasonable person under the circumstances *would* consent. If that were the standard, the surgeon would not have to seek the patient's consent at all, but only to assess what the hypothetical reasonable person would do in similar circumstances.

b. This argument appears to invoke the privilege discussed in the introduction, to extend a surgery already in progress if the conditions encountered require it, without sewing up the patient to obtain consent. As the introduction indicates, courts have established a limited privilege to extend surgery within the area of the initial incision to remedy *unanticipated* problems revealed by the surgery. Langone's counsel will doubtless make much of the following language from one of the leading cases, *Kennedy v. Parrott*, 90 S.E.2d 754, 759 (N.C. 1956):

> In major internal operations, both the patient and the surgeon know that the exact condition of the patient cannot be finally and definitely

diagnosed until after the patient is completely anesthetized and the incision has been made. In such case the consent — in the absence of proof to the contrary — will be construed as general in nature and the surgeon may extend the operation to remedy any abnormal or diseased condition in the area of the original incision whenever he, in the exercise of his sound professional judgment, determines that correct surgical procedure dictates and requires such an extension. . . .

Despite this strong language, Langone's argument may well fail. This is not a situation in which an unexpected condition first becomes apparent during surgery. The example indicates that bone deterioration requiring a full replacement is common in patients with Seaman's problem. Thus, it would be practical for Langone to discuss this foreseeable scenario in advance with the patient and obtain consent to the replacement if required. Through this procedure, the demands of good health care and the patient's autonomy can both be served. By failing to discuss this scenario with Seaman, Langone has foreclosed Seaman's opportunity to choose for himself.

c.   Langone is certainly right that this consent form is broad enough to encompass extension to a full hip replacement. The question, of course, is whether a court will enforce a consent clause this broad. Certainly, one can hypothesize circumstances under which the court would *not* enforce the clause. Suppose, for example, that Langone waltzed into Seaman's room an hour before the surgery was scheduled, described the surgery as routine, and indicated that Seaman just had to "complete a few forms" before they could proceed. On these facts, most courts would conclude that Seaman's signature does not manifest a meaningful consent to this unexplained extension of surgery. The privilege of consent is based on the patient's "willingness in fact" (Restatement (Second) of Torts §892(1)) that the touching occur; cursory presentation of a form on a clipboard, in the coercive context of imminent surgery, would not fill the bill.

On the other hand, the circumstances might indicate that Seaman signed this form with a full understanding that a full replacement might be done. If Langone spent an hour with him explaining the details, possible extensions, and complications of the procedure, a court would likely conclude that his signature on the form reflected a meaningful consent to the more extensive surgery, in light of the parties' prior discussions. But it is certainly unwarranted to conclude that the consent form avoids liability simply because it is broad enough on its face to encompass what Langone actually did. See B. Furrow, S. Johnson, T. Jost, R. Schwartz, Liability and Quality Issues in Health Care 426 (1997) (summarizing study that concludes that consent forms "played an insignificant role" in the medical decision making process, and were generally treated as a mere ritual confirming a decision already made).

This case should be distinguished from "informed consent" cases. Here, the issue is whether Seaman consented to a hip replacement at all.

By contrast, in informed consent cases the patient admits that she consented to the procedure performed, but claims that the doctor did not provide her with sufficient information about the risks and consequences to make a proper judgment about whether to consent. Informed consent cases are generally viewed as negligence cases — based on failure to live up to the professional standard of care in disclosing risks — while cases in which the patient claims that the procedure was not authorized at all are still analyzed under battery law and the consent privilege.

You're the Doc

14a.   In this example the patient effectively delegates the decision making to his doctor, on the ground that the doctor knows best how to treat his condition, and should use her best judgment in doing so. There is no bar to a patient making this choice, if it is deliberately made. Presumably, the autonomy to make decisions about one's body also includes the right to allow someone else to do it for you: That principle is frequently honored in various substituted consent situations, in which a patient designates a family member to make health-care decisions for him if he is incapacitated. Naturally, a court would look for signs of coercion or misunderstanding in reviewing a situation such as the one in the example, but absent such problems Seaman's delegation of the decision is probably effective.

b.   This case may be different. While Seaman has apparently delegated to Langone the authority to make some decisions concerning his treatment, presumably there is a limit to her authority. Surely Langone could not give him a new nose or install a pacemaker while Seaman is anesthetized.

The scope of Seaman's consent will be construed in the context of the discussions between him and Langone, and the purpose of his treatment. The jury will have to decide, as a matter of fact, whether Langone would reasonably have understood Seaman's consent to extend beyond repair of the hip to performance of a different procedure in the same general surgical field. A major consideration will presumably be whether the artery problem was contributing to Seaman's symptoms. If it was, the inference is stronger that Seaman meant to authorize Langone to deal with it as well as the anticipated bone problem. If it was not, Dr. Langone's act might be held an unrelated procedure which she could not reasonably conclude that Seaman had authorized.

Damned If You Do ...

15. In the typical "emergency privilege" case, the physician is privileged to provide emergency treatment if the patient is unable to consent, if good medical practice calls for immediate treatment, and if the reasonable person would consent to it. If Willis's wife had not been available, Langone would have been privileged to proceed with the operation under

this emergency privilege. But Willis's wife *was* available and refused to consent. What should Langone do?

Many sources suggest that the consent of a relative to medical treatment of an incompetent patient is effective and is widely relied upon in medical practice. See, e.g., *Shine v. Vega*, 429 Mass. 456, 466 (1999); Curran, Hall & Kaye, Health Care Law, Forensic Science, and Public Policy 1020 (4th ed. 1990) (noting "universal" use of spouse as substitute decision maker in such cases). However, in the usual case, the spouse *gives* consent, so there is no conflict between what the physician wishes to do and the spouse's choice. Consequently, the decision is not often challenged. If it were, it is not entirely clear that spousal consent would protect the defendant from liability. See *Gravis v. Physicians and Surgeons Hosp. of Alice*, 427 S.W.2d 310 (Tex. 1968) (suggesting that husband does not have automatic authority to consent for wife).

Unlike the usual case, Dr. Langone and Mrs. Willis are at odds on whether to operate. If we assume that a spouse has the authority to consent to treatment of her incompetent husband, then it seems that she should also have the authority to *refuse* to consent: It hardly seems logical that the relative's decision should be honored only when she agrees with the doctor. Consequently, it appears that Langone would have to desist, since she would commit a battery if she operated without permission. This would doubtless be very difficult for the surgeon to accept, if she views immediate surgery as necessary. It is one thing for the patient himself to make treatment decisions that the physician deems unwise, but it is another to see the patient's health jeopardized by the decision of a relative with no medical expertise (and even, perhaps, with motives unrelated to the patient's health).

Langone's lawyers very likely would advise her on these facts that she should not go forward in face of Willis's refusal, but should go to court to seek a judicial determination of her right to proceed. While the courts usually honor a patient's right to refuse treatment, they are a good deal more likely to put aside the decision of a family member, which may not accurately reflect the patient's own views. (Here, for example, the fact that surgery gives Mrs. Willis "the creeps" should not determine whether surgery should be performed on Mr. Willis.)

A number of states have enacted statutes that expressly authorize relatives to consent for an incompetent patient. See, e.g., Ark. Stat. §20-9-602; Miss. Code Ann. §41-41-3; Idaho Code §39-4303. Some of these statutes give health providers immunity if they follow the relative's decision. See, e.g., Ariz. Rev. Stat. tit. 36, §36-3231. Most do not address the situation in which the relative unreasonably refuses to consent. But see the Arkansas statute, which provides that the court may consent to treatment if a person authorized to consent for another has refused. See §20-9-604(a)(1). Under a provision such as this the court could supersede Mrs. Willis's decision not to allow surgery. The same result would likely be reached on common law principles in a state that had no statute on point.

PART TWO

The Concept of Negligence

4

That Odious Character: The Reasonable Person

Introduction

Surely the most common basis for tort liability is negligent conduct. This chapter is about the meaning of negligence.

Let's begin by clarifying our terminology. Courts often speak of a "claim for negligence." In this sense, negligence is a tort with four elements: (1) a duty of reasonable care, (2) breach of that duty, (3) causation, and (4) resulting damages. A plaintiff must prove all four of these elements to "recover on a claim for negligence." But courts also use the term "negligence" in a related but more limited sense, to refer to the failure to live up to the standard of due care. In this sense, "negligence" refers to the *second element* of a claim for negligence, breach of the standard of due care. To say that the defendant "was negligent" is to say that he failed to exercise reasonable care under the circumstances.

Since courts do not always distinguish these two meanings of "negligence," students often get confused between the tort of negligence and the concept of negligence as a breach of the standard of due care. A defendant may be negligent without necessarily being "liable for negligence" (if, for example, the plaintiff does not suffer damages from the defendant's failure to exercise due care). It is important to distinguish the *tort* of negligence from the second *element* of that tort. This chapter is about the latter meaning, the failure to live up to the standard of reasonable care.

The Standard of Reasonable Care

The basic premise of negligence law is that we generally owe our fellow citizens a duty to exercise reasonable care in the conduct of our own affairs. This duty does not require that we avoid all injury to others, but only that we avoid injuring others by carelessness. That duty is breached (element #2 of a negligence claim) by failing to exercise reasonable care.

> Negligence is the omission to do something which a reasonable man, [sic] guided upon those considerations which ordinarily regulate the conduct of human affairs, would do, or doing something which a prudent and reasonable man [sic] would not do.

Blyth v. Proprietors of the Birmingham Waterworks, 156 Eng. Rep. 1047, 1049 (1856). See also Restatement (Second) of Torts §283 (to avoid being negligent, actor must act as "a reasonable man [sic] under like circumstances.") While the *Birmingham Waterworks* case goes back a century and a half, you could go into courtrooms across the United States and hear juries in negligence cases instructed in very similar terms today—though the reference would be to the gender-neutral "reasonable person."

Who is this "excellent but odious character,"[1] the Reasonable Person? He is a model of propriety and common sense, a person of sound judgment who acts at all times with "ordinary prudence, ... reasonable prudence, or some other blend of reason and caution." Prosser & Keeton §32, at 174.

> He is an ideal, a standard, the embodiment of all those qualities which we demand of the good citizen ... He is one who invariably looks where he is going, and is careful to examine the immediate foreground before he executes a leap or bound; who neither stargazes nor is lost in meditation when approaching trapdoors or the margin of a dock; ... who never mounts a moving omnibus and does not alight from any car while the train is in motion, ... and will inform himself of the history and habits of a dog before administering a caress; ... who never drives his ball till those in front of him have definitely vacated the putting-green; ... who uses nothing except in moderation, and even while he flogs his child is meditating only on the golden mean.[2]

Odious indeed, the Reasonable Person is a fiction, an impossible creature who always exercises proper self-restraint and weighs appropriately not

---

1. A. P. Herbert, Misleading Cases in the Common Law 12 (7th ed. 1932).
2. Herbert, supra n.1, at 9-11.

only his own interests, but those of others as well in regulating his affairs.

How the Reasonable Person Thinks

The reasonable person standard seems self-evident, even tautological: Of course we should all act reasonably to avoid injury to others. But the standard is also desperately vague. It hardly projects the majesty of The Law to admit that every year hundreds of millions of dollars in damages turn on such a homespun, common sense idea of fault. Yet, courts obviously cannot prescribe more specific rules in advance as to what is reasonable in every situation: The variety of human experience is much too great to allow such a catalogue of proper behavior. It is possible, however, to describe in a general way the factors that the reasonable person considers before acting, and how he weighs those factors.

First, in deciding whether a course of conduct is appropriate, the reasonable person considers the *foreseeable risks of injury* that that conduct will impose on the community. This does not suggest that Mr. Reasonable avoids all conduct that creates risks to others: We all accept the fact that people must act, and that most activities impose some risk on the community. But the reasonable person considers those risks in light of the *utility* of the conduct. Restatement (Second) of Torts §291. For example, lighting a fire in dry woods near a town imposes a risk that the fire will spread. It may be reasonable to impose that risk to prevent a brush fire from spreading, but not to toast marshmallows. Similarly, rapid release of a large volume of water from behind a dam imposes a risk of downstream property damage or personal injury. That risk might be reasonable to prevent a collapse of the dam, but not to lower the water level to facilitate dredging.

The reasonable person also considers the *extent* of the risks posed by her conduct. Restatement (Second) of Torts §293. Conduct may be reasonable if it threatens minor property damage, but unreasonable if it creates a risk of serious personal injury. The dam release, for example, might be appropriate if it risks minor flooding of grazing land but not if it threatens to drown campers down river. Placing a gas tank in a particular place on a truck might be reasonable if it poses a risk of stalling the engine, but unreasonable if it could cause the tank to explode in a collision. And, since a risk is greater if it exposes many to a risk of injury than if it endangers a few, our odious paragon considers that too.

The reasonable person also considers the *likelihood* of a risk actually causing harm. It often makes sense to do a useful thing that imposes low-probability risks, but may not if the risk is greater. Placing the gas tank in a particular place may be reasonable if it risks a one-in-a-million explosion, but not if one in a thousand will blow up. Distributing a vaccine may be a reasonable choice if an adverse reaction will happen to one patient in ten thousand, but not if one in ten will suffer it. Restatement (Second) of Torts §293(d).

Our Model of Propriety also considers whether *alternatives* to her proposed conduct would achieve the same purpose with lesser (or greater) risk. Restatement (Second) of Torts §292(c). If a live vaccine poses a risk of serious injury to one patient in ten thousand, but a dead vaccine achieves the same protection with injury to only one in a million, it may be unreasonable to use the live vaccine. On the other hand, if there is no alternative to the live vaccine, the one in-ten-thousand risk may be reasonable, given the benefit to the other nine thousand nine hundred and ninety-nine users.

It must also be admitted that this obnoxious paragon of ours is a little bit cold-blooded: He also considers the *costs* of various courses of action in determining what is reasonable. He does not take every precaution which might reduce the risk of injury, but only those which are "worth it" in the sense that the injuries avoided outweigh the cost of the extra precaution. If it would cost fifteen dollars to add a kill switch to a fifty dollar skill saw, and the switch would prevent a hand injury to one in 20,000 users but would also substantially impede the operation of the saw, it would likely be reasonable to leave off the switch. Adding the switch would increase the costs of the machine by $300,000 for each injury avoided ($15/saw × 20,000 saws) and reduce its efficiency for all users. The "trade-off" to avoid one hand injury doesn't seem worth it.

Similarly, if a live vaccine that risks side effects to one in 10,000 costs $1 per dose, while a dead vaccine that will only injure one patient in 100,000 costs $25, the drug manufacturer may be "reasonable" to market the live form, even though it will mean, statistically speaking, nine more injured kids per 100,000 users. This economic dimension to reasonableness analysis is hard to swallow—one of those kids might be yours—but there is little question that it exists. Otherwise we would all drive tanks instead of vulnerable automobiles.

The "Hand Formula"

While it is useful to identify the factors the reasonable person considers in contemplating action, it is more difficult to specify exactly how he weighs those factors, or what conclusion is reasonable on a given set of facts. One estimable jurist, Judge Learned Hand, endeavored to do so in the famous case of *United States v. Carroll Towing Co.*, 159 F.2d 169 (2d Cir. 1947). Judge Hand postulated that the defendant's duty in controlling its barge in that case was

> a function of three variables: (1) The probability that [the barge] will break away; (2) the gravity of the resulting injury, if she does;

(3) the burden of adequate precautions. Possibly it serves to bring this notion into relief to state it in algebraic terms: if the probability be called P; the injury L; and the burden B; liability depends upon whether B is less than L multiplied by P; i.e., whether B is less than PL.

Id. at 173. This celebrated "Hand formula," B < PL, is meant to suggest not only the factors the Reasonable Person considers, but how he balances those factors in reaching a judgment. The reasonable person, Hand postulates, takes a precaution against injury if the burden of doing so is less than the loss if the injury occurs multiplied by the probability that the injury will occur. To illustrate, suppose that a safety catch costs $20 per machine, that one in 100 of the machines will cause an injury without the catch, and that the likely damages from the injury if it happens are $1,000. The Hand formula suggests that the reasonable person will not attach the safety catch. It will cost $2,000 to put the guard on 100 machines, but will only prevent $1,000 in injury costs. On the other hand, if the guard cost $5 per machine, the formula would compel the conclusion that the reasonable person would add it.

The Hand formula has been applauded particularly by economic theorists, who see negligence law as a means of regulating social conduct to promote efficiency. See, e.g., R. Posner, A Theory of Negligence, 1 J. Legal Stud. 29, 32-34 (1972). But it is also very easy to criticize. What, for example, does "L" really mean in the formula? A single risk, such as a bald tire on the defendant's car, could cause a wide variety of losses, from a broken axle to a nine car collision with multiple fatalities. How is the reasonable person to apply the formula where such a range of "L"s is possible? And, of course, *valuing* even a known loss is a very speculative business. How is the defendant, in deciding whether to drive on the bald tire, to assign a value to a serious personal injury if he does not know the age, employment, susceptibility to pain, family circumstances or other characteristics of his future victim? Similarly, assigning probabilities to particular types of risks is a highly speculative business. The defendant may have a vague sense that bald tires are a bad idea, but that is a far cry from assigning a meaningful quantitative value to "P" in the Hand formula.

The formula, standing alone, also fails to consider other possibilities, such as adopting an entirely different method of achieving a given result. It may be prohibitively expensive to design an alarm system which would eliminate a small risk of a release of a poisonous gas used in a certain manufacturing process. If so, the Hand formula suggests that it is reasonable to conduct the operation without such a system. But the reasonable person would also consider other alternatives: It may be possible to change the process to eliminate the gas entirely, and ordinary prudence may dictate that course if the danger cannot otherwise be adequately reduced. In other cases where precautions to eliminate a risk are too expensive, the only reasonable choice may be to *forgo the conduct entirely*, a possibility not accounted for in Hand's calculation.[3]

Such criticisms of the Hand formula are valid, but they may miss the point. Judge Hand never viewed his formula as a mechanical solution to the complex human problem of reasonableness. He made no attempt to quantify the elements of the formula in *Carroll Towing*, and suggested elsewhere that it is in fact impossible to do so. *Moisan v. Loftus*, 178 F.2d 148, 149 (2d Cir. 1949). But Judge Hand's formula does highlight basic factors that the reasonable person considers in making choices about risk-creating conduct. In an intuitive, impressionistic way, reasonable people do consider, in deciding upon a course of conduct, the extent of the risks posed by that conduct, the type of injury likely to result from those risks, the utility of the conduct, and the cost of avoiding the risk. Juries in negligence cases will not be instructed in strict Hand formula terms ("the reasonable person takes precautions against risk if the burden of doing so is less than the probability of an injury multiplied times the loss that will be suffered if the risk materializes"). But a jury might well be instructed that, in considering whether the defendant acted reasonably, they should consider the likelihood of an accident happening, the burden of taking precautions to prevent an accident, the utility of the conduct, and the nature and extent of the injuries likely to result if an accident occurs.[4]

Applying the Reasonable Person Standard: The Relevance of Personal "Circumstances"

While the reasonable person is a fictitious construct, people are not. Each individual possesses unique physical and mental characteristics. How can this artificial, uniform standard of good judgment account for our individuality — or should it?

To some extent, the negligence standard does account for the personal characteristics of the actor. One's duty is to act as a "reasonable person

---

3. Other more global criticisms have been leveled at the formula as well. For example, the formula appears devoid of any moral content, suggesting that tort law is a purely economic calculation rather than a system to compensate victims, to punish unacceptable conduct, or to deter injurers. Beyond that, of course, lies the plain fact that people simply don't think in formulas, and won't be made to by judges.

4. The draft Third Restatement of Torts expressly endorses Hand formula analysis in determining negligence: "Primary factors to consider in ascertaining whether the person's conduct lacks reasonable care are the foreseeable likelihood that it will result in harm, the foreseeable severity of the harm that may ensue, and the burden that would be borne by the person and others if the person takes precautions that eliminate or reduce the possibility of harm." Restatement (Third) of Torts: Liability for Physical Harm (Basic Principles) (Tentative Draft No. 1, 2001) §3.

under the circumstances." Some individual characteristics of the actor are considered part of "the circumstances" in determining reasonableness. For example, it is generally held that a person with a physical disability is required to act as a reasonable person *with that disability* would act. Thus, it is not negligent for Lear, a blind person, to walk the streets, though he will occasionally bump into others. The blind have to live in the same world as the rest of us, and it is reasonable for them to impose the risk of occasional sidewalk collisions (and more serious motor vehicle accidents as well) in order to do so. It might be a closer case if Lear ventured forth without a cane, but the important point is that his conduct will be judged against that of other actors in the same "circumstances," not against the population at large.

While allowance is made for physical disabilities, no allowance is made for the "circumstance" that a person lacks good judgment, is hasty, awkward, or perennially oafish. This was well settled in the torts classic, *Vaughan v. Menlove,* 132 Eng. Rep. 490 (1837), in which poor Menlove argued that he had exercised his judgment to the best of his ability, and should not be held liable just because his "best" wasn't very good. If Lear is not held to the standard of a sighted person, why should Menlove be held to the standard of a person with good judgment? Isn't his obtuseness a "circumstance" that the law should take into account as well?

In the courts of heaven, Menlove's argument will doubtless weigh heavily, but as a legal standard his suggested test (whether he "had acted honestly and bona fide to the best of his own judgment" (id. at 493)) would obviously be a disaster. Had Menlove's test been adopted, we would not have one standard of care for negligence, but a million. We would not try the defendant's *conduct* in negligence actions, but his character and intelligence. The perennially careless would enjoy the right to endanger their neighbors with impunity. By sticking with the "reasonable person under the circumstances" test, the courts have provided instead an objective test that allows impartial application, avoids subjective judgments about individual character, and allows some measure of prediction about the consequences of conduct.

This same refusal to consider individual personality is illustrated in the treatment of the mentally ill. The traditional rule, still generally accepted, is that the mentally ill are held to the same standard as everyone else, despite the "circumstance" of their illness:

> Unless the actor is a child, his insanity or other mental deficiency does not relieve the actor from liability for conduct which does not conform to the standard of a reasonable man [sic] under like circumstances.

Restatement (Second) of Torts §283B. This is a harsh, perhaps indefensible rule. It holds a mentally ill adult to a standard that any psychology student will tell you he cannot meet. But it is at least consistent with

Menlove, in the sense that it is based on a refusal to make the standard a subjective one, to account for individual personality in administering the negligence system. These rules send the same message to those who, due to mental illness or weak intelligence, may have trouble meeting the objective standard: "Since the law will not hold you to a lesser standard, you will have to curtail your activity or exercise particular self-restraint (or be restrained by others) in order to avoid liability."

This treatment of the mentally ill and those of weak judgment confirms that the reasonable person standard is a legal judgment, not a moral condemnation. Morally, we could hardly fault a Menlove for a judgment which was the best he could do, or a mentally ill defendant for conduct that was compelled by delusion or neurosis. But for legal purposes, we need a standard that defines "fault" in some predictable, universal way. The "reasonable-person-under-like-circumstances" test provides a neutral instrument for deciding disputes, not a value judgment about a person's character.

Given the refusal of negligence law to account for mental deficiencies, the application of the "reasonable person" standard to children may seem inconsistent. Children are *not* held to the adult standard of care, but rather the standard of a "reasonable person of like age, intelligence, and experience under like circumstances." Restatement (Second) of Torts §283A. Unlike the unitary adult standard of care, this child standard clearly *does* make allowance for their mental ability and development. The rationale is that children have to *learn* to be careful, and ought not be exposed to tort liability for conduct that is reasonable in light of their stage of development during the learning process. Adults, however, have had 18 years to become "reasonable"; if they don't make it by that age, they probably never will. They must then suffer the liability consequences or adopt a low-risk lifestyle to avoid causing injury to others.

The child standard does not mean that children cannot be found negligent. There is little doubt that most children of ten have developed the judgment to understand that setting a fire can burn a building, or shooting an arrow at a playmate can put out an eye. In many respects a child of sixteen is as capable of due care as an adult (in crossing streets, stacking lumber, or playing football, perhaps) and will effectively be required to meet the adult standard of care. In addition, a good many cases hold children who engage in certain high risk activities primarily engaged in by adults, such as driving, to the adult standard of care. See D. Dobbs, The Law of Torts 298-302.

Applying the Reasonable Person Standard: The Relevance of External "Circumstances"

While the personal characteristics of the actor are sometimes relevant to determining whether she acted reasonably, the external circumstances in which she acted are always relevant. Decisions about conduct are not made in a classroom or an armchair, they are made in the hurly burly of everyday events, in the factory, on the road, in the operating room. The reasonableness of the defendant's decision is always judged in relation to the unique context or "circumstances" in which she made it.

For example, a defendant may make a decision in the second before an impending accident that he would not have made if he had time to weigh the choices more carefully. In judging that decision, the jury should consider whether the decision was reasonable in light of the "circumstance" that the defendant had to act in a split second. The so-called emergency doctrine means no more than this, that in judging the reasonableness of conduct in an emergency, the "circumstance" that the defendant must act quickly is relevant.

Other circumstances are also relevant. It is relevant that the defendant acted as others customarily do in like circumstances. The fact that conduct is generally engaged in by those in a particular trade or profession at least suggests that such conduct is acceptable. For example, if a roofer is injured in a fall from the roof of a two-story building, it is relevant on the issue of his negligence that roofers ordinarily do not wear safety harnesses in reshingling two story buildings (or that they do). If most roofers consider that an acceptable risk for the extra freedom of movement or time savings involved, it may well be that they are right.

However, while relevant, evidence of custom is not dispositive. In some circumstances, custom and reasonableness may diverge dramatically. To save costs, out of inertia, tradition, or for other reasons, a practice may continue long after thoughtful analysis would compel its rejection, or a new precaution may be ignored despite its obvious benefits. Seat belts offer a good example. Aware of the proven safety advantages of seat belts, our odious paragon doubtless buckles up every time he motors forth, although a substantial segment of the population refuses to follow his pious example.[5] Similarly, if some enterprising roofer develops a new easy-snap, no-hassle safety harness, it may be that the reasonable roofer would use it. Even if it is hard to teach old roofers new tricks, they may be unreasonable to follow the older custom under changed circumstances.

Another "circumstance" that commonly colors the reasonableness of conduct is whether a statute requires a particular course of action under the circumstances. Generally speaking, the reasonable person obeys the

---

5. Ironically, courts and legislatures have gone to considerable lengths to avoid the ineluctable conclusion that it is unreasonable to drive without buckling up. See, e.g., D. Westenberg, Buckle Up or Pay: The Emerging Safety Belt Defense, 20 Suffolk U. L. Rev. 867, 885, 923-943 (1986) (detailing statutes limiting use of evidence of failure to wear seat belt to prove negligence). These attitudes may be changing, however. See Restatement of the Law (Third) Torts: Apportionment of Liability §3 cmt. b (failure to wear seat belt treated as negligence).

law; thus, evidence that the defendant ignored a statutory standard will frequently suffice to establish that he was negligent. This problem, proving negligence based on violation of statute, is explored further in the next chapter.

A further relevant circumstance is whether the actor has acted as an expert in a particular field. If you have a tax accountant prepare your taxes for you, you justifiably expect a higher level of knowledge and judgment than if your bookkeeper or your neighbor does. If you entrust your yacht to a licensed merchant marine captain, she should have a higher level of skill than a beach bum. This does not mean that persons with specialized knowledge are held to a higher *standard* of care than others: Their standard, like that of others, is reasonable care under the circumstances. But the fact that an actor is a professional or assumes the role of an expert in an activity is a "circumstance" that colors the meaning of reasonableness.

The facilities or resources available to the actor are also relevant to the reasonableness analysis. It may be reasonable to perform exploratory surgery in a community where less invasive methods of diagnosis are unavailable, but not in an area were they are. It may be reasonable for a general practitioner to litigate an antitrust case in northern Maine, where antitrust lawyers are hard to come by, but not in Washington, D.C., where one is found on every block.

Beyond these recurring types of relevant circumstances, there are the utterly miscellaneous facts of every individual case to be considered. Facts about weather, about what the parties knew, about how they observed events, about the condition and behavior of animals, vehicles, computers, or machines, about the purposes the actors hoped to achieve by their conduct and alternative ways they might have done so. Reality is infinitely diverse, and each case is unique. It is up to the parties to bring out the circumstances that conditioned the actors' choices, and argue the reasonableness of those choices in light of the flesh and blood context in which they were made. It is exactly this multifariousness of *facts* that requires the *legal standard* of negligence to be so frustratingly general, and makes the practice of negligence law interesting.

The examples below explore the factors involved in the negligence calculus, and the process by which they are weighed.

EXAMPLES

Burdens and Benefits

1.   Costard, owner of a large estate, throws an all day party for a few hundred of his close friends. During the day, some of his guests wander through the woods and come to an abandoned quarry on the property, which has filled up with water. They opt for a dip. Trinculo is injured when he dives

into the quarry and hits his head on a submerged promontory only three feet under the surface. He sues Costard for negligence.

Costard argues that he was not negligent, since, though the injury was foreseeable, filling in the quarry was prohibitively expensive. In Hand formula terms, the burden was too great given the relatively low risk of injury to a wandering entrant on the property, which is normally not open to outsiders. What is the problem with this argument?

2. Suppose that, instead of a quarry, an abandoned well existed on the property, covered with some boards placed there a few years ago and now beginning to rot. Trinculo, wandering the grounds, does not see the well, which is covered with autumn leaves. He falls through, is injured and sues Costard for negligence. Is he likely to prove negligence?

3. The town of Stratford is given a piece of vacant land adjacent to a quiet residential street. Since there is considerable demand for recreational space, and little open space in town, they build a baseball field on the parcel. The edge of the field is thirty feet from the road. In the course of a game, Feste hits a high foul ball, which is caught by the wind and angles into the street. Glendower, driving by, suddenly sees the ball coming, instinctively swerves away from it, and is injured when his car turns into a ditch. He sues the town for negligence in locating the field where it did. Do you think the jury will find the town negligent?

Risks and Reasonableness

4. The Leadville Railroad Company is putting in a new rail line. The line will cross Elm Street, a moderately busy street. The railroad's planners have to decide between a grade crossing (where the street simply crosses the tracks) and an overpass. Based on long experience they can predict that, even with gates and flashing lights, there will be (statistically speaking, anyway) two accidents at a grade crossing on a street like this every ten years. If they build an overpass for the street, the presence of the rail line will not cause any accidents. However, it will cost $12 million for the overpass, compared with $20,000 to install a grade crossing.

The planners opt for the grade crossing. Feste is seriously injured when he fails to see the gate coming down and drives across the track in the path of an approaching train. Is the railroad negligent?

5. One of the early classics of negligence law is *Blyth v. Proprietors of the Birmingham Waterworks*, 156 Eng. Rep. 1047 (1856). In *Blyth*, the plaintiff's basement was flooded by a Birmingham Waterworks water line, which burst during a cold spell. Due to the cold, the frost had "penetrated to a greater depth than any which ordinarily occurs south of the polar regions." Id. at 1049. The court held that the waterworks was not liable

for failing to place their pipes deep enough in the ground to avoid bursting in such a frost.

   a. Suppose that there had been a frost this bad 75 years ago. Would the waterworks be negligent for failing to set the pipes deep enough to withstand such a frost?

   b. Suppose that there had been a frost this bad the year before, but it was the only one in recorded history and was considerably worse than any other recorded year. Would the waterworks be negligent if it continued to place its pipes at the shallower depth?

   c. Let's think about *Blyth* in Hand formula terms. Suppose that placing the pipes one foot down would avoid most, but not all, flooding damages to abutters. It would cost the waterworks an extra $20 million to place the pipes two feet down, but the waterworks engineers can predict with confidence that going the extra foot would avoid $5 million in flooded basement damages to homeowners. What would the reasonable waterworks company do?

   d. Assume that, after doing the calculation just described, the Waterworks lays its pipes at the one foot level. Two years later, a highly unusual, deep frost bursts a pipe and Blyth's basement is flooded. Is the waterworks liable to Blyth?

   e. Assume that tort law holds waterworks companies strictly liable for all damages caused by their operations (that is, they must pay if the system causes damages, whether they conducted their operations with due care or not). Assume further that the waterworks had placed their pipes one foot down, knowing that in highly unusual years some pipes could burst and flood basements. In an unusual frost, a pipe bursts and floods Blyth's basement. Who pays?

   f. Assume that strict liability applies, and that the waterworks knows that it will be strictly liable for all flooding damages from its system. If the numbers given in Example 5c apply, at which level would the waterworks place its pipes?

A True Story: Judge Hand at the Roller Rink

6.   Once upon a time, a Torts professor took his daughter roller blading. Kids of all ages were speeding around the rink, some more in control than others. To his dismay, the prof noticed that there was a wall around the rink, about three feet high, made of concrete blocks. Having always sought to emulate that odious paragon, the Reasonable Person, the prof approached the rink manager. "Why don't you hang some mats on the inside of that wall? One of these kids could lose control, go into the wall head first, and suffer serious injury." The manager coolly replied, "it hasn't happened in 17 years."

The next day, Jane, a nine-year-old daredevil, stumbles and goes into the wall, suffering a serious head injury.

- a. Identify the Hand factors — probability, loss, and burden — in Jane's case.
- b. If you were arguing those factors in front of a jury, which party would you think had the stronger argument?

Fudd and Foreseeability

7.   Falstaff, anxious to get to a pub, passes a driver on a curve, and collides with Bottom coming the other way. Sued for negligence, Falstaff argues that he was not negligent, because the road was little traveled, and it was very unlikely that a car would come around the curve at the time he was in the wrong lane. Judge Fudd instructs the jury as follows:

> If you find that it was more probable than not that a car would be traveling in the opposite lane and collide with the defendant's car, then you should find that the defendant violated the standard of reasonable care in passing as he did.

What is wrong with Fudd's instruction? Can you write a more accurate one?

8.   Barnardine, a roofer, is working on the roof of a townhouse on a narrow city street. Like most roofers, he is not wearing a safety harness, though effective safety harnesses are available. He is startled by a flying pigeon, steps back, and falls from the roof, hitting Elbow, a passing pedestrian.

In Elbow's negligence action, Judge Fudd instructs the jury as follows:

> If you find that it was customary in the trade for roofers to work on roofs such as the one in question without safety harnesses, then you must find that the defendant was not negligent for failing to wear a safety harness at the time of the accident.

- a. Which party will object, and why?
- b. Assuming that the evidence that most roofers don't use safety harnesses is admitted, how should Judge Fudd instruct the jury with regard to that evidence?

A Duty of Much Care

9.   Gobbo, a gas station attendant, has just started a cigarette break when Mariana drives up for gas. He goes out to fill her gas tank with the cigarette in his mouth. Annoyed by a persistent bee, he takes a swipe at it and knocks the cigarette out of his mouth. It falls near the nozzle of the hose, causing an explosion that injures Mariana. She sues him for negligence.

At trial, her counsel asks the judge to instruct the jury that Gobbo, in dispensing the gas, owed her a duty of extreme care, due to the explosive nature of gasoline. Should the judge give the instruction?

An Almost Perfect Record

10. Dr. Quince operates on Peasblossom to remove a bony growth from her lower spine. During surgery, he accidentally contacts her spinal cord, causing partial paralysis of her left leg. Peasblossom sues him for negligence.

At trial Quince seeks to establish that he exercised due care in surgery by offering evidence that he has an almost perfect record as a back surgeon. He has performed over 370 similar surgeries, and only twice come into contact with the spinal cord. His counsel argues that this proves that he is a careful surgeon.

    a. Does this evidence establish that Quince complied with the standard of reasonable care?

    b. How should Judge Fudd instruct the jury as to the standard of care Dr. Quince was required to meet in operating on Peasblossom?

    c. How is the jury to know what due care requires in this case?

Menlove in Reverse

11. Dogberry has been skiing since he was four, has participated in several skiing competitions, and is generally acknowledged to be a first class skier. One morning, he is executing a turn on a moderate ski run, loses control, and slides backwards into Portia, breaking Portia's ankle. She sues him for negligence. At trial, Portia argues that the jury should be instructed that Dogberry must exercise the level of care that would be exercised by "the reasonable expert skier under the same circumstances." Should the instruction be given?

An Elementary Example

12. Falstaff heads home after drinking nine beers at the local pub. Much the worse for wear, he is proceeding along at 28 miles per hour, just below the speed limit, within his lane of traffic, when a pickup truck, going the other way, makes a sharp stop in the opposite lane. Moth, a boy of five, is leaning over the side of the bed of the pickup and is thrown out immediately in front of Falstaff's left front wheel. Falstaff runs him down and is sued for negligence. Leaving aside possible contributory negligence of Moth, would Falstaff be liable?

EXPLANATIONS

Burdens and Benefits

1. Costard has tried to take charge of the negligence analysis here by looking at one possible means of addressing the risk and applying the

Hand formula with only that in mind. The argument might hold water (so to speak) if filling in the quarry were the only possible means of dealing with the risk. But other, less burdensome "B"s exist here. Costard could have fenced the quarry, or posted signs warning of the danger of rocks beneath the surface. The burden of taking these alternative precautions is much lower, and the balance of risk against cost of prevention is a great deal closer on these facts. This is not to say that Trinculo will necessarily win, but that it is important for his counsel not to let Costard frame the negligence issue only in terms of a prohibitively expensive precaution, since other means of prevention are possible.

2.   In this case, Costard's negligence is clear because the burden of prevention is so low. Even filling in the well would likely be an appropriate precaution to eliminate the risk of serious injury from falling in. But much less would prevent most accidents. Building a fence around the well or capping it with a solid concrete cover would eliminate the risk at a clearly acceptable cost. Surely our Paragon of Propriety, the reasonable person, would have done so.

3.   Stray foul balls like Feste's are certainly foreseeable; indeed, even an accident like Glendower's is foreseeable. But foreseeable risk is not the end of the analysis. The reasonable man eschews unreasonable risks, but not all risks. If the risk here was low enough, in relation to the utility of the activity, it is not negligent for the town to impose it.

Here, that may well be the case. The facts suggest that there was little open land and a need for recreational facilities in the town. The town sited the field with a substantial margin beside the road. Certainly, a few fouls will still reach the road, but, since it is a quiet street, most will not hit a car. Those that do will not usually cause much damage. In view of the value of the field to the citizenry, the lack of alternative sites, the relatively low risk of accidents, and the minimal damage likely if an accident does take place, the town's choice is probably reasonable.

One lesson of this example is that plaintiffs do not always win negligence suits just because an accident actually happens. The test is not whether injury was caused, or even whether injury was foreseeable, but whether the defendant's conduct was reasonable in view of *all* the circumstances, including the possibility of injury, the utility of the conduct, the alternatives available, and others.

The example also illustrates that the peculiar circumstances of every individual case really do matter. This case might come out differently if there were more alternatives to the site, if the space outside the foul line were only ten feet, or if the road was a busy high-speed freeway. *Facts* are ever so important to negligence cases, because each fact colors the "circumstances" against which the defendant's conduct must be judged.

Risks and Reasonableness

4.   My students often conclude that a defendant who foresaw a risk of injury but failed to prevent it will be found negligent. However, negligence law does not hold actors to that stringent standard. In this case, the railroad could foresee injuries if it chose a grade crossing, but went ahead anyway, based on the great expense of eliminating the risk and the small number of injuries likely to be caused by the grade-crossing option. This may well be a reasonable decision, even though the railroad knows, on an actuarial basis, that its decision will cause injuries to others. The railroad is not required to eliminate all risk of injury from its operations, only to conduct it with reasonable care. If the planners drew a reasonable balance here between risk and the expense of eliminating it, the decision to use a grade crossing will not be deemed negligent.

Analyzing the railroad's decision in Hand formula terms suggests that the decision may well be reasonable. If we assume that two injuries will be caused in a decade, that the average injury cost will be $500,000,[6] and that the overpass will last 30 years, the injury cost will be $3 million, compared to the $12 million cost of averting the six likely accidents. In social terms, the investment to prevent these accidents may be more than society — through the mechanism of tort law — is willing to require.

It is true that the analysis here involves valuing human suffering against economic cost, but negligence law routinely involves such heartless but practical balancing. For example, the automobile causes immense human suffering, yet we accept — indeed, seem at times to worship — the automobile for the convenience it brings. It is not negligent to drive, even though resulting accidents are a statistical certainty. "There is essential truth ... in the saying that the law of negligence privileges actors to kill and maim people carefully." Harper, James & Gray, §16.9 p. 478.

5a.   Here again, the waterworks is not necessarily negligent for failing to take precautions against this risk. Once in 75 years is a very small risk. A frost like that may not happen for another 75, or another 150. Even if it does happen again, the flooding damages are likely to be small compared to the cost of placing the pipes deeper. So the reasonable operator might very well choose to ignore this very small risk in planning the water system.

b.   Logically, it shouldn't make any difference if the freak frost was 75 years ago or last week. In either case, the waterworks is on notice of this unusual risk, but the question remains whether they must act to avert it. As long as it is a very unusual risk, and as long as it will be very expensive to eliminate it, the decision not to eliminate it is probably reasonable.

---

6. Yes, I know, this figure is bound to be a wild approximation. The actual accidents could be anything from a minor fenderbender with no personal injuries to a school bus full of seriously injured children.

Of course, if the waterworks engineers had reason to believe that last year's frost shows that such frosts were becoming *more* common (if, for example, woolly mammoths have recently appeared in the streets of Birmingham), then the risk would be a more important factor in the equation. But if their best judgment is that the recent deep freeze was indeed off the charts, they may reasonably view it as too remote a risk to warrant expensive precautions.

c.   The Hand formula indicates that the reasonable waterworks company should not place the pipes lower. In economic terms, it is not reasonable to invest $20 million to avoid $5 million in economic losses. So, if we use Hand's formula as the measure of reasonableness, the waterworks company is not negligent for laying the pipes at the one foot level.

d.   Assuming that the decision not to guard against this frost was a reasonable judgment on the part of the waterworks, it is not liable to Blyth. The whole point of a negligence liability rule is that you pay if your conduct was unreasonable, but not if it was reasonable, *even though others suffer harm from your reasonable conduct.*

The irony of this example, of course, is that the waterworks saves $20 million by imposing $5 million in losses on the homeowners! Because negligence law tells the waterworks that it doesn't have to take precautions against this unusual risk, it doesn't. If the risk comes to pass, and floods Blyth's basement, the waterworks isn't liable to compensate Blyth, because it wasn't negligent.

e.   The difference between strict liability and negligence is that under strict liability the actor who causes harm pays the resulting damages, even if he acted with due care. Under this rule, the waterworks would have to pay for Blyth's flooded basement, even if it made a reasonable judgment not to avoid the risk of extreme frosts. Under negligence law, the cost of accidents often falls on an innocent victim — like Blyth in the last example — as long as the person causing the harm acted with due care.

f.   This example asks how the waterworks' conduct would be different if we change the governing tort principle to strict liability. A large organization like a waterworks, which expects to be around for a long time, may very well consider liability rules in planning its operations. Indeed, according to economic theorists, one of the goals of tort law is to design rules that will encourage socially desirable planning *in advance*, not just redistribute a loss after it happens.

In this case, however, the waterworks' conduct wouldn't be different at all. Using the figures in Example 5c, the rational waterworks would still put the pipes at the one foot level. This would save $20 million. If a freak frost occurs, they will have to pay $5 million to homeowners, but that makes more sense than spending $20 million to save $5 million.

So here, the choice of the strict liability rule over a negligence rule does not affect the rational economic actor's level of precautions. However, it *does* make a difference: It requires the actor to internalize the accident costs it causes, even though it reasonably chose not to prevent them. There's something to be said for that result, both in economic terms and in person-in-the-street fairness terms. But strict liability is not the law in most accident cases. Negligence is.

A True Story: Judge Hand at the Roller Rink

6a.   This really is a classic Hand formula situation, isn't it? There is evidence of P — that the probability of an accident was quite low. "It hadn't happened in 17 years." Intuitively, I would have estimated that P was much higher: The combination of youthful exuberance, frequently coupled with inexperience and speed, suggests that accidents would be more common. Frankly, I think the rink was beating the odds.

There is also evidence about L, the likely loss if an accident happens. Of course, L could be low, a skinned knee or bruised shoulder, perhaps. But really serious accidents, possibly leading to profound brain injuries, are also quite predictable — and of course, those are the ones likely to end up in court.

On the other side of the formula, (B), the burden of prevention is also very low: For a few hundred dollars the rink could pad that wall and drastically reduce the risk of a serious injury.

b.   While the jury can't quantify the Hand formula terms, they could, in an impressionistic way, analyze this case intelligently in Hand formula terms. Can't you just hear Jane's lawyer's closing argument to the jury:

> An accident like Jane's was an obvious, very serious risk. They should have seen it coming and known that when it came it was likely to be a head injury, the most serious kind. All they had to do to prevent this from happening to Jane was to put some padding on the walls. The cost would be negligible — a few hundred bucks to avoid a catastrophic injury. The reasonable operator would have done it. They should have done it. If they had, Jane would be OK and we wouldn't be here today. You should send them a clear message to give safety a higher priority in running their business.

I would sure rather argue this case for the plaintiff than the defendant, wouldn't you? It would have taken so little to avoid the harm. Even if the accident was unlikely, the formula clearly suggests that that odious Reasonable Person would have taken precautions.

Fudd and Foreseeability

7.   Fudd has grievously confused the burden of proof with the standard of care. His instruction suggests that Falstaff was negligent only if the accident was "more probable than not." In fact, Falstaff's act may have been negligent even if an accident was very unlikely.

In a civil case, the plaintiff must convince the jury that it is more probable than not that each of the elements of the claim is true. Here, most juries would conclude that it was more probable than not that Falstaff *was negligent*, even though the probability that his conduct would cause an accident was quite low. As the Hand formula suggests, a risk does not have to be *likely* to happen before the reasonable person avoids it. The reasonable person avoids even small risks if the resulting injuries, if they occur, are likely to be great. Since the damages from a head-on collision with an on-coming car are likely to be grievous, the reasonable driver in Falstaff's circumstances would not take that risk, even if it was a very small risk. In Hand formula terms, while P is low, L is very great, and B, the burden of avoiding the risk, is very low: Falstaff need only wait for a clear stretch of road before passing.

Opinions in negligence cases often state that conduct was negligent because injury was the "natural and probable consequence" of the defendant's act. This is promiscuous language; "probable" here really means *foreseeable*. A risk may be foreseeable, and worth avoiding, even though the chances are a great deal less than 50 percent that it will actually come to pass.

The Honorable Fudd would be better advised to instruct the jury along these lines:

> If you find that the defendant passed on the curve without being able to tell whether a car was coming the other way, and that the risk of a collision was sufficiently foreseeable that a reasonable person in the defendant's circumstances would not have acted as he did, then you should find that the defendant breached the standard of due care.

This instruction requires the jury to engage in the same balancing process that the Reasonable Person does, to weigh risks and advantages to determine what Falstaff *should have done* and then to compare that to what he actually did. In effect, the jury first decides what the standard means in the context of the facts (what is "reasonable" under *these* circumstances) and then decides whether the defendant acted that way or not.

8a.   Elbow's counsel will object to Fudd's instruction, because it requires the jury to find that Barnardine was not negligent if he did what is customarily done in the trade. This instruction would elevate custom to a rule of law: Whatever is done in a trade or profession would automatically constitute due care, thus delegating to roofers the decision about what due care means on a roof. For various reasons, real roofers may not behave the way the reasonable roofer would. As Judge Learned Hand so eloquently explained:

> [A] whole calling may have unduly lagged in the adoption of new and available devices. It never may set its own tests, however persuasive be its usages. Courts must in the end say what is required . . . .

The T. J. Hooper v. Northern Barge Corp., 60 F.2d 737, 740 (2d Cir. 1932). Consequently, evidence of custom, what is usually done in a trade or profession, is admissible at trial—the jury is allowed to hear such evidence. However, they still must determine whether what was done, customary or not, comports with the negligence standard itself—ordinary care under the circumstances.

b.   Judge Fudd should tell the jury that they can consider the evidence of what is customary in the roofing trade, but that they are not bound to find Barnardine reasonable if he did what most roofers do:

> There has been evidence introduced at trial about the extent to which roofers wear safety harnesses in working on jobs like the one that gave rise to this claim. If you find that it was customary in the trade to use a safety harness, or not to wear one, you may consider this evidence in determining whether the defendant acted reasonably under the circumstances that gave rise to this claim.

This instruction allows the jury to consider custom evidence, but indicates that the question for the jury is whether the defendant's conduct was reasonable under the general due care test.

If I represented Elbow, I would ask Judge Fudd to give the following further instruction:

> If you find that it was customary for roofers not to wear a safety harness, you may still find that the defendant was negligent for failing to do so. The standard you must apply is reasonable care under the circumstances, not what is generally done in the trade.

This instruction makes the point a little more emphatically from the plaintiff's point of view. However, the judge might refuse to give it. It basically repeats the general instruction above, and is perhaps a bit argumentative as well.

A Duty of Much Care

9.   The judge should refuse the instruction. Negligence law holds defendants to a duty of reasonable care under the circumstances, not different duties depending on the degree of risk of each activity. The jury should be instructed that Gobbo owed Mariana a duty of reasonable care under the circumstances.

However, the circumstances here involve a high risk of injury. Reasonable care in the dispensing of gasoline undoubtedly requires a greater *amount* of care than dispensing ice cream sodas. But this is not a different *standard* of care, it is just what the reasonable person would do under *these* circumstances. It would be perfectly appropriate for the judge to instruct the jury as follows:

> If you find that dispensing of gasoline involves a high risk of explosion, and that the reasonable person in the defendant's circumstances

would have known or should have known of that risk, then the defendant was required to exercise a high level of care commensurate with the high risk involved in that activity.

This instruction may be only subtly different from the one Gobbo's counsel requested, but it is different in an important respect: It states that the reasonable person, acting under the usual due care standard, exercises a higher *amount* of care if the circumstances involve high risk. The requested instruction wrongly suggests that a different *standard* of care applies.

The jury very likely won't catch the subtle distinction between these two instructions: They will just pick up on the fact that the defendant was required to be very careful. But getting the instruction right is still important, especially to Mariana. If the inaccurate one is given, her verdict may be reversed on appeal. The correct instruction will communicate much the same message to the jury, but without the risk of reversal for legal error.

An Almost Perfect Record

10a.   In baseball, .300 is a good batting average, and Quince is batting nearly a thousand. This tends to show that Quince is a careful doctor. If I were choosing a doctor, such information would make me more likely to choose Quince.

But this case is not about whether Quince is a careful doctor: It is about whether he exercised due care *on this occasion*. We are not testing his general virtue or his career accomplishments, we are testing his conduct in one particular operation. It is no answer to Peasblossom that Quince was careful in all those *other* cases; she claims—and is entitled to—the exercise of reasonable care in the performance of *her* operation.

On the other hand, how can we hold Quince to a standard of perfection? We all make mistakes, and Quince makes fewer than most. How can we condemn him if the knife slips once?

Well, we aren't condemning him. A finding of negligence is not a moral judgment passed upon a person, or a finding of incompetence, but a post hoc evaluation of a single event against an abstract standard set up by the law. Since that is all that we are doing, evidence of Quince's batting average, that he usually meets the standard of care in his operations, is beside the point, just as evidence that he had made mistakes on other patients would not establish that he was careless in Peasblossom's operation. See Fed. R. Evid. 404 (evidence of character generally inadmissible "for the purpose of proving action in conformity therewith on a particular occasion").

b.   Judge Fudd should not give the usual reasonable-care-under-the-circumstances instruction on the element of negligence. Here, the defendant was acting as a professional, a lumbar surgeon. By doing so, he has undertaken to apply the skill of a specialist, and will be required to meet that standard in Peasblossom's case. Fudd should instruct the jury along the following lines:

> In performing the operation that gave rise to this claim, the defendant was acting as a specialist in the area of surgery. In determining whether the defendant was negligent, you must decide whether, in performing the operation, he committed some act that the reasonably competent physician engaged in the practice of surgery would not have done, or failed to do some act that the reasonably competent physician engaged in that specialty would have done.[7]

c.   The average jury is made up of a cross-section of individuals with varying educational backgrounds, professions, experiences, and values. Few, if any, will know anything about lower lumbar surgery. They are in no position, based on their general knowledge, to say what reasonable care requires in such operations.

Thus, the parties will have to educate the jury not only about what the defendant did, but also about what the standard of reasonable care required under the circumstances in which he did it. Each side will offer expert evidence (doubtless from lumbar surgeons in Peasblossom's case) as to the proper way to perform surgery of this type. The jury will have to determine, after assessing on the conflicting testimony of these experts, what the reasonable surgeon does in such cases. Having determined that, they will then have to decide whether Quince failed to meet that standard.

In many cases, the jury's life experience suffices to allow them to determine what reasonable care means without the testimony of experts. Jurors can pass judgment on the reasonableness of driving a car, operating simple machinery, controlling children in a classroom, crossing the street, or climbing a ladder, based on their general knowledge. But a great many cases require expert evidence in order for the jury to determine the standard of reasonable care. The proper way to reinforce a bridge, to pilot an ocean vessel, to analyze a financial statement, to ride a race horse, to land a 747, or to treat a drug overdose, to name a few examples, are beyond the common experience of jurors. In such cases, trial must include an expensive "battle of the experts" on what reasonable care demands in those circumstances.

---

7. A good many states still apply a "customary practice" standard of care to doctors. See, e.g., *Purtill v. Hess*, 489 N.E.2d 867, 872 (Ill.1986) (same reasonable care as "reasonably well qualified physician" in same or similar medical community). This standard essentially equates what doctors generally do with acceptable medical practice, contrary to the more limited role that custom usually plays in proving reasonable care. (see Example 8.) However, the general reasonable physician standard reflected in this instruction appears to be gaining ground. See P. Philip, The Role of the Jury in Modern Malpractice Law, 87 Iowa L. Rev. 909, 913-917 (2002).

Menlove in Reverse

11.   Portia can make a pretty good argument for holding Dogberry to the standard of care of an expert: He is a highly experienced skier who is probably capable of better control than your basic weekender on the slopes. Why should he be held to a lesser standard of care than he is able to meet?

There is some force to the argument, but there are also problems with it. First, it tends (like Menlove's argument) to destroy the uniformity of the standard of care. If the argument were accepted, the jury would have to ascertain in each case just how good the defendant was at what he did before deciding what standard to apply to him. Should the jury "grade" the defendant as "expert," "very good," "good," or "average" before determining what standard he must meet? Suppose he is a sub-par skier? Ratcheting the standard of performance *up* for the able seems to imply lowering it for the less able as well, yet *Menlove* certainly indicates that the court will not do that. If the goal is a single objective standard, it appears to make sense to stick to the reasonable-person-under-the-circumstances test for Dogberry, at least when he is engaging in ordinary maneuvers engaged in by skiers with a wide range of abilities.

It would be different if Dogberry were *acting as an expert* at the time of the injury. For example, if Dogberry were a member of the ski patrol in the course of a rescue, he would be acting as an expert and should be held to that standard. But in this example Dogberry is just skiing, like everyone else on the slopes, and should be held to the same standard of care as the reasonable skier under the circumstances. Similarly, a trucker driving his car to the movies may be an "expert" driver, but will be held to the general reasonable person standard for ordinary driving. See *Fredericks v. Castora*, 360 A.2d 696, 698 (Pa. Super. 1976) ("to vary the standard according to the driver's experience would render the application of any reasonably uniform standard impossible").

The result here is not entirely clear, however. Some authorities suggest that Dogberry should be held to the standard of an expert in this example. See Restatement (Third) of Torts Liability for Physical Harm (Basic Principles) §12; see also Harper, James & Gray, §16.6, at 415-421. As a practical matter, of course, if the evidence shows that Dogberry is highly experienced, the jury is likely to demand more of him anyway, whether or not they are instructed to do so.

An Elementary Example

12.   This chapter began by drawing the distinction between negligent conduct and liability on a negligence claim. We end with the same distinction. Falstaff was clearly negligent here in the sense that he breached the standard of due care by driving drunk. He failed to act as a reasonable

person under the circumstances would. That satisfies Element #2 of the cause of action for negligence.

But the *tort* of negligence has three other elements, and one of those is causation. Here, the facts suggest that Falstaff was not negligent in the way he handled the car, even though he was drunk. He was in his lane, driving below the speed limit. Because Moth fell right in front of the car, there was nothing he could have done to avoid hitting him; even if he had been sober, the accident would have happened the same way. Liability for negligence turns not just on *being* negligent, but upon negligent conduct *causing* injury.

But Falstaff's negligence did cause the harm, didn't it? He was negligent to be on the road *at all* while drunk, and his driving caused the accident. This argument proves too much. On this theory, Falstaff would be liable to Moth if he had bald tires, worn windshield wipers, or a loud muffler, and had the same accident, even though none of these conditions contributed in any way to the injury.

In order for a negligent act to be considered a cause of the plaintiff's injury, the risk that makes the conduct negligent must lead to the harm. Driving while drunk is negligent because it impairs the ability to control the car: It is only when this impairment contributes to the occurrence of the accident that the negligence becomes a "cause" of resulting harm. Falstaff would be liable if Moth fell far enough in front of the car that an unimpaired driver could have braked in time, and Falstaff failed to brake because of his inebriation. On those facts his negligence would have affected the outcome, and the causation requirement — Element #3 — would be established. See generally Chapter 7 on cause in fact.

5

Borrowing Standards of Care: Violation of Statute as Negligence

Introduction

As the previous chapter indicates, the plaintiff in a negligence case must prove four elements, duty, breach, causation, and damages, in order to recover in a negligence case. To establish the second element, breach of the duty of care, or negligence, the plaintiff must show that the defendant failed to act with reasonable care, to behave as the ordinary prudent person would under like circumstances.

This reasonable person standard has been criticized as too vague to provide any meaningful guidance to the jury in evaluating the defendant's conduct. Juries are supposed to find facts, not to establish the rules of law that determine whether the defendant is liable. Arguably, the negligence standard is so broad that it licenses the jury to find as they please, without constraining them by meaningful legal rules.

On the other hand, how can the rule be any more specific? The variety of human experience, the range of circumstances that may cause injury, is so great that it would be impossible for courts to formulate specific rules in advance to govern liability for all careless conduct. Since it is impossible to "particularize" the negligence standard, the jury is usually instructed under the reasonable person formula. The jurors are left to use their common sense, experience, and, where appropriate, expert testimony, to pass judgment on the defendant's conduct under this very general standard.

While courts cannot elaborate specific negligence rules to define how parties should behave in all circumstances, *legislatures* routinely enact statutes establishing standards of care for common situations. This chapter considers the role that such statutes play in proving the second element of a claim for negligence, that a party breached the standard of care or "was negligent."

Legislative Standards of Conduct

Legislatures very commonly enact statutes that establish standards of care for private conduct. Many such statutes govern that ubiquitous, highly practical, but potentially lethal instrumentality, the automobile. Here are some hypothetical, but typical, examples:

> No person shall make a turn onto or off of a public way without signaling his or her intention to turn, either by hand or by an electrical signal device. West Dakota Ann. Laws Title V, §12.

> No person shall drive a motor vehicle without a muffler or other suitable device to control excessive noise. West Dakota Ann. Laws. Title V, §212.

> No person shall drive an unlighted vehicle upon any public highway during the period from one-half hour after sunset until one-half hour before sunrise. West Dakota Ann. Laws Title V, §94A.

> The driver of a vehicle on any public highway, traveling in any direction, shall stop before reaching any bus marked "school bus" and exhibiting flashing red lights. Said driver shall not proceed until the bus resumes motion or the lights are no longer flashing. West Dakota Ann. Laws Title V, §74.

Many statutes establish standards of care in other areas as well:

> No person shall enter upon or be employed upon the premises of an active construction site without wearing a construction helmet. West Dakota Ann. Laws Title IX, §111.

> No person shall leave a refrigerator, freezer, or similar appliance in any unsecured area accessible to children, whether for disposal or otherwise, without detaching the door from said appliance. West Dakota Ann. Laws Title XXIX, §51.

> Every owner or lessor of property used for rental purposes shall maintain every outside stair and porch in sound condition and good repair. West Dakota Ann. Laws Title XVII, §19.

> No person shall operate any mobile piece of heavy construction equipment unless said equipment is equipped with a beeper which sounds at all times while such equipment is operating in reverse. West Dakota Ann. Laws Title XXIII, §123.

Statutes like these are intended to promote safety by establishing standards of conduct for particular situations. They are legislative commands which, if applicable, every citizen is bound to obey. Usually, such safety statutes establish a small criminal penalty for violations of the standard, but do not say anything about whether violation of the statutory standard establishes negligence in a civil action for damages. Not surprisingly, however, persons injured due to a violation of such a statute usually claim that the defendant was negligent for failing to comply with the statutory standard of care.

Suppose, for example, that Bourjailly drives past a stopped school bus with flashing lights and hits Hellman, a child alighting from the bus. If the school bus statute above applies, Hellman will argue that Bourjailly should be found negligent because he violated the statute. Or suppose that Updike is injured by a falling object on a construction site, and sues the contractor. If the helmet statute quoted above applies, and if Updike was not wearing one, the defendant would argue that Updike's violation of the statute proves, in and of itself, that he failed to live up to the standard of due care.

Arguments for and Against the Negligence Per Se Rule

There are some good arguments that a violation of a statute should be treated as negligence per se, that is, negligence in itself. Where the legislature has decreed that certain precautions must be taken, or that certain acts should not be done, a person who violates the statute has ignored the standard of care established by the legislature. Arguably, reasonable people don't do that.

In addition, if the jury is permitted to find that the defendant acted with due care, despite his violation of a statutory standard of care, the jury is being licensed to disregard the command of the legislature. Suppose, for example, that the jury finds that Updike was not negligent in failing to wear a helmet. Doesn't this ignore the legislature, the voice of the people, which has barred such conduct? Shouldn't the standard of conduct enforced by the courts be the same as that established by the legislature, so that court decisions in negligence suits will reinforce rather than contradict the policy of the legislature?

There is much logic to these arguments, but the negligence per se cases vividly illustrate Justice Holmes's famous maxim, "The life of the law has not been logic; it has been experience." O. W. Holmes, Jr., The Common Law 1 (Little, Brown 1881). Automatic adoption of general legislative standards has proved too rigid. While it may be generally true that the reasonable person obeys the law, it is not always true. In unusual circumstances, it may be reasonable to disregard the statute, as where a driver swerves across the center line to avoid a child in the street, or stops in a no stopping zone to attend to a seriously ill passenger. In other cases, it may be impossible to obey the law, despite the best will in the world, as where blizzard conditions overwhelm efforts to keep a street clear. Imposing liability in cases like these, simply on the ground that the defendant violated the statute, would look more like strict liability than liability based on fault.

Another argument against automatic adoption of the legislative standard is that most statutes that establish standards of care say nothing about what role the legislative standard should play in a tort action for damages. Since the legislature has not provided that violation of the statutory standard of care automatically establishes negligence, it is fair to infer that courts have some discretion to "borrow" that standard selectively.

Last, it is doubtful that the legislature intended blind adherence to statutory standards regardless of the circumstances. Legislators tend to be practical people, and practical people recognize that there are circumstances in which the ordinary rules do not pertain. If asked, no legislator who voted for a statute requiring drivers to keep to the right would testify that she intended them to run down small children in order to fulfill the statutory command, or to smash into a stalled oil delivery truck.

Common Approaches to Borrowing Statutory Standards

Some early cases appear to hold that violation of a statutory standard of care always constitutes negligence per se. Under this approach, if the defendant violated the statute, the jury would be required to find her negligent, without regard to any excuse she might offer. One of the classic cases, *Martin v. Herzog*, 126 N.E. 814 (N.Y. 1920), might be read to stand for this position,[1] and early cases from other jurisdictions appear to agree. See, e.g., *Decker v. Roberts*, 3 A.2d 855 (Conn. 1939); *O'Bannon v. Schultz*, 169 A. 601 (Conn. 1933); cf. *Zeni v. Anderson*, 243 N.W.2d 270, 281 (Mich. 1976) (noting that the negligence per se rule bars evidence of excuse). Under this approach, the only way the defendant could avoid liability would be to show that the statute did not apply under the circumstances (see, e.g., *Tedla v. Ellman*, 19 N.E.2d 987 (N.Y. 1939)), or that the violation, while admittedly negligence, did not cause the plaintiff's injury.

---

1. However, even *Martin*, despite its strong language, intimated that the violation in that case established negligence per se because it was "wholly unexcused." 126 N.E. at 815.

However, as Holmes's maxim portends, increased experience with the negligence per se doctrine has led virtually all courts to soften this Draconian stance. Most courts have adopted one of the following approaches, which allow the jury to *consider* the violation of a statutory standard of care in determining negligence, but avoid making it automatically determinative.

A. Negligence Per Se with "Excuse"

The most common formula is to hold that an unexcused violation of a relevant statute is negligence per se, but that the party who violated the statute may offer evidence of an excuse or justification for violating it. Suppose, for example, that Hellman tries to prove that Bourjailly was negligent by showing that he passed the stopped school bus in violation of the statute. Suppose further that Bourjailly produced no explanation for the violation. On these facts, the jury would be instructed that, if they find that Bourjailly violated the statute, they must find that he was negligent. If, however, Bourjailly produced evidence of a sufficient reason for violating the statute, the jury would be free to conclude that the violation was "excused," and would not, in and of itself, establish negligence.

The Restatement (Second) of Torts adopts this approach to the problem. Section 288A provides that an excused violation of a statute is not negligence per se. Section 288A offers the following examples of acceptable excuses:

a.   incapacity (e.g., the actor is a minor unable to comply with the usual standard of care)

b.   lack of knowledge of the need to comply (e.g., where a driver's tail light goes out while he is driving and before he has the opportunity to discover it)

c.   inability to comply (e.g., where a blizzard makes it impossible to comply with a statute requiring a railroad to keep its fences clear of snow)

d.   emergency (as where a driver swerves across the center line to avoid a child in the street)

e.   compliance poses greater risk than violation (as where a pedestrian walks with her back to the traffic due to unusually heavy traffic going the other way)

Under the Restatement, these listed excuses are not exclusive; Bourjailly would be free to offer some other reason for the violation as well. Restatement (Second) of Torts §288A cmt. a.

Under the Restatement approach, Bourjailly would be deemed negligent if he violated the school bus statute and offered no evidence of an acceptable excuse. However, if he did present evidence of an excuse, the plaintiff's effort to prove negligence simply by proving a violation of the statute would fail. The jury would be instructed to determine whether Bourjailly acted reasonably under all the circumstances, including his violation of the statute, the reasons offered for noncompliance, and others. That sounds a good deal like a general reasonableness inquiry.

B. "Presumption" of Negligence

Some jurisdictions hold that proof of a statutory violation creates a "presumption" that the violator was negligent. The violator is still free, however, to rebut the presumption by showing that the reasonable person would have acted as he did. It is not clear that there is much difference between this approach and the Restatement approach. Under each, the plaintiff may use evidence of a statutory violation to establish negligence. Under each, the defendant may offer evidence of a good reason for her conduct. If she does not offer such evidence, the violation of the statute establishes her negligence. If she does, the jury is left to assess her conduct under a reasonable person standard, considering both the requirements of the statute and the violator's reasons for violating it.

Under both the Restatement and the presumption approaches, most courts hold that the burden of proof remains on the plaintiff.[2] The plaintiff can prove negligence by proving violation of a relevant safety statute, if the defendant does not offer evidence of an adequate reason for the violation. If evidence of an excuse *is* offered, the burden remains on the plaintiff to convince the jury that, in light of the violation and the reasons offered, the defendant did not behave as a reasonable person would under the circumstances. See, e.g., *Moughon v. Wolf*, 576 S.W.2d 603, 604-605 (Tex. 1978) (where plaintiff proves statutory violation and defendant offers evidence of excuse, plaintiff bears the burden to convince the jury that defendant's conduct was negligent under the reasonable person standard).

C. Evidence of Negligence

The third common approach is to treat violation of a statutory standard of care as evidence of negligence. Under this approach, evidence that the defendant violated a statute is admissible at trial. The jury may consider it along with all the other evidence that the defendant did or did not exercise ordinary care. They may be persuaded (on that evidence alone, or

---

2. A few cases appear to shift the burden of proof to the defendant to prove due care, once a violation of statute has been shown. See, e.g., *Resser v. Boise-Cascade Corp.*, 587 P.2d 80, 84 (Or. 1978) (once violation is shown, burden shifts to violator to prove that he nevertheless acted reasonably). It is not always clear, however, whether these courts mean that the burden to produce evidence of excuse shifts to the defendant, or the actual burden of proof.

along with other evidence) that the defendant was negligent. But they are not compelled to find him negligent, *even in the absence of rebutting evidence from the defendant*.

This is meaningfully different from the per se and presumption approaches. Under those approaches, if no excuse is offered, the judge should instruct the jury that they must find the defendant negligent, if they find that she violated the statute. Under the evidence-of-negligence approach, proof of an unexcused violation would support a finding of negligence by the jury, but they would still be free to find that the defendant was not negligent, *even if no excuse were offered*. It is certainly conceivable that a jury would refuse to find negligence despite the violation: For example, a jury might well find that driving 57 m.p.h. on a clear dry day on a rural interstate highway is not negligence, even if the speed limit were 55 and the defendant had no excuse. Under the evidence-of-negligence approach, the jury would be free to reach that conclusion. Under the presumption or per se approaches, however, this violation would establish negligence unless an excuse were offered.[3]

The Requirement of Relevance

As the foregoing section indicates, evidence of the violation of a statutory standard of care is usually admissible, and can be conclusive, on the negligence question. However, such evidence may not be used to establish breach of the duty of care unless the statute establishes a *relevant* standard of care. If Bourjailly causes an accident by turning into the path of Perelman's oncoming car, common sense tells us that it is irrelevant that he violated a statute requiring him to curb his dog, or even one requiring working windshield wipers (assuming the weather was dry at the time of the accident). Allowing evidence of these violations might prove that Bourjailly was a generally negligent person, but would not show that his negligence caused this particular accident.

Courts frequently state that a statute is only relevant in establishing negligence if it is meant to protect persons like the plaintiff from the type of harm which actually occurred. The dog curbing statute was not aimed at preventing intersection collisions, but the turn signal statute quoted at p. 94 clearly was enacted to protect other drivers from collisions with turning vehicles, exactly the type of accident which resulted from Bourjailly's failure to comply with the statute. This statute establishes a relevant

---

3. It is sometimes said in the cases that violation of a relevant statute establishes "*prima facie* evidence of negligence." This sounds very much like the "evidence of negligence" approach, but most courts that use this phrase actually appear to apply the presumption of negligence approach. See, e.g., *Zeni*, 243 N.W.2d at 276, 283, in which the court appears to use the presumption and prima facie evidence language interchangeably.

standard of care, because it was meant to protect drivers like Perelman from the type of harm — turning accidents — that resulted in this case. Prosser & Keeton, §36, at 222-226.

This requirement is nicely illustrated by one of the classic cases on the point. In *Gorris v. Scott,* 9 L.R.-Ex. 125 (1874), the plaintiff's sheep were washed overboard while being transported by sea. The plaintiff tried to establish the carrier's negligence by proving that it had violated a regulation requiring that animals on shipboard must be kept in pens of a certain size. Had the defendant complied with the statute, the plaintiff argued, the sheep would not have been washed overboard.

The court refused to find negligence on the basis of the violation. The regulation, the court concluded, was not meant to protect animals from being washed overboard, but rather to prevent the spread of disease by preventing overcrowding. Since it was not aimed at preventing the type of harm that occurred, it did not establish a standard of care relevant to the circumstances, and could not be used to establish the shipper's negligence.

Another case which nicely illustrates the point is *Kansas, Okla. & Gulf Ry. Co. v. Keirsey,* 266 P.2d 617 (Okla. 1954), in which the plaintiff's cow entered a railroad right of way and ate itself to death. The plaintiff claimed that the railroad was negligent per se, because it had violated a statute which required it to maintain fences to prevent animals from straying onto the right of way. The court refused to find negligence based on the violation, since the statute was aimed at protecting farm animals from being hit by trains, not from eating too much grass.

Courts will also refuse to treat violation of a statute as negligence if the statute was not intended to protect the class of persons to which the plaintiff belongs. See Restatement (Second) of Torts §286(a). For example, a building code might be intended to protect building occupants, not workers involved in the construction of the building. If so, the court would likely refuse to apply the building code standards to determine negligence in an action by a worker injured during construction, since the legislature was thinking about a different group with a different set of expectations and different opportunities to protect themselves. Thus, the statute is not relevant on the question of proper precautions during construction. Another nice example is a firefighter injured fighting a fire in a building that lacks sprinklers required by statute. The court might well refuse to allow the firefighter to establish negligence based on the lack of sprinklers, since the statute was meant to protect occupants, not emergency personnel.

If the defendant successfully argues that the statute was not aimed at the type of harm the plaintiff suffered, or at protecting persons in the plaintiff's situation, violation of the statute will not be given per se effect. That does not mean that the plaintiff must lose the case. All it means is that she cannot prove the second element of her claim — breach of the standard of care — by proving a violation of the statute: Instead, she must shoulder the usual burden to show negligence under the reasonable person standard discussed in the previous chapter.

The Persuasive Force of the Negligence Per Se Argument

It is easy to see why the negligence per se argument is attractive to lawyers. If Hellman can prove that Bourjailly was negligent just by showing that he violated the school bus statute, it substantially eases her burden of proof. It is a lot easier to prove that he didn't stop for the bus than to prove that his conduct was careless under the vague ordinary-prudence-under-the-circumstances standard. In addition, proving that Bourjailly violated the statute brands him as a "lawbreaker" in the eyes of the jury, which can't do his case a lot of good. Thus, using the violation to establish negligence has great tactical value for Hellman. Similarly, if the contractor in the second example can prove that Updike was negligent simply by showing that he wasn't wearing a helmet, its defense looks a good deal stronger than it would under a general negligence standard.

The use of statutory standards to prove negligence also reduces the likelihood that the jury will decide the case on grounds unrelated to the merits. A jury sympathetic to the injured Updike in the helmet case might be tempted to ignore his negligence and find for him anyway. It will be harder for them to do that if they are instructed that they *must* find him negligent if they find that he did not wear a helmet. Indeed, if it were undisputed that Updike had no helmet on, the court might take the negligence issue from the jury entirely, on the ground that the undisputed and unexcused violation of the statute establishes his negligence as a matter of law.[4]

All this appears complex, but is pretty much a matter of common sense in actual operation. Perhaps the following examples will help.

EXAMPLES

Some Relevant Questions

1. A good place to start in any negligence per se situation is to ask whether the statute was intended to protect the plaintiff from the type of harm which she actually suffered. In which of the following cases do you think the court would find the statutory standard relevant to the plaintiff's claim?

---

4. Even if instructed that the violation constitutes negligence, the jury in a comparative negligence jurisdiction would still have to determine Updike's percentage of negligence.

a. Porter, the town dog officer, quarantines a dog who had bitten a child. The officer allows the owner to take the dog after a week, in violation of a quarantine statute that requires him to hold the dog for 14 days. The next day, the dog runs in front of Jones's car. Jones swerves to avoid the dog and is injured.

b. Oliver, a seven-year-old child, finds an abandoned refrigerator in a vacant lot, crawls in to hide, and suffocates. In an action for his death, the estate tries to prove the owner's negligence by showing violation of the statute quoted on p. 94, requiring removal of doors from appliances left in places accessible to children.

c. Welty hits Capote broadside when she is driving down Main Street and fails to see Capote pulling out into the street at an intersection. Capote alleges that Welty was negligent because she violated the statute quoted above at p. 94, requiring a working muffler on all motor vehicles.

d. O'Neill leaves his dirt bike on the front porch of a general store while he goes in to buy some candy. When he comes out, he mounts the bike, rides off the end of the porch, and is seriously injured. He sues the store owner, claiming that she was negligent for violating a building code provision that requires "a wall or protective railing at least 36 inches high enclosing every porch more than 30 inches above the ground."

e. Welty is driving east on Main Street when a school bus coming in the other direction stops. Since she can see that the only child around is already stepping into the bus, Welty drives on. As she passes the bus, she hits Capote's car coming out of a side street. Capote claims that Welty's negligence is established by her violation of the statute quoted on p. 94, requiring traffic to stop when school buses do. How should the court rule?

f. Austin, riding her bicycle down the street, approaches a truck parked in a loading zone. To clear the truck, she steers further into the street, and is hit by a passing motorist. She alleges that Porter, the owner of the truck, was negligent for violating a statute that limits parking in the loading zone to one-half hour during morning hours. Porter's truck had been there for nearly two hours.

2. After reading about the various ways in which the defendant may excuse a statutory violation, it may seem that the negligence per se doctrine is a toothless tiger. The plaintiff can use it to suggest negligence, but the defendant can rebut it, so it all comes down to general reasonableness anyway. Here are a few cases that illustrate that the doctrine can make a big difference in a negligence case. In each case, ask yourself why the per se negligence doctrine will make an important difference in the outcome.

a. Salinger is driving east on a rural West Dakota highway when Ginsberg comes toward him from around a curve, driving astride the center line of the road. Their cars collide and Ginsberg is killed. Salinger sues Ginsberg's estate for negligence. To prove that Ginsberg failed to exercise due care, he testifies that Ginsberg violated a statute that requires vehicles to keep to the right of the center line.

b. Salinger is injured when Ginsberg's car turns in front of him while he is driving down Maple Street. He seeks to establish Ginsberg's negligence by proving that Ginsberg failed to signal his turn, as required by the statute quoted on p. 94. Ginsberg claims that he did signal before turning.

c. Perelman hits Woolf, a construction worker, while backing up a large bulldozer. Perelman was watching carefully, but (as he knew) the beeper on the bulldozer was broken, and had been for five days. The statute on p. 94, requiring a beeper on heavy construction equipment, applies.

3. Williams, a painter, is painting the exterior wall on a new five-story building. Although a statute requires that hardhats be worn on all active construction sites, Williams was not wearing one. He is injured when a two-by-four falls on him from a higher floor. Williams claims that he lacked "knowledge of the need to comply" (Restatement (Second) of Torts, §288A(b)) with the statute, since he was unaware of the statute. Will this excuse the violation?

Statutory Enlightenment

4. Cheever owns a three-unit apartment building in Oakley, West Dakota. He fails to replace a burnt out light bulb in the upstairs hall, and O'Connor, unable to see the steps, trips and falls down the stairs. She sues him for negligence, and offers to prove his negligence by showing that he violated West Dakota Stat. Ann. Title XVI, §31, which requires landlords to maintain adequate lighting in all common areas of their buildings.

a. Does the statute establish a standard of care relevant to the case?

b. Assume that Cheever defends by offering evidence that the light was not out; thus, he does not offer any reason for failing to replace the bulb. Assuming that West Dakota applies the negligence per se doctrine, should the judge direct a verdict for O'Connor on the negligence issue?

c. Assume again that Cheever claims the light was on, and that West Dakota applies the negligence per se doctrine. How should the judge instruct the jury on the negligence issue?

d. If there were no statute establishing a relevant standard of care in this case, how would the judge instruct the jury on the negligence issue?

e. Assume now that West Dakota takes the position that violation of a relevant statute is admissible evidence of negligence rather than negligence per se. If O'Connor claims that Cheever violated the statute, how should the judge instruct the jury on the issue?

5.   Assume again that O'Connor relies on the violation of the lighting statute to prove Cheever's negligence. Cheever testifies that he was aware of the burnt-out bulb, but had asked Porter, another tenant, to replace it and Porter had told him that he would do it right away.

    a. Assume that West Dakota applies the negligence per se with excuse approach, but that it only recognizes the five excuses listed in the Restatement (Second) of Torts §288A (see p. 97). How will the negligence issue be resolved?

    b. Assume that the Restatement (Second) of Torts §288A is applied, but that other excuses may also be offered for violating the statute. How would the negligence issue be resolved?

    c. Assume that West Dakota applied the "presumption of negligence" approach. How would the negligence issue be resolved?

6.   Assume that Cheever's building is in a high crime area. Calisher, accosted on the street by a robber, runs into his building to escape. Because the light is out, she stumbles over a child's tricycle and is injured. In a negligence action, can she rely on his violation of the lighting statute to establish negligence?

Judge Fudd Rules Again

7.   Calisher runs a small, low-budget theater in the round. Wharton, a patron, is injured when her seat collapses during a performance, evidently because a bolt sheared off underneath it. In her negligence action against Calisher, Wharton introduces evidence that Calisher had violated West Dakota Ann. Laws Title XIX, §21A, which requires that theater owners have their premises inspected and certified annually by the city building inspector.

    a. Assume that West Dakota follows the evidence of negligence approach. Judge Fudd instructs the jury, in part, as follows:

> If you find that West Dakota Ann. Laws Title XIX, §21A is intended to protect a class of persons including the plaintiff from the danger of injuries such as that suffered by her, and that the defendant violated that statute, then you are instructed that the violation is evidence, along with all the other evidence in the case, that you may consider in determining whether the defendant was negligent.

    Can you spot a fundamental flaw in Judge Fudd's instruction?

    b. Assuming that the statute establishes a relevant standard of care, what other basic problem do you see in Wharton's case?

Negligence Per Se, or Negligence Per Cent?

8.   One more variation on Cheever's lightbulb woes. Let's assume that the case takes place in a comparative negligence jurisdiction. Under comparative

negligence, the jury not only decides whether the parties were negligent, they also assign percentages of negligence to all parties who caused the accident. The plaintiff's damages are then reduced to account for her negligence. For example, if the jury found the defendant 60 percent negligent and the plaintiff 40 percent negligent, the plaintiff would recover 60 percent of her damages. (For a detailed treatment of comparative negligence, see Chapter 23.)

Assume that O'Connor sues Cheever in a state that applies comparative negligence, and that Cheever has no excuse for violating the lighting statute. What would be the effect of the negligence per se doctrine in the case?

The Goose and the Gander

9.   A West Dakota statute requires a fence at least four feet high around private pools. Beverly has such a pool, with a four foot fence. Allen, a child of seven, climbs over the fence, jumps into the pool, and drowns. Allen's parents sue Beverly for negligence in failing to prevent children from entering the pool area.
       a. What will Beverly argue in her defense?
       b. How should the court rule on the defense?

EXPLANATIONS

Some Relevant Questions

1a.   Clearly, this statute is aimed at protecting people from being bitten by diseased dogs, not at preventing dogs from running into the street, which could happen no matter when the dog is released. Since the statute is not meant to protect against the *type of harm* suffered by Jones, the court will not allow her to prove Porter's negligence by showing this violation.

       b.   This statute was clearly aimed at exactly the risk that caused the harm here: A child getting caught in the appliance when the door closes on her. In the absence of an excuse, the violation of this statute would establish negligence in a per se or a presumption jurisdiction.

       c.   In order to invoke the muffler statute to prove Welty's negligence, Capote will have to demonstrate that it was aimed, at least in part, at preventing the type of accident that took place here. At first glance, the statute appears aimed at preventing excessive noise from passing cars. But it is entirely plausible that it was also aimed at assuring that drivers could *listen* for traffic hazards as well as see them. A statute may be aimed at preventing a variety of evils. So long as one purpose of the statute is to avert the type of injury suffered by the plaintiff, the violation should be considered relevant to the negligence issue.

Often there is little legislative history to assist in determining what risks the legislature was trying to prevent by the passage of a statute. The court must infer the statute's purposes primarily from the provisions of the statute itself. Thus, courts exercise a good deal of judgment in determining whom the statute was meant to protect, and from what hazards.

Of course, Welty's violation of the muffler statute would only establish liability if it *caused* the accident. Her noisy muffler would be irrelevant unless her inability to hear contributed to the accident. The evidence might show, however, that Capote had blown his horn to warn Welty, but that she was unable to hear due to the muffler noise. If so, Welty's violation of the muffler statute would be a cause of the accident.

d.   This example is based on *Matteo v. Livingstone,* 40 Mass. App. Ct. 658 (1996). In *Matteo,* the court held that when building code provisions "prescribe protective walls or rails, the consequence they are designed to prevent is that a person will fall off accidentally. Such regulations do not have as their object preventing bicycle acrobatics." 40 Mass. App. Ct. at 661. The court upheld the trial judge's refusal to allow the statute to be admitted in evidence to establish the store owner's negligence.

The regulation at issue in *Matteo* was not a statute, but a regulation promulgated by a state agency. Some courts refuse to give per se effect to local ordinances or administrative regulations, even if they apply the doctrine to statutes promulgated by the state legislature. Harper, James & Gray, §17.6, at 642. Such enactments are promulgated by bodies with fewer resources to investigate, and do not represent as broad-based a judgment about proper conduct as a vote of the state legislature. Other states, however, give per se effect to ordinances and regulations as well. But this regulation was clearly not aimed at the type of harm the plaintiff suffered anyway.

e.   This statute was obviously aimed at protecting school children from injury, not other drivers. On that rationale, the Supreme Court of Rhode Island held on similar facts that violation of the statute could not be used to establish negligence. *Paquin v. Tillinghast,* 517 A.2d 246 (R.I. 1986).

However, the fact that the violation of the statute would not establish Welty's negligence does not mean that it is irrelevant in this case. It may be, for example, that Capote pulled out because he expected Welty to stop for the bus, as the statute required her to do. If so, Capote could prove those facts in order to show that Welty was negligent for failing to do what the reasonable person would do under the circumstances. But this is quite different from equating negligence with violation of the statute, as the per se approach does. Rather, the statute would be introduced here to prove that, in light of the normal expectations of drivers, Welty was negligent under the usual reasonable person standard.

f.   This statute is aimed at assuring access to adequate parking for deliveries, not at preventing the type of accident Austin has suffered here. Austin does not claim the truck was too far out into the street, but only that it was *there*. She could just as well have suffered the same accident if the truck had only been there for ten minutes. Indeed, if Porter had left on time, another truck would likely have been there anyway. This statute is irrelevant to the case; Porter's violation of it should not be considered by the jury on the negligence question. See *Capolungo v. Bondi*, 224 Cal. Rptr. 326 (Cal. App. 1986).

2a.   Under either the per se or presumption approaches, Salinger's evidence of the violation will, if the jury believes it, establish Ginsberg's negligence, unless evidence of an adequate excuse is offered. Here, Ginsberg is not around to offer exculpatory evidence. He may have had a good reason for the violation, but if the proof is not offered, the presumption governs. The doctrine is very powerful in cases like this, where the violator is unable to offer the countervailing evidence that would rebut the presumption.

b.   Here, instead of trying to prove a good reason for violating the statute, the defendant claims that he did not violate it. It is a little hard for the defendant to play both sides of the street (no pun intended) in these cases. Usually, she will have to either try to explain a violation or deny that it took place. If she stakes her case on the factual contention that she did not violate the statute, and the jury finds that she did, that finding will determine the negligence issue: Under either the negligence per se or presumption approach, the violation establishes negligence, in the absence of any evidence of an acceptable excuse.

c.   Here, the defendant violated the statute, which was clearly intended to prevent the type of accident which took place, and just has no acceptable excuse. In a per se or presumption jurisdiction, the evidence that the beeper was not working will establish Perelman's negligence. The fact that he looked carefully will not avert a required finding of negligence, because the jury is not free to make a general finding on the negligence issue: If it finds that the statute was violated, and Perelman has no excuse, it must find that he breached the duty of due care.

This will doubtless be the situation in many negligence per se cases: The defendant simply has no excuse for the violation of the statute. In such cases, the statutory negligence doctrine provides a powerful weapon for the plaintiff, since it establishes the most ambiguous element which she must prove to recover: breach of the duty of due care.

3.   No way. We are all held to know the law. Subsection (b), allowing an excuse where the violator lacks knowledge of the need to comply, deals with the situation where the violator does not know *facts* that would make her aware of the violation, such as not knowing that a turn indicator is

broken. The judge would not even allow Williams to offer this evidence, since the excuse is insufficient as a matter of law.

Statutory Enlightenment

4a.   The lighting requirement in the statute is clearly aimed at protecting tenants like O'Connor from the type of harm that she has suffered — injury while trying to negotiate the stairs in the dark. Thus, it establishes a standard of care relevant to the case, and it is appropriate to consider that standard in resolving the negligence issue.

   b.   The judge should not direct the verdict, even if the negligence per se doctrine applies. The violation of the lighting statute only establishes Cheever's negligence if the light *was* out. Whether it was out is a factual issue the jury must decide. Thus, the jury still has an important role to play, even in a negligence per se jurisdiction. But their task will be much more circumscribed than it would be under a general reasonable care standard, since they need only decide whether Cheever violated the statute. If he did, and offers no excuse, his negligence is established under the negligence per se doctrine.

   c.   The judge should instruct the jury along the following lines:

> Under West Dakota law, the violation of a statute intended to protect against the type of harm suffered by the plaintiff establishes negligence. If you find in this case that the defendant violated West Dakota Ann. Laws Title XVI, §31, by failing to provide adequate lighting in the hallway of the building, then you must find that the defendant was negligent.

Note that the judge would not instruct the jury on the effect of an excuse for the violation, since Cheever has not offered such evidence. He has staked his case on the position that he did not violate the statute.

   d.   If there were no statute relevant to the case, the judge would instruct the jury to consider whether Cheever was negligent under the usual reasonable person standard:

> Negligence is the failure to use that degree of care that an ordinary prudent person would use under the circumstances. If you find that the defendant exercised the degree of care that an ordinary prudent landlord would exercise in maintaining the common areas of the building, then you should find that he was not negligent. If you find that the defendant failed to exercise the degree of care that an ordinary prudent landlord would exercise in maintaining the common areas of the building, you should find that he was negligent.

It is not hard to see why O'Connor would prefer to see the jury given the instruction in Example 4c. That instruction narrows the issue from the general "throw-it-to-the-jury" due care standard to a very specific fact question, and requires the jury, if it finds the light was out, to find for

O'Connor on the critical issue of negligence (assuming no evidence of excuse is offered). Thus, the adoption of the statutory standard of care substantially eases her burden of proof. It also brands Cheever as a "wrongdoer," which may color the way the jury looks at other issues in the case.

e. The judge should give the jury a general negligence instruction, such as the instruction in Example 4d. She should then add a further instruction along these lines:

> If you find that the defendant violated West Dakota Ann. Laws, Tit. XVI, §31, requiring adequate lighting in the common areas of apartment buildings, you may consider that violation together with all the other evidence in the case in determining whether the defendant failed to exercise reasonable care under the circumstances.

This instruction would leave it to the jury to consider the statutory duty along with all the evidence in deciding whether Cheever was negligent. The jury could conclude, under the ordinary reasonable person standard, that he was negligent. On the other hand, the jury would also be free to conclude otherwise, even if it finds that the light was out. This more flexible rule gives a good deal more latitude to Cheever to persuade the jury that he acted reasonably under all the circumstances, even if he violated the statute.

5a. On these facts, the trial judge should probably direct a verdict for O'Connor on the question of negligence. Cheever has admitted that he did not comply with the statute, so the only question is whether he has an adequate excuse for noncompliance. Relying on his tenant's assurance does not appear to meet any of the five categories of permissible excuses in §288A: Cheever is not a minor; he is not unable to replace the bulb; he was aware of the need to do so; no emergency intervened, and compliance did not pose any risk. Thus, if these are the only permissible excuses, Cheever has none, and his negligence is established by his admission that he violated the statute.

b. The Restatement allows the violator to prove one of the five listed categories of excuses, but also allows proof of others not listed. Restatement (Second) of Torts §288A cmt. a. Under the Restatement, presumably the jury would be allowed to consider whether Cheever's reliance on his tenant was an adequate excuse for the violation. Thus, the jury would have to decide, in light of the violation and cheerer's excuse, whether he exercised reasonable care.

c. In a presumption state, proof of the violation establishes negligence, unless the violator offers evidence of an excuse. Here, Cheever has offered evidence of an excuse. Unless the offered excuse were patently insufficient, it would be for the jury to evaluate the adequacy of that excuse. Thus, as under the Restatement, the case would go to the jury.

6. To be relevant, a statute must not only protect against the harm suffered by the plaintiff, but must also be intended to protect a class of persons to which the plaintiff belongs. Certainly, the lighting statute was meant to prevent stumbling over obstacles in the dark, but it is questionable whether it was meant to protect *Calisher* from such risks. It was doubtless aimed at protecting tenants, and probably guests as well ... maybe even meter readers. But it hardly seems that it was meant to protect passersby who enter unexpectedly to avoid a robbery. Thus, arguably, Calisher cannot use the statute to show a standard of care relevant *to her.*

Judge Fudd Rules Again

7a. The problem here is that the jury is not the proper body to decide whether the standard of care established in the statute is relevant — Judge Fudd is. The jury is there to try the case, not the statute. When Wharton offers evidence of the violation at trial, the judge will have to decide whether the statute was meant to protect parties in the plaintiff's position from the type of harm suffered. If the judge concludes that the statute establishes a standard that is relevant to the case, evidence that it was violated will be admitted; otherwise, the jury will hear nothing about it.

b. Wharton may be able to convince the jury that the inspection statute was meant to prevent injuries by identifying safety problems on the premises. But she will still have a hard time establishing that the violation of the inspection statute *caused* her injury. It is extremely unlikely that an inspection would have revealed that a bolt in the chair was about to shear off. Presumably, most of the bolt is not even visible, and it may be impossible to spot this type of metal fatigue from a visual inspection anyway. It is doubtful that the inspector would get down and look underneath the chairs; probably she would check for major risks such as blocked aisles, inadequate emergency lighting, or broken sprinklers. Thus, Calisher will argue that, even if the required inspection had been done, the bolt problem would not have been detected. If this is so, the violation is not an actual cause of Wharton's injury.

That does not mean that Wharton must lose: It simply means that she must fall back on the general negligence standard to establish Calisher's negligence. She might well prove that Calisher was negligent in other ways. Perhaps she continued to use the seats beyond their useful life or after other similar accidents. Perhaps she was notified of this type of risk by the manufacturer, but failed to repair the seats. Maybe she replaced the bolt herself with one too small for the task. Any of these might show that Calisher was negligent under the usual reasonable person standard.

Negligence Per Se, or Negligence Per Cent?

8.   At common law, negligence was an all-or nothing decision. If the plaintiff was negligent, for example, she lost, under the doctrine of contributory negligence. If the defendant was negligent, she was fully liable for the damages, unless the plaintiff was negligent as well. Thus, the negligence per se doctrine had particular force, because in many cases it required the jury to find a party negligent.

Under comparative negligence, however, a finding that one or both of the parties was negligent has a less profound impact on the outcome. For example, even if the jury is instructed, under the negligence per se doctrine, that they must find Cheever negligent for failing to replace the lightbulb, *the percentage of negligence* they attribute to him based on the violation is still up to them. If they don't think he was particularly faulty, they might ascribe 3 percent to him and 97 percent to O'Connor, which is pretty close to letting Cheever off the hook entirely.

However, the negligence per se doctrine still has a powerful impact in cases where the jury ascribes *no negligence* to the plaintiff. If Cheever violated the lighting statute, the jury would have to find him negligent under the per se doctrine. If O'Connor was not negligent at all, the jury must then ascribe 100 percent of the fault to Cheever, even if they don't think he was "very negligent" for violating the statute. Thus, the doctrine still forces the jury in these cases to find the defendant fully liable for the plaintiff's injury.

In addition, the doctrine still has important persuasive force in comparative negligence cases, since it may lead the jury to ascribe a large percentage of fault to a party who has failed to follow an established statutory standard.

The Goose and the Gander

9a.   Of course, Beverly will argue that "what is sauce for the goose is sauce for the gander": If failure to comply with a statute constitutes negligence, *compliance* with a statute ought to constitute due care. Here, the statute required a four foot fence. That, Beverly will argue, is the measure of due care, and she should be found "careful per se" for complying with the statute.

b.   The argument has an immediate appeal to it but has generally been rejected. Standards of care imposed by the legislature are often minimum standards, intended to avoid the most dangerous practices but not to immunize persons who do the minimum from liability where more precaution is appropriate. It may be that it is unreasonable to ignore the minimum standards set by the legislature, but it does not follow that the reasonable person takes *only* those minimum precautions. See Restatement

(Second) of Torts §288C (compliance with statutory standard "does not prevent a finding of negligence where a reasonable man would take additional precautions"). For example, a four foot fence around a pool may suffice in some areas, but in others where many children live a reasonable person might conclude that a four foot fence is insufficient to prevent them from entering.

Speed limits provide another good example of this point. In setting a limit, the legislature may have concluded that it is dangerous to exceed a particular speed, but that does not imply that it is always reasonable to travel at that speed. In fog, snow, or heavy traffic, a much slower speed may be called for and a rule that compliance with the posted limit absolves the defendant would be inappropriate.

6

A Phrase in Latin: Res Ipsa Loquitur

Introduction

The last chapter considered the use of statutory standards of care to prove that the defendant breached the duty of due care or "was negligent." This chapter considers another means of proving negligence, through the mystic doctrine of res ipsa loquitur.

Sometimes proving negligence is straightforward. Suppose that Cisneros goes to the neighborhood garage to have the wheels of his Maserati balanced. After driving away, the right front wheel falls off. Cisneros gets out and looks around, but is only able to find three of the lug nuts that hold the wheel on. He returns to the station, where another customer tells him that he saw the mechanic leave the other lug nuts off. Negligence? No problem: What happened is clear from direct evidence, the testimony of the other customer, and a jury would almost certainly conclude that the mechanic was negligent in failing to replace all the lug nuts.

Would that all negligence cases were so easy. If they were, few negligence cases would be tried, because cases in which liability is clear almost always settle before trial. The cases that reach the trial stage are likely to present substantial disputes of fact, in which proof of essential elements — particularly negligence — is more problematic.

The Difference Between Direct and Circumstantial Evidence

In the Maserati example, Cisneros produces compelling evidence of the mechanic's negligence, direct testimony from a witness who observed the negligent act. However, negligence need not always be proved by direct evidence. In many cases, plaintiffs will have to rely on "circumstantial" evidence, that is, evidence of facts from which a jury could *infer* that the defendant was negligent. Cisneros might, for example, return to the garage and find two Maserati lug nuts sitting next to the wheel balancing apparatus. This might suffice to allow a jury to infer negligence on the part of the mechanic. The argument runs like this: If the wheel fell off shortly after Cisneros drove away, and if two Maserati lug nuts were sitting at the garage, and if Cisneros could only find three at the scene, it is likely that the mechanic only refastened three. Common experience tells us that leaving some of the lug nuts off creates an unreasonable risk that the wheel will come loose. Therefore, it appears probable that the mechanic was negligent in failing to secure the wheel.

Cisneros might have to rely on even less compelling circumstantial evidence to establish negligence. He might only be able to prove that the wheel fell off shortly after he left the garage, and that he was unable to locate all the lug nuts at the scene of the accident. This does not directly show that the mechanic failed to refasten them, but it again suggests (though less forcefully than the last scenario) that the likely explanation of the accident is the failure to refasten all the lug nuts. A jury could still reasonably infer from the facts Cisneros *has* proved that the accident more probably than not happened because the lug nuts were not refastened or were improperly fastened. Thus, proof of the circumstances allows an inference of further facts which would establish the mechanic's negligence.

Circumstantial evidence is commonly used in proving all sorts of tort cases. The plaintiff offers evidence of a pile of freshly cut maple logs in the defendant's backyard to establish that the defendant cut down his maple trees. Scratches or paint scrapings on the defendant's fender are offered to establish that it was his car that hit the plaintiff's. Evidence of large, unexplained deposits in defendant's bank account is offered to establish that he converted the plaintiff's funds. In each case, evidence of one fact is offered because it tends to establish another.

The "banana peel cases" offer a classic example of the use of circumstantial evidence to establish negligence. The plaintiff slips on a banana peel on the supermarket floor, and sues for his injuries. To establish negligence, he must show that the banana peel was there long enough that store employees should have seen and removed it. It would be ideal to introduce direct evidence, say, three customers who saw it on the floor over the course of several hours before the accident. Such direct evidence isn't likely to be available, however. If three customers had seen it, one would likely have told someone about it, or picked it up. (Similarly, in the Maserati case, if another customer had seen the lug nuts left off, he would likely have said something to the mechanic and averted the accident.)

Absent such direct evidence, banana peel plaintiffs usually offer circumstantial evidence to prove that the banana peel was on the floor long enough that store employees should have seen and removed it. The plaintiff will testify that the banana peel was black, or gritty, or trampled flat. From such facts, a jury could reason as follows: Most people don't hold onto old banana peels; they throw them away immediately after eating the banana. Therefore, if a black and gritty banana peel was on the floor, it was probably on the floor long enough to *turn* black and gritty. Common experience suggests that this takes an hour or so, and that's long enough that an employee should have found it and picked it up. Similarly, if the banana peel had been trampled, the jury could infer that it had been stepped on repeatedly over a period of time. Such evidence does not exactly provide an airtight case, but it will often be the best that the plaintiff can do, and may well convince a jury that it is "more probable than not" that the defendant was negligent.

From Circumstantial Evidence to Res Ipsa Loquitur

If circumstantial evidence is one step away from direct testimony, the classic doctrine of res ipsa loquitur is a further step beyond the traditional use of circumstantial evidence. The doctrine originated in the famous case of *Byrne v. Boadle*, 159 Eng. Rep. 299 (1863), in which the unfortunate plaintiff was hit on the head by a flour barrel which fell from the defendant's second story window. While there was no evidence of what caused the flour barrel to fall on Byrne's boodle, the court allowed him to recover. "Res ipsa loquitur," the court opined, "the thing speaks for itself."

Dean Prosser offers the following whimsical response to this tautological logic: "*res ipsa loquitur, sed quid in infernos dicet?*" ("The thing speaks for itself, but what the hell did it say?") Prosser, Wade, and Schwartz, 10th ed., 231. Well, the *Byrne* judges took it to say that flour barrels don't just fall out of windows on their own; that when they do fall, the most likely reason is the negligence of the person in control of the premises. Thus, even though the plaintiff cannot offer direct or circumstantial evidence of exactly what caused the barrel to fall, he should be allowed to reach the jury on the issue of negligence by proving the circumstances of the accident itself, because they "bespeak negligence" even without a more specific showing of the chain of events.

There is nothing particularly mystical or sophisticated about this idea. As Lord Shaw quipped: "If that phrase had not been in Latin, no one would have called it a principle." *Ballard v. North British R. Co.*, 1923 Sess. Cas. 43 (1923). Res ipsa is not really a separate principle, but rather a special form of circumstantial evidence. The underlying rationale of res ipsa loquitur, as of circumstantial evidence in general, is that facts can sometimes be inferred from other facts. In a case like Cisneros's tire problem, the circumstantial evidence allows the jury to infer *a particular negligent act*, failure to replace the lug nuts. In res ipsa loquitur cases, the circumstantial evidence allows the jury, based on evidence about the accident itself, to infer that it must have resulted from *some negligent act* by the defendant. In *Byrne v. Boadle*, for example, the circumstantial evidence that the barrel had fallen from the defendant's second story window sufficed to allow a jury to conclude that some negligent act by the defendant had caused it to fall.

Here are some other examples of cases in which the plaintiff might use res ipsa loquitur to establish negligence.

- A railway company hires a contractor to install a temporary boarding platform for trains, and it collapses under Feinstein shortly after it is put into use. Even if the collapse makes it impossible to produce evidence of the exact cause, a jury might well infer that negligent construction caused the collapse.
- A brick falls from a roof where a chimney is being repaired and hits the plaintiff. Here again, the plaintiff may not be able to demonstrate what caused the brick to fall; indeed, the workers may not be able to either. Again, however, a jury might fairly infer that the brick probably fell due to some negligent act by the workers.
- An elevator stops abruptly between floors, throwing the plaintiff to the floor.

In each of these cases, there is no showing of exactly how the accident happened, but the fact that it happened at all suggests that someone was probably negligent.

A Critique and a Defense

We saw in Chapter 4 that the plaintiff must prove all the elements of a negligence claim in order to hold the defendant liable. Arguably, courts that apply res ipsa loquitur play fast and loose with the negligence element of the claim, since they allow the jury to find for the plaintiff without proving any specific negligent act. In the platform case, for example, if the plaintiff merely offers evidence that the platform fell shortly after it was constructed, he has not "proved" any particular negligent act by the contractor. Similarly, in the brick case, evidence that the brick fell while the defendant's employees were working on the roof does not prove what negligent act (if any) caused it to fall. The jury cannot determine exactly what caused the brick to fall on the basis of such general evidence. How then, are they to know that there was negligence involved at all?

Well, they don't *know* that negligence was involved, of course. On the other hand, they don't *know* what caused the accident in the Maserati example, either; they simply make a reasonable estimate of the probabilities based on what they do know. Similarly, in res ipsa loquitur cases, the jury may not be able to reconstruct the sequence of events, but they may be able to make an educated inference that, whatever it was, it probably involved the defendant's failure to exercise due care in some respect. The inference may not be infallible, it may not be satisfying to the ruthlessly syllogistic mind, but it is accepted by the legal system as sufficient to satisfy the "more probable than not" standard of proof in negligence cases. Courts, as practical institutions, must face the fact that irrefutable proof is seldom available in practical affairs, that the system is imperfect by its nature and must settle for a reasonable balance of the probabilities. "Res ipsa by its nature deals with mysteries and the efforts of imperfect legal processes to unravel them." M. Shapo, Principles of Tort Law 255.

Consider the alternative. The judicial system could send Byrne away empty handed, explaining the result to him thus:

> Sorry, Byrne, about your busted boodle. But we aren't willing to make Boadle pay you unless you show that he did something wrong. You haven't met your burden of proof, because you haven't shown us what specific act Boadle did that was negligent. Unless you produce such evidence, you are not entitled to recover.

This reasoning sounds pretty good, but it doesn't comport with most people's sense of elementary fairness. Most people *would* make the inference that Boadle or his employees must have done something negligent for that barrel to get loose, even if we don't know exactly what it was. Similarly, most people would infer that the platform collapse was caused by faulty construction, or that the brick fell because of negligence. The res ipsa loquitur doctrine allows juries to make the same inference of negligence that most of us would make from our common experience.

The "Foundation Facts" in a Res Ipsa Case

Not every plaintiff can get to the jury by intoning the magic Latin, however. For the res ipsa doctrine to apply, the circumstances must support an inference of negligence:

> There must be reasonable evidence of negligence. But where the thing is shown to be under the management of the defendant or his servants, and the accident is such as in the ordinary course of things does not happen if those who have the management use proper care, it affords reasonable evidence, in the absence of explanation by the defendants, that the accident arose from want of care.

Scott v. London & St. Katherine Docks Co., 159 Eng. Rep. 665, 667 (1865). This early statement of the doctrine remains essentially intact. Most courts hold that the plaintiff can make a case for the jury under res ipsa loquitur by showing *first* that he was injured by an accident that would not ordinarily happen without negligence and *second* that the negligence is more likely than not attributable to the defendant, rather than to the plaintiff or a third party.

A. The Requirement that the Accident Ordinarily Would Not Happen Without Negligence

The first "foundation fact" is that the accident is of a type that ordinarily does not happen without negligence. Many accidents would not support an inference that negligence was involved. It is doubtful that a court would allow the jury to infer negligence from the fact that the plaintiff trips going down the defendant's stairs, or that the defendant's car skids into plaintiff on a rainy day. There are common explanations for such occurrences which do not involve negligence. But many other accidents, by their very nature, do support an inference of negligence. For example, most courts would conclude that the following accidents probably would not have occurred without negligence:

- a newborn baby is matched to the wrong mother in the maternity ward
- an airplane disappears without a trace in good weather
- a chunk of glass or a tack is found in a can of spinach
- oil spills from a tank truck on the highway

In each of these cases, common knowledge suggests that this is probably not an "accident" in the pure sense of the word; that someone's careless conduct is the likely explanation. That is not to say that negligence is the *only conceivable* explanation for the accident. It is always possible to hypothesize other causes — for example, terrorism in the airplane case, or an undiscoverable defect in the tank truck case. But the plaintiff's burden of proof in a negligence case is not to eliminate all possible alternative causes of his injury. His burden is to show that the *more probable* cause was negligence. In the example cases just given, a jury might reasonably conclude that it was.

B. The Requirement that the Negligence, If Any, Is Attributable to the Defendant

The second "foundation fact" in a res ipsa case is that the negligence is attributable to the defendant. It is not enough to show that someone's negligence probably caused the harm. The evidence must point to the defendant as the negligent party. Often this is obvious, as where a load of cement drops from the defendant's crane, or a scaffold just erected by the defendant falls. In these examples, the defendant is in control of the source of the accident and responsible for its safe operation. If an accident bespeaks negligence in these cases, it very likely bespeaks the defendant's negligence.

This attribution requirement is more difficult, however, where a product causes injury after leaving the defendant's hands. A frequent example is the explosion of a bottle of soda or beer in the hands of a consumer. Many courts have concluded that beverages bottled under pressure should not explode unless someone was negligent in filling or handling the bottle. Thus, the probably-would-not-happen-without-negligence element is met. But in these cases the bottle may have been handled by the distributor, the retailer, and the consumer after it left the bottler's hands. Thus, it is harder to show that the negligence, if there was any, was the bottler's.

The cases often state that this attribution requirement is not met in a res ipsa loquitur case unless the instrumentality that caused the harm was "under the defendant's control" at the time of the accident. This formula is clearly too narrow. For example, in the glass-in-the-spinach case, the canner was clearly not in "control" of the can when the plaintiff ate the spinach and was cut by the glass. Yet it is highly likely that the glass got in the can when the spinach was canned. Thus, a jury could reasonably infer that the negligence, if any, is attributable to the canner. Similarly, the collapsing railroad platform may not be in the "control" of the contractor who built it at the time of the collapse, but it is very likely that the negligence took place at the time of construction and is therefore attributable to the contractor. Although this "control" language is often found in the cases, most courts have not taken it so literally as to preclude use of res ipsa in such obviously appropriate cases.[1]

The formulation of the res ipsa loquitur doctrine in the Second Restatement of Torts nicely avoids the misleading "control" language:

> (1) It may be inferred that harm suffered by the plaintiff is caused by negligence of the defendant when
>> (a) the event is of a kind which ordinarily does not occur in the absence of negligence;
>> (b) other responsible causes, including the conduct of the plaintiff and third persons, are sufficiently eliminated by the evidence. . . .

Restatement (Second) of Torts §328D. Under this statement of the doctrine, the plaintiff may invoke res ipsa loquitur even if the defendant did not have exclusive control of the source of the harm, so long as

---

1. *Kilgore v. Shepard Co.*, 158 A. 720 (R.I. 1932), is an oft-cited case in which the court took an overly rigid approach to the "control" issue. In *Kilgore*, the plaintiff was injured when she sat down in a chair at the defendant's store and it collapsed under her. Although the cause of the collapse was very likely negligent maintenance of the chair, the court refused to apply res ipsa loquitur. Taking the control element too literally, the court concluded that the foundation elements of res ipsa were not established, since the plaintiff, not the defendant, was in control of the chair at the time of the accident.

the plaintiff can demonstrate that the negligence was likely that of the defendant rather than himself or other parties.

The Effect of the Plaintiff's Conduct

Courts often state that there is a third requirement for the application of res ipsa loquitur: that "the event must not have been due to any voluntary action or contribution on the part of the plaintiff." *Reber v. United States*, 941 F.2d 975, 978 n.1 (9th Cir. 1991). This is confusing, because it suggests that a plaintiff who was partially at fault in causing an accident can never prove the defendant's negligence through a res ipsa loquitur inference.

That isn't so. Often, the circumstances will support an inference that a defendant was negligent, even if the plaintiff was too. Suppose, for example, that a contractor sets up a scaffold on the outside of a building, and it starts to topple. Merlini, rushing to a meeting inside the building, sees it sway, but dashes underneath, figuring that she can get inside before the scaffold falls. She doesn't make it, and is injured. Clearly, Merlini's negligence contributed to her injury. But shouldn't res ipsa still be available to prove negligence of the contractor in causing the initial collapse? A scaffold should not collapse unless there is negligence in erecting it. And, if there was negligence, it was almost certainly the negligence of the contractor. Merlini should be able to use res ipsa to establish the contractor's negligence, whether she was negligent in rushing underneath or not. Her subsequent negligence should be accounted for under comparative negligence analysis, not by barring her from proving the other party's negligence through res ipsa loquitur.

This supposed third requirement is really only a corollary of the second: It is meant to reemphasize that the plaintiff must show that the negligence that created the initial danger (whatever it was) is attributable to the defendant rather than to her. If it is equally probable that the plaintiff's negligence created the danger, she has not "brought the negligence home to the defendant." But when the circumstances show that the negligence that created the initial danger was probably the defendant's, res ipsa should be available, even if the plaintiff was negligent in reacting to the danger. In the scaffold case, for example, there is a strong res ipsa loquitur case that the *collapse* was caused by the defendant's negligence. Merlini should be able to invoke res ipsa on that issue, even though she was negligent in running under the scaffold.

The Effect of the Doctrine at Trial

Even if a case is tried, a judge has the power to refuse to submit it to the jury if there is no credible evidence in support of one or more of the elements of the plaintiff's claim. Frequently, the defendant will argue that the judge should take the case from the jury (by "directing a verdict" for the defendant[2]) since the plaintiff has not produced proof of a specific negligent act by the defendant. The crucial impact of res ipsa loquitur is that it allows the plaintiff's case to go to the jury even though he has not proved a specific act of negligence. Naturally, plaintiffs are very keen to avoid directed verdicts and reach the jury; thus, the res ipsa doctrine is very popular with the plaintiff's bar.

If the plaintiff establishes the "foundation facts" discussed in the preceding section, the judge will allow the case to go to the jury. It will then be up to them to decide whether the accident was more probably than not the result of the defendant's negligence. They are free to infer that his negligence caused the accident, but they are also free to conclude, based on the evidence presented, that the defendant's negligence is *not* the more likely explanation. The doctrine, in other words, permits the jury to infer negligence, but it does not require them to. Some cases suggest that res ipsa loquitur shifts the burden of proof to the defendant, or creates a presumption of negligence which requires a finding of negligence if not rebutted. Most courts hold, however, that the doctrine merely provides evidence sufficient to support an inference that the defendant was negligent, but does not compel a finding for the plaintiff even where there is no rebuttal evidence. See Restatement (Second) of Torts §328D(3) & cmt. m.

Instructing the Jury on Res Ipsa Loquitur

Logically, it would seem unnecessary to confuse the jury by giving them specific instructions about res ipsa loquitur. It should suffice to tell them that the plaintiff must prove the defendant's negligence by the preponderance of the evidence, and that they are free to infer negligence or not, as they choose, from the evidence presented. The risk of resting on such general instructions, however, is that the jury will take a more technical view of the plaintiff's burden than the courts do, and find for the defendant simply because the plaintiff has not shown the exact cause of the accident. Thus, courts usually give specific instructions detailing the "foundation facts" for res ipsa loquitur and the effect of finding those foundation facts. Here is an example adapted (not quite *verbatim*) from a Minnesota case:

> When an accident is such that it would not ordinarily have happened unless someone was negligent, and if the thing which caused the accident is shown to have been under the exclusive control of the defendant at the time that the negligent act, if any, must have happened, then you are permitted to infer from the mere fact that the accident happened and the circumstances surrounding it that the defendant was negligent.

---

2. For a discussion of directed verdict practice, see J. Glannon, Civil Procedure: Examples and Explanations 409-417 (4th ed. 2001).

See *Bossons v. Hertz Corp.*, 176 N.W.2d 882, 886 (Minn. 1970). Note how this instruction tracks the elements of the doctrine. It tells the jury that they *may* conclude that the defendant was negligent, *if* they find that it was the type of accident that does not ordinarily happen without negligence, and that the thing which caused it was under the defendant's control at the time of the negligence. (This instruction, like many currently in use, does include the dubious "exclusive control" language, which has raised problems when taken too literally. However, it focuses on control at the time of the likely negligence rather than at the time of the accident.)

The Defendant's Case

The res ipsa doctrine may warm the hearts of plaintiff's counsel, but it places the defendant in a very difficult position. How is he to refute the plaintiff's proof of negligence, where plaintiff hasn't proved any specific negligent act? Certainly, the most effective way to rebut a res ipsa loquitur case is to prove the actual cause of the accident. For example, proof that the station platform collapsed because the transit authority was tunneling underneath it will completely undermine (excuse the pun) the res ipsa inference.

Short of that, the defendant can attack each of the foundation facts necessary to support res ipsa loquitur. He may question the second foundation fact by showing that other persons mishandled the product that caused the injury after it left his hands (e.g., the retailer in the exploding beverage case). He may undermine the required showing that the type of accident does not ordinarily happen without negligence, by showing other common, non-negligent causes of this type of accident. A chain is only as strong as its weakest link; if the jury is not convinced that each of the foundation facts is established, it should refuse to infer the ultimate fact of negligence. If the defendant's proof on either of these points is strong enough, the judge may even direct a verdict for him, on the ground that the jury could not reasonably conclude that the proper foundation for the res ipsa doctrine has been established.

When the defendant does *not* have evidence of the exact cause of the accident, he may try to refute the res ipsa inference by proving that he generally exercised due care. In the case of the glass in the spinach, for example, the canner might produce evidence of the careful quality control measures it takes to avoid objects getting into the cans. The airline in the lost plane example might produce evidence of its careful training, maintenance, and inspection procedures. This does not conclusively eliminate negligence as the cause, but it could influence the jury's thinking about the probabilities. On the other hand, this can backfire: The more careful the defendant's procedures, the less likely that an accident would happen if they had in fact been followed. Thus, such proof could lead the jury to conclude that, had the procedures been followed, there would not have been an accident at all. For a fine example of this, see G. Fricke, The Use of Expert Evidence in Res Ipsa Loquitur Cases, 5 Vill. L. Rev. 59, 70-72 (1959), quoting cross-examination of a defendant's expert that very effectively showed that the accident could not have happened unless the usual precautions were not taken.

The cases often suggest that the plaintiff should be able to rely on res ipsa loquitur because the defendant has better access to evidence of the cause of the accident than the plaintiff does. It is certainly true that the doctrine creates a strong incentive for the defendant to produce any evidence it has that will rebut the inference that its negligence caused the accident. However, most courts do not restrict the doctrine to cases in which the defendant has better access to proof. See Restatement (Second) of Torts §328D cmt. k; D. Dobbs, The Law of Torts §160. Often, the defendant has no better chance of explaining the accident than the plaintiff does. In the disappearing plane case, or the glass-in-the-spinach case, for example, the airline or the canner may have no idea what caused the accident, or any way of finding out. Yet the likely explanation of the accident may still be negligence. In such cases, the defendant should not be able to avoid res ipsa simply by showing that it knows no more about the cause of the accident than the plaintiff does.

The following examples should help you to understand the types of cases in which the res ipsa doctrine applies, and how this mystic doctrine assists the plaintiff in getting to the jury in those cases.

EXAMPLES

Victims of Circumstance

1.   In which of the following cases do you think plaintiff could reach the jury by invoking res ipsa loquitur?

    a. Lindsey's front tire blows out while he is driving down Sunset Boulevard. He sues Firewall Tire, the manufacturer of the tire.

    b. LaGuardia is injured while making a delivery to Acme Manufacturing Company's warehouse. He was raising a rolling garage door upward when the door stuck in the metal track and bounced back on his head. He offers evidence of multiple hammer marks on the track and a distortion in the shape of the track to show that Acme had negligently maintained the door.

    c. Young, a three-year-old toddler, comes home from day care. Throughout the evening, he complains of a sore arm. His parents finally take him to the emergency room, where an x-ray reveals that his arm is broken. The parents sue the day care center for negligence.

d. Brown, a five-month-old baby, comes home from day care. Throughout the evening she shows obvious discomfort on her left side. Her parents take her to the emergency room, where x-rays reveal that her left arm is broken. The parents sue the day care center for negligence.

e. Flynn is walking past a high-rise hotel when a beer mug falls on his head from one of the balconies above. He sues the hotel for negligence.

f. While entering an interstate highway, Daley is injured when a stray Volkswagen engine suddenly appears in the roadway in front of him, causing him to crash. There is no sign of an ailing Volkswagen to be found in the area. Daley sues his insurance carrier, under a policy provision allowing recovery from the insurer for injuries negligently caused by an unidentified motorist.

g. White is injured when a large truck backs into a propane tank, causing an explosion. Lindsey, the trucker, claims that he hit the tank because Wagner, another trucker, waved him back too far. Wagner claims that the truck jumped suddenly at the last moment, presumably because Lindsey hit the accelerator instead of the brake. White sues them both, and invokes res ipsa loquitur.

Possibly Probable Negligence

2. Consider again Example 1c above, in which Young, a three-year-old toddler, came home from day care with a broken arm. Suppose that the only evidence before the court is the evidence of Young's injury. Suppose further that the judge recognizes that there is a good deal of uncertainty about the more likely cause of the accident. He believes that negligence of the day care center may have been involved, but doubts that it was the *more likely* cause. Perhaps he views negligence as a 40 percent likelihood, and an accident resulting from the toddler's general exuberance a 60 percent likelihood. Should the judge direct a verdict for the day care center, or allow the case to go to the jury?

Firming Up the Foundation

3. Alioto makes up a yummy salad for lunch. He throws in some lettuce, a tomato, a can of artichokes, some mushrooms, and some sliced turkey. Then he pours Newton's Own Natural Russian Salad Dressing over the top. While enjoying the salad, Alioto bites into a piece of glass and breaks a tooth. He sues Newton's.

a. Which of the foundation facts poses a problem here?

b. How might Alioto strengthen the argument for applying res ipsa loquitur to the case?

4.   Ulner undergoes leg surgery by Dr. Eastwood to correct an arterial problem in his thigh. After the operation, he notices that he has decreased sensation along the left side of the leg, which gets worse over the ensuing weeks. He sues Eastwood for negligence.

    a. What foundation fact raises problems in applying res ipsa loquitur to this case?

    b. In addition to the basic facts described above, Ulner presents a medical expert, who testifies that reduced sensation "does not ordinarily occur" as a result of the type of surgery Ulner had, if ordinary care was exercised. Should Ulner's case go to the jury on a res ipsa loquitur theory?

    c. Assume that Ulner's expert testifies that nerve damage of the type he suffered would not happen unless the surgeon was negligent. Dr. Eastwood then offers an expert who testifies that such loss of sensation may result from a number of causes, including the underlying medical problem, poor post surgical nursing care, unavoidable surgical abrasion of the nerve, or negligence. Given the contradictory expert testimony as to the likelihood of negligence, should the judge allow the case to go to the jury on a res ipsa theory?

    d. Suppose that after Ulner's expert testifies that the damage would not ordinarily occur without negligence, Dr. Eastwood takes the stand. He testifies that the surgery was unremarkable, that he followed standard procedure, and that he definitely did not touch, cut, or pinch any of the surrounding nerves. At the close of his evidence he moves for a directed verdict. How should the judge rule?

    e. Assume instead that Dr. Eastwood takes the stand and testifies that during the surgery an artery in Ulner's leg began to hemorrhage, due to an unanticipated weakness in the artery wall. To prevent a life threatening loss of blood, Eastwood was forced to clamp off the artery, which was directly in contact with the major nerve in the left side of the leg. This procedure risks damage to the nerve, but is unavoidable when such surgical complications arise. This evidence is confirmed by the surgical notes and by the assisting physician. After offering this evidence (which is not contradicted by the plaintiff), Dr. Eastwood moves for a directed verdict. Should it be granted?

Not for Attribution

5.   Should the court apply res ipsa loquitur in the following cases?

    a. Feinstein rents a dry cleaning shop from Bradley. The shop is destroyed by fire in the middle of the night. Investigation indicates that the fire began near or along the wall between the office and the cleaning area, but there is no explanation as to the cause. Bradley sues Feinstein for negligently burning the shop.

    b. Bradley, a guest at the Fontainbleau hotel, leaves his suite for dinner. A half hour later there is a fire in the room. The evidence indicates that the fire started in a sofa in the sitting room of the suite. The hotel sues Bradley for negligence.

6.   Atkins's house is destroyed in a fire following an explosion in a closet in the cellar. He offers evidence that two weeks before the fire the gas company had installed a new gas line to his water heater, located in the closet. He argues that this evidence suffices to allow the jury to find negligence based on res ipsa loquitur.

    a. Would this evidence suffice to get to the jury on a res ipsa theory?

    b. After Atkins produces this evidence, the gas company puts on its case. Its evidence indicates that Atkins had taken the door off the closet and stored various combustible materials in the closet before the explosion, that no one had smelled gas during the two weeks before the fire, that Atkins had been working around the heater an hour before the fire, and that the wind was blowing at 80 miles an hour outside at the time of the explosion. Should the case go the jury on a res ipsa loquitur theory?

7.   Young is hit by a piece of wood that falls from the open third floor of a construction site. At the time, Koch and Alioto, two employees of the Wagner Construction Company, the framing subcontractor, were the only workers on that floor.

    a. Unable to discover exactly what caused the board to fall, Young sues Koch and Alioto. Can he invoke res ipsa?

    b. Young has an easy alternative here; what is it?

Fudd Ipsa Loquitur

8.   Assume that Judge Fudd tries the case described in Example 5b, in which the hotel fire started in a couch in the defendant's room. Judge Fudd, after brushing up on his res ipsa learning, gives the following instruction to the jury:

> If you find that the fire in this case was not likely to have happened in the absence of negligence, and that the negligence, if there was negligence, was most likely that of the defendant, then these facts give rise to an inference of negligence on the part of the defendant.

What is the problem with the Honorable Fudd's instruction?

9.   Farmer Jones decides to take a break from the spring plowing. He turns off the ignition and gets off his new tractor. Suddenly, the tractor unaccountably starts up with Jones standing next to it. Jones, perhaps ill-advisedly, jumps for the driver's seat to stop it, is thrown off and injured. He sues International Tractor Company, the manufacturer, alleging negligence in

causing his injuries. At trial, he proves the above facts, and argues that he should get to the jury based on res ipsa loquitur.

The defendant asks Judge Fudd to give the following jury instruction:

> No inference of negligence by the defendant is permitted, unless the plaintiff has shown that the injury-causing occurrence was not due to any contribution or voluntary activity on the plaintiff's part.

Should Judge Fudd give the instruction?

EXPLANATIONS

Victims of Circumstance

1a. As the introduction states, res ipsa loquitur only applies where the nature of the accident indicates that it would not ordinarily happen without negligence. Most courts would probably hold that a tire blowout does not satisfy this requirement. Tires can blow out from a number of causes, including over- or underinflation, glass or other sharp objects in the road, excessive wear, a Chicago-sized pot hole, and probably others as well. Of course, it could result from a defect in the tire, but given all the other potential causes, this accident is probably not the type that "ordinarily does not happen without negligence."

b. This isn't really a res ipsa case. LaGuardia has simply used circumstantial evidence to show a *particular negligent act*. The hammer blows and twist in the track indicate that the track had been damaged and someone had tried to fix it. From this a jury could infer that the repair had been poorly done, and that the distortion in the track had caused the door to stick and bounce back at LaGuardia.

In a res ipsa case, the plaintiff usually doesn't have evidence of the particular cause of the accident. Rather, he tries to show that the general circumstances of the accident suggest that it wouldn't have happened if the responsible party had been careful. The plaintiff argues, "Hey, I can't explain just what happened here, but it's reasonable to infer that the defendant must have done *something* careless, or this accident wouldn't have happened." LaGuardia doesn't have to fall back on such general proof, since he has evidence — albeit, circumstantial evidence — of the specific act of negligence that caused his injury.

c. Surely any parent can testify to the fact that many toddlers are more enthusiastic than careful. They try new things, fall down a lot, bump into things. It seems quite credible that an active three-year-old would fall off a swing, trip, or get hit hard enough to break an arm, even if the day care personnel were exercising due care in supervising him. Thus, it is at least doubtful that a jury could infer negligence of the day care center from the mere fact of this accident. See, e.g., *Ward v. Mount Calvary*

Lutherun Church, 873 P.2d 688 (Ariz. App. 1994), which refused to apply res ipsa on similar facts.

d. Although three-year-olds get around very well and consequently take some pretty hard knocks, a five-month-old can hardly navigate at all. It seems improbable that Younger could manage to break her arm all by herself; it is much more likely that someone dropped her, or left her unattended on a changing table. This case seems a much stronger candidate for application of res ipsa loquitur.

e. This accident is not likely to happen without someone's negligence. The problem is in attributing the negligence to the hotel owner. It is quite likely that a guest, rather than an employee, knocked the mug off a balcony railing. While hotels have a duty to exercise due care in controlling the conduct of guests, the hotel cannot have guards in every room to interdict every careless act of its guests. Thus, res ipsa will probably fail here because it is impossible to show that the negligence, if there was any, was attributable to the defendant.

f. This is a good res ipsa case. When an engine is found in the middle of an expressway, it probably didn't walk there. The facts strongly suggest that the engine must have fallen from a truck. Clearly, that shouldn't happen if the hauler has exercised reasonable care in securing the load.

But what of the second foundation fact — ascribing the negligence to a particular person? Here, Daley is relieved of the problem posed by the second res ipsa requirement. Under the policy provision, the insurer is liable as long as his accident was caused by the negligence of some unidentified motorist. Here the facts provide reasonable proof of that.

g. When I gave this fact pattern on an exam, a number of students said that White should invoke res ipsa, since he is unable to tell which defendant's negligence caused the collision. However, this is not a res ipsa case. First, to invoke res ipsa the plaintiff must show that the negligence, if any, was likely that of a particular defendant. Here, there are two, and White simply isn't sure which one was at fault. Res ipsa does not allow White to simply point the finger at multiple defendants and argue, "Hey, someone did it, so I can sue them all, prove that somebody was negligent, and recover." White still bears the burden of attributing the probable negligence to a particular person.

In addition, this is not really an unexplained accident. It is clear what happened: The truck backed into the tank. The only problem is the conflict in the evidence as to which of two negligent acts caused it. That's simply a question of who is telling the truth. Suppose, in *Byrne v. Boadle*, that Boadle had testified that a delivery person for another company had been in the shop and dropped the barrel, but the delivery person testified that Boadle had dropped it. On these facts, their Lordships would not have thrown any legal Latin at the problem. They would simply have left it to the jury to decide who was telling the truth.

Possibly Probable Negligence

2.   This example raises a tough but important question. Here, it is a debatable proposition whether the accident was more probably the result of negligence or pure accident. The judge puts the probabilities at 40 percent negligence/60 percent pure accident, but recognizes that others (in particular, the jury) might disagree. Should he let the jury decide, or direct a verdict for the defendant on the ground that one of the foundation facts (that the accident "ordinarily would not have happened without negligence") has not been established?

Presumably, if the jury could reasonably conclude that the accident "ordinarily would not happen without negligence," they should be allowed to decide. They are the factfinders, so presumably they decide the *foundation facts* as well as the ultimate issue of negligence. If they agree with the judge that negligence is not the more probable explanation, they should find for the defendant. But if they conclude that the accident does bespeak negligence (and that the negligence is likely attributable to the defendant) they would be entitled, under res ipsa, to make an inference that the defendant was negligent.

Put another way, the judge's role is not to make findings himself that the foundation facts are established, but rather to determine whether the jury reasonably could conclude that those facts are proved. If there is evidence from which the jury could find that the plaintiff has established the foundation facts, they must be given the opportunity to do so, and (if they do) to decide whether to make the further inference that the defendant was negligent.

Firming Up the Foundation

3a.   It seems very likely that glass would not have ended up in Alioto's salad unless someone was negligent. The problem in the case, of course, is to decide whose negligence it was. The glass could have come from the mushrooms, the lettuce, the artichokes, perhaps even the sliced turkey, as well as from the salad dressing. It may also have fallen into the salad from a shelf or the kitchen counter. Thus, the circumstances do not of themselves demonstrate that the negligence is attributable to Newton's.

b. Alioto may be able to shore up his res ipsa foundation against Newton's by eliminating the other possible sources of the glass. He may be able to testify that he washed the lettuce, drained, washed, and cut up the artichokes, rubbed each mushroom before cutting it into the salad, and sliced the turkey on a clean cutting board. He may also be able to testify that he washed the counter before making the salad. Depending on the particulars, such testimony could lead the jury to eliminate the other items in Alioto's lunch as the source of the glass, leaving Newton's the likely culprit.

It is quite common for plaintiffs to offer testimony to eliminate the negligence of others, including themselves, so as to satisfy the requirement that the negligence be attributable to the defendant. In an exploding bottle case, for example, the plaintiff will try to show careful handling by the retailer and himself, in order to prove that the negligence was likely that of the bottler. In a disappearing airplane case, the plaintiff will offer testimony that the weather was clear to bolster the inference that negligence, not weather, caused the plane to crash.

4a.   If there was negligence at all in this case, it was very likely attributable to Dr. Eastwood. However, it is not at all clear that this side effect results from negligence. It is very doubtful that a jury could conclude, from their general knowledge, that decreased sensation after thigh surgery bespeaks negligence of the surgeon. Thus, the jury is not in a position, based on the mere fact of the injury, to determine that the foundation for the res ipsa inference is established.

b.   Ulner's expert testifies that nerve damage does not usually result when the type of surgery Ulner had is carefully performed. However, it does not follow, just because this side effect doesn't usually occur, that when it occurs it probably results from negligence. There are many side effects of surgery that occasionally happen despite the exercise of due care. Surely, negligence should not be inferred just because such side effects are rare. For example, surgical patients rarely get infections from careful surgery, but this does not mean that, if a patient does get infected, the surgeon was probably negligent. In a small percentage of cases, it just happens anyway, despite all reasonable precautions.

Many courts state that res ipsa applies to "the type of injury that ordinarily would not occur if reasonable care had been used." *Wick v. Henderson*, 485 N.W.2d 645, 649 (Iowa 1992). However, this language is misleading. It is one thing to say that the type of accident does not ordinarily happen when the actor is careful. It is another to say that, *when the accident does occur*, it is more likely than not that negligence was the cause. Tire blowouts do not ordinarily happen if car owners are careful, but it does not follow that when tires *do* blow out, it is probably the result of negligence. People do not ordinarily fall down on the sidewalk, but when they do, it does not follow that negligence is the likely cause.

A better statement of this requirement is that the accident "would not ordinarily happen without negligence." (Note that Ulner's expert did not testify to that.) Res ipsa requires that the accident not only be unusual, but that it be unlikely to happen unless someone failed to exercise due care. If Ulner's expert testified that nerve damage does not occur in this type of surgery *unless the surgeon was careless*, his testimony would provide an evidentiary basis for the jury to conclude that his injury probably resulted from negligence. On that testimony, Ulner would be allowed to reach the jury on a res ipsa theory.

c. Here, Ulner's expert has provided testimony that would support the first "foundation fact." However, Dr. Eastwood has offered expert testimony that contradicts that testimony. Presumably, it is for the jury, as the factfinders, to resolve this conflict in the evidence. If they believe Ulner's expert, they may conclude that injuries of this type most likely result from negligence. They could then make the further inference that this one in fact *did* result from Dr. Eastwood's negligence. Compare Example 2. If they are convinced by Eastwood's expert, they will conclude that negligence is not the most likely explanation, and find for the defendant.

d. Eastwood's motion should be denied. Ulner's evidence suggests that this type of outcome likely results from negligence of the surgeon. Eastwood then testifies that he did not make the type of mistake which would likely explain Ulner's complications. If the jury believes Eastwood's testimony, they will presumably refuse to make the inference permitted by the res ipsa loquitur doctrine. They are free to do that, but they are also free to disbelieve Eastwood's testimony and make the res ipsa inference based on the evidence that such results usually do result from negligence of the surgeon, and the further fact that the injury did in fact occur. On this state of the evidence, the case is for the jury.

e. The res ipsa loquitur doctrine allows a jury to conclude that an unexplained accident more than likely happened due to negligence. But here, the defendant has offered an uncontradicted, fully corroborated explanation that the injury occurred without negligence. Unless there is some basis to conclude that the witnesses are lying, this accident is no longer unexplained, and there is no need for the jury to estimate the probabilities concerning an unexplained occurrence. Thus, res ipsa would no longer have a role, and the judge would likely direct a verdict for the defendant.

If there were some basis in the evidence for the jury to disbelieve Eastwood's testimony concerning the ruptured artery, they would be entitled to do so. If they did disbelieve it, and the proper res ipsa foundation had been laid, they would be free to infer that negligence caused the problem.

Not for Attribution

5a. Most courts would probably refuse to allow this case to go to the jury on the basis of res ipsa. Ordinary experience suggests that there are a number of possible causes for this fire which do not involve negligence of the tenant, including electrical problems, a customer's smoldering cigarette, vandalism, or mechanical problems. The fire may be attributable to the operator's negligence: She could have spilled cleaning fluids, left oily rags near the wall or left a pressing machine on. But it seems doubtful, where the fire occurs overnight and cannot be directly tied to the cleaning machines, that it can reasonably be inferred that one of these is the more likely cause.

b. Although this is another fire case, it is a much better candidate for application of res ipsa loquitur. Here, the evidence indicates that the fire started in a sofa, not a usual place for fires absent someone's negligence. In addition, it started shortly after Bradley left the room, which supports the inference that, if negligence led to the fire, it was his. See *Olswanger v. Funk*, 470 S.W.2d 13 (Tenn. App. 1970) (approving use of res ipsa loquitur in a similar case).

In this case, further evidence may strengthen the inference of Bradley's negligence. If he locked the room, for example, this tends to eliminate vandalism as an alternative explanation. If Bradley is a smoker, that would greatly strengthen the inference that he had caused the fire.

6a.   Atkins has probably produced enough evidence to go to the jury on res ipsa. His evidence shows that the accident happened shortly after the gas company worked on the heater, that the fire resulted from an explosion, and that the explosion took place in the area where the gas company had done the work. A reasonable jury could infer from these facts that the accident probably resulted from a gas leak, and that the leak was probably caused by faulty work in installing the gas line. Atkins's case is hardly iron-clad, but it supports a reasonable inference of negligence.

Of course, the gas company was not "in control" of the heater or the gas lines at the time of the explosion. But under the Restatement formulation of res ipsa this is not necessary. Atkins must simply show that the negligence is probably attributable to the gas company.

b. Sometimes res ipsa seems to leave defendants at the mercy of the jury as long as some inference of negligence can be made. But this example, based on an actual case, *Nutting v. Northern Energy, Inc.*, 874 P.2d 482 (Colo. App. 1994), illustrates that defendants, through aggressive discovery, are often able to muster substantial evidence to undermine the foundation facts. In *Nutting*, the plaintiffs had to admit that they had been working around the heater, weakening the inference that the negligence, if any, was the gas company's. In addition, the weather records suggested yet another explanation for the fire — that the force of 80-mile-per-hour winds had caused a downdraft, blowing the burner flame outward, and igniting the combustible materials stored in the closet. On this state of the evidence, the court held that the plaintiffs had not made a case for one of the res ipsa foundation facts: that the negligence, if any, was likely attributable to the defendant. Consequently, the court refused to give the jury a res ipsa instruction.

7a. This case resembles *Byrne v. Boadle*, the flour barrel case that gave rise to the res ipsa doctrine. As in *Byrne*, it seems fairly clear that a jury could find, based on their own experience, that this accident would not ordinarily happen without negligence. Someone must have left the board too near the edge of the building, or dropped it in the course of the work, or *something*.

The problem is the other foundation requirement, attributing the negligence to a particular defendant. Granted, it is probably attributable to *one of the defendants*, but it is not clear which one. Even where the plaintiff relies on the general inference of negligence permitted by res ipsa, it must be an inference of a particular person's negligence, not just someone's. Otherwise, Young could simply sue all possibly negligent parties and argue that one of them must have been negligent.[3] On these facts, most courts would refuse to send the case to the jury on a res ipsa theory.

b. Young can rely on res ipsa loquitur in this case if he sues Wagner Construction Company. The accident is of a type that ordinarily would not happen without negligence. Wagner, as an employer, is liable for the negligence of any of its employees in the course of the work. See Chapter 21. Thus, it is liable regardless of which employee caused the board to fall. Even though Young could not invoke res ipsa against Koch or Alioto, he could show that the negligence must be attributable to someone for whom Wagner is responsible.

Fudd Ipsa Loquitur

8. Fudd's instruction tells the jury that, if they find the foundation facts established, "these facts give rise to an inference of negligence on the part of the defendant." This suggests to the jury that they *should* make the inference that Bradley was negligent if they find the foundation established. Most courts hold that res ipsa permits, but does not require a jury to infer negligence where the foundation facts are shown. The instruction would be much improved if the Honorable Fudd told the jury that, if they find the foundation facts are established, they *may* but are not required to infer that the defendant was negligent.

One may well wonder if such subtle distinctions in a complex verbal instruction have any real meaning for a jury. If the jury understands the

---

3. *Ybarra v. Spangard*, 154 P.2d 687 (Cal. 1944), appears to hold that the plaintiff can do just that. However, *Ybarra* has not been generally accepted outside of the unique context (surgery on the unconscious patient) in which it arose. Even in that context, it may be a dubious proposition that the defendants should bear a burden of explanation which they probably cannot meet. See D. Seidelson, Res Ipsa Loquitur — The Big Umbrella, 25 Duq. L. Rev. 387, 446-450 (1987).

res ipsa instruction at all, they may well understand it as Judge Fudd mistakenly phrased it, to mean that they should find for the plaintiff if they find the foundation facts established. Jury instructions play an ironic role in the trial of cases. When they are correct, it is not clear that the jury understands them or pays them undue attention. But when they are wrong, the losing party is very likely to appeal on the ground that the jury was given the wrong rules for decision. Thus, it may be more important not to get the instructions wrong than it is to get them right.

9.   As the Introduction notes, you will very frequently see language of this sort in the statement of the res ipsa loquitur requirements. See, e.g., *Stillman v. Norfolk & W. Ry. Co.*, 811 F.2d 834, 837 (4th Cir. 1987). The rationale is apparently that, if the plaintiff contributed to the accident, the inference that the negligence leading to it was the defendant's is undermined. In addition, res ipsa dates from the era of contributory negligence, when any negligence by the plaintiff barred recovery even if the defendant was negligent.

In this case, however, Jones should be able to invoke res ipsa loquitur even if he was a partial cause of his injury. Although Jones may have been negligent *after* the tractor started, for jumping on board, there is nothing to suggest that he contributed in any way to causing it to start. Thus, his conduct does not undermine the inference that any negligence that led to the tractor starting up was International's. Brand new tractors should not roar into life on their own. When they do, a jury could reasonably infer that the manufacturer was negligent. The fact that Jones *reacted negligently* to the risk should not bar him from using res ipsa to establish the initial negligence of International. If Jones reacted negligently to the situation, and thus contributed to his own injury, this can be accounted for under comparative negligence by reducing his recovery.

Thus, in instructing the jury, Judge Fudd should separate the issue of International's negligence in causing the initial problem from Jones's negligence in reacting to it. He should instruct the jury that they could infer negligence of International based on res ipsa loquitur, and further instruct them that, if Jones's subsequent conduct was also negligent, they should account for that under comparative negligence principles. See, e.g., *Giles v. City of New Haven*, 636 A.2d 1335 (Conn. 1994) (allowing plaintiff to invoke res ipsa in a similar situation under comparative negligence).

This point is a bit confusing, but important, since comparative negligence has become the law in most states. So let me describe another example. In *Cramer v. Mengerhausen*, 550 P.2d 740 (Or. 1976), the plaintiff was having a tire changed at a repair shop when the truck started to slip off the jack. He grabbed the back of the truck, to try to keep it from sliding forward, and was injured when the truck fell. The court held that plaintiff could invoke res ipsa, even if he had been negligent as well, to establish the initial negligence of the repair person, since trucks shouldn't fall if properly jacked. If plaintiff was negligent in reacting to the situation, this could be accounted for under comparative negligence by assigning him a percentage of negligence and reducing his damages accordingly.

PART THREE

The Causation Enigma

7

Reconstructing History: Determining "Cause in Fact"

Introduction

As previous chapters have indicated, the common law has developed a consistent set of elements — duty, breach, causation, and damages — that plaintiffs must prove in order to recover in a negligence action. This chapter addresses basic aspects of the very difficult — and fascinating — third element, causation. The next chapter addresses several complex causation issues frequently encountered in the Torts course.

No writer could venture into the mysteries of causation without profound trepidation. In a philosophical sense, the causes of any event may be traced back to the dawn of time, and the consequences of the most trivial act ripple forth in all directions to irrevocably change the world. Every cause has its own causes, and every consequence, consequences.

This is fancy language and causation is a profound problem. We could think about it for years and perhaps at the end be little closer to understanding it. Yet one of the majesties of the law is that it must answer the unanswerable: It must decide, *today*, between plaintiff and defendant, and lacks the luxury of indefinite speculation. Consequently, judges must settle for some working approaches to thorny problems like causation, approaches that are no doubt imperfect, perhaps not even fully intellectually consistent, and always subject to refinement and eventual change.

Although causation is a complex problem, fundamental fairness obviously requires that a defendant be held liable only for injuries he actually caused. If Jones, an electrician, wires Smith's house, and leaves exposed wires in the wall, which cause a spark and burn down the house, Smith's loss is a direct result of Jones's negligence. It would not have happened if Jones had been careful, and it did happen because Jones wasn't careful. It seems fair to shift the loss from the blameless Smith to the careless Jones. However, if the house burns down because Smith's toddler starts the fire, Jones did not cause the harm and should not pay, even if he was negligent in wiring the house.

To assure that liability will only be imposed where the plaintiff's loss is fairly attributable to the defendant's conduct, courts have developed two causation requirements, causation *in fact* and *proximate* or legal causation. Cause in fact, the subject of this chapter, requires that, as a factual matter, the defendant's act contributed to producing the plaintiff's injury. Proximate causation, considered in Chapter 9, deals with limits on liability for remote or unexpected consequences of tortious conduct.

It is often quite clear from the events themselves that the defendant's negligence was the cause in fact of an injury. Suppose, for example, that Wright drops a sheet of plywood from a building onto Sullivan's car, obscuring her ability to see the road, and she crashes into a parked car. There is little doubt that Wright's negligence "caused" the accident. Sullivan will doubtless testify that she swerved off the road *because* the plywood obscured her view. The accident would not have occurred otherwise. Similarly, if Darrow, a lawyer, draws a will for a client and fails to include one of the intended beneficiaries, it is clear that this omission is the cause in fact of the beneficiary's inability to take under the will. Common sense tells us that the problem happened because the beneficiary was left out, and would not have happened if she had been included. We would all accept that Darrow's mistake "caused" the beneficiary's damages, and so would any court.

In other cases, we could all agree, philosophers included, that the defendant's negligence did not cause the plaintiff's injury. Suppose that Pei's truck hits Gaudi on Maple Street. Investigation shows that the truck was carefully driven and in good working order, except that the windshield wipers were broken. However, the weather was dry at the time. No court will hold Pei liable for the accident because of the broken wipers. The wipers weren't needed; the accident would have happened the same way if they had been working. Even though Pei was negligent, his negligence was, in the language of the torts trade, "negligence in the air," negligence irrelevant to the injury that Gaudi suffered, and therefore not actionable.

The Traditional Test: "But For" Causation

Traditionally, courts have used the "but for" test to determine whether the defendant's act was a cause in fact of the plaintiff's harm. Under the "but for" test,

> [t]he defendant's conduct is a cause of the event if the event would not have occurred but for that conduct; conversely, the defendant's conduct is not a cause of the event if the event would have occurred without it.

Prosser & Keeton, 266. Under this approach, the court asks whether the plaintiff would not have suffered the harm "but for" the defendant's negligence. In other words, if we go back and replay the accident, but take away the defendant's negligent act, would plaintiff have escaped injury? For example, in Pei's windshield wipers case, if the wipers had been working at the time of the accident, Gaudi would still have been injured in exactly the same way. So, Pei's negligence in failing to fix the wipers is not a "but for" cause of the harm. We cannot say that, but for the broken wipers, the accident would not have happened.

The plywood case, on the other hand, satisfies the "but for" test. But for the falling plywood, which obscured Sullivan's view of the road, she would not have swerved and hit the car. If we take Wright's negligence in dropping the plywood out of the scenario, the accident doesn't happen. Because the accident would not have happened without Wright's act, that act is a "but for" cause of the harm. Consequently, cause in fact is satisfied.

Another way of saying this is that the defendant's act must be a "sine qua non" of the plaintiff's injury. Sine qua non means "without which it is not; an indispensable requisite" (*Ballentine's Law Dictionary*, 1182 (1969)), that is, that the injury would not have happened without the defendant's act. Again, the test invites us to look at what *did* happen and compare it to what *would have* happened if defendant had not been negligent. If the injury would not have resulted without the defendant's negligence, then the negligence is a sine qua non of the injury, and the cause-in-fact element is met.

Let's apply the "but for" test to two more straightforward examples. (We'll see more complicated ones soon enough.) Suppose that Rios, a pharmacist, mistakenly fills Paul's prescription for an antidepressant with pills that can lead to seizures. Paul takes the pills and has a seizure resulting in injuries. "But for" causation is clear: Paul had the seizure because Rios gave him the wrong pills. But for Rios's mistake, Paul would not have had the seizure. Rios's negligence is a cause in fact of Paul's injury.

Now the other example. Suppose that Mancuso works in a factory using a high-speed band saw. Phillips had removed the saw blade guard, which is meant to prevent workers' hands from contacting the blade. Mancuso is cutting a piece of plastic on the saw and has a severe allergic reaction to the plastic fumes. Here, although Phillips may have been negligent in removing the guard, his negligence is not a "but for" cause of Mancuso's injury. Presumably, the fumes would still have wafted up to Mancuso's nose if the saw had a guard, so the accident would have happened the same way if Phillips had not been negligent. His act is not, therefore, a cause in fact of Mancuso's injury.

The Problem of Multiple "But For" Causes

Accidents very frequently result from more than one negligent act. Suppose, for example, that the Edison Company negligently attaches a transformer to a light pole, and Gaudi negligently backs into the pole, knocking the loose transformer down on a child waiting for the school bus. Assume that the transformer would not have fallen, even though Gaudi hit the pole, if it had been tightly secured. Similarly, assume that the transformer would not have fallen, even though it was loose, if Gaudi had not negligently hit the pole.

If this is so, Edison might argue as follows: "Yes, it is true that I was negligent, but even though I was, the accident would not have happened unless Gaudi was, too. Even if the transformer was loose, it wouldn't have fallen unless he hit the pole. So Gaudi is the cause of the accident, not me." Of course, Gaudi can make a similar argument: "Well, I may have negligently hit the pole, but if the transformer were adequately secured it would not have fallen. So Edison's negligence is the cause of the harm, not mine."

Neither argument is sound. While it is true that either defendant's negligent act was not enough to cause the accident alone, each act was a necessary antecedent to the harm. Each cause contributed to the accident; if we take away the negligence of either defendant, the accident would not have happened, even assuming the negligence of the other. In cases like this, *both* negligent acts are causes of the injury under the "but for" test.

Put another way, it is no defense for one negligent actor that someone else's negligence also contributed to the accident. There is no requirement that the defendant's act be the *sole* "but for" cause of the injury, only that it be *a* "but for" cause.

> [A] tortfeasor is liable for all damage of which his tortious act was a proximate cause. "[He] may not escape this responsibility simply because another act—either an 'innocent' occurrence such as an 'act of God' or other [tortious] conduct—may also have been a [concurrent] cause of the injury."

Richards v. Owens-Illinois, Inc., 928 P.2d 1181, 1185 (Cal. 1997), quoting from *American Motorcycle Assn. v. Superior Court,* 578 P.2d 899, 903

(Cal. 1978). Thus, Edison cannot avoid liability because the transformer would not have fallen if Gaudi hadn't hit it. Although the loose transformer was not the sole cause of the accident, it was a "but for" cause because if Edison had not been negligent there would not have been an accident. The same is true for Gaudi.

This point is important enough to merit another illustration. Suppose Olmstead, a mason, is building a chimney on top of a city townhouse while pedestrians are using the sidewalk below. Richardson, the general contractor, was required to place a protective scaffold with a roof over the sidewalk to protect pedestrians from falling objects during construction, but failed to do so. Olmstead drops a brick and it injures Wren who is walking on the sidewalk. On these facts, the negligent acts of both Richardson and Olmstead are "but for" causes of the harm. The accident would not have happened if Olmstead had not dropped the brick. It also would not have happened (even if Olmstead dropped the brick) if Richardson had put up the scaffold.

This logic applies both to negligent acts that take place at different times, as in the Edison example, and to negligent acts that take place simultaneously. Suppose that Sullivan is driving down the street without looking carefully, and that Pei runs a stop sign coming out of a side street. Sullivan hits Pei, and his car careens into a pedestrian. The jury finds that the accident would not have happened if Pei had not run the stop sign. They also find that (even assuming Pei's negligence) the accident wouldn't have happened if Sullivan had been keeping a proper lookout. On this reasoning, both drivers' negligent acts are "but for" causes of the accident. Take away either one, and the accident would not have happened. Each is a sine qua non of the harm, since that harm would not have happened without the negligence of each.

Problems in Applying the "But For" Test: Reconstructing History

In the cases described above, applying the "but for" test is easy. In many cases, however, it involves a complex and speculative exercise, because we can never know for sure what would have happened if history had been different. Suppose, for example, that a motorcyclist is killed when he pulls out in front of a bus that is going seven miles per hour over the speed limit. Or, suppose that the plaintiff suffers chest pains and his doctor fails to diagnose it as a heart attack and provide suitable emergency treatment. Last, suppose that a landlord fails to provide a fire escape, and the tenant dies in a fire.

In each of these cases, we know that the defendant was negligent, but we don't know whether things would have come out differently if the defendant had not been negligent. If the bus had been driving at the speed limit, could it have stopped before hitting the cyclist? If the doctor had provided timely treatment, would the patient have survived or died anyway? If there had been a fire escape, would the tenant have reached it and escaped the fire? The defendant should not be held liable in such cases if the harm would have taken place regardless of the negligence. However, to determine whether the defendant's negligence affected the outcome, the jury must not only decide what actually happened, but must also speculate about a hypothetical alternative version of events: What would have happened if the defendant had not been negligent. In such cases, the "but for" test

> challenges the imagination of the trier to probe into a purely fanciful and unknowable state of affairs. He is invited to make an estimate concerning facts that concededly never existed. The very uncertainty as to what might have happened opens the door wide for conjecture.

W. Malone, Ruminations on Cause in Fact, 9 Stan. L. Rev. 60, 67 (1956).

However, while the "but for" inquiry involves a speculative comparison between actual events and hypothetical alternatives, that comparison still must be made, in order to distinguish consequences that would have happened anyway from those that were brought about, in whole or in part, by the defendant's negligent conduct. After all, the defendant's argument in these cases has much force: "I should not be held liable, even if I was negligent, unless my negligence made a difference, actually led to the plaintiff's injury."

Although this type of counterfactual inquiry is inherently speculative to some degree, the parties may be able to produce evidence that makes it less so. Evidence in the fire-escape case that the decedent died at the window certainly strengthens the inference that he would have used an available fire escape. In the motorcycle example, the distance between the bus and the cycle when the cyclist pulled into the street will be critical in determining whether the excessive speed of the bus made a difference. Expert evidence about stopping distances at various speeds will also make the jury's task less speculative. In the heart attack example, the medical evidence may establish fairly clearly that the plaintiff would have recovered with prompt treatment, or, conversely, that death was inevitable even with immediate care. Although we can never achieve certainty about cause in fact, the jury can usually make a reasoned judgment as to whether the negligence contributed to the outcome.[1]

---

1. For an example of just how difficult such counterfactual analysis can be, consider the case of a plaintiff attacked by an emotionally unstable mental patient taking Prozac. Plaintiff claims that the drug caused the assailant's assaultive conduct, yet the very reason the patient was on the drug was for emotional problems. Even if the plaintiff shows that Prozac can cause aggressive behavior, it is a speculative enterprise indeed to show that it, rather than the patient's underlying condition, caused her assault.

Some Complications: The "Substantial Factor" Test

"But for" analysis has been the traditional basis for analyzing cause in fact in negligence cases.[2] Cause in fact will virtually always be established if the "but for" test is met. Harper, James & Gray, §20.02, 91-92. However, there are a few quirky situations in which the "but for" test leads to unsatisfactory results, yet courts still think the defendant should be treated as a cause of the harm. In these situations, courts have created exceptions to the "but for" approach. Remember, however, that these *are* exceptions; in most circumstances, the defendant whose conduct was not a "but for" cause of the harm will not be liable.

One situation in which courts have created an exception to the "but for" rule is where two defendants act negligently, and either's act would suffice to cause the plaintiff's injury. Suppose, for example, that two motorcyclists roar past the plaintiff's horse and wagon, scaring the horse and injuring the plaintiff. See *Corey v. Havener,* 182 Mass. 250 (1902). In this situation, the plaintiff cannot establish cause in fact under the "but for" approach. Defendant One will argue that his act was not *necessary* to cause the harm, since the noise of the other cycle was *sufficient* to scare the horse even if Defendant One had not been there. Defendant Two will make the same argument. Since, conceptually, neither act is a sine qua non ("without which it is not") of the harm, both would get off under the "but for" test.

The court wrestled with this sufficient-but-not-necessary dilemma in *Anderson v. Minneapolis, St. P. & S. S. M. Ry. Co.,* 179 N.W. 45 (1920), in which two fires merged into one and burned the plaintiff's property. Only one of the fires was due to the defendant's negligence. It was impossible to say that but for the defendant's fire, the defendant's barn would still stand, because the other fire would likely have caused the damage anyway. Yet the defendant's culpable act clearly contributed, and it seemed fair to hold him liable for it.

In *Anderson,* the court resolved the dilemma by applying a different, less stringent, test of causation. The court held that the defendant would be a cause in fact of the damage if the jury found that its act was "a material or substantial element" in producing it. 179 N.W. at 46, 49. Under that test, the defendant was held liable even though the property would probably have been burned by the other fire anyway. This "substantial factor" test clearly leaves more leeway to the jury in assigning causal responsibility for the harm. Unlike the "but for" test, the substantial factor test is a matter

---

2. For a sophisticated discussion of "but for" causation, and a suggested alternative (but basically consistent) test, see R. Wright, Causation, Responsibility, Risk, Probability, Naked Statistics, and Proof: Pruning the Bramble Bush by Clarifying the Concepts, 73 Iowa L. Rev. 1001, 1018-1023 (1988).

of degree. The jury must make an intuitive judgment both as to what degree of causation is "substantial" and whether the defendant's negligence reaches that level. See Robertson, Powers, Anderson & Wellborn, Torts (2d ed. 1998), 141 ("substantial factor" test "incorporates no particular mental operation but appeals forthrightly to instinct"); see also, for a more jaundiced view, B. Black & D. Hollander, Unravelling Causation: Back to the Basics, 3 J. Env. Law 1, 10 (1993) ("substantial factor" test allows jury "to do essentially what it pleases").[3]

In the unusual situation illustrated by *Anderson,* the "substantial factor" test has gained wide acceptance. See Restatement (Second) of Torts, §431(a). However, it is important to understand that the "substantial factor" test is an *alternative* approach to cause in fact for those unusual situations in which the "but for" test does not yield satisfactory results. On exams, students often run the facts through both tests, as though both must be satisfied in any case. This reflects understandable confusion. Remember that, generally speaking, plaintiff must show that the defendant's act was a "but for" cause of the harm. Only in unusual situations like *Anderson,* where the traditional analysis breaks down, will the court allow the more amorphous showing that the defendant's negligence was a substantial factor in causing the harm. See Robertson, Powers, Anderson & Wellborn, 141-142.

Despite the origin of the substantial factor test, as an exception to the usual "but for" approach, some courts now hold that the substantial factor test should be used to determine cause in fact in all cases, not just anomalies like *Anderson.* See, e.g., *Mitchell v. Gonzales,* 819 P.2d 872, 878-879 (Cal. 1991). However, even under a substantial factor instruction, the defendant should not be held liable (except in *Anderson*-type multiple-sufficient-cause cases) if the harm would have occurred even if she had not been negligent. See Restatement (Second) of Torts, §432(1) (an actor's negligence is not a substantial factor in causing harm if the harm would have been sustained even if the actor had not been negligent);[4] see also Prosser & Keeton 267-268 (in almost all situations, defendant's conduct will not be a substantial factor if the harm would have occurred without it). So, the "but for" test is alive and well for most situations. If the defendant is not a "but for" cause of the harm, he will generally not be liable, unless the situation involves a twist like *Anderson* or *Summers* (discussed immediately below).

---

3. Because the "substantial factor" test requires the factfinder to make a judgment about how much causal contribution is "enough," it arguably melds the actual causation inquiry with proximate cause analysis. See R. Wright, Causation in Tort Law, 73 Cal. L. Rev. 1735, 1782-1783 (1985). ("[T]he question of limiting liability due to the *extent* of contribution rather than to the absence of *any* contribution, is clearly a proximate-cause issue of policy or principle, rather than an issue of actual causation (contribution to the injury).")

4. For a review of the debate about the relation between the two tests, see Wright, 73 Cal. L. Rev. at 1781-1784.

More Complications: Shifting the Burden of Proof

Summers v. Tice, 199 P.2d 1 (Cal. 1948), illustrates another situation in which the "but for" test yields unsatisfactory results. In *Summers,* the two defendants fired their shotguns, and a pellet from one or the other injured the plaintiff's eye. Both defendants were negligent, but it was impossible for the plaintiff to show that it was "more probable than not" that either defendant's pellet had hit him: It was a 50/50 proposition that either defendant's shot had hit the eye. Under "but for" analysis, the plaintiff would lose.

The California Supreme Courts was unwilling to see the plaintiff lose in *Summers.* It was clear that both defendants had committed the same act, that both were negligent, and that one or the other had injured the plaintiff. Given those facts, the court concluded that it would be unfair to let both of them off the hook simply because plaintiff was unable to pinpoint which hunter's shot had caused the harm. Instead, the court shifted the burden of proof to each defendant to show that he had *not* caused the harm. The defendants, of course, were no more able to prove whose shot hit the plaintiff than he was. So, the result was that both were liable for the injury.

Summers v. Tice stands for the proposition that, where two (or perhaps more) defendants commit substantially similar negligent acts, one of which caused that plaintiff's injury, the burden of proof shifts to each defendant to show that he did not cause the harm. If they cannot make that showing, both will be held liable for the plaintiff's loss. This fairly narrow proposition has been followed by a number of courts. Others, however, have rejected *Summers* entirely, leaving the plaintiff to establish causation under the traditional "but for" test. See, e.g., *Leuer v. Johnson,* 450 N.W.2d 363 (Minn. App. 1990).

However, be careful not to take this case to stand for more than it does. *Summers* does *not* hold that every time the plaintiff sues more than one defendant, the burden of proof shifts to the defendants on the issue of causation. That is much too broad a reading of the case. *Summers* addresses a narrow anomaly in which "but for" analysis fails; it is not a general abdication of plaintiff's burden on the causation element of a negligence claim.

Suppose, for example, that Corbusier is injured when a light pole collapses on him as he walks down the sidewalk. There is evidence that Van der Rohe may have backed into the pole earlier in the day, and evidence that Wren did some excavating next to the pole the day before. The plaintiff cannot march into court, citing *Summers v. Tice,* and shift the burden of proof to each of these defendants to show that his negligence did not cause the pole to fall. This case is very different from *Summers.* First, in *Summers,* the two defendants were both found to be negligent. Naturally, the principle of the case could not apply until Corbusier proves that both

Van der Rohe and Wren were negligent. Second, Corbusier alleges quite different acts of negligence against Van der Rohe and Wren. In *Summers,* the defendants did exactly the same thing, so the chances were equal that either caused the harm, and there was no logical way to decide who had caused it. In more typical multi-defendant cases like Corbusier's, the jury has some basis for making a more-probable-than-not finding of who caused the harm (or finding that they both did under traditional "but for" analysis). Consequently, the court is unlikely to invoke the burden-shifting approach of *Summers.*

Reconstructing History: Practical Proof Problems in Establishing Cause in Fact

In many cases the act that caused the injury is clear, but the plaintiff faces a difficult causation problem in identifying the actor who did that act. Suppose in the plywood example that three subcontractors were working on the floor from which the plywood fell. Although the falling plywood clearly caused Sullivan's injury, Sullivan will have the very practical causation problem of proving who dropped it. Or, suppose that Fleming is injured when a crowbar she is using snaps in half, sending a splinter of steel into her eye. Here again, the mechanism that caused the harm is clear, but Fleming faces a formidable problem in proving who made the crowbar, since crowbars look pretty much alike and may not carry any identifying marks. Or, suppose a fan throws a beer bottle from the stands at a football game, injuring a player. Negligence and causation are clear, but it may simply be impossible to identify who threw the bottle.

The causation issue in these who-done-it cases is not *conceptually* difficult, but poses the difficult practical problem of identifying the proper defendant. If we had an omniscient observer (we'll call him Solomon) and a time machine, we could send him back to re-view the relevant events and solve these identification problems. Without Solomon, however, plaintiffs must do the best they can to prove that the defendant was the negligent actor. In the real world of law practice, plaintiffs often lose cases because they cannot prove that the defendant committed the negligent act. In many other cases, the plaintiff never brings suit in the first place because she simply can't identify the negligent party. Students generally come to the Torts course with the preconception that a person who is hurt always recovers damages, but any torts practitioner will attest that practical realities often prevent worthy plaintiffs from recovering at all.

The examples below illustrate basic problems in determining cause in fact. In approaching them, assume that the "but for" test applies, except in situations such as *Anderson* and *Summers,* in which it yields unsatisfactory results.

EXAMPLES

Causation and Consequences

1.   Malone, a carpenter, is hired to rebuild some seats at the local high school football stadium. He finds a plug near the scoreboard to plug in his power saw. The outlet has outdated wiring, lacking a third grounding wire to discharge static electricity. But Malone's homemade extension cord had only two prongs as well; it lacked the third grounding prong that plugs into the third wire in a modern outlet to discharge static electricity. He plugged in the saw, turned it on, and was electrocuted.

   a. Assuming that the school district was negligent for having the outdated wiring, is its negligence a "but for" cause of Malone's death?

   b. Would its negligence be deemed a cause of Malone's death under a substantial factor test?

   c. Can you think of a twist in the facts (assuming Malone survived to testify) that might change the result in this case?

2.   Gray, a cabinetmaker, is driving his delivery truck on the interstate when it suffers a freak blowout and jackknifes to a halt across the three lanes of traffic. Harper, another driver who is tuning the radio dial instead of looking where his car is going, doesn't see the truck until too late and applies his brakes hard, swerving into the next lane. James, a third driver who is combing his hair in the little mirror on the visor fails to brake and hits Harper, sending Harper's car careening into Gray's truck, causing injuries to Gray. Who is liable to Gray?

3.   Gray is taken to the hospital, where Dr. Green negligently sets his arm. Consequently, it must be rebroken a week later and set again, causing Gray considerable pain and medical expense. Which actors are "but for" causes of the injuries to Gray?

Nature and Negligence

4.   Corbusier, driving down a country road, comes around a curve and encounters a deep puddle due to recent heavy rains. He tries to stop, but his brakes have been so poorly maintained that he cannot control the car. The car swerves to the left and hits Saarinen driving in the opposite direction, causing serious injuries. Is Corbusier liable under the "but for" test?

5.   Dobbs is driving carefully to the store for a quart of milk when Fletcher pulls out of a side street without looking and crashes into Dobbs, who swerves into Schwartz on the sidewalk. Which driver's conduct is a "but for" cause of Schwartz's injuries?

6.   Dobbs is driving to the store without his glasses, which he really ought to be wearing to drive safely. Fletcher pulls out of the side street without looking. Dobbs sees him too late, they collide, and Dobbs suffers a concussion in the resulting collision. What are the "but for" causes of the accident?

Revisionist History

7.   Haines, a student, is beaten and robbed in a college dormitory. Investigation determines that the assailant, Gibbs, had been admitted to the dorm to visit another student. Haines sues the college, alleging that it was negligent in failing to hire enough security officers to assure adequate security.

    a. What is the nature of Haines's problem in proving causation in this case?

    b. What will the college argue on the causation issue?

    c. What will the plaintiff's counterargument be?

    d. If you represented the plaintiff, would you prefer that the jury be instructed under the "but for" or substantial factor test for causation?

8.   Smith applies to Jones, the Chief of Police, for a permit to carry a handgun. A statute requires Chief Jones to check with the state Department of Public Safety to determine whether an applicant has a criminal record before issuing the permit, and to refuse the permit if the applicant has a record. Jones fails to do so and issues the permit. Three days later, Smith shoots Doe on the street with the gun. Doe sues Chief Jones for negligence.

    a. Assume that Smith had no criminal record. Is cause in fact established?

    b. Assume that Chief Jones fails to check, and issues the permit to Smith even though he has a criminal record. Can the plaintiff prove cause in fact?

Pestiferous Problems

9.   Smith and Jones, two farmers, both sell tomatoes that have been sprayed with Icthar, a banned pesticide, to a local market. The market puts the tomatoes out, together, in a bin. Wren buys one and gets sick from the pesticide.

    a. If Wren sues the farmers, what type of causation problem will he face?

    b. How does the problem compare to the problem in *Anderson v. Minneapolis, St. Paul & St. Marie R.R. Co.*, the two fires case?

    c. Can this problem be solved by use of the "substantial factor" test?

    d. How will this case come out under *Summers*?

    e. What is the best argument *against* the *Summers*'s court's solution to this type of problem?

But for Judge Fudd

10.   Ortega is injured when he slips on a pencil on the office floor. The floor had been swept early that morning. The only other employees in the office that day are Chu, Abbrezio, and Tate. Ortega sues all three for his

injury. Prior to trial, Ortega requests the following jury instruction on cause in fact at trial:

> If you find that the defendants Chu, Abbrezio, and Tate were at the office on the day in question, but that the plaintiff is unable to establish which of them dropped the pencil that caused her injury, you should find each of the defendants jointly liable for the injury. However, if any of the defendants establishes by a preponderance of the evidence that he did not drop the pencil, you should not find that defendant liable.

Should the Honorable Fudd so instruct the jury?

11. Markosky's oncoming car negligently swerves into Osteen's. One second later, Jagger, following Osteen too closely, plows into Osteen's car. When the dust settles, Osteen has a serious back injury. The problem, of course, is to determine which impact caused the injury.

    a. How is this case like *Summers v. Tice*?

    b. How does it differ from *Summers*?

    c. What are the court's options for choosing a causation rule for this case?

A Conundrum for Fun

12. Two farmers negligently start fires on a windy day, to burn brush off of their fields. Both fires escape, Farmer Jones's fire a bit ahead of Farmer Smith's. Jones's fire burns toward Menlove's barn, which burns to the ground. Just after it burns, Smith's fire arrives.

    a. Who is liable under the "but for" test?

    b. Who is liable under the substantial factor test?

    c. Applying a little common sense, who should be liable to Menlove?

An Elemental Example

13. Wright negligently runs down Morales in the street. Morales dies of his injuries. However, Morales had a terminal disease from which he was expected to die within a matter of weeks. Did Wright cause Morales's death? Should he be held liable, and if so, for what?

EXPLANATIONS

Causation and Consequences

1a.   The district's negligence is a "but for" cause of Malone's death if its failure to have a third grounding wire made a difference in the way the accident happened. It didn't; if there had been a third wire, it would not have grounded the saw, because Malone's extension cord had no third prong to deliver current into the grounding wire and avoid the shock. So, the accident would have happened the same way if the district had not been negligent. Consequently, even though the district *was* negligent, it is not liable, since it did not cause the harm. See *Grain Dealers Mutual Insurance Co. v. Porterfield*, 695 S.W.2d 833 (Ark. 1985). Remember, proving negligence only gets you part way there; the negligent act must cause the plaintiff's injury to support recovery.[4.1]

b. Although some courts purport to apply the substantial factor test in analyzing all actual cause issues, this should make no difference in Malone's case. If the injury would still have happened even without the defendant's negligence, it will not generally be deemed a substantial factor in causing that injury. Cases like *Anderson* are exceptions, for unusual circumstances like the two-sufficient-cause case and some others we will take up in the next chapter. Generally speaking, no "but for" causation, no substantial factor causation either. If Malone would have died even if the district had had a third grounding wire in the system, the lack of such a wire is not a substantial factor in causing his death. Indeed, it is not a factor at all.

c. If Malone survived, he might testify that he only used his old two-prong extension cord because he saw that the outlet had no grounding wire. Why bother to use a grounded extension cord if it wasn't going to make any difference? On these facts, Malone could show that the lack of a grounding wire in the system did lead to the injury, because, had the grounding wire been there, he would have used the appropriate cord and avoided the injury. This would show that history would have been different but for the negligence of the district.

2. In this example Harper's negligence and James's are both "but for" causes of the accident, because each contributed to causing Gray's injuries. But for Harper's sharp stop, which sent him into James's lane, James would not have hit him. But for James's failure to watch the road, he would have avoided hitting Harper and knocking his car into Gray's truck. Each contributed to causing a single, indivisible injury to Gray, and each is liable for the entire injury.

3. Under "but for" analysis, Harper and James are both "but for" causes of Gray's initial injury, and of his additional injuries due to Green's malpractice. But for each of their negligent acts, Gray would not have been in the hospital to begin with, and would not have suffered the additional injury due to Green's mistake. Consequently, they have caused the initial injury and the malpractice damages as well.

Dr. Green, however, is not a cause of the turnpike accident. It would have happened the same way if we remove his negligence from the scenario.

4.1. Of course, Malone was negligent here too, for not having the right extension cord. If the district's negligence were a "but for" cause of the harm, his negligence would reduce his recovery under comparative negligence.

He is, of course, a "but for" cause of the injuries from resetting the arm. But for his failure to set it properly the first time, this enhanced injury would not have happened. So, he may be liable for the enhanced injuries but not those resulting from the initial collision.

As we will see in later chapters, the traditional response of the common law to situations where more than one tortfeasor causes an injury is to hold them all liable for the plaintiff's damages. In this case, Harper and James would be liable for Gray's initial injury. Harper, James and Green would be liable for the extra damages due to Green's missetting of the arm.

Nature and Negligence

4.   This accident is caused by both Corbusier's negligent maintenance of his car and the puddle that created the dangerous condition in the road. Although only one of these causes is due to Corbusier's negligence, that negligence is still a "but for" cause of the harm. The accident would not have happened if Corbusier had not been negligent. True, it would not have happened, *even if Corbusier was negligent*, if the puddle had not been there, but that does not exonerate him. It is not a defense for him that other circumstances, whether natural or negligent, also contributed to the accident, if his negligence was one of those causes.[5]

5.   This example makes a very basic point. Clearly, both Dobbs's and Fletcher's driving are "but for" causes of the accident. If Dobbs hadn't gone for milk, the accident wouldn't have happened; if Fletcher hadn't pulled out of the side street, the accident wouldn't have happened. However, the fact that they both *caused* the accident doesn't mean that they will both be liable to Schwartz. Dobbs caused the accident by nonnegligent conduct, while Fletcher was a negligent cause. In a tort case, the plaintiff must show that the defendant's *tortious conduct* caused the harm, not just that his act caused it. In analyzing cause in fact, then, be careful to ask the right question — whether the defendant's negligence caused the harm, not just whether his conduct caused it.

6.   In this example, the plaintiff's negligence is one of the "but for" causes of the accident, along with the negligence of the defendant. There's nothing unusual about that; it's just another multiple-cause case. Sometimes two parties are negligent and cause injuries to a third party, as in the typical joint tortfeasor situation like the Edison example in the

---

5. In addition to the puddle, there are many other nonnegligent causes of this accident. Saarinen's decision to drive caused it; the construction of the two drivers' cars caused it; the invention of the wheel caused it. Clearly, Corbusier should not be able to exonerate himself by showing that there were such other contributing factors.

introduction. At other times, two actors are negligent and their negligence causes injury to *one of them*, as in this case.

If the plaintiff's negligence is one of the "but for" causes of an accident, tort law has to decide what to do about that. As a matter of policy, we might decide to bar a plaintiff who was causally negligent from recovery entirely — the rule of contributory negligence. Or, we might reduce the plaintiff's damages to account for his negligence — the rule of comparative negligence. Last, we might hold the defendant fully liable anyway — the rule of strict liability. But these choices have nothing to do with the basic *factual* question of whose negligence caused the accident: It is perfectly clear under "but for" causation that both Dobbs and Fletcher did.

Revisionist History

7a.   The causation problem here is to determine whether the defendant's negligence affected the result, that is, whether the plaintiff would have been assaulted if the college had provided adequate security. It requires the factfinder to compare what did happen to what *would have happened* absent the defendant's negligence.

b.   The college will argue that it should not be held liable, even if security was inadequate, because any inadequacy in security did not cause the assault. It will argue that having more security officers would not have affected the outcome, because the student did not slip into the dorm illegally; he was admitted through the ordinary procedures.

There is certainly force to this argument. Gibbs did not break into the dorm, he entered openly for a legitimate reason. Consequently, inadequate security did not affect Gibbs's ability to get into the dorm. Even if there had been additional officers available, they would not have barred his entry and prevented Gibbs's actions.

c.   Haines will argue that, even if the inadequate security did not "cause" Gibbs's entry, it still caused the harm because, had Gibbs known that the campus was well patrolled, he would have feared being caught and therefore would not have attempted the crime. This illustrates the speculative role of the jury in this type of case, in which they must try to get into Gibbs's mind and decide what he would have done under different circumstances.

d.   Under the "but for" test, the jury could only find causation if it concluded that Gibbs would not have committed the assault if security had been better. The substantial factor test, however, would allow the jury to find for the plaintiff on the causation issue if they concluded that inadequate security was a substantial factor in causing Gibbs's assault. This is clearly less demanding than the "but for" standard. The substantial factor instruction is less clear-cut, and thus leaves the jury more leeway to conclude that inadequate security contributed in a meaningful way to Gibbs's decision, without resolving the harder question of whether Gibbs would have acted the same way if security had been stronger.

8a.   This is another case that requires the jury to compare what actually happened to what would have happened if the defendant had not been negligent. Here, Jones's negligence in failing to check Smith's criminal record was not a "but for" cause of Doe's injury. Had he checked, he would have discovered that Smith had no record; consequently, he would have issued the permit anyway. Thus, Doe cannot show that, but for Jones's failure to check the record, Smith would not have obtained the gun permit and shot Doe. Although that failure was negligent, it was not causal negligence.

b.   The argument for causation is a great deal stronger in this case. If Jones had checked, he would have discovered that Smith had a record and refused the permit. But for his failure to check, the permit would not have been issued.

However, Smith might have carried the gun without the permit and shot Doe anyway. Perhaps the evidence would even show that he would have. But the evidence might also lead the jury to conclude that Smith would not have carried a gun without a permit, and that Doe would therefore not have been shot. The plaintiff need not show that Smith could not possibly have shot Doe without the permit; she need only convince the jury that it is more probable than not that she would not have been injured but for the defendant's negligence. Though there is certainly a measure of speculation involved, one can imagine facts on which the jury could reasonably reach that conclusion here.

Pestiferous Problems

9a.   These facts are closely analogous to the facts of *Summers v. Tice*, in which two hunters fired at a bird and shot from one of the guns injured the plaintiff. Here, as in *Summers*, we know what caused the harm — eating the tomato laced with pesticide — but we need to know whose tomato it was. It is a proof problem that Solomon could easily solve if he went back and watched the events carefully enough. But we don't have a Solomon and we don't have any way of determining which farmer's tomato Wren ate.

b.   In *Anderson*, there were two causes of the harm, either of which was sufficient to produce it. Each defendant could argue that its negligence was not a "but for" cause of the harm, because the negligence of the other would have caused it anyway. However, each was clearly a sufficient cause of the fire. Here, by contrast, there was only one cause of the harm: Wren only ate one tomato, supplied by one of the farmers but not by the other. The problem — probably an insuperable one, as a practical matter — is identifying which defendant's tomato was the "but for" cause of his illness.

    c.   Using a substantial factor test for causation does not resolve this problem. Even under this test, there was only one "substantial factor" that caused the injury. The basic problem of tracing the tomato remains.

    d.   In *Summers*, the court resolved the dilemma posed by cases like this by shifting the burden of proof to the defendants, since they were both negligent. This does not solve the identification problem; it simply places the risk of nonidentification on the defendants. Since the farmers here are no more able to show whose tomato caused the harm than the plaintiff, they will both be held liable, and will end up splitting the loss under contribution principles if both are solvent. This resolution of the dilemma may lack intellectual elegance, but it does provide a kind of rough and ready justice that courts must often settle for in real disputes.

    e.   The best argument against the *Summers* solution is that it guarantees that a defendant who did not cause any harm to the plaintiff will be held liable for her damages. Since neither farmer will be able to prove that Wren did not eat his tomato, each will be held jointly and severally liable. Presumably, one will pay Wren, and then seek contribution from the other, so they will end up splitting the damages. But Wren only ate one tomato, so only one farmer caused her any harm. Admittedly, the other was negligent, but traditional tort doctrine says that's not enough to support liability: The defendant's negligence must *cause injury* to support liability. Not so under *Summers v. Tice.*

    While this is a departure from the traditional rules, it is one that a number of courts find more acceptable than the alternative: sending the plaintiff away empty-handed.

But for Judge Fudd

10. If I put this on my exam many students would say that Judge Fudd should give the requested instruction, since the case is vaguely like *Summers v. Tice*. They would justify that conclusion with reasoning like this: "If the plaintiff is unable to determine which defendant caused the harm, the court will shift the burden of proof to the defendants to show that they didn't cause it."

    This is Fudd-led analysis, because this case differs from *Summers* in important respects. First, in *Summers*, the plaintiff had proved that both defendants were negligent. Here, she hasn't proved that any of them were; she could have dropped the pencil herself. If it was one of the defendants, well, it was *one* of the defendants, and the others didn't do anything negligent. There is no justification for shifting the burden of proof to the defendants every time plaintiff sues more than one. This would be a major change in American tort law, one even the California court didn't make! The burden remains on Ortega to prove who dropped that pencil.

But, how can she ever meet that burden of proof? Maybe she can't. But there is no rule of tort law that says injured plaintiffs must always win. The basic rules say she wins only if she proves all elements of her negligence claim, and — *Summers* or no *Summers* — the uncertainty of making that proof *generally falls on her.*

11a.   The case is like *Summers* in that plaintiff can prove that both defendants were negligent. It is also like *Summers* in that plaintiff may be unable to establish by a preponderance of the evidence which defendant caused her injuries.

b.   The case differs from *Summers* in that here, unlike in *Summers*, causation is not necessarily an either/or proposition. In *Summers*, plaintiff's eye was hit by one pellet, either Tice's or Simonson's. One defendant had caused no harm at all; the other had caused the entire injury. In Osteen's case, one collision may have caused the entire injury, but it is also possible — indeed, likely — that the first collision caused some and the second collision caused some more.

This type of case (in which two negligent defendants have probably contributed to an injury, but it is difficult or impossible to determine how much of the injury was caused by each) is much more common than the pure *Summers v. Tice* scenario. Osteen's case, unlike *Summers*, poses a proof problem that commonly arises in the practice of tort law.

c.   The court could take a number of approaches to this apportionment problem. One would be to stick to the traditional rules: make Osteen prove how much injury each defendant caused. If she couldn't, she loses. She may not be able to muster the necessary proof, but if not, that's life in the big city. As indicated in the introduction, lots of plaintiffs go without compensation because they simply can't find the proof.

A second approach is to shift the burden to the defendants, once plaintiff establishes that they were both negligent, to show that they did not cause the injury, or to show what part of it they did cause. Most courts have taken this approach to this apportionment dilemma. If the plaintiff proves that both defendants were negligent, and that she suffered an injury difficult to apportion, the burden shifts to the defendants to show which part they caused. If they can't separate the damages, they are held jointly liable for them all. Restatement (Second) of Torts, §433B.

A Conundrum for Fun

12a.   The "but for" test exonerates both farmers. We cannot say that, "But for Farmer Jones's fire, Menlove would not have lost his barn," because Smith's fire would have burned it if Jones's hadn't gotten there first. We cannot say that Smith's fire is a "but for" cause, either. Clearly, the barn would have burned anyway even if Smith had never lit his fire.

b.   Any sensible jury should conclude that Jones's fire was a substantial factor in burning Menlove's barn. It *did* burn the barn, without any help from Smith's fire.

Presumably, Smith's fire was *not* a substantial factor in causing the loss — it made no contribution at all to the demise of Menlove's beloved barn. It certainly could have if it had had the chance, but the barn was gone when it got there.

c.   This conundrum involves what might be called the preempted cause, one that is sufficient to cause the harm, but never actually comes into operation. Smith's fire would have done the job, but didn't, because the other fire caused the loss first. Having the capacity to cause the loss ought not to substitute for actually having caused it. Jones, whose negligence caused the damage, should be liable for it, even though the "but for" test fails. Smith, who didn't cause it, shouldn't be liable, even though his negligence would have caused the harm if Jones had not preempted him.

This is like the case of Villain, who poisons his enemy's drink. Just as Enemy puts it to his lips, he is shot by Desperado. Villain tried to cause Enemy's death, and his means were sufficient to the purpose. But the poison never came into operation, since Enemy died without drinking. We might punish Villain for attempted murder at criminal law, but he is not the cause of Enemy's death.

An Elemental Example

13.   Of course Wright caused Morales's death; the example basically says so. Morales died of his injuries, not of the terminal disease. But for the accident, Morales would have been alive; because of the accident, he died. Wright is a tortfeasor and liable for Morales's death.

The fact that Morales was terminally ill is relevant, however, to the fourth element of the negligence claim, *damages*. The measure of damages in Morales's case will be the loss caused by Wright's tort. But for Wright's negligence, Morales would have lived, but only for a few weeks. Wright will be liable, but the damages for wrongful death will be limited by Morales's short life expectancy.

8

Risks Reconsidered: Complex Issues in Establishing Factual Cause

Introduction

Most law students think of proximate cause as the Heartbreak Hill of the Torts marathon, the toughest problem in a course replete with tough intellectual issues. However, the real action today is in the cause-in-fact arena, where tort law is constantly butting heads against an intractable problem: the limits of human knowledge about cause and effect. There is a world of difference between a defendant causing injury to a plaintiff, on the one hand, and the plaintiff *proving* that she did, on the other. This chapter, for those of you courageous enough to press on, addresses a number of cutting edge factual causation issues often encountered in the Torts course—and increasingly, in the practice of tort law.

Causation in DES Cases: Who Done It?

The first complex causation problem is illustrated by the DES cases. DES is a drug that was widely prescribed for several decades to prevent miscarriage, but which has subsequently been shown to cause various medical problems in the daughters of women who took it during pregnancy. Because DES was marketed in chemically identical form by over 200 companies, a plaintiff injured by DES exposure faces a very difficult cause-in-fact problem: Even if all companies were negligent for marketing the drug, only one of them — the manufacturer that manufactured the DES pills her mother took — caused her injuries.

This is an enormously difficult proof problem, but there is nothing *conceptually* hard about it. The chemical that injured the plaintiff is known. The problem is simply a matter of "who done it." If we could summon Solomon, our omniscient time traveler, he could solve this problem easily enough, by going back to watch the relevant events and jotting down the name of the manufacturer on the bottle.

Sometimes the plaintiff can solve it, too. She may be able to identify the manufacturer if her mother recalls the shape, color, or brand of DES she took.[1] In many cases, however, the evidence will show that the mother took DES, but not which manufacturer's pill it was. In such cases, the plaintiff will be unable to establish that a particular manufacturer caused her injury. If she is held to the usual burden to prove causation, she must lose.

While this result appears inexorable under traditional tort theory, the California Supreme Court in *Sindell v. Abbott Laboratories*, 607 P.2d 924 (1980), found it unacceptable. To avoid this outcome, the court fashioned the "market share" theory, which allows the plaintiff to sue a number of manufacturers and — assuming they are found at fault — hold each liable for part of the plaintiff's damages. Under the *Sindell* approach, each manufacturer's share of the liability is determined by the proportional share of DES it sold in the relevant market area.

Sindell does not solve the cause-in-fact problem, it redesigns it. Instead of asking who caused the particular plaintiff's damages, it asks who contributed to the creation of a general risk of injury, and distributes the damages among those risk creators in proportion to the amount of risk each created. It is entirely clear under *Sindell* that defendants will be held liable to a plaintiff *even though they did not cause her any harm*. If Sindell sues six manufacturers who sold DES in the relevant market, but her mother only took one brand of DES, five of them will be held partially liable without having caused the injuries for which she sues.

On the other hand, if all DES daughters sued all manufacturers under the market share approach, the manufacturers would, theoretically, pay in proper proportion to the injuries they caused. A manufacturer who made 10 percent of the DES sold would be held liable for 10 percent of each plaintiff's injuries. Since it actually caused *all* the injuries suffered by

---

1. The plaintiff hit a snag with this approach in *Krist v. Eli Lilly & Co.*, 897 F.2d 293 (7th Cir. 1990). Her mother testified repeatedly, under the defendant's examination, that the DES she had taken was a "little red pill." The defendant then introduced evidence that it had indeed sold DES in a little red pill, but that it had done so only *after* the mother's pregnancy.

10 percent of DES daughters, this should work out about right in the aggregate. Of course, all plaintiffs will not sue all defendants for their DES injuries, nor have all states (or even a majority) adopted the market share theory. Consequently, while in theory there is logic to the market share approach, its effect is rather haphazard in practice.

Market share liability looks more like a legislative solution to the causation problem than a judicial one: The court fashions a remedy that encompasses not only the party that actually caused the plaintiff's harm but also other parties who contributed to the general risk that harmed her. While it serves several of tort law's basic goals—compensation for the plaintiff and deterrence of negligent conduct—it arguably goes beyond the traditional role of courts in tort cases, by holding parties liable who caused no harm to the plaintiff before the court. But complex problems of modern life have forced courts to fashion such nontraditional remedies in a variety of contexts. While it is easy to criticize the California court's approach, the alternative—leaving plaintiffs without a remedy for negligent conduct, and defendants without an incentive to avoid it—isn't very satisfying either. In lawsuits, unlike philosophy classes, courts have to decide. Refusal to refashion traditional doctrine in cases like *Sindell* usually means that the plaintiff loses.

Since *Sindell*, courts have created some interesting variations on the market share approach. Here are three.

- In *Martin v. Abbott Labs.*, 689 P.2d 368 (Wash. 1984), the Washington Supreme Court held that a plaintiff may sue one DES manufacturer only. (Of course, she is free to sue more if she wishes.) If she proves that that manufacturer sold the drug in the relevant market area (that is, where her mother purchased the drug), and that DES caused her injuries, that defendant will be liable for the plaintiff's injuries.

  However, the defendant may implead (that is, bring into the action) other DES makers. If it does, all makers before the court are *presumed* to have equal market shares. Thus, the plaintiff need not shoulder the difficult burden of establishing market shares. If the defendants offer no proof as to market share, they will each be held liable for a pro rata share of the plaintiff's damages. (If, for example, five are joined, each would be severally liable for one-fifth of the plaintiff's damages.) Any defendant that establishes that it had a smaller market share will pay according to that share. If this happens, the shares of the other defendants go up, so that plaintiff still recovers 100 percent of her damages.

- In *Abel v. Eli Lilly & Co.*, 343 N.W.2d 164 (Mich. 1984), the Michigan Supreme Court adopted an approach to DES liability modeled on *Summers v. Tice*. The court held that a plaintiff may recover by joining all defendants who might have sold the drug ingested by her mother. Any defendant may avoid liability by proving that it did not manufacture the DES that injured the plaintiff. Any maker who does not make such proof is *jointly and severally liable* to the plaintiff for her entire damages.

- The New York Court of Appeals has taken the most radical approach to market share liability. In *Hymowitz v. Eli Lilly & Co.*, 541 N.Y.S.2d 941 (1989), the court held that a plaintiff who proves that she was injured by her mother's ingestion of DES recovers from any defendant who participated in the *United States* market for DES. Recovery is in proportion to national market share. If less than all makers are before the court—which will virtually always be so—the plaintiff will recover less than full damages, since each maker pays only in proportion to its market share.

What makes New York's approach radical is that it uses national market share, *and bars any maker from proving that it did not make the DES that injured the plaintiff*. Suppose, for example, that Acme Drug Company proves that it never sold DES in New York, where the plaintiff's mother bought the drug. Or suppose it proves that its DES pills were blue, and the plaintiff's mother testifies that the pills she took were red. Under *Hymowitz*, Acme pays in proportion to its national market share, even though it conclusively establishes that it did not cause the plaintiff's injury:

> It is merely a windfall for a producer to escape liability solely because it manufactured a more identifiable pill, or sold only to certain drugstores. These fortuities in no way diminish the culpability of a defendant for marketing the product, which is the basis of liability here.

541 N.Y.S.2d at 950.

This quotation from *Hymowitz* is enormously ironic. Common law courts for centuries have premised liability on causing the plaintiff's harm. Yet the *Hymowitz* court fairly casually concludes that it is "merely a windfall" to allow the defendant to avoid liability by showing it did no harm to the plaintiff!

Market share liability is a controversial doctrine. Many courts have refused to adopt any variant on *Sindell*. Rhode Island, for example, rejected it in a one-page rescript opinion. "We are not willing to adopt the market-share doctrine which has been accepted in the State of California in *Sindell v. Abbott Laboratories, Inc.* . . . We are of the opinion that the establishment of liability requires the identification of the specific defendant responsible for the injury." *Gorman v. Abbott Laboratories*, 599 A.2d 1364, 1364 (R.I. 1991). See also *Mulcahy v. Eli Lilly & Co.*, 386 N.W.2d 67, 75 (Iowa 1986) ("awarding damages to an admittedly innocent party by means of a court-constructed device that places liability on manufacturers who were not proved to have caused the injury involves social engineering more appropriately within the legislative domain").

The examples that follow illustrate the application — and some of the problems — of the market share approach to actual causation. The explanations begin on p. 172.

EXAMPLES

Share, or Share Alike?

1. Sindell sues nine DES makers in California. At trial, she introduces some proof that the drug was that of Acme Drug Company. In the alternative, she relies on the market share theory. If the jury concludes that Acme made the drug her mother took, what should it do?

2. Sindell sues four DES makers in California. At trial, she establishes that all defendants were negligent for marketing DES, and that their individual market shares were as follows: D1 10 percent, D2 20 percent, D3 30 percent. D4 proves that it sold no DES in the relevant market at the time. The jury finds Sindell's damages to be $100,000. Under the *Sindell* approach, how much should each defendant pay?

3. On the facts of Example 2, what happens if D2 is unable to pay its share of the total liability?

4. You represent Sindell, and have decided to proceed on a market share theory in California. What problems would you foresee in proving the market shares of the various defendants?

Absent Tortfeasors

5. Assume that Sindell's mother bought DES in New York, and Sindell sues there after *Hymowitz.* One defendant, the Acme Drug Company, establishes that it never sold DES in New York, but that it did have a 10 percent share of the national market for DES at the relevant time. Is it liable?

6. Assume that Sindell sues in New York after *Hymowitz.* Assume that the Acme Drug Company proves that it did not sell DES at all at the time that Sindell's mother took the drug, but the plaintiff establishes that it did have a 20 percent share of the DES market two years later. How should its liability be determined under *Hymowitz?*

7. Assume that Sindell sues one DES maker, the Acme Drug Company, in Washington State (Washington's approach to market share liability is described on p. 161). Acme brings three others, Beta, Gamma, and Phi Corporations, into the suit. Phi establishes that it never sold DES in the relevant market. Beta establishes that its share of the market was 6 percent. The other defendants offer no evidence on their market shares. Under the

approach adopted by the Washington Supreme Court in *Martin*, what would each defendant owe?

8.   Suppose on the facts of Example 7, that Acme proved its share was 15 percent, Beta proved its was 6 percent, Gamma proved its share was 10 percent, and Phi proved it had no market share. How much would each defendant pay under the Washington market share approach?

9.   On the facts of Example 7, what would the plaintiff recover under the Michigan approach (p. 161), assuming again that she cannot prove which manufacturer sold the DES taken by her mother? Assume that the plaintiff's damages are $100,000.

Causation in Multiple Exposure Cases

A somewhat different problem is posed by cases of multiple exposure to a dangerous substance such as asbestos. Suppose, for example, that Corbusier worked as a pipe insulator in a shipyard for 30 years and was exposed over those years to various asbestos products sold by six companies. These products might include insulating materials, fireproofing, floor and ceiling tiles, and others. Eventually, he contracts asbestosis, a disease of the lungs which has been definitively linked to breathing asbestos fibers.

As in the DES cases, there is no problem here in ascertaining the mechanism that caused the harm. As the name indicates, abestosis is a "signature disease"; medical experts can determine from a physical examination that Corbusier got his disease from asbestos exposure.[2] The problem here is another who-done-it problem, but of a different sort. Here *all* the defendants exposed the plaintiff to the injury-causing agent.

If it were clear that *cumulative* exposure to all the asbestos was necessary to cause Corbusier's disease, the "but for" test would dispose of this problem. The plaintiff could argue that, but for the negligence of each defendant, he would not have gotten asbestosis. Each would be liable under traditional causation principles.

In most cases, however, the evidence will *not* show that each defendant's product was essential to causing the disease. The plaintiff's expert will testify that breathing asbestos causes asbestosis and that the more you breathe, the greater the chances of contracting the disease, but that a fairly brief exposure can suffice. She will be unable to state in Corbusier's case how much was necessary, though she will state with certainty that asbestos exposure caused the harm. On these facts, each defendant can argue that "but for" causation is not established because, even if its product had not

---

2. Asbestos exposure also causes diseases, including cancer, that are not signature diseases (i.e., they have other causes as well, some known and some not known). In these cases, the plaintiff faces both a who-done-it problem and a what-done-it problem in establishing factual causation.

been at the site, Corbusier would have contracted asbestosis from the other defendants' products anyway.

In this type of multiple exposure case, most courts have invoked the "substantial factor" test for cause in fact. The jury is left to consider, based on the evidence of each defendant's contribution to the risk, whether its product was a substantial factor in causing Corbusier's disease. If the exposure to Company #6's product was minimal, the jury may conclude it did not meaningfully contribute to the harm. But if Company #6's product was there on a consistent basis and its asbestos particles were more than a minimal percentage of the exposure, they would be free to conclude that it had "caused" Corbusier's disease, even though he probably would have contracted it from the other manufacturers' products anyway. The test allows the jury to find the defendant liable if it contributed significantly to the *risk* of plaintiff's injury:

> We therefore hold that . . . in a trial of an asbestos-related cancer case, the jury should be told that the plaintiff's or decedent's exposure to a particular product was a substantial factor in causing or bringing about the disease if in reasonable medical probability *it contributed to the plaintiff or decedent's risk of developing cancer.*

Rutherford v. Owens-Illinois, Inc., 941 P.2d 1203, 1206 (Cal. 1997) (emphasis added).

Using the "substantial factor" test in such cases is hardly an intellectually rigorous solution to the problem. "The [substantial factor] test has become a default, resorted to when nothing else works, and juries are afforded virtually no guidance as to how much of a causal connection is necessary to satisfy the test." G. Boston, Toxic Apportionment: A Causation and Risk Contribution Model, 25 Envtl. L. 549, 630 (1995). The jury cannot determine which asbestos particles actually injured the plaintiff. Even Solomon with his time machine would have tough sledding trying to reconstruct the etiology of the disease. So the question is, what should tort law do in the absence of better knowledge about causation? On balance, holding the defendants liable under the substantial factor approach, based on meaningful contribution to a general risk, is probably more satisfactory than denying liability simply because the other manufacturers' asbestos might have caused the disease anyway.

EXAMPLES

Substances and Substantial Factors

10. Are the asbestos cases more like *Summers v. Tice* (discussed in the previous chapter at p. 147) or *Anderson v. Minneapolis, St. Paul and St. Marie R.R. Co.* (discussed in the previous chapter at p. 145)?

11. Why not use a market share approach to liability in the asbestos cases?

12. Suppose the plaintiff proves exposure to the asbestos products of five defendants, and the jury concludes that each was a "substantial factor" in causing his asbestosis. What would the plaintiff recover from each defendant?

13. Suppose that the evidence shows that Asbestos Products, Inc. contributed about 4 percent to the asbestos particles in the work area where the plaintiff worked during his years of exposure to asbestos. Should it be held liable to the plaintiff? Suppose it contributed one-tenth of 1 percent?

Comparing Causation

14. Five mining companies release salt water into various streams that flow into Farmer Jones's pond. Over a period of time, the salt level rises to the point where his fish die.

    a. How is this like the asbestos cases?

    b. How would you argue that this is different from the asbestos cases?

Causation in Toxic Exposure Cases

A third thorny cause-in-fact problem arises in cases like the Agent Orange case, which involve exposure to toxic chemicals. The Agent Orange plaintiffs were veterans who were exposed to dioxin in Vietnam and subsequently developed a number of skin diseases they claimed were caused by the exposure. Medical science can sometimes establish that persons who have been exposed to toxic substances are more likely to contract certain diseases, but such evidence will not always establish causation in tort cases. Suppose, for example, that epidemiological studies demonstrate that individuals exposed to quasimegamethane are more likely to contract liver cancer. The studies might show, perhaps, that there are 10 cases of liver cancer per 100,000 among the general population, but 14 cases per 100,000 among those exposed to quasimegamethane. Suppose further that Wren was exposed to quasimegamethane and that he subsequently contracts liver cancer.

There are two problems with using this evidence to prove that quasimegamethane caused Wren's cancer. First, although liver cancer is *correlated with* exposure to quasimegamethane, this does not necessarily prove that quasimegamethane has the capacity to *cause* liver cancer. Here is a nice example to prove the point: Although production of pig iron in the United States and the birth rate in Great Britain follow the same linear increase, it is relatively clear that the one did not cause the other![3] Similarly, exposure to quasimegamethane could be correlated to liver cancer

---

3. B. Black & D. Lilienfeld, Epidemiologic Proof in Toxic Tort Litigation, 52 Fordham L. Rev. 732, 755 (1984) (citing G. Snedocor & W. Cochran, Statistical Methods, 189 (6th ed. 1967)).

for many reasons, even though it did not cause the cancer. Perhaps the lives of factory workers are more stressful for economic reasons, so that they smoke more. Or perhaps they had poorer nutrition as children, and this increases their rate of liver cancer.

If studies are carefully done to correct for such extraneous factors, they may establish that quasimegamethane *can* cause liver cancer.[4] Doubtless, epidemiologists would accept strong correlations based on careful studies as proof of causal capacity. However, even assuming that the plaintiff establishes causal capacity, there remains the further question whether quasimegamethane caused *Wren's* cancer. The statistics given show that people also get liver cancer *without* being exposed to quasimegamethane. Indeed, of the 14 cancer victims in the group exposed to the toxin, presumably 10 contracted cancer from other causes: There is no reason to believe that the rate of cancer from background causes would be lower in the exposed group. Thus, even if quasimegamethane *can* cause liver cancer, this does not show that it *did* cause Wren's.

In the first two situations discussed in this chapter, the mechanism of harm was clear but the identity of the proper defendant was problematic. In these cases, by contrast, the mechanism of harm is itself uncertain both on the general level ("Can quasimegamethane cause liver cancer?") and on the particular level ("Did quasimegamethane, rather than one of the other possible causes, cause Wren's cancer?"). This is a what-done-it problem, and a very difficult one indeed.

Sometimes the plaintiff in these cases can provide evidence to link her disease to a particular toxic agent. The medical evidence may establish that the agent can cause the disease, and that it runs a different course in patients who contract it from that agent, or that these patients have unique symptoms that support an inference that the agent induced it. She might show that the disease appears after an unusual latency period if it is caused by the defendant's chemical, and that hers did as well, or that the diseased cells actually look or act a little differently if they are caused by the chemical. Evidence of this sort allows the jury to infer that *this plaintiff* contracted the disease from the exposure instead of other known causes for which the defendant is not responsible.

In other cases, however, the plaintiff is only able to show that she was exposed to a toxic chemical and that persons exposed to it contract the disease at an increased rate. Some courts would refuse to allow a jury to find the defendant liable based solely on such proof. Even if statistical evidence establishes a general causal relationship between the chemical and the disease, this does not establish that *this* plaintiff contracted the

---

4. In the Agent Orange cases, the plaintiffs were ultimately unable to surmount even the first hurdle, proving that Agent Orange had the capacity to cause their illnesses.

disease from the exposure. See, e.g., S. Gold, Causation in Toxic Torts: Burdens of Proof, Standards of Persuasion, and Statistical Evidence, 96 Yale L.J. 376, 379-380 (1986). If courts require "particularistic evidence" that the individual plaintiff's disease was caused by the chemical rather than background causes, the plaintiff may lose even though the exposure caused by the defendant substantially increased their risk of getting the disease.

This is a very tough problem. Some commentators have suggested a risk-creation approach to it, analogous to *Sindell's* approach to DES liability. Under this approach, the manufacturer would be liable to each liver cancer victim who had been exposed to quasimegamethane for a proportion of her damages, reflecting the probability that the exposure caused the disease. See, e.g., D. Rosenberg, The Causal Connection in Mass Exposure Cases: A "Public Law" Vision of the Tort System, 97 Harv. L. Rev. 849, 859 (1984) (advocating proportional liability in toxic exposure cases).

Most courts have not adopted a proportional approach, however, or automatically imposed or rejected liability based on statistical probabilities derived from epidemiological evidence. Instead, courts have generally admitted careful studies in evidence as relevant to the question whether the toxic substance is capable of causing the plaintiff's disease (general causation) and whether it actually did cause it (specific causation). Courts then look to expert testimony about the individual plaintiff that may undermine or strengthen the inference of causation based on the statistics. A plaintiff may bolster her case, for example, by showing (in addition to a statistical increase in disease due to exposure to the substance) that she lacks genetic factors suggesting alternative causes, that she has not engaged in other conduct (such as smoking) likely to lead to the disease, that she had extensive exposure to the toxic agent, or that the disease appeared within an expected "latency period" after exposure to the agent. Such testimony by the medical witnesses or experts supports an inference, beyond bare statistical likelihood, connecting the plaintiff's exposure to her injury. Courts are likely to find such "particularistic evidence" sufficient to allow the plaintiff's case on causation to go to the jury.

EXAMPLES

Science and Solomon

15. Quinn worked for 11 years at Acme Company's plant. During those years his hands often came into contact with the chemical pseudomonomethane. After he left Acme, he developed skin cancer on his hands. He believes that the cancer was caused by his exposure to pseudomonomethane. However, since pseudomonomethane is a rare chemical, no

epidemiological studies have been done to determine whether it causes cancer. How will Quinn prove that Acme is liable?

16. Employees of Beta Corporation are exposed to quasimegamethane during their employment there, and later contract liver cancer. Suppose that a careful epidemiological study shows that exposure to quasimega-methane increases liver cancer rates by 40 percent. The disease strikes 10 people per 100,000 in the general population, but the study shows that 14 per 100,000 persons exposed to quasimegamethane contract liver cancer.

    a. If Nunez, one of the employees, sues for damages, should she be allowed to recover based on the study?

    b. Assume that the jurisdiction would not allow recovery to a plaintiff based on this evidence, unless she presented some proof that her individual disease was caused by quasimegamethane. If 14 Beta employees with liver cancer sued Beta and the study is the only evidence they have, how many would recover?

    c. Based on the scientific evidence, how many of these 14 plaintiffs can we deduce were harmed by exposure to quasimegamethane?

    d. If we view deterrence and compensation as major goals of the tort system, what is the problem with denying recovery to these plaintiffs?

17. Suppose we allow each of these plaintiffs to prove her case based on the study, and send each case to the jury with a "substantial factor" instruction. What should the jury do? What would you do if you were on the jury?

18. What would happen in these 14 cases if we used a percentage-risk approach to the problem, under which each plaintiff recovers in proportion to the risk that her disease was caused by Beta's conduct?

Double Indemnity

19. Suppose that the epidemiology study shows that exposure to quasi-megamethane increases the risk of liver cancer by more than two? Suppose, for example, that there are 10 cases per 100,000 in the general population, but 23 cases per 100,000 in the population of persons exposed to quasimegamethane. If 14 employees sued Beta for causing their cancer, how many would likely recover?

20. Suppose that Nunez produces a credible expert who testifies, with supporting evidence from the medical literature and her own experience, that liver cancer, when caused by quasimegamethane, attacks a particular part of the liver and follows an unusual disease pattern. Surgery shows that Nunez's disease follows this pattern. However, assume that the epi-miological studies indicate that quasimegamethane only increases the risk

of liver cancer by 20 percent. Should Nunez be allowed to get to the jury on the issue of whether quasimegamethane caused her disease?

Causation in Loss-of-a-Chance Cases

Another difficult cause in fact problem is illustrated by medical malpractice cases in which the defendant's negligence has reduced a plaintiff's chances of survival or cure. In *Herskovits v. Group Health Cooperative of Puget Sound*, 664 P.2d 474 (Wash. 1983), for example, the decedent died of lung cancer. The evidence indicated that he had a 39 percent chance of surviving with prompt diagnosis of his cancer, but that the defendant's negligent delay in diagnosing it reduced his survival chance to 25 percent. The suit was for wrongful death.

Naturally, the defendant in cases like this will argue that he did not "cause" the harm. It is impossible to say that Herskovits would have lived but for the delay in diagnosis, since, even if his cancer had been promptly diagnosed, chances were better than even (61/39) that he would have died.

This loss-of-a-chance causation problem, like other "but for" dilemmas, requires the factfinder to compare what did happen to what would have happened if the defendant had not been negligent. This is a very speculative endeavor: The statistics suggest that the outcome *might* have been different absent the defendant's negligence, but probably would not have been.[5] Yet the plaintiff takes little solace from these cold statistics. She still feels she has lost something very valuable, a significant chance that her husband would still be with her. In *Herskovits*, for example, the late diagnosis deprived the decedent of a 14 percent chance to survive.

The majority in *Herskovits* held that the causation issue should go to the jury under a "substantial factor" instruction. This is not a very satisfactory solution to a vexing problem: How can the jury possibly place Herskovits in the 14 percent group that would have lived with earlier diagnosis, as opposed to the 61 percent who were doomed either way? The substantial factor approach simply licenses the jury to find for the plaintiff on intuitive grounds, despite the likelihood that the negligence did not change the outcome.

There is an obvious relationship between this loss-of-a-chance problem and the toxic chemicals problem just discussed. There, the epidemiological evidence established an increased risk of harm, but could not show whether the chemical had injured the individual plaintiff. Here, the statistical survival evidence establishes that the defendant's negligence decreased

---

5. Even Solomon with his time machine couldn't help much with this one. Going back to watch the events wouldn't answer the real question: What *would have happened* if the doctor had diagnosed the cancer at an earlier stage?

the plaintiff's chance of survival, but cannot resolve the issue of whether she would have survived if promptly diagnosed.

Here, as there, some scholars have suggested a proportional approach to the problem: If a defendant reduced the decedent's chance of survival by 15 percent, she should be held liable for 15 percent of the wrongful death damages. See J. King, Causation, Valuation, and Chance in Personal Injury Torts Involving Preexisting Conditions and Future Consequences, 90 Yale L.J. 1353 (1981). In this group of cases, unlike the toxic exposure cases, this percentage solution has caught on with the courts. A good many have chosen to treat the injury as the *lost chance*, and allow the jury to value the damages in proportion to the chance lost due to the defendant's negligence.

This solution is subject to the same objection here as in the toxic exposure cases: It overcompensates in every case in which the decedent would have died anyway, and undercompensates in every case where the delayed diagnosis caused the death. The examples below explore the implications of the loss-of-a-chance approach.

EXAMPLES

Chance Occurrences

21. Sven goes to Dr. Kildare complaining of indigestion and tightness of the chest. Kildare negligently fails to diagnose a heart attack. Later that day, Sven goes to the emergency room and is diagnosed and treated for a heart attack. However, he dies three days later.

The medical testimony establishes that Sven had a 40 percent chance of recovery had he been diagnosed when he first saw Kildare. However, once he went to the emergency room, the progress of the heart attack had reduced his chance of recovery to 15 percent. Sven's survivors sue Kildare for wrongful death.

    a. If the court retains the traditional "but for" approach to causation, how will the case come out?

    b. If the court sends the case to the jury under a "substantial factor" instruction, how will it come out?

    c. If the court applies the "lost chance" approach to the case, how will it come out?

22. Assume that Dr. Kildare made the same mistake on 100 patients, and the survivors of the patients who died sued in each case.

    a. How many would recover under the traditional causation standard?

    b. How many would recover under the loss of chance approach?

23. Assume that the medical testimony is that Sven would have had a 60 percent chance of recovery with prompt treatment, which was reduced to 40 percent due to the delay. Sven dies and his family sues Kildare.

a. What will happen if the court applies the traditional causation standard?

b. What will happen if the court applies the loss of chance approach?

Judge Fudd's Dilemma

24. Yamato goes to Dr. Kildare, complaining of a lump in her breast. Kildare fails to take a biopsy. Later, after the lump has grown, Yamato goes to Doctor Rivera, who finds an advanced malignant tumor. The tumor is removed, and no sign of cancer is found in the surrounding tissue. However, Rivera advises Yamato that, because of the advanced stage of the tumor, she has a 50 percent risk of a recurrence. Had the tumor been taken out earlier (when she went to Kildare) the risk would have been 20 percent. Yamato sues Kildare, in a jurisdiction that has adopted the lost chance approach to damages. Should the Honorable Fudd dismiss the case?

EXPLANATIONS

Share, or Share Alike?

1.   Obviously, the jury should find Acme liable for her full damages and dismiss the claims against the other manufacturers. The market share theory provides a back-up alternative where the plaintiff cannot prove which maker caused the harm. If the jury finds that one defendant caused it, that defendant should pay, and the others should not.

2.   Under *Sindell*, where the plaintiff sues defendants representing "a substantial share" of the market, they are liable in proportion to their market shares, unless a defendant proves that it did not sell DES in the relevant market. Since D4 has made that showing, it is not liable. The other three, however, are liable for their market shares.

So what do they pay? There are two possibilities: They could each pay an appropriate proportion of $100,000, the total damages. Under this approach, D1 would pay 10/60ths of $100,000, D2 would pay 20/60ths, and D3 would pay 30/60ths. Sindell would recover fully, though she only sued four makers and there are many more out there who could have supplied the drug.

Alternatively, *Sindell* may be interpreted to require each defendant to pay its market share percentage times the total damages. Here are the numbers:

D1 pays 10 percent of $100,000 = $10,000
D2 pays 20 percent of $100,000 = $20,000
D3 pays 30 percent of $100,000 = $30,000
Sindell recovers $60,000.

It was unclear after *Sindell* which of these methods the California Supreme Court intended. In *Brown v. Superior Court of San Francisco*, 751 P.2d 470 (Cal. 1988), the court opted for the second. Under this approach, plaintiff does not recover her full damages, because the defendants found liable do not absorb the market shares of absent defendants.

3.   The point of *Sindell* is that each maker would pay in proportion to the risk it created by marketing DES. Each is only *severally* liable for its share of the market; it is not liable for other defendants' shares. Thus, if D2 cannot pay, plaintiff loses this part of the judgment.

4.   The first problem you would face is defining the market. Is the market the particular pharmacy plaintiff's mother bought from? The town where she lived? The metropolitan area? Or the state? The individual pharmacy seems like the best choice, but this information may not be available. If a local area is used, there will be serious proof problems: For example, many drug makers may have sold DES to wholesalers, who redistributed the drug to pharmacies. They may have filled orders with DES from various manufacturers, and may well have no remaining records of what was sold where. The same proof problems are likely if a state market area is used. To make matters worse, the plaintiff's mother may have bought the drug in a distant state. Thus, actually *proving* a market area under *Sindell* could be extremely complicated and expensive.[6]

Doubtless, this entered into the thinking of the New York Court of Appeals in choosing a national market area. The total national sales of various makers will be easier to reconstruct. And, once it has been done in a few cases, the parties in later cases will likely stipulate the market shares, thus dramatically simplifying the trial of most market share cases.

Absent Tortfeasors

5.   Yes, it is. Even though Acme conclusively establishes that it could not have caused the plaintiff's injury, it will pay 10 percent of her damages. New York has chosen to impose damages based on the amount of risk each maker created, *nationally*, even where it is clear that some of them created no risk to the plaintiff personally. That is why defendants cannot exonerate themselves under *Hymowitz* by showing that they did not make the drug taken by the plaintiff.

6.   This example introduces another problem posed by the market share approach: Manufacturers entered and left the market for DES at various times. Here, Acme created a risk of DES injuries, but not at the time the

---

6. "The administrative costs of determining each defendant's market share have been distressingly disproportionate to the compensation provided." Restatement (Third) of Torts: Liability for Physical Harm (Basic Principles) (Tentative Draft No. 2, 2002) §28, cmt. o.

plaintiff's mother ingested the drug. If a court decides to base liability on risk creation, rather than specific causation of the plaintiff's injury, it seems that Acme ought to pay in this case. Under *Hymowitz*, it pays even if it was not in the market at the particular *place* where the drug was sold. Why shouldn't it pay here, even though it was not in the market at a particular *time*, so long as it contributed to the overall risk posed by the sale of DES? As the *Hymowitz* court held, "[W]e choose to apportion liability so as to correspond to the overall culpability of each defendant, measured by the amount of risk of injury each defendant created to the public-at-large." 541 N.Y.S.2d at 950.

If we are looking to the "overall culpability" of each defendant, it seems we ought to look at the total DES sold by each defendant over the entire period DES was marketed, and convert that to a percentage of the total DES sold by all makers during that entire period. Acme would pay that percentage, even though it did not sell DES at the time plaintiff's mother took it. Under this logic, Acme could be held liable, though it never sold DES in New York and never sold it anywhere when plaintiff's mother took the drug.

7.   Phi Corporation owes nothing. By proving it did not participate in the Washington market at the relevant time, it establishes that it did not cause the plaintiff's injury. In Washington (unlike in New York), this bars recovery.

Beta owes plaintiff 6 percent of her damages. Under the Washington scheme, makers who prove their market shares pay in proportion to those shares.

The dicey part of the analysis concerns Acme and Gamma. Since they have not presented proof of their market shares, they are presumed to have equal market shares, and to have the entire market except for Beta's 6 percent. Thus, they are each presumed to have 47 percent of the market (one half of 94 percent). Each will pay 47 percent of the plaintiff's damages.

Note several points about this: First, under the Washington approach, the plaintiff doesn't bear the burden of proof on market share; the defendants do. If they don't shoulder that burden, they are presumed to have equal shares of the market. Second, unlike in California, the plaintiff recovers fully, since the market shares of defendants who don't prove their actual share expand to cover the shares of makers who were not sued. Third, in Washington a plaintiff can sue just one maker. Defendants then have a strong incentive to implead other makers, to reduce their presumptive market shares.

8.   Here, the defendants have overcome the presumption of equal shares, so each would pay according to its market share. Acme would pay 15 percent, Beta 6 percent, Gamma 10 percent, and Phi would pay nothing. Plaintiff would recover only 31 percent of her damages. However, if she

could locate one defendant unable to establish its market share, that defendant would be liable for the remaining 79 percent.

9.   Under Michigan's approach, all makers who can't prove that they were not in the market are jointly and severally liable for the plaintiff's full damages. Thus, Acme, Beta, and Gamma would be jointly and severally liable to Sindell for $100,000. Under contribution principles, of course, they will ultimately share the loss.

There is language in *Abel*, however, that suggests that the plaintiff must sue "all the possible defendants" to invoke this form of market share liability. 343 N.W.2d at 174. This is based on the rationale of *Summers v. Tice*, 199 P.2d 1 (Cal. 1948), which held that all negligent parties must be before the court before shifting the burden of proof. In the DES context, this requirement will be almost impossible to meet, since many DES makers are out of business, have been bought out, or have gone bankrupt.

Substances and Substantial Factors

10.   These cases are closer to *Anderson* than to *Summers*. In *Summers* there was only one cause, but the plaintiff was unable to prove which hunter it was. In *Anderson*, there were two sufficient causes of the harm, and the defendant argued that he should get off because the plaintiff would have suffered the same harm if his fire had not been present. The harm was "overdetermined," in the sense that, if the one fire hadn't caused it, the other would have.

Similarly, in the asbestos exposure cases, the plaintiff's injury is also overdetermined. If any one defendant's asbestos had not been at the worksite, others would probably have sufficed to cause the plaintiff's disease anyway. The problem is, if we let any one defendant off the hook on this basis, they all get off. *Anderson's* substantial factor approach avoids that unpalatable result.

11.   In the DES cases, all defendants marketed exactly the same product, and the plaintiff's mothers (presumably) only took one defendant's pill. The problem is simply identifying which defendant made the offending product. It can be said, with approximate fairness, that each created risk to the public in direct proportion to its market share.

In the asbestos cases, however, the plaintiff's injury was usually caused by cumulative exposure to the asbestos in the products of several defendants. In addition, asbestos products are quite different, and impose quite different risks. For example, in some products the asbestos is permanently fixed in tiles or other adhesives, and is seldom released into the atmosphere. In others, however, the particles are "friable," that is, easily broken up and released, posing a much greater risk.

Last, asbestos exposure takes place over time, often decades. Over such long periods asbestos products entered and left the market, or a particular workplace. Thus, it would be virtually impossible to reconstruct a single "market" for asbestos. For these reasons, courts have generally rejected market share analysis in asbestos cases.

12. If the jurisdiction retains joint and several liability, under which each defendant that caused the harm is fully liable, the plaintiff could recover his entire damages from any one of the five defendants.[7] This is marked contrast to market share liability, which holds each defendant severally liable only in proportion to its percentage of the market.

13. Under the substantial factor standard, this defendant probably could be held liable. Most courts have not set a threshhold minimal percentage requirement for finding a defendant liable under the substantial factor test. Indeed, it would be hard to ascertain such a percentage, given the variety of asbestos products involved, the differences in their toxicity, and the great difficulty in reconstructing working conditions decades after the fact. Some courts have required the plaintiff to establish that they worked regularly in proximity to the defendant's product to get to the jury against that defendant. See, e.g., *Sholtis v. American Cyanamid Co.*, 568 A.2d 1196 1206-1208 (N.J. Super. Ct. App. Div. 1989). Other courts have rejected even this requirement, in light of evidence that a minimal exposure can cause asbestosis.[8]

At some point, however, a defendant's contribution to the risk may become so small that it is inappropriate to hold it liable, even though it did contribute to the risk that caused the injury. The substantial factor test allows the jury to reach that result; they can simply conclude, if Asbestos Products contributed one-tenth of 1 percent of the asbestos, that its product was not a "substantial factor" in causing the plaintiff's disease, and render a verdict in its favor.

The draft Third Restatement of Torts would reach the same result by a different analysis. It would conclude that such a trivial contribution to the risk is not a legal cause of the resulting harm. Thus, it would reject liability on proximate cause grounds rather than actual cause grounds. The drafters reason that this defendant's product may in fact be an actual cause, though a minor one. The reason to exonerate Asbestos Products is that its conduct was a trivial contributing factor, which is a judgment about the appropriate contours of legal responsibility, not a judgment about factual causation. See Restatement (Third) of Torts Liability for Physical Harm (Basic Principles) (Tentative Draft) 29, cmt. q.

---

7. In most states, if Defendant #1 paid the judgment, it would have a right to contribution from the other defendants, so that the judgment would be redistributed among them all.

8. See B. D. Masi, Comment, The Threshold Level of Proof of Asbestos Causation: The "Frequency, Regularity and Proximity Test" and a Modified *Summers v. Tice* Theory of Burden-Shifting, 24 Cap. U. L. Rev. 735, 748-751 (1995).

Comparing Causation

14a. This case is like the asbestos exposure cases, in that all the defendants have contributed to the exposure that caused the plaintiff's harm. All released salt into Jones's pond, though perhaps in varying amounts.

b. In the asbestos cases, any one of the defendants' asbestos could have caused the harm even if the others were not present. We don't know—and never will—which defendant's asbestos actually caused it, or if they all did together. In this case, by contrast, the facts suggest that the harm resulted from the *cumulative* exposure to salt, so we can say that they all contributed to cause an indivisible harm: When the combined discharges reached a certain level, the fish died. Thus, the defendants would probably all be liable even under a "but for" standard. If the court uses a substantial factor standard, a jury would probably find them all liable. However, if one of them released very little salt into the water, it might get off under the substantial factor test.

Science and Solomon

15. Quinn probably won't recover from Acme. He bears the burden of proof, yet the evidence to tie the chemical to his disease simply doesn't exist. Scientists can't study everything, and they simply hasn't gotten around to pseudomonomethane. In the absence of proof that it causes cancer, it is hard to see how Quinn can win, even if the chemical really did cause it.

As the introduction suggests, Quinn will probably offer medical testimony that his cancer was caused by exposure to pseudomonomethane. Although courts have noted that scientific studies are not always necessary to support a finding of causation (*Ferebee v. Chevron Chemical Co.*, 736 F. 2d 1529, 1535-1536 (D.C. Cir. 1984)), her expert will have to support her view on some accepted medical basis. If she could show that the symptoms are different if linked to pseudomonomethane, that would allow an inference of causation. But they probably aren't, or, if they are, no one has shown that they are, since there are no studies on the drug. She might make the causal link by showing that the disease progresses differently, or appears sooner, or whatever, but how will she make such a showing without supporting scientific studies?

How about the fact that Quinn's disease appeared after his exposure to pseudomonomethane, and in the area where he sustained that exposure: Would that suffice to allow the jury to infer causation? Probably not; this is a "post hoc, ergo proper hoc" argument: Because it occurred after the exposure, it must have been caused by the exposure. The argument has some force, but may not suffice to make a prima facie case. See, e.g., *Conde v. Velsicol Chemical Corp.*, 804 F. Supp. 972, 1020-1023

(S.D. Ohio 1992), in which the plaintiffs showed that their home was treated with Chlordane, that they became sick after the exposure, and that their symptoms abated when they moved out of the house. The court held that they had not established that Chlordane caused their injuries, in the absence of medical evidence that chlordane could cause the symptoms they alleged. But see *Alder v. Bayer Corp.*, 61 P.3d 1068, 1089-1090 (Utah 2002) (temporal sequence, together with other evidence, supported proof of causation).

16a. Here, there is no individual proof that any plaintiff's disease was caused by quasimegamethane, as opposed to the general background causes of liver cancer. Solomon might be able to go back and find the answer, but logically there is no way for the jury, based on the study, to conclude that Nunez's disease was more likely caused by quasi-megamethane than by the other, nontortious causes of the disease. Indeed, chances are 10 out of 14 that it was caused by something other than the defendant's conduct. If the only proof before the court was the statistical increase, it seems that a verdict should be directed for Beta.

b. If particularized proof is needed, none of these plaintiffs will recover. Each plaintiff will face the same problem, lack of individualized proof that *her disease* resulted from the defendant's conduct. The 40 percent increase in disease associated with exposure to quasimegamethane is not sufficient (even in a purely statistical sense) to establish that any plaintiff's disease was "more probably than not" caused by the exposure. (To establish that, as a matter of statistics, the increase would have to exceed 100 percent; exposure would have to more than double the risk of contracting the disease.)

c. The studies show that 4 out of every 14 cases of liver cancer in persons exposed to quasimegamethane are caused by that exposure (the 14 cases minus the 10 expected from general causes). Thus, statistically speaking, we can say that 4 of these plaintiffs' injuries were caused by Beta's conduct.

d. If each of these plaintiffs loses her case for lack of particularized proof that her cancer was caused by the chemical, neither of these goals is served. Refusing recovery to each of these plaintiffs will lead to "under-deterrence" of tortious conduct, since Beta caused four cases of liver cancer, but is held liable for none. In addition, four deserving plaintiffs who suffered injury from Beta's conduct go without compensation.

17. This is not a viable solution to the causation enigma. There is simply no way for the jury to reach a reasoned verdict using a substantial factor test. They should probably, if acting rationally, find for the defendant in each case, since there is no logical way to conclude that its conduct probably caused any one of these cases of liver cancer.

More likely, they will find for the plaintiffs in all 14 cases, since Beta was negligent and caused harm to some. If so, then Beta's conduct will be overdeterred, since they probably only caused 4 cases of the disease. In addition, the 10 plaintiffs who contracted the disease from background causes instead of quasimegamethane will be overcompensated.

18. Under this approach, the manufacturer should pay each plaintiff 4/14ths of her damages. If each plaintiff suffered $100,000 in damages, each would recover $28,571.

Arguably the manufacturer would pay the "right" amount in damages under this formula. The study shows that it caused 4 of these cases of liver cancer, for a total in damages of $400,000. It ended up paying 14 plaintiffs $28,571 each, which comes out to $400,000. Thus, this approach works well in terms of deterrence.

However, it does not work so well in serving tort law's compensatory purpose. Ten of these plaintiffs collect $28,571 too much, while four of them (those actually harmed by defendant's chemical) collect $71,429 too little.

Double Indemnity

19. In this example, the study shows that exposure to the chemical more than doubles the risk of contracting liver cancer. Thus, the jury can reasonably conclude — at least statistically speaking — that it is more probable than not that the exposure caused each plaintiff's disease. It seems likely that a court would allow the jury to find for each of the 14 plaintiffs on this evidence. See, e.g., *Merrell Dow Pharmaceuticals, Inc. v. Havner*, 953 S.W.2d 706, 715-717 (Tex. 1997); *Deluca v. Merrell Dow Pharmaceuticals, Inc.*, 911 F.2d 941, 958-959 (3d Cir. 1990) (suggesting that doubling of the "relative risk" might satisfy more-probable-than not standard under New Jersey law).

This result is not inexorable, however. The plaintiff has still only presented purely statistical proof, not any evidence about her won disease. Some courts would probably still deny recovery, absent particularized proof about each individual plaintiff's disease, such as testimony about the extent, nature, and duration of the plaintiff's exposure to quasimegamethane, the exact nature of each plaintiff's symptoms, or the absence of other risk factors for the disease.

If the court allows each plaintiff to recover based on the study alone, the defendant will pay some plaintiffs who did not get the disease from exposure to its chemical. Presumably some of these cases (roughly 10 out of 23) were caused by other causes, not by quasimegamethane.

20. In the last example, the statistical evidence demonstrated that exposure to quasimegamethane more than doubled the risk of contracting liver

cancer. In this example, however, the studies alone would certainly not support a finding that Nunez "more probably than not" contracted the disease from exposure to quasimegamethane, since exposure only increases the risk of liver cancer by 20 percent.

But here, while the statistics suggest that exposure to quasimegamethane only increases the risk of getting liver cancer by 20 percent, Nunez has evidence that strongly suggests that she is one of that 20 percent. The fact that the disease originated in an unusual spot, and followed an unusual pattern characteristic of quasimegamethane poisoning, provides "particularistic" evidence that Nunez contracted liver cancer from that chemical. Even if the studies suggest that people exposed to quasimegamethane are not very likely to contract liver cancer, they also support a conclusion that the agent is *capable of causing* liver cancer, and does so in about 20 percent of the cases. And Nunez has clinical evidence suggesting that it did lead to her disease. Thus, even though exposure to quasimegamethane does not "double the risk," her diagnostic evidence, together with the epidemiological evidence of "general causation," would likely suffice to make a submissible case that exposure to quasimegamethane caused her disease.

Chance Occurrences

21a. Under the traditional approach, Sven's survivors would not recover. The chances are better than even that he would have died even if Kildare had diagnosed him immediately. Thus, a jury could not rationally conclude that it is "more probable than not" (the standard of proof in a civil case) that Sven would have survived with prompt treatment. If the medical evidence is to be believed, he probably wouldn't have.

b. Who knows what the jury will do if the judge instructs them under the substantial factor test? They may take a sober look at the case, conclude that he probably would have died even if treated immediately, and find for Kildare. But they may also decide that Kildare injured Sven by depriving him of a very significant chance of recovery, and find Kildare liable. If they do; it appears, if the court follows *Herskovits*, that Kildare would be liable for full wrongful death damages.

c. Under the lost chance approach, the jury would determine the chance that Sven lost due to Kildare's negligence, and value that. To do this, they would determine full wrongful death damages and discount them by the percentage chance Sven lost due to Kildare's negligence. If damages for his death were $100,000, they would find Kildare liable for $25,000 (25 percent × $100,000).

22a. Presumably, all plaintiffs would lose, since none can show that their decedent's death was more probably than not due to the negligence of

Kildare. The irony, of course, is that with a hundred cases, we can say (with statistical confidence, anyway) that Kildare caused 25 deaths.

b. Under the lost chance approach, the survivors in each suit would recover $25,000 (assuming, again, that damages in each case were $100,000). There will be 85 suits (remember, statistically speaking, 15 percent of Kildare's victims will survive even with delayed diagnosis). Kildare will pay $25,000 × 85, or $2,125,000 in damages.

If we could identify the 25 patients who died due to delayed diagnosis, each family would recover $100,000 from Kildare. So he would pay 25 × $100,000, or $2.5 million. So he saves a little, but pays something like the full damages he has caused.

Once again, however, the approach looks dubious in light of tort law's compensatory goals. If all 100 families sue, 60 of them recover $25,000, even though Kildare caused no harm to their decedents — the 60 who would have died even with prompt diagnosis. The other 25 families, who have each suffered $100,000 in damages, recover only a quarter of that.

23a. Here, Sven's family can presumably carry their burden of proof under the traditional more-probable-than-not causation standard. Sven would "probably" (60 chances out of 100) have recovered if diagnosed promptly.

However, note that in this example Kildare deprived Sven of a smaller chance of recovery than in the prior examples. It is at least quizzical that Sven's family would only be entitled to a percentage recovery in Example 21c, yet here, because the numbers hover around the 50 percent mark, his family recovers full wrongful death damages.[9] At least one court has recognized that it is awkward to allow full recovery in a case like this, and opted for a lost-chance approach even though the initial chance of recovery exceeded 50 percent. See *DeBurkarte v. Louvar*, 393 N.W.2d 131 (Iowa 1986).

b. A jurisdiction that applies the loss-of-chance approach in cases like Example 21, where the plaintiff's initial chance of recovery was less than even, to be consistent should also apply the loss-of-chance approach in a case like this. If the court so holds, recovery under the loss-of-chance approach will be less generous than under the traditional rule: Sven's family will recover 20 percent of wrongful death damages rather than full damages.

---

9. If we assume that Kildare reduced the chances of recovery of 100 patients from 60 to 40 percent, the families of all who died — there should be 60 of them — would recover under the traditional standard. Statistically speaking, however, he would only have injured 20 patients.

Judge Fudd's Dilemma

24. In this example, the plaintiff has incurred a 30 percent increased risk of *future* harm due to Kildare's negligence. However, she has not yet sustained the injury itself, just incurred the risk. How can the plaintiff sue without having suffered an injury?

If a court adopts the loss-of-chance approach to cases like those just discussed, it is really compensating the plaintiff for incurring the risk, not for the disease itself. Thus, it ought not to matter that the risk is a future risk instead of a past risk. In both cases, the injury is the exposure to risk. To be consistent, shouldn't Judge Fudd allow Yamato to recover 30 percent of the damages she would incur from a recurrence of the cancer?

The cases in this chapter illustrate that some courts have recognized risk exposure as a harm in several contexts. Yamato's counsel should argue that she has been harmed by being exposed to the risk of future disease, and is entitled to recovery for the harm. See, e.g., *Cudone v. Gebret*, 821 F. Supp. 266 (D. Del. 1993) (approving submission of an increased risk claim to the jury under Delaware law).

Many courts would probably refuse to do this, even if they had adopted the lost-chance approach. After all, the plaintiff has not suffered the actual underlying harm — malignancy — just a risk of it. These courts might hold Yamato's suit premature, but allow her to sue later if her cancer recurs. Then, the case becomes a regular lost-chance case.

What would happen if the court allowed recovery, and then Yamato later did have a recurrence? Presumably, she would be barred from a second action, under traditional principles of res judicata. Even if she could bring one, presumably her recovery should be a loss-of-chance recovery (since the late diagnosis only increased the risk by 30 percent) and she would already have received that in her earlier action.

9
Drawing a Line Somewhere: Proximate Cause

Introduction

One of the nice things about the inch is that virtually everyone who has anything to do with one agrees about what it is. While it is a purely human construct, an *idea*, we have achieved such wide consensus about its meaning that we can use the term effectively without wasting energy arguing about its definition. This is probably true for the vast majority of concepts we manipulate through language. If it weren't, language wouldn't communicate much and people would rebel and vote in a new one.

Unfortunately, proximate cause is the exception that proves the rule (please excuse the pun). A great deal of confusion persists about what the term "proximate cause" is meant to convey. Students find this very frustrating: Justifiably, you would like some answers, some solid ground on which to base an understanding of a difficult concept.

Yet, if exact definition eludes us (as it does, of course, for other useful concepts, like "negligence" or "justice") we can still achieve a working knowledge of the problem sufficient for most purposes. This chapter seeks such a working knowledge of "proximate cause."

The Crux of the Problem

Despite differences in approach to proximate cause, all courts agree that the crux of the problem is that defendants cannot be held liable for every consequence of their conduct, even if that conduct is negligent. Here are a few examples in which courts would likely balk at imposing liability:[1]

- Defendant store owner leaves a box lid on the sidewalk. Plaintiff stumbles over it, skins her knee, and stops to get first aid. Consequently, she misses her train and gets a later one. She is injured when that train crashes into another at a crossing.
- Defendant, a restaurant owner, leaves a box of rat poison on a shelf near the stove that is used to store food. Although the owner had no reason to expect it, the poison explodes due to heat from the stove, injuring a customer.
- Defendant drives negligently, and collides with plaintiff, causing him injuries. Plaintiff is taken to the hospital, where he is further injured three days later when the hospital burns.
- Defendant leaves his car unlocked, with the keys in the ignition. A terrorist steals the car, loads it with explosives, and sets off an explosion at a foreign embassy, injuring a passerby.

In each of these cases, the defendant was negligent, yet most courts, perhaps all, would deny recovery, on the ground that the plaintiff's injury is too unusual, too far removed from the type of harm to be anticipated from the defendant's negligence to warrant imposing liability.

It is important to emphasize at the outset that this is not based on a lack of *actual* causation. If the only issue were cause-in-fact, the defendant would likely pay in all of the examples, since her conduct was a necessary antecedent of the plaintiff's harm in each. If the store owner had not left out the box lid, the pedestrian would have gotten the earlier train and would not have been injured in the crash; if the restaurant owner had not placed the poison on the shelf, it would not have exploded, and so on. Indeed, unless actual causation is found, there is no need to consider issues of proximate cause at all. If the defendant was not a cause-in-fact of the harm, the court will dismiss the case without reaching the complex policy question of whether liability should follow. For this reason, courts often describe the proximate cause problem as one of "legal cause," to emphasize that the issue is whether liability should be imposed, not whether the defendant's act was a cause-in-fact of the plaintiff's harm. "An actual cause question asks, 'What happened?'; a legal cause question asks, 'What shall be done about it?'" C. Morris, On the Teaching of Legal Cause, 39 Colum. L. Rev. 1087, 1089 (1939).

Certainly, courts must impose some further limit on liability, apart from the cause-in-fact requirement. Otherwise it is too easy to come up with absurd hypotheticals. Reynolds, not looking where he is going, bumps

---

1. Many of the examples in this chapter are drawn from cases discussed in Judge Robert Keeton's helpful book, Legal Cause in the Law of Torts (1963).

Carpenter on the sidewalk, knocking her down. Carpenter then walks to the corner and meets Dias, an old boyfriend, crossing the other way. They have dinner, end up at Dias's apartment, and Carpenter contracts a venereal disease. Reynolds's negligence is a necessary historical antecedent of the harm; had he not delayed Carpenter, she would not have spotted Dias, and so on. Yet no system could countenance holding Reynolds liable for Carpenter's disease. As a matter of policy, the relation between the negligence and the injury is too tenuous the consequence too out of proportion to the fault, to make Reynolds pay.

Here's another example that makes the point.[2] A doctor negligently performs a vasectomy. As a result, the patient later fathers a child. At the age of six, the child sets fire to the plaintiff's garage. Here, as in the last case, the doctor's negligence is clearly a "but for" cause of the plaintiff's loss. If he had done the operation right, the patient could not have conceived a child, etc. If the defendant were held liable for all injuries caused by her negligence, the doctor would pay here. But no court would hold the doctor liable for this. All courts agree that a line must be drawn, *somewhere*, to limit liability for the consequences of a negligent act. The problem, of course, is how to define that limit.

Efforts to Define Proximate Cause

Courts have labored for over a century to articulate such a definition, to draw a defensible line between consequences of negligence that are actionable and others too remote to support liability. Perhaps it is a mistake to try; proximate cause decisions, even within a single jurisdiction, often appear inconsistent or hard to predict based on previous precedents. It may be like pornography of which Justice Stewart said that perhaps he could not define it, but "I know it when I see it." *Jacobellis v. Ohio*, 378 U.S. 184, 197 (1964). Most courts, however, have felt obliged to try to define some proximate cause limits, in order to guide litigants and lower courts in future cases.

A. An Early Approach: The Direct Cause Test of *In Re Polemis*

An early proximate cause case, *In Re Polemis and Furness, Withy & Co.*, 3 K.B. 560 (1921), held that the defendant is liable if his conduct is the "direct cause" of the plaintiff's injury, as opposed to a "remote" cause. In *Polemis*, a workman dropped a board into the hold of the plaintiff's ship, which caused a spark and ignited petrol vapors in the hold, destroying the

---

2. This example is taken from Dobbs & Hayden, Torts and Compensation (4th ed. 2001) 216.

ship. Although the explosion was deemed unforeseeable, the court held that the defendant was liable, since the negligent act of its employee was the "direct cause" of the harm. Although the English court questioned *Polemis* in *Overseas Tankship (U.K.) Ltd. v. Morts Dock & Engineering Co., Ltd. (The Wagon Mound)*, A.C. 388 (1961), direct cause language still appears in some proximate cause cases.

The problem with the direct cause test is that it is "not responsive to the decisions either as a test of inclusion or exclusion." Seavey, Mr. Justice Cardozo and the Law of Torts, 52 Harv. L. Rev. 372, 389 (1939). In other words, it simply does not explain the results in real cases. It is often more restrictive than the cases: Since "directness" suggests the lack of a later cause after the defendant's negligence, it suggests that liability would be cut off where subsequent conduct contributes to the accident. Yet courts often conclude that the defendant should be liable despite intervening forces. For example, where one driver is negligent and another then negligently fails to avoid the accident, the first driver would typically be held liable, even though a later, independent act of the other driver also led to the accident. But if this is direct, just what does direct mean?

In other cases, we would all agree that the defendant's act led directly to the harm, yet we would not think she should be held liable. The act of the restaurant owner in leaving the rat poison near the stove appears to be a direct cause of the explosion in that case. The placement of the poison led it to become hot and blow up. Yet many courts would be uncomfortable imposing liability for that unexpected consequence of the owner's negligence. Thus, it is hard to escape the conclusion that "direct" is just a word rather than a method of analysis. It does not in itself help judges or juries to draw the line between consequences the defendant should be held responsible for and others he should not.

B. Perhaps as Good as It Gets: Foreseeability/Scope of the Risk

Perhaps the most helpful approach to proximate cause considers whether the defendant, at the time that he acted, could foresee the risk that injured the plaintiff. Under this foreseeability/scope of the risk approach, the court considers what the risks were that made the defendant's conduct negligent in the first place. If the defendant should have anticipated a particular risk at the time he acted, and he negligently failed to avert that risk, he would be liable if that risk caused the plaintiff's harm. See Restatement (Second) of Torts, §281, cmt. c.

For example, in the terrorist bombing case, a reasonable driver should realize that leaving the keys in the car creates a risk that children would be injured tampering with the car, that a thief would take it and drive negligently, or that vandals would damage it. But it hardly seems that the reasonable person should foresee a terrorist using the car to dynamite an embassy. Under the scope-of-the-risk approach, the defendant would not be liable, since the risk that caused the harm was not a risk he should have anticipated when he committed the negligent act.

Similarly, where a driver drives too fast, she should foresee that a collision could follow, injuring another motorist. But only the most bleakly neurotic pessimist who drove too fast would anticipate that her victim would be injured in a hospital fire three days later.

This foreseeability/scope of the risk approach to proximate cause has the virtue that it provides an analytical basis for consistent decision making. It relates the scope of liability to the faulty aspect of the defendant's conduct, and gives us a question to ask about that conduct, rather than relying on a phrase like "direct cause" or an intuitive guess in limiting liability. The judge or jury can ask what unreasonable risks the defendant should have anticipated at the time she acted, and compare those risks to the injury that actually occurred.[3]

Here's a little torts role-play you can use to apply the scope of the risk analysis to proximate cause problems. Imagine that at the time the defendant acted, that obnoxious, self-righteous, odious character, the Reasonable Person, was standing next to him. Imagine that the defendant is about to do the unreasonable act that gives rise to the plaintiff's injury. As he presses his foot to the accelerator, or drops the box lid on the sidewalk, or exits his car without taking the keys, what would that odious paragon say to him? In the speeding case, he would doubtless warn him that he might cause an accident, with resulting personal injury to himself or others, or property damage from a collision. However, obsessive though he may be, the odious character would not warn him not to speed, because his victim might end up suffering burns in a hospital fire. In the box lid case, the Reasonable Person would warn the storeowner, as he dropped the lid to the sidewalk, that a pedestrian might stumble over it and fall, or drop a valuable package, or even fall down the adjacent stairs. But even the odious character would not say "Tsk! Tsk! Don't drop that box lid! A pedestrian might fall over it, suffer an injury, end up getting a later train, and be injured in a train wreck!"

Varieties of Foreseeability: Wagon Mound *and* Palsgraf

The two most famous proximate cause cases, *Overseas Tankship (U.K.) Ltd. v. Morts Dock & Engineering Co., Ltd. (The Wagon Mound)*, 1 All

---

3. The Third Restatement of Torts endorses the "risk rule" approach. Restatement (Third) of Torts: Liability for Physical Harm (Basic Principles) §29 (Tent. Draft No. 3, 2003).

E.R. 404 (1961), and *Palsgraf v. Long Island R.*, 162 N.E. 99 (N.Y. 1928), both exemplify a scope-of-the-risk approach to the proximate cause problem.

In *Palsgraf*, the defendant's conductors were negligent in assisting the rushing passenger onto a moving train, causing him to drop a package. Although there was no reason for the conductors to suspect it, the package contained firecrackers, which exploded, overturning some scales a distance away. The scales fell and injured the reluctantly famous Mrs. Palsgraf.

Although the railroad's employees were evidently negligent in *Palsgraf,* the railroad argued that their negligence only posed a foreseeable risk of injury to the passenger or his package, not to Mrs. Palsgraf. Justice Cardozo, writing for the majority, held that the duty to avoid injuring others extends only to those risks the actor should anticipate from her negligent act. Here, the unreasonable risk created by the conductors' conduct was that the passenger or his package would be injured, not Mrs. Palsgraf. Since the conductors would not have anticipated injury to her from their conduct, they owed no duty to avoid the injury and were not negligent in relation to her. Since she was an "unforeseeable plaintiff" to whom no unreasonable risk was to be anticipated, Mrs. Palsgraf was denied recovery.[4]

In *Wagon Mound,* the defendant's oil fouled the waters around the plaintiff's dock, where welding was in progress. Because of its high ignition point, the oil was unlikely to burn, but it did, through a strange concatenation of circumstances found in the case to be unforeseeable. Other injury to the dock, however, *was* foreseeable, and in fact took place: the fouling of the docks by the oil. The dock owner argued that, since the defendant could foresee *some* injury to the dock, it was liable for *all* injury which actually resulted.

The Privy Council held that the plaintiff could only recover for the injuries that the defendant should have anticipated at the time it released the oil into the water. It would be liable for fouling the slips of the plaintiff's dock, a foreseeable consequence of releasing the oil, but not for the unforeseeable fire which destroyed the dock itself.

Some Guideposts in the Wilderness

Although proximate cause can never be reduced to a test that mechanically resolves all the cases, there are some fairly well-established principles that at least help to narrow the issues.

First, and most fundamentally, if the plaintiff's injury is truly beyond the type of harm to be expected from the defendant's conduct, the

---

4. Another way to look at this is to say that there is no doctrine of "transferred negligence" analogous to that of transferred intent in intentional tort cases. See G. Williams, The Risk Principle, 77 Law Q. Rev. 179, 185-190 (1961).

plaintiff will virtually always go uncompensated. A basic sense of justice demands that liability should not extend to consequences radically different from those to be anticipated from an act, and courts — whatever language they use — will find a way to reach that result. In the venereal disease hypo, for example, the court may dub Carpenter's disease too remote, unforeseeable, or beyond the risk that made the conduct negligent, but one way or another, it will reason to a judgment for the defendant.

Conversely, it is worth noting that most tort cases pose no legal cause problem because the harm suffered is exactly the type to be expected. In the run-of-the-mill motor vehicle case, for example, there is no question that a collision is the type of harm to be anticipated, and that, if the other elements are proved, the defendant must pay. Like *Erie* problems in civil procedure, the close cases are excruciatingly hard, but the great majority of the cases are not hard at all.

Second, where a particular type of injury to the plaintiff is foreseeable, the defendant is liable for the injury sustained, even though it is more serious than might have been anticipated. If, for example, Goodhart knocks Gregory down, causing small lacerations, he is liable if Gregory contracts an infection and becomes seriously ill, or if he is a hemophiliac and dies from loss of blood. If Goodhart injures Bohlen in an auto accident, disabling him for six months, he must pay the value of Bohlen's lost wages, whether he is a day laborer or the CEO of a Fortune 500 company. It is said that the defendant "takes the plaintiff as he finds her." The fact that she is more susceptible to injury than the average person, has a "thin skull," so to speak, is not a defense to liability. If Goodhart could foresee personal injury to Bohlen, he is liable for the personal injury actually caused, not some hypothetical average ordinarily to be expected from the act.

Third, the cases distinguish unforeseeable consequences of a negligent act from consequences that are foreseeable but take place in an unusual manner. This foreseeable-injury-in-an-unforeseeable-manner principle is nicely illustrated by *United Novelty Co. v. Daniels,* 42 So. 2d 395 (Miss. 1949). In *Daniels,* the defendant allowed its employee to clean some machines with gasoline in a small room heated by a heater with an open flame. A rat, drenched with gas, ran from under one of the machines over to the heater, caught fire, and ran back to the machine, causing an explosion which killed the employee. The court concluded that, while the manner in which the accident took place was unusual, an explosion was exactly the type of accident to be anticipated from using a volatile, flammable liquid in a small room with an open flame. The defendant was held liable.

There is something to this distinction. The exact sequence of events in every accident is unique, but in most the general nature of the damage threatened was foreseeable. Distinguish from the rat case, for example, the terrorist bombing hypo at the beginning of the chapter. In the rat case, the general nature of the accident threatened by the conduct actually took place. In terms of the risk rule, the risk of an explosion of the vapors, causing personal injury to the employee, was the very risk that made the defendant's conduct negligent. But in the terrorist case, the general nature of the risk to be expected from leaving the keys in the car was far afield from that which injured the passerby at the embassy.

The trick, of course, is in making the distinction: In many cases the line between unforeseeable consequences and unforeseeable manner is fine one, if indeed a defensible line can be drawn at all. Consider, for example, *Doughty v. Turner Mfg. Co.*, 1 Q.B. 518 (1964). In *Doughty*, the plaintiff was standing next to a vat of molten liquid when the cover of the vat was negligently knocked into it. Nothing happened at first, but several minutes later there was an explosion within the vat, caused by a chemical reaction of the lid with the liquid. The plaintiff argued that the defendant's employees negligently created a risk that he would be splashed by the liquid, and that, indeed, he *was* injured by splashing (when the explosion threw the liquid out of the vat) though in an unusual manner. The court, however, held that he was injured by a different risk, the risk of an unforeseeable chemical reaction causing explosion, not physical splashing from the dropping of the cover. I think the case was rightly decided, but it turns on a nice distinction indeed.

Fourth, an injury does not have to be *likely* or *probable* in order to be foreseeable in proximate cause analysis. Many acts are culpable even though they pose a relatively small risk of injury. If Smith throws a flower pot out a third story window without looking, there may be only a 10 percent chance that someone will be hit. But this conduct is clearly negligent, because it poses an unreasonable risk of injury to passersby. No court in the country would deny liability in such a case on proximate cause grounds. "Foreseeability is not to be measured by what is more probable than not, but includes whatever is likely enough in the setting of modern life that a reasonably thoughtful person would take account of it in guiding practical conduct." Harper, James & Gray, §18.2, 657-659. Similarly, the Reasonable Person stops at a rural railroad crossing, even though it is rarely used: In Hand formula terms, the risk of a train appearing may be low, but the extent of injury if it does is great, and the burden of avoiding the harm is slight.

Superseding Cause

In a good many proximate cause cases, the defendant argues that, even if she was negligent, a later act supersedes her negligence and "breaks the causal chain." An example from the casebooks is *Derdiarian v. Felix Contracting Corp.*, 434 N.Y.S.2d 166 (1980). In *Derdiarian*, the defendant contractor was working in an excavation in the traveled roadway, and failed to erect a barrier (such as a truck or concrete blocks) to protect workers from traffic. Dickens, an epileptic who had failed to take his medication, suffered a seizure, lost control of his car, and careened into the excavation, throwing Derdiarian into the air, where his body ignited from a kettle of hot enamel in use for the repairs.

Derdiarian involves a typical scenario in which the "superseding cause" argument is raised. *First*, the defendant is negligent (failure to erect the barrier); *second*, some other act happens after the defendant's negligence (Dickens's passing out due to failure to take meds), and *third*, the two acts together lead to an injury to the plaintiff (Derdiarian's accident). The defendant in *Derdiarian* argued that the bizarre subsequent events leading Dickens's car to enter the work area "superseded" its negligence. Consequently, "there was no causal link" (434 N.Y.S.2d at 159) between its failure to erect a barrier and the worker's burns.

In actual cause analysis, of course, this argument does not hold water. The company's negligence in failing to provide a barrier was clearly a "out for" cause of Derdiarian's injury. If the company had provided a proper barrier, Derdiarian would not have been injured, even if Dickens lost control of his car. The contractor's real argument is that Dickens's subsequent negligent act of driving without taking his meds, and the bizarre sequence of events that it engendered, should "cut off its liability," should cause the court to place the loss on the later actor instead of on the contractor.

Such multiple cause cases don't require any different analysis than other proximate cause problems. If we apply scope-of-the-risk analysis to *Derdiarian*, the outcome is clear: Working in the middle of a busy street poses a risk that a vehicle will enter the worksite. This is the foreseeable risk that makes it reasonable to put up a barrier. "A prime hazard associated with [omitting the barrier] is the possibility that a driver will negligently enter the work site and cause injury to a worker.... Id. at 170. This is the risk that injured Derdiarian. The contractor should be liable — and it was held liable — even though later negligence of Dickens caused the vehicle to enter the worksite. As to the quirky details of the accident — Dickens' epilepsy, the vat of molten enamel — the court correctly noted that "the precise manner of the event need not be anticipated." Id. at 170.

So what kind of later events would a court find a "superseding cause" that "cuts off" the liability of the previously negligent party? Generally speaking, courts will not hold the negligent party liable when bizarre, unforeseeable events give rise to a risk different from the one the defendant should have anticipated. "Highly improbable and extraordinary intervening forces are generally found superseding and preclude liability." J. Diamond, L. Levine & M. Madden, Understanding Torts 219. In other words, these cases are just a special instance of the more general principle, that actors are not liable for truly unforeseeable harm.

In rewriting this chapter, I searched some treatises for cases in which a defendant, though negligent, got off based on "superseding cause." While many cases are cited in which the argument was raised, the defendant's argument prevailed in few. In *Cleveland v. Rotman*, 297 F.3d 569 (7th Cir. 2002), the court refused to hold a lawyer who had allegedly provided negligent tax advice liable for the subsequent suicide of his client, dubbing the suicide "an independent intervening event that broke the chain of causation." Id. at 572. And here's a hypo in which the argument would fly: Ace Taxi Service is called by Costas, waiting at a park for a ride. It negligently fails to send a driver, and Costas is injured by a tornado that strikes the park. The dangers the taxi company should foresee from failing to send a car do not include the risk of tornados; a court would very likely dub this one a "superseding cause."

The superseding cause argument is frequently made in cases involving subsequent intentional acts by third parties, including criminal acts. In one of the classic superseding cause cases, *Watson v. Kentucky and Indiana Bridge & R.R. Co.*, 126 S.W. 146 (1910), for example, the defendant railroad negligently spilled gas in a street, and it was subsequently ignited by a match thrown by Duerr. The court held that if Duerr had thrown the match negligently, the railroad would be liable for the fire, but if he had done it intentionally, his deliberate criminal act would cut off the railroad's liability, since it was "not bound to anticipate the criminal acts of others." 126 S.W. at 151. The argument for this result seems to be that the deliberate act of arson is unforeseeable as a matter of law, and that the greater culpability of a criminal act should lead the court to place the responsibility on the criminal actor rather than the actor whose prior negligence contributed to the harm.[5]

In many circumstances, however, criminal acts are foreseeable, and indeed, are the very risk that require the reasonable person to take precautions. In another of the classic cases, *Ilines v. Garrell*, 108 S.E. 690 (Va. 1921), a train passed the plaintiff's stop, and then let her off a mile down the line, in an area known to be frequented by vagrants. While walking back to her stop she was assaulted. The court summarily dismissed the railroad's argument that the assault was a superseding cause: "The very danger to which this unfortunate girl fell a victim is the one which would at once suggest itself to the average and normal mind as a danger liable to overtake her under these circumstances." 108 S.E. at 694. When the risk of criminal conduct is foreseeable, it will not "cut off" the liability of a defendant who negligently exposes the plaintiff to that risk.

> If the likelihood that a third person may act in a particular manner is the hazard or one of the hazards which makes the actor negligent, such an act whether innocent, negligent, intentionally tortious, or criminal does not prevent the actor from being liable for harm caused thereby.

---

5. "A view common in the 19th and early 20th century was that the deliberate infliction of harm by a 'moral being,' who was adequately informed, free to act, and able to choose, would 'supersede' the negligence of the first actor." D. Dobbs & P. Hayden, Torts and Compensation (4th ed. 2001) 234.

Restatement (Second) of Torts §449. This principle is frequently applied in cases involving negligent security at hotels and apartment complexes.

An Economics Perspective on the Foreseeability/Scope of the Risk Approach

Economic analysis provides an interesting defense of the scope-of-foreseeable-risks approach to proximate cause. Economists view tort law as a means to control activity *prospectively*. They advocate rules of liability that will encourage people to act in socially desirable ways. If tort law holds a person liable for certain risks of his conduct, presumably the actor will take care to avert those risks, since he will bear their costs if an injury occurs:

> These [liability] rules tell decision makers that, under certain conditions, they will be forced to bear the costs of their activities to others. The effect of such rules is to give rational decision makers an incentive to incorporate the costs to others into their decisions about whether to engage in the activity, and hence, to create a situation in which the activities chosen by the rational decision maker are efficient from an aggregate point of view.

B. Zipursky, Rights, Wrongs, and Recourse in the Law of Torts, 51 Vand. L. Rev. 1, 46 (1998). However, the rational actor can only consider the liability consequences of risks that he can foresee. Imposing liability for unforeseeable risks will not affect his choices:

> *Palsgraf* stands for the proposition that the tort law does not require an individual to consider, in selecting her activity, costs to persons to whom harm is not reasonably foreseeable. Unforeseeable harm cannot be internalized because, by definition, the decision maker could not have have foreseen it. Imposing liability where there is no fore-seeability will "confer no economic benefit; it will merely require a costly transfer payment."

Id. at 46. In economic terms, a rule that an actor must pay for unforeseeable harms will not affect the actor's choices about activities that impose risk. If we make him pay for unforeseeable injuries caused by his conduct, it will not make the world any safer or more efficient: An actor cannot plan his conduct in light of risks he does not anticipate. Instead, "hanging over defendants' heads the specter of liability for harm from risks they cannot anticipate might conceivably produce socially unwarranted overdeterrence." J. Page, Torts Proximate Cause (2003) 103. So, economic analysis argue, there is little point to a liability rule that makes him pay damages for such risks.

If you think economic analysis of tort law is a lot of hooey, the basic point can be rephrased in more general normative terms: We impose liability because we think the actor should have acted differently. But we can't really "blame" an actor for acting in a certain way unless he would anticipate that doing so would cause harm. If the injury that results could not be anticipated, it doesn't seem "fair" to hold him liable for it.

Harm Inside the Circle of Foreseeability

Although courts will find a way to avoid imposing liability for unforeseeable injuries, it does not follow that the converse is always true, that is, that a defendant must pay whenever he causes *foreseeable* harm. In some situations, for various reasons of policy, courts also refuse to hold defendants liable for injuries that could be foreseen.

Consider the case in which the shopkeeper dropped the box lid, delaying the plaintiff, who was later injured in a train wreck. Doubtless, her harm falls outside the circle of foreseeability, at point A on Figure 9–1, and the court will refuse to impose liability for it. The court will likely explain its decision on the ground that the shopkeeper's act was "not the proximate cause" of the injury because it could not be foreseen.

Well enough. But now let's consider some types of cases that pretty clearly fall *inside* the circle of foreseeability, but in which courts still refuse to hold the defendant liable. One example is the case of secondary economic losses as a result of a negligent act. Suppose that Goodhart negligently causes a factory fire that injures Green, an employee, but also shuts down the factory for three months. It is obviously foreseeable that a fire would cause injury to a worker in the factory, and Goodhart will be liable for this foreseeable injury. However, while it seems equally foreseeable that the fire could cause a shutdown, so that the employees would suffer lost wages, most courts would deny recovery for the workers' lost wages during the shutdown.

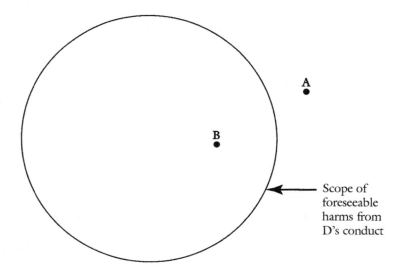

Figure 9–1. The Circle of Foreseeability

This economic loss to the workers pretty clearly falls at point B on Figure 9–1, within the circle of foreseeability, just as Green's personal injury does. Thus, courts that deny recovery for such secondary economic losses cannot credibly do so based on lack of proximate cause. Generally, courts reason that the burden of liability for such secondary economic losses is too great. (Imagine, for example, the potential liability if Goodhart had burned down a bridge, interrupting the business affairs of an entire town.) See generally Harper, James & Gray, §25.18A. However, while the denial of recovery in such cases has nothing to do with proximate cause, the cases frequently state that the defendant's conduct was "not the proximate cause" of the secondary losses. The use of proximate cause language in cases like these is unfortunate, but widespread.

New York's early rule limiting recovery for damages by fire provides another example of a court limiting liability, for policy reasons, for harm within the circle of foreseeability. In *Ryan v. New York Central Railroad Co.*, 35 N.Y. 210 (1866), the New York court restricted liability for fire damage to the first adjacent property burned. The *Ryan* court dubbed the burning of further properties "not the immediate but the remote result of the negligence of the defendants." Id. at 212. This conclusory proximate cause analysis, to borrow Dean Prosser's language in a related context, is "moonshine and vapor."[6] Anyone could foresee that a fire would burn beyond the next lot. The true rationale for the rule was the crushing burden such liability would impose, and the general availability of fire insurance as an alternative source of protection:

> To sustain such a claim as the present, and to follow the same to its legitimate consequences, would subject to a liability against which no prudence could guard, and to meet which no private fortune would be adequate... To hold that the owner must not only meet his own loss by fire, but that he must guarantee the security of his neighbors on both sides, and to an unlimited extent, would be to create a liability which would be the destruction of all civilized society.

Id. at 216.[7]

Unfortunately, courts that restrict liability for harm *within* the circle of foreseeability, for reasons of policy, often mask their decisions in proximate cause language as the *Ryan* court did in talking about "remote" and "immediate" causes. Cases involving liability for serving alcohol to intoxicated patrons provide another example of such obfuscatory rhetoric. Early liquor liability cases refused to hold barkeeps liable for liable serving intoxicated patrons who caused motor vehicle accidents, on the ground that the

---

6. W. Prosser, Proximate Cause in California, 38 Cal. L. Rev. 369, 376 (1950).

7. Most states have rejected the rigid limits of the *Ryan* rule. New York has modified it as well. See Prosser, Wade & Schwartz, Cases & Materials on Torts (9th ed. 1994) 292.

drunk driving, not the service of liquor, was the "proximate cause" of the injury. Yet few acts are more foreseeable than a drunk driving home from a roadside bar. The real thrust of these cases (since repudiated in many jurisdictions) was a policy decision to place liability for obviously foreseeable harm on the more blameworthy of two negligent parties.

The law of torts would be tidier if the courts would use *duty* analysis when they deny recovery for harm within the circle of foreseeability, for other policy reasons, and use *proximate cause* analysis in cases involving unforeseeable harm. Frequently, courts do use duty analysis to limit liability for foreseeable harm. (See pp. 204–205 for several examples.) But many other cases that deny recovery for policy reasons — as in the economic loss and drunk driving cases — use proximate cause language instead. One of the great challenges in reading these cases is to cut through promiscuous foreseeability references to determine whether some other policy is actually driving the decisions.

The following examples illustrate the basic issues involved in proximate cause cases. In analyzing them, assume that the court adopts a scope-of-the-risk approach to the proximate cause issues, unless otherwise noted.

EXAMPLES

Revisionist History

1. Bingham is running for a Long Island Railroad train that is about to pull out of the station. He is carrying a small package wrapped in brown paper. Two conductors, seeing the train start to leave, reach out to help Bingham onto the train, and one clumsily knocks the package onto the tracks. Alas, the package contains an antique music box which Bingham had just had valued at $5,000. The music box is demolished upon landing. Is the railroad liable under a foreseeability/scope-of-the-risk approach?

2. Bingham is running for a Long Island Railroad train that is about to pull out of the station. He is carrying a small package wrapped in brown paper. Two conductors, seeing the train start to leave, reach out to help Bingham onto the train, and one clumsily knocks the package onto the tracks. Alas, the package contains fireworks, which explode upon impact. A certain Mrs. Falsgraf, running to the same train immediately behind Bingham, is injured by the explosion.

    a. Is the railroad liable for her injuries?

    b. Assume, on the facts of Example 2a, that Mrs. Falsgraf sued Bingham. Would Bingham be liable for her injuries?

    c. Assume that the conductors negligently jostle Bingham, causing him to drop the package to the platform. It explodes, the passengers on the crowded platform panic and run, knocking down Mrs. Falsgraf 30 feet away. Would the railroad be liable to Falsgraf?

d. Assume, on the facts of *Palsgraf*, that Mrs. Palsgraf had sued the passenger. Would the court have denied recovery on proximate cause grounds?

Judge Fudd Does the Foreseeable

3. The Bentham Construction Company excavates a deep foundation for an office building in downtown St. Louis, immediately adjacent to a main street. Beale, a Bentham crane operator, sets down a load of iron beams in the street, on the edge of the excavation, but his touch is off and the load lands heavily, causing the wall of the excavation to collapse. The landslide breaks a large water main under the street, flooding the foundation.

Bentham's employees were not aware that the water main was there.

The owner sues for the damage caused by the flooding. Judge Fudd instructs the jury, in part, as follows:

> If you find that the defendant's employees were unaware that the water main was under the street, then you must find that any negligence of Bentham's employees in causing the collapse was not the proximate cause of the plaintiff's damages.

What is wrong with Judge Fudd's instruction?

4. Consider the distinction discussed in the Introduction between foreseeable injuries that happen through an unusual sequence of events (for which a defendant will be held liable) compared to injuries that happen through an unforeseeable mechanism of harm (for which they often will not). In which category would you put the following cases?

a. A train collides with a car at a railroad crossing, due to negligence of the engineer. The car is thrown into a track switch, throwing the switch and turning the train onto a side track, where it collides with a boxcar. Fletcher, a passenger, is injured by the collision with the boxcars.

b. Hill was repairing a "fender," made of piles driven into a stream bed below a bridge. He pried two piles apart and inserted a brace to hold them apart while he was inserting another pile. At this point a tug came along and hit a pile further along the fender, jarring the successive piles, causing the brace to fall out and the piles to spring back together. Hill's leg was trapped between them. He sued for his injuries.

c. In *Lewis v. Kehoe Academy*, 346 So. 2d 289 (La. App. 1977), a day care center negligently allowed a child to ingest rat poison. As a result, a small bruise the child later suffered was greatly accentuated, leading welfare authorities to conclude that the child had been abused, and to remove the child from the custody of his guardians.

Fudd Tries Again

5.   Corletti, a passenger on the way to an Italian festival, is assisted onto a Long Island Railroad train by a conductor. The conductor jostles him roughly, and he drops a package, which contains fireworks. The package explodes, causing burn injuries to Corletti.

Judge Fudd, who is handling the case, must determine whether the issue of proximate cause should be decided by the judge or the jury.

  a. Which party do you think would prefer to have the jury decide the proximate cause question?
  b. Suppose that Judge Fudd proposes to send the Corletti case to the jury, with the following instruction:

> If you find that, when the conductor assisted the plaintiff onto the train, he should have foreseen an unreasonable risk of injury to him from that act, then you should find that the conductor's negligence was a proximate cause of his resulting injury.

What change would you recommend in the Honorable Fudd's instruction?

The Thin Shell Rule?

6.   Keeton is driving along the road when his nose starts to run. He reaches over to the floor of the passenger's seat for a tissue and his car crosses the center line into the path of a gasoline truck. The truck swerves to avoid a collision, hits a wall and springs a leak. Gasoline pours out, percolates down into the public water supply, and triggers a $1 million environmental clean-up by county health officials. The county sues Keeton to recover its costs. Assuming that Keeton was negligent, is his conduct a proximate cause of the clean-up?

Risky Business

7.   On March 16, 2004, the Gregory Railroad Company accepts electric motors from Pollack for shipment. Because Pollack needed the motors as components for a finished product, he required, and the railroad agreed, to make delivery of the goods within ten days. Through the negligence of the railroad, shipment of the goods is delayed for five days. On March 30, while in transit on board a Gregory freight train, the goods are damaged in a flood. Is the railroad liable under the "risk rule"?

8.   On October 15, 2004, the Gregory Railroad accepts a shipment of apples to deliver for Pollack. Because the weather is cool and frost could spoil the apples, Pollack requires that the apples be delivered within four days. Gregory delays, and the apples are spoiled by freezing on October 23. Is the railroad liable?

Afterthoughts

9.   Consider, in the following cases, whether the later event should be treated as a superseding cause, "cutting off" the original negligent party's liability.

    a. Hart negligently repairs Mendoza's brakes. As Mendoza is driving
       along a main highway, Ellsworth negligently pulls out without
       looking, in front of Mendoza. Mendoza applies the brakes, but
       they fail, and the cars collide. Mendoza sues Hart for her injuries.

    b. Mendoza is injured in the accident and taken to the hospital with
       a broken arm. The arm is negligently set by Dr. Zipursky, causing
       additional injuries. Mendoza sues Hart and Ellsworth for her inju-
       ries, including the injuries from Zipursky's malpractice.

    c. In *Merhi v. Becker*, 325 A.2d 270 (Ct. 1973), a union gave a party
       with unlimited beer, but negligently failed to provide adequate
       security. Becker drank a lot of beer and got into two fights. A half
       hour later he got his car and drove it at one of his adversaries, but
       injured the plaintiff instead.

    d. Icarus Airlines negligently fails to fill all the fuel tanks on a passen-
       ger plane. Consequently, the plane is forced to land on a Pacific
       Island. Morris, a passenger, is injured when a volcano on the island
       erupts while they are refueling. Is the airline's negligence a proxi-
       mate cause of Morris's injury?

    e. Apex Alarm Company installs a security system in Smith's home. The
       alarm is designed to sound at the Apex office if the system is activated
       by an intruder. The Apex employee on duty then calls the police
       department, which ideally nabs the culprit at the scene of the crime.

         On a balmy June evening, a burglar breaks a window at
       Smith's home. This should activate the alarm system, but due to
       negligent rewiring at the Apex office, it fails to go off. The burglar
       makes off with Smith's valuables, and Smith sues Apex. Apex
       moves for summary judgment on the ground that the burglar's
       intentional criminal act supersedes its negligence in wiring the
       alarm improperly. How should the court rule?

You Be the Judge

10. Consider this case:

> A dredger, though warned of a gas main in the area, negligently
> breaks it while dredging. A factory a mile away, supplied with gas
> through the main, suffers damage to its equipment and loss of pro-
> duction due to the sudden loss of power.

Would you characterize this case as one involving unforeseeable harm, or
foreseeable harm in an unusual manner, or one inside the "circle of foreseeability" for which liability would be denied anyway?

EXPLANATIONS

Revisionist History

1.   Whether the railroad is liable under the foreseeability/scope-of-the-risk rule depends on how broadly you define the risk the defendant must foresee. Arguably, the presence of an expensive antique was not a risk that the conductors should have foreseen, and therefore they were not negligent for failing to foresee it. But most courts would define the risk more generally. They would conclude that the risk that makes the conductor's act negligent is the risk that either the passenger or his belongings would fall and be injured. When one of those risks causes the injury, the defendant is liable, because it is a risk that she should have anticipated and averted.

The fact that the package contained a valuable antique goes to the *extent* of the risk rather than its nature. The nature of the unreasonable risk that the conductors should have anticipated was damage to personal property from falling, and that was the risk that led to the harm. As in the "thin skull" cases, it should not be a defense for the railroad that the conductors did not know the contents of the package. They could foresee that Bingham would be carrying a package, that it might fall if they were not careful, and that the content — whatever they were — might be damaged if it fell. Where damage of the general type sustained was foreseeable, courts usually hold defendants liable for the damage *actually* caused, even if that is greater than one might ordinarily expect.

2a.   There are some obvious differences here from the facts of *Palsgraf*. Here, because Mrs. Falsgraf is next to Bingham, personal injury to her is foreseeable: The package could fall on her foot and injure her, or the conductor or the passenger could hit her, causing her to fall to the platform or even under the train. Palsgraf will argue that, on these facts, the conductors could foresee a risk of personal injury to her. Consequently, she is a foreseeable plaintiff and should recover for her injuries.

However, the court will probably not accept this argument. True, the conductors could foresee personal injury of one sort to Mrs. Falsgraf — from falling or being hit by the package — but they could not foresee injury of the sort that actually occurred — explosion. Most courts would conclude that the injury she suffered arose from a different risk than those the railroad could anticipate, and would therefore deny recovery. See e.g., the *Doughty case*, described above at pp. 178-179.

Example 1 illustrates that the proximate cause analysis must avoid defining the foreseeable risk too *specifically*. This example shows that the court may also go awry if it defines the risk too *generally*. If the defendant need only foresee "personal injury" of some sort, the plaintiff who tripped over the box lid, missed her train and was injured when the later train crashed could recover. The box lid left on the sidewalk created a risk of personal injury, she suffered personal injury, ergo liability. Yet this analysis would be too broad in both cases. The court must focus on the particular types of harm to be anticipated from the defendant's act. At the same time, as Example 1 illustrates, it must avoid getting bogged down in the idiosyncratic "details" of the accident.

b.   Mrs. Palsgraf's case against Bingham is distinguishable from her case against the railroad. Since Bingham *knows* that the package contains fireworks, he is aware of the risk of explosion. Most courts would conclude that he is negligent for bringing fireworks into a crowded place, precisely because they might be detonated by some kind of incident such as the scenario here. Since the risk of an explosion is one of the risks that makes his conduct negligent, most courts would hold him liable to those injured when an explosion actually takes place.

c.   Under the scope-of-the risk approach, the railroad should probably not be held liable to Mrs. Falsgraf on these facts. When the conductors acted, they could anticipate Bingham falling or dropping his package, but they had no reason to anticipate an explosion that would trigger a stampede among the passengers. Not even that odious character, the Reasonable Person, would warn them of such a consequence from jostling a passenger. Since they could not anticipate the general nature of the risk that injured Falsgraf, they should not be liable to her under the scope-of-the-risk approach.

d.   In the *Palsgraf* case, Mrs. Palsgraf was not directly injured by the blast, but by a set of scales some distance from the explosion, which were knocked over on her foot. Yet it does not seem unusual that a bystander, even at some distance, should be injured by flying debris if an explosion takes place. The details are unique — as they always are — but the general nature of the accident is within the scope of the risk to be anticipated.

Suppose you went up to the Reasonable Person and asked her whether she would anticipate that, if a package of explosives exploded in a public place, a bystander might be injured by an object dislodged by the blast. Doubtless, our odious character would view this as foreseeable, even if she could not tell you that the object would be a set of scales. Since this is a foreseeable risk of carrying explosives in a train station, the passenger would likely be held liable to Mrs. Palsgraf.

Judge Fudd Does the Foreseeable

3.   Judge Fudd's instruction requires the jury to find for the defendant if they find that its employees did not know that the water main was there. Presumably, his reasoning is that, if its employees were unaware of the water main, they had no reason to foresee the risk of water damage.

This is seriously Fuddled reasoning. If actual knowledge were required, a Menlove who threw a flower pot out the third story window without looking would not be liable if it hit a pedestrian. The important question is what Beale, the employee who dropped the beams, could *foresee* as a consequence of his negligence, not what he knew would happen. Surely, if that odious Reasonable Person had been there when Beale dropped the beams, he would have smugly explained to Beale that underground utilities *might* be under the street and that, if they were, they might rupture if the excavation collapsed. Since this was one of the risks that made Beale's act negligent, he should be liable, even if he was not sure what utilities actually ran under the street.

4a.   In the early case from which this example is drawn,[8] the court denied recovery, based on lack of foreseeability.

> That an automobile should suddenly appear upon a railroad track and be struck by an approaching train is not a matter of unusual occurrence, and is one that might reasonably be anticipated; but that such a collision should result in the automobile being thrown against a switch stand in such a manner as to open the switch is a possibility so remote as to be beyond the realm of events reasonably to be anticipated. This being true, the independent agency so intervening must be treated as the sole proximate cause of the injuries. . . .

133 N.E. at 140. However, this court almost certainly was seduced by the quirky "details" of the accident. While the particular sequence of events was certainly bizarre, the general nature of the harm — injury to the passenger when a collision throws him from his seat — is a foreseeable risk of negligently driving the train at a crossing. Most modern courts would look to the general nature of the risk threatened by the engineer's negligence, and hold the railroad liable on these facts.

b.   This Rube Goldberg scenario seems pretty idiosyncratic. But one of the basic risks of negligent piloting of the tug was that it would hit the fender and injure a worker working on it. That's just that what happened. If the defendant had to foresee the particulars, such as the brace getting dislodged and trapping the plaintiff's leg, defendants would seldom be liable, even though they could foresee the general risks of their conduct. This one should go in the foreseeable injury/quickly facts category.

c.   This case is best characterized as unforeseeable harm through a different mechanism of harm. The risk the reasonable person would anticipate from exposing the child to poison is the risk of physical injury from poisoning, not the risk of deprivation of custody through misinterpretation of bruising. In addition, the reasonable actor would anticipate harm to the child from leaving the poison around, not to his guardians. As in *Palsgraf*, harm to them from this negligent act is unforeseeable. The complaint in *Lewis* was dismissed for lack of proximate cause.

---

8. *Engle v. Director General of Railroads*, 133 N.E. 138 (Ind. App. 1921).

Fudd Tries Again

5a. It is frequently said that whether the defendant's negligence was a proximate cause of the plaintiff's injury is a question of fact for the jury. Surely the plaintiff will breathe a sigh of relief if the judge decides that the issue is one of fact, and sends it to the jury. In general, the jury won't have the foggiest idea of what proximate cause means. Imagine yourself, after a few classes on the concept in Torts class, trying to apply the concept effectively to a real case. The jury must do so based on a vague, general instruction such as this:

> A proximate cause of an injury is that which in a natural and continuous sequence, unbroken by an independent intervening cause, produces the injury, and without which the injury would not have occurred. It need not be the only cause, nor the last nor nearest cause. It is sufficient if it occurs with some other cause acting at the same time, which in combination with it, causes the injury.[9]

One study of jurors' understanding of proximate cause instructions concluded that all they take from an instruction like this is that "proximate cause [is] just a fancy way of saying causation." C. Mikell, Jury Instructions and Proximate Cause: An Uncertain Trumpet in Georgia, 27 Georgia St. Bar J. 60, 63 (1990). They have no real concept of it as a separate limit on *legal responsibility* apart from actual causation.

The lesson of this for defense lawyers is that they must win the proximate cause battle in front the judge, by convincing her that, as a matter of law, the defendant's act was not the proximate cause of the plaintiff's injury. This is a realistic prospect; in many cases the judge will grant summary judgment for the defendant, concluding as a matter of law that the plaintiff's injury was unforeseeable. If she lets the issue go to the jury, the plaintiff has probably won the proximate cause battle.

b. Judge Fudd's instruction misses the mark. He has instructed the jury that if the conductor should have anticipated injury to Corletti from his act, he is liable to him for the injury he sustains. This instruction is too broad, though you could find similar instructions in use in various states today. Surely the conductor could anticipate injury to Corletti from jostling him as he gets on the train: He might fall under the train, or fall down and get a bruise. But the conductor would not foresee explosion injuries, and it is very unlikely a court would hold him liable for them.

Here is a less fuddled instruction:

> If you find that, when the conductor assisted the plaintiff onto the train, he should have foreseen an unreasonable risk of injury to plaintiff *of the general nature that actually took place*, then you should

---

9. Adapted from the New Mexico Model Jury Instruction UJI 13-305.

find that the conductor's negligence was a proximate cause of plaintiff's resulting injury.

If Judge Fudd had added the italicized language to the instruction, he would probably have concluded that, as a matter of law, the jury could not find it satisfied. The mechanism of harm that injured Corletti — explosion — was quite different from the risks the conductor might have expected from helping him onto the train.

The Thin Shell Rule?

6.   When I used this example on my exam, many students argued that Keeton's negligence was not the proximate cause of the clean-up, on the ground that he would not have anticipated such an expensive consequence of his act. However, it is very doubtful that a no-proximate-cause argument is going to get Keeton off the hook. Certainly, an accident with an on-coming vehicle is exactly the risk the odious Reasonable Person would announce, "like a town-crier in Pompci,"[10] as he saw Keeton dive for the tissue. And, if such an accident happens, it is entirely foreseeable that one of the vehicles could be damaged and leak. It is unfortunate for Keeton that that vehicle was a gasoline truck, and that the resulting damage is so extensive, but that fact is a detail of the accident. The general nature of the risk that caused the harm is the risk Keeton should have anticipated. Let's hope he's well insured.

Risky Business

7.   This is a recurring fact pattern that has spawned contradictory holdings in the cases. But the result under the risk rule seems clear. The risk that made the railroad's delay negligent was the risk that Pollack would suffer commercial losses, not the risk that, if the motors were shipped later rather than sooner, they would be damaged in transit by a flood. That risk is presumably the same whether they are in transit from March 16 to March 26, or March 21 to March 31, for all we know from the facts. Thus, the risk of flood was not a risk that made it negligent to delay the shipment. Under the risk rule, the railroad should not be held liable.

8.   This example contrasts nicely with the last. Here, the railroad agreed that the apples would be shipped immediately, and was presumably aware, or should have been, that delay posed a risk that the apples would be spoiled by cold weather. Thus, one of the risks that made the delay negligent here was the risk of freezing as the weather got colder, and it was exactly this risk that caused the damage. (Couldn't you just see that self-righteous Reasonable Person wagging her finger at the railroad superintendent and warning,

---

10. Dylan Thomas, A Child's Christmas in Wales (New Directions 1954) 4.

"Those apples may freeze if you don't ship them soon ...") Consequently, the railroad would likely be held liable for the resulting damage. See *Fox v. Boston and Maine Railroad Co.*, 19 N.E. 222 (Mass. 1889).

Afterthoughts

9a. This is the typical "joint tortfeasor" case in which two actors are negligent at different times, and the two negligent acts combine to cause the plaintiff's injury. If Hart could argue that Ellsworth's negligence "superseded" his, there would be no law of "joint tortfeasors"; only the party who was negligent last would be liable, even though the negligence of each was a "but for" cause of the plaintiff's injury.

This is clearly not the law. One of the foreseeable risks of driving is that other drivers will be negligent. Thus, Hart cannot argue that Ellsworth's subsequent negligence "cuts off" his liability — one of the primary purposes for efficient brakes is to respond to the foreseeable risk of emergencies due to negligent driving.

b. Clearly, Hart's negligence and Ellsworth's negligence are "but for" causes of Mendoza's malpractice injury. If negligence of a driver on the road is foreseeable, why not negligence of a doctor practicing her profession? Virtually all courts hold that a tortfeasor who causes injury can anticipate that the victim might suffer further injury from medical treatment. Thus, the original tortfeasor is also liable for the subsequent malpractice.

Of course, Dr. Zipursky is *not* liable for the original injury, since he is not a "but for" cause of that injury. He is liable only for the additional injury caused by his negligent treatment.

c. Surely, one of the risks of supplying unlimited beer to guests at a party is that fights will arise. Most people won't get mad enough to run someone down, but the general risk of aggressive conduct is one of the risks that makes such conduct negligent, absent adequate security (or, probably, with it). In *Merli*, the court noted that

> neither foreseeability of the extent nor the manner of the injury constitutes the criteria for deciding questions of proximate cause. The test is whether the harm which occurred was of the same general nature as the foreseeable risk created by the defendant's negligence.

325 A.2d at 273. Here, the general nature of the risk — uncontrolled aggressive conduct — was clearly foreseeable. The union was held liable though it did not foresee that Becker would resort to using his car as a weapon.

d. In this example, borrowed from V. Schwartz, K. Kelly of D. Pactlett, Torts Cases and Materials (10th ed. 2000) 324., virtually any court would conclude that the airline's negligence was not the proximate cause of Beale's injury. Injury from an erupting volcano is not a foreseeable consequence of failing to fill all the fuel tanks. Under the risk approach, leaving the fuel out creates an unreasonable risk that the plane would have to ditch in the water or make an emergency landing, but not that the plane would land on an island at the time of a volcanic eruption. The court will deny recovery to Beale for this bizarre occurrence.

Many courts would hold that the eruption of a volcano near the airport where the plane was forced down was such an unexpected later event that it "supersedes" the negligence of the airline. But labeling the eruption a "superseding cause" is more a conclusion than a helpful method of analysis. The court must still separate superseding causes from others which do not cut off liability. Most courts do so on the basis of the extraordinary or unforeseeable nature of the subsequent events.

In this example, Apex was negligent in rewiring the system, but a later, deliberate criminal act of a third person leads to the plaintiff's injury. The issue is whether this act "supersedes" the negligence of Apex, so as to cut off its liability for the theft.

Subsequent intentional acts may cut off liability in some cases. A nice example is the owner who allowed a child trespasser into its building, only to have the boy maliciously usher a visitor into an unguarded elevator shaft. See *Cole v. German S. & L. Soc.*, 124 F. 113 (8th Cir. 1903). No one, not even a law professor, would anticipate such a twisted sense of humor. But other intentional acts are entirely foreseeable. Here, Apex was hired to avert the very type of act which caused Smith's loss. It hardly seems appropriate to take his money to protect him from theft, and then when it fails to do so, to deny that such theft was foreseeable! Since illegal entry by a burglar is clearly one of the hazards that makes it negligent to wire the system improperly, Apex's motion for summary judgment should be denied. See Restatement (Second) of Torts, §449 (quoted at p. •••).

You Be the Judge

10. In the case from which this example is drawn, the court held that, while injury to persons or property from the escaping gas would be foreseeable, injury to the plaintiff's business was not.

> [T]he damage arising from the loss of natural gas supply, in turn causing the shutdown of electric turbines, in turn causing a loss of electric power vital to the aluminum reduction process, with the ultimate result being substantial damage to equipment and product-in-process, goes beyond the pale of general harm which reasonably might have been anticipated by negligent dredgers.

Consolidated Aluminum Corp. v. C.F. Bean Corp., 833 F.2d 65, 68 (5th Cir. 1987). With all due respect, this conclusion is dubious. It seems eminently foreseeable that the interruption of gas service will cause many commercial losses to nearby businesses. In fact, such secondary economic losses fall so clearly within the circle of foreseeability, and are claimed so frequently in tort cases, that courts have developed the "economic loss doctrine" to address them.

This case is an example of a court misusing foreseeability analysis to limit liability for other reasons. As stated in the introduction, courts often limit liability for clearly foreseeable harm for other policy reasons. Doubtless, the court denied liability because of the extreme burden that liability for secondary economic losses would impose in a case like this: If the dredger were liable to this plaintiff, it would be liable to all those who suffered from the interruption in service. It is certainly understandable that courts will refuse to impose overwhelming liability for secondary consequences of negligence. But it does little for clarity of analysis to mask this policy conclusion in the guise of foreseeability.

Couldn't the court, with stronger justification, have written as follows, relying on the economic loss doctrine:

> It is hardly unforeseeable that severing a major gas supply line (of which the defendant had been informed) will interrupt the flow of energy to a nearby manufacturer dependent upon that supply line, causing injury from the sudden disruption of complex manufacturing sequences and loss of products in process. However, given the magnitude of the losses that could flow from even a single interruption of such service, we think the burden of liability for such secondary losses too great to impose on the negligent tortfeasor.

PART FOUR

The Duty Element

10

The Elusive Element of Duty: Two Principles in Search of an Exception

Introduction

It is hornbook law that the plaintiff in a negligence case must prove four elements in order to recover: duty, breach, causation, and damages. Even if the defendant was negligent, and that negligence caused injury to the plaintiff, the defendant will not be liable unless he also owed the plaintiff a duty of care. This chapter addresses the elusive element of duty.

It hardly seems that this should be a problem: Don't we all owe a duty to *everyone* not to injure them by our own negligence? Such a universal duty of care would simplify negligence law considerably: It would effectively eliminate the duty element from the plaintiff's burden of proof, since a duty of care would always exist. Although such a broad rule is tempting, courts have not been willing to impose a universal duty of due care. Courts have often refused to hold defendants liable, even though they have caused clearly foreseeable harm to the plaintiff. Here, for example, are some situations in which many courts would deny recovery even though harm was to be anticipated from the defendant's conduct.

a.   Adler visits city hall to pay a traffic ticket. While walking up the stairs, he sees a pen lying on the edge of one of the stair treads. He fails to pick it up, and Skinner later falls on it, breaking a leg.

b. Federal Safety Insurance Company provides fire insurance for industry. To reduce claims, Federal inspects the premises of the companies it insures for fire hazards before issuing a policy. Federal Safety inspects Rainbow Paint Company's factory, but neglects to enter a small room in which oily rags have been left in a pile. A week later, Skinner, an employee at the plant, is burned in a fire started by those rags. He sues Federal for failing to prevent the fire by seeing that the rags were removed.

c. Reik is driving down a rural highway and witnesses an accident in which White drives into a tree. Unwilling to get involved, she drives on. White is not found for an hour, and his injuries are aggravated by the delay in receiving treatment.

d. Dr. Rogers treats Jung for an infectious form of hepatitis. He is aware that Jung is a professional dancer. However, he makes no effort to warn other dancers who may have contact with Jung. Klein, a member of Jung's dance troupe, contracts hepatitis from Jung.

In each of these examples, the actor was (we will assume) negligent, and that negligence caused the plaintiff's damages. Yet many courts would refuse to allow recovery in these cases, on the ground that the actor did not owe a duty of care to the plaintiff.

Why Courts Impose Duties, or Refuse to Impose Them

Tort duties are not like chemistry's Periodic Table of Elements. Nature's elements (they tell me) have a physical existence quite apart from anything we might think about them. Chemists have identified them, but (with perhaps a few high-tech exceptions) they have not created them. Tort duties, on the other hand, do not exist in nature; they are *made up* by judges because they conclude that a duty *ought* to exist under the circumstances. "[L]egal duties are not discoverable facts of nature, but merely conclusory expressions that, in cases of a particular type, liability should be imposed for damage done." *Tarasoff v. Regents of the Univ. of California*, 551 P.2d 334, 342 (Cal. 1976). "[I]t should be recognized that 'duty' is not sacrosanct in itself, but is only an expression of the sum total of those considerations of policy which lead the law to say that the plaintiff is entitled to protection." Prosser & Keeton at 358. If a court concludes that society will be better off if store owners exercise due care to assist injured customers, it will create such a duty; if a court concludes that bystanders should not be legally bound to render aid in an emergency, it will refuse to create a duty to intervene, and so on.

This fundamental fact of tort life is not something to be embarrassed about: Determining the legal rights and obligations of the parties is the most fundamental task of judging. "The scope or extent of duty in any case can only be resolved by the learning, experience, good sense and judgment of the judge — the molding of law in response to the needs of the environment." L. Green, Duties, Risks, Causation Doctrines, 41 Tex. L. Rev. 42, 45 (1962). On the other hand, it is not particularly satisfying to students simply to tell them that the duty issue is difficult and judges have to decide it. Understandably, you want more guidance about such an important issue.

Though the duty issue is complex, some guidance is possible. To begin with, we can identify major factors that judges consider in deciding whether to impose a duty in a given case. These factors include the judge's sense of morality, the foreseeability and extent of the likely harm from the defendant's conduct, the burden that the new duty will impose on the defendant, alternative ways of protecting the plaintiff's interest, the increased safety likely to result from imposing the duty, the chilling effect the duty may have on defendants' conduct, administrative problems for the courts in enforcing the duty, problems of proof, and others.

Certainly, the foreseeability of harm weighs heavily in favor of imposing a duty on the actor, since it makes basic good sense that a defendant "should" avoid foreseeable injuries to others. For example, it is highly foreseeable that a mental patient who threatens to kill a relative will do so if released from custody, or that a parent will suffer traumatic shock if a negligent driver hits his child. Where resulting harm is so likely to follow, the argument is persuasive that the court should impose a duty of care to prevent it.

The moral argument is also strong in many duty cases. Most people would believe that it is "right" for an employer to go to the aid of an injured worker, or a doctor to take steps to assure that an HIV infected patient does not engage in unsafe sexual practices. This argument is particularly persuasive if the defendant is uniquely positioned to prevent harm. The psychiatrist who releases a patient who has threatened a relative, for example, may be the only one in a position to warn the relative. The police officer who stops a drunk driver is uniquely placed to prevent that driver from causing an accident.

Other factors, however, weigh against imposing a duty of care, even if harm is foreseeable and avoidable. Courts hesitate to create duties that impose excessive burdens on actors. A court might, for example, refuse to impose a duty on school officials to supervise school children at bus stops. Such a duty would impose an expensive burden on school districts, which can be fulfilled as well, if not better, by parents. Similarly, many courts have refused to impose a duty of care on municipalities to properly inspect private property. Here too, the burden on municipalities would be exceedingly broad, and the risk can be averted by owners. Similarly, a court refused to hold that a hospital has a duty to warn all patients of the risks of medications, on the ground that the duty would be too broad, and that it can be better fulfilled by the patient's doctor. *Kirk v. Michael Reese Hosp. & Medical Ctr.*, 513 N.E.2d 387, 396-397 (Ill. 1987).

Administrative problems of enforcing the duty may also influence the court's judgment. For many years, courts denied liability for infliction of emotional distress on the ground that the risk of fraudulent claims and excessive litigation was too great. Similarly, they rejected claims for injury to fetuses partly on the ground that it would be extremely difficult to prove that the defendant's conduct was the cause of the injury.

In other cases, the chilling effect of imposing the duty has counseled hesitation. In *Eiseman v. State*, 511 N.E.2d 1128 (N.Y. 1987), the court refused to hold that a college had a duty to control the acts of a parolee admitted to a college enrichment program. The court was unwilling to create a duty that would force colleges to place discriminatory restrictions on the very persons the program was meant to assist in reintegrating into society. Similarly, some courts have refused to impose a duty on theater operators to prevent violence by viewers of violent movies, to avoid chilling activity protected by the First Amendment. See, e.g., *Yakubowicz v. Paramount Pictures Corp.*, 536 N.E.2d 1067, 1071-1072 (Mass. 1989).

Policies established by the legislature will also influence the court's duty analysis. Courts that have imposed a tort duty on the police to arrest drunk drivers have noted the firm legislative policy of controlling drunk driving. See *Irwin v. Town of Ware*, 467 N.E.2d 1292, 1302 (Mass. 1984). Similarly, the *Tarasoff* court, in concluding that the psychiatrist had a duty to warn, rejected the argument that it would impair doctor/patient confidentiality in part because a statute rejected the privilege in situations involving danger to third persons. 551 P.2d at 346-347.

Other policy considerations may also be relevant to the duty analysis, depending on the facts of each case. In most, no single factor will be determinative, the judge will balance many to reach a conclusion. As an advocate, you may not always be able to predict that conclusion, but you can learn to identify factors relevant to the duty analysis, and to formulate arguments for or against imposing a duty based on those factors.

In many common situations, decades of precedent have defined fairly clearly the extent to which the courts will recognize a duty of care. The remainder of this introduction addresses common situations in which courts impose such a duty—or refuse to. However, it is important to remember that the duties described are not immutable truths; they are pragmatic policy judgments that may be reconsidered by future judges as society and public attitudes evolve.

First Principles: Torts and the Couch Potato

I find it useful to analyze tort duties in terms of two basic principles, each liberally qualified with exceptions. The first principle is that courts generally refuse to impose liability for doing nothing. If Adler, a couch potato, spends all of his time on the sofa watching TV, he is in an excellent position to avoid tort liability. Indeed, as a Torts professor, I would advise you to do just that. People get into tort suits in the weirdest of ways, but they have little to fear from being inert.

This long held view of the common law, that there is no liability for the failure to act, is illustrated by the hypothetical of the callous bystander who watches a blind man walk into a busy street and fails to call out a warning. Our moral sense is repulsed by the illustration, yet in most states the bystander still has no *legal* duty to act to protect another, and therefore is not liable for failing to do so. Similarly, a sunbather who watches a child going under the waves has no duty to dive in the water, throw her a life ring, or even notify a nearby lifeguard:

> The fact that the actor realizes or should realize that action on his part is necessary for another's aid or protection does not of itself impose upon him a duty to take such action.

Restatement (Second) of Torts §314. According to the Restatement,

> The origin of the rule lay in the early common law distinction between action and inaction, or "misfeasance" and "non-feasance." In the early law one who injured another by a positive affirmative act was held liable without any great regard even for his fault. But the courts were far too much occupied with the more flagrant forms of misbehavior to be greatly concerned with one who merely did nothing, even though another might suffer serious harm because of his omission to act. Hence, liability for nonfeasance was slow to receive any recognition in the law.

Restatement (Second) of Torts §314 cmt. c.

Although torts scholars usually cite this no-duty-to-act principle with embarrassment, there are some substantial policy arguments to support it. The defendant whose act (misfeasance) endangers the plaintiff has "created a new risk of harm to the plaintiff, while by 'nonfeasance' he has at least made [the plaintiff's] situation no worse, and has merely failed to benefit him by interfering in his affairs." Prosser & Keeton at 373. Other defenders of the principle emphasize the infringement on individual liberty posed by coercing services from unwilling bystanders,[1] and the difficulty of defining the duty if it is to be imposed. For example, how great an effort would the defendant have to make? Would a bystander have to dive in after the child if he could not swim? *Which* bystanders would have the

---

1. Consider the case posed by Professor Epstein in his defense of the rule:

   > X as a representative of a private charity asks you for $10 in order to save the life of some starving child in a country ravaged by war. There are other donors available but the number of needy children exceeds that number. The money means "nothing" to you. Are you under an obligation to give the $10?

   R. Epstein, A Theory of Strict Liability, 2 J. Legal Stud. 151, 198-199 (1973).

duty—a whole beachful? Would bystanders be required to subordinate important interests of their own to effectuate rescue (for example, postpone visiting a seriously ill relative to assist at an accident scene)?

These objections are probably not insurmountable; most European countries impose a limited duty to aid, as does the state of Vermont. See Vt. Stat. Ann. tit. 12 §519. Yet most American courts have not rejected the no-duty-to-act rule outright. Instead they have nibbled away at it by carving out exceptions (discussed below at pp. 217-220).

Second First Principles: Risk Creation as a Source of Duty

The second broad duty principle complements the first: Those who do act, who choose to engage in activities that create a risk of injury to others, *do* have a duty to exercise care to avoid injuring others. If Bruner drives his car negligently and hits Gilligan, he has set loose a dangerous force that creates a risk to others. If Freud is reroofing his garage and drops his hammer on a pedestrian, that also creates a new risk of harm. If Chef Adler bakes a quiche with spoiled ingredients, causing food poisoning, he too has set in motion a new force capable of causing harm. These defendants, unlike the bystander in the nonfeasance cases, have "created new risks" by their activities which have caused injury.

Far and away the largest proportion of negligence cases—perhaps 90 percent—involve situations like these, in which defendants have let loose dangerous forces that have caused injury. In these cases, the defendant's choice to engage in risk-creating conduct for his own benefit imposes the reciprocal duty to exercise due care toward those who may foreseeably be injured by that conduct. The law tolerates, indeed, encourages, activity, including activities that impose risks of injury on others. But it has long recognized that those who unleash such forces owe a duty to others to keep that risk to a reasonable level.

In most cases, risk creation is the obvious basis of the duty to exercise due care. Duty is probably the least frequently contested element of a negligence claim, because most negligence cases arise from active conduct, and it is clear that the actor owed a duty to exercise due care toward those who might foreseeably be injured by it. For example, the duty issue is seldom raised in highway accident cases, since we all understand that we owe a duty of due care to others in driving a car. Similarly, it is clear that a utility company that erects a telephone pole owes a duty of care to anyone who might foreseeably be injured if it falls.

In analyzing duty issues, it is important to keep in mind these two divergent first principles—on the one hand, the bystander who has not created any risk and who declines to get involved, and, on the other, the actor whose conduct creates a risk of injury. However, these two paradigms do not, unfortunately, resolve all the cases. For various policy reasons, courts have spawned exceptions to both principles. As discussed below, a person who has done nothing may sometimes be held liable for failing to act. And, at times, a person who has created a risk will *not* be held liable, even though her risk-creating activity leads to foreseeable injury.

Exceptions to the No-Duty Rule: Duties of Affirmative Action

Let's look first at some exceptions to the no-duty-to-act rule. Courts have not hesitated to create "affirmative duties" to act for the protection of another where some policy justifies departing from the no-duty rule. When such a duty of affirmative action is found, the actor may not defend on the basis that "I just didn't want to get involved": The law imposes a duty to get involved.

A. Duty Based on a Special Relationship to the Victim

Courts often impose a duty to aid based on a preexisting relationship between the defendant and the person who needs assistance. See Restatement (Second) of Torts §§314A, 314B. Here are some typical examples in which courts have imposed a duty to act for the protection of another due to a "special relationship" to the plaintiff:

- A train conductor sees a passenger being assaulted by another, but fails to come to the victim's aid.
- A factory owner fails to assist an employee who is trapped in an elevator in the course of his employment.
- School officials note that a child is feverish but fail to seek medical care for the child.
- A prison inmate complains repeatedly to a guard of stomach pains, but the guard fails to take any steps to get him medical help.

In each of these situations, the defendant is not the source of the injury producing conduct. The school officials, for example, did not cause the child's fever, nor did the train conductor assault the passenger. However, because of the defendant's relationship to the victim in these cases, the courts impose a duty on the defendant to take affirmative steps to minimize or avert the harm. In the factory example, the duty is based on the fact that the employer is uniquely situated to mitigate the harm and that the employee is on the premises for the benefit of the employer. The duty in the school case is based on the fact that school officials take charge of children with knowledge of their need for protection. The duty to prisoners is premised on taking charge of the prisoner and depriving him of the ability to act for his own protection. See Restatement (Second) of Torts §320 cmt. b.

B. Duty Based on a Special Relationship to the Perpetrator

A second category of special relationship exceptions to the no-duty rule involves situations in which courts impose a duty to control one person to prevent him from injuring others. Examples include the duty of a parent to control a child in certain circumstances (Restatement (Second) of Torts §316) and the duty of an employer to control an employee. Restatement (Second) of Torts §317. The Restatement imposes a similar duty on one who takes charge of another with "dangerous propensities":

> One who takes charge of a third person whom he knows or should know to be likely to cause bodily harm to others if not controlled is under a duty to exercise reasonable care to control the third person to prevent him from doing such harm.

Restatement (Second) of Torts §319. This exception, which applies primarily to those in charge of mental patients or prisoners, reflects the courts' conclusion that the defendant accepts a duty of care by taking charge of a person who poses a risk of injury. The employer's duty to control an employee is presumably based on the benefit the employer derives from the activities of the employee. In addition, as noted above, the defendant in those situations is often uniquely positioned to prevent the harm.

Perhaps the most famous affirmative duty case, *Tarasoff v. Regents of the Univ. of California*, 551 P.2d 334 (1976), was decided on the basis of this special relationship principle. The *Tarasoff* court concluded that the psychiatrist's relationship to a dangerous patient gave rise to a duty to warn the patient's intended victim that the patient had threatened to kill her. This particular application of the special relationship approach has been controversial. Because of the burden this duty imposes on defendants, some courts have refused to extend it beyond situations involving a threat to a particular victim. See *Leonard v. State*, 491 N.W.2d 508, 512 (Iowa 1992) (holding psychiatrist owes no duty to members of general public in discharging patient).

C. Duty Based on Innocent Creation of the Risk

Another set of exceptions to the no-duty rule involves situations in which the defendant, without negligence, creates the risk that causes injury to the plaintiff. See Restatement (Second) of Torts §321, which provides:

> (1) If the actor does an act, and subsequently realizes or should realize that it has created an unreasonable risk of causing physical harm to another, he is under a duty to exercise reasonable care to prevent the risk from taking effect.

The Restatement gives the example of a driver whose truck suddenly becomes disabled on the road and fails to warn on-coming traffic. Restatement (Second) of Torts §321 illus. 3. Under §321, the driver, though not negligent, is the author of the risk, and owes an affirmative duty to warn other drivers of the danger. Similarly, under Restatement (Second) of Torts §322, an actor who has injured another, even without negligence, has an affirmative duty to render assistance to prevent further harm to the injured party. For example, if Freud hits Adler, a pedestrian, with his car and knocks him into the street, §322 requires Freud to take reasonable steps to protect Adler from further injury.

These exceptions to the no-duty rule are presumably based on the risk creation rationale. Even though Freud was not negligent, he has, by his risk-creating conduct for his own purposes, placed Adler in a position of danger. To require him to go to Adler's aid "is simply requiring [a person] to minimize the consequences of risks which society gives him a privilege to create." F. James Jr., Note, Scope of Duty in Negligence Cases, 47 Nw. U. L. Rev. 778, 804 (1953).

This duty to help persons injured or placed in peril by the actor without negligence illustrates the way in which duties evolve. While §322 of the Second Restatement takes the position that innocently placing another in peril gives rise to a duty, §322 of the First Restatement of Torts, published 31 years earlier, limited the duty to persons "made helpless by *tortious* conduct" (emphasis added). What changed in the intervening years to make judges willing to impose a duty to assist, even if the actor had not been negligent? Perhaps the New Deal and the Second World War tempered the rampant individualism of the nineteenth century. Perhaps the increased frequency of automobile accidents played a part. Perhaps the lessening of a moralistic focus on fault, and increased emphasis on risk creation and cost avoidance as bases for liability, have contributed. For whatever reasons, as society has changed, so has the scope of duty.

D. The Gratuitous Services Exception

Another widely recognized exception to the no-duty-to-act principle arises where the defendant, though under no initial duty to do so, goes to the aid of another:

> One who, being under no duty to do so, takes charge of another who is helpless adequately to aid or protect himself is subject to liability to the other for any bodily harm caused to him by

(a) the failure of the actor to exercise reasonable care to secure the safety of the other while within the actor's charge, or

(b) the actor's discontinuing his aid or protection, if by so doing he leaves the other in a worse position than when the actor took charge of him.

Restatement (Second) of Torts §324. This exception is illustrated by the bystander who sees a pedestrian hit by a car, and goes to the pedestrian's assistance, but negligently causes further injury to her by handling her roughly or using clearly inappropriate first aid techniques.

Ironically, this exception to the no-duty principle imposes the risk of tort liability on the bystander who makes the worthy choice to render assistance. Once Smith decides to "get involved," he assumes a duty of care, although, had he simply stood by or walked away, he would have incurred no liability. See Restatement (Second) of Torts §314. Presumably, the rationale is that the actor, while virtuous, is still a risk creator in rendering assistance, and should not be licensed to mishandle the victim with impunity.

Exceptions to the Risk Creation Rule: Duty as a Limiting Factor in Negligence Cases

This introduction began by describing two "first principles": that there is no general duty to act for the benefit of another, and that those who choose to act owe a duty to others to use due care in such conduct. Then, we explored some exceptions to the no-duty principle, situations in which courts have imposed a duty on one person to act for the benefit of another. Now, let's consider some exceptions to the second "first principle," that persons who choose to engage in risk-creating activity owe a duty of care to others who might foreseeably be injured by that activity.

One school of thought argues that there should be *no* exception to this second "first principle": Those who engage in risk-creating activities should be liable for all injuries foreseeably caused by their negligence. The argument traces its roots to the following statement in *Heaven v. Pender*, 1881-1885 All E.R. Rep. 35, 39 (1883).

> [W]henever one person is by circumstances placed in such a position with regard to another that any one of ordinary sense who did think would at once recognise that, if he did not use ordinary care and skill in his own conduct with regard to those circumstances, he would cause danger of injury to the person or property of the other, a duty arises to use ordinary care and skill to avoid such danger.[2]

---

2. See also Restatement (Second) of Torts, §302, cmt. a: "In general, anyone who does an affirmative act is under a duty to others to exercise the care of a reasonable man to protect them against an unreasonable risk of harm to them arising out of the act."

Despite the intuitive appeal of this statement, no court accepts it without qualification. Liability for all foreseeable injury from negligent conduct would impose too heavy a burden on defendants in some situations. Sometimes, the extent of this burden leads courts to restrict liability for foreseeable harm by holding that the defendant "owed no duty" to the plaintiff.

Many casebooks illustrate the point with two classic limited duty problems, duties to the unborn and duties to avoid inflicting emotional distress. In each of these areas, courts have drawn the circle of duty considerably more narrowly than the limits of foreseeable harm. For example, many early cases held that a defendant who injured a fetus (e.g., by negligently hitting the mother with a car), was not liable, because there was "no duty to the unborn." See, e.g., *Magnolia Coca Cola Bottling Co. v. Jordan*, 78 S.W.2d 944, 945-950 (Tex. 1937), overruled, *Leal v. C. C. Pitts Sand & Gravel Inc.*, 419 S.W.2d 820, 822 (Tex. 1967). In these cases, there was no doubt that the defendant's risk-creating conduct had caused the injury. Nor was there doubt that the injury was foreseeable. The early cases denied liability for policy reasons, including the difficulties of proving the cause of prenatal injury, reluctance to treat fetuses as "persons" in the absence of statutory authority, and the risk of fraudulent claims.

More recently, many courts have recognized a duty of care to the unborn in at least some circumstances. This is not because the defendant's conduct is any different or the plaintiff's injury any more foreseeable. Modern courts, for various reasons of policy, are simply more willing to impose a duty in such cases. Doubtless two reasons for the shift are the improved ability to trace the source of fetal injury and the wide availability of insurance for such claims.

Similarly, early cases refused to allow recovery for infliction of emotional distress unless the plaintiff suffered a physical impact. For example, recovery was denied where the plaintiff, narrowly missed by a speeding car, suffered serious fright and a resulting heart attack. Here again, it was often clear that the defendant had created the risk and that the risk had caused foreseeable injury to the plaintiff. Yet the courts refused to recognize a duty here, out of fear of fraudulent claims and greatly increased litigation. Recent cases have broadened this duty as well, but liability for negligent infliction remains considerably narrower in most states than the all-foreseeable-risks principle argued for in *Heaven v. Pender*. See Chapter 11, which analyzes in detail claims for negligent infliction of emotional distress.

Courts have similarly limited the duty of care in many other types of cases, based on policy considerations unique to each situation. Some examples include liability for serving alcohol to intoxicated patrons, liability of lawyers to beneficiaries for negligent drafting of a will, liability of accountants to parties (other than their clients) who rely on their opinions, liability for secondary economic losses and the liability of landowners for injury to entrants on their land. In these and other situations, courts often refuse, for policy reasons, to impose liability even though the defendant has caused foreseeable harm to others.

The Relation of Duty to Proximate Cause

Much confusion exists as to the distinction between the duty element in negligence cases and proximate cause limitations on liability. It may help, however, to distinguish two types of limitations that courts place on liability: First, limiting liability to the foreseeable consequences of the defendant's negligent act, and second, denying liability for consequences that *are* foreseeable, for the types of policy reasons discussed in this chapter.

Courts very frequently use the concept of *proximate cause* to limit liability to the foreseeable consequences of a negligent act. Consider, for example, the hypothetical in which the defendant leaves the ignition key in his car, and it is stolen by a terrorist and used to bomb an embassy. The defendant may well owe a duty not to leave his car open to theft, particularly in an area where teenagers congregate. Yet the result here is so idiosyncratic, so beyond the scope of harm to be expected, that most courts would refuse to hold the defendant liable for the bombing damages. The rationale here is that liability should be limited to the circle of foreseeability, the consequences that the defendant could reasonably anticipate at the time he acted.

By contrast, courts often use the *duty* concept to deny liability for consequences that *are* foreseeable, as in the early emotional distress and fetal injury cases. These courts refused to impose liability for policy reasons, and found the duty concept a proper tool for limiting recovery much more narrowly than foreseeability analysis would.

Unfortunately, this distinction between duty and proximate cause analysis is not consistently honored in the cases. The issue in *Palsgraf*, for example, was foreseeability, yet Justice Cardozo used duty analysis to reject Mrs. Palsgraf's claim, while Justice Andrews's dissent concluded that she was owed a duty and analyzed the case in proximate cause terms. In other cases courts use proximate cause language in placing policy limits on liability for clearly foreseeable harm. For example, earlier cases held that a barkeep who served liquor to an intoxicated patron was not "the proximate cause" of her drunk driving, though nothing could be more foreseeable than a drunk driver causing an accident.

When they make me the King of Torts, my first decree shall be that courts must always use proximate cause analysis to bar liability for unforeseeable harm, and duty analysis to impose policy limits on liability for harm that *is* foreseeable. But in our motley kingdom as it stands today, we have to live with the fact that the two concepts are sometimes used interchangeably. Even if the courts' duty and proximate cause analysis is not always consistent, however, it will still be helpful to keep in mind the above distinction between refusing to impose liability for unforeseeable consequences (the classic proximate cause situation), and refusing, for policy reasons, to impose liability for ones that are foreseeable (the classic duty limitation).

EXAMPLES

Matters of Principle

1.   On a breezy morning after a storm, Ellis leaves his house to walk to the train station. As he passes the house of his neighbor, Klein, he notices a tree limb in the road opposite her driveway. Pressed for time, he continues on his way to catch his train. Klein is injured when her car hits the limb as she backs out of the driveway. She sues Ellis for failing to warn her of the danger. Ellis moves to dismiss Klein's complaint, on the ground that, as a matter of law, he had no duty to Klein under the circumstances.
    a. Should this case be analyzed under the no-duty principle (and its exceptions) or the risk creation principle (and its exceptions)?
    b. Will the motion be granted?

2.   Muller, while tearing down an old shed with a friend, Ehrlich, negligently knocks out a post which supports the upper floor. The floor falls on Ehrlich, who suffers a concussion. She is taken to the hospital and kept for observation overnight. During the night, the hospital wing catches fire, and she is burned. She sues Muller for her injuries.
    a. Is this a risk creation case or a no-duty case?
    b. How should the court rule if Muller moves to dismiss the claim for the burns?

Limited Duties

3.   Reik decides to go boating. She goes down to the local marina, rents a rowboat from Lake Rentals, and takes her family out in the boat. An hour after they get out onto the lake, the wind comes up, the boat capsizes, and Reik is drowned.

Her estate sues Lake Rentals for wrongful death. The complaint alleges that Lake was negligent in failing to supply adequate life vests, in renting a boat that was not seaworthy for the lake, and in failing to warn her that strong winds were expected that afternoon.
    a. Which theory is likely to be challenged on no-duty grounds?
    b. How do you think it will be resolved?

4.   Consider the example from the Introduction in which Dr. Rogers treats Jung, a professional dancer, for hepatitis, but fails to warn his dance troup that he has a disease that can be spread through physical contact. Klein, one of his dance partners, contracts hepatitis and sues Dr. Rogers. Naturally, Klein, in arguing that Rogers owed her a duty of care, relies on

Tarasoff v. Regents of the University of California, 551 P.2d 334 (1976), which held that a therapist had a duty to warn a homicide victim that a mental patient had threatened to kill her.[3]

    a. You represent Rogers. How would you argue that the duty created in *Tarasoff* should not be extended to this case?

    b. You represent Klein. If the court refuses to recognize a duty to warn her, what more limited duty argument might still support recovery?

Her Spouse's Keeper?

5.   Antell, an alcoholic, injures Freud while driving drunk. Freud learns that Antell had been drinking at home all day before the accident. Antell's wife had threatened to take away his car keys (usually left hanging on a hook in the kitchen when not in use) but had failed to do so. Freud sues Mrs. Antell for negligence, and she moves to dismiss.

    a. Should this case be analyzed under the no-duty principle (and its exceptions) or the risk creation principle (and its exceptions)?

    b. How should the court rule on the motion?

6.   Suppose instead that Antell had a history as a child abuser. His wife notes that two neighborhood girls are spending a lot of time with Antell, but does nothing about it. The girls are sexually abused and sue her for failing to intervene or warn their families of her husband's propensities.

    a. Once again, should the duty argument for suing Mrs. Antell be based on risk creation or a special relationship?

    b. What are the strongest arguments against a duty here?

The Priest and the Levite

7.   Dr. Rogers, a doctor in general practice, is driving to work one morning on a quiet country road. He witnesses a single-car accident in which the driver, Jung, hits a tree, opens the driver's side door and falls to the ground. Anticipating a busy morning at the office, he drives on. Jung suffers permanent injuries which would have been considerably less severe if he had received prompt treatment. He brings a negligence action against Rogers.

    a. Did Dr. Rogers cause any injury to Jung?

    b. Will the court dismiss the case for lack of duty?

    c. How do you think the court would rule if Rogers recognized Jung as a patient he had treated for ulcers, yet still failed to stop?

---

3. See, e.g., 551 P.2d at 340, where the court holds that, "[w]hen a therapist determines, or pursuant to the standards of his profession should determine, that his patient presents a serious danger of violence to another, he incurs an obligation to use reasonable care to protect the intended victim against such danger. The discharge of this duty may require the therapist to ... warn the intended victim or others likely to apprise the victim of the danger...."

8.   Assume, on the facts above, that Dr. Rogers *did* stop to help Jung. In an effort to make him more comfortable, he moves Jung over onto the grass. However, because Jung's leg was broken, the move caused serious additional damage to Jung's leg. Jung sues Rogers for negligence. Rogers moves to dismiss on the basis that he owed no duty of care to Jung. How will the court rule on the motion?

9.   Suppose, on the facts of Example 7, that Klein happens by and sees Jung lying unconscious on the ground. She moves Jung off the road and then, realizing that Jung is severely injured, she becomes upset and drives away. Jung suffers serious injuries from loss of blood, which could have been avoided had Klein remained with him and bound up his wound. Would Klein be liable to Jung under §324 of the Second Restatement?

10.   While Skinner is driving down a West Dakota street a mudflap from a truck blows onto his windshield. Skinner instinctively ducks, and his car swerves onto the sidewalk, pinning Klein, a pedestrian, against a building. Skinner gets out and tries to extract Klein by pushing the car. Instead, the car rolls farther forward, aggravating Klein's injury. Klein sues Skinner for negligently causing the increased injury.

Skinner moves to dismiss based on West Dakota's Good Samaritan statute, which provides in part that "A person who, without a duty to do so, renders emergency care at or near the scene of an emergency, gratuitously and in good faith, is not liable for any civil damages as a result of any act or omission by the person rendering the emergency care, unless the person is grossly negligent." How should the court rule on Skinner's motion?

Remy's Revenge

11.   As the introduction notes, a common duty problem in tort law involves whether a duty of care is owed to unborn children. Early cases generally rejected such a duty, but more recent cases tend to recognize it. For example, most courts today would recognize that drivers owe a duty of care to unborn children, so that a driver who negligently injures a pregnant woman, leading to injuries to the fetus, would be liable for those injuries.

A recent case involves a fascinating twist on this problem. In *Remy v. MacDonald*, 440 Mass. 675 (2004), an unborn child was injured in an auto accident, and sued for her injuries. The twist was that she sued her mother, who was driving one of the cars.[4] Fifty years ago, this suit would have been barred by parental immunity. But that doctrine has been abrogated in most states, including Massachusetts. If Remy's mother had delivered her, and

---

4. Why would she sue her mother, rather than the other driver? Most likely, the other driver had limited insurance, so the child (suing through her father) sought to reach the mother's insurance policy as well to obtain full compensation. (There is always the possibility, too, that the accident was caused solely by the mother's negligence.)

caused injuries to her while driving home from the hospital, Remy could have recovered from her mother for those injuries. And, as just noted, if she were injured while in utero by the negligence of the other driver in the accident, she could have recovered from the other driver after being born. So why not, putting these two principles together, recover from her mother for her pre-natal injury due to the mother's negligence?

    a. What principle is in play here, the special relationship principle or the risk creation principle?

    b. What are the arguments *against* recognizing that the mother owed her fetus a duty of reasonable care?

12. Bettelheim, a bar owner, is working behind the bar when a distraught citizen runs in to call the police to stop a robbery out on the street. Bettelheim refuses to allow him to use the phone. Couch, the victim of the robbery, is then stabbed by his assailant and sues Bettelheim for his injuries.

    a. Which of our two principles should we start from in analyzing this case?

    b. Should Bettelheim be held liable?

Judge Fudd Does His Duty

13. Jack, a convicted murderer, escapes while being transported to court by Freud, a prison guard, and attacks White on the street while trying to steal his car. White sues Freud for his injuries. Judge Fudd instructs the jury in part as follows:

> If you find that the defendant had charge of Jack at the time of the incident, and that Jack was likely to cause harm to others if not controlled, then you may find that the defendant owed a duty to the plaintiff to prevent the attack by Jack on the plaintiff.

Can you spot two fundamental problems with Judge Fudd's instruction?

EXPLANATIONS

Matters of Principle

1a. This case should be analyzed under the first principle, that there is no general duty to act for the protection or aid of another. Ellis has not created a risk to Klein; Mother Nature is responsible for that. The question is whether, for one reason or another, the court will impose a duty on Ellis to take affirmative steps to protect Klein from a risk he did not create.

    b. As the introduction suggests, the general rule is that Ellis is not his neighbor's keeper. He is under no legal duty to aid another simply because she may need it, because it would be easy or morally appropriate, or because the risk to the other person is great. Archaic though the rule may seem, it is alive and well. The court will grant Ellis's motion, on the ground that he owed no duty to Klein, unless she can establish some basis for an exception to the no-duty principle.

The facts here do not suggest a basis for such an exception. Ellis has not created the hazard, so the most likely basis for avoiding the effect of the general rule is to argue that a special relationship between him and Klein supports a duty to aid her. The only source of such a relationship in this case is the fact that Ellis and Klein are neighbors. But in a society that puts a premium on individualism, it is very doubtful that a court would transform neighborliness into a legally enforceable duty. Becoming a neighbor is not like taking charge of a pupil or running a train service. People hardly expect that they have assumed any degree of care for their neighbors, whom they may like, loath, or ignore as the case may be.[5]

While imposing such a duty might lead to a marginal decrease in injuries, it would also create potentially intrusive relationships between abutters who may have no interest in anything but being left alone. Can't you just imagine the busybody next door coming over weekly with a list of dangerous conditions you should abate immediately, for your own good? Those dead limbs should come off your trees; that big flower pot on the railing could fall; you need a safer lid on your well; you ought to trim those bushes at the end of your driveway, and so on. It's enough to make the no-duty rule look halfway respectable!

2a. This case is clearly based on Muller's risk-creating conduct. Muller's active conduct in demolishing the shed has created a risk of injury to Ehrlich, and she has suffered injury from that risk.

b. This example illustrates the distinction between existence of a duty and the *extent* of liability in a situation where a duty clearly exists. Any court would conclude that Muller owed Ehrlich a duty of care in working on the shed, and that he is liable for her concussion. He engaged in risk-creating conduct, and Ehrlich's injury results from it. It was foreseeable that, if the floor collapsed, the collapse would cause personal injury, and it did.

However, many courts would refuse to hold Muller liable for Ehrlich's burns, since the risk that she would be burned in a fire at the hospital was unforeseeable. To me, this is best explained in proximate cause terms, as a refusal to hold a defendant liable for bizarre consequences. Yet many courts would conclude, following Cardozo's approach in *Palsgraf*, that Muller "owed no duty" to Ehrlich to prevent this type of harm, since being burned in a hospital fire was not one of the foreseeable risks of knocking out the porch post.

Whichever formula the court uses, the crux of the matter here is that courts are unwilling to extend liability for risk-creating conduct beyond

---

5. For a provocative feminist critique of the no-duty rule, clearly rejecting the result in examples like this, see L. Bender, A Lawyer's Primer on Feminist Theory and Tort, 38 J. of Legal Ed. 3, 33-36 (1988).

the circle of foreseeable risk. They sometimes draw the liability limit *short* of foreseeability, but very seldom impose liability *beyond* its bounds.

Limited Duties

3a. The estate's third theory raises the most difficult duty question. Lake Rentals engaged in risk creating conduct by renting the boat to Reik: It would clearly create unreasonable risks if it rented her a boat that wasn't seaworthy, or that lacked adequate life vests. However, it is more of a stretch to argue that they assumed a duty to warn her about the weather.

b. While Lake Rentals clearly engaged in risk creating conduct by renting Reik a boat, there must be some limits to the duty it has assumed. Must it, having rented the boat, instruct Reik in safe methods of rowing? Must it warn her of submerged rocks on the other side of the lake? Must it explain to her that putting all passengers on one side of the boat will cause it to tip, or that in cold water one might die of hypothermia before reaching shore? If the court imposes a duty to warn of the weather, these cases will follow hard upon. At the same time, boaters are in as good a position as Lake Rentals to check the weather before they take to the lake. In the case from which this example is drawn, the court held that the marina had no duty to monitor the weather and warn of expected winds. The court emphasized that the duty would be "unwieldy" and that boaters are equally able to ascertain these matters for themselves. *Leach v. Mountain Lake*, 120 F.3d 871, 873 (1997).

Note that here the plaintiff's injury is clearly foreseeable to the defendant. It should hardly be surprising to Lake Rentals that a small boat will founder in high winds, especially if it knew the winds were coming. Liability is denied, not for lack of proximate cause, but because the judicial system is unwilling to impose a duty to prevent the harm.

4a. There is some force to the argument that *Tarasoff* supports recovery for Klein. Rogers has assumed a duty of care by accepting Jung as a patient, and he was uniquely placed to prevent the harm. Imposing a duty to warn on Rogers would perhaps reduce the risk that Jung would infect others, just as warning Tarasoff might have prevented her death.

However, there is a strong argument that imposing a duty to warn Klein is an unwarranted extension of *Tarasoff*. In *Tarasoff*, the psychiatrist was aware of a risk to a particular person. Here, the risk is to a large, ill-defined class of persons. Would Rogers be required to seek them out or to obtain a list of all possible dance partners? Who else would he be required to warn? In addition, there is a significant difference between Jung in this case and the mental patient in *Tarasoff*. Presumably, Jung has no desire to infect others, and can take steps to avoid doing so. By contrast, the patient in *Tarasoff* had every incentive to conceal the risk he posed from his intended victim.

In addition, imposing a duty to warn would seriously breach the confidentiality of the doctor/patient relationship. Rogers would have to reveal Jung's disease to a large group of persons, not just to one individual.

A few cases have imposed a duty to warn members of a patient's family of a communicable disease. See, e.g., *Shepard v. Redford Community Hospital*, 390 N.W.2d 239 (Mich. Ct. App. 1986) (duty to child who died of meningitis where hospital had failed to diagnose and treat mother's meningitis); *Safer v. Estate of Pack*, 677 A.2d 1188 (N.J. Super. 1996) (duty to inform member of patient's family of genetic risk). Compare *Lemon v. Stewart*, 682 A.2d 1177 (Md. Ct. Spec. App. 1996) (no duty to inform family members that patient was HIV positive); *Gammill v. United States*, 727 F.2d 950 (10th Cir. 1984) (doctor owed no duty to warn friends who contracted hepatitis while babysitting for children of infected patient); see generally Annot., 3 A.L.R. 5th 370 (1992). But this example entails a considerable expansion of the duty that most courts would hesitate to approve.

b. Since courts are naturally hesitant to create broad new duties, plaintiff's counsel should argue for the narrowest duty that will serve her purpose. Here, Klein can argue that Rogers had a duty to *warn the patient* of the risk of spreading the disease through contact. This duty is not subject to the same objections as the wider duty to warn third parties: It is easily performed while treating the patient, involves no breach of confidentiality, and places no burden on Rogers to identify persons at risk. Consequently, this duty has been much more widely accepted. See, e.g., *Reisner v. Regents of the University of California*, 37 Cal. Rptr. 2d 518 (Cal. App. 1995) (third party later infected by patient may sue hospital for failure to inform patient of HIV infection).

Of course, if Klein relies on this narrower duty, she will face a further problem: causation. She will have to establish that Jung, if warned, would have avoided the contacts through which he gave Klein the disease. Even if warned, Jung might not have acted on the advice, since his livelihood was as stake.

Her Spouse's Keeper?

5a. This case should be analyzed under the no-duty principle and its exceptions. This is not a case in which Mrs. Antell has created the risk that injured Freud. The direct risk-creating conduct was her husband's — the supremely antisocial act of driving while intoxicated. If she is liable for it, it will have to be based on some affirmative duty to avert that risk.

b. This motion should be granted unless some exception to the no-duty principle applies. Naturally, the special relationship exceptions spring to mind as a promising source of such a duty; what relation is "special" if not marriage?

Marriage is indeed sacred, but it is not an automatic source of vicarious liability for the torts of one's spouse, nor have courts concluded that tying the knot gives rise to a duty to control an errant spouse. Even though it would have been easy and socially beneficial for her to palm the keys, most courts would conclude that Mrs. Antell is not liable to Freud for failing to do so. Cf. *Andrade v. Baptiste*, 411 Mass. 560 (1992) (wife had no duty to prevent husband from storing weapons in home she owned, though she knew of his serious drinking problem). See also *Grover v. Stechel*, 45 P.3d 80 (N.M. App. 2002) (mother supporting adult son owed no duty to protect third party from his violent tendencies).

Plaintiffs in cases like this will have a better chance of recovering under the risk creation principle. Suppose, for example, that Mrs. Antell had provided her husband with keys to her car and he was driving that car at the time of the accident, or she had insisted that he drive to the store for more disks for her laptop. On these facts, she would have participated in the creation of a foreseeable risk, and could be held liable for doing so.

6a. Here again, Mrs. Antell did not create the risk that the girls would be abused; her husband did. The tort claim against her is premised not on something she did, but on her failure to act, the failure to warn or prevent the abuse. The plaintiffs will have to argue that she had a special relationship to her husband, the perpetrator, that imposed a duty on her to act to prevent the abuse.

b. There are several strong arguments against imposing a duty in these circumstances. If the court imposes such a duty, it suggests that Mrs. Antell must, if she has reason to suspect abuse, watch and confront her husband, or denounce him to others based on a suspicion that he might commit child abuse. Even child abuse reporting statutes usually are triggered by knowledge of actual abuse, not just knowledge of a risk. Imposing such a duty is hardly likely to promote marital harmony.

Another argument against imposing the duty is that recognizing the duty will lead to many slippery slope problems, much as the *Tarasoff* decision has in an analogous context. If the court imposes a duty on these facts to warn the girls' families, it would be short step to impose a duty in the example of the intoxicated spouse. In that case, as here, the wife was aware of a risk, but failed to take steps to prevent that risk of injuring a third party. Further, if this duty to act is recognized, *which* neighbors would the spouse have to warn? All of them, or only those with children? For what distance? And, if the duty is recognized, the court will have to confront cases in which defendants other than spouses, such as roommates or neighbors, are sued for failing to prevent abuse. And, suppose that the suspicion proves erroneous? In *Schmitz v. Ashton*, 3 P.3d 184 (Ariz. App. 2000), the defendants suspected a father of abuse and warned his neighbors. The father then sued them for defamation and intentional infliction of emotional distress and recovered a substantial verdict. It isn't hard to predict that many such difficult cases will follow if this duty is recognized. This prospect might lead a court to avoid these murky waters entirely by refusing to recognize a duty at all, despite the reprehensible nature of child abuse.

Despite these arguments, the New Jersey Supreme Court, in *J.S. v. R.T.H.*, 714 A.2d 924 (N.J. 1998), held that a spouse owes a duty to take reasonable steps to prevent child abuse, or to warn of the risk, if the spouse "has actual knowledge or special reason to know of the likelihood of his or her spouse engaging in sexually abusive behavior against a particular person or persons." Id. at 935. The court relied on the "strong public policy of protecting children from sexual abuse," and on the fact that a New Jersey statute requires reporting of child abuse, even by spouses. But see *Sacci v. Metaxas*, 810 A.2d 1119 (N.J. Super. App. Div. 2002), which refused to extend the duty recognized in *R.T.H.* to require a wife to warn a shooting victim of the risk that her husband, who had violent propensities, might kill him.

The Priest and the Levite

7a. Rogers certainly did not cause Jung's injury from running into the tree, but he may be a but-for cause of the aggravation of the injury. If Jung's injuries would have been less severe with prompt treatment, Rogers's failure to stop is a but-for cause of the aggravation. Certainly if Rogers had a duty to help Jung (for example, if Jung were a student in his charge), a court would have no problem concluding that he had caused the aggravated injuries by his failure to aid.

b. This is also a nonfeasance case, in the sense that the defendant Rogers has not created the risk to Jung or done anything to cause his initial injury. The question is whether a court will impose a duty on Rogers, due to his awareness of Jung's need for assistance or his ability to render it.

Most courts would conclude that this falls squarely under the no-duty principle, that a bystander owes no duty to aid another unless the bystander has placed the victim in peril or has a previous relationship with the victim that supports a finding of duty. Since Rogers, as a doctor, is obviously in a superior position to help Jung, there is a strong moral argument that he should stop. The cases, however, do not find a duty to aid based on the fact that the defendant would be good at it.

If duties are based on public policy, why shouldn't the court jettison the special relationship theory and impose a duty on Rogers frankly based on common sense? Courts can create whatever duties they wish; the special relationship concept is simply a rationale for the court's decision to do so. Imposing a duty on doctors to assist accident victims should lead to an overall increase in societal welfare, since more victims would get timely professional assistance — so why not go for it?

Maybe courts should. Maybe they will some day. But most courts remain unwilling to press strangers into service by creating such a duty. Instead, many states have sought to encourage bystanders to assist by passing statutes that limit their liability for injuries they may cause while rendering aid. Typically, such "good samaritan" laws immunize those who assist in an emergency from liability for negligence, though not for grossly negligent or reckless conduct. See Kan. Stat. Ann. §65-2891 (1993) (health care providers only).

c. In this example Rogers is still guilty of nonfeasance, so the issue is whether the court would find that his prior treatment of Jung imposes a duty on Rogers to succor him on the roadside. If Rogers were Jung's banker, no court would conclude that he had assumed a duty to aid Jung under these circumstances. But Rogers is Jung's doctor. Shouldn't that support a duty to help him?

Probably not. It hardly seems that either Rogers or Jung would expect that Rogers had accepted such a duty by his unrelated prior treatment of Jung. Suppose Rogers had treated Jung six years ago? Or suppose Rogers were an allergist; would *that* impose a duty to treat Jung's leg at the accident scene? Or suppose Jung was not physically injured at all, but trapped in his car? On balance, it seems difficult to impose or define a legal duty based on this limited prior relationship.

8.   This case is squarely addressed by §324 of the Second Restatement, quoted at pp. 219-220. Once Dr. Rogers decides to intervene, the Restatement takes the position that he must exercise due care in assisting Jung. Because he has assumed a duty of care, the motion will be denied. Rogers is now a risk creator, an actor whose negligent conduct may foreseeably injure Jung. It hardly seems appropriate that he should be immune from liability no matter how badly he bungles the rescue. On the other hand, as Prosser so eloquently puts it:

> The result of all this is that the Good Samaritan who tries to help may find himself mulcted in damages, while the priest and the Levite who pass by on the other side go on their cheerful way rejoicing.

Prosser & Keeton at 378. Good Samaritan statutes provide a middle ground in such cases, by limiting the rescuer's liability to grossly negligent or reckless conduct.

Section 324 does not say, however, that Dr. Rogers is liable for *any* injury he causes in rescuing Jung. Rather, it imposes on Rogers a duty of due care in the course of his rescue. If Rogers had no reason to know that Jung's leg was broken, moving him was probably a reasonable choice. If so, he would not be liable to Jung, even though his assistance caused further injury. Similarly, on my exam one year, I had Cleveland, a rescuer, roll an accident victim over to check his breathing. In doing so, he aggravated the victim's cracked rib. However, Cleveland probably made a reasonable choice to roll the victim over, if he didn't know about the cracked rib, and maybe even if he did, since breathing is rather important. If Cleveland's conduct was reasonable, he is not liable, even if he caused further injury to the victim.

9.   In this case Klein, a bystander with no duty to aid Jung, elects to come to his aid. The Restatement takes the view that Klein's laudable decision to act gives rise to at least a minimal duty of care to Jung, though she owed him none before. On the other hand, Klein's duty should presumably be limited: Her admirable conduct should not obligate her to pay Jung's hospital bills or take him home and tend to him until he recovers.

Section 324 of the Restatement tries to walk this line, by imposing only a limited duty on the rescuer. Section 324(a) requires her to use reasonable care while she assists Jung, but §324(b) provides that she may stop assisting, even if Jung could use more help, as long as she doesn't leave him "in a worse position that when [she] took charge of him." Here, Klein has not left Jung in a worse position than he was in before; he is in a safer position out of the road.

Jung might argue that Klein did not "secure his safety" (§324(a)) because she did not bind up his wound. Comment g to §324 states that the bystander's choice to intervene "does not require him to continue his services until the recipient of them gets all of the benefit which the actor is capable of bestowing." But the same comment also states that the actor must "act with reasonable consideration for the other's safety."

The drafters probably intended to require Klein to use reasonable care for the victim's safety *while she chooses to continue her aid*, but to leave her free to discontinue her services at any time. This conclusion follows from the basic assumption that the victim's need for services does not create a duty to render them. The opposite reading, that §324 imposes a duty on the rescuer to continue aid until the victim is "safe," would create a positive duty to continue aiding the victim for an uncertain period. Section 324(b) only holds the rescuer who chooses to discontinue aid liable if she leaves the victim in a worse position. The drafters did not intend to impose on a rescuer the duty to continue giving assistance until the victim no longer needs any.[6]

---

6. The draft Third Restatement of Torts might change the result in this example. It provides that if the injured person is "in imminent peril of serious bodily harm," the rescuer must "exercise reasonable care with regard to the peril before terminating the rescue." Restatement (Third) of Torts: Liability for Physical Harm (Basic Principles) (Tentative Draft No. 4, 2004) §45(b). It isn't clear whether Jung's further injury from loss of blood constitutes "imminent peril of serious bodily harm." The drafters may have meant that the rescuer must take care to avert further harm from an *outside source*. An example given in the draft is a rescuer who tows a swimmer half way to shore and then lets go of the swimmer.

10. The court should deny the motion. The purpose of Good Samaritan laws is to encourage bystanders who are not obligated to render assistance to do so anyway, by giving them a measure of protection from liability. Such statutes are not intended to grant immunity to persons who *already have a duty* to render assistance. Skinner's risk creating conduct (driving) caused the original injury to Klein. Under the Second Restatement, he has a duty to come to her aid, whether or not he was negligent in causing the accident. Restatement (Second) Torts §322. Thus, he was not "gratuitously" assisting Klein, but fulfilling a duty to assist her under the circumstances. The court would probably conclude that he is not protected by the Good Samaritan statute. See, e.g., *James v. Rowe*, 674 F. Supp. 332 (D. Kan. 1987).

Remy's Revenge

11a. Although there could hardly be a more "special" relationship than that between a mother and her unborn child, this is actually a risk creation case. The child's argument is not that her mother failed to protect or rescue her from some danger from a third party, but rather that she (the child) was injured due to her mother's negligent driving. Remy's mother engaged in risk-creating conduct, did so negligently, and injured the plaintiff. Our second "first principle"—that those who impose new risk on others owe a duty to act reasonably in creating that risk—applies, unless the court makes an exception to it.

b. On first blush, this case seems like a slam dunk. Relevant case law already established that parents owe a duty of care to their children and are not immune from suit by them. The cases also establish that those who injure children in utero are liable for those injuries. It seems an obvious next step to combine the two principles and hold the mother liable. Indeed, the *Remy* court stated that "[t]here is ... no question that, had the plaintiff been born at the time of the accident, even if only one hour of age, she would have been able to recover" for injuries suffered due to her mother's negligence. 440 Mass. at 681.

There are some powerful arguments, however, for refusing to impose a duty in these circumstances. In the *Remy* court's words:

> [D]uring the period of gestation, almost all aspects of a woman's life have an impact, for better or for worse, on her developing fetus. A fetus can be injured not only by physical force, but by the mother's exposure, unwitting or intentional, to chemicals and other substances, both dangerous and nondangerous, at home or in the workplace, or by the mother's voluntary ingestion of drugs, alcohol, or tobacco. A pregnant woman may place her fetus in danger by engaging in activities involving a risk of physical harm or by engaging in activities, such as most sports, that are generally

not considered to be perilous. A pregnant woman may jeopardize the health of her fetus by taking medication (prescription or over-the-counter) or, in other cases, by not taking medication. She also may endanger the well-being of her fetus by not following her physician's advice with respect to prenatal care or by exercising her constitutional right not to receive medical treatment.

440 Mass. at 678-679. In view of these considerations, the court feared that recognizing such a duty

would present an almost unlimited number of circumstances that would likely give rise to litigation. Courts would be challenged to refine the scope of such a duty, including the degree of knowledge expected of a mother in order to pinpoint when such a duty would arise (e.g., at the point of pregnancy; at the point of awareness of pregnancy; or at the point of awareness that pregnancy is a possibility) or the particular standard of conduct to which a reasonably careful pregnant woman, in a single case, should be held.

440 Mass. at 678.[7]

In light of these concerns, the court refused to recognize a duty owed by the mother to her unborn child. The case presents a dramatic example of a court creating an exception, for reasons of social policy, to the second "first principle," that we all owe a duty of care to those injured by our risk-creating conduct. Typically, however, the *Remy* court notes five other cases on the point, two refusing to recognize the duty and three that allowed recovery.

12a. The analysis here must begin with the no-duty principle. White was not injured by any risk created by Bettelheim. The threat is from his assailant, and Bettelheim is asked to act to prevent the harm by helping to summon aid.

b. It is hard to fashion an argument for liability in this case based on the recognized exceptions to the no-duty principle. Bettelheim has no relation to either the perpetrator of the accident or to Couch. The owner of a bar, a place of public accommodation, might owe a duty to Couch if he were injured in the bar, or if he were a patron, but he was not. While the conduct appears gratuitously obnoxious, it does not appear actionable.

The California Court of Appeals, however, ruled otherwise in *Soldano v. O'Daniels*, 190 Cal. Rptr. 310 (Cal. Ct. App. 5th Dist. 1983). The *Soldano* court recognized the prevalence of the no-duty rule embodied in §314 of the Second Restatement, and admitted that it would be "stretching the concept beyond recognition" (190 Cal. Rptr. at 314) to find any special

---

7. Interestingly, the court hardly mentioned another factor counseling hesitation, the constitutional right of a woman to terminate a pregnancy.

relationship between the barkeep and the injured plaintiff. It then openly rejected the no-duty rule based on an analysis of various policies California cases have considered in determining duty issues.[8]

The *Soldano* case may portend the abandonment of the no-duty principle, long tort law's ugly duckling. However, reaction to the case does not suggest any rush to bury the rule. See, e.g., *Clarke v. Hoek*, 219 Cal. Rptr. 845, 852 (Cal. Ct. App. 1st Dist. 1985) (suggesting more limited reading of *Soldano* and that California Supreme Court has reaffirmed the no-duty rule since). Indeed, the ALR annotation on *Soldano* may win the prize for the shortest annotation ever: Nineteen years after *Soldano* was decided, it still included only *one* case — *Soldano* itself! See 37 A.L.R. 4th 1196 (1985 & Supp. 2004). If this is the wave of the future, it is still a long way from shore.

Judge Fudd Does His Duty

13. The first problem with Fudd's instruction is that it tells the jury to decide whether Freud owed a duty to White or not ("[Y]ou may find that the defendant owed a duty. . . ."). Unlike the other elements of a negligence claim, duty is a question of law. It is up to courts to define enforceable legal duties, not juries. If Judge Fudd's language were proper, the jury would be left to create the substantive law of torts in each case, by determining the extent of the defendant's duty anew in every trial. Consequently, there would not be one standard for liability, but a different one for each case. *Au contraire*, the judge should instruct the jury as to the duty owed in each case. If none is owed under the circumstances, the case should never go to the jury at all.

The second problem with the instruction is equally basic: Fudd's language implies that Freud had a duty to *prevent* the attack. This would be a duty indeed, a duty of absolute protection of White no matter what the circumstances. The law seldom imposes such a stringent burden, although it does at times impose greater or lesser duties than the duty of due care. In this situation, as in most, the Restatement describes the duty as a duty to *exercise reasonable care* to prevent injury from the dangerous person. Restatement (Second) of Torts §319.

---

8. "These factors include: 'the foreseeability of harm to the plaintiff, the degree of certainty that the plaintiff suffered injury, the closeness of the connection between the defendant's conduct and the injury suffered, the moral blame attached to the defendant's conduct, the policy of preventing future harm, the extent of the burden to the defendant and consequences to the community of imposing a duty to exercise care with resulting liability for breach, and the availability, cost, and prevalence of insurance for the risk involved.'" 190 Cal. Rptr. at 315 (quoting *Rowland v. Christian*, 443 P.2d 561, 564 (Cal. 1968).

11

Vicarious Displeasure: Claims for Indirect Infliction of Emotional Distress and Loss of Consortium

Introduction

Hamlet hit the nail on the head when he complained of the "thousand natural shocks that flesh is heir to."[1] Even in a "civilized" society such as ours, life is fraught with stresses, anxieties, fears, and sorrows. Many are indeed natural shocks, the inevitable concomitants of unfolding human experience from birth to death (and let's not forget adolescence either). Much emotional distress, however, is inflicted upon us by other people as well, either deliberately or carelessly.

We live in a culture that attempts a legal response to most problems, probably too many problems, so it should not prove surprising that courts have been asked to fashion a remedy for emotional distress as well. This chapter considers the approaches courts have taken to one of tort law's most

---

1. W. Shakespeare, Hamlet, act 3, sc. 1.

intractable problems, claims for indirect infliction of emotional distress. It then contrasts such claims with another type of claim for emotional injuries, loss of consortium.

Claims for indirect infliction of emotional distress (frequently referred to as "bystander" claims) are based on emotional trauma suffered by one person who witnesses or learns of an injury to another. Here are some examples:

- A worker at a construction site sees a co-worker crushed under a dump truck.
- A father, watching from the living room window, sees his child hit by a car which careens over the curb and onto the front lawn.
- A wife suffers emotional distress from watching her husband's health decline due to medical malpractice.
- A parent learns by telephone that his son has just suffered a serious injury in a fire negligently caused by the defendant.
- The wife of a comatose patient visits him at the hospital and discovers that he has just been severely bitten by rats.

In each of these cases, the person who suffers direct physical injury from the defendant's negligence obviously has a claim for those injuries. However, those who witnessed or soon learned of the injury may also seek damages for emotional distress resulting from the traumatic experience of either witnessing that injury or learning of it. Such claims are referred to as claims for "indirect infliction" of emotional distress because they are asserted by bystanders who suffer emotional injury indirectly due to the direct physical injury to another.

The distress in such cases is often both foreseeable and severe. Thus, the plaintiff will frequently be able to establish that the defendant's negligence was an actual and proximate cause of his emotional damages. Consequently, courts which have sought to limit liability for indirect infliction of emotional distress have usually used duty analysis to do so. Many courts have held that defendants owe no *duty* to avoid inflicting emotional distress on bystanders, or only owe such a duty in very limited circumstances. That is why this chapter, which seems to deal primarily with a type of damages, appears in the duty section of the book.

It is not hard to see why courts are reluctant to impose a duty to avoid indirect infliction of emotional distress. Several important factors relevant to duty analysis suggest caution in creating such a duty. *First*, the very foreseeability of such distress argues for restraint. For every victim who suffers negligent physical injury, a number of bystanders may suffer emotional distress:

> It would be an entirely unreasonable burden on all human activity if the defendant who has endangered one person were to be compelled to pay for the lacerated feelings of every other person disturbed by reason of it, including every bystander shocked at an accident, and every distant relative of the person injured, as well as all his friends.

Prosser & Keeton, §54, at 366.

Second, courts are reluctant to impose a duty to persons who have no relationship to the defendant. While the defendant usually has some immediate interaction with the direct victim of his negligence—the child hit by the car, the patient diagnosed, the worker actually hit by the dump truck—he usually has had no contact with bystanders who suffer indirect emotional distress. He may not know who they are, where they are, or how many of them there are.

Third, judges are justifiably concerned about the impact that creating a duty will have on the administration of justice. Recognition of indirect infliction claims could clog the courts with suits over trivial unpleasantries better dealt with by "a certain toughening of the mental hide." C. Magruder, Mental and Emotional Disturbance in the Law of Torts, 49 Harv. L. Rev. 1033, 1035 (1936). In addition, courts have feared the specter of fraudulent claims. It is easy enough for a plaintiff to carry on about how distressed he was by the defendant's conduct, and even to believe it after a while. It is difficult to verify such claims, or to attribute the plaintiff's distress to the defendant's conduct, as opposed to the thousand natural shocks that take their toll on us all.

Thus, for many years courts severely limited indirect infliction claims, lest such claims open a Pandora's box of woes for both courts and defendants. However, the compelling nature of the suffering inflicted on indirect victims has led to a gradual recognition of some claims for indirect infliction of emotional distress. How can a court refuse recovery to a father who watches a driver negligently run down his child and suffers a heart attack on the spot? Many courts, unable to turn such sympathetic plaintiffs away, have created a duty to avoid inflicting emotional distress, at least in limited circumstances.

Once a court opens this box a crack, however, it is very hard to close it on other equally sympathetic indirect victims. The history of the law in this area has been a constant struggle to define some limiting principle that will allow recovery for deserving victims without throwing the courts open to a flood of litigants upset over something that the defendant did to someone else. (Other useful metaphors for the jurisprudence in this area might be a series of defense lines by a retreating army, or successive walls of sandbags holding back a flooding Mississippi.) Indirect infliction claims are a useful study, because they vividly illustrate the difficulty of establishing satisfactory limits to a duty once it has been recognized. The effort of courts to limit indirect infliction claims has led to tortured line-drawing, evasive distinctions, and some of the least intellectually defensible doctrine in the annals of tort law. Emotional distress seems to be one of those areas in which courts cannot solve a legal problem, only decide cases.

The Historical Approach to Emotional Distress Claims

Courts have long awarded emotional distress damages in negligence cases if the defendant causes direct physical injury to the plaintiff. For example, if Marat's car knocks DuBarry down, DuBarry may recover for any physical injury sustained and for any emotional distress from the accident as well. Restatement (Second) of Torts §456; Prosser & Keeton, §54, at 362-363. This would include pain and suffering resulting from the physical injury, emotional distress resulting from disfigurement or physical impairment (such as a facial scar or a limp), and any other demonstrable emotional damages.

This principle, that recovery for emotional distress was proper if the plaintiff also suffered physical injury, became known as the "impact rule." Emotional distress damages were often described as "parasitic": They could be added on if the plaintiff suffered a traditional physical contact from the defendant's negligence, but could not sustain an action on their own. If Marat's car narrowly missed DuBarry, he could not recover, even if he was badly frightened by the near miss, since he suffered no "impact."

The impact rule was tort law's first effort to keep the flood of emotional distress claims at bay. While it defined a limit, many courts found it an intellectually indefensible one. The plaintiff was allowed full recovery for emotional distress if the defendant barely touched him, but denied recovery if the defendant inflicted the same degree of distress (or much more) but just missed hitting the plaintiff. Even if the emotional distress *led* to a physical illness (for example, if DuBarry suffered a heart attack from fear of being hit by Marat's car), recovery was barred if there was no physical impact upon which to piggyback the distress damages. The obvious artificiality of this rule invited courts to evade it by literal application. In *Porter v. Delaware, L. & W. R.R.*, 63 A. 860 (1906), for example, the court found the impact requirement satisfied where the plaintiff got dust in her eyes, and therefore allowed full recovery for emotional distress from the accident. A recent example is *Conder v. Wood*, 716 N.E.2d 432 (Ind. 1999), in which the plaintiff pounded on the side of a truck to alert the driver that her companion had fallen under the wheels. The court concluded that the pounding constituted an impact, making her eligible to recover for emotional distress due to the injury to her companion.

Although the impact rule was no "hymn to intellectual beauty,"[2] it did address some of the policy concerns relevant to duty. It alleviated fears

---

2. "[A]s law is an instrument of governance rather than a hymn to intellectual beauty, some consideration must be given to practicalities." *Newman-Green, Inc. v. Alfonzo-Larrain R.*, 854 F.2d 916, 925 (7th Cir. 1988), *rev'd on other grounds*, 490 U.S. 826 (1989).

of fraudulent claims, perjured (or at least, exaggerated) testimony and excessive damages based on jury sympathy. It premised liability on an objective fact that could be proved or disproved, and, in a rough sort of way (all right, a *very* rough sort of way), filtered out frivolous claims while allowing the most serious ones to proceed. A few courts still apply the rule, at least in some types of cases. See, e.g., *Jordan v. Atlanta Affordable Housing Fund, Ltd.*, 498 S.E.2d 104 (Ga. Ct. App. 1998).

The "Zone-of-Danger Rule"

The impact rule bars recovery in most indirect infliction cases, because these claims are generally asserted by bystanders who were not directly involved in the accident. Some courts, unwilling to turn all bystander plaintiffs away, have adopted alternative tests to define the duty in indirect infliction cases. Some allow a bystander to recover for emotional distress if he was in the "zone of danger," that is, if he was close enough to the defendant's negligent conduct to be placed at risk of physical injury, even though he was not actually touched. Under the zone-of-danger rule a mother walking next to a child hit by a negligent driver would recover for emotional distress due to witnessing injury to her child, since she might have been hit herself.

The rationale for the zone-of-danger approach is that the defendant owes these bystanders a duty of care because they are within the area of the risk created by his conduct, and hence injury to them is foreseeable. This rationale derives from Justice Cardozo's proximate cause analysis in *Palsgraf v. Long Island R.R. Co.*, 162 N.E. 99 (N.Y. 1928). Since injury to the bystander is foreseeable, the argument goes, the defendant has a duty to avoid injury — either physical or emotional — to him.

The zone-of-danger rule compensates a limited class of indirect victims, a class that is reasonably likely to be seriously affected by the accident. However, like other limiting principles in this area, it is easier to criticize than to justify. The father who watches from the house as his wife and child cross the street will suffer just as much distress if the child is hit as the mother will. In addition, his presence is foreseeable, though he is not within the zone of risk of physical injury. Yet, because he is out of range of the car, he is barred from recovery under the zone-of-danger rule, no matter how manifest his distress may be. The line drawn is basically arbitrary. In the words of a leading decision on emotional distress, it suffers from "hopeless artificiality." *Dillon v. Legg*, 441 P.2d 912, 915 (Cal. 1968).

Limited Foreseeability: The Dillon Rule

The arbitrariness of the zone-of-danger rule has led other courts to seek a more flexible approach to indirect infliction claims. Many states have found such an approach in the California Supreme Court's decision in *Dillon v. Legg*. In *Dillon*, a mother suffered emotional distress from seeing her daughter fatally injured by a car while crossing the street. The *Dillon* court held that defendants have a duty to avoid infliction of emotional distress that is reasonably foreseeable, including infliction of such distress on indirect victims. However, the court established three factors to be considered in determining whether such distress was foreseeable:

> 1) whether plaintiff was located near the scene of the accident as contrasted with one who was a distance away from it; 2) whether the shock resulted from a direct emotional impact upon the plaintiff from the sensory and contemporaneous observance of the accident, as contrasted with learning of the accident from others after its occurrence; 3) whether plaintiff and the victim were closely related, as contrasted with an absence of any relationship or the presence of only a distant relationship.

441 P.2d at 920.

Although *Dillon* purports to establish a foreseeability standard based on the above factors, the *Dillon* rule, like the impact and zone-of-danger rules, also bars recovery to many bystanders whose distress is foreseeable. For example, the first factor implies that a close relative would be barred if she was not present at the scene of the accident, though it is virtually inevitable that close relatives will suffer severe distress when a family member is injured. The second factor implies that a plaintiff who is summoned to the scene after the accident cannot recover, though the potential for severe distress is still great. And the third factor suggests that a stranger, friend or co-worker would not recover, though it is surely foreseeable that anyone could suffer traumatic distress from witnessing massive injury to another.

Requiring Further Corroboration: Resulting Physical Injury

Some courts that apply the zone-of-danger or *Dillon* approaches to indirect infliction claims *also* require that the plaintiff suffer some physical symptoms *as a result of* the emotional distress caused by the defendant's conduct. This "resulting-physical-injury" requirement is intended to provide additional corroboration that the plaintiff's claim is genuine. See *Payton v. Abbott Labs.*, 437 N.E.2d 171, 180 (Mass. 1982) (resulting-physical-injury rule "will serve to limit frivolous suits and those in which only bad manners or mere hurt feelings are involved, and will provide a reasonable safeguard against false claims"). California initially suggested that resulting physical injury must be shown along with the *Dillon* factors, but later abandoned this additional requirement. See *Hedlund v. Superior Court of Orange County*, 669 P.2d 41, 47 n.8 (1983). Other courts have adopted the *Dillon* guidelines for indirect infliction cases without requiring resulting physical injury. See, e.g., *Paugh v. Hanks*, 451 N.E.2d 759 (Ohio 1983).

It is important to distinguish the resulting-physical-injury approach from the impact rule. The impact rule allows a plaintiff who sustains a direct physical impact (from the defendant's car, for example) to recover for emotional distress. The resulting-physical-injury rule, on the other hand, allows the plaintiff who is missed by the car, but frightened by the near miss, to recover for emotional distress *if* the emotional distress itself leads to some form of physical injury, such as a heart attack.

Some courts have imposed other corroborative requirements along with one of the above approaches. Some require the plaintiff to prove "serious" or "severe" distress in order to recover. *Camper v. Minor*, 915 S.W.2d 437, 446 (Tenn. 1996). Others require expert testimony to establish the existence of the distress. *Kinard v. Augusta Sash & Door Co.*, 336 S.E.2d 465, 467 (S.C. 1985). Some cases have refused recovery, even if the distress is genuine, unless the *direct* victim of the accident suffers serious injury. *Clohessy v. Bachelor*, 675 A.2d 852, 864 (Conn. 1996).

On the other hand, some courts have adopted very broad standards for indirect infliction claims. Several courts allow indirect plaintiffs to recover if they prove that they suffered objective symptoms of a physical injury or psychic disability as a result of the distress suffered from witnessing injury to the direct victim. See D. Dobbs, The Law of Torts 837-838. And at least one court has held that indirect infliction plaintiffs may recover simply on a showing that severe emotional distress was reasonably foreseeable from the defendant's negligent act. *Wages v. First Natl. Ins. Co. of America*, 79 P.3d 1095 (Mont. 2003).

A Distinction with a Difference: Distress Distinguished from Distress

An injury to one person is likely to cause a variety of emotional reactions in others. A bystander who witnesses traumatic injury to a family member may suffer acute emotional shock from the unexpected, wrenching experience of witnessing serious physical injury to a loved one. She may also experience feelings of grief, loss, sympathy or sadness due to the fact that the immediate victim has been injured or killed.

Although the general term "emotional distress" (or "mental anguish") is often applied to both of these types of injuries, they are meaningfully different. The shock of witnessing the accident is sudden and traumatic, aggravated by the very fact that it is unanticipated, so that one can make no emotional preparation to sustain it. Consider, for example, the gruesome facts of *LeJeune v. Rayne Branch Hosp.*, 556 So. 2d 559 (La. 1990), in which the wife of a comatose patient came into his room shortly after he had been bitten all over by rats. There is a fundamental difference between the impact that kind of horror scene engenders and the grief or sadness one experiences from knowing that a loved one has suffered an injury and must cope with its consequences.

It is the first type of emotional distress — the trauma of witnessing a horrific event or injury — which gives rise to a claim for indirect infliction of emotional distress. This cause of action does *not* compensate for general feelings of grief, loss, or empathy for an injured person. See, e.g., *Frame v. Kothari*, 560 A.2d 675, 678 (N.J. 1989) (claim applies to "the observation of shocking events that do not occur in the daily lives of most people," such as "bleeding, traumatic injury and cries of pain"); *Thing v. La Chusa*, 771 P.2d 814, 828 (Cal. 1989) ("the impact of personally observing the injury-producing event ... distinguishes the plaintiff's resultant emotional distress from the emotion felt when one learns of the injury or death of a loved one from another, or observes pain and suffering but not the traumatic cause of the injury"). While watching a loved one suffer is surely one of life's most gut-wrenching experiences, it is one of the "natural shocks" that we all must bear when a loved one suffers. Most courts do not allow emotional distress claims for such general grief and suffering of third parties.

Because indirect infliction claims are based on the sudden shock of witnessing injury, factors like those cited in *Dillon*, which emphasize proximity to the traumatic events themselves, make sense as limiting factors. Proximity to the accident, actually witnessing it, and being closely related to the victim, all tend to increase the traumatic impact of witnessing serious injury. By contrast, liability has usually been denied where relatives learn of an injury at a distance, or even observe an injured family member after the fact. Similarly, where relatives of a direct victim suffer emotional distress, but the victim has not suffered a traumatic accident, recovery is usually denied. In *Frame*, for example, the direct victim was allegedly injured due to medical malpractice by the defendants. Although relatives witnessed his suffering, they did not witness a sudden traumatic injury to him. Their claims for indirect infliction of emotional distress were denied. See *Frame*, 560 A.2d at 680 (a misdiagnosis "normally does not create the kind of horrifying scene that is a prerequisite to recovery"). Accord: *Finnegan v. Wisconsin Patients Compensation Fund*, 666 N.W.2d 797, 808, 811-812 (Wis. 2003).

Another Distinction, and Another Difference: Loss of Consortium

When one person suffers physical injury due to a defendant's negligence, relatives of the victim will also suffer a third type of emotional damage, "loss of consortium." This term refers to the impairment of a relative's opportunity to relate to the party directly injured by the defendant. The classic loss of consortium claim is brought by the spouse of a person whose physical injury prevents him or her from enjoying the usual satisfactions of the marital relationship. If, for example, Josephine is seriously injured due to Robespierre's negligence, her injury may interfere drastically with her ability to relate to her spouse. The injury may interfere with recreational activities the couple shared, the division of labor within the household, the sexual society they shared, and the comfort, affection, advice, and moral support that ideally flow from marriage. These associational losses, the "constellation of companionship, dependence, reliance, affection, sharing and aid" (*Hopson v. St. Mary's Hosp.*, 408 A.2d 260, 261 (Conn. 1979) (quoting *Brawn v. Kistleman*, 98 N.E. 631 (1912)), which derive from the marital relationship, are generally referred to as "loss of consortium" or "loss of society."

Like indirect infliction, loss of consortium compensates an emotional loss to one party due to a direct injury to another. But the two claims compensate very different losses, and may frequently be brought in the same suit. Loss of consortium does not stem from a sudden traumatic experience, but from the impairment over a period of time — perhaps years or decades — of the opportunity to relate to the injured spouse. While a large component of the loss is emotional, it is not a claim for shock or trauma from witnessing the injury. Indeed, it is entirely immaterial to a consortium claim whether the consortium plaintiff witnessed the accident.

Loss of consortium also differs subtly from grief and sadness. Loss of consortium compensates for the inability to relate to the direct victim, not for general feelings of sadness or empathy for him. While grief and sadness tend to fade over time, the impairment of the relationship may persist as long as the injury does. In theory, a jury should consider only the interference with the relationship in determining consortium damages, not the general grief a spouse feels due to injury to his partner. Obviously, however, it is easier for lawyers to draw conceptual distinctions between these types of emotional losses than it is for juries to separate them in reaching a damage award.

The Evolution of Loss of Consortium Claims

The history of consortium claims has not been the common law's finest hour. Under early doctrine the wife owed her husband services. Where injury to the wife impaired her ability to render them, the husband had a cause of action against the tortfeasor for that impairment. The wife, however, had no corresponding claim, since at common law the husband had no duty to render services to her. Prosser & Keeton, §125, at 931.

Gradually, the concept of "services" was broadened to encompass not only loss of services, but also emotional losses, including affection, comfort, companionship, and sexual society. Despite the obvious reciprocity of these emotional blessings of marriage, the claim remained limited to the husband until 1950, when the court in *Hitaffer v. Argonne Co., Inc.*, 183 F.2d 811, 813-819 (D.C. Cir. 1950) rejected the common law analysis and granted consortium recovery to the wife as well. Most courts quickly followed suit in granting equal consortium rights, though a few ironically equalized them by eliminating the husband's right rather than extending it to wives. Prosser & Keeton, §125, at 932. In most states today both spouses have a right to full recovery for loss of consortium due to injury to the other.

While spousal consortium claims are well established, there is no consensus on the right of parents or children to claim consortium losses. Historically, the common law accorded a father the right to his children's services, and authorized a claim for the loss of those services where the child was injured. Prosser & Keeton at 934. But no claim existed for interference with the emotional relationship with a child. Since the broadening of spousal consortium rights, some states have allowed claims by parents for loss of "filial consortium" when their child is injured. Many courts, however, have rejected such claims. There is a similar split of authority on claims for loss of consortium brought *by* children whose parents have been injured by a tortfeasor. Some states have recognized such claims, but the majority of those that have addressed the issue have rejected those claims as well, choosing to restrict consortium recovery to spouses only. See *Mendillo v. Board of Education of East Haddam*, 717 A.2d 1177, 1193-1194 (Conn. 1998) (reviewing the decisions going both ways).

If judges were writing on a blank slate, most would probably find a small child's relationship to a parent at least as worthy of protection as the spousal relationship. It is difficult to imagine a more serious loss than the support, advice, comfort, and education that a parent provides over a child's early years. However, unlike spousal consortium claims, which have been recognized in a limited way for many years, there was no historical precedent for consortium claims for loss of a parent. Approving such claims would represent a new burden on defendants (and insurers). That burden would often be substantial, since parents often have several children, while only the most adventurous have multiple spouses. Thus many courts have refused to create a duty to avoid loss of parental society, even though the logical case for doing so may be stronger than for spousal consortium. For the same reason, courts have not extended the consortium cause of action to other close relatives such as siblings.

The examples that follow are intended to help you distinguish the types of claims discussed in this chapter and to understand the varying standards courts have applied to them.

EXAMPLES

Unnatural Shocks

1.   Marat is shaken up but not injured when the car she is riding in, driven by her husband De Sade, collides with a car negligently driven by Robespierre. De Sade suffers gruesome injuries and is in severe pain. Marat brings suit against Robespierre for the distress she suffers from seeing her husband seriously injured in the accident.

    a. Would Marat recover in a state applies the impact rule?

    b. Would she recover in a state that applies the zone-of-danger rule?

    c. Would she recover in a state that applies the *Dillon* approach?

2.   Assume that Marat was driving to work with a friend, Blanc, instead of her husband when the accident took place. She suffers severe emotional distress from witnessing serious injury to Blanc.

    a. Would she recover under zone-of-danger rule?

    b. Would she recover under the *Dillon* approach?

    c. Would she recover under the impact rule?

3.   Cardet, an elementary school student, falls asleep on the school bus on Friday afternoon. The driver completes his route, returns the bus to the parking area, and locks it, without noticing the student. She is not found for almost two days, driving her parents to distraction. Under which rules for indirect infliction would her parents recover for their distress?

Hard Cases Make Sad Law

4.   As indicated in the introduction, efforts by courts to establish defensible limits on a defendant's duty to avoid indirect infliction of emotional distress have led to arbitrary decisions and seemingly indefensible distinctions. The following examples illustrate some typical problem cases under the various rules. Consider how each should be resolved under the applicable standard.

    a. Roget is walking with his daughter on the sidewalk when a car careens off the road from behind them and hits the girl. Roget sues for his emotional distress from seeing her seriously injured. May he recover under the zone-of-danger rule?

    b. Carnot is visiting his wife in the hospital when she has cardiac arrest. Two nurses rush to the bedside to attempt to revive her. His wife is clearly in great pain, although she survives. Later, Carnot learns that the nurses negligently used a type of resuscitation technique that is dangerous for a patient with her illness, thereby greatly exacerbating her pain. He sues for his distress at witnessing the episode. What result if the zone-of-danger rule applies? What result if the *Dillon* standards apply?

    c. Cordet hears a crash and comes running out as a small child, evidently her son, is hit by a car, flies through the air and lands on a lawn across the street. She suffers a cerebral hemorrhage and dies. Her estate sues for indirect infliction. However, it turns out that the child is not her son. How should this case be decided under the *Dillon* approach to indirect infliction?

    d. Cordet hears a screech of brakes while weeding the flower beds and turns to see a car careening off the street right at her son. Terrified, she faints. As it turns out, the car missed little Johnny, but she suffers severe traumatic neurosis from the incident and sues the driver. What result under *Dillon*?

    e. Carnot hears shouts and sirens from his neighbor's yard, and races over in time to see his son lying beside his neighbor's pool, very close to death from drowning while paramedics struggle to revive him. He collapses in distress and later sues the neighbor (who had left the pool gate open) for negligent infliction. What result if the *Dillon* approach applies?

    f. Danton witnesses an accident in which his wife is seriously injured when hit by Roget's car. As a result of the incident, he experiences anxiety, sleeplessness, and loose bowels for several months. He sues Roget for indirect infliction of emotional distress. What result in a jurisdiction that applies the *Dillon* factors, but also requires resulting physical injury?

    g. Consider the example given at the beginning of the chapter, in which a parent learns by phone that her son has just been badly burned in a fire negligently started by the defendant. What result under *Dillon*?

Consortium Compared

5.   DeFarge's adult daughter Belle is seriously injured in an auto accident while driving with DeFarge. Belle is hospitalized for three months, and is left with a permanently disfigured left leg. Which of the following claims will support recovery, and under what theories (i.e., indirect infliction or loss of consortium)?

    a. DeFarge claims damages for the loss of Belle's company during the time Belle is hospitalized.

    b. DeFarge is knocked unconscious from the accident. She wakes up in the hospital and suffers severe distress when told of the extent of her daughter's injuries.

    c. DeFarge claims damages due to the fact that Belle is withdrawn, quiet, and unwilling to go out in public due to humiliation at her disfigurement.

d. DeFarge claims damages for Belle's inability to play tennis with her due to her disability.

e. DeFarge claims damages for the depression she suffers as a result of watching Belle trying to cope with the disability caused by the accident.

f. As a result of her injuries, Belle is unable to work, and consequently unable to contribute to the rent of the apartment she shares with her mother. DeFarge claims damages for these lost payments.

g. Marlene, Belle's twin sister, was also in the car at the time of the accident. She is slightly injured, but is extremely upset from seeing Belle seriously injured at the scene. She claims damages for indirect infliction of emotional distress and for loss of consortium due to Belle's inability to participate in many activities they previously enjoyed together.

6. Assume that DeFarge was not in the car with Belle when Belle was injured. Could DeFarge still sue for loss of consortium with Belle?

7. What kinds of evidence will the consortium plaintiff submit at trial to allow the jury to assess damages for a claim for loss of consortium with a spouse?

Another Distinction that Makes Another Difference

8. In what important respect do *all* of the following emotional distress cases differ from the ones previously analyzed in this chapter?

- Plaintiff was negligently diagnosed with cancer. It turned out that she had an easily treated viral infection.

- Plaintiff was a passenger in a plane that dove suddenly, 35,000 feet, toward the ground. The pilot regained control at 5,000 feet and landed safely.

- Plaintiff, a health care worker, was negligently stuck with a used hypodermic needle, and suffered severe distress from fear of contracting AIDS.

- Plaintiff was informed by his physician that he was sterile. It turned out not to be true.

- Plaintiff is traumatized when a huge cement truck loses control and narrowly misses hitting her.

- Plaintiff is trapped in an elevator negligently repaired by the defendant, and suffers extreme anxiety and claustrophobia.

An Elementary Example

9. DuBarry is driving down Rue Street when she has a sudden heart attack. Her car careens off the street and hits Louis, who is seriously hurt.

Antoinette, Louis's wife, witnesses the accident from the sidewalk and sues for indirect infliction. Will she recover if the jurisdiction applies the *Dillon* approach to indirect infliction claims?

EXPLANATIONS
Unnatural Shocks

1a. Although Marat was not injured, she did sustain an impact from the accident. Under the impact rule, a plaintiff who suffered a physical impact to her person was allowed to recover for emotional distress as well as physical injury. However, this example goes a step beyond the usual impact case, since the plaintiff who suffered an impact seeks recovery for distress caused by injury to another person.

The impact rule is based on the premise that physical contact corroborates the likelihood of actual emotional distress. That premise seems justified where the distress is "parasitic" to the impact itself, that is, where the distress is suffered due to the accident and the injury. But it is more attenuated to conclude that Marat has suffered genuine distress due to injury to her husband simply because she also sustained an impact in the accident. The rule seems a poor fit for indirect infliction cases.

However, some courts have allowed recovery for indirect infliction of emotional distress under these circumstances. In *Binns v. Fredendall*, 513 N.E.2d 278 (Ohio 1987), for example, the court allowed recovery to a passenger who suffered emotional distress due to injuries to the driver. The court noted the difficult proof problem of separating her distress from the accident itself (which is compensable along with her own injuries under the impact rule) from the additional distress she suffered due to the injury to the driver. The court also suggested that, since impact is basically a corroborative factor, once it is satisfied the door is open to all emotional damages from the accident, not just those directly flowing from the impact to her. For another case with a full discussion of this twist on the impact rule see *Pieters v. B-Right Trucking, Inc.*, 669 F. Supp. 1463 (N.D. Ind. 1987) (also allowing recovery).

b. Marat was in the zone of danger in this case, that is, she was herself at risk of physical injury from the defendant's conduct. Thus, she can recover for the emotional distress she suffers from witnessing injury to her husband under the zone-of-danger approach. Courts that apply the zone-of-danger rule reason that defendants can foresee injury to persons who are in danger of physical injury from their negligence. Thus, the defendant owes such persons a duty of care and is liable to them even if they only suffer emotional distress.

However, some states that follow the zone-of-danger approach require that the indirect infliction plaintiff *also* suffer physical injury as a result of the emotional distress. See, e.g., *Rickey v. Chicago Transit Auth.*, 457 N.E.2d 1, 4-5 (Ill. 1983). Marat would not recover in such a state since she did not suffer physical injury from her distress. The *impact* she suffered in the accident would not satisfy this requirement; the physical injury must be caused by the *distress*, not by the accident itself.

However, Marat would probably recover in this state anyway under the impact rule: Most courts view standards like the zone-of-danger rule or *Dillon* standards as an expansion of traditional grounds for recovery, rather than a new, exclusive standard. Since Marat satisfies the impact rule, she would likely recover on that ground even in a zone-of-danger state. It is worth remembering this subtle point, that the plaintiff can probably still recover her emotional damages as "parasitic" if she suffers impact, even if she does not satisfy the state's "liberalized" standard for indirect infliction claims *in the absence of* impact.

c. The *Dillon* approach would probably also support recovery on these facts. Marat satisfies all three of the *Dillon* requirements for "foreseeability." She was present at the time of the accident, witnessed it, and is a close relative of DeSade. Robespierre might argue that Marat did not witness the accident unless she was actually looking at her husband at the time of the collision, but it is doubtful that the court would be that rigid about the requirement that the plaintiff observe the accident. Presumably, realizing that the accident was taking place would suffice. See *Bliss v. Allentown Pub. Library*, 497 F. Supp. 487, 488-489 (E.D. Pa. 1980) (rejecting the argument that the plaintiff should be denied recovery because she was looking in the other direction at the moment the accident occurred).

Although the basic *Dillon* factors would support recovery on these facts, some courts have imposed the additional requirement that the plaintiff's emotional distress result in physical injury as well. See, e.g., *Champion v. Gray*, 478 So. 2d 17 (Fla. 1985). In a state that takes this view, Marat would have to demonstrate resulting physical injury from her emotional distress in order to recover.

2a. The zone-of-danger analysis is no different here than in Example 1. However, the driver here is not a member of the plaintiff's family; does the zone-of-danger approach still apply?

Nothing in the zone-of-danger test itself suggests that it only allows recovery to members of the direct victim's family. Nor does the logic of the test, which is based on the fact that the defendant could foresee injury to those near the victim. However, it is very doubtful that recovery would be allowed to non-family members. Even though distress is clearly foreseeable in a case like this, allowing recovery would greatly expand the scope of liability. It is likely that the balance of burdens and benefits (the "practical politics" of tort law Justice Andrews notes in his *Palsgraf* dissent[3]) is

---

3. *Palsgraf v. Long Island R.R. Co.*, 162 N.E. 99, 103 (N.Y. 1928).

likely to weigh against extending a duty to bystanders unrelated to the primary victim. See Minzer, Nates, et al., Damages in Tort Actions, §5.03[2][c] (most courts have rejected bystander claims by non-family members under all theories). Similarly, the construction worker who witnesses a co-worker's injury — or, *a fortiori*, a stranger — will likely be denied recovery, even if she was nearly hit herself. Yet, even this levee against the flood may be giving way in some jurisdictions. See *Bray v. Marathon Corp.*, 588 S.E.2d 93 (S.C. 2003), which allowed the plaintiff to recover for distress from witnessing the death of a co-worker.

b. Two of the factors established in *Dillon* are clearly met here: Marat witnessed the accident and was at the scene. However, it is not clear that the third factor, a close relationship to the injured party, is met, since the plaintiff and the driver were friends, not relatives. Thus, the example poses two issues under the *Dillon* approach. *First*, is each of the factors a *prerequisite* to recovery, or only a consideration in making a case-by-case assessment of the foreseeability of serious emotional distress? And *second*, is friendship a close enough relationship to satisfy the third *Dillon* factor?

The *Dillon* court did not hold that all three criteria must be satisfied to allow recovery. Rather, it suggested that they were relevant "factors" in the foreseeability analysis. 441 P.2d at 921. However, the California Supreme Court subsequently held that each of the *Dillon* factors must be satisfied to support recovery for indirect infliction. *Thing v. La Chusa*, 771 P.2d 814, 829-830 (Cal. 1989). In other words, *Thing* converts the *Dillon* factors from relevant considerations to absolute prerequisites to recovery. The court in *Thing* acknowledged that it was "arbitrary" to require each factor, but concluded that "drawing arbitrary lines is unavoidable if we are to limit liability and establish meaningful rules for application by litigants and lower courts." 771 P.2d at 828.

While the California court now requires all three factors to be present, other courts continue to view the *Dillon* factors as relevant rather than essential. See, e.g., *Paugh v. Hanks*, 451 N.E.2d 759, 766 (Ohio 1983). Marat would obviously have a better chance of recovery in a state that views the factors as guidelines rather than absolute prerequisites to recovery.

If a "close relationship" is required, will friendship satisfy it? Most cases involve recovery for family members, and it seems very doubtful that the courts will go beyond the family sphere in allowing recovery. Several California cases have refused to do so. See *Kately v. Wilkinson*, 195 Cal. Rptr. 902, 905-907 (Cal. App. 1983) (emotional distress recovery denied under *Dillon* analysis for witnessing injury to close friend, but allowed on product liability theory); *Elden v. Sheldon*, 758 P.2d 582 (Cal. 1988) (refusing to allow indirect infliction claim resulting from injury to cohabiting lover of accident victim); but see *Dunphy v. Gregor*, 642 A.2d 372 (N.J. 1994) (allowing recovery to unmarried cohabitant fiancee of victim);

Graves v. Estabrook, 818 A.2d 1255 (N.H. 2003) (same); *Paugh v. Hanks*, 451 N.E.2d at 766-767 (blood relationship not necessarily required).[4] Doubtless, the advent of same-sex marriage and civil unions in several states will spawn further cases probing the relationship requirement.

c. Example 1a indicates that some courts have allowed recovery for distress due to injury to another person under the impact rule. However, it is likely that many courts would refuse to extend indirect infliction claims to cases like this, in which the negligent infliction plaintiff is not a close relative of the injured party, for the same policy reasons already discussed. But, typically, there's a case that allowed recovery on similar facts. See *Conder v. Wood*, 716 N.E.2d 432 (Ind. 1999).

3. Although it is hard to imagine a scenario more likely to inflict emotional distress than this, Cardet's parents are unlikely to recover under any of the common approaches to indirect infliction claims. They have not suffered an impact. They are not within a zone of physical danger. And the *Dillon* factors are not satisfied, since they have not witnessed traumatic injury to their child.

Cases like this have repeatedly defeated the efforts of courts to develop consistent standards for recovery for emotional distress. After the court establishes a purportedly clear rule such as zone-of-danger or *Dillon*, a case like this comes along, which cries out for relief but doesn't fit the rule. Very frequently, the court then writes a confusing decision that blurs the lines but comes out "right."

For example, some California courts have allowed recovery in indirect infliction cases that don't meet the *Dillon* standards if the defendant owed a "direct" duty to the bystander. See, e.g., *Huggins v. Longs Drug Stores California, Inc.*, 14 Cal. Rptr. 77 (Cal. Ct. App. 1992) (concluding that parents who administered improper dose of medication to infant could recover for distress resulting from injury to infant, despite failure to meet *Dillon* test, since pharmacist owed them direct duty to provide proper dosage).[5] Some cases have purported to use a straight foreseeability standard in hard cases, which certainly would favor recovery here, but would lead to a dramatic increase in such claims, and difficult issues as to the limits of foreseeability. See, e.g., *Masaki v. General Motors Corp.*, 780 P.2d 566, 575-576 (Haw. 1989) (recovery allowed based on foreseeability though parents did not witness the accident); but see *Kelley v. Kokua Sales and Supply*, 532 P.2d 673 (Haw. 1975) (recovery denied where decedent

---

4. Although *Paugh* viewed the close relationship as only a factor, not a prerequisite to recovery, a subsequent Ohio case denied recovery to a plaintiff who witnessed the electrocution death of a friend. *Smith v. Kings Entertainment Co.*, 649 N.E.2d 1252 (Ohio Ct. App. 1994).

5. This dubious holding was overruled by the California Supreme Court. 862 P.2d 148 (1993). But many other equally dubious holdings in hard emotional distress cases have not been.

died of a heart attack in California upon being informed of his relatives' death in Hawaii). See also *Wages v. First Natl. Ins. Co. of America*, 79 P.3d 1095 (Mont. 2003) (requiring only that severe distress be foreseeable from the negligent act).

Hard Cases Make Sad Law

4a. In this example Roget is in the zone of danger but does not know it, since the car approached from behind. Must he be *aware* of the risk to himself in order to recover for distress at the injury to his daughter? The logic of the zone-of-danger test would not seem to require this; the rationale is that the defendant can foresee injury to Roget because he is close to the accident, so it is not unreasonable to hold the defendant liable if Roget suffers emotional distress rather than physical injury.

This seems like the right answer, and many courts would probably so hold. However, some zone-of-danger cases suggest that the bystander plaintiff must *both* be in the zone *and* fear for his own safety before he can recover for distress at injury to another. See, e.g., *Rickey v. Chicago Transit Auth.*, 457 N.E.2d 1 (Ill. 1983).

b. A court that sticks by the zone-of-danger rule will provide no relief on these facts. Carnot is simply not in any physical danger. His distress at witnessing his wife's suffering is foreseeable and doubtless severe, but this arbitrary line cuts him out.

It is unclear whether Carnot would recover if the *Dillon* standards applied. Carnot suffered emotional distress from witnessing his wife's medical crisis, but at the time he was not aware that it resulted from negligence on the part of the nurses. Must he be aware that the injury is being caused by negligence, if he satisfies all the *Dillon* criteria? Logically, such awareness seems unnecessary. The gravamen of the indirect infliction claim is traumatic distress caused by the defendant. This comes from witnessing the injury, whether the bystander realizes that it results from negligence or not. This logic was followed in *Mobaldi v. Board of Regents*, 127 Cal. Rptr. 720, 727-728 (Cal. App. 2nd Dist. 1976), which allowed recovery on analogous facts.

Indeed, it seems unnecessary that the indirect infliction victim witness the defendant's negligent act at all. The mother who sees a car hit her child suffers the same degree of distress whether it resulted from the driver's negligence or that of a mechanic who failed to properly repair the brakes two weeks earlier. Yet it is not clear that recovery will be allowed in cases of antecedent negligence. Typically, there are cases going both ways. See *Love v. Cramer*, 606 A.2d 1175, 1178 n.4 (Pa. Super. 1992), *appeal denied, Cramer v. Love*, 621 A.2d 580 (indicating that Pennsylvania law requires bystander to witness the negligent act); compare *Kearney v. Philips Indus., Inc.*, 708 F. Supp. 479 (D. Conn. 1987) (allowing recovery where bystander only witnessed resulting injury, not the negligent act that caused it).

c.   This change in the facts challenges the line drawn in *Dillon*. In *Dillon* the direct victim actually was the bystander's child; here, Cordet mistakenly thought he was. The impact on Cordet could still be traumatic; indeed, in the case upon which this example is based (*Barnes v. Geiger*, 446 N.E.2d 78 (Mass. 1983)) the bystander really did suffer a cerebral hemorrhage and die. If the defendant's duty to bystanders were based solely on foreseeability, it seems clear that this plaintiff would recover. But in this area, as in others, public policy frequently requires that the limits of the defendant's duty be drawn well short of foreseeability. Although the Massachusetts courts use an approach much like *Dillon*, *Barnes* denied recovery, emphasizing the practical need to limit liability:

> Daily life is too full of momentary perturbation. Injury to a child and the protracted anguish placed upon the witnessing parent is, on the scale of human experience, tangible and predictable. Distress based on mistake as to the circumstances is ephemeral and will vary with the disposition of a person to imagine that the worst has happened. We are unwilling to expand the circle of liability . . . to such an additional dimension, because to do so expands unreasonably the class of persons to whom a tortfeasor may be liable.

Id. at 81. Whenever courts draw a line like this, ivory tower academics (who don't have to decide the case) will argue that the line is arbitrary. Such caviling is easy; of course the line is arbitrary. Still, it must be drawn.

d.   Here again, foreseeability and practical politics suggest different results. It is obviously foreseeable that a mother would be traumatized by seeing her child nearly killed by a car. Yet allowing recovery would again expand the ambit of liability substantially. The *Barnes* court would deny recovery on these facts: "Whether the mistake be as to the identity of the victim . . . or the gravity of the injury, the anxiety, perforce, is transitory, and a 'fleeting instance of fear or excitement' . . . does not present a set of circumstances against which a tortfeasor can fairly be asked to defend." 446 N.E.2d at 81. Some courts have required that the direct victim suffer serious injury if bystanders are to claim for indirect infliction (see, e.g., *Portee v. Jaffee*, 417 A.2d 521, 527-528 (N.J. 1980)), but others have not. See *Paugh v. Hanks*, 451 N.E.2d at 767 (direct victim need not suffer actual physical harm).

e.   This example tests the limits of the *Dillon* requirement that the indirect victim witness the injury. Many cases have turned on whether the relative must be on the scene, see or hear the accident, arrive immediately, or simply see the injured victim in pain. Recovery has usually been denied where relatives learn of an accident later, but this case is closer, since Carnot arrives in the immediate aftermath of the accident.

The Introduction to this chapter distinguished between grief at injury to another and the trauma of witnessing a shocking event. Here, the parent has suddenly come upon the child in a desperate condition immediately after being pulled from the pool, amid frantic efforts to revive him. This is a sudden, terrible shock. It does no violence to the *Dillon* requirement of witnessing the injury to hold it met here. The court so held in *Nazaroff v. Superior Court*, 145 Cal. Rptr. 657 (Cal. Ct. App. 1978), but *Nazaroff* was overruled in *Thing v. La Chusa*, 771 P.2d at 830, which held that the bystander plaintiff must actually witness the injury-causing event itself in order to recover. Courts have drawn various fine distinctions in applying *Dillon*'s "contemporaneous observance" requirement. See, e.g., *Brooks v. Decker*, 516 A.2d 1380 (Pa. 1986) (recovery denied to father who rushed to the scene, saw the ambulance arrive, saw his son's bicycle on the ground, and accompanied his injured son to the hospital); *Stump v. Ashland, Inc.*, 499 S.E.2d 41 (W. Va. 1997) (recovery allowed where plaintiffs were at the scene and knew victims were being harmed by fiery crash, but their view was obscured by flames); *Gabaldon v. Jay-Bi Prop. Mgmt. Inc.*, 925 P.2d 510 (N.M. 1996) (bystander must either be there when the injury occurs or arrive before emergency medical personnel). One of the most liberal cases is *Ferriter v. Daniel O'Connell's Sons, Inc.*, 413 N.E.2d 690 (Mass. 1980), which allowed recovery where plaintiffs did not witness accident but rushed to the hospital and saw the seriously injured victim there.

f.   Danton satisfies the three basic *Dillon* factors, but must also show that he has suffered "physical injury" as a result of the distress from witnessing the accident. In most cases the bystander plaintiff does not suffer dramatic physical injury such as a heart attack or cerebral hemorrhage. Yet, if the courts require resulting physical injury, plaintiffs will try to come up with something. Many tedious, unsatisfactory cases consider whether headaches, upset stomach, loose bowels, depression, social withdrawal, insomnia, perspiration, muscle tension, loss of appetite, and other general complaints satisfy the "resulting physical injury" standard.

Because such symptoms are subjective and hard to disprove, the resulting physical injury requirement has failed miserably as a bright line test to corroborate distress. In the same way that skeptical courts turned the impact requirement into a token, they have eviscerated the "resulting physical injury" requirement by finding vague complaints sufficient. See *Sullivan v. Boston Gas Co.*, 605 N.E.2d 805 (Mass. 1993) (discussing range of symptoms that satisfy the requirement, and approving virtually any evidence that corroborates plaintiff's claim of distress). As with the other requirements, however, some courts have taken a tougher line. See, e.g., *Muchow v. Lindblad*, 435 N.W.2d 918, 921-922 (N.D. 1989) (loss of sleep and weight insufficient).

g.   This case will fail under the *Dillon* standard, since the parent was not on the scene and did not witness the accident. See, e.g., *Harmon v.*

Grande Tire Co., 821 F.2d 252 (5th Cir. 1987). This result makes sense, if recovery is to be limited to the trauma of witnessing the injury itself, as opposed to the sudden grief of learning that a loved one has been injured. Yet this parent *has* suffered a traumatic experience, which is foreseeable and attributable to the defendant's conduct. The nice distinctions made by the indirect infliction rules will make little sense to this plaintiff in light of the emotional suffering the defendant has inflicted upon her. If she lives in Montana, she has a good shot at recovery, however. See *Wages*, 79 P.3d 1095 (Mont. 2003).

Consortium Compared

5a. This is a proper element of a loss of consortium claim. DeFarge does not seek damages for the shock of witnessing injury to Belle, but for the interference with her ability to associate with Belle while she is hospitalized *after* the accident. However, this claim is for loss of "filial consortium," that is, for interference with the relationship to a child. As the introduction states, courts are divided on whether parents may recover for loss of consortium with a child. Many have refused to allow such claims.

b.   This is a claim for distress at the thought that Belle has suffered serious injury. In one sense, it looks like an indirect infliction case, since DeFarge is distressed due to the injury of another. But it is not based on sudden shock at the scene of the accident itself, but the distress and grief of learning that her daughter has been injured. She would experience the same grief if she had not been with her at the time of the accident, and learned of it at home. This does not meet any of the usual tests for indirect infliction of emotional distress.

Arguably, this is like Example 1a, in which a passenger who suffered impact in an accident sought emotional distress damages from witnessing injuries to the driver. However, in that example the plaintiff saw the injuries immediately at the scene. Here, DeFarge passed out so she did not perceive the injury to Belle.

c.   The example here is ambiguous. Does DeFarge seek damages for *Belle's* emotional reaction of withdrawal from social activities, or for the loss of her own (DeFarge's) opportunity to engage in such activities with Belle? If the claim is for Belle's social withdrawal itself, this is an element of Belle's negligence claim, not DeFarge's. Plaintiffs who suffer physical injury are always entitled to prove their full damages, including emotional damages like Belle's, that result from or accompany physical injury. Chapter 15, p. 345.

If DeFarge seeks damages for loss of the opportunity to engage in social activities with Belle as they did previously, or to relate to her due to her emotional withdrawal, this would be a proper element of a loss of consortium claim in states that recognize filial consortium. Note again that the injury claimed is the on-going impairment of DeFarge's relationship with Belle after the accident, not the trauma of witnessing the accident itself.

d.   This chapter considers consortium claims together with indirect infliction claims because both are injuries to one person as a result of a separate injury to another. But consortium claims are substantially broader than infliction of emotional distress claims, since loss of consortium compensates a variety of losses due to impairment of the relationship to an accident victim, including interference with social and recreational aspects of the relationship. The loss of the opportunity to play tennis with Belle, while not strictly a form of emotional distress, is a loss the jury may consider in valuing DeFarge's consortium claim.

e.   This is not an indirect infliction claim — at least, not in the sense in which the courts have recognized them. It stems from DeFarge's sadness at seeing her daughter cope with a disability, not from witnessing the injury that gave rise to it. Nor is it, strictly speaking, within the ambit of a loss of consortium claim. It is not a claim for Belle's inability to do things with DeFarge, or to relate to her emotionally and socially. It is a form of grief distinct from either of the claims addressed in this chapter.

As previously noted, the legal distinction between DeFarge's depression from watching Belle struggle with disability and the emotional impairment of their relationship due to Belle's injury may be too subtle for most juries. Their award for emotional damages is likely to be a general one, based on their overall impression of the impact Belle's injury has had on DeFarge.

f.   This is obviously not a claim for emotional distress, nor is it properly recoverable on a loss of consortium claim. Even if DeFarge loses rent due to Belle's injury, she may not sue the negligent driver for it. Belle will recover directly for her lost future wages in her negligence action against the other driver. If DeFarge could recover for the contributions Belle would have made to the rent from her future wages, the defendant would be made to pay the same loss twice.

It is not unusual for third parties to suffer substantial secondary losses as a result of an injury. If Belle is an indispensable executive, for example, her company may suffer serious economic losses from her absence. Generally speaking, however, courts have refused to allow recovery for these types of derivative losses to others. See generally, Harper, James & Gray, §25.18A, at 619-623.

g.   Marlene has a better claim than DeFarge for indirect infliction of emotional distress, since she was in the car and saw Belle's injuries at the scene. This would probably state a claim for indirect infliction under the impact rule (see Example 1a) and the zone-of-danger rule. It would also probably satisfy the *Dillon* factors, since siblings have generally been considered close enough relatives to recover under *Dillon*.

However, Marlene will almost certainly not recover for loss of consortium, since most courts have denied consortium recovery to siblings. Once again, this has nothing to do with foreseeability; impairment of Marlene's relationship to her sister is highly likely when Belle is seriously injured. It is another example of the practical need to keep liability within manageable limits.

It is not surprising that most courts have extended indirect infliction claims to siblings but barred their claims for loss of consortium. Cases in which siblings witness traumatic injury to accident victims are unusual. But many seriously injured accident victims will have siblings who suffer loss of consortium. Thus, allowing sibling recovery for indirect infliction does not expand liability substantially, while allowing sibling recovery for loss of consortium clearly would.

6.   Yes, she could, if the jurisdiction recognizes claims for loss of consortium with a child. DeFarge's claim is not for the trauma of witnessing the injury; it is for the interference with her ability to relate to Belle caused by Belle's injury. DeFarge suffers this interference equally, whether she witnessed the injury or not. In most cases, consortium plaintiffs will not have witnessed the underlying injury to the direct victim. But this is irrelevant to recovery for loss of consortium.

7.   If the jury is to assess damages for loss of consortium, it has to have a sense of what the consortium plaintiff has lost. Thus, evidence about the quality of the relationship between the direct victim and the consortium plaintiff before and after the accident is relevant and admissible. The jury will hear evidence about how the spouses related to each other, their recreational activities together, the closeness of their relationship, their social life and sex life, their division of functions within the home, and the impact the injury has had on all these aspects of their marriage. Consider, for example, this description of the consortium evidence in a case involving injury to a 48-year-old husband:

> [The wife's evidence indicated that] (1) he had a life expectancy of 24.7 years; (2) she took care of him after his release from the hospital; (3) their social life had been sharply curtailed; (4) prior to the accident the husband had helped with cooking and assorted household tasks on an average of 15-20 hours per week, but he could no longer do so; (5) after the accident he was moody, depressed and "really changed"; (6) she had to wait on him "like waiting on a baby"; and (7) she takes medicine daily as a result of the emotional strain his attitude and conduct cause her.

Minzer, Nates, §11.02[3] at 11-21.

This is powerful and emotional evidence that may have a significant impact on the jury.[6] And, typically, the consortium claim will be heard

---

6. For descriptions of representative cases and awards, see Minzer, Nates, Damages in Tort Actions, §11.02[3].

with the personal injury claim of the direct victim, in a single trial. No defendant can be enthusiastic about the jury hearing all this. Thus, the assertion of consortium claims ups the ante for the defendant, and may drive up the settlement value of the case.

Another Distinction that Makes Another Difference

8.   In each of these cases, the plaintiff suffered emotional distress due to fear of an injury to *herself*, rather than fear of or witnessing injury to another. These are often referred to as "direct infliction" cases, as opposed to "bystander" cases, in which the plaintiff seeks recovery after witnessing injury to another. In Example 3, for example, in which Cardet is unintentionally locked in the school bus, she would likely suffer emotional distress as a direct victim, just as her parents would as indirect victims.

The standards applicable to direct infliction cases are even less clear than those for indirect infliction. Courts have not even consistently made the distinction between direct and indirect infliction, or recognized that standards developed in one context may not work in another. A few courts continue to apply the impact rule to such cases. Some apply the zone-of-physical-danger rule. Some may focus on resulting physical injury, or on whether the defendant owed the plaintiff a preexisting duty. A few appear only to require that distress be foreseeable and serious. See generally Minzer, Nates, §5.02.

Originally, I contemplated including a separate chapter on direct infliction. Efforts to draft one, however, convinced me that as a result of the utterly disorganized state of the case law on the subject, a separate chapter would spawn more frustration than enlightenment.

An Elementary Example

9.   This example is deceptively simple. The *Dillon* factors are clearly met, since Antoinette is closely related to the direct victim, witnesses the accident and is close at hand. However, satisfying the *Dillon* factors merely proves that DuBarry *owed Antoinette a duty* to avoid negligently inflicting emotional distress upon her. It does not show that DuBarry breached that duty of care, and the facts here suggest that she didn't. She did not drive negligently, but was overtaken by a sudden illness that prevented her from controlling her car at all. See, e.g., *Cohen v. Petty*, 65 F.2d 820 (D.C. Cir. 1933) (no liability when driver fainted from sudden illness).

Students often get so caught up in the special standards for allowing indirect infliction claims that they forget that those standards only address the issue of whether a duty of care is owed. These are still claims for negligence, and that means that all four elements of a negligence claim must be proved to recover. In other words, the special standards for indirect infliction claims are not a separate set of elements which support recovery in themselves, but rather prerequisites to establishing *one* of the usual elements of a negligence claim, duty. If they are met, the plaintiff must still shoulder the burden of proof on the other three as well. Here, DuBarry will fail to establish that old stand-by, Element #2, breach of the duty of due care.

12

Caveat Actor: Strict Liability for Abnormally Dangerous Activities

Introduction

Many students come to law school with the belief that an actor who causes injury to another is *always* liable for that injury. However, in cases governed by negligence law, this is not the case. Recovering in an action for negligence requires proof that the defendant breached the duty of due care. Since many accidents result from unexpected circumstances, unknowable mechanical defects, weather conditions or other nonnegligent causes, injured parties are often unable to recover, even though another person caused their injuries.

In *Cohen v. Petty*, 65 F.2d 820 (D.C. Cir. 1933), for example, the plaintiff was denied recovery where the defendant suffered a sudden fainting spell, lost control of his car and injured the plaintiff. The plaintiff lost in *Cohen* because the defendant did not owe her an absolute duty to avoid injuring her, but only a duty to *exercise reasonable care* to prevent injuries from his driving. Where injury results despite the exercise of reasonable care, that duty has not been breached, and the injured party cannot recover under a negligence standard.

However, the negligence standard is not the only possible basis for imposing tort liability. In some situations tort law imposes either more demanding or lesser duties of care on actors. For example, many courts hold that common carriers owe their passengers "the highest degree of care," clearly a more stringent standard than negligence. See Prosser & Keeton at 208-209. In other situations, courts hold that a defendant owes a lesser duty than the exercise of reasonable care. For example, many courts hold that a landowner only owes a trespasser a limited duty to avoid willful or wanton injury. D. Dobbs, The Law of Torts 592-593.

This chapter deals with situations in which the law imposes a very heavy duty on actors, a duty to avoid injury to the plaintiff entirely or pay for any resulting injuries. When such a duty exists, the defendant is liable regardless of the care with which she conducts the activity. The liability flows not from carelessness, but from the very choice to conduct the activity at all. Such "strict liability" is not premised on fault in the conventional sense of the term, but on the policy choice to place accident losses from the activity on the actor rather than on its victims. The defendant, it is said, "acts at her peril" in conducting such activities. No matter how much care she takes to avoid injuries to others, she will be held "strictly liable" if such injuries result.

Some History

Although strict liability is often thought of as a controversial recent development in the law of torts, all early common law causes of action were apparently "strict." Liability was imposed simply for injuring another, regardless of fault. C. Peck, Negligence and Liability Without Fault in Tort Law, 46 Wash. L. Rev. 225, 225-226 (1971). In the last 150 years, however, fault has come to the fore in the law of torts. Today, most tort claims require either intentional conduct or negligence.

Despite that predominance, strict liability has continued to apply in some areas. For example, keepers of wild animals have long been held strictly liable for injuries caused by them. If Springsteen keeps a boa constrictor in his apartment and Boa escapes through a heating duct and injures Neville, Springsteen is liable, even if he took every precaution to prevent Boa's escape:

> A possessor of a wild animal is subject to liability to another for harm done by the animal to the other, his person, land or chattels, although the possessor has exercised the utmost care to confine the animal, or otherwise prevent it from doing harm.

Restatement (Second) of Torts §507(1). Under §507(1), Springsteen's duty is not just a duty of extreme care, it is a duty to prevent the injury entirely or pay the resulting damages. If the injury results, precautions are no defense.

The rationale for imposing strict liability for keeping wild animals is easy enough to see. Keeping a wild animal in a community is an uncommon, unnecessary, and highly dangerous activity. Given the low utility, inappropriate location, and high risk of such activity, it might be appropriate to ban it entirely; doubtless many communities do. If such conduct is tolerated, strict liability makes good sense for several reasons. *First,* those who are tempted to keep a tiger or two will hopefully give serious thought to the risk of liability. Some may decide to forgo the questionable pleasures of tiger keeping rather than risk the broad liability it may entail. *Second,* those who simply can't do without a tiger will at least take all possible precautions to restrain them, in order to avoid liability. *Last,* under strict liability the tiger's victims will at least be compensated for injuries resulting from an arguably frivolous or even antisocial choice by the owner.

There is an obvious analogy between this arcane doctrine of strict liability for wild animals and the broader strict liability doctrine that traces to *Rylands v. Fletcher,* 1 Ex. 265 (1866), *aff'd,* 3 H.L. 330 (1868). The defendant in *Rylands* had introduced a dangerous force—a large body of water—onto his land, which escaped unexpectedly and injured his neighbor's property. There was no evidence that the defendant had been negligent in his efforts to contain the hazard, but the court held that the keeping of this metaphorical tiger supported strict liability for the resulting damage:

> We think that the true rule of law is that the person who, for his own purposes, brings on his land, and collects and keeps there any thing likely to do mischief if it escapes, must keep it in at his peril, and if he does not do so, he is prima facie answerable for all the damage which is the natural consequence of its escape.

Rylands v. Fletcher (1861-1873), All E.R. 7. (Blackburn, J., Exchequer Chamber opinion). Unfortunately, the decision in *Rylands* was not clearly premised on the very sensible policy underlying the wild animal cases. Although neither nuisance nor trespass directly applied,[1] the rationale of *Rylands* appeared to limit such liability to activities on land of the defendant that injure land of an abutter. In addition, Lord Cairns, in the House of Lords opinion, appeared to narrow Blackburn's rationale still further. He suggested that strict liability only applied to "non-natural" uses of land (*Rylands v. Fletcher* at 339), evidently referring to unusual activities that are out of place in the area where the defendant chooses to conduct them.

Regardless of these doctrinal complexities, the underlying spirit of *Rylands* is to impose strict liability on those who (like tiger keepers) impose grave and truly unusual risks on the community. In the century

---

1. Trespass did not lie, because the injury was not direct. Neither did nuisance, because the injury resulted from a single incident, rather than a continuing interference with the plaintiff's use and enjoyment of his property. See Prosser & Keeton at 545.

since *Rylands,* the doctrine of strict liability for abnormally dangerous activities has shed much of the doctrinal baggage of its origins in *Rylands,* and come to focus increasingly on this factor. *Rylands* contained the kernel of an idea that has grown to much greater proportions since.

If an activity poses such high risk, one might ask why it is not simply banned entirely. Life is risky enough without people blowing off dynamite, spraying the unsuspecting with pesticides, and terrorizing them with tigers. Legislatures often *do* ban dangerous activities under particular circumstances or in particular places. But many activities that pose unusual risk are also unusually productive: Try clearing the way for a road with a pick and shovel sometime, and you will gain a renewed appreciation for the social value of dynamite. Strict liability allows such socially useful activities, but requires them to bear the accident costs associated with them.

The Current Doctrine

Today, many jurisdictions accept the principle that actors should be held liable without fault for injuries resulting from activities that pose an unusually high risk of injury. The Second Restatement formulation of the doctrine, which is widely followed, is as follows:

> One who carries on an abnormally dangerous activity is subject to liability for harm to the person, land or chattels of another resulting from the activity, although he has exercised the utmost care to prevent the harm.

Restatement (Second) of Torts, §519(1). The rationale offered in the Restatement is heavily reminiscent of the policy underlying the wild animal cases:

> The liability arises out of the abnormal danger of the activity itself, and the risk that it creates, of harm to those in the vicinity. It is founded upon a policy of the law that imposes upon anyone who for his own purposes creates an abnormal risk of harm to his neighbors, the responsibility of relieving against that harm when it does in fact occur. The defendant's enterprise, in other words, is required to pay its way by compensating for the harm it causes, because of its special, abnormal and dangerous character.

Restatement (Second) of Torts, §519 cmt. d.

Although only hinted at in the Restatement, current economic concepts of cost avoidance and loss spreading also support strict liability for high risk activities. Strict liability encourages those who conduct high risk enterprises to avoid costs in two ways. *First,* the threat of liability will encourage actors to forgo these risky activities entirely. Because it makes the actor pay for all injuries associated with the activity, strict liability encourages her to consider alternative ways of achieving the same goal: Perhaps the same cellar can be dug with a backhoe instead of blasting.

Thus, imposing strict liability may lead to less high risk activity and fewer accident losses from it. See Restatement (Third) of Torts: Liability for Physical Harm (Basic Principles) (Tent. Draft No. 1), §20 cmt. b; M. Geistfeld, Should Enterprise Liability Replace the Rule of Strict Liability for Abnormally Dangerous Activities? 45 UCLA L. Rev. 611, 652-658 (1998).

Second, because actors who conduct abnormally dangerous activities must compensate even for blameless injuries, strict liability encourages them to reduce the cost of accidents by taking extra precautions. Thus, the threat of liability will make high risk activities safer, though it cannot make them completely safe.[2]

Third, economic analysts (and, increasingly, courts) argue that losses should be placed on the party who can most easily *spread the costs* of the enterprise by adding the cost of compensation for accidents resulting from the activity to the price of the product. This policy also supports strict liability for abnormally dangerous activities. A blasting company, for example, can spread the cost of blasting accidents (including nonnegligent accidents) by purchasing liability insurance to pay the damages. It will redistribute this cost to consumers of its service by raising the price of its product. *Chavez v. Southern Pacific Transp. Co.,* 413 F. Supp. 1203, 1209 (E.D. Cal. 1976). By contrast, if the cost of a blasting injury falls on the victim, she will have no means of reducing its impact by spreading the loss to others.

Of course, the increased cost of blasting due to strict liability may lead to a reduction in the amount of blasting done, but if so, this is because the price, adjusted to include the accident costs it imposes, *reflects the true cost of the activity.* Generally, economists consider such "internalization" of the costs of an enterprise (requiring it to "pay its way") a good thing, rather than imposing the injury costs of the enterprise on accident victims who derive no benefit from it. Under a negligence regime, unlike strict liability, the costs of *nonnegligent* accidents are externalized to their victims, since those victims cannot recover these costs from the defendant.

Defining Abnormally Dangerous Activity

The toughest issue for the courts has been determining which activities should be subject to strict liability. The First Restatement of Torts confined strict liability to "ultrahazardous activities." Restatement of Torts, §519. The

---

2. Economic analysts may dispute this, on the ground that the rational economic actor takes the same level of precautions under strict liability or negligence: That is, she will take precautions to the point where the expense of the precautions outweighs the projected liability for the activity. See R. Posner, Tort Law: Cases and Economic Analysis 4-5. My intuition tells me, however, that if *I* kept a tiger, and knew I had to pay for any resulting injuries, I would keep it *very* carefully indeed, regardless of what the economic literature says about the efficient level of precautions.

Second Restatement, however, applies strict liability to "abnormally dangerous" activities, which appear to encompass a somewhat broader range of activities. Restatement (Second) of Torts, §519. Section 520 of the Second Restatement sets forth six factors that courts should consider in deciding whether to impose strict liability:

> In determining whether an activity is abnormally dangerous [and hence, subject to strict liability], the following factors are to be considered:
> (a) existence of a high degree of risk of some harm to the person, land or chattels of others;
> (b) likelihood that the harm that results from it will be great;
> (c) inability to eliminate the risk by the exercise of reasonable care;
> (d) extent to which the activity is not a matter of common usage;
> (e) inappropriateness of the activity to the place where it is carried on; and
> (f) extent to which its value to the community is outweighed by its dangerous attributes.

Like so many other current legal tests, these "factors" do not provide a mechanical means of deciding whether strict liability applies:

> [A]ll [of the factors are] to be considered, and are all of importance. Any one of them is not necessarily sufficient of itself in a particular case, and ordinarily several of them will be required for strict liability. On the other hand, it is not necessary that each of them be present, especially if others weigh heavily.

Restatement (Second) of Torts §520 cmt. f.

Factors (a), (b), and (c) in §520 are closely related. All three emphasize that strict liability should apply to activities that pose unusual risks to the community. Most human activities pose some risk of injury, but strict liability is reserved for those that pose a high risk of injury (factor (a)), that threaten particularly serious or widespread injury (factor (b)), and from which the risk cannot easily be reduced (factor (c)). These, in other words, are activities that, whatever their social usefulness, are particularly dangerous, and cannot be made completely safe despite the exercise of due care.

The American Law Institute is currently engaged in drafting a *third* Restatement of Torts. The Third Restatement's proposed provision on strict liability for abnormally dangerous activities gives even greater emphasis to the irreducibly dangerous nature of the activity. See Restatement (Third) of Torts: Liability for Physical Harm (Basic Principles) (Tentative Draft No. 1) §20, which provides that an activity is abnormally dangerous if it "creates a foreseeable and highly significant risk of physical harm even when reasonable care is exercised by all actors." See also id. at cmt. b, g. A fine article on strict liability suggests that this factor, the inability to make the activity reasonably safe by exercising due care, is the crucial factor in virtually all strict liability cases. G. Boston, Strict Liability for Abnormally Dangerous Activity: The Negligence Barrier, 36 San Diego L. Rev. 597, 628-639 (1999).

Cases in which courts have applied strict liability illustrate the types of risks referred to in subsections (a) to (c) of §520. Strict liability has been applied to blasting, large artificial ponds for retention of mining wastes, crop dusting, fumigation, storage of large quantities of gasoline, rockets, experimental aircraft, and use of radioactive materials. Each of these activities involves forces or substances capable of causing extensive damage if not properly controlled. Each usually goes forward without mishap, but can misfire badly without negligence. The risk of such activities may differ only in degree from other activities, but the extra risk has been enough to convince courts to apply strict liability to them.

Abnormal Danger: The Effect of "Common Usage"

Where the unusual risk emphasized in the first three subsections is *not* present, strict liability will probably not apply. However, even if the first three factors *are* met, strict liability will not necessarily apply under the Second Restatement formula. Section 520 contains three more factors that the court must consider, suggesting that strict liability will sometimes not apply even if the activity involves unusual risk.

For example, subsection (d) of §520 requires the court to consider whether the activity is a "matter of common usage." A classic example is driving. Doubtless, more people are injured in a week by the automobile than are injured in a decade by blasting. Yet, because it is so common (and so useful), courts have not applied strict liability to driving. Recovery for motor vehicle accidents still requires a showing of negligence, and many innocent victims who cannot make that showing go uncompensated.

If an activity poses unusual risk to others, why should the plaintiff be put off with the explanation that the danger is a common one? One reason is historical: This "common usage" factor traces to Lord Cairns's requirement in *Rylands* that the injury result from a "non-natural" use. Whatever His Lordship actually meant by this,[3] many courts have concluded that strict liability only applies if the defendant's use of his property

---

3. The phrase is enigmatic at best; virtually any human economic activity is "non-natural" by definition. Most courts have read the phrase to refer to an unusual or inappropriate use. Prosser & Keeton at 545-546. But Lord Cairns may have meant only that the defendant had introduced a force onto his property (there, an accumulation of water) which did not occur there by operation of nature. See F. H. Newark, Non-Natural User and *Rylands v. Fletcher*, 24 Modern L. Rev. 557 (1961).

is unusual or extraordinary as well as dangerous. See Restatement (Third) of Torts: Liability for Physical Harm (Basic Principles) (Tentative Draft No. 1) §20, reporter's note p. 331; Prosser & Keeton, §78, at 546. This suggests that an activity might give rise to strict liability in an area where it is common, but not in another where it is rare. Some cases bear this out: One court refused to impose strict liability for drilling an oil well in rural Oklahoma (*Sinclair Prairie Oil Co. v. Stell*, 124 P.2d 255 (Okla. 1942)), but another held a defendant strictly liable for drilling one in downtown Los Angeles. See *Green v. General Petroleum Corp.*, 270 P. 952 (Cal. 1928) (relying primarily on trespass theory).

Another rationale for the "common usage" factor is that activities that are common, such as driving or building excavation, often involve creation of *reciprocal* risks between actor and victim. The plaintiff who is hit by a car at one time probably travels by car herself at other times, and thus imposes a similar risk of injury on others. By contrast, those who conduct unusual activities such as fumigation or blasting impose hazards on the community that are generally not imposed on them by similar activities of others. See G. Fletcher, Fairness and Utility in Tort Theory, 85 Harv. L. Rev. 537, 543-548 (1972). It is not surprising that courts impose strict liability on actors who impose a risk on the community disproportionate to the general risks they are exposed to themselves.[4]

The proposed Third Restatement section on strict liability for abnormally dangerous activities not only retains the "not-a-matter-of-common-usage" requirement, but elevates its importance, by making it the sole additional requirement along with the inability to make the activity safe by exercise of due care:

§20. Abnormally Dangerous Activities

(a) A defendant who carries on an abnormally dangerous activity is subject to strict liability for physical harm resulting from the activity.

(b) An activity is abnormally dangerous if:

---

4. This rationale may help to explain the difference in the common law's treatment of wild and domestic animals. Keeping a wild animal involves an unusual danger seldom matched by similar activity of one's neighbors. Large dogs, on the other hand, are a common risk. A great many more people are bitten by dogs than by tigers but under the common law they were required to prove negligence in order to recover.

It also illuminates the Second Restatement's treatment of ground damage from aircraft, which obviously impose a nonreciprocal risk on persons and property on the ground. The Restatement would hold aviation operators strictly liable for ground damage caused by aircraft, but not for damage to those (including passengers) who actually take part in the aviation activity. Restatement (Second) of Torts §520A. This provision has not, however, met with general acceptance by the courts. See, e.g., *Crosby v. Cox Air. Co.*, 746 P.2d 1198 (Wash. 1987).

(1) the activity creates a foreseeable and highly significant risk of physical harm even when reasonable care is exercised by all actors; and
(2) the activity is not a matter of common usage.

Abnormal Danger: "Inappropriateness" of the Activity

Under the Second Restatement factors, the "inappropriateness of the activity to the place where it is carried on" is also relevant in determining whether to impose strict liability. Restatement (Second) of Torts §520(e). This factor will weigh heavily in favor of strict liability if an activity is carried on in an inappropriate place. For example, a company that processes volatile chemicals will more likely be held strictly liable if its factory is located in a densely populated area than in sparsely populated countryside.

However, it is unlikely that courts will *reject* strict liability for high risk activity simply because the defendant chose an *appropriate* locale for the activity. For example, it is entirely appropriate to blast for a new road in the location where the road is to go; indeed, there is no other appropriate locale. But most courts impose strict liability for blasting anyway. Similarly, it is "appropriate" to store mining wastes in retaining pools near the mine, but the court is unlikely to be persuaded that strict liability is unwarranted simply because it is stored there. See, e.g., *Cities Service Co. v. State*, 312 So. 2d 799, 803-804 (Fla. Dist. Ct. App. 1975) (imposing strict liability on similar facts, despite argument that location was appropriate). See Third Restatement draft, §20 cmt. k; see also G. Boston, Strict Liability for Abnormally Dangerous Activities, 36 San Diego L. Rev. 597, 662 (1999) (cases on this factor are "all over the map"). Thus, the fact that the activity could have been carried on elsewhere with less risk to the community will strengthen the case for liability, but choosing an appropriate site will probably not, by itself, preclude application of strict liability. See Prosser & Keeton at 555 (doubting that appropriate location should preclude strict liability for unusually dangerous activities).

In some cases, however, the fact that the activity is located in an appropriate area, *together with other factors,* may tip the balance away from strict liability. In *Turner v. Big Lake Oil Co.*, 96 S.W.2d 221 (Tex. 1936), for example, the Texas court refused to impose strict liability for impounding salt water in rural areas as part of an oil drilling operation. In rejecting strict liability, the court emphasized the rural nature of the area, the need for such facilities due to the lack of rainfall, the common usage of retaining ponds associated with oil drilling, and the great importance of the oil industry to the state. *Turner* at 165-166.

Abnormal Danger: Importance of the Activity to the Community

The most controversial factor in the §520 calculus is the last, "the extent to which its value to the community is outweighed by its dangerous attributes." This suggests that a particularly important local industry may escape strict liability, even though it imposes great risk on the community. It also suggests that an actor would be strictly liable for the same activity in a location where there are many industries (and any one is therefore expendable) but not in another where the community depends heavily on the activity.

This factor was apparently included to avoid burdening locally important but economically fragile industries with the extra expense associated with strict liability. It has been criticized by many (including the later editors of Prosser's own treatise — see Prosser & Keeton at 555), as reintroducing a "Hand formula" negligence analysis into strict liability doctrine. See *Koos v. Roth,* 652 P.2d 1255, 1261-1262 (Or. 1982) (refusing to consider value to the community in determining liability standard).[5] Professor Boston's review of the cases suggests that this factor is rarely more than a throw-in. G. Boston, Strict Liability for Abnormally Dangerous Activities: The Negligence Barrier, 36 San Diego L. Rev. 597, 664 (1999). The Third Restatement would eliminate it from the definition of abnormally dangerous activities. If this factor ever influences the outcome, it is probably when the activity has *little* value to the community. For example, a court might be more willing to impose strict liability for stunt flying, which has marginal social value, than on some other type of aviation activity that has an important economic impact on the community.

Recap and Closing Comments

The Second Restatement's multi-factor approach to determining strict liability has been embraced by most courts that have considered it. This is no surprise. Courts like multi-factor tests, because they give judges guidance, but leave them the flexibility to decide pretty much as they like. This suggests the downside of such tests: They promote litigation, because they tend to be less determinate, leaving parties room to argue about whether strict liability should apply. And they tend to defeat predictability, because they are inherently indeterminate.

Fundamentally, the cases tend to sort themselves out around this crucial issue: Is this activity so inherently dangerous that the level of risk will

---

5. Evidently Dean Prosser himself viewed the requirement as marginal, and included it largely for political reasons. See *Koos* at 1262 n.5 (quoting Prosser's remarks from proceedings of the American Law Institute).

remain high despite conscientious, reasonable efforts to reduce it. If that is *not* true, if reasonable care can make the activity generally safe, courts will not impose strict liability. See *Indiana Harbor Belt R. Co. v. American Cyanamid Co.,* 916 F.2d 1174, 1177 (7th Cir. 1990); see generally G. Boston, Strict Liability for Abnormally Dangerous Activities: The Negligence Barrier, 36 San Diego L. Rev. 597, 653-659 (1999). If it *is* true, if the activity poses grave risk of injury that even the reasonable care required in dealing with dangerous activities will not substantially control, strict liability will probably apply, no matter how the later factors in the test shake out. The defendant's best argument to avoid strict liability in such cases is that the activity is one of "common usage."

The draft Third Restatement recognizes the centrality of these two factors to the analysis. See Restatement (Third) of Torts: Liability for Physical Harm (Basic Principles) (Tentative Draft No. 1) §20 (strict liability applies to activity that poses "highly significant risk of physical harm even when reasonable care is exercised" and "is not a matter of common usage"). While courts may continue to invoke the Second Restatement test, they will probably decide future cases — as they have past ones — almost entirely on the two factors emphasized in the Third Restatement.

Abnormally dangerous activities are not the only example of strict liability in American tort law. The most common is strict products liability, which holds a manufacturer or seller strictly liable for injuries resulting from the sale of defective products. Strict products liability is based on different rationales than strict liability for abnormally dangerous activities and requires proof of different elements. This burgeoning area of tort law is taken up in the next two chapters.

The following examples illustrate the application and the limits of strict liability for the conduct of abnormally dangerous activities. In analyzing them, assume that the principles of the Second Restatement apply unless otherwise indicated.

EXAMPLES

Clearing the Air

1.   Franklin Pest Control Company is called in to fumigate an apartment house. The process calls for spraying the premises with Vikane, a toxic chemical that kills bugs. Unfortunately, Vikane is also toxic to people.

Prior to spraying the building, Ciccone, an employee of Franklin, carefully investigates to be sure that the chemical fumes can not spread through the party wall into the adjacent apartment building. She is assured that the party wall is an impenetrable fire wall, and her own inspection confirms this. Unfortunately, a crack, almost impossible to find, exists in the wall. The chemical fumes spread through the wall and overcome Prince in the next building.

Prince sues Franklin for his injuries. The company argues that it took all reasonable precautions and had no reason to suspect that the fumes could travel into Prince's building. Assume that the court concludes that fumigation is a strict liability activity, and agrees that the company's conduct was reasonable. Is Franklin liable to Prince?

A Dull Fthudd

2. Franklin Company's tank truck delivers Vikane to an apartment building for use in the fumigation. The driver carefully backs up to the loading dock, checking his mirrors and beeping as he goes. Unfortunately, Jackson, a child, runs impulsively behind the truck and is hit. Jackson sues Franklin Co. for his injuries. At trial, Judge Fudd instructs the jury as follows:

> I instruct you that the process of fumigation with Vikane is a strict liability activity. If you find that the plaintiff's injury took place in the course of the defendant's fumigation activities, then the defendant may be found liable without proof of negligence.

a. By instructing the jury that strict liability applies to the activity of fumigation, Judge Fudd has decided that question as a matter of law. Was that proper?

b. Who will object to Fudd's instruction, and why is it improper?

3. On the facts of Example 1, Prince sues Ciccone, the employee who sprayed the Vikane, for his injuries. Should the court apply a negligence or strict liability standard in determining liability?

Driving to Endanger

4. Neville is driving a Petrosur Oil Company tank truck containing gasoline south on Interstate 591 when Dean, driving a pick-up truck, cuts in front of him. Neville swerves to the right to avoid a collision and tips over. The tank car ruptures, and the gasoline explodes and injures Hendrix, who was driving north in the opposite roadway. Hendrix sues Petrosur for damages, and claims that Petrosur is strictly liable for his injuries.

a. Would strict liability apply under the holding of *Rylands v. Fletcher*, quoted on p. 265?

b. If the Second Restatement applied, would Neville be barred from relying on strict liability because the activity did not take place on the land of the defendant?

c. Under both the First and Second Restatement, it is relevant whether the activity is a "matter of common usage." Is transportation of gasoline a matter of common usage?

d. Would strict liability apply under the Second Restatement?

5. Based on the facts in Example 4, Petrosur claims that it is not liable, even if gasoline hauling is a strict liability activity, since the accident resulted from the negligence of Dean. How should the court rule?

6. Assume that after the truck fell over, but before the gasoline exploded, a state trooper was stationed in the road waving down vehicles before they reached the scene. Hendrix, in a hurry and thinking there was just an ordinary accident, ignores the trooper, proceeds up the road and is injured when a spark from his car ignites the gasoline vapors from the overturned truck. Petrosur claims that liability should be reduced or denied due to Hendrix's contributory negligence. How should the court rule?

7. Baez Construction Company is engaged in the construction of a sky-scraper in a small but growing city. A worker drops a plank from the seventh floor and injures a passing pedestrian. Is Baez strictly liable?

Crying over Spilled Pseudomonomethane

8. Ronstadt Plastics Company has a major plant in a suburban area near Nashville. As part of its process for manufacturing certain plastic toys, Ronstadt keeps a large tank of pseudomonomethane on its property. Pseudomonomethane is not explosive, caustic, or flammable. It is easy to work with and essential to Ronstadt's manufacturing process. However, it has been identified as a very potent carcinogen if ingested.

While one of Ronstadt's delivery trucks is arriving at the plant, it loses its brakes (non-negligently, we will assume), and careens off the road and into the tank. The tank is knocked over, and pseudomonomethane spills on the surrounding earth. The chemical migrates underground and enters the city's water supply, requiring the closing of its wells. The city sues for damages, and argues that Ronstadt is strictly liable for the damage to its water supply. How should the court rule?

Cause for Concern

9. Guthrie Hospital uses hydromegasulfate, a highly explosive chemical, in several sophisticated medical applications. Because the chemical is so explosive, Guthrie stores it in a heavy gauge tank on its grounds, two hundred feet behind the hospital.

One morning, the cashier at the hospital is held up at gun point. He alerts the police, who respond and chase the culprit out the back door. An officer fires a warning shot, which unfortunately hits the tank on a rico-chet. The tank explodes, injuring Dean, who was emptying trash into a nearby dumpster. Assuming that the storage of hydromegasulfate is a strict liability activity, is Guthrie strictly liable for Dean's injury?

10. One of the most famous strict liability cases is *Foster v. Preston Mill Co.*, 268 P.2d 645 (Wash. 1954). In *Foster*, the plaintiff ran a mink farm.

Mink, it seems, are of "exceedingly nervous disposition." *Foster*, 268 P.2d at 648. When the defendant conducted blasting operations to build a road several miles from the plaintiff's farm, many of the mother mink were so upset by the noise that they killed their young. The farmer sued, but the defendant was not held liable. Why not?

EXPLANATIONS

Clearing the Air

1. Franklin can hardly be faulted here for the way in which it conducted its operation. Ciccone investigated carefully, and only proceeded after she was satisfied that it was safe to do so. If liability turned on a showing of negligence, Prince would not recover.

However, liability does *not* turn on a showing of negligence, since strict liability applies. Prince may recover by showing that his injury was caused by the defendant's conduct of the activity, no matter how carefully it was done. Franklin is liable, since its use of the toxic chemical caused his injuries.

The defendant's plea, "but we didn't do anything wrong!" has considerable appeal, but it does not carry the day in a strict liability case. (If it did, it wouldn't be very strict, would it?) The basis of strict liability is not fault, but the choice to engage in the activity in the first place. Because of the nature of that activity, courts place the damages flowing from that choice on the actor, rather than those who suffer injury, even blameless injury, from it. See *Old Island Fumigation, Inc. v. Barbee,* 604 So. 2d 1246, 1247-1248 (Fla. Dist. Ct. App. 1992) (imposing liability on similar facts "regardless of the level of care exercised in carrying out th[e] activity"); but see *Dow Chemical Co. v. Ebling,* 723 N.E.2d 881 (Ind. App. 2000), reversed on other grounds, 753 N.E.2d 633 (2001) (rejecting strict liability for pesticide use under Second Restatement test).

A Dull Fthudd

2a. Judge Fudd may be on the dull side at times, but he has quite properly decided the applicable liability standard as a matter of law. The decision to impose strict liability is a policy decision as to the nature of the duty owed in the conduct of the activity. This is a question of law for the court, just as the existence of a duty of care is an issue of law in a negligence case. If the jury were allowed to decide whether fumigation is a strict liability activity, they would not only be applying the rules of law, but *making* them as well. This is the court's job. Restatement (Second) of Torts §520 cmt. l.

Of course, the judge's decision whether or not to apply strict liability will require Judge Fudd to take evidence and weigh the facts under the six-part analysis in §520. Fudd will have to consider how toxic Vikane is, how quickly it spreads, whether it is easily detected, alternative means of fumigation, the value to the community of the activity, and other factors. Although facts must be considered (just as they must be, for example, in deciding whether a duty is owed to avoid emotional distress to a bystander in a negligence case), it is the court which must balance the Restatement factors in deciding whether strict liability is appropriate.

b. Franklin, the defendant, will object to the instruction, because it suggests that it is strictly liable for any injury that takes place in the course of fumigation. It makes sense, though, doesn't it, to confine strict liability to the types of risks that make the activity abnormally dangerous. Although Jackson was injured while Franklin was in the general course of its fumigation activities, he was not injured by the peculiar risk that makes fumigation "abnormally dangerous." His injury arose from related, ordinary activity incident to fumigation. Delivering Vikane by truck is no more likely to cause this kind of accident than delivering topsoil or lumber or collecting garbage by truck. Fumigation is not a strict liability activity because of the risk of truck accidents, but rather due to the risk of Vikane poisoning, which has nothing to do with this case.

The Second Restatement explicitly bars strict liability for such collateral injuries:

> §519(2). This strict liability is limited to the kind of harm, the possibility of which makes the activity abnormally dangerous.

This provision would also bar strict liability if a Franklin employee poked a resident in the eye with the chemical applicator, or an employee of a blasting company dropped a box of dynamite caps on the foot of a passerby.

3. The question here is whether an employee who conducts abnormally dangerous activity is strictly liable for resulting injuries, as well as the enterprise for which she works. The Second Restatement is ambiguous on the point: It makes "one who carries on an abnormally dangerous activity" strictly liable. Restatement (Second) of Torts §519.

Certainly, Ciccone participated in the creation of the unusual, nonreciprocal risk that injured Prince. But so did the secretary who made the appointment for the fumigation, the driver who delivered Vikane to the apartment building, and the workers who dug Rylands' reservoir. If individual negligence is not required, it is hard to know which individuals who participated in some manner in creating the risk would be subject to strict liability.

In addition, the rationale for strict liability suggests that it is the *enterprise* undertaking the activity that should be strictly liable, not employees who carry out the operation. The owner or corporation makes the decision to conduct the abnormally dangerous activity and derives profit from doing so. It is in a position to decide how much fumigation it will undertake, whether alternative safer products should be used, the precautions that will be taken, and how to insure the risk or spread the risk of loss through the price of the service. Strict liability is meant to place the loss on those who make such decisions about the activity. See Restatement (Second) of Torts §519 cmt. d (stating that "the defendant's enterprise" should be required to pay its own way through strict liability). Although there is little authority on the point, it appears that Franklin, not Ciccone, should be held strictly liable for Prince's injury; your author has found no case imposing such liability on the employee.

Driving to Endanger

4a. Petrosur would not be liable under *Rylands*, since the accident did not arise from conduct of an activity on the defendant's property that caused injury on surrounding property. *Rylands* dealt only with dangerous activities on the land of one person, which "escaped" and caused injury on the land of another. Indeed, the later English cases rather rigidly confined *Rylands* to this situation. In *Read v. J. Lyons & Co.*, 1947 A.C. 156 (1947), the court held that *Rylands* did not apply to a case in which a government inspector was injured on the premises of the defendant's munitions plant, since there was no "escape" from the defendant's property!

b. Although *Rylands* tied strict liability to land use, there is nothing in the Second Restatement that suggests such a limitation. Section 519 imposes strict liability if the activity is abnormally dangerous and causes harm to the *person, land, or chattels* of another. Clearly, these prerequisites can be met in many situations that do not arise directly from land use by either the actor or the injured party. Comment e to §520 specifically states that it does not limit strict liability to activity on the defendant's property. Thus, strict liability could apply in Hendrix's case even though the accident did not arise from an abnormally dangerous use of real property. Accord: Restatement (Third) of Torts: Liability for Physical Harm (Basic Principles) (Tentative Draft No. 1) §20 cmt. d.

Note, too, that the damage in this case is personal injury, not property damage as in *Rylands*. Under the Restatement, however, strict liability encompasses personal injury claims as well as property damage claims. See Restatement (Second) of Torts §519(1).

c. Most people would say, based on common sense, that hauling gasoline on an interstate highway *is* a matter of common usage. It happens every day, all over the country. It would be hard to take a trip of any length on an interstate without seeing several gasoline trucks along the way.

However, this phrase may refer not to how visible the activity is, but to the number of people who engage in the activity. See, e.g., Restatement (Second) of Torts §520 cmt. i (noting that use of explosives, while frequent, is "carried on by only a comparatively small number of persons . . ."). If this is the test, gasoline hauling looks a lot less "common." It is a highly specialized activity performed by a relatively small number of entities. Similarly, tens of thousands of buildings may be fumigated every year; in this sense fumigation is "common." (A quick look at the Boston Yellow Pages indicates that there are about 150 fumigation companies in the Boston area alone.) But it is still a specialized activity carried on by a small number of experts in the field, rather than an every day activity that ordinary people undertake. In this sense it imposes an unusual, non-reciprocal risk and may be found not a matter of "common usage." *Luthringer v. Moore*, 190 P.2d 1, 8 (Cal. 1948).

However, the fact that only specialists engage in an activity is not dispositive. The draft Third Restatement suggests that activities that are common, such as electric and gas transmission, are in "common usage," even though they are conducted by a small number of specialized personnel, in part because the benefits of the activity are widely enjoyed in the community. "The appeal of strict liability for an activity is stronger when its risks are imposed on third parties while its benefits are concentrated among a few." Restatement (Third) of Torts: Liability for Physical Harm (Basic Principles) (Tentative Draft No. 1) §20, cmt. j. Given this non-obvious conception of "common usage," some courts would doubtless conclude that transportation of gasoline is a matter of common usage.

d. Obviously, there is no mechanical way to answer this question. Whether strict liability applies to Hendrix's case will depend on a balancing of the six factors in §520, and different courts might balance them differently. Under the first three factors an activity is "abnormally dangerous" if it poses a high risk of serious harm that cannot be eliminated by reasonable care. Gasoline transportation is likely to satisfy these factors. Although it does not usually cause injury, the stuff is highly flammable; when it does explode, resulting injuries are likely to be severe indeed. The risk can certainly be kept down by reasonable care, but explosions still happen, as this one did.

The fourth factor in §520 requires the court to consider whether the activity involved is a matter of common usage. Under the Second Restatement common usage is only a *factor to be considered*, along with the others, in determining whether strict liability should apply. Compare §520(b) of the First Restatement (activity must not be a matter of common usage). If the other factors weigh heavily in favor of strict liability, Petrosur could be held strictly liable even if gasoline hauling is deemed "common." Some courts would probably view gasoline hauling as a specialized, unusual activity under this factor, but others probably would not. See Example 4c above.

The last two factors in the Second Restatement analysis do not support strict liability. Gasoline transportation is appropriate to an interstate highway, which is probably the safest place to haul it; and the availability of gasoline is obviously of great value to the community.

In *Siegler v. Kuhlman*, 502 P.2d 1181 (Wash. 1972) the court applied strict liability to the transportation of gasoline. While the court adopted the provisions of the Second Restatement, its opinion concentrated almost exclusively on the extreme risk that gasoline hauling poses. This suggests that in some cases, the risk factors are alone sufficient to support strict liability, even if the other factors weigh against it. For example, the *Siegler* court was unimpressed by the argument that major highways are an "appropriate" place for gasoline hauling:

> That gasoline cannot be practically transported except upon the public highways does not decrease the abnormally high risk arising from its transportation.

502 P.2d at 1187. Despite the balancing required under the Second Restatement, *Siegler* and some other courts appear to take the common-sensical position that, if an activity is not just dangerous, but damned dangerous, the enterprise ought to pay regardless of its common use or social value. See also *Koos v. Roth*, 652 P.2d 1255, 1261-1262 (Or. 1982) (emphasizing importance of the extraordinary danger of the activity and questioning the relevance of the last three Second Restatement factors).

5.   In Example 1, the defendant argued that it should not be held liable, since it conducted the activity with reasonable care. Petrosur's defense here goes a bit further. It argues that, not only was it *not* negligent, but that someone else *was*. The accident was caused by Dean's negligent driving. Since there is a faulty cause of the accident, Petrosur argues, the party at fault should bear the liability.

This defense is unlikely to prevail. The accident was caused not only by the negligence of Dean, but also by the unusual risk that gasoline hauling imposes on the community. If Dean had hit an ordinary car, he might have caused injury to an occupant of that vehicle, but not an explosion that would injure Hendrix many feet away. The accident results in part from the peculiar risk Petrosur has imposed on the community. It is not unreasonable to apply strict liability even though the accident was *also* caused by a third party's negligence. See Restatement (Second) of Torts §522(a). But see *Seigler* at 1188 (Rosellini, J., concurring) (majority should not be read to apply strict liability where third party's negligence causes accident).

Looked at another way, one of the risks of hauling gasoline around the countryside is that the hauler may encounter a negligent driver, leading to an accident that triggers a dangerous explosion. As long as drivers remain human, that risk is impossible to eliminate. Under strict liability, the actor who chooses to engage in the activity that poses this risk is liable for any resulting injuries.[6]

6.   Many courts have held that the plaintiff's contributory negligence is not a defense to a strict liability claim. Harper, James & Gray, §14.5.

---

6. Of course, Dean will be liable as well. The fact that Petrosur is strictly liable does not affect Hendrix's right to sue Dean for negligence.

"The reason is the policy of the law that places the full responsibility for preventing the harm resulting from abnormally dangerous activities upon the person who has subjected others to the abnormal risk." Restatement (Second) of Torts §524 cmt. a. Other authorities suggest that, since strict liability is not based on negligence, plaintiff's negligence should not be relevant either. Posner suggests that, under economic analysis, contributory negligence is not recognized as a defense because only the enterprise, not the plaintiff, is in a position to control or reduce the risk. Posner, Economic Analysis of Law 178 (4th ed. 1992). Last, it has been questioned how, assuming comparative negligence applies, one is to compare negligent conduct with the defendant's nonnegligent conduct of an abnormally dangerous activity.

None of these explanations seems entirely satisfying. The rule "involves the seemingly illogical position that the fault of the plaintiff will relieve the defendant of liability when he (the defendant) is negligent, but not when he is innocent." Prosser & Keeton at 565. In this case, Hendrix could have avoided injury entirely by use of due care, even though the injury stemmed from a strict liability activity. In terms of accident prevention, it makes sense to give him an incentive to do so. The draft Third Restatement therefore would recognize a plaintiff's negligence as a damage-reducing factor in strict liability cases. Restatement (Third) of Torts: Liability for Physical Harm (Basic Principles) (Tentative Draft No. 1) §25.

Courts have been less sympathetic to the plaintiff who *deliberately* exposes himself to the risk posed by a strict liability activity. (That is probably not the case here, because Hendrix, although he ignored the trooper, did not fully comprehend the danger ahead.) The Second Restatement would bar a plaintiff from recovery in a strict liability case if she "knowingly and unreasonably subject[s] [her]self to the risk of harm from the [abnormally dangerous] activity." Restatement (Second) of Torts §524(2). However, the Third Restatement rejects this approach in favor of treating even a plaintiff's deliberate choice to encounter the danger as a form of comparative negligence, which reduces the plaintiff's recovery rather than fully barring recovery. Restatement (Third) of Torts: Liability for Physical Harm (Basic Principles) (Tentative Draft No. 1) §25. This is in accord with current treatment of assumption of risk in both negligence cases (see p. 501) and strict products liability cases (see p. 317).

7. The construction of high rise buildings certainly imposes risks on the community, including the risk of objects falling from high above the street. Although this building may be unusually high for the area, the court will probably not impose strict liability. The risk of falling objects is a common one, as is construction activity in general. Many engage in it in the community, and many are subject to it. In addition, although such activity may cause serious harm, it does not pose the extreme risk of an explosion or a

dam collapse, which may injure many or wipe out an entire community. Last, most of the risks of ordinary construction work can be reduced to a minimum by precautions in the course of the work.

Other arguably dangerous but very common activities have similarly been shielded from strict liability. For example, courts have not generally applied strict liability to distribution of water, electricity, or natural gas. See, e.g., *New Meadows Holding Co. v. Washington Water Power Co.*, 687 P.2d 212, 217 (Wash. 1984) (natural gas transmission).

Crying over Spilled Pseudomonomethane

8.   In this case, pseudomonomethane carries the potential for very widespread harm if it gets into the water supply. However, unlike volatile agents like nitroglycerine or gasoline, it has no unusual tendency to cause an accident. The example suggests that the likelihood of an accident taking place from storing pseudomonomethane is no higher than from storing molasses, water, or anything else. Thus, factor (a) of §520 does not appear to apply.

Nor is there is any indication that the risk of damage from storing pseudomonomethane is irreducible. Restatement (Second) of Torts §520(c). Careful handling will not *absolutely eliminate* the risk of a spill, but it seems unlikely that subsection (c) means that, since there are few activities from which the risk of harm can be completely eliminated. Presumably, it applies where, despite due care, there remains an unusual risk of an accident that simply cannot be eliminated. This is true of the activities in the earlier examples — fumigation with poisonous gas, transportation of gasoline, storage of explosive chemicals — but it is not true of storing pseudomonomethane, which is not explosive, volatile, or flammable. This chemical is very nasty *if* it escapes (see §520, subsection (b)), but it is no more likely to escape than many other relatively innocuous substances.

In *Indiana Harbor Belt R. Co. v. American Cyanamid Co.*, 916 F.2d 1174 (7th Cir. 1990), the court, in overruling a district court decision imposing strict liability for a spill of a highly toxic chemical during shipment, relied heavily on factor (c). The court (speaking through Judge Posner, a leading advocate of economic analysis of tort doctrine), emphasized that courts make defendants strictly liable to encourage them to relocate activities, to substitute other, less hazardous ways of accomplishing the task, or to reduce the extent of the activity. 916 F.2d at 1177. Where the risk can be substantially controlled by due care, Posner concludes, such extreme measures are not called for, and strict liability should not be imposed. 916 F.2d at 1179.

It seems likely that other courts, however, would impose strict liability even though a toxic chemical is not unusually likely to escape. In

Rylands, the court spoke of a thing "likely to do mischief if it escapes" without suggesting that the force had to be one that is especially likely to escape. Some courts appear to focus primarily on the extent of the threat *if the chemical does escape*. See, e.g., *State, Department of Envtl. Protection v. Ventron*, 468 A.2d 150, 157 (N.J. 1983); Harper, James & Gray, §14.5, at 224; see also Restatement (Second) of Torts §520 cmt. g:

> If the potential harm is sufficiently great, however, as in the case of a nuclear explosion, the likelihood that it will take place may be comparatively slight and yet the activity be regarded as abnormally dangerous.

The rationale for strict liability supports placing the pollution loss from an accident like this on the operator, who creates and uses chemicals that pose a risk of widespread injury, is able to take steps to reduce the risk or substitute safer alternatives, and can insure against the risk it imposes on the community. Some legislatures have imposed strict liability for the costs of cleaning up toxic discharges. See, e.g., N.J. Stat. Ann. §58:10-23.11g(c). Such statutes reflect the same policy underlying common law strict liability, that the risks associated with unusually hazardous activities should be borne by the industries that generate them.

Cause for Concern

9.   In this case, the plaintiff's injury results from the hazardous activity, but the intervening act that causes the explosion is (at least arguably) unforeseeable. Were this a negligence case, most courts would conclude that the storage of the chemical was not the proximate cause of the resulting harm. So the example poses the issue of whether proximate cause limitations applicable to negligence cases apply to strict liability claims as well.

The Second Restatement would allow recovery in strict liability cases even if an unexpected act intervened:

> The reason for imposing strict liability upon those who carry on abnormally dangerous activities is that they have for their own purposes created a risk that is not a usual incident of the ordinary life of the community. If the risk ripens into injury, it is immaterial that the harm occurs through the unexpectable action of a human being, an animal or a force of nature.

Restatement (Second) of Torts §522 cmt. a. This reasoning makes sense. In this case, the hospital chose, for its own purposes, to impose the explosion risk on the community. The premise of strict liability is that it is fair to impose the unavoidable losses from such high risk activities on the actor rather than the victim.

However, some cases reject the Restatement view, and deny recovery where the accident results from unforeseeable events, natural disasters or intentional acts of third persons, even though the risk that makes the activity abnormally dangerous causes the injury. See *Smith v. Board of County Commissioners*, 146 N.W.2d 702, 704 (Mich. Ct. App. 1966), *aff'd*, 161 N.W.2d 561 (1968) (excessive rainfall); Restatement (Third) of Torts: Liability for Physical Harm (Basic Principles) (Tentative Draft No. 1) reporter's note pp. 432-446.

Such holdings illustrate the firm grip that the fault concept holds on the judicial mind. Negligence law limits liability to foreseeable accidents because the defendant is not negligent in failing to foresee the unforeseeable. But the basis for strict liability is unusual risk, not fault. The defendant is held liable for introducing a risk into the community that poses extreme danger if it miscarries, regardless of why it miscarries. Since the source of liability is creating the risk itself, imposing foreseeability limitations seems an unwarranted "judicial retreat from the logic of strict liability." J. Fleming, The Law of Torts 319 (7th ed. 1987). See also Harper, James & Gray, §14.5, at 225-232 (arguing persuasively against foreseeability limitations on strict liability).

10. Arguably, the defendant's conduct in this case was not the proximate cause of the plaintiff's harm. Blasting would foreseeably cause concussion damages, or hurl rocks on neighboring property, but it seems well beyond anticipation that it would cause the damages in this case. However, this in itself might not suffice to prevent recovery. *First*, as Example 9 explains, the Restatement view is that strict liability should not be limited to foreseeable harm. See Restatement (Second) of Torts §522 (actor liable even if harm is caused by "unexpectable ... action of an animal ..."). *Second* (though I didn't say so in the example), in *Foster* the plaintiff had *told* the defendant that his blasting was causing the mink to kill their young, and only sought damages for those killed after giving notice, 268 P.2d at 646-647. Thus, it is hard to argue that the harm was unforeseeable.

The better ground for denying strict liability in this case is that the type of harm caused was not the type that made defendant's conduct abnormally dangerous. Blasting creates a serious, irreducible risk of concussion, throwing of debris, and vibration of structures, not the scaring of mink. Under the Restatement (and the reasoning of *Foster*), strict liability is limited to the type of harm that makes the conduct abnormally dangerous. See Restatement (Second) of Torts §519(2); *Foster*, 268 P.2d at 647. Thus, the court refused to apply a strict liability standard to the case.

Even if the court refused to impose strict liability, wouldn't the defendant be liable on a negligence theory, since it was on notice of the risk? The testimony showed that to suspend blasting operations until the whelping season was over would have cost the defendant a full year of logging and required it to shut down its mill. In light of this, and the unusual sensitivity of the mink, the plaintiff evidently declined to proceed on a negligence theory.

13

Strict Products Liability: Basic Theories of Recovery

Introduction

The term *products liability* refers to claims for injuries caused by commercial products. Examples of such cases abound: A plaintiff is injured by a snowblower that lacks an adequate blade guard; a user of a prescription medication suffers an adverse side effect; a passenger in a car is injured when the brakes unaccountably fail; a child is caught under an electric garage door. This chapter addresses the basic theories of recovery available to such plaintiffs, with an emphasis on the cause of action for "strict products liability."

Background: Products Liability Theories Other Than Strict Liability

The recognition of "strict liability" for injuries due to defective products was one of the most dramatic developments of twentieth-century tort law. But why did it happen? Why weren't negligence law and other traditional remedies deemed adequate to remedy this class of tort claims?

A. Negligence Claims

Plaintiffs have long pleaded negligence claims in actions for injuries caused by products, and still do. But there are some significant hurdles to negligence recovery in products liability cases. For many years, the concept of "privity" barred negligence claims against manufacturers. The privity requirement, relied on in the oft-cited case of *Winterbottom v. Wright*, 152 Eng. Rep. 402 (Ex. 1852), held that a seller of goods only owed a duty of care to the purchaser of a product. Under *Winterbottom*, if a manufacturer sold a defective stagecoach to a transit company, and a passenger was injured due to a defect in the coach, the manufacturer was not liable. The manufacturer was only "in privity" with its direct buyer, the transit company, and therefore only owed a duty of care to the transit company. The same principle applied if the defect caused the coach to veer off the road into a pedestrian: The lack of privity between the pedestrian and the manufacturer precluded recovery.

However, the privity requirement was rejected in *MacPherson v. Buick Motor Co.*, 217 N.Y. 382 (N.Y. 1916), and virtually all courts today would follow *MacPherson*. See Restatement (Second) of Torts, §395 cmt. a. Courts now hold that a manufacturer owes a duty of care to all those who may foreseeably be injured by its products. Id., cmt. h, i. So, if that were the only problem with the negligence remedy, courts might not have felt the need to deploy other remedies to deal with product injuries.

But there are other problems with negligence claims for product injuries. It is often difficult to prove that a manufacturer's negligence led to the defect that injured the plaintiff. Even with good quality control, a small number of units of a product may come off the assembly line with defects. Although a plaintiff can invoke res ipsa loquitur, the jury may deny negligence recovery, accepting the defendant's argument that although it used due care such defects may still occur.

Another problem with negligence liability is that it will frequently provide no remedy against the available defendant. Suppose that a Colorado manufacturer's table saw is marketed through a chain of wholesalers, and ultimately sold to the plaintiff by a hardware store in Indiana. If the plaintiff is injured using the saw in Indiana, the manufacturer might not be subject to personal jurisdiction there. See *Asahi v. Superior Court*, 480 U.S. 102 (1987). The hardware store, which clearly would be subject to jurisdiction in Indiana, would very likely not be liable in a negligence action. It simply sold a product it bought from a wholesaler, probably without ever taking the saw out of its box or doing anything to prepare it for use. It is hard to see in such a case what act of the retailer falls below the standard of due care.

B. Breach of Express Warranty

Plaintiffs have also invoked several contractual theories of recovery for injuries due to product defects. One such theory is breach of express warranty under Article 2 of the Uniform Commercial Code. Section 2-313 of the Code allows recovery if a seller makes specific representations about the qualities of a product, and the buyer is injured due to the failure of the goods to fulfill those representations. This sounds pretty good, but is frequently a limited remedy. First, it only applies when specific representations were made to the buyer about the product feature that caused the injury. Statutory notice provisions, which require the buyer to notify the seller of the breach within a short time or be barred from recovering on the warranty, may also limit the remedy. See, e.g., *Greenman v. Yuba Power Products, Inc.*, 377 P.2d 897, 900 (Cal. 1963) (noting notice requirement under California statute). Traditionally, the buyer also had to prove that she had relied on the warranty, but under the Uniform Commercial Code reliance is presumed. See §2-313, cmt. 3. And, of course, the claim only arises if the feature that was the subject of the warranty causes the injury. If the seller warrants that a vehicle "has excellent brakes," and it doesn't, a plaintiff could sue for breach of the warranty if the brakes fail, but not if some other defect in the product causes her injury.

C. Breach of Implied Warranty of Merchantability

Another, somewhat broader contractual theory supporting recovery for injuries from product defects is breach of the "implied warranty of merchantability." In most states today this remedy is governed by the Uniform Commercial Code, which provides that a seller warrants (among other warranties) that its goods are "fit for the ordinary purposes for which such goods are used." UCC §2-314(c). This warranty arises by operation of law; it is not based on any representations of the seller. Thus, a plaintiff may recover by showing that the defendant was a dealer in goods of that kind, sold the goods, that they were not fit for the ordinary purposes for which they were sold, and that she suffered personal injury as a result of their unfitness for that purpose.

The implied warranty remedy approaches a strict liability cause of action, since the warranty arises automatically and allows recovery without any showing of negligence or misrepresentation by the seller. However, it also has limitations. First, it can be disclaimed, if it is done clearly. UCC §2-316. Second, the Code contains alternative provisions that states may adopt concerning who may recover for breach of the implied warranty. One alternative limits recovery to "any natural person who is in the family or household of his buyer or who is a guest in his home...." In a state that adopts this version of the section, the class of potential plaintiffs is quite limited. Injured employees, bystanders, or passengers in the buyer's car, for example, would not be within the scope of this warranty. Third, the warranty claim requires timely notice of the breach to the seller.

D. Misrepresentation

Another potential source of recovery for persons injured by products is the tort of misrepresentation. The plaintiff establishes a misrepresentation claim by showing that the defendant made a public misrepresentation (either intentionally, recklessly, negligently, or innocently) about a fact material to the transaction, that the plaintiff acted in reliance on that misrepresentation, and that she suffered injury because the product was not as represented by the seller. Restatement (Second) of Torts, §402B; Restatement (Third) of Torts: Products Liability §9.

One advantage of the misrepresentation claim is that the plaintiff may recover even if the product is not defective, as long as failure to live up to the representations led to the plaintiff's injury. If an all-terrain vehicle, for example, has a tendency to tip in certain situations, but the seller represented that it would not, the buyer could sue for misrepresentation, even if there was no defect in the vehicle. But the plaintiff must establish that she was actually aware of the seller's representation, and relied upon it in deciding to make the purchase or in using the vehicle.

Like the other remedies described, misrepresentation is a limited remedy. The most obvious limit is that there must have been an inaccurate representation by the seller about the particular characteristic of the product that led to the plaintiff's injury. If no relevant representation was made, the plaintiff has no claim. Another problem with the misrepresentation remedy is that it may not support recovery by third parties such as bystanders.

The Development of Strict Liability for Defective Products

In the mid-1960s, courts began to recognize a broader approach to products liability — strict liability for product defects. The seminal case was *Greenman v. Yuba Products, Inc.*, 377 P.2d 897 (Cal. 1963), in which Justice Traynor held a manufacturer strictly liable for an injury caused by a defective product. *Greenman* held that strict liability was appropriate in order "to insure that the costs of injuries resulting from defective products are borne by the manufacturers that put such products on the market rather than by the injured persons who are powerless to protect themselves." Id. at 901.

Since *Greenman*, courts have articulated several policy reasons for imposing strict liability on manufacturers for injuries caused by their products. The increasing sophistication of products makes it difficult for consumers to assess their risks, emphasizing the need for manufacturers to do so. The lack of any personal relationship between manufacturers and consumers means that buyers cannot rely on such relationships to assure quality. Instead, they must rely on information provided by the distant manufacturer. In addition, manufacturers encourage purchase of their products by extensive advertising. Courts have viewed such aggressive efforts to stimulate sales as fairly involving a quid pro quo: that manufacturers stand behind their products when they cause injuries. Other courts have argued that manufacturers should be held liable for injuries from defective products because they can redistribute that liability, through insurance, to all users of the product. Thus, the price of the product will reflect its true cost, rather than "externalizing" accident costs to innocent victims. In addition, the risk of liability will encourage manufacturers to make their products safer and to discover and disclose product risks that the consumer might not recognize. See generally Dobbs & Hayden, Torts and Compensation (4th ed. 2001) 626-629.

Shortly after *Greenman*, strict products liability gained momentum when the American Law Institute added §402A to the Second Restatement of Torts. The Restatements of the Law are drafted by the American Law Institute (ALI), an organization of eminent lawyers, scholars, and judges. The goal of the Restatements is to restate and clarify areas of the common law. The ALI, of course, has no authority to pass statutes or decide cases; thus, the adoption of §402A, endorsing strict liability for defective products, did not "create a cause of action" for strict liability. However, the Restatements are frequently influential, and it is doubtful that any provision in a Restatement has had more impact on courts than §402A. The Reporter for the Second Restatement was Dean William Prosser, the dean of Torts scholars of his day. His "restatement" of strict products liability in §402A, along with the *Greenman* case, virtually created the tort of strict products liability.

Restatement (Second) of Torts, section 402A.

Special Liability of Seller of Product for Physical Harm to User or Consumer

(1) One who sells any product in a defective condition unreasonably dangerous to the user or consumer or to his property is subject to liability for physical harm thereby caused to the ultimate user or consumer, or to his property, if

(a) the seller is engaged in the business of selling such a product, and

(b) it is expected to and does reach the user or consumer without substantial change in the condition in which it is sold.

(2) The rule stated in Subsection (1) applies although

(a) the seller has exercised all possible care in the preparation and sale of his product, and

(b) the user or consumer has not bought the product from or entered into any contractual relation with the seller.

Let's tease out the elements of the claim created by §402A. It authorizes recovery

1. by a *user or consumer*
2. from *a seller*,
3. who is *engaged in the business of selling the product*
4. for *physical harm*
5. caused by a *defective product*
6. that is *unreasonably dangerous*.

Note that §402A says nothing about how the product came to be defective and dangerous. Fault is not — on the face of §402A, anyway — an element of the claim, which is why the commentary to §402A declares that it creates "strict liability, making the seller subject to liability to the user or consumer even though he has exercised all possible care in the preparation and sale of the product." Section 402A cmt. a. However, in practice, courts have construed §402A to require proof of fault in many products liability cases, making many such claims almost indistinguishable from a negligence claim. (More to come on this below.)

The claim for strict products liability defined in §402A was quickly adopted in many states. Some courts simply adopted §402A verbatim as their law of strict products liability. "If ever a Restatement reformulation of the law were accepted uncritically as divine, surely it is section 402A of the Second Restatement of Torts." D. Owen, Defectiveness Restated: Exploding the "Strict" Products Liability Myth, 1996 U. Ill. L. Rev. 743, 744 (footnotes omitted).[1]

Types of Product Defects

Under §402A, a manufacturer is liable for injuries resulting from the "defective condition" of its products. Such product defects usually fall into one of three categories: manufacturing defects, design defects, and warning defects.

A. Manufacturing Defects

Cases based on manufacturing defects present the most straightforward type of products liability claims. In these cases, the plaintiff alleges that

---

1. Professor Owen indicates that only five states "never did succumb to the new religion" of strict products liability. 1996 U. Ill. L. Rev. at 745.

the product was defective because it did not meet the manufacturer's own specifications for the product. Suppose, for example, that a medical instrument has a structural defect due to contamination in the steel, and breaks while in use during an operation, injuring the patient. The gravamen of the plaintiff's claim is that the instrument was defectively manufactured — it did not come off the assembly line as the manufacturer intended. Or, a computer hard drive is somehow miswired, so that it catches fire when turned on. Again, the problem alleged is that the computer failed to meet the manufacturer's own design, and was consequently defective and dangerous.

Today, manufacturing defect claims are the only true "strict" products liability claims recognized in most states. The plaintiff recovers by showing that the product does not meet the manufacturer's own specifications for the product, and as a result the product was dangerously defective. If the product does not match the product specifications, it does not matter how the defect occurred. The plaintiff need not show that negligence led to the defect, or that the manufacturer should have discovered the defect. She need only establish that the defect existed, made the product unreasonably dangerous, and caused her injury. For example, if it turns out that the steel used in the medical instrument had an undetectable flaw when it was purchased by the manufacturer, the manufacturer would still be liable. The basis of the liability is selling the defective product, not faulty conduct that leads to the defect. It is commonly said that "the gravamen of the claim is the condition of the product, not the conduct of the defendant."

B. Design Defects

A product can also be defective if its design makes it unnecessarily dangerous to the user. A power saw, for example, may be quite safe with a blade guard, but invite risk of serious injury without one. A punch press with an exposed switch may lead to accidents when it is inadvertently started, while a recessed switch would eliminate the risk. Probably the lion's share of products liability claims are based on the theory that the product was defectively designed because it failed to eliminate the risk of injuries from its use. Frumer & Friedman, Products Liability §11.03[1][c].

Surely, however, a manufacturer should not be liable simply because its product involved *some* risk of injury. If so, auto makers would be liable for all motor vehicle injuries, knife manufacturers would pay for all cut fingers, and drug sellers would pay for even the most unexpected and unavoidable side effects of their medications. These products involve some risk of injury, but are often not *unreasonably* dangerous. Since many products cannot be functional without imposing some level of risk, products liability law needs some standard for distinguishing acceptable designs from those that pose unacceptable risks. "The goal of both design engineers and the law should be to promote in products an ideal *balance* of product usefulness, cost and safety." D. Owen, Defectiveness Restated: Exploding the "Strict" Products Liability Myth, 1996 U. Ill. L. Rev. 743, 754 (footnote omitted).

Section 402A provides that a product is "unreasonably dangerous" if it is "dangerous to an extent beyond that which would be contemplated by the ordinary consumer who purchases it, with the ordinary knowledge common to the community as to its characteristics." Restatement (Second) of Torts, §402A cmt. i. A good many courts have applied this test, which focuses on the consumer's expectations about the product. Others, however, have used a risk/utility balancing approach to design defect cases. Under this approach, the factfinder decides, applying a number of factors, whether the product's design represents a fair balance between the cost of designing the product to prevent the risk of injury, the effect the redesign would have on the utility of the product, and the extent of the risk that the product poses.

> [I]n evaluating the adequacy of a product's design pursuant to this latter standard, a jury may consider, among other relevant factors, the gravity of the danger posed by the challenged design, the likelihood that such danger would occur, the mechanical feasibility of a safer alternative design, the financial cost of an improved design, and the adverse consequences to the product and to the consumer that would result from an alternative design.

Barker v. Lull Engineering, 573 P.2d 443, 455 (Cal. 1978).

The choice between the consumer expectations test and the risk/utility test has been a hotly disputed one. While many courts have applied §402A's consumer expectations test, the drafters of the ALI's Third Restatement of Torts: Products Liability, adopted in 1997, chose to endorse the risk/utility test. Restatement (Third) of Torts, Products Liability, §2(b) and cmt. d.

Ironically, while plaintiffs' advocates tend to favor the consumer expectations approach, that test does not always support broader liability than the risk/utility approach. Some products might meet consumer expectations but not satisfy the risk/utility test. A consumer might, for example, think a machine with an exposed switch was a reasonable design, or not have thought anything about it one way or the other. However, if the switch could easily be relocated to avoid inadvertent start-ups, the design might fail the risk/utility test. In *Halliday v. Sturm, Ruger & Co.*, 792 A.2d 1145 (Md. 2002), the plaintiff argued that simple design changes in a hand gun would have prevented the death of a three-year-old child, who was killed playing with the gun. But the court, applying the consumer expectations test, held that the product had functioned exactly as expected, and was not defective, even if a simple redesign would have prevented the accident. The *Halliday* court's choice to invoke the consumer expectations test doomed the plaintiff's case, while a risk/utility test might have gotten the case to a jury.

Yet the consumer expectations test has several advantages plaintiffs embrace. It is more intuitive, leaving more leeway to the jury to make a common sense evaluation of the product. And, proving a design defect under this approach does not require the plaintiff to demonstrate a safer way to design the product. She need only show that the product was less safe than a reasonable consumer would expect. This may allow the plaintiff to establish her claim without hiring an expensive expert witness to testify about alternative designs that would have eliminated the danger that injured the plaintiff. In some cases, a product may not live up to consumer expectations, even though it cannot be redesigned to be safer. Consumers may reasonably anticipate that a product will function safely (and the manufacturer's advertising may create such expectations), although it in fact poses serious risks that the consumer would not anticipate. An interesting article on the controversy between the tests (H. Bowbeer, T. Cavanaugh & L. Stewart, *Timmy Tumble v. Cascade Bicycle Co.*: A Hypothetical Case under the *Restatement (Third)* Standard for Design Defect, 30 U. Mich J.L. Ref. 511 (1997)) offers the example of a dirt bike with a shock absorber that fails in certain circumstances. A consumer might well expect the bike to function more safely than it does, yet be unable to suggest a redesign that would eliminate the risk. If so, it might be defective under the consumer expectations test, even if there is no feasible safer alternative design.

The Third Restatement endorses the risk/utility approach to design defects, but also requires the plaintiff to establish that "a reasonable alternative design" would have eliminated the risk that injured the plaintiff. Restatement (Third) of Torts, Products Liability, §2(b). This can be an imposing evidentiary problem, involving evidence of costs of materials, production techniques in a specialized industry, complex price calculations, and analysis of the collateral effects of the hypothetical alternative design on function and marketability of the product.[2] The evidence must show that "the suggested alternatives are not only technically feasible but also practicable in terms of cost and the over-all design and operation of the product." *Wilson v. Piper Aircraft Corp.*, 577 P.2d 1322, 1327 (Or. 1977).

If the plaintiff cannot demonstrate a reasonable alternative design that would eliminate a product risk, then the product is presumably not defective under the Third Restatement approach. Yet it may still pose more danger than consumers would expect. In such cases the design would be

---

2. The Third Restatement throws a bone to consumer-expectations advocates, however, by providing that consumer expectations about product dangers are relevant to the risk/utility analysis in a design defect case. Restatement (Third) of Torts: Products Liability, §2 cmt. g.

defective under the consumer expectations test, but not under the Third Restatement. Some detractors of the Third Restatement argue that the consumer expectations approach is preferable because some products — such as cigarettes and asbestos — may be unreasonably dangerous even if they cannot be designed to be safer. Others endorse the risk/utility test in general, but argue that the plaintiff should be able to prove that a design is defective, because it poses excessive risk, even if she cannot demonstrate a feasible alternative design that would eliminate the danger.

Some courts have held that a product is defective if it fails *either* the consumer expectations test or the risk/utility test. See, e.g., *Barker v. Lull Engineering Co.*, 573 P.2d 443 (Cal. 1978); cf. Ohio Rev. Code §2307.75A (statute providing that product design is defective if it fails either test). If Maryland accepted that position, the *Halliday* plaintiff could have argued that even if the gun was as safe as a consumer would expect it to be, it was defective, because it could have been made safer without impairing its function.

Cases since the adoption of the Third Restatement (in 1997), with its strict risk/utility approach to design defect claims, including the reasonable-alternative-design requirement, have been mixed. Certainly, there has been nothing like the broad acceptance that greeted §402A. Some courts have rejected the requirement that the plaintiff in a design defect case establish a reasonable alternative design. See, e.g., *Delaney v. Deere and Co.*, 999 P.2d 930, 945 (Kan. 2000). Others have continued to apply the consumer expectations test, rejecting the risk/utility test entirely. *Guilbeault v. R.J. Reynolds Tobacco Co.*, 84 F. Supp. 2d 263, 267 (D.R.I. 2000).

Regardless of which test a state adopts, design defect claims will generate a vigorous defense from manufacturers. A manufacturing defect claim alleges that a single unit of a product was defective, because something went awry in the manufacturing process. When the plaintiff claims that the product design is defective, a lot more is at stake, since a design defect claim asserts that all units of the product are defective. A finding that the product's design is unreasonably dangerous suggests that the product should not be marketed at all, unless it is redesigned to reduce the risk of injury.

C. Defects Due to Failure to Warn

The third common type of strict products liability claim involves failure to warn the user of dangers associated with a product's use. Many products are safe if used as intended, but pose risks of injury if not properly used. A hay baler may pose a risk of entangling the user if the gears are not disengaged before clearing obstructions. A drug may pose a risk of adverse reactions if taken with alcohol. A solvent may prove useful and safe, if the user wears gloves while applying it, but cause serious allergic reactions to exposed skin.

In such cases, the user is often the "cheapest cost avoider": She can avoid the risk posed by the product at a low cost, by taking precautions in using it, while redesigning the product to eliminate the risk would be considerably more costly — or impossible. However, if the user is to avoid the risk, she must have clear directions and warnings to allow her to do so. Thus, a product may be safe enough with the appropriate warnings and directions, but unreasonably dangerous without them. Plaintiffs frequently allege that a product, though reasonably designed, was defective for failure to provide such warnings of the dangers posed by its use.

What dangers does a manufacturer have the duty to warn users about? Because each case turns on its facts, it is hard to articulate a standard other than that of reasonable care. The manufacturer should consider the extent of the risk, the likelihood that it will arise, the user's likely understanding about the danger, the means available to convey a warning, the likelihood that too many warnings will decrease the effectiveness of each, and other factors in deciding which warnings to give. The Second Restatement suggests that a consumer should be warned if a danger is "not generally known, or if known is one which the consumer would reasonably not expect to find in the product." Restatement (Second) of Torts §402A cmt. j. The Restatement (Third) of Torts: Products Liability throws similar language at the problem: "[W]arnings must be provided for inherent risks that reasonably foreseeable product users and consumers would reasonably deem material or significant in deciding whether to use or consume the product." Section 2, cmt. i; see also id., first paragraph (detailing factors the court should consider in assessing the adequacy of a warning). This language, studded with references to reasonable conduct, suggests that "strict" liability for failure to warn turns basically on a reasonableness standard. "In effect, warning claims are negligence claims, as a number of courts agree." D. Dobbs, The Law of Torts 1005 (footnote omitted).

If a warning is required, it must be an *adequate* warning, that is, one calculated to clearly alert the user to the danger and how to avoid it.

> [T]he warning must plainly describe the *Nature* of the risk; its *Severity*, its *Scope*; and the means of *Avoidance.* . . . To illustrate, the Nature of the risk might be conveyed by language like, "Radioactive," "Live Electricity," "Poisonous." Severity could be described by language such as "2000 Volts," "Severe Burns if Used Without Protective Clothes," "No Antidote." Scope might be stated by, for example, "Unprotected Exposure Causes Chronic Respiratory Illness." Means of Avoidance could be explained by language like "A Facemask Must be Worn," or "If Contact With Skin Or Eyes, Irrigate with Water For 20 Minutes and Seek Medical Attention Immediately."

J. Diamond, L. Levine & M. Madden, Understanding Torts, 2000. Here again, the jury will likely be instructed to assess the adequacy of the warning under a general reasonableness analysis.

A product may also be defective because it provides inadequate directions for use or assembly. Directions are different from warnings, and both may be required. In *Midgeley v. S.S. Kresge Co.*, 127 Cal. Rptr. 217 (1976), for example, a telescope, which was safe if properly assembled, caused injury to the plaintiff's eye, because the sun filter was not properly installed. The court held the telescope was defective without proper instructions for installing the sun filter.

The Second and Third Restatement Approaches Compared

The Third Restatement of Torts: Products Liability, adopted in 1997, "restates" strict products liability law in somewhat different terms than §402A. First, it explicitly categorizes products liability claims as manufacturing defect claims, design defect claims, or failure to warn claims. Section 2(b). It also adopts the risk/utility test for design defect claims, rather than §402A's consumer expectations test. Id. In addition, it requires the design defect plaintiff to establish that a reasonable alternative design was available. Id.

The Third Restatement also takes the position that there should be one unified claim for injury due to product defect, replacing the melange of claims that courts have recognized based on negligence, warranty, and strict liability. Thus, liability under the Restatement would exist, no matter what theory the plaintiff asserted in her complaint, only if the liability standard of Restatement (Third) §2 was met. See §2 cmt. n. This too does not reflect settled law. In many states, a claim for strict products liability, whether based on case law or a state products liability statute, may be asserted along with other claims based on negligence or breach of warranty. See, e.g., *Singer v. Federated Dept. Stores, Inc.*, 447 N.Y.S.2d 582 (N.Y. Sup. 1981); *Nicolodi v. Harley-Davidson Motor Co., Inc.*, 370 So. 2d 68 (Fla. App. 1979) (discussing products liability cases brought on multiple theories).

It is not at all clear that the Third Restatement will be widely accepted. Its standard for design defects, in particular, has met fierce opposition from plaintiff advocates. Since its publication, a number of courts have continued to endorse the consumer expectations test, or have applied risk/utility analysis without the reasonable-alternative-design requirement. It is likely that many courts will also continue to allow plaintiffs to try their cases on negligence, warranty, and strict liability theories simultaneously. Indeed, §402A remains the law in many states today, though frequently embellished with local quirks and quiddities.

The Third Restatement has been criticized for attempting to establish a new products liability regime, rather than "restating" current doctrine. This criticism may be accurate, but it is also ironic: When Dean Prosser drafted §402A of the *Second* Restatement, it was directly supported by only one case! While Restatements are generally meant to clarify and organize accepted doctrine, they have on occasion pushed the law into dramatically new channels. Section 402A is probably the most striking example of a Restatement taking the law in a new direction rather than summarizing accepted principles.

Statutory Changes to Products Liability Law

For the most part, strict products liability law, like most tort law, is *state* law.[3] The principles of strict products liability developed through the common law process, that is, by decisions in individual cases. The right to recover on a strict products liability claim, the types of defects that would support recovery, and the applicable defenses were established through judicial opinions. Statutes in the strict products liability area were rare.

Recently, however, many states have supplemented or displaced their common law principles of products liability by enacting statutes that define and limit products liability claims. These statutes may address myriad issues, including limitations periods in products liability cases; definitions of product defect; the relation of product liability claims to other available theories; the effect of plaintiff's fault, misuse, or assumption of the risk; the state-of-the-art defense; privity requirements (or the lack thereof); limitations on the liability of sellers; the nature of the warnings required; limits on particular claims (such as tobacco or firearms cases); punitive damages; the effect of compliance with safety statutes; and many other issues. Some states have attempted to simplify products liability litigation by creating an *exclusive statutory tort remedy* for injury from defective products. See, e.g., Conn. Gen. Stat. §52-572n(a). In such states, a plaintiff sues under the statute, and cannot assert additional common law claims asserting negligence, breach of implied warranty or other product liability theories.[4] This chapter reviews general principles of products liability doctrine, but remember that the devil is in the details, and the product liability details may very well be covered by statute in your state.

---

3. Congress does have authority to regulate interstate commerce. United States Constitution, Article I, §8, clause 3. Interpreted liberally, this could support a good deal of federal tort legislation. But so far Congress has not broadly regulated tort law through the Interstate Commerce Clause.

4. For a lengthy compendium of state products liability statutes, see Frumer & Friedman, Products Liability, Vol. 8 App. C.

How Strict Is "Strict Products Liability"?

If strict liability means that the defendant is liable for causing an injury without fault, only manufacturing defect cases satisfy that definition in most states today. In manufacturing defect cases (almost certainly the least common of the three categories),[5] the manufacturer is liable simply for selling a product that turns out to be defective, without proof of any fault.

In design defect cases, however, the plaintiff must establish that the product design was inadequate, under a standard that looks much like a negligence test. Under a risk/utility standard, the jury must decide whether the manufacturer made a reasonable trade-off, in designing its product, between risk and the expense of preventing that risk. This "Hand formula" type assessment of the design decision is very close to the reasonable person standard of negligence law. Arguably, design defect liability is "strict" if a court uses the consumer contemplation test, which theoretically only considers the nature of the product sold, rather than the defendant's conduct in designing it. But this too can be conceptualized as negligence, the unreasonable choice to market a product that does not satisfy consumer expectations for safety.

Similarly, in warning cases, the question basically comes down to whether the manufacturer made a reasonable choice in deciding not to warn, or in the nature of the warnings it provided. Thus, while courts frequently refer to "strict products liability," a strong case can be made that, in all but manufacturing defect cases, Dean Prosser's dramatic §402A remedy has become a negligence claim with a good many specialized rules, but a negligence claim nonetheless.

In working through the examples below, assume that §402A of the Second Restatement applies, unless otherwise indicated.

EXAMPLES

Parameters of Strict Products Liability

1. In each of the following cases, there is an issue as to whether strict liability under Restatement (Second) §402A would apply. Can you spot the problem in each?

   a. Menendez buys an Acme framing machine for use in his picture framing business. For some reason, the machine repeatedly breaks down, leading Menendez to suffer delays and lose business.

---

5. One study concluded that design defect claims constituted 75 percent, and warning claims, 18 percent of strict products liability claims. See Owen, Montgomery & Keeton, Products Liability and Safety — Cases and Materials (3d ed. 1996) 24.

b. Fun & Fitness Gyms provides exercise facilities for busy professionals with fancy jobs. It buys an exercise machine from Ace Equipment Company, but decides it is too small for its purposes and buys a bigger model. It sells the smaller machine to Florio, a customer. Florio is injured when the machine tips over while he is using it in his basement. He sues Fun & Fitness under §402A.

c. Paramount Construction Company buys a concrete mixing truck directly from Constantine Truck Bodies, a manufacturer of trucks. Due to a design defect, sand added to the mix escapes into the gears that turn the mixer, destroying the mixer. Paramount brings suit against Constantine under §402A.

d. Merriman goes to Scott Motors, the local Ford dealership, to test drive a new Ford. She takes it for a spin, but when a car stops short in front of her and she hits the brakes, they fail. She is injured, and sues Scott Motors, claiming a design defect in the brakes under §402A.

e. Argento Electric installs wiring in Porazzo's house. One of Argento's electricians strips the insulation too far back off a wire, causing a fire that extensively damages the house. Porazzo sues Argento Electric under §402A.

Responsibility Without the Blame

2. Computex Corporation manufactures computers. It sells a computer to Tech Store, a computer products store, which resells it to Gutierriez. She takes it home and plugs it in. It catches fire, and the fire damages her home.

Investigation reveals tiny teeth marks on the wires inside the computer — mice had evidently gotten in at some point during the manufacturing process and chewed off some insulation, allowing a short circuit that started the fire. Gutierriez sues Tech Store and Computex on a strict products liability theory. Will either defendant be liable to her?

3. Gutierriez brings a strict liability claim against Computex, on a manufacturing defect theory. In a second count in her complaint, she seeks recovery on a negligence theory. Is this proper?

4. Assume that investigation reveals that the offending mouse must have gotten in at Tech Store's retail store, rather than during the manufacturing process. Which defendant, if either, would be liable to Gutierriez under §402A?

5. Assume instead that the fire resulted from a printed circuit board inside the computer. Computex had bought the circuit board from Allied Wiring Corporation and installed it, without alteration, in the computer. Somehow, the circuit board had been misprinted, leading to the fire. Who would be liable to Gutierriez under §402A?

Designs and Defects

6.   In *Pouncey v. Ford Motor Co.*, 464 F.2d 957 (5th Cir. 1972), the blade of a radiator fan broke off, striking Pouncey in the face. Examination revealed (according to the plaintiff's expert, anyway) a high level of impurities in the steel in the blade, which would tend to make it more prone to breakage. Is this a manufacturing defect case or a design defect case? Why do we care?

7.   Algren develops a taste for Smirnoff Vodka in college. She becomes an alcoholic, her husband leaves her, and she loses her job. She sues Smirnoff's, alleging that its vodka is defective and unreasonably dangerous because it can lead to alcoholism.

   a. Under §402A, how do you think the court would go about rejecting Algren's claim that vodka is defective and unreasonably dangerous?

   b. Algren sues instead for failure to warn that consumption of vodka may lead to addiction. What result?

8.   Perini purchases a Honda motorcycle, and is injured in a collision with a car. When he was hit, the motorcycle fell over, and his right leg, under the cycle, was crushed. He sues, claiming that the cycle should have had crash bars that would have protected his legs in a crash of this type.

   If you represented Perini, and had the choice to sue in a jurisdiction that would apply the consumer expectation test to this design defect case, or alternatively, one that would apply the risk/utility test, which would you think preferable for your client's case?

Liability for Failure to Warn

9.   Durabrand Power Tools makes a stamping machine for metal fabricators. The machine has an on/off switch away from the stamping area, but no guard to protect the operator's hands from entering that area. Such a guard could be included, but it would reduce the speed of production somewhat. On the bed of the machine, directly in front of the operator, is a warning label, in large red letters: WARNING: KEEP HANDS FROM STAMPING AREA TO AVOID SERIOUS INJURY OR AMPUTATION! Gainor, using the machine, is distracted by a co-worker. She turns, and her hand drifts into the stamping area and is seriously injured. What is the best argument that Durabrand should be liable under principles of strict products liability?

10. Parker purchases an electric hedgeclipper from his local hardware store, Acme Hardware Company. The clipper was purchased fully packaged from Garden Products, Inc., the manufacturer, with directions inside and various warnings on the clipper itself as well as in the directions. Acme never opens the box, but sells the clipper to Parker still in the

package. Parker is injured using the clipper when the clipper dips into a puddle and Parker receives a shock. Neither the directions nor the clipper provided any warning about the danger of shock through this type of occurrence.

Parker sues Acme Hardware, alleging strict liability for failure to warn. Assuming that there should have been a warning about this risk, will *Acme Hardware* be liable to Parker?

Limits of the Duty to Warn

11. Lawrence Ladder Company makes step ladders. Paoli buys a Lawrence ladder for use in painting his house. As he is trying to reach a high point on the side of the house, he puts one foot on the next-to-the-top step of the ladder, and the other on the little paint shelf opposite to it. The paint shelf collapses, and Paoli falls. He sues Lawrence, alleging that it failed to warn him of the danger of climbing on the paint shelf. Lawrence argues that it owes no duty to warn consumers of dangers from the *misuse* of its products. Will its argument prevail here?

12. Juarez buys a set of oversized wheels for her pick-up truck. The tires bear a label stating that they should not be installed on a truck larger than a certain size. Plaintiff installs the tires on hers, even though it is larger than the specified size. She is injured when the truck rolls over in an emergency stop. Juarez brings a products liability claim, arguing that the warning on the tires was inadequate. Is it?

Material Risks

13. Leahy Pharmaceuticals develops a new drug for depression, called Perzac. Leahy tests the drug thoroughly for three years before placing it on the market, and discovers several side effects, but no hint of any psychiatric side effects. It markets Perzac, warning of several side effects but not of a 3 percent risk that the drug may cause a psychotic reaction. Collier takes Perzac, has a psychotic reaction, and brings suit against Leahy, alleging it is liable for selling Perzac without a warning of the danger of psychotic reactions.[6]

    a. Leahy argues that it is not liable, because the benefits of the drug justify marketing it, even if it does cause an adverse reaction in some patients. What would Collier argue to counter this argument?

---

6. Leave aside for the moment the question of *who* must be warned of the risks from the drug. Under the "learned intermediary doctrine, drug manufacturers can frequently discharge the duty to warn of drug risks by warning the medical providers who prescribe them.

b. Leahy argues that it is not liable, because only 3 percent of patients experience the adverse reaction, too small a percentage to merit a warning. How do you think the court would rule on this argument?

Elements, Elements

14. Daniel suffered respiratory injuries when Shroeder, a co-worker in a restaurant, poured chlorine bleach instead of cleaning fluid into a deep fat fryer. Shroeder testified that he was in a hurry, grabbed the bottle by mistake, and poured it into the fryer. The chlorine vaporized, injuring Daniel's lungs. She sued the manufacturer of the bleach, alleging that the label on the bleach bottle should have contained a warning against exposing it to heat. What problems do you anticipate Daniel will have in proving her failure-to-warn claim?

EXPLANATIONS

Parameters of Strict Products Liability

1a. Section 402A allows recovery for "physical harm" caused by defective products that are unreasonably dangerous. Here, Menendez has not suffered physical harm — meaning, generally, personal injury or damage to property. He has suffered loss of business due to the failure of the machine to perform as expected. Section 402A was not intended to cover this type of claim. Fundamentally, this loss is a commercial loss due to the failure of the goods to live up to contractual expectations. Courts have generally held that the buyer should be left to contractual remedies for the failure of the product to meet contractual requirements. See Frumer & Friedman, Products Liability, §13.07[2].

b. The problem here is that Fun & Fitness is not "engaged in the business of selling such a product." Its business is providing exercise facilities, not selling exercise equipment; this sale was an aberration, rather than its regular business. Section 402A limits liability to sellers who are in the business of selling the product that caused the injury.

> The basis for the rule is the ancient one of the special responsibility for the safety of the public undertaken by one who enters into the business of supplying human beings with products which may endanger the safety of their persons and property, and the forced reliance upon that undertaking on the part of those who purchase such goods.

Restatement (Second) of Torts, §402A cmt. f. Most of the rationales for strict liability do not apply to a situation like this. Fun & Fitness is not in a position to spread the cost of this product injury, since it neither regularly makes nor sells exercise equipment. It is not in a position to improve the design of the equipment, in any direct way, since it doesn't design them. It doesn't advertise or promote the sale of exercise machines, so it cannot be said to have induced the sale or promoted reliance on its expertise.

c.   Here, the damage caused by the product defect is to the product itself. There's a fair argument that this constitutes "physical harm thereby caused to the ultimate user or consumer, or to his property." Restatement (Second) §402A. After all, the defect did cause physical harm to the user's property, the truck itself. However, most courts applying §402A have held that when a defect causes injury to the product itself, rather than to other property, the owner is limited to contractual remedies. The Third Restatement also takes this position. Restatement (Third) of Torts (Products Liability) §21 cmt. d.

d.   Under §402A it is proper to sue a retailer as well as a manufacturer. Scott Motors is a "seller . . . engaged in the business of selling such product," so it is a proper defendant under §402A. But Merriman's problem here, if it is one, is that there hasn't been a sale. Merriman is a customer, but not yet a buyer when she is injured. Section 402A speaks of "one who sells any product . . ." and here Scott hasn't sold it yet. However, it is unlikely that a court would take this literally, when the product was offered for sale by a seller. The rationale for strict liability involves the distribution of products that impose risks on users. This product has done that, even though it has not yet been purchased. Requiring sale to the consumer smacks of the old privity requirement; §402A, by contrast, allows recovery by many plaintiffs who never bought anything from the defendant. ("It is not even necessary that the consumer have purchased the product at all. He may be a member of the family of the final purchaser, or his employee, or a guest at his table, or a mere donee from the purchaser." Restatement (Second) §402A cmt. l.) Thus, Scott probably won't prevail on the argument that it is not liable because the sale never transpired. For a case rejecting the argument, see *Rivera-Emerling v. Fortunoffs of Westbury Corp.*, 721 N.Y.S.2d 653, 654-655 (App. Div. 2001).

e.   The problem here is that the claim does not arise from the sale of a defective product. It arises from faulty installation, which is the provision of a service. Section 402A creates a remedy for dangerously defective products, not for faulty rendition of services. Porazzo will likely have to look to other remedies, either under contract or negligence law.

The issue would be closer if Argento's electricians installed defective wiring, manufactured by Superior Electric, and a defect in the wire caused the fire. Clearly, Superior would be liable under §402A, as a seller (to Argento) of the defective wire. But would Argento be a "seller" on those facts? Surely the cost of the wire is incorporated into its contract price for the work, so in some sense it is a seller of the wire. But the sale is incidental to Argento's main work — electrical installations. Similarly, a plumber may provide a gasket for sealing gas lines when installing a new gas stove. Doubtless, a charge for this will appear on the plumber's bill, but most courts would hold that the plumber is not primarily "engaged in the business of selling such product" (Restatement (Second) of Torts, §402A(1)(A)) and therefore not liable under §402A. See, e.g., *Cafazzso v. Central Medical Health Services, Inc.*, 668 A.2d 521 (Pa. 1995) (medical providers not strictly liable for defect in prosthetic device implanted during surgery).

Responsibility Without the Blame

2.   Both Computex and Tech Store will be liable to Gutierriez under §402A. They each are in the business of selling computers, and both sold one that was defective and unreasonably dangerous, and led to physical harm to Gutierriez's house. Computex, of course, did not sell it to Gutierriez, but that isn't required under §402A: Manufacturers and intermediate sellers (such as wholesalers) are liable to consumers injured by the products they sell, as well as the retailer who directly deals with the consumer. Privity is not a requirement.

In this case, neither Computex nor Tech Store did anything negligent; the mouse was the guilty party. Although the defect here is neither a failure of the manufacturing materials nor misassembly, the manufacturer and retailer are still liable. It is enough under §402A to establish that the seller sold a defective product. The plaintiff need not establish that the product was defective due to negligence.

This case would come out the same way under the Restatement (Third) of Torts: Products Liability. Under §2(a) of the Products Liability Restatement, sellers are strictly liable for manufacturing defects in their products, "even though all possible care was exercised in the preparation and marketing of the product." Several of the rationales for strict liability support this result, including the manufacturer's ability to spread the cost of accidents from product defects through price, the incentive that liability will give manufacturers to inspect products carefully, and the inability of the consumer to protect herself from such defects.

3.   In many states, it is proper to assert multiple tort theories for recovery in a products liability case. The adoption by courts of a cause of action for strict products liability was meant to expand plaintiffs' remedies, not to bar their resort to traditional causes of action that might also apply. A plaintiff might sue for negligence, breach of implied warranty, breach of express warranty, misrepresentation, and strict products liability, if the evidence supports each theory.

The elements of a negligence claim and a manufacturing defect claim are slightly different. On her negligence claim, Gutierriez will have to establish that Computex failed to exercise reasonable care in making or inspecting the computer. As Example 2 illustrates, she doesn't have to show that to recover on a strict liability claim for defective manufacture. Often, there will be little point to asserting the negligence claim if strict liability applies, but in some states statutes of repose or limitations or other defenses might defeat one claim but not the other.

As the Introduction indicates, some states have passed products liability statutes that create an exclusive remedy for injuries from defective products. Because claims for misrepresentation, negligence, and strict liability overlap in some respects, but differ in others, some states have sought to simplify products liability cases by limiting the plaintiff to a single "products liability" claim. See, e.g., N.J.S.A. 2A:58C-1b(3), *Canty v. Ever-Last Supply Co.*, 685 A.2d 1365 (N.J. Super. 1996) (New Jersey Products Liability Act signaled intention of legislature to replace common law negligence theories in products liability area with statutorily defined cause of action). In these states, Gutierriez would have a single claim defined by the statute.

4. In this case, Tech Store would be liable but Computex would not. Computex sold the product, but it was not defective when it left Computex's control. It is not strictly liable for defects that occur later. Similarly, it would not be strictly liable for a defect that arose from shipping or weather damage after the product was shipped. The product was defective, however, when it was sold by Tech Store, so it would be liable to Gutierriez under either §402A or the Third Restatement, §2(a).

5. This is another manufacturing defect case, but here the defect is in a component Computex purchased and incorporated into its finished product. Computex will be liable for the fire. The defective component made the finished product defective, since it was unreasonably dangerous and led to the fire. Again, Computex did not do anything "wrong," but is strictly liable for the damage caused by its defective product.

Both Allied Wiring and Tech Store will also be liable to Gutierriez under §402A, since they also sold the defective product that led to the fire. Allied sold the defective printed circuit board. As a seller, it remains responsible for damages caused by that product, even if it is incorporated into a finished product and resold to a consumer. See, e.g., *Jenkins v. T & N P.C.*, 53 Cal. Rptr. 2d 642, 645 (Cal. App. 1996).

Designs and Defects

6. You can't really answer this question without more information. If the blade that broke was like all blades on Ford radiator fans — if they all had the same level of impurities in the steel — this is a design defect case. Pouncey would argue that Ford's design choice to use that type of steel in its fans was inappropriate, in light of the risks of failure of the blades. If, however, discovery revealed that the level of impurities in this fan blade

was an aberration, the case would be a manufacturing defect case, since the fan blade did not conform to Ford's own design specifications for the product.

Classifying the case matters, because if it is a manufacturing defect case, the plaintiff need not shoulder the expensive burden of proving that the design was defective, under risk/utility analysis or a consumer expectations standard. (What consumer really has any expectations at all about this?) It need only show that the fan did not conform to manufacturing specifications, and that the resulting defect led to Pouncey's injury. If that is true, Ford would be "strictly" liable for Pouncey's injury.

7a. It appears that Algren's claim is based on design defect rather than manufacturing defect. She does not claim that the vodka was adulterated in some way, but that vodka, in its intended form, is unreasonably dangerous. If the claim were accepted, Smirnoff would be liable to all alcoholics, since they marketed the product in an unsafe form.

The court will almost certainly reject Algren's argument, based on the fact that vodka, while it has risks, cannot be made safer without fundamentally altering its nature. It would be great if we could have unlimited vodka without hangovers or addiction. But that isn't one of the choices. If products liability law dubs alcohol defective and unreasonably dangerous because it poses risks, it condemns the entire product, since it can't be redesigned and still be vodka. While courts might be willing to brand some such products unreasonably dangerous (cigarettes and asbestos are two possible candidates) they have generally been unwilling to assume the role of arbiters of public conduct in this way. Consequently, courts have seldom concluded that products that pose risks, but cannot serve their intended purposes without those risks, are defective.

> Good whisky is not unreasonably dangerous merely because it will make some people drunk, and is especially dangerous to alcoholics; but bad whiskey, containing a dangerous amount of fusel oil, is unreasonably dangerous. . . .

Restatement (Second) of Torts, §402A cmt. i. The Third Restatement takes a similar position. Restatement (Third) of Products Liability, §2 cmt. d. Under the consumer expectations test, the product passes muster because consumers understand its dangers and accept them as inseparable from the product itself. Under a risk/utility test, vodka is not defective, since it can't be redesigned to be completely benign and still be vodka; there is no reasonable alternative design.

b.   Since the court will not likely hold that vodka is "defectively designed," Algren tries a failure to warn theory. Even if it is reasonable to market a product that poses risks, a manufacturer may be liable for failure to warn users of risks from its use. But here the risk is so generally known that the court will almost certainly hold that a warning is unnecessary, simply because there is no duty to tell people what they already know. In *Garrison v. Heublein, Inc.*, 673 F.2d 189 (7th Cir. 1982), the court rejected the failure to warn argument in an alcohol case on this theory.

It might be different if the risk were less generally understood. For example, until recently the effect of alcohol on unborn children was not general knowledge, though it was likely understood by medical personnel and distillers. A claim for failure to warn of potential damage to fetuses might have prevailed in those circumstances. This risk is one that cannot be eliminated. While it may not warrant a ban on alcoholic products, it is appropriate to warn pregnant women of this risk, so they can avoid it.

8.   The consumer expectations test very likely would be less favorable in this case. Most consumers would probably recognize the risk that a motorcycle will be knocked over, and that if it is, a rider's leg may be crushed underneath it. They would probably be surprised to learn that cycles can be fitted with crash bars that offer protection against leg injuries. Thus, the cycle without such crash bars probably comports with most consumers' expectations.

However, a fair case can be made by design experts that the cycle could be made safer with little effect on its operation. In a jurisdiction that applies the risk/utility approach, this evidence might establish that the cycle was defective, even though it was as safe as most consumers would expect it to be. See *Camacho v. Honda Motor Co., Ltd.*, 741 P.2d 1240 (Colo. 1988), in which the court splits on the proper test to use in a case with similar facts.

Liability for Failure to Warn

9.   Gainor should argue that a warning was an insufficient response to the danger posed by the machine. Instead, the manufacturer should have eliminated the risk altogether by designing a guard that would prevent the operator's hands from entering the stamping area. Although a guard would have slowed production somewhat, under a risk/utility analysis this loss in production speed is likely outweighed by the increased safety. It is foreseeable — indeed, almost inevitable — that an operator's hands will end up in the stamping area now and then, due to some form of accident, the temptation to adjust the work despite the danger, or sheer inadvertence, as in Gainor's case. If that is true, the machine is probably defective if it lacks a guard.

Assuming that a reasonable design required a guard, Durabrand's argument that it provided a *warning* of the danger likely will not avoid liability. Interestingly, §402A appeared to endorse the defendant's argument here. See §402A cmt. j (product not defective if a warning was given, and a product could be safely used if the warning was heeded). Courts, however, have generally rejected cmt. j, as does the Third Restatement.

Restatement (Third) of Torts, Products Liability, §2 cmt. l (when safer design is possible, warning not adequate alternative). The manufacturer should not be able to avoid liability for a defective design by giving notice of the danger it should have designed out of the product. It would frequently be cheaper for the manufacturer to warn of a defect in its product than to redesign the product to make it reasonably safe. If a warning were a defense to design defect liability in such situations, it would undermine the incentive to make products safer. Thus, the court will almost certainly reject the argument that the warning is a proper substitute for a safer design.

10. The Introduction notes that since a reasonableness standard governs products liability claims for failure to warn, many authorities question whether there is really a difference between negligence and strict liability in failure to warn cases. This example illustrates one significant difference. Surely, if Parker sued Acme Hardware for negligence, he would lose. They didn't do anything negligent. They just bought a packaged product from a presumably reputable manufacturer and resold it to a customer. It was Garden Products that was negligent. But under §402A, Acme is a "seller," and would be liable if the warning is inadequate. It will likely have an action against Garden Products for indemnification, but Parker will still be able to sue the local seller for his injury. See, e.g., *In Re Shigellosis Litigation*, 647 N.W.2d 1, 5-6 (Minn. App. 2002); *Crowe v. Public Building Commission of Chicago*, 383 N.E.2d 951, 952 (Ill. 1978).

A number of states now limit the plaintiff's right to sue downstream sellers, either by statute or judicial decision. Indiana, for example, limits products liability claims to the manufacturer of the product or component that caused the injury, unless the manufacturer is not subject to personal jurisdiction in the action. Ind. Code §34-20-2-3, §34-20-2-4 (2003). See also Del. Code, tit. 18, §7001(b). These statutes reflect the view that the manufacturer, who designs the product, fabricates it, and decides what warnings to give, should bear liability for injuries it causes. In states that allow suit against the retailer, the retailer will have a right of indemnification — reimbursement — from the manufacturer if it is held strictly liable to the plaintiff.

Limits of the Duty to Warn

11. The example raises the question of whether manufacturers can be strictly liable for failing to warn a consumer about the dangers of various ways she might misuse their products.

In *Greenman v. Yuba Power Products, Inc.*, Judge Traynor spoke of strict liability for a product's "intended" use. 377 P.2d 897, 901 (Cal. 1963). Similarly, §402A refers to dangers in "normal handling and consumption." Restatement (Second) of Torts, §402A cmt. h. Since consumers can come up with all kinds of ridiculous ways to misuse a product, Lawrence's argument that it should not be required to warn Paoli of the dangers posed by unintended uses is a credible one.

The case law, however, has generally recognized a duty to warn of *foreseeable* misuses that result from human nature acting upon opportunity. It is highly foreseeable that a user, stretching to reach the top of a window, will be tempted to gain some altitude by putting one foot on that paint shelf. If it is dangerous to do so, that danger can be averted by a warning. Many courts have held that defendants have a duty to warn of such foreseeable misuses. Frumer & Friedman, Products Liability, §12.05; see generally D. Owen, Defectiveness Restated: Exploding the "Strict" Products Liability Myth, 1996 U. Ill. L. Rev. 743, 780-781. It is likely that this approach will continue in jurisdictions that adopt the Third Restatement, which imposes liability for "reasonably foreseeable uses and risks." Restatement (Third) of Torts, Products Liability, §2 cmt. l.

Of course, Paoli may be *negligent herself* for trusting her weight to the paint shelf without inquiry. If so, her negligence can be taken into account under principles of comparative negligence or assumption of risk, rather than concluding that the manufacturer had no duty to warn of this misuse. (This is analyzed in detail in the next chapter.) If the manufacturer can avoid serious and foreseeable accidents from such foreseeable misuse by printing a warning on the shelf, products liability standards should encourage it to do so.

12. This notice is almost certainly inadequate. Arguably, it isn't a warning at all; it's an instruction about how to use the product. It is frequently insufficient to simply instruct consumers not to use a product in a particular way. A true warning should inform the consumer of the nature and extent of the risk posed by ignoring the instructions. As one court stated,

> it may be doubted that a sign warning, "Keep off the Grass," could be deemed sufficient to apprise a reasonable person that the grass was infested with deadly snakes. In some circumstances a reasonable man might well risk the penalty of not keeping off the grass although he would hardly be so daring if he knew the real consequences of his failing to observe the warning sign...."

Post v. American Cleaning Equip. Corp., 437 S.W.2d 516, 520 (Ky. 1968). Without a sense of the reason for obeying instructions, people have a human tendency—whether reasonable or not—to ignore them if obedience is inconvenient. To really affect consumers' behavior, a warning must convey the nature and gravity of the risk of ignoring instructions. "Warning! Use of these tires on trucks heavier than 2000 pounds may cause serious injury or death from rollover accidents!" would be an obviously more effective warning.

Material Risks

13a. This argument is easily refuted. Leahy Pharmaceuticals argues that the benefits Perzac provides to most users makes it reasonable to market the drug, even if a few users suffer side effects. But Collier hasn't challenged Leahy's decision to market Perzac. He claims that while it was reasonable to market the drug despite the small risk of psychotic reactions, users *should have been warned* about that risk. When a drug is widely beneficial, yet presents risks to some users that cannot be eliminated, warnings give users the information they need to make choices about the product. If Collier had been warned of the risk of psychotic episodes, she could have made an informed decision whether to run that risk or avoid the product. Because the drug had no warning of the risk of a psychotic reaction, Collier was unable to make that choice.

So, Leahy can't defend the failure to warn claim on the ground that its choice to market Perzac, despite the risk, was a reasonable one. A manufacturer must be reasonable both in choosing to market a drug that poses risks, and in informing users about the risks it cannot eliminate from that product. See Restatement (Third) of Products Liability, §2 cmt. k.

b.   Leahy's argument here is that it had no duty to warn of the risk, because it was a small one. Many cases consider whether a risk was sufficiently substantial to merit a warning. In deciding whether a warning of a particular hazard should be given, courts have taken a general reasonableness approach, considering such factors as the gravity of the risk, how likely it is, whether the user will already be aware of it, and whether adding another warning to the product would decrease the effectiveness of *other* warnings. Because warnings are easy to provide, they will usually be warranted if the risk is one the ordinary consumer would want to know about. While the need for a particular warning is usually a question of fact, it is likely that a manufacturer should warn of a serious reaction suffered by 3 percent of users.

In the medical malpractice area, some courts hold that a patient should be warned of all risks she would consider material in deciding whether to undergo the procedure. See, e.g., *Scott v. Bradford*, 606 P.2d 554 (Okla. 1979). Logically, a similar standard might be applied to products liability failure to warn claims, but has apparently been invoked only occasionally. See D. Dobbs, The Law of Torts 1006.

Elements, Elements

14. One problem Daniel faces is convincing a jury that this type of misuse of the product is sufficiently likely that the defendant should have warned about it. Manufacturers can't warn about *everything*, since excessive

warnings tend to undercut the impact of each one.[7] Nor can manufacturers anticipate every preposterous manner in which people will, in the fullness of time, misuse their products.

Assuming that Daniel could convince a jury that a warning of this risk was needed, she faces another elemental problem: causation. Given Shroeder's testimony, it appears that even if the label had warned about this risk, Shroeder never would have read it, since he grabbed the bottle in haste and poured without examining the label. Products liability plaintiffs, like other tort plaintiffs, must establish that the defendant's defective product was a "but for" cause of her harm, that is, that the injury would not have happened if the product had not been defective. See Chapter 7, pp. 141 ff. Here it seems likely that the injury would have happened the same way even if the manufacturer had provided an adequate warning to keep the bleach away from heat, since Shroeder would not have read it. Don't lose sight of the fact that causation must always be proved in a products liability case, as in other tort cases.

Defendants frequently raise this argument when the plaintiff admits that she did not read the label or directions on a product. Courts have sometimes resolved the problem by creating a presumption that an adequate warning (perhaps with exclamation points, red capital letters, or a skull and crossbones, or prominently placed) *would* have been read. But even this helpful presumption may be rebutted when the evidence indicates — as it probably does here — that an adequate warning would not have come to the user's attention.

---

7. The defensive tendency to overwarn in order to limit liability has been referred to as "warnings pollution." D. Owen, Defectiveness Restated: Exploding the "Strict" Products Liability Myth, 1996 U. Ill. L. Rev. 743, 766.

14

More Products Liability: Common "Defenses" to Strict Products Liability Claims

Introduction

The previous chapter considered the elements a plaintiff must establish to recover on a claim for "strict products liability."[1] We saw that strict products liability allows an injured party to recover against a *seller* for *personal injury or property damage* caused by *defective* products. We also saw that proof that a product was defective depends on the type of defect alleged. A plaintiff who claims injury from a manufacturing defect may recover by proving that the product was dangerously defective, but need not prove that negligence by the manufacturer led to the defect. However, in design defect and failure to warn cases, the plaintiff must make a showing that looks very much like negligent conduct by the manufacturer.

---

1. This chapter uses the term *strict products liability* to refer to claims under §402A of the Second Restatement of Torts, §2 of the Third Restatement of Torts (Products Liability), or similar state law, authorizing recovery for injuries caused by defective products.

This chapter considers a number of "defenses" that are commonly asserted in strict products liability cases to defeat liability. The word "defense" is in quotation marks because several of these issues are probably not, strictly speaking, affirmative defenses. The term *affirmative defense* refers to evidence offered by a defendant that may avoid liability, even though the plaintiff proves the basic elements of her claim. Several of the issues covered here are true affirmative defenses, including comparative negligence and assumption of the risk. But others, such as the state-of-the-art "defense," the argument that a danger was "open and obvious," and the "defense" of misuse, might better be characterized not as defenses, but as challenges to the plaintiff's ability to make a prima facie case of product defect.

While the issues reviewed in this chapter arise in products liability cases in every state, their treatment varies considerably from one state to another. For example, a plaintiff's negligence may bar a products liability recovery entirely in one jurisdiction, reduce it in others, and have no effect at all in others. This chapter emphasizes basic arguments that defendants commonly raise in products cases to avoid liability, and the various approaches the states have taken in analyzing those arguments. Remember that tort law is state law, so every state makes its own. Thus, states may, and do, take different approaches to defenses in strict products liability cases.

The Effect of Plaintiff's Negligence

Let's start with a true affirmative defense, contributory or comparative negligence. In strict products liability cases, as in traditional negligence cases, defendants frequently argue that the plaintiff should be barred from recovering because her own negligence contributed to her injury. For example, suppose that Accu-Cut Corporation makes a saw with a blade that tends to stick if used to cut stock that is thicker than one inch. Ramirez, the plaintiff, uses the saw and senses that something isn't right, but continues to work. On one cut, the saw sticks and the board kicks back, injuring Ramirez. The saw may well be defective, because it tends to throw the work back (or because of failure to warn not to use it for thicker cuts). However, Ramirez may also have contributed to his injury, by continuing to cut the stock despite this problem.

A. The Background: Treatment of Plaintiff's Fault in Negligence Cases

In cases brought on a negligence theory, such "contributory negligence" by a plaintiff barred her entirely from recovery in most states, until the 1960s. Since then, however, contributory negligence has been replaced in most states by comparative negligence. Under comparative negligence, a plaintiff whose negligence contributed to an injury may still recover, but her recovery will be reduced by the percentage of fault the jury attributes to her. If, for example, Ramirez sued Accu-Cut on a negligence theory, and the jury concluded that Ramirez was 30 percent at fault for continuing to use the saw for thick cuts, his damages would be reduced by 30 percent. In a good many states, Ramirez would be barred from any recovery if his negligence reached a certain level — either 50 or 51 percent.

B. Evolution of Treatment of Plaintiff's Fault in Strict Products Liability Cases

When §402A was added to the Restatement (Second) of Torts, in 1965, contributory negligence — which fully barred the negligent plaintiff from recovery — was the general rule in *negligence* cases. However, the drafters concluded that contributory negligence should not bar recovery on a strict products liability claim. Restatement (Second) of Torts, §402A cmt. n. Strict liability was thought of as a different type of liability, intended to place the risk of injury from defective products on the seller, even if the plaintiff's negligence was also a cause of her injury. Early cases under §402A followed comment n, refusing to bar plaintiffs in strict products liability cases even if their negligence was a factor in causing their injury. See Prosser & Keeton on Torts (5th ed.) 712.

However, as states abandoned the complete bar of contributory negligence in negligence cases, in favor of comparative negligence, litigants inevitably began arguing that comparative negligence principles should apply to strict products liability claims as well. Indeed, in many products liability cases, the plaintiff asserts both a negligence claim and a strict products liability claim, based on the same underlying conduct of the defendant. It seems odd that the plaintiff's negligence would reduce her recovery on the negligence count, but be ignored on the strict liability count in the same case.

One argument against applying comparative fault to strict products liability claims is that it requires the jury to compare apples and oranges. In a negligence case, the jury compares the defendant's negligence to the plaintiff's. But how do you compare a defendant's *strict liability* for selling a defective product to the plaintiff's *negligence* in using it? These are conceptually different types of conduct: The defendant's liability arises without any fault at all (at least, in manufacturing defect cases), while the plaintiff's fault is based on negligence.

On the other hand, reducing recovery for a plaintiff's fault furthers several goals of tort law. It encourages care by plaintiffs, and causes negligent plaintiffs to share the loss caused in part by their negligence. The common sense of this approach has led many states to apply comparative fault to strict products liability claims as well as negligence claims. In these states, the jury is instructed to assign a percentage of causal responsibility to the seller-defendant, for selling the defective product, and to the plaintiff, for her negligence in using the product. If the jury finds the seller 70 percent responsible, for example, and the plaintiff 30 percent responsible, the plaintiff will recover 70 percent of her damages. Although it may be a bit conceptually messy to assign percentages of "responsibility" to these different types of conduct, experience indicates that juries manage to do it reasonably well, and apportioning responsibility in such cases probably serves the goals of tort law better than ignoring the plaintiff's fault entirely.[2]

Because the jury compares strict liability to negligence in such cases, some states now call their statutes comparative "responsibility" statutes rather than "comparative negligence" statutes. See, e.g., Tex. Civ. Prac. & Rem. Code Ann. §33.001 ("proportionate responsibility"); see also Restatement (Third) of Torts: Apportionment of Liability, Topic 1 (entitled "Basic Rules of Comparative Responsibility"). Others still call their statutes "comparative fault" schemes, but define fault broadly, to include the sale of a defective product. The Arkansas comparative fault statute, for example, applies to "any act, omission, conduct, risk assumed, breach of warranty, or breach of any legal duty which is a proximate cause of any damages sustained by any party." Ark. Code Ann. §16-64-122. The broad phrase "breach of any legal duty" surely includes strict liability for selling a defective product. Similarly, the Maine comparative fault statute applies to a "breach of statutory duty or other act or omission that gives rise to a liability in tort." 14 Me. Rev. Stat. Ann. §156. This too would include a strict products liability claim.

Note that adopting comparative negligence in strict products liability cases has a very different impact than adopting it in negligence cases. States switched to comparative negligence in negligence cases to allow plaintiffs *some recovery,* even if they were partly responsible for their own injury. Under the harsh contributory negligence doctrine, a plaintiff whose negligence contributed at all to her injury recovered nothing. Under comparative negligence, a negligent plaintiff now recovers reduced damages. But switching to comparative negligence for strict products liability claims often leads to a smaller recovery for plaintiffs. Under the approach of §402A cmt. n, the products liability plaintiff *recovered fully despite her negligence.* Switching to comparative responsibility principles in strict products liability cases means that a negligent plaintiff will recover less than before, because her negligence (ignored before) will reduce her damages.

---

2. As Judge Richard Posner has wryly observed, the law "is an instrument of governance, not a hymn to intellectual beauty." *Newman-Green, Inc. v. Alfonzo-Larrain R.,* 854 F.2d 916, 925 (7th Cir. 1988).

Today, the effect of a plaintiff's negligence in a strict products liability case varies from state to state. A few states still adhere to the approach of comment n, that a plaintiff's negligence is irrelevant to a strict products liability claim. In these states, a negligent plaintiff recovers fully despite her negligence in using the product. "A strong majority"[3] of states, however, now treat such negligence as a partial defense to a strict products liability claim. A negligent plaintiff's damages will be reduced by the percentage of fault the jury assigns to her. If the applicable comparative fault statute bars a plaintiff from recovery if she is 50 percent or more at fault, the same rule is applied to strict products liability claims. Last, at least one state, North Carolina, treats contributory negligence as a full defense to a strict products liability claim. Any negligence of the plaintiff bars her from recovery entirely. See *Nicholson v. American Safety Utility Corp.*, 488 S.E.2d 240, 244 (N.C. 1997).

Assumption of the Risk

Just as the adoption of comparative negligence has spread from negligence cases to strict products liability cases, it has also affected the treatment of another traditional defense, assumption of the risk. To understand current approaches to assumption of the risk in strict products liability cases, we need to recall how that defense has evolved in negligence cases.

A. The Background: Treatment of Plaintiff's Assumption of Risk in Negligence Cases

Fifty years ago, most courts held that a plaintiff who recognized a risk and made a deliberate choice to encounter it was barred from recovering from the defendant who created the risk, even if the defendant was negligent in creating the risk. See Restatement (Second) of Torts, §496A. Suppose, for example, that Quentin, an obviously intoxicated driver, offered Tanaka a ride, and Tanaka accepted and was later injured due to Quentin's negligent driving. Under the concept of assumption of the risk, a negligence claim by Tanaka would be barred by his deliberate choice to accept the risk of driving with Quentin. See id., illus. 2. The idea was that the plaintiff's deliberate choice to proceed in the face of clear knowledge of the danger constituted a kind of consent to the risk posed by the defendant's conduct, even if it had been negligently created by the defendant. See generally Chapter 22, infra.

The advent of comparative negligence has altered the treatment of assumption of the risk in negligence cases. Today, many states that have comparative negligence regimes treat a plaintiff's conscious choice to encounter

---

3. Restatement (Third) of Products Liability, §17 cmt. a.

a risk as a form of negligent conduct. Thus, the jury will be instructed to assign the plaintiff a percentage of fault for deliberately encountering the risk, just as they do for other forms of plaintiff's negligence. Consequently, assumption of the risk, like other forms of plaintiff's negligence, becomes a partial defense to a negligence claim rather than a complete bar to his recovery. In the drunk driving case, for example, the jury might find Tanaka 30 percent at fault for choosing to ride with Quentin, and Quentin 70 percent at fault for driving while intoxicated. If so, Tanaka would recover 70 percent of his damages. In states that treat a plaintiff's deliberate choice to engage in the risk as comparative negligence, the separate defense of assumption of the risk is abolished. See, e.g., Mass. Gen. Laws ch. 231, §85; see generally D. Dobbs, The Law of Torts 539.

A few states, however, continue to treat conscious assumption of the risk as a separate and full defense to a negligence action, even though they otherwise apply comparative negligence to account for a plaintiff's negligence. See, e.g., *Kennedy v. Providence Hockey Club, Inc.*, 376 A.2d 329 (R.I. 1977); see generally V. Schwartz, Comparative Negligence, §9.03. This is clearly a minority position, but you should keep in mind that despite the strong trend toward applying comparative negligence, not all states have abolished the separate assumption of the risk defense.

B. Evolution of Treatment of Assumption of the Risk in Strict Products Liability Cases

With assumption of the risk, as with plaintiff's negligence, the evolution of the law in negligence cases has affected strict products liability claims as well. When the American Law Institute adopted §402A, it took the position that a plaintiff's deliberate assumption of the risk (unlike contributory negligence) should bar her from recovery entirely.

> [T]he form of contributory negligence which consists in voluntarily and unreasonably proceeding to encounter a known danger, and commonly passes under the name of assumption of risk, is a defense [to liability] under this Section as in other cases of strict liability. If the user or consumer discovers the defect and is aware of the danger, and nevertheless proceeds unreasonably to make use of the product and is injured by it, he is barred from recovery.

Restatement (Second) §402A cmt. n. Strict products liability cases initially followed this approach. See, e.g., *Johnson v. Clark Equipment Co.*, 547 P.2d 132 (Or. 1976); Annot., Products Liability: Contributory Negligence or Assumption of Risk as a Defense under Doctrine of Strict Liability in Tort, 46 A.L.R.3d 240 §5 (1972).

In recent years, however, a good many states that have adopted comparative negligence, and treat assumption of risk as a form of negligence in *negligence* cases, have adopted the same approach for *strict products liability* claims as well. That is, they now treat a plaintiff's conscious choice to encounter the risk posed by a defective product as a form of comparative fault. See, e.g., Iowa Code Ann. §668.1 (applying comparative negligence to "unreasonable assumption of risk"); Utah Code Ann. §78-27-37(2) (same). The Restatement (Third) of Torts: Products Liability adopts this position — that assumption of the risk should be treated as a form of plaintiff's "responsibility" that reduces rather than bars recovery. "The majority position is that all forms of plaintiff's failure to conform to applicable standards of care are to be considered for the purpose of apportioning responsibility between the plaintiff and the product seller or distributor." Restatement (Third) of Torts: Products Liability §17 cmt. d.

Once again, however, the law is not uniform on the point. Some states continue to treat a plaintiff's conscious assumption of the risk as a complete defense in strict products liability cases. See, e.g., *Tafoya v. Sears Roebuck & Co.*, 884 F.2d 1330, 1341 (10th Cir. 1989) (applying Colorado law); *Fiske v. MacGregor Div. of Brunswick*, 464 A.2d 719, 727-729 (R.I. 1983); see generally Restatement (Third) of Torts: Products Liability §17, reporter's note to cmt. d, p. 263. So, though it is frustrating to students, who would like to know "what the law is," the law again varies from state to state. A plaintiff's conscious assumption of the risk posed by a defective product will reduce her recovery in many states, but in a few it still stands as a complete defense. In these latter states, a plaintiff who doesn't recognize the danger posed by a product, but should (i.e., who is negligent, but has not consciously assumed the risk), will have her damages reduced to account for her negligence. A plaintiff who recognizes the danger and proceeds to use the product, however, will recover nothing.

The "Defense" of Misuse

While cases sometimes refer to a "misuse defense," misuse of a product may affect a strict products liability claim in several ways. Sometimes misuse defeats the plaintiff's prima facie claim, because it indicates that the product was not defective; in other cases, it constitutes a form of plaintiff misconduct that reduces or bars recovery.

Let's start with misuse that defeats the plaintiff's initial proof of a strict products liability claim. Sometimes people use a product in truly unforeseeable ways, ways so unusual that the manufacturer, when it made the product, would not reasonably have anticipated them. In these cases, a court (or a jury) may find that the product was not defective, even though it was dangerous when used as the plaintiff did, because it was never designed to be put to that use. In *Venezia v. Miller Brewing Co.*, 626 F.2d 188 (1st Cir. 1980), for example, the plaintiff sued the manufacturer of a beer bottle that shattered when he threw it against a telephone pole, injuring his eye. The court held that the manufacturer could not be held liable for the plaintiff's injury, because beer bottles are not designed to withstand such "use."[4] A court might hold the same way if the plaintiff inhaled spark plug cleaner to get high, or used a revolver to drive a nail.[5] In these examples,[6] the plaintiff's "misuse" is not an affirmative defense, but rather prevents the plaintiff from establishing a prima facie case. She cannot establish that the product was defective, since she does not show that it was used for a purpose the manufacturer intended or should have foreseen. Such a use is "so unusual that the average consumer could not reasonably expect the product to be designed and manufactured to withstand it." *Findlay v. Copeland Lumber Co.*, 509 P.2d 28, 31 (Or. 1971).

It is conceptually tidier to view such misuse as defeating the plaintiff's proof of her prima facie case, rather than as an affirmative defense. However, courts often hold that the plaintiff loses in such cases due to a "misuse defense," and several states have adopted statutes that expressly make "misuse" an affirmative defense. See, e.g., Ariz. Rev. Stat. §12-683(3); Conn. Gen. Stat. §52-5721. It is important to recognize, however, that in cases like this the plaintiff loses entirely, since the manufacturer was not bound to make its product safe for an unforeseeable use.

In other strict products liability cases, the plaintiff's injury may be caused by a defect in the product, but also by her own misuse of it. Take, for example, the plaintiff who stands on the paint shelf of a step ladder. This is not the intended use of the shelf, but it is a foreseeable one. Consequently, the maker of the ladder probably has a duty to warn against that use. The plaintiff may well convince a jury that the ladder was defective without a warning of this. But it is also true that the reasonable person should know better than to stand on the paint shelf. Doing so is a negligent misuse by the user.

In cases like this ladder example, the plaintiff has used the product in a foreseeable manner, and may be able to prove that it was defective. The defendant, however, pleads the plaintiff's negligent misuse as an affirmative defense. ("Even if the ladder was defective for lack of a warning about standing on the paint shelf, you were negligent too, since the reasonable person would realize that it was dangerous to stand on it.") The treatment

---

4. For a ridiculous example of this unforeseeable use concept, consider *May v. Gillette Safety Razor Co.*, 464 N.E.2d 401 (Mass. App. Ct. 1984). In *May*, the plaintiff swallowed a razor blade. His estate sued Gillette, alleging that it was not (as it was represented) made of stainless steel, and therefore did not show up on an x-ray! The court refused recovery, on the ground that a razor blade is not defective even if it will not show on an x-ray. Gillette was not bound to design a razor blade with this use in mind. (We never do find out, from the brief rescript opinion, how the decedent managed to swallow the blade.)

5. See *Jimenez v. Sears, Roebuck and Co.*, 904 P.2d 861, 872 (Ariz. 1995) (Martone, J., concurring).

6. For more examples of radical misuse, see D. Owen, S. Madden & M. Davis, Madden & Owen on Products Liability (3d ed.) 58-60.

of this type of misuse varies, as explained above in discussing comparative negligence. Some jurisdictions ignore a plaintiff's negligence in strict products liability cases. If she is injured in one of those states, the plaintiff's misuse in stepping on the shelf will not affect her strict products liability claim against the manufacturer. Other jurisdictions, a clear majority now, treat such negligent misuse by a plaintiff as a form of comparative fault, and reduce her recovery to account for it. In those states, the plaintiff would be assessed a percentage of fault for misusing the shelf as a step, and her recovery would be reduced by that percentage.[7]

But suppose that the plaintiff fully appreciated the danger of misusing the product, and proceeded to misuse it that way anyway? For example, the plaintiff realizes that a table saw should have a guard, and that hers does not, but uses it anyway, confident that she can avoid injury. Here, the plaintiff's "misuse" could be characterized as conscious assumption of the risk, the deliberate choice to encounter a risk created by the defective product. And here again, the effect of such deliberate misuse will vary from state to state. Some states still treat such deliberate misuse as a complete defense, as §402A recommends. Other states—now most—treat it as a form of plaintiff's fault.

Misuse of a product may undermine a plaintiff's strict products liability claim in yet another way: She may misuse a product in such an unexpected way that she loses based on ordinary proximate cause analysis. Here's a classic example. In *Daniell v. Ford Motor Co.*, 581 F. Supp. 728 (D.N.M. 1984), the plaintiff deliberately locked herself in a car trunk, intending to commit suicide. She then changed her mind, but was unable to get out, because the trunk lid had no inside release. The car may have been defective for lack of a release, but the court held that even if it was defective, Ford would not be liable for such an unforeseeable occurrence as the plaintiff's failed suicide attempt. In this case, the bizarre nature of the plaintiff's misuse barred recovery even if she proved that the product was defective.

Products liability law would be conceptually cleaner if courts stopped treating the concept of "misuse" as a separate defense in products liability cases. The term adds little that isn't better accounted for by other concepts. When the plaintiff uses a product for an unforeseeable purpose, courts could simply hold that she has failed to prove that the product was defective. When the product is defective, but the plaintiff contributes to her injury through negligent or deliberate misuse, courts could address that conduct through the affirmative defense of plaintiff's fault or assumption of risk. See D. Dobbs, The Law of Torts 1026. If the misuse led to a completely unforeseeable type of harm (as in the *Daniell* case), the court could resolve the case under traditional proximate cause analysis.

---

7. In jurisdictions that bar a plaintiff from recovering if her negligence exceeds 50 percent, she might lose entirely.

However, under current strict products liability law, the term *misuse* is frequently invoked, in each of the forms discussed above. The term is enshrined in statutes in some states as well. So the concept is certain to remain important in strict products liability cases. To understand its use, you need to recognize the different roles that the plaintiff's misuse may play: that it may defeat proof of defect, establish an affirmative defense to the claim (or partial defense), or establish that the resulting harm was unforeseeable.

The Open and Obvious Danger "Defense"

Another argument defendants raise in product liability cases is that the danger that injured the plaintiff was "open and obvious." Suppose that a cook gets cut while using an Accu-Cut knife, and sues Accu-Cut for failing to warn him of the danger of cuts. Accu-Cut will no doubt argue that it is not liable for failure to warn, because the risk of being cut by a knife is open and obvious. This is another phrase that is loosely used. Sometimes the fact that a danger is obvious is no defense at all. In other cases in which a danger is obvious and cannot be eliminated from the product, obviousness defeats a plaintiff's prima facie case for failure to warn, since there is no need to warn people of dangers they fully understand.

Distinguish two types of open and obvious dangers: ones that can't be designed out of a product, and ones that can. Suppose Sno-Begone Company markets a snow blower on which the snow-throwing blades are completely exposed. The owner stumbles against the blades and is injured. The danger of the exposed blades may be obvious, but the snow blower is still unreasonably dangerous, because this obvious danger *should have been designed out*. Because it is easy to add a shield over the blades, this design fails either the consumer expectations test or the risk/utility test. Since that is true, Sno-Begone cannot avoid liability by claiming that the danger was open and obvious. Although the danger is obvious, it should not be there at all. Sno-Begone cannot avoid liability by arguing that while its product design was unreasonably dangerous, it was obviously so. If this argument worked, manufacturers would not have a duty to design reasonably safe products. And the more egregiously dangerous the design was, the less risk the manufacturer would run of being held liable. When the danger can be eliminated at a reasonable cost, it should be, whether it is obvious or not. Sno-Begone should not be permitted to avoid liability by claiming that the danger posed by its machine was blatant.

Compare the knife case. The danger of cutting a finger with a sharp knife is obvious. But here, the risk is not the result of a design flaw; to do its job, a knife must be sharp. Although the knife poses a risk of cuts, it is not an unreasonable risk, and can't be eliminated without undermining the utility of the product. So the design of the knife is not defective, despite the danger of cuts.

However, the plaintiff may argue that even if the knife had to be sharp, it should have included a warning of the risk of cuts. "If you couldn't design this risk out of the knife, at least you *could have warned me about it.*" In other words, the plaintiff is thwarted on her design defect theory, and tries a failure to warn theory instead. Here, the obviousness of the danger plays a different role. If a danger is obvious, there is no need to warn about it, because people know about obvious dangers (whichever they are, but they surely include cuts from knives). So, the plaintiff will lose on her *design defect* claim, because the danger is inseparable from the product, reasonably designed. And she will lose on her *failure to warn* claim, because the manufacturer has no duty to warn people of dangers they already understand.

Just One More: The State-of-the-Art "Defense"

Here's one more "defense" that is probably not logically a defense at all. During the formative period of strict products liability law, the 1960s to the 1980s, a hotly disputed issue was whether a product was defective if it posed dangers that were unknown at the time of sale, and could not reasonably have been discovered through investigation and testing. Suppose, for example, that a drug manufacturer marketed a drug, after reasonable testing, without any reason to anticipate that it might cause an allergic reaction. However, after widespread use by large numbers of patients, it became clear that the drug leads to an allergic reaction in a small percentage of users. If a user who suffered a reaction brought suit on a strict products liability theory, the manufacturers would argue that given the state of the art at the time they sold the drug — that is, the state of scientific knowledge about its risks — they had no reason to anticipate this type of injury. It would be unfair, they argued (and still argue, vehemently), to hold them liable for marketing a drug that posed a risk they could not recognize when they marketed it.

Under a negligence standard, this seems right. But in those heady days when §402A swept the nation, the thinking was that strict liability was *not* negligence liability; it was *strict* liability, based on the seller's distribution — with or without fault — of a defective product. Arguably, if the drug lacked a warning of a dangerous side effect, or if its design entailed an unacceptable risk of injury, it was defective, whether or not the seller could have known of the defect.

While one treatise suggests that rejecting the state-of-the-art defense would impose a duty that "could only be met, perhaps, by hiring Merlin, the magician of Arthurian legend, who lived backwards,"[8] several of the rationales for strict liability support liability for such unknowable defects.

---

8. Frumer & Friedman, Products Liability, §12.02[4].

These include the ability of the manufacturer to insure and distribute the loss, reliance by consumers on the safety of products, and the incentive that liability provides to ferret out product risks. In the early days of §402A, several courts, convinced by these arguments, rejected the state-of-the-art defense in strict products liability cases, holding instead that manufacturers were liable for failure to warn of unknowable dangers of their products. See, e.g., *Beshada v. Johns-Mansville Products Corp.*, 447 A.2d 539, 546-547 (N.J. 1982).

However, most of the more recent cases have rejected this position, concluding that manufacturers are not liable for failing to warn of a danger unless they knew or should have known of the need for a warning. *Vassallo v. Baxter Healthcare Corp.*, 696 N.E.2d 909 (Mass. 1998); *Fibreboard Corp. v. Fenton*, 845 P.2d 1168 (Colo. 1993); F. Vandall, Constricting Products Liability: Reforms in Theory and Practice, 48 Vill. L. Rev. 843 (2003). Even New Jersey, which started the brouhaha by rejecting the state-of-the-art defense in *Beshada*, subsequently endorsed it in *Feldman v. Lederle Labs.*, 479 A.2d 374 (N.J. 1984). Once again, however, there are contrary holdings. See *Shanks v. Upjohn Co.*, 835 P.2d 1189 (Alaska 1992) (rejecting state-of-the-art defense) and *Sternhagen v. Dow Co.*, 935 P.2d 1139 (Mont. 1997), a comprehensive opinion rejecting the defense despite its recognition in the Third Restatement of Torts.

While the state-of-the-art argument is frequently referred to as a defense, it may be conceptually clearer to conclude that the manufacturer has not committed a tort by selling a product that posed an unknowable risk of injury. This characterization matters, because if this is an element of the plaintiff's prima facie case rather than a defense, she will have the burden to establish that the manufacturer should have been aware of or discovered the danger before selling the product. Once again, the state of the law is mixed: Some states have treated it as a defense, and others have simply placed the burden on the plaintiff to establish that the risk could have been discovered by the seller. See D. Dobbs, The Law of Torts 991.

There are many other interesting defensive issues in products cases, including preemption of state products liability law by federal law, the "learned intermediary" doctrine, the government contractor defense, and others. Those, however, are grist for an advanced products liability course. For now, let's focus on sorting out the five basic issues discussed above.

EXAMPLES

Some Apples and Oranges

1. Ortney sues Pretoria Motor Company for injuries she suffered when the brakes on a Pretoria sedan she was driving suddenly locked, causing an accident in which she was injured. Prior to the accident, Ortney had noticed

that the brakes seemed "a little sticky," but had not taken the car in to have them checked. Ortney's complaint asserts a strict liability claim based on defective design of the brakes. Pretoria claims that Ortney was negligent, since she did not have the car serviced after noticing brake problems.

    a. If the jury found that the brakes were defectively designed, but also that Ortney was negligent for failing to have them checked, what judgment would the court enter, in a jurisdiction that applied §402A of the Second Restatement of Torts?

    b. How would this case be submitted to the jury in most jurisdictions today, and how would the judgment be fashioned based on the jury's findings?

2.   Suppose, in Ortney's case, that Pretoria had raised the defense that Ortney had assumed the risk of the defective brakes. Assume that the jury concluded that Ortney fully understood the risk posed by the brakes and chose to use the car anyway.

    a. What judgment would result if the approach of §402A applied?

    b. What judgment would result in most jurisdictions today?

3.   On the same facts, Ortney sues Pretoria on two theories. In Count One she alleges that Pretoria negligently designed the brakes. In Count Two, she alleges that Pretoria is strictly liable for selling the car with defective brakes.

    a. Is it possible that she could recover on both theories?

    b. Assume that Pretoria pleads, as a defense to each of Ortney's claims, that she was contributorily negligent for failing to have the brakes checked. The jury finds that the brakes were defective, but that Ortney was also negligent. If the approach of §402A applied to the strict liability claim, what judgment would result on each of Ortney's claims?

A Tough Question and a Tough Choice

4.   Hedgepeth drives an oil delivery truck for a home heating oil business. When he tries to make a delivery to a West Dakota customer one morning, the pump on his truck doesn't function properly. He climbs on top of the truck and loosens the cap on the fill pipe, to allow some air into the tank and to facilitate pumping. As he does so, he slips on the rounded surface of the tank and falls. He sues TankCraft, the manufacturer of the tank, for his injuries, claiming that the tank was defectively designed because there is no flat surface on top to walk on when servicing the tank. TankCraft claims that Hedgepeth, who testified in his deposition that the surface of the tank was sometimes "real slick" from spilled oil, assumed the risk of slipping when he climbed onto the tank.

    Since TankCraft does business in both West and East Dakota, Hedgepeth's lawyer could file his suit in either state. Assume that West Dakota treats assumption of the risk as a full defense to a strict products liability claim, but does not bar or reduce recovery if the plaintiff is negligent. Assume that East Dakota treats both assumption of the risk and plaintiff's negligence as forms of comparative fault that reduce recovery. Hedgepeth's lawyer concludes that whichever state hears the case would probably choose to apply its own products liability law to the case. In which state should Hedgepeth's lawyer file suit?

Use and Misuse

5. Pahti, an unhandy fellow, buys a can of paint to paint the living room of his apartment. When he gets home he realizes that he doesn't have a screwdriver to open the lid. So he uses a paring knife instead. Unfortunately, the blade of the knife breaks as he pries at the lid, and a piece goes into his eye. He sues Accu-Cut, the manufacturer of the knife, on a strict liability/design defect theory. What is the manufacturer's best argument to avoid or reduce liability?

6. Carlino bought a pair of pajamas and glued white cosmetic puffs all over them to make a Halloween costume. While wearing the costume, she reached up above the stove and was burned when the puffs ignited.

    a. What strict liability theory might Carlino assert in an action against Acme Cosmetics, the manufacturer of the puffs?
    b. What defenses should Acme assert? How would you expect the court to rule on them?

The "Open and Obvious" Defense

7. Clancy is riding in the cargo area of a Ford pick-up truck when it collides with another vehicle. He is thrown from the truck and injured. He sues Ford, claiming that the truck bed should have included a warning that persons riding in the truck bed could be injured when thrown from the vehicle in a collision.

8. Let's revisit the situation in Example 9 from Chapter 13, in which Durabrand designed a stamping machine without a guard to prevent the operator's hands from getting caught in the machine, although a guard was feasible. Suppose that Durabrand did not provide a warning of the risk of injury to the user's hands from entering the stamping area. Gainor's hand drifted into the stamping area, she was injured, and she sues Durabrand on a strict products liability. She asserts that the product was defectively designed, and that Durabrand was liable for failing to warn her of the danger posed by the open stamping area.

    a. Durabrand argues that the design of the stamping machine was not defective, because the danger from putting her hands in the work area was "open and obvious." Consequently, since Gainor was clearly aware of the danger, Durabrand is not liable when she ignores the danger and suffers injury. Assuming that the danger is obvious to an ordinary user, does this prevent Gainor from proving a *design defect* claim?

b. Durabrand moves for summary judgment on Gainor's *failure to warn* claim, arguing that it had no duty to warn her of a danger that was obvious to the user. How should the court rule?

c. Durabrand argues that if the machine was defective, Gainor assumed the risk of getting her hands caught in the machine, and is therefore barred from recovery even if the machine was defective. How would this argument affect Gainor's recovery in most states today?

Unknowable Dangers

9. Let's revisit another example from Chapter 13, Example 13, in which Leahy Pharmaceuticals marketed Perzac for depression, without warning of the danger of a psychotic reaction. It subsequently turns out, after wide use by hundreds of thousands of patients, that it can cause such a reaction in a very small number of patients. Leahy argues that it is not liable for failing to warn of this risk, because it did not know about it, despite reasonable care in making and testing Perzac. How is the court likely to rule on this argument?

The State of Judge Fudd's Art

10. Pollard sues General Motors Corporation, claiming that he was injured in an accident driving a GM car because it did not have an airbag. GM argues that airbag technology had not been developed at the time Pollard bought his car, so it could not have been used to reduce collision injuries.

a. How is GM's state-of-the-art argument here different from the state-of-the-art argument in the last example?

b. Assume that Judge Fudd instructs the jury as follows:

> If you find that at the time the defendant marketed the car that was involved in the plaintiff's accident, no manufacturer provided airbags in its sedans, then the defendant is not liable for failing to provide airbags.

If you represented the plaintiff, why would you argue that Judge Fudd's instruction is defectively designed?

11. Bernstein's hair catches fire while using a Holden Products hair dryer. Investigation reveals that the solder on an electrical connection in the hair dryer was contaminated, melted, and caused a short circuit, causing the temperature of the hair dryer to increase dramatically. In Bernstein's strict products liability action, Holden argues that such contamination can happen in the manufacturing process but that it is exceedingly rare, and that

there is no known process for detecting it. Judge Fudd instructs the jury that if the defect could not have been detected under the state of the art at the time of the sale, Holden is not liable for Bernstein's injury. What is wrong with the Honorable Fudd's instruction?

Fish or Fowl? A Too Hard Hypothetical

12. Acme Chemical sells a solvent used for removing oil from metal. The solvent causes a serious rash if it comes in contact with the skin. However, the risk of this rash can't be eliminated if the solvent is to do its job. Acme places a boldface warning on the container that the user should always wear rubber gloves to avoid the risk of a serious rash. Trask reads the label, but he can't find his rubber gloves. In a hurry to finish a job, he uses the solvent without gloves, and suffers the rash. He sues Acme for his injury. The state applies comparative fault principles in strict products liability claims, and treats a plaintiff's conscious assumption of the risk as a form of comparative fault.

   a. If you represented Acme, what would you argue to defeat recovery?
   b. If you represented Trask, what would you argue to keep his case alive?
   c. Suppose that Trask had not read the label. How should his case come out?

EXPLANATIONS

Some Apples and Oranges

1a. Under §402A, the plaintiff's negligence—unless it constituted conscious assumption of the risk—was not a defense to a strict liability claim. Thus, Ortney would recover her full damages, despite her negligence in failing to have the brakes checked. For a dramatic example of this approach, which ignores the plaintiff's fault on a strict products liability claim, see *Kimco Development Corp. v. Michael D's Carpets*, 637 A.2d 603, 605-607 (Pa. 1993). In *Kimco*, a store ordered carpet backing and piled it all the way up to the ceiling. It ignited from the heat of the lights, leading to a serious fire. The jury found the store 80 percent at fault in causing the fire, but also found that the seller had failed to warn that the product was flammable. The court held that the store could recover fully for its fire loss, since the store's negligence was not a defense to its strict products liability claim for failure to warn.

b.   In most (though not all) jurisdictions today, the jury would be asked to find whether the brakes were defectively designed and also whether Ortney was negligent in failing to have the brakes checked. If they found that the design was defective, but that the plaintiff was also negligent in failing to have the brakes checked, they would assign percentages of fault to Pretoria for selling the defective product and to Ortney for her negligence. A judgment would then be entered based on these percentages of fault. For example, if they found Ortney 20 percent at fault and Pretoria 80 percent, Ortney would recover 80 percent of her damages.

2a.   Section 402A ignored a plaintiff's contributory negligence, but treated assumption of the risk as a complete defense to a strict liability claim. Thus, if Ortney fully appreciated the dangerous condition of the brakes, but chose to take a chance and use the car anyway, she would be barred from any recovery under the §402A approach. Needless to say, this made a rather subtle distinction — between a negligent failure to check the brakes and a clear appreciation that they posed a particular danger — critical in a strict products liability case. If the jury found only the first — negligent conduct but no deliberate choice to encounter the risk — the plaintiff recovered fully. If they found that the plaintiff understood the risk and consciously encountered it, she lost entirely.

b.   Today, in most jurisdictions, even full appreciation of the danger posed by a defective product is not a complete defense to liability. The jury would be asked to assign a percentage of fault to Ortney for her choice to drive with knowledge of the danger. (Naturally, they might assign a higher percentage of fault for such a deliberate choice than they would for driving with vague concerns about the brakes.) Ortney's damages would be reduced to reflect her fault in deliberately using the car with awareness of the risk posed by the defective brakes.

3a.   Yes, it is possible. A product will frequently be defective due to negligence of the manufacturer in designing it. Indeed, if the risk/utility test applies to the design defect claim, it seems likely that a finding that the design was defective (because the manufacturer had not properly balanced risk and utility) would usually support a finding that the manufacturer was negligent as well. If the jury finds that the design was unreasonably dangerous, they presumably also would find that Pretoria was negligent for using that design.

b.   If the jury found that the brakes were defective because Pretoria was negligent in designing them, Ortney would recover on her negligence claim. However, if the jurisdiction applied comparative negligence, her negligence would reduce her recovery on the negligence claim. For example, if the jury had found Ortney 20 percent negligent, she would recover a judgment for 80 percent of her damages on the negligence count. (In a contributory negligence jurisdiction, she would lose entirely.)

However, the jury's finding that she was negligent would have no effect on the strict liability count. Under the approach of §402A, contributory negligence was not a defense to a strict liability claim, so Ortney would recover fully on the strict liability claim. The judge should enter judgment on the negligence claim for 80 percent of Ortney's damages, but on the strict liability count for 100 percent of those damages. Of course, the plaintiff could not recover twice (or almost twice) by recovering on two theories. But she could choose to enforce the strict liability judgment for her full damages and thus recover fully despite her negligence.

This anomaly — that the same events could lead to judgments for different amounts based on the same conduct — is eliminated in jurisdictions that apply comparative fault to strict products liability claims. The plaintiff's negligence is treated the same way on the strict liability count and the negligence count, as a damage-reducing factor rather than as a full defense.

A Tough Question and a Tough Choice

4.   This is the kind of tactical decision that litigators often face in trying to serve their clients' interests. The problem is that it is not clear whether Hedgepeth will be found to have assumed the risk of his injury by climbing on the tank, even though it was sometimes "real slick." If the jury concludes that he fully appreciated this danger, and chose to encounter it, he will lose entirely under West Dakota law, based on the assumption of risk defense. If, on the other hand, the jury concludes that he was simply negligent for disregarding a risk that the tank would be slippery, he would recover fully, with no deduction for his negligence, since West Dakota does not reduce recovery in strict products liability cases based on a plaintiff's contributory negligence. So West Dakota is either the best or the worst choice, depending on the subtle factual distinction between consciously assuming a specific risk and acting negligently without fully appreciating the consequences of that choice.

If Hedgepeth sues in East Dakota he will probably recover something. The assumed East Dakota law treats plaintiff's fault as a damage-reducing factor, whether the jury characterizes his conduct as assumption of risk or negligence. So this is the conservative choice. But, the jury might find him pretty careless for walking on top of the tank, so this could mean a substantially reduced recovery.

There is no "answer" to this question. It is a difficult judgment to make, based on counsel's assessment of the likelihood that a jury would label Hedgepeth's conduct as assumption of the risk. Adventurous lawyers might "roll the bones," by suing in West Dakota. The more timid would likely opt for the safer course and sue in East Dakota.

Products liability cases often involve connections to multiple states. The product may have been designed in one state, manufactured in another, sold in a third, and caused injury in a fourth. In such cases, the court in which the case is filed must decide, under complex choice-of-law principles, which state's products liability law to apply to the case. The plaintiff's lawyer will have to consider which states could hear the case (i.e., which would have personal jurisdiction over the manufacturer) and make a careful assessment of those states' choice-of-law rules and substantive products liability rules, in order to choose the court likely to apply the most favorable products liability principles to his case.

Given the complexity and flexibility of choice-of-law rules, however, this assessment will be an educated guess at best. If Hedgepeth sues in East Dakota, he can't be sure that the East Dakota court will apply its own products liability law to the case. That court, applying its choice-of-law rules, might conclude that the case has stronger connections to West Dakota and apply its products liability law instead, even though the case is heard in an East Dakota court.

Use and Misuse

5.   The knife manufacturer might argue that Pahti was negligent to use a paring knife to open a can of paint. However, in some jurisdictions, a plaintiff's negligence is not a defense at all, and in most, it is only a partial defense, under comparative negligence rules. A better argument would be that Pahti had used the knife for an unforeseeable purpose for which it was never intended. If the court (or the jury) finds that this is true, Accu-Cut would not be liable at all. To recover on a strict products liability theory, Pahti must prove that the knife was defective when used for the purpose for which it was intended, or at least for a purpose that Accu-Cut should have anticipated that it would be used for. If this is an unforeseeable misuse (which it probably is), the knife is not defective, even though it was unfit for that use.

Surely this limitation on strict liability makes sense. Accu-Cut, in designing knives, can't be expected to contemplate its use for a screwdriver, a splint, or other idiosyncratic uses that might occur to a buyer. They are entitled to focus on the risks and utility of the knife as a knife, and perhaps for other closely related, foreseeable uses. A knife can't be all things to all people; if manufacturers had to design products for all possible uses, they could never design a decent knife.

6a. Carlino might argue that the puffs were defectively designed because they were flammable. However, it seems doubtful that cosmetic puffs, generally used individually for applying or removing cosmetics from the skin, are defective even if they are flammable. A stronger argument (though still somewhat shaky) is that Acme could foresee this type of misuse, and therefore should have included a warning with the puffs of the danger that they would catch fire. Acme need not design its puffs for that use, the argument goes, but it should at least warn people of the danger of that foreseeable misuse.

b.   Acme might argue that Carlino was contributorily negligent for using the puffs for a Halloween costume. This argument would be based on misuse as a form of negligence. However, a jury might find that she *wasn't* negligent for doing so, in light of the low risk of igniting one's clothes. And, if she was negligent, that would not necessarily reduce her recovery, since in some states contributory negligence is not a defense to strict products liability claims. (In other states, however, her negligence would reduce recovery in proportion to her fault.) Acme might also argue that Carlino was negligent for getting too close to the stove. If she was, the effect of that negligence, as just stated, varies from state to state.

However, Acme's best argument is that gluing the puffs onto a Halloween costume is not a foreseeable misuse of the product. Again, this is not really an affirmative defense, but an argument that Carlino cannot establish an element of her prima facie case: that the puffs were used for a purpose for which they were intended, or a foreseeable misuse. If they are put to some truly bizarre alternative purpose, they are not defective if they fail to serve that purpose safely. In *Trivino v. Jamesway Corp.*, 539 N.Y.S.2d 123 (N.Y. App. Div. 1989), on which this example is loosely based, the trial court granted summary judgment for the manufacturer, but the appellate court reversed, holding that it was a jury question whether this use of the puffs was an unforeseeable misuse.

Last, Acme might argue that the danger of the puffs igniting was obvious. If so, a warning would not be necessary, since users would be aware of it. The *Trivino* court held that this, too, was a jury question, so the plaintiff survived the summary judgment motion.

The "Open and Obvious" Defense

7.   While manufacturers have a duty to warn users of the dangers of their products, including the dangers of misuse, they do not have to warn of dangers that the user would already know about. It is probably foreseeable that consumers will misuse the cargo area of a pickup truck as a passenger compartment, but surely the danger of being thrown from the open bed of a pickup truck is "open and obvious." The duty to warn extends to dangers that the consumer would not readily understand from her common knowledge. Here, the obviousness of the danger obviates the need to warn of it, because the user very likely already knows about it. In *Maneely v. General Motors Corp.*, 108 F.3d 1176, 1180 (3d Cir. 1997), on which this example is based, the court rejected the plaintiff's claim on this ground.

Naturally, there will be close questions as to when a danger is obvious. Does the manufacturer, for example, have a duty to warn of the danger of choking on a marshmallow? A Montana trial judge held that this danger was obvious, but in *Emery v. Federated Foods, Inc.*, 863 P.2d 426 (Mont. 1993), the appellate court reversed, on the ground that whether the danger was obvious was a jury question. A Michigan appellate court held that a manufacturer had a duty to warn of the risk of diving into the shallow end of its pool (see *Glittenburg v. Wilcenski*, 435 N.W.2d 480 (Mich. App. 1989)) but was reversed by the Michigan Supreme Court. It held (but with a dissent!) that the manufacturer owed no duty to warn of this danger, because it was open and obvious. *Glittenburg v. Doughboy Recreational Industries*, 491 N.W.2d 208 (Mich. 1992).

8a. In this example Durabrand designed a machine that posed an unreasonable risk of injury to users. Since the danger could be substantially eliminated by a guard, the design is defective. Durabrand argues, however, that it is not liable because the danger posed by the machine was "open and obvious" to users.

In Example 9 from Chapter 13, Durabrand warned of the danger of hands getting caught in the machine. However, this warning did not avoid liability, since the danger could have been eliminated by a better design. If it was liable in that case, it surely should be liable here too, where its design is unreasonably dangerous and it does not warn of the danger. The machine is defective because the danger should not exist at all: The machine should be designed with a guard that eliminates the danger. Durabrand should not be allowed to defend a design defect claim by arguing that it designed an *obviously* dangerous product. The machine should not have been marketed in that form at all. If Durabrand's argument were accepted, it would mean that the more egregious the danger of its product, the greater the protection it would enjoy from design defect liability.

b. Durabrand's "open and obvious" defense to the failure to warn claim is more credible. There is no duty to warn of obvious dangers; if the danger here was indisputably obvious, Durabrand might get summary judgment on the failure to warn claim. In many cases, however, whether the danger was obvious will be a factual question appropriate for the jury to decide.

So here, the open and obvious defense might defeat a failure to warn claim, but the obviousness of the danger does not defeat the claim for defective design, based on the theory that the danger should have been designed out of the product. Indeed, the obviousness of the danger strengthens the argument that it was defectively designed.

c. As the Introduction indicates, most states have now folded the concept of assumption of the risk into their comparative negligence schemes. Thus, the jury would be instructed to assess Gainor's knowing choice to use the machine despite the clear danger posed by the exposed stamping blades and determine whether to assign her a percentage of fault for making that choice. Her recovery would be reduced to reflect the percentage of fault assigned to that choice.

Some states, however, do not recognize the assumption of the risk defense in the workplace context, on the theory that employees don't really have a choice about completing workplace tasks with the equipment supplied to them. See, e.g., *Johansen v. Makita U.S.A., Inc.*, 607 A.2d 637, 642 (N.J. 1992).

Unknowable Dangers

9.   As the Introduction indicates, some cases have held that a product is "defective" if it lacks warning of a danger, even if the manufacturer had no reason to know of that danger when it marketed the product. See, e.g., *Beshada v. Johns-Mansville Products Corp.*, 447 A.2d 539, 546-547 (N.J. 1982). The logic for this is that strict products liability is based not on the conduct of the manufacturer, but on the unreasonable risk posed by the product. If such a danger turns up, the consumer has been exposed to it whether or not the manufacturer could have anticipated it.

However, most courts today would accept Leahy's argument that it is not liable for "unknowable" dangers posed by its product, as long as it had conducted reasonable testing before marketing the drug. These courts hold that if the risk could not have been anticipated based on the state of scientific knowledge and reasonable testing at the time of sale, the manufacturer is not liable for injuries resulting from that risk. See, e.g., *Potter v. Chicago Pneumatic Tool Co.*, 694 A.2d 1319 (Conn. 1997); *Barton v. Adams Rental, Inc.*, 938 P.2d 532, 539 (Colo. 1997); Restatement (Third) of Products Liability, §2 cmt. a (product only defective if dangers reasonably foreseeable at time of distribution). Acceptance of the state-of-the-art defense is one of several ways in which "strict" products liability has converged with negligence law in the post-§402A era.

The State of Judge Fudd's Art

10a.   The prior example involved a claim of failure to warn of the side effect of a drug. A drug may not be defective, even if it poses a risk of side effects, if an adequate warning is given of those side effects, so users (and their doctors) can make adequate judgments about whether to use them. But a manufacturer cannot warn of a danger it doesn't know exists.

In this case, by contrast, the argument is that given the technology available at the time the defendant sold the car, it was not feasible to design an effective airbag. Just as it should not be liable for failing to warn of risks it could not anticipate, the manufacturer argues, it also should not be held liable for omitting safety devices that were not technologically feasible at the time of manufacture. This argument is based on the same underlying premise, that the limits of scientific and technical knowledge should be considered in determining the manufacturer's liability for product injuries. Courts that accept the state-of-the-art defense are likely to accept it in both the warning and design contexts.[9]

b.   Judge Fudd's instruction suggests that the car was not defective for failure to provide an airbag unless at least one other manufacturer was using them when it sold the car to Pollard. This is not an accurate instruction, even in a jurisdiction that recognizes the state-of-the-art defense. That defense provides that a manufacturer is not liable for failure to include a safety feature if, in light of the technology available at the time it sold the product, it would not have been aware of the need for the feature, or had the technical means to provide it. This argument, that "no manufacturer would have been aware of the need for this, or been able to provide it," is quite different from the argument that "no manufacturer *was doing it* at the time I sold the product." As Judge Learned Hand opined in a different context, "a whole calling may have unduly lagged in the adoption of new and available devices." *The T.J. Hooper*, 60 F.2d 737, 740 (2d Cir. 1932). The state-of-the-art argument is that an adequate safety device *could not* reasonably have been provided at the time of sale, not that no manufacturer was doing so. See generally D. Dobbs, The Law of Torts 1032-1033.

On the other hand, evidence that no other manufacturer provided airbags is certainly probative on the issue of feasibility. As in negligence cases, this type of evidence is admissible, but not dispositive. See Restatement (Third) of Products Liability, §2 cmt. d.

11.   The problem here is that Judge Fudd has imported the state-of-the-art defense from the design defect/warning context and applied it to a manufacturing defect case. The gist of the state-of-the-art defense is that a manufacturer cannot be faulted if the design of its product is reasonably safe, in light of the technology available at the time it designed and sold the product. Similarly, the trend in the cases applies the state-of-the-art defense to failure to warn claims as well: A manufacturer does not have a duty to warn of product risks it could not have discovered, in the exercise of reasonable care and pre-sale investigation, before it sold the product.

Here, however, Holden's argument is that there was no technologically feasible way to detect this type of manufacturing defect, and consequently, it should not be held liable for failing to detect it. The argument isn't a bad one; Holden is in some sense just as "blameless" for failing to

---

9. It seems axiomatic that a state that follows the Third Restatement of Products Liability would accept the state-of-the-art defense in design defect cases. The Third Restatement requires the plaintiff, in order to prove a design defect, to show that a reasonable alternative design existed that would have eliminated the danger. Restatement (Third) of Products Liability, §2(b). The essence of the state-of-the-art argument is that no safer design was feasible at the time of manufacture.

detect this problem as it would be for failing to institute a design that wasn't technologically feasible. Yet, Professor Dobbs suggests that "knowability of risks is logically no part of the manufacturing defect case." Dobbs, The Law of Torts 1033. Manufacturing defect cases, are, after all, the last bastion of "true" strict liability in the products area. Holden's argument would probably not prevail in most jurisdictions. However, several products liability statutes appear to apply the state-of-the-art defense even to manufacturing defect cases. See Iowa Code §668.12; Ky. Rev. Stat. §411.310. Others, however, make clear that the defense only applies to design defect and warning claims. Miss. Code Ann. §11-1-63.

Fish or Fowl? A Too Hard Hypothetical

12a. Here, Trask has misused the solvent, by ignoring the warning. What effect should Trask's misuse have on his claim? Should it bar it, or reduce his recovery? Acme should argue that Trask cannot show that its solvent was defective, because used as directed it is safe. It could not design the risk of the rash out of the product, and it warned users of that risk. It will argue that it has the right to expect users to use products according to adequate instructions and warnings. If the product is safe when so used, Acme argues, the product is not defective, so Trask cannot make a prima facie case of strict products liability. And the necessary warning was given. What more can it do? If, in spite of all that, it is liable for Trask's injury, it seems like a form of absolute liability; it is held liable no matter what it does if the product causes injury.

b.   Trask would doubtless argue that it is foreseeable that users will sometimes ignore the warning and use the solvent without gloves. Since such misuse is foreseeable, the product is defective if it is dangerous for that use. Trask's recovery should be reduced to reflect his fault in ignoring the need for gloves, but not barred entirely. Even if his choice would constitute conscious assumption of the risk, the example states that the relevant law treats assumption of risk as a form of comparative fault, so Trask's recovery should be reduced, not barred. Under this approach, Trask might still recover substantial damages.

Most courts would hold, I think, that when Acme provides a product that is reasonably safe when used as directed, and warns of dangers that cannot be designed out of the product without undermining its function, the product is not defective. On this logic, Trask should lose entirely. Otherwise, Acme is liable despite offering a reasonably safe product, and providing adequate warnings of the irreducible dangers associated with its use.

> Where warning is given, the seller may reasonably assume that it will be read and heeded; and a product bearing such a warning, which is safe for use if it is followed, is not in defective condition, nor is it unreasonably dangerous.

Restatement (Second) of Torts, §402A, cmt. j. See *Uptain v. Huntington Lab. Inc.*, 723 P.2d 1322 (Colo. 1986). Some states also have statutes that deny recovery if the plaintiff ignores adequate product directions or warnings. See, e.g., Ariz. Rev. Stat. §12-683; N.C. Gen. Stat. §99B-4(1).

However, a few cases have treated the plaintiff's failure to follow directions in such circumstances as a form of comparative fault. See, e.g., *Barnard v. Saturn Corp.*, 790 N.E.2d 1023 (Ind. App. 2003), which, despite finding that the decedent ignored adequate warnings, held that his fault should be assessed under the comparative negligence statute.

c.   Assuming that Trask would lose if he had read the label, on the ground that the product was not defective, he also should lose if he didn't read the label. The logic in the first case is that the solvent is not defective, so long as an adequate warning is given, so Trask cannot make out a strict products liability claim. If that is true when he reads the label, it is equally true when he doesn't.

PART FIVE

Damages for Personal Injury

15

Personal Injury Damages: The Elements of Compensation

Introduction

Plaintiffs bring lawsuits for a variety of reasons, but when the cause of action is in tort, the reason is almost always to obtain monetary compensation for the injury.

We might well pause for a moment to ask whether this makes sense. If Krutch runs down Gray, breaking Gray's leg, why should the legal system respond by ordering Krutch to pay money to Gray? Aren't there other responses that would make more sense? Perhaps the court should order Krutch to perform services for Gray, take a driving course, or publicly acknowledge responsibility. Or maybe the court should provide social services to Gray, or retraining, or visits from neighbors, or who knows what.

Such responses to personal injury might be more creative than the impersonal transfer of dollars from the defendant (or his insurer) to the plaintiff. But the fact is that the usual balm the law provides to personal injury plaintiffs is money. Such payments are called "compensatory damages," and it is sometimes said that they are intended to "repair[] plaintiff's injury or . . . mak[e] him whole as nearly as that may be done by an award of money." Harper, James & Gray, §25.1, at 493.

Clearly this goal is an idle dream in many cases: No amount of money could possibly compensate an active, healthy adult rendered paraplegic in an auto accident, a child disfigured by severe burns, or a patient brain-damaged by excessive anesthesia. These plaintiffs can never be put back in their pre-injury position, and none of us would incur their injuries for any sum. However, while money damages may seem an inadequate response to such injuries, they do help. A paraplegic with a two million dollar trust fund is a lot better off than he would be with no money and impaired earning power, and a remedy that provides the trust fund is, if imperfect, still a good deal better than nothing. And so tort law endeavors to provide the injured plaintiff a sum of money adequate to *compensate* him, though certainly not to *restore* him to his pre-injury position.[1]

The Single Recovery Rule

Perhaps the most fundamental point to grasp about tort damages is that the plaintiff must seek compensation for all his losses from the tort in a single trial. That is, he must prove both past damages and any future losses he is likely to experience from the injury—such as future medical expenses, lost wages, or medical complications—at the time of trial. The rationale for the rule is not hard to discern. Without it, cases would have to be reopened every time the plaintiff incurred further losses due to an injury, to allow recovery for those additional losses. There is simply no way the judicial system could entertain such repeated claims; it is hard enough to provide even a single hearing for the numbers of cases that confront the courts today.

While this "single recovery rule" makes administrative sense, it places the plaintiff in a difficult, at times untenable position. As the sage has noted, "the art of prediction is very unpredictable . . . particularly when it pertains to the future."[2] It is often very difficult to anticipate whether the plaintiff will need future operations, have his work life expectancy shortened, or incur a further disability due to his injury. Under the single recovery rule, however, the plaintiff must make just such predictions about events that may lie far in the future—and prove them by a preponderance of the evidence.

---

1. Two other types of damages, nominal damages and punitive damages, are not addressed in this chapter. Nominal damages may sometimes be granted if the plaintiff proves the elements of a tort but has suffered no actual damages. Punitive damages are sometimes awarded in tort cases to punish the defendant for particularly egregious conduct, and to deter such conduct in the future. Punitive damages may be awarded in addition to compensatory damages.

2. This bon mot, like so many others, has been attributed to Yogi Berra, but I don't have an official citation.

Even if such future problems *may* arise, they may not be sufficiently likely to support a damage award under the single recovery rule. Most courts hold that the plaintiff can recover for future consequences of an injury if he proves that they are "reasonably probable" (Minzer, Nates, eds., Damages in Tort Actions §9.06[5][a]), but an award may not be based on "mere conjecture or speculation." Id. If the plaintiff might need future surgery, but probably will not, most courts would not allow him to recover damages for it. If, then, he actually does require the surgery, he will be barred by the single recovery rule from bringing a second suit for the losses associated with that surgery. Similarly, if the plaintiff cannot prove that the injury will prevent him from working, he will not receive damages for future lost earning capacity. If in fact he is unable to return to work, that loss will go uncompensated.

Of course, this can work both ways: The plaintiff might prove that he is likely to require future surgery, and recover damages for it, but then do better than expected and not require surgery. If so, he will have received damages for a loss he ultimately did not incur, but will not have to return the damages recovered for that future risk.

The Elements of Compensatory Damages

The three usual components of compensatory damages are medical and related expenses, lost earnings and earning capacity, and pain and suffering. Let's examine each of these in a little more detail.

A. Medical Expenses

The plaintiff is entitled to compensation for all medical costs of diagnosing and treating the injuries resulting from the tort, such as doctor and hospital bills, medicines and special therapeutic equipment, rehabilitation therapy, travel for medical treatment and on-going nursing care. These services are incurred to cope with the consequences of the accident, and their cost should be shifted to the tortfeasor who caused the injury rather than borne by the victim.

Past medical expenses are often fairly easy to calculate. The plaintiff can submit medical and hospital bills and offer expert testimony to prove the reasonable value of these losses. But even such tangible economic losses as medical costs become extremely difficult to calculate if they will extend for a significant period into the future. Under the single recovery rule, the plaintiff must offer proof of what his future medical expenses will be, years or decades before they occur, and the jury must attach dollar sums to these future expenses based on the evidence before them.

For example, if the jury concluded that the plaintiff would probably require future surgery to relieve muscle problems related to a burn injury, they would have to determine the proper sum to compensate him for the medical expenses of that operation, even though it might occur twenty years down the road. They would also have to value the associated pain, any resulting loss of earnings, the costs of rehabilitation, and so forth. Needless to say, any sum the jury awards for such future contingencies would be charitably viewed as a rough approximation. Measuring such damages may not be "a leap in the dark, but it is certainly a leap into the deep dusk of twilight." D. Dobbs, Law of Remedies, Practitioner Treatise Series, vol. 2, §8.1(1), at 361 (2d ed. 1993).

B. Lost Earnings and Earning Capacity

The second component of compensatory damages is lost earnings and earning capacity. Lost earnings refers to *past* income losses due to the injury, that is, earnings lost between the time of injury and the time of trial. Clearly, if the plaintiff was out of work for ten weeks because of the injury, the tortfeasor should compensate him for the wages lost as a result. Lost earning *capacity* refers to loss of *future* earning potential. If the injury will prevent the plaintiff from going back to work for a period of time, it has affected his ability to continue to earn money in the future. Under the single recovery rule, he must be compensated at trial for this future loss.

Lost earnings, like past medical expenses, can usually be calculated fairly accurately, based on the plaintiff's earnings record for the period immediately prior to the accident, evidence of his likely advancement had he not been injured, and evidence concerning changes in the salary structure of his employer up to the time of trial. But future earning capacity is seldom so easily assessed. First, the jury will have to determine how long the plaintiff would have worked if he had not been injured. This may depend on the type of work he did, his life expectancy, state of health *prior to* the injury, and level of interest in his work. Other factors that might have led him to retire early must also be considered, such as a spouse's retirement, an unrelated medical condition which could cause him to move to a different climate, or an anticipated inheritance.

Second, the jury will have to determine what type of work the plaintiff would have done if he had not been injured. For plaintiffs with a long-established work history, this may be clear, but in other cases it is not. Maybe the plaintiff was working as a secretary for a year to pay off some loans, but planning to enter business school the year after. Maybe he graduated magna cum laude from Berkeley, but was working as a truck driver for a while as a lark. Maybe he was earning $150,000 as a partner in a law firm, but hated his work passionately and would not have lasted another six months. (Imagine the difficulty defense counsel would have proving that crucial but subjective fact.) To compound the problem, suppose that he was not working at all when injured, but likely would have returned to the work force at some point. Or consider the case of a plaintiff five years old at the time of the injury, with no work history, educational history, or other basis for estimating his future income potential.

Even if it is reasonably clear what work the plaintiff would have undertaken, the jury will have to decide what his salary would have been during those years. Ideally, this projection would include such factors as prior advancement in his job, the projected future fortunes of his employer, the general state of the sector of the economy in which he worked, the prospects that he would have been promoted or moved to a more lucrative position with another employer, possible alternative employment he may be able to find after his injury, and doubtless many others unique to each plaintiff's circumstances.

In addition, if the plaintiff is really to be fully compensated for future lost earnings, the jury should consider fringe benefits, such as health insurance, a company car, educational credits, bonuses, and stock options. And how about retirement? If the defendant's tortious conduct has deprived the plaintiff of the opportunity to build a retirement fund partially funded by the company, this benefit should also be calculated. Here again, in assessing such damages, the jury is called upon to make judgments that would intimidate the most experienced actuary.

C. Pain and Suffering

The third component of damages, "pain and suffering," can cover a lot of ground. It certainly includes physical pain from the impact of an accident, but it also includes on-going pain from a wound, or long term discomfort from a permanent condition such as a limp or weakened back. It also includes the pain of medical procedures (such as surgery, grafting, or physical therapy) to treat the injuries.

Beyond these obvious connotations, the phrase also includes many other types of mental suffering from the consequences of the injury, such as the humiliation, anguish, or embarrassment suffered from living with permanent disfigurement, the frustration of dealing with disability caused by the injury, the fright associated with a traumatic accident, fear of a recurrence of the accident, or depression induced by the injury and its consequences. Thus, "pain and suffering" is a catch-all term that can encompass almost any kind of subjective reaction to the accident or its consequences. "[T]he unitary concept of 'pain and suffering' has served as a convenient label under which a plaintiff may recover not only for physical pain but for fright, nervousness, grief, anxiety, worry, mortification, shock, humiliation, indignity, embarrassment, apprehension, terror or ordeal." *Capelouto v. Kasier Found. Hosp.,* 500 P.2d 880, 883 (Cal. 1972).

Obviously, such sensations are highly subjective; there is no scale or mathematical process jurors can use to reach a dollar figure to compensate the plaintiff for them. They must simply pick a number based on their sense of the severity of the loss the plaintiff has suffered. Consider, for example, the following fairly typical instruction on pain and suffering damages:

> In assessing damages, if you have occasion to do so, the law allows you to award to plaintiff a sum that will reasonably compensate him for any past physical pain, as well as pain that is reasonably certain to be suffered in the future as a result of the defendant's wrongdoing.
>
> There are no objective guidelines by which you can measure the money equivalent of this element of injury; the only real measuring stick, if it can be so described, is your collective enlightened conscience. You should consider the evidence bearing on the nature of the injuries, the certainty of future pain, the severity and the likely duration thereof.
>
> In this difficult task of putting a money figure on an aspect of injury that does not readily lend itself to an evaluation in terms of money, you should try to be as objective, calm and dispassionate as the situation will permit, and not to be unduly swayed by considerations of sympathy.

G. Douthewaite, Jury Instructions on Damages in Tort Actions 274 (1988). Basically, this instruction throws the matter to the jury without guidance, but with a plea for them to be objective even if there are no objective guidelines to apply!

Loss of Enjoyment of Life

In addition to the unpleasant sensations and emotions usually associated with the concept of pain and suffering, tort victims also frequently suffer loss of the opportunity to engage in many of life's pleasurable activities. If his leg is maimed in the accident with Gray, Krutch will doubtless suffer the physical pain and mental anguish generally associated with such injuries. But he may also lose the ability to play tennis, to take walks in the woods, to carry his son to school, to dance, or to enjoy many of life's other common, pleasurable experiences. These functional impairments go beyond the usual connotations of "pain and suffering," but are also common consequences of serious injuries.

Such impairments are often profound—perhaps the most profound—consequences of physical injury. Imagine, for example, that Krutch's most cherished activity is playing the violin, and that he suffers a hand injury that prevents him from doing so. Or suppose that the accident destroys his sense of sight or taste. Certainly, these are grievous losses above and beyond the sensation of physical pain or fear immediately stemming from the injury.

Many courts describe these losses, aptly enough, as "loss of enjoyment of life."[3] Most courts recognize that such losses are compensable, but the cases are split over whether damages for loss of enjoyment are analytically a type of "pain and suffering" or a separate element of compensatory damages. Some courts treat loss of enjoyment as a form of pain and suffering: The mental suffering that comes from the plaintiff's realization that he can no longer engage fully in life's pleasure. Courts that take this approach will refuse to give the jury a separate instruction on "loss of enjoyment" damages, on the ground that it duplicates the pain and suffering instruction and invites the jury to compensate the plaintiff twice for the same losses. See *McDougald v. Garber*, 536 N.E.2d 372, 375-377 (N.Y. 1989).

Other courts have recognized loss of enjoyment as a distinct category of compensable damages. See, e.g., *Thompson v. National R.R. Passenger Corp.*, 621 F.2d 814, 824 (6th Cir.), *cert. denied*, 449 U.S. 1035 (1980), in which the court concluded that "pain and suffering compensates the victim for the physical and mental discomfort caused by the injury; and loss of enjoyment of life compensates the victim for the limitations on the person's life created by the injury." See also *Boan v. Blackwell*, 541 S.E.2d 242, 243-245 (S.C. 2001). Courts that take this view allow the trial judge to instruct the jury separately on loss of enjoyment of life. Plaintiffs' counsel naturally prefer such a separate instruction, since it emphasizes the distinct nature of loss of enjoyment damages and invites the jury to consider them apart from a general pain and suffering award.

It is probably not of great consequence whether loss of enjoyment is characterized as part of pain and suffering or as a separate component of compensatory damages. The important thing is that everyone — the lawyers, the judge, and the jury — understands that, whatever called, such restrictions on the plaintiff's "ability to function as a whole person" (*Canfield v. Sandock*, 563 N.E.2d 1279 (Ind. 1990)) are proper elements in the assessment of damages. Plaintiff's counsel may introduce evidence of all the ways in which the plaintiff's injury has impaired his ability to engage in activities he previously enjoyed. Where such evidence is offered, the judge should explain to the jury that they

---

3. Another term currently in vogue is *hedonic* damages. This concept is related to loss of enjoyment damages, but endeavors to measure the general value of living itself, rather than focusing on loss of the enjoyment of particular activities. See D. Dobbs, Law of Remedies, Practitioner Treatise Series, vol. 2, §8.3(5), at 443-444 (2d ed. 1993).

are entitled to compensate the plaintiff for these losses, in addition to the physical pain and emotional distress traditionally associated with "pain and suffering."

The Elusive Concept of "Disability"

Although all states recognize the basic categories of damages discussed above, some courts may use different terms, such as "disability" or "permanent impairment" in discussing compensatory damages. These terms often overlap with several concepts already discussed, particularly loss of enjoyment and lost earning capacity.

In its strictest sense, "disability" or "permanent impairment" refers to the injured party's *condition*, not to the losses suffered as a result of that condition:

> Disability and permanent injury refer to states of ill health that preclude an injured person from carrying on normal activities of life in the manner which would have been possible had the injury in question not occurred.

Minzer, Nates, §402[2][c]. While this definition sounds similar to loss of enjoyment, it is more accurate to view loss of enjoyment as the *consequence* that flows from the plaintiff's disabled condition. For example, the loss of a leg is an impairment or disability. The loss of the opportunity to engage in activities as a result of that disability—running marathons, hiking, or whatever—constitutes a consequential loss of enjoyment for which damages may be awarded.

However, many courts use the terms "disability" and "permanent impairment" loosely as the equivalent of "loss of enjoyment of life." These courts will instruct the jury that they may assess damages for the plaintiff's "disability," but will obviously not instruct separately on loss of enjoyment damages: It would allow double counting to instruct the jury to award damages for both disability and loss of enjoyment. See P. Hermes, Note, Loss of Enjoyment of Life—Duplication of Damages versus Full Compensation, 63 N.D. L. Rev. 561, 579 (1987).

There is also frequent confusion between "disability" and lost earning capacity. Here again, the *condition* of being disabled leads to the *consequence* of lost earning capacity. If the jury is instructed to award damages for lost earning capacity, the instructions should make clear that they should not award the same losses under a separate "disability" instruction, even though the earnings loss stems from the disability. On the other hand, it is quite possible to have disability without loss of earning capacity: If Krutch is a computer programmer who loses a leg in an accident, for example, he might return to work in a few weeks with little or no loss of salary. Yet clearly he has suffered a permanent, serious disability—in the sense of interference with enjoyment of life—that should be compensated.[4]

Economic vs. Noneconomic Damages

The elements of damages discussed above are often grouped into *economic* and *noneconomic* damages. Lost earnings, lost earning capacity, and medical and other out-of-pocket expenses are considered *economic* or *tangible* damages, since they are actual dollar losses that can be calculated. By contrast, pain and suffering and loss of enjoyment are *noneconomic* or *intangible* damages which the jury has no mathematical or accounting basis for valuing. (Infliction of emotional distress and loss of consortium also generally fall into this category.)

The distinction between economic and noneconomic damages has become increasingly important in recent years. A good many legislatures, reacting to large increases in insurance costs, have enacted caps on noneconomic damages such as pain and suffering and loss of consortium. For example, Idaho Code §6-1603 provides:

> (1) In no action seeking damages for personal injury, including death, shall a judgment for noneconomic damages be entered for a claimant exceeding the maximum amount of two hundred and fifty thousand dollars ($250,000).[5] . . .

Other states have enacted caps on noneconomic damages in particular types of cases, such as medical malpractice:

> (a) In any action for injury against a health care provider based on professional negligence, the injured plaintiff shall be entitled to recover noneconomic losses to compensate for pain, suffering, inconvenience, physical impairment, disfigurement and other nonpecuniary damage.
> (b) In no action shall the amount of damages for noneconomic losses exceed two hundred fifty thousand dollars ($250,000).

Cal. Civ. Code §3333.2. Needless to say, statutes of this type do not warm the hearts of the plaintiff's bar, since they reduce plaintiffs' recoveries and counsel's contingent fees. They represent a legislative compromise between

---

4. A few cases hold that permanent disability is compensable as a per se loss, apart from any loss of enjoyment, pain and suffering, or lost earning capacity that results from it. See *Thompson v. National R.R. Passenger Corp.*, 621 F.2d 814, 824 (1980). The *Thompson* court reasoned that "permanent impairment" compensates the plaintiff "for the fact of being permanently injured whether or not it causes any pain or inconvenience" while loss of enjoyment compensates for "the limitations on the person's life created by the injury." Id. But this appears to be an isolated view. See Dobbs, Law of Remedies, Practitioner Treatise Series at §8.1(1) n.6.

5. Section 6-1603 provides for annual adjustments to the cap to reflect general changes in wage levels.

the ideal of full compensation and the reality of limited resources. The debate about such compromises has been heated, and continues to be. A major indictment of damage caps is that they limit the recovery of those who need it most: Plaintiffs with lesser injuries recover fully for their intangible damages, while those most seriously injured may recover only a fraction of their intangible damages.[6]

While the terminology courts use in analyzing compensatory damages may vary, the fundamental inquiry does not. The jury must assess the plaintiff's situation after the injury compared to his situation before. They must consider his physical and emotional suffering from the injury, his lost opportunities, both economic and personal, as a result of the injury and the economic costs of dealing with the injury. From this analysis they are to distill a sum of money damages to "compensate" him for all losses he has suffered or will suffer in the future from the injury. The examples below explore these damage issues in the context of particular cases.

EXAMPLES

The Art of Prediction

1. Mendel, a 25-year-old truck driver, is injured in a traffic accident and rendered permanently paraplegic. He sues the other driver. If you represented Mendel, for what types of future medical and therapeutic expenses would you seek compensation?

2. Assume that Mendel only suffers a concussion in the accident. He has minimal medical expenses, but testifies that he has developed tinnitus, or ringing in the ears, as a result of the impact. Tinnitus is a recognized medical condition, but it is very hard to corroborate its existence by medical tests. Mendel testifies that the ringing is always there, that it is a constant irritant, that it has made him irritable and difficult with his family. He continues to work as a construction worker, but the condition interferes with his ability to concentrate on many leisure activities, such as card playing or reading. It also makes it very difficult for him to get to sleep, so that he is always tired.

Assume that liability is clear, and that medical costs and lost earnings are negligible. The defendant's insurer offers $35,000 to settle Mendel's claim. If you represented Mendel, would you take it?

3. Audubon, a 42-year-old naturalist, is seriously injured in an accident involving his car and Darwin's. The evidence at trial indicates that Audubon is totally disabled. Due to his injury, his life expectancy has been

---

6. A good argument can be made that a *floor* on intangible damages would be more fair. This approach would bar recovery for intangible losses where the economic loss (and therefore, presumably, the underlying physical injury itself) is minor, but preserve full recovery to victims of catastrophic injury.

shortened from 31 years to 20 years, and his work life expectancy from 25 years to zero. Stated another way, before the accident Audubon could have expected, based on statistical tables, to live to the age of 73, and work to the age of 67. However, due to his injuries he will now likely live only to the age of 62, and will not return to work. The evidence also indicates that he will continue to endure pain, embarrassment, and other psychic injuries from the accident until his death.

    a. If Darwin is found liable, for what time period should the jury assess damages for Audubon's lost earning capacity?

    b. Assuming that Audubon will continue to experience pain and mental anguish from the accident as long as he lives, for what period should the jury assess damages for pain and suffering?

    c. Should the jury award damages to Audubon for the shortening of his life span?

    d. For what period should the jury award damages for loss of enjoyment of life?

The Single Be-Fuddlement Rule

4. Muir, a shipyard worker, contracts asbestosis, a respiratory disease caused by exposure to asbestos. He sues General Yards, the shipyard, for negligently failing to warn him of the danger of working with asbestos. At trial, he produces evidence of the pain and suffering he suffers from the disease, his medical expenses, and his impaired earning capacity. He also offers expert testimony that 20 percent of those who contract asbestosis later go on to develop cancer as well, and of the likely medical effects of this type of cancer. Counsel for General Yards objects to all evidence relating to the cancer risk. What is the basis of the evidentiary objection and how should Judge Fudd rule on it?

Unpredictable Predictions

5. Beebe is a college graduate with a degree in economics. She is also a mother of three. She worked as an administrative assistant at a college until her first child was born. Now, she has three children and does not work outside the home. She is injured in an auto accident and permanently disabled. If she sues the other driver, should she recover for lost earning capacity?

6. Thoreau, a 12-year-old child, is thrown from an off-road vehicle and sustains serious injuries. As a result, he is left with a limp and permanent weakness in his right arm and leg. Thoreau had never worked prior to the injury.

    a. In an action against the manufacturer of the vehicle, could Thoreau recover for loss of earning capacity?

   b. Assume (through it is unlikely on these facts) that the jury found
      that Thoreau would be unable to work at all due to the injury.
      What evidence would be relevant to ascertaining the value of his
      lost earning capacity?
   c. Assume that the jury concludes that Thoreau would have earned
      $900,000 as a laborer over his work life expectancy, had he not
      been injured, and that, due to his injury, he will not be able to do
      any kind of heavy work. Should they award him that sum as
      damages for lost earning capacity?

Missing Elements

7.   Agassiz, a 79-year-old retired botanist, is hit by a concrete block
which falls from the fifth floor of an apartment house. He is rendered permanently unconscious by the blow, and is maintained in a comatose state
by various invasive procedures such as breathing and feeding tubes. Prior
to the accident, Agassiz lived on his pension and social security, which he
continues to receive. The medical bills for his treatment are truly impres-
sive; luckily, they are covered by Medicare and his supplemental health
insurance.
   a. Should Agassiz recover for pain and suffering?
   b. Should he recover for loss of enjoyment of life?
   c. Should Agassiz recover for the medical expenses for treatment of
      his injury?
   d. Should he recover for lost earning capacity?

An Emotion Motion

8.   Watson is seriously burned in an intersection accident between a car
in which he is riding as a passenger and a dump truck driven by Muir.
One of the two vehicles ran a red light, causing the collision. As a result
of the accident, he is hospitalized for many months, is severely disfigured,
suffers on-going pain and a variety of humiliating and depressing side
effects of his injuries. He will also require continuing treatment, including
many operations, for the rest of his life. He sues for his injuries.
      As trial approaches, one of the lawyers moves to "bifurcate" the trial,
that is, to try the issue of liability first, and have the jury decide whether
Muir negligently caused the accident before presenting evidence to the
jury on Watson's damages.
   a. Which lawyer probably made the motion, and why?
   b. What are the arguments in favor of granting the motion?
   c. What are the arguments against granting the motion?
9.   Assume that Watson's case goes to trial on liability and damages. At
trial, Watson's counsel seeks to introduce evidence that Agassiz, a plaintiff

in another recent lawsuit, received a jury award of $5.3 million in damages for burns. Should the evidence be admitted?

EXPLANATIONS

The Art of Prediction

1. You are probably not an expert in the medical treatment of paraplegia—though you might become one if you represented Mendel. But it is not hard to imagine the wide variety of medical problems that may result from paraplegia, and are likely to continue or worsen throughout the patient's life. Mendel, at 25, has a very long life expectancy, even if it is diminished somewhat by the injury. Over the years, he will likely require operations to cope with the consequences of his immobility, including, perhaps, plastic surgery to deal with sores on his body. He will need long-term physical therapy to preserve as much mobility as possible. He will need vocational training and counseling, sexual counseling, home care, special equipment, and home modifications to accommodate his condition. He will likely be hospitalized from time to time for more intensive care. He will need continuous medical monitoring and prescription medications, and may develop a variety of diseases that must be treated as well. He is likely to require psychotherapy as well to assist in adjusting to his disability. For a fuller discussion of the medical consequences of paraplegia, see Minzer, Nates, §126.

Naturally, Mendel himself knows little or nothing of all this, and probably does not want to think about it. His counsel must develop the proof based on Mendel's past treatment, current condition, and expert medical and actuarial testimony. Counsel must learn a great deal about the day-to-day effects of her client's condition, including such unglamorous realities as bowel and bladder control, bed sores, and muscle atrophy. Medical specialists will testify about the likely course of treatment his condition will require over the years, the probable prognosis for his long-term health, likely complications and corrective surgery, and the types of ongoing nursing and therapeutic services and medicines he will need. An accountant or economist will also testify as to the likely costs of such care, extrapolating out years or decades into the future, depending on the plaintiff's life expectancy.[7]

The defendant will likely present opposing experts on these issues, who reach substantially different conclusions concerning the required

---

7. These experts will command substantial fees for their assistance in trial preparation and for their testimony. In the ordinary case, the fee will be advanced by plaintiff's counsel as part of the costs of suit. Ultimately the plaintiff will have to repay her counsel for these expenses (ranging perhaps into five figures) out of the judgment the defendant pays.

treatment and its projected cost. Ironically, the members of the jury, probably unschooled in either medical care or accounting, will then have to assign a sum to this element of damages based on their assessment of the evidence.

2.   This is typical of the type of judgment attorneys must make all the time about the value of tort cases. Actually, it is simpler than most: Since negligence is admitted, Mendel's counsel does not have to consider the risk that he will be unable to establish that crucial element. In addition, since earnings and medical costs are negligible, the only real issue is the value of the intangible damages for tinnitus.

Of course, Mendel's counsel does have to consider whether the jury will believe his client. Since the symptoms cannot be corroborated by objective measures, Mendel's testimony will be critical. If the jury concludes that he is making up the injury, they may find against him even though the defendant admits negligence: You have to prove all four elements to recover for negligence, including damages.

If we assume that Mendel is credible, and that the testimony of family and co-workers corroborates his story, the question then becomes what the injury is "worth." As the introduction states, there is no objective measure for such intangible damages, so it becomes very difficult to predict the number a jury will attach to it. Any settlement will be based on educated guesses of counsel as to what would happen if they went to trial. As an indication of how uncertain the damages may be, I gave the facts of Mendel's case to my Torts class, and asked the students to decide, individually, what they would award if they were on the jury. The figures ranged from twenty thousand dollars to over half a million dollars.[8]

If Mendel's counsel concludes that the jury would award $50,000 for this, he might still settle for $35,000. He has to consider the costs of trial and the risk that the jury will disbelieve his client. On balance, it might be a reasonable choice to accept. Obviously, if counsel expects a considerably higher verdict at trial — as the figures from my class suggest he might — he should hesitate to accept the insurer's offer.

3a.   The goal of tort damages is to "place the victim in the same position he would have been in if he had not been injured." If Audubon had not been injured, he would have had income up until the age of 67. Due to the accident, all of those earnings are lost. Most courts would hold that Audubon can recover for lost earning capacity based on his *pre-accident* work life expectancy, even though he is not now able to work, and will (statistically speaking) die eight years before he would have retired.

---

8. A fair number of students reached their awards by calculating a sum for each minute, hour or day that Mendel must live with the problem. One student gave two cents per minute; another allotted $10,000 per year; a third, a dollar an hour. The resulting awards were in the $300,000 to $500,000 range given Mendel's life expectancy.

Arguably, calculating the future wages for the entire period overcompensates Audubon somewhat. If he had not been injured, he would likely have had his income for his full work life expectancy but would also have expended a large part of that on his living expenses. For the period from age 62 to 67, however, Audubon will not incur those expenses, due to his premature death (again, statistically speaking). It would be more accurate to require the jury to deduct the living expenses for that period from the earnings. Sounds a bit cold-blooded, though, doesn't it? Darwin's counsel may hesitate to raise the argument, since it sounds like he is trying to take advantage of the fact that the accident has shortened Audubon's life expectancy.

b.   Damages for pain and suffering compensate the victim for having to endure physical and psychic pain, humiliation, and anguish caused by the injury. The award should be based on the period during which he will actually experience pain and suffering. In Audubon's case, he will have to endure these (again, statistically speaking) for 20 more years. Pain and suffering damages should be awarded for his 20 year post-accident life expectancy, not based on his pre-accident life expectancy.

c.   This is an interesting issue. It is hard to deny that the loss of 11 years of life is grievous. It seems that Audubon ought to be compensated for that. On the other hand, if Audubon had been killed in the accident, he would have received no compensation for his lost years: Wrongful death actions compensate the *survivors* for their losses, not the decedent for his. See Chapter 17. But then, one of the rationales for the rule in death cases is that you cannot compensate the dead. Audubon is still alive. If we award him damages for his lost years, he can at least live out the years he has left a bit more pleasurably.

The courts are split on whether loss of life expectancy is a proper element of damages. English courts have allowed limited recovery for reduced life expectancy, but most American courts have denied it. See Minzer, Nates, §8.39. Several cases have recognized this as compensable, however, and there may be a trend in this direction. See e.g., *Alexander v. Scheid*, 726 N.E.2d 272, 280 (Ind. 2000); *Morrison v. Stallworth*, 326 S.E.2d 387, 393 (N.C. Ct. App. 1985).

Even courts that deny recovery for lost life expectancy per se will often allow the jury to consider, as a part of pain and suffering, the mental anguish the plaintiff suffers from the *realization* that he will likely die before his time. In addition, since Audubon's lost earning capacity is assessed on the basis of his pre-accident life expectancy, this element of his "lost years" will be considered in assessing damages.

d.   This is another interesting question. Loss of enjoyment damages compensate the plaintiff for her inability to participate in activities that she enjoyed prior to the accident. The types of losses included are legion, from walks in the park to playing softball with the kids to sky diving to bocci to sitting on the front porch and watching the world go by. Had the accident not taken place, Audubon would have engaged in whatever activities he fancied for as long as he was able, in many cases up to the end of his life. Due to the accident, he can no longer do so. The loss of enjoyment damages should be assessed with regard to his pre-accident life expectancy, not his reduced expectancy after the accident.

If a court accepts this view and allows damages for loss of enjoyment based on Audubon's pre-accident life expectancy, this recovery will also partially substitute for a separate award for the lost years themselves. Naturally, a large part of the value of Audubon's lost 11 years is the enjoyment of the activities and sensations of life during that period. If the jury can compensate for this loss, they are effectively invited to compensate for the lost years themselves. There may be a technical distinction — they are not supposed to give an award for the loss of life per se — but it is one which is likely to elude most juries.

The Single Be-Fuddlement Rule

4.   Doubtless, General Yards has objected to the evidence because it only indicates a 20 percent chance that Muir will develop cancer. Most courts hold that plaintiffs are entitled to recover for future injuries that are "reasonably probable" (Minzer, Nates at §9.06[5][a]), but 20 percent does not meet this standard. If Muir's evidence is insufficient to prove that cancer is a probable consequence, the jury should not hear it.

Obviously, Muir is in a very difficult position here. If he sues for his asbestosis damages, he will not recover any cancer damages in that action, and under the single recovery rule, he may be barred from bringing a second suit if he develops cancer later. Some courts have reached this conclusion under the single recovery rule. See, e.g., *Gideon v. Johns-Mansville Sales Corp.*, 761 F.2d 1129, 1136-1137 (5th Cir. 1983) (under Texas law, plaintiff must recover for present harm and all future consequences that will probably develop in the future). If Judge Fudd presides in such a jurisdiction, he should deny admission of the cancer evidence and Muir would recover nothing for this risk.[9]

Other courts, however, have recognized an exception to the single recovery rule, on the ground that cancer is a separate disease giving rise to a separate cause of action. See, e.g., *Pustejovsky v. Rapid-American*

---

9. Even in such a jurisdiction, Muir may be able to recover for the present fear that he will contract cancer in the future. Some courts have viewed this as a separate form of mental distress which, if reasonable, is compensable. See generally D. Dobbs, Law of Remedies, Practitioner Treatise Series §8.1(4), at 392-393.

Corp., 35 S.W.3d 643, 647-654 (Tex. 2000) (declining to follow *Gideon*); *Mauro v. Raymark Indus., Inc.*, 561 A.2d 257, 262-263 (N.J. 1989). These courts would allow Muir to sue again if he contracts cancer in the future. If the Honorable Fudd presided in a state that takes this view, he would *still* deny admission of the cancer evidence in the initial action, but Muir would be able to recover for cancer in a later suit if he develops it.

This latter approach relieves the plaintiff from the difficulties of proof posed by the single recovery rule, but it has several serious implications. First, it will multiply litigation, since plaintiffs who have already sued for asbestosis will be entitled to sue again. In addition, this approach seriously erodes the single recovery rule, since plaintiffs will make the same argument in other types of cases where further complications of an injury arise that were not compensated in the original suit.

There is a third possibility in such cases. The court could award damages to the plaintiff in the initial action for her *increased risk* of developing cancer. For example, if the risk is 20 percent, the jury could determine the damages that the plaintiff will incur if cancer develops, and award her 20 percent of that. This tracks the approach taken by some courts in loss-of-a-chance cases, and shares some of the same problems discussed with regard to that approach in Chapter 8, pp. 170-171, 180-182.

Unpredictable Predictions

5.   Although she was not working outside the home prior to the accident, Beebe certainly should receive damages for lost earning capacity. The fact that she was not working at the time does not mean that she would not have worked later. The odds are very good that a woman in her position would return to the work force when her children were older, if only to help with the staggering cost of college. Beebe's capacity to do so has been destroyed, and she is entitled to compensation for that. Estimating her lost earning capacity, of course, will be difficult, since she has little in the way of a track record on which to predict her earning potential. The jury will simply have to do their best based on testimony about her background, interests, and opportunities, and economic testimony concerning wage trends for the kind of work she would likely have undertaken in later years.

Beebe would be entitled to an award for loss of earning capacity even if she testified that she had no intention to work in the future, since the injury has deprived her of the *option* to work, should circumstances require her to do so. "The theory is that the injury has deprived the plaintiff of a capacity he would have been entitled to enjoy even though he may never have profited from it." *Hunt v. Bd. of Supervisors of the La. State Univ.*, 522 So. 2d 1144, 1152 (La. Ct. App. 1988).

6a. Surely Thoreau should not be denied recovery for loss of earning capacity simply because he has no earnings history. It would make no sense to refuse recovery to a child plaintiff who is injured before starting to work, and therefore loses *all* his potential earnings, while an adult who only lost part of his would be fully compensated for that loss. The jury should compensate Thoreau for his lost future earning capacity, even though it is exclusively a *future* loss and he has no earnings history.

While it is clear that Thoreau has a right to recover for lost earning capacity, it is less clear whether he has actually lost earning capacity, and, if so, how much. His partial disability would certainly interfere with his earning capacity if he were likely to become a manual laborer, but the interference might be minimal if he becomes a computer programmer or a stock broker. At the time of trial, Thoreau had no earnings history, no profession, probably no special skills or interests upon which to base a prediction of what work he would have chosen absent the injury. Thus, it will be very difficult for the jury to determine whether he has lost earning capacity. Yet they must decide, and might well conclude that an injury of this magnitude is likely to reduce his earning power. If they do, they may award damages, in some roughly appropriate amount, to compensate for the loss.

b.   In arriving at a figure, the jury must decide what Thoreau was likely to have earned if he had not been injured, which turns on the kind of work he would have chosen. To predict this, the jury may consider such factors as Thoreau's character, his health and physical skills, his record in school, his IQ, his background (including his parents' occupations and education), the likelihood that he would have finished high school and gone on to college, and his interests, as well as government statistics about earnings for different occupations and education levels. On the basis of such factors, the jury must determine Thoreau's pre-accident earning capacity. The result will of course be a gross approximation, but on balance preferable to denying compensation for a very serious economic loss.

Ironically, Thoreau's award may be higher if the evidence shows that he was academically deficient or less intelligent. If he shows strong intellectual ability, he may have lost little earning capacity, since he can still perform the work he would likely have chosen if he had not been injured. By contrast, a plaintiff with weaker academic skills would more likely make his living through some form of manual labor. A disabling injury would have a greater impact on his earning capacity and lead to a greater award.

Issues like future earning capacity often present very delicate problems of proof for defense counsel. Consider the issue of lost earning capacity for a 14-year-old boy killed by a police officer in the course of arrest. The jury has just heard the tearful testimony of the boy's mother about how diligent he was and how he hoped to grow up to be a firefighter. Now, counsel for the officer must present proof that the decedent had a long history of juvenile delinquency, truancy, failure at school, and general bad character, and that his most likely future was one of crime and incarceration. This evidence is clearly relevant to the issue of lost earning capacity, but it requires considerable skill to place it before the jury without alienating them.

c.   The jury's calculation of Thoreau's loss begins rather than ends with the determination of what he would have earned. Thoreau's lost earning capacity cannot be measured solely by what he could have earned *before* the injury. The jury must make a separate assessment of what he can earn *after* the injury. While Thoreau won't be able to do heavy manual labor, he may still be able to perform many other kinds of work. If he can work, his award for lost earning capacity should be based on the difference between his earning potential before and after the injury. Thus, the jury should consider what type of work Thoreau will be able to do with his disability, and determine the amount he is likely to earn from that work. They should then subtract that amount from the $900,000 he would have earned to determine the damages for lost earning capacity.

Once the jury has determined an amount for lost earning capacity, they will have to reduce this figure to "present value." Since Thoreau will receive the award today to compensate for losses over a number of years, the amount must be reduced to account for the interest Thoreau can earn on the award over the years. This present value concept is considered in the next chapter.

Missing Elements

7a. Agassiz has suffered a very serious injury, but a number of the usual elements of compensatory damages will not apply to his case. The facts suggest that he was rendered unconscious immediately by the blow. If so, he has not suffered any conscious pain and suffering. Most courts hold that a plaintiff must be conscious to recover for pain and suffering, since pain and suffering compensates subjective discomfort resulting from the injury, and unconscious patients do not experience these symptoms. See D. Dobbs, Law of Remedies, Practitioner Treatise Series §8.1(4), at 388.

This basic fact of damages doctrine has led to strained, sometimes unseemly efforts by plaintiffs' counsel to prove that the victim was conscious, if only for a second, since such proof opens the door for the jury to award damages for this highly subjective element.

b.   Agassiz has lost the ability to enjoy virtually all of life's pleasures. If that isn't loss of enjoyment, what is? Interestingly, the cases are divided on the question of whether a comatose patient can recover for loss of enjoyment. A leading New York case denies recovery, on the ground that the unconscious patient cannot benefit in any way from an award for loss of enjoyment, and consequently such an award would serve no compensatory purpose:

> Simply put, an award of money damages in such circumstances has no meaning or utility to the injured person. An award for the loss of enjoyment of life "cannot provide [such a victim] with any consolation or ease any burden resting on him . . . He cannot spend it upon necessities or pleasures. He cannot experience the pleasure of giving it away."

McDougald v. Garber, 536 N.E.2d 372, 375 (1989) (quoting *Flannery v. United States*, 718 F.2d 108, 111 (4th Cir. 1983), *cert. denied*, 467 U.S. 1226 (1984).

This holding has been controversial. For one thing, there can be no doubt that the plaintiff has suffered a grievous loss: Basically, he has lost *all* of life's enjoyment, whether he is aware of it or not. Had the plaintiff been totally disabled, but remained aware of it, he would have received full compensation for loss of enjoyment. It hardly seems appropriate that an even more seriously injured plaintiff should receive nothing for this loss. In addition, tort victims sometimes do obtain recoveries that they cannot enjoy, as where the estate of a decedent recovers damages in a survival action for predeath pain and suffering.

Other courts have allowed loss of enjoyment damages to comatose plaintiffs, on the theory that the loss of life's pleasures is an objective loss suffered by the plaintiff, whether or not he subjectively comprehends or experiences it. See, e.g., *Eyoma v. Falco*, 589 A.2d 653, 658-662 (N.J. Super. 1991); *Flannery v. United States*, 297 S.E.2d 433, 438-439 (W. Va. 1982); see generally Minzer, Nates at §8.40.

c.   This fairly simple question requires a complex answer. There is in the law of damages a quizzical doctrine called the "collateral source rule," which frequently holds the defendant responsible for losses to the plaintiff even though those losses are actually paid by a third party. For example, if a plaintiff incurs $5,000 in medical bills, but her health insurer pays most of it, she is still entitled, under the collateral source rule, to collect the full $5,000 from the defendant. Similarly, if plaintiff loses $30,000 in wages, but is compensated by his disability insurance policy for the loss, the defendant must still pay $30,000 for the loss.

This bewildering rule is often justified on the ground that the defendant should not obtain a windfall from the plaintiff's foresight in obtaining (and paying for) insurance protection against these losses. See generally D. Dobbs, Law of Remedies §8.6(3), at 494-498. Whether or not this rationale is convincing, the rule has been applied to many types of collateral source payments, including medicare, private insurance, continuation of wages by the plaintiff's employer, unemployment compensation, worker's compensation, and others. See generally Minzer, Nates at §17.00 ff.

Although the collateral source rule has been very widely applied, it has also been widely criticized, since it compensates plaintiffs for losses that they do not actually incur. Many recent statutes have limited the rule in an effort to control insurance costs, at least for certain types of cases or certain types of collateral benefits. See, e.g., Mich. Laws Ann. §600.6303 (1994) (requiring reduction of damages for collateral payments, adjusted for premiums plaintiff paid to obtain collateral source protection). If Agassiz's case were governed by the Michigan statute, he would recover very little despite the very substantial expense of his medical care.

d.   Although lost earnings and earning capacity are basic elements of tort damages, Agassiz will presumably not recover anything for this category of damages. Agassiz has not lost his pension or social security income: They are still paid to him after his injury, just as they were before. If he has not suffered a loss of these items due to the accident, the defendant need not compensate for them.

Even if the collateral source rule applies in Agassiz's jurisdiction, Agassiz will still have no claim for these lost benefits. The collateral source rule bars the defendant from taking advantage of the fact that plaintiff's loss from the injury has been compensated by a third party. But Agassiz is entitled to be paid his pension and Social Security regardless of his state of health, and will continue to be paid them despite the injury. Thus he hasn't lost these benefits; the collateral source rule is irrelevant to this element of his damages.

In the final analysis, Agassiz's case is troubling. He has suffered catastrophic injury, yet most of the big ticket elements of compensation — pain and suffering, loss of enjoyment, and lost earnings — will hardly figure at all in his damages. Depending on the status of the collateral source rule, he may not even be compensated for medical costs.

An Emotion Motion

8a. The motion will virtually always be made by defendant's counsel. If the trial is bifurcated, and liability is tried first, the jury will hear the evidence about the collision, the relative positions of the vehicles, the skid marks, their speed, and so on, and then go out and deliberate on the issue of which party ran the red light. If they find that Muir was not negligent, the trial will be over: Watson can't recover if Muir wasn't negligent. Defendant's counsel would very much prefer that the jury decide this relatively mundane issue without hearing the emotionally charged evidence about Watson's frightful injuries and continuing suffering. Who could hear such testimony and not want to do something for him? Who could dispassionately consider closely conflicting liability evidence without visions of the debilitated Watson haunting the deliberations? Jurors understand that Watson will go away empty handed if they find that Muir was not negligent. It seems almost too much to ask of them to set aside the testimony about Watson's injuries in deciding that question.[10]

b. There are several strong arguments for bifurcating trials in such circumstances. The first has already been suggested, that the jury will be more objective about the liability issues if they have not heard extensive testimony about Watson's grievous injuries. Another is that trying liability first can save a great deal of time. The damages testimony in Watson's case will be extensive, probably including expert witnesses, treating physicians and other health professionals, medical actuaries, and Watson himself. If the jury finds that Muir was not negligent, all the time devoted to hearing that extensive damages testimony will be saved. Further time will be saved in closing arguments and in instructing the jury if the trial is bifurcated, since only the liability issues need be considered and argued during the liability phase of the trial.[11]

c. One argument against bifurcation is that the same witnesses may testify on both liability and damages issues — for example, the plaintiff and the eye witnesses to the accident. The trial may lose coherence if these witnesses are called, examined on liability issues, and then recalled later to testify on damages. In addition, the plaintiff's injuries are sometimes relevant to the liability issues. For example, the location of Muir's injuries may assist the jury in deciding how the collision took place. In a surgical malpractice case, the nature of the plaintiff's neurological injuries may assist the jury in determining whether she received excessive anesthesia.

The decision to bifurcate the trial rests in the discretion of the trial judge, which is unlikely to be reversed on appeal. Traditionally, many judges favored letting plaintiffs try their cases as they please, and then sending the whole case to the jury. In an age of judicial management and overcrowded dockets, however, the efficiency and fairness arguments for bifurcation have begun to find more favor in the courts. See, e.g., 22 N.Y. Uniform Trial Ct. Rules, §202.42[a] (judges encouraged to bifurcate liability and damages issues in personal injury cases).

---

10. "Plaintiff in this case seeks damages for physical injuries, death and pain and suffering on behalf of himself and his deceased wife and children. In support of such damages, he will offer detailed evidence of extreme pain and suffering, including burning flesh and screams of pain. Courts in this Circuit have recognized that 'evidence of harm to a plaintiff, regardless of the cause, may result in sympathetic jurors more concerned with compensating plaintiff for his injury than whether or not defendant is at fault.'" *Zofcin v. Dean*, 144 F.R.D. 203, 205 (S.D.N.Y. 1992) (quoting from *Buscemi v. Pepsico, Inc.*, 736 F. Supp. 1267, 1272 (S.D.N.Y. 1990)).

11. Even if the jury finds the defendant negligent, bifurcation can save time, since, once liability is established, the likelihood of settlement increases dramatically.

9.   The introduction to this chapter emphasizes the subjective, unguided nature of the jury's decision on the intangible aspects of damages. Wouldn't it reduce this subjectivity somewhat if juries were able to compare awards made by other juries in similar cases?

Perhaps it would, but the evidence will almost certainly be excluded. To understand why, ask yourself what *Muir's* counsel would do if the judge admitted it. Naturally, she would want to distinguish Agassiz's case from Watson's, by showing that Agassiz's injuries were worse than Watson's, for example, or that he had a longer life expectancy than Watson. She would also cast about for other burn cases in which juries had awarded substantially *less*. Each party would expect the other to reveal the cases they planned to use before trial, and the parties would then do discovery and prepare evidence about them all. Pretty soon, the court would be trying not one burn case, but twenty.

Even if Agassiz's case were closely comparable to Watson's, the damage award in Agassiz's case is not an objective measure of the proper award. It is simply *another jury's* effort to value an inherently ambiguous loss. It is difficult to see why the Watson jury should give it any more credence than they would to their own judgment on the point.

On the other hand, giving the jury guidance about a reasonable range of verdicts would certainly improve the system; currently, they receive essentially no guidance in determining intangible damages. The only method of controlling damage verdicts is for judges to order a remittitur — to give the plaintiff a choice between accepting a lesser amount or facing a new trial. This provides some protection against extreme awards, but still leaves a wide range of discretion to the jury. A number of commentators have suggested that juries should receive a list of verdicts in similar cases, with information about the injuries in those cases and the amounts awarded. See, e.g., O. Chase, Helping Jurors Determine Pain and Suffering Awards, 23 Hofstra L. Rev. 763 (1995). See also *Jutzi-Johnson v. United States*, 263 F.3d 753, 759-760 (7th Cir. 2001) (suggesting that trier of fact should be informed of awards in similar cases to avoid "standardless, unguided exercise of discretion").

16

Astrological Calculations: Valuing Future Damages

Introduction

I dedicate this chapter to Rick, my old backpacking partner. Rick is an astronomer, and accustomed to working with large numbers. Sometimes, while our legs were getting a workout in the White Mountains, I would give his brain a little exercise as well. For example, while winter hiking once, I asked, "Rick, how many snowflakes do you think there are in New Hampshire today?" Here's how Rick came up with the answer:

Rick: Well, how big is New Hampshire?

Me: Oh, I don't know, about 60 miles by 150.

Rick: O.K., that's about 9,000 square miles. A mile is about 5,300 feet, so a square mile would have 5,300 times 5,300 square feet, which is roughly 28 million square feet. Multiply that by 9,000, and you get about 250 billion square feet in New Hampshire.

Now, how deep do you think the snow is in New Hampshire these days?

Me: Gee, Rick, it varies quite a bit. We didn't see much down south, but there's as much as three feet in parts of the mountains.

Rick: Well, the mountains cover only about a quarter of the state. How does a foot sound for an average?

Me: I'd say that's about right.

Rick: All right then, if there are 250 billion square feet of surface area in the state, we're talking the same number of cubic feet of snow. Now, how many snowflakes do you think there might be in a cubic inch?

Me: That's hard to say, Rick ... maybe a thousand?

Rick: I would have said 400, so we'll split the difference. That's 700 to the cubic inch, and there are about 1,700 cubic inches to the foot, so that's ah, 1.2 million snowflakes to the cubic foot. We'll round that off to a million. Multiply that times 250 billion, and you get 250 to the 16th power, or 250 quadrillion. So there you are, there are 250 quadrillion snowflakes in New Hampshire.

Me: Gee, Rick, that's a lot of snowflakes.

Rick was a good mathematician, and there was nothing wrong with his calculations. The problem, of course, lay in our *assumptions*, which were flagrantly, even joyously approximate.[1]

As the last chapter indicates, the same is often true in assessing future damages for such items as medical expenses and lost earning capacity. In projecting future wages, for example, the jury must often make assumptions, based on little relevant information, about the plaintiff's expected work life, the nature of his future employment, his prospects for advancement, future increases in productivity in his occupation, and others. Consequently, in assigning a dollar value to the loss, the jury will often have to reach a sum certain by multiplying uncertainties.

This chapter deals with some of the actuarial problems in assigning a sum to be paid today to compensate for damages to be suffered in the future. Although these appear to be largely accounting problems susceptible of mathematical solutions, they turn out, like Rick's snow calculations, to be based on some frequently dubious assumptions. The purpose of the chapter is to illustrate those assumptions, and the basic approaches lawyers use in valuing future damages. While the chapter is full of numbers, have no fear; it is the underlying legal principles, not the particular numbers, which you should understand.

Astronomical Hypotheticals

Two simple examples will illustrate the problems of assessing future damages. In the first, Kepler, an 83-year-old black man, retired from the banking business, is severely injured in an automobile accident, and the jury determines that he will need medical care for the rest of his life. In

---

1. On another trip, I noted the striking fact that the forest floor was covered with fallen trees, but we never saw a tree fall while hiking. We figured out how long we would have to walk to see a tree fall, but I don't remember the numbers.

the second, Hubble, a 59-year-old white woman who worked part-time in a machine shop, is disabled in an accident while working with a metal press. The jury concludes that she will not need future medical care, but that she will never work again.

In both cases, it is obvious that the jury will have to begin by determining the period over which the plaintiff's loss will be suffered. In Kepler's case, that will be his life expectancy; in Hubble's, her work-life expectancy. Life and work-life expectancy tables provide a starting point for making these determinations. These tables, compiled by insurers or government agencies, provide statistical averages of the number of years a person of a given age will live or work. Here is an example of a life expectancy table.[2]

Table 16-1: Life Table — Black Male

Age	Life Expectancy
76-77	8.9
77-78	8.5
78-79	8.1
79-80	7.7
80-81	7.3
81-82	7.0
82-83	6.7
83-84	6.3
84-85	6.0

Based on the table, Kepler, if he were the hypothetical average black male of age 83, could expect to live 6.3 more years.[3] Of course, no one is truly "average"; each of us is a unique individual. Kepler, for example, has permanent injuries from the accident that may shorten his life span considerably. It would be superficial to assume that he will live 6.3 years, and unduly rigid for courts to require juries to use the average figure. Thus, while such tables are admissible, the parties are free to introduce evidence that the plaintiff has a longer or shorter life expectancy. But the tables provide a good starting point, especially in cases, such as the wrongful

2. The table is based on statistics from the National Center for Health Statistics website, http://www.cdc.gov/nchs/products/pubs/pubd/lftbls/lftbls/htm (last visited May 5, 2004).

3. Use of race- and/or sex-based life expectancy and work-life expectancy tables has been criticized. See M. Chamallas, A Woman's Worth: Gender Bias in Damage Awards, Trial (Aug. 1995), 38-43. Their use has been approved, however, in analogous contexts. See *Manufacturers Hanover Trust Co. v. United States,* 775 F.2d 459 (2d Cir. 1985) (use of sex-based table approved in calculating value of reversionary interest in trust).

death of an infant, in which there is little evidence other than such tables from which to predict life expectancy.

Similar tables are available to estimate the future work-life expectancy of Hubble:

Table 16–2: [4] Work-Life Expectancies for White Women

Age	White Women	Active	Inactive
55	6.3	7.7	3.3
56	5.6	7.1	2.8
57	5.0	6.6	2.4
58	4.5	6.1	2.1
59	3.9	5.6	1.8
60	3.4	5.2	1.6
61	3.0	4.8	1.3
62	2.5	4.5	1.1

After the accident, of course, Hubble has *no* work-life expectancy; that is the whole point of her damage action. However, in estimating her wage loss, a table of this sort provides a starting point for estimating how long she *would have worked* if she had not been injured. As a 59-year-old woman, the table indicates that Hubble (who was "active" in the labor force before her injury) had a work-life expectancy of 5.6 years. However, as with life expectancy, the parties are free to argue that her actual work-life expectancy was higher or lower, and the jury may so find. In Hubble's case, the table may be pretty accurate, since she is close to the end of her work life. But it requires many snowflake assumptions to apply such tables to a disabled child, for example.

Let's assume for the sake of argument that the jury finds Kepler's life expectancy to be four years (less than average due to his injury) and Hubble's work-life expectancy to be six, just about the average for her age. We can roughly calculate each plaintiff's loss by multiplying the estimated yearly loss (fraught, of course, with its own flaky assumptions) by the number of years it will be suffered. If Kepler will need $25,000 a year in medical treatment, the loss is roughly $100,000; if Hubble made $10,000 per year, she should receive $60,000.

---

4. This table is based on data in J. Ciecka, et al., A Markov Process Model of Work-Life Expectancies Based on Labor Market Activity in 1997-98, 9 J. Legal Econ. 33 (1999-2000).

Accelerating the Future: The Concept of Present Value

A moment's thought, however, suggests that these awards may overcompensate both plaintiffs. The jury awards a sum today (i.e., the day of the verdict) to compensate the plaintiff for losses she will suffer next year, or three years from now, or 33 years from now. Kepler will not need $100,000 this year, nor would Hubble have earned $60,000 this year if she had not been injured. In each case the loss is spread over a period of future years, though the award is made at the beginning of the period.

The problem is that a dollar in the hand is worth two — or more — in the bush, or, put in more rigorous terms, the value of a dollar received today is greater than the value of a dollar that *will be received* in five years. Suppose, for example, that Hubble receives $10,000 in 2004, to compensate her for $10,000 in wages that she will lose in 2009. She can invest that $10,000 for the intervening five years, so that she will have a considerably larger sum in 2009 than the $10,000 that will be lost in that year. We all probably went to law school to avoid numbers, but it is important to understand this at least in a general way. Here's a simple illustration of the point, based on the assumption that Hubble will earn interest at 8 percent on her award:

Table 16–3

Jan 2004	Receives $10,000	
Jan 2005	Has $10,000 + $800 interest	= $10,800
Jan 2006	Has $10,800 + $864 interest	= $11,664
Jan 2007	Has $11,664 + $933 interest	= $12,597
Jan 2008	Has $12,597 + $1,008 interest	= $13,605
Jan 2009	Has $13,605 + $1,088 interest	= $14,693

As Table 16–3 indicates, the difference is very substantial, almost half again the $10,000 that the jury expects Hubble to lose in 2009. Clearly, the time value of money must be taken into account in awarding such future damages. This is done by a process known as "discounting the award to present value," that is, reducing the $10,000 future loss to a figure that, if invested conservatively for the five years, will yield $10,000 in the year of the expected loss. If the jury concluded, for example, that Hubble would lose $14,693 in wages in 2009, and that safe investments for the five-year period would earn 8 percent, they should award $10,000 to compensate for that future loss. As Table 16–3 shows, if she receives $10,000 in 2004 it will grow to $14,693 in 2009 if 8 percent interest rates are assumed.

Once again, actuarial charts, called "present value tables," are available to calculate the present value of a dollar to be received in the future at various interest rates. Here is an example of a chart for calculating present value.

Table 16–4[5]

Years Until Sum Is Due	Present Value of $1 at 2.00%	4.00%	6.00%	8.00%	10.00%
1	.98039	.96154	.94340	.92592	.90909
2	.96116	.92456	.89000	.85734	.82645
3	.94232	.88900	.83962	.79383	.75131
4	.92384	.85480	.79209	.73503	.68301
5	.90573	.82193	.74726	.68058	.62092
6	.88797	.79032	.70496	.63016	.56447

This table makes it easy to calculate the sum needed today to yield a dollar in a future year at a given interest rate. For example, if the jury wants to compensate Hubble for a one dollar loss three years from now, and they conclude that the interest rate will be 4 percent during that period, they should award her $.88900. If they wish to compensate her for a one dollar loss five years hence, and they find that interest rates will average 8 percent, they should award her $.68058, or 68-and-a-fraction cents. If they want to compensate her for a $10,000 loss five years in the future, they should give her (10,000 × .68058), or $6805.80. If Hubble receives that amount in January 2004, and invests her award wisely (a flaky assumption in itself), here's what should happen to it:

Table 16–5

Jan 2004	Receives $6805.80
Jan 2005	Has $6805.80 plus $544.46 interest ($7350.26)
Jan 2006	Has $7350.26 plus $588.02 interest ($7938.28)
Jan 2007	Has $7938.28 plus $635.06 interest ($8573.34)
Jan 2008	Has $8573.34 plus $685.87 interest ($9259.21)
Jan 2009	Has $9259.21 plus $740.74 interest ($9999.95)

As this table shows, the $6805.80 "present value" figure is simply $10,000 (minus a few cents for rounding off), projected backwards to account for the interest Hubble will earn on it over the following five years.[6]

---

5. Figures based on a similar chart in Minzer, Nates; Damages in Tort Actions, at §108.32.

6. This calculation is itself oversimplified: it assumes interest compounded yearly, while it may be compounded more frequently on many investments.

Clearly, the jury—who must fashion an award for Hubble's future loss—are not likely to know a thing about discounting, present value, and the like. They need to be educated on these actuarial concepts, and the lawyers must do so through expert witnesses. In a case with large future damages, the plaintiff will introduce expert testimony from an economist, who will offer an opinion on matters such as Hubble's likely future income had she not been injured, and the rates of interest she could earn on a damage award to replace those future earnings. The expert will also give her opinion as to the proper sum to replace the future wage loss, or a range of estimates based on different assumptions about Hubble's work-life expectancy and future interest rates.

The defendant's lawyer will cross-examine Hubble's expert, challenging the various assumptions she has used concerning future wages and discount rates. The defense may also offer its own expert, who will go through a similar exercise ... doubtless concluding that a lower figure should replace the future loss.

It is then up to the jury to decide. They may accept the plaintiff's expert's figure—or the defendant's. Or, they may view the plaintiff's figure as too generous and the defendant's as too stingy, and award something in the middle. What they will probably *not* do, however, is to try to go through detailed calculations themselves in selecting their damage award. They will probably recognize that the process is inherently a little flaky, and make a rough judgment based on the experts' presentations instead.

As a lawyer, you will need to understand these actuarial matters well enough to prepare an expert to testify, and to expose doubtful testimony by cross-examining the other side's economic experts. So it is worth a little brain strain to try to understand what is going on with calculations like these. Try your hand at the following present value calculations based on our example plaintiffs. (The explanations begin on p. 378).

EXAMPLES

Back to the Future

1. The jury in the Hubble case, deliberating on January 1, 2004, concludes that she will lose $6,000 per year in wages due to the disability and that she would have worked for six more years if she hadn't been injured. If the jury finds that Hubble can safely expect to earn interest at 6 percent on her award, how much should they award for the lost earnings? (Use Table 16–4 (on p. 370) and assume that each year's wages are received at the end of the year in which they are earned.)

2. Kepler seeks recovery for the future costs of physical therapy required due to his injury. The jury finds that he will spend $2,000 per year on physical therapy for the next two years. They further find that interest rates will

be 10 percent for those years. How much should they award for the cost of
the physical therapy?

3.   Suppose that Galileo incurs an injury that will cause him to lose 25 years
of future wages. At trial, the experts produce evidence that interest rates
have varied dramatically over the past three decades — as in fact they have.
The jury then retires and calculates that Galileo would have earned
$350,000 in future wages. They also conclude that interest rates are likely to
behave in the future much as they have in the past — that is, they will fluctu-
ate, perhaps between 4 and 10 percent. How should they discount Galileo's
wage loss to present value? If *you* were on that jury, what would you do?

Speculating Precisely: Adjustment
for Future Inflation

It may seem a bit snowflaky to have the jury make speculative assessments
of future earnings or expenses and then massage those numbers through
adjustments like present value. Such fine-tuning suggests a level of precision inconsistent with the astrological assumptions underlying projections
of future losses — sort of like tiptoeing on quicksand. Yet recent cases have
required considerably more precision in adjusting the jury's speculative
figures. For example, the courts increasingly hold that damages for future
losses should also be adjusted to take account of inflation.

Suppose, for example, that Hubble will lose $10,000 in wages in
2004 and that inflation is running at 4 percent. The jury may well find
that Hubble would have received cost of living increases to keep her salary
at the same level in terms of real buying power. Thus, her wages for the
six future years would actually be as follows:

Table 16–6

Wages for 2004	$10,000
Wages for 2005	$10,000 + $400 = $10,400
Wages for 2006	$10,400 + $416 = $10,816
Wages for 2007	$10,816 + $433 = $11,249
Wages for 2008	$11,249 + $450 = $11,699
Wages for 2009	$11,699 + $468 = $12,167

If inflation is to be considered in assessing Hubble's wage loss, it
appears that the jury should first calculate her wages for each future year
by adjusting them upward for inflation, and *then* discount the adjusted
sums to present value. Clearly, this will yield a higher figure than calculating present value without considering inflation. For example, based on
Table 16–4, the present value (in 2004) of Hubble's wage loss for the
year 2009, assuming a 6 percent interest rate, is .74726 × $10,000, or

$7472.60, if the future wage is not adjusted for inflation. If inflation is considered, however, the present value will be .74726 × $12,167 (the inflation-adjusted wage), or $9091.91. Accounting for inflation thus provides a considerably larger award in present dollars.

Traditionally, courts ignored inflation in calculating future losses, on the ground that it was too speculative to consider. However, the high inflation rates of the 1970s caused many courts to reconsider this somewhat unrealistic approach. The purpose of compensatory damages, after all, is to put the plaintiff in the position she would have been in if she had not been injured. If she had not been injured, her wages would doubtless have risen due to future inflation. Thus, most courts now allow the jury to take inflation into account in calculating damages, using one of several approaches. For example, the plaintiff's expert may do what I have done above in Table 16–6, that is, increase each future year's wages to account for inflation, and then discount the inflation-adjusted figures to present value. See *Jones & Laughlin Steel Corp. v. Pfeifer*, 462 U.S. 523, 543-544 (1983).

Another way to account for inflation is the "total offset" method, which assumes that the rate of inflation and the rate at which the award will earn interest will be roughly equal over the future years. See, e.g., *Beaulieu v. Elliott*, 434 P.2d 665, 671-672 (Alaska 1967).[7] On this assumption, the increase for inflation and the decrease for discounting to present value cancel each other out. Thus, the jury is simply instructed to calculate the award without increasing the future wage figures to reflect inflation *or* reducing the award to present value. This quizzical approach, which adjusts for two variables by adjusting nothing, has the considerable virtue of simplicity: The jury need not get into the complexities of projecting inflation and interest rates or discounting to present value.

A third method is to calculate present value by a discount rate based on the anticipated difference between inflation and interest rates. As a historical matter, interest rates tend to run between 1 and 3 percent above inflation; thus, the "real" earning power of money is 1 to 3 percent. Courts that use the "real interest rate" approach reason that discounting future losses by a figure in this range automatically accounts for both interest earned and inflation. See generally *Pfeifer*, 462 U.S. at 541-549. For example, assume that the jury finds that inflation will run at 5 percent and interest rates at 8 percent for the period of the future loss. Instead of increasing the wage figures by 5 percent to account for inflation and then decreasing them by 8 percent to present value, this approach accounts for both effects in one step, by calculating the loss in present dollars and

---

7. *Beaulieu* has been partially superseded by statute. Alaska Stat. §09.17.040 (requiring reduction of future economic damages to present value unless parties agree to apply *Beaulieu*).

discounting each year's loss by 3 percent, the differential between the inflation rate and the interest rate.

The following examples illustrate the application of these methods of accounting for inflation.

Inflated Expectations

4.   Assume that Hubble will loss $10,000 (in 2004 dollars) in wages for each year from 2005 to 2009. Assume also that the jury finds that inflation will run at 4 percent, and that interest rates will average 6 percent.
   a. How much should the jury award Hubble for this loss under the total offset method?
   b. How much should the jury award if it adjusts the award for inflation and then reduces it to present value? (Use the figures in Table 16–6 to save some calculations.)
   c. How much should the jury award under the "real interest rate" approach?

5.   Assume that Kepler will require $4,000 (in 2004 dollars) worth of physical therapy in each year from 2005 to 2009.
   a. Should the jury also take account of inflation in calculating this award?
   b. Assume that inflation is running at 4 percent and interest rates are 6 percent. If you represented Kepler, what argument would you make that the court should use a higher inflation rate in calculating the award for physical therapy?

Speculating More Precisely: The Effect of Taxes

Perhaps this brief excursion into the astrology of predicting future damages[8] has already convinced you to strike personal injury law from

---

8. As a former English major, I felt it wise to have an economist read this chapter. He was not taken with my astrology metaphor:

> As a thin-skinned economist, I object to comparing economic forecasting with astrology. Your basic point, with which I strongly agree, is that the forecasts are bound to have large errors sometimes, as no one can perfectly forecast the future. But the presence of large errors in forecasts for a particular individual does not mean either that the individual forecasts are random, or that they do not predict well for the population of individuals over long periods of time. Astrology? This comparison makes it seem as if the forecast for an individual contains no information about the individual's future earnings. I don't think that's correct.

Well, maybe I do overstate the case a bit. Certainly, I would be a lot more comfortable with these types of figures if they were forecasting the *average* future earnings of a large population rather than the *actual* earnings of Hubble.

your list of possible specialties. But recent cases require still further refinements of future damage calculations. Most notably, some courts now require juries to factor the effects of taxes into their calculations.

Traditionally, courts have not instructed juries to take account of taxes in calculating personal injury awards, even for such elements as wages, which would have been subject to tax if they were earned in the regular course. One reason for this reluctance is the complexity of taking taxes into account. As one court opined, "The average accident trial should not be converted into a graduate seminar on economic forecasting." *Doca v. Marina Mercante Nicaruguense* S.A., 634 F.2d 30, 39 (2d Cir. 1980). Considering the effect of taxes introduces many additional variables, such as future tax rates, exemptions, and deductions. For many years, courts concluded that this additional complexity, even if conceptually justified, was too flaky to get into.

There are actually two aspects to the tax problem. First, there is the question of the taxation of *the judgment itself*, the dollar sum the plaintiff receives from the defendant if she wins the lawsuit. Under the Internal Revenue Code, tort awards "received...on account of personal physical injuries or physical sickness" are not taxable income. 26 U.S.C. §104(a)(2). Thus, the plaintiff will receive the full amount awarded, even if part or all of the award is for future wages that clearly would have been subject to tax if they had been earned in the normal course. Suppose, for example, that Hubble is awarded $47,000 for lost future wages. Under §104(a)(2), she will not be required to report any part of that sum as income for tax purposes, so long as her damages are for physical injury or sickness. She will pocket the entire sum — less the considerable expenses and legal fees incurred to achieve the recovery.

Traditionally, courts refused to instruct the jury that the award is not taxed, even if a party asked the court to do so. Courts reasoned that the tax consequences of the judgment were none of the jury's business; their task was simply to calculate the amount of the loss.[9] Here again, however, some courts have rejected the earlier approach and approved instructions that the award is not taxable, to help the jury understand the consequences of the calculations they are making. See, e.g., *Norfolk & Western Ry. Co. v Liepelt*, 444 U.S. 490, 496-497 (1980).

---

9. Here is Justice Blackmun's reason for opposing the instruction: "The required instruction...does not affect the determination of liability or the measure of damages. It does nothing more than call a basically irrelevant factor to the jury's attention, and then directs the jury to forget that matter." *Norfolk & Western Ry. Co. v. Liepelt*, 444 U.S. 490, 502 (1980) (Blackmun, J., dissenting). See also *Rego Co. v. McKown-Katy*, 801 P.2d 536, 539 (Colo. 1990) ("it is beyond the court's province to caution the jurors against every erroneous belief they may hold").

An Interim Question

6.   Which party, plaintiff or defendant, is likely to request an instruction to the jury that the award will not be subject to taxes?

The second aspect of the tax issue is whether the jury, in calculating the future wages the plaintiff would have received, should consider the fact that the plaintiff, had she earned the wages in due course, would have actually received only her *net* wages after taxes. Defendants have argued that using gross earnings to estimate future wage losses overcompensates the plaintiff, since she would have received substantially less because of the taxes due on those wages. For example, if Hubble would have earned $10,000 per year in the five remaining years of her work life expectancy, she might have paid something like $1,500 of each year's income in taxes. Thus, her net pay would only have been about $8,500 in each of those years. If the goal of compensatory damages is to "put the plaintiff in the position she would have been in but for the injury," it seems like the $8,500 figure should be used.

The argument certainly appears sound, since we all know that taxes take a considerable bite out of our gross pay. However, as with inflation adjustments, factoring income taxes into the equation complicates the jury's task considerably, and moves us further into the realm of snowflake speculation. Here are a few of the factors which must be considered in predicting future taxes:

- Future tax rates. The top rate for federal income taxes was 31 percent in the late eighties, but more than twice that at the beginning of the decade. What tax rate should the jury choose for future years?
- Deductions. Will the plaintiff have children, marry (or divorce), have large medical expense deductions due to his injuries or other illnesses?
- Gross income. Since federal tax rates are progressive, a couple's tax rate will depend on both spouses' income. Should the jury hear evidence on the plaintiff's *spouse's* future income, in order to ascertain the rate of tax on their joint income for future years?
- Other taxes. Should social security, medicare, and other taxes be considered? How about state taxes? If so, should evidence be allowed as to whether the plaintiff will move to another state with a higher state tax, or with none?
- Other income sources. Should the jury hear evidence of the plaintiff's (or his spouse's) prospects of a large inheritance, which would raise his tax bracket in future years? Should it predict the future value of his stock portfolio for the same purpose?

Obviously, these and other factors could vastly complicate the trial of damages, without necessarily resulting in a more precise conclusion as to the proper damage figure. Thus, many courts concluded, and a fair number still do, that future taxes are "too speculative" to consider in valuing future wages. See the annotation, Propriety of Taking Income Tax into Consideration in Fixing Damages in Personal Injury or Death Action, 16 A.L.R. 4th 589 §8. Other cases, however, have allowed consideration of the tax impact, especially since the Supreme Court approved this practice in *Liepelt*. These courts recognize the uncertainties inherent in predicting taxes, but point out that many *other* factors are speculative too, so why should one more be ignored! It is not surprising that, having once tiptoed into these actuarial quicksands, it is hard for courts to refuse to consider factors, like taxes, which clearly do affect the plaintiff's actual loss.

The argument for considering the effect of taxes is especially strong in assessing damages for *past* lost wages. If the trial takes place five or six years after the injury, the jury will have to calculate the lost wages for the period between injury and trial, as well as for future years. The factors affecting the plaintiff's tax liability for this past period are relatively easy to ascertain, and thus the argument for considering taxes is strong. If taxes are deducted for past wages, however, it weakens the argument for ignoring taxes on future income.

For the stout of heart, the following example illustrates how taxes may be taken into consideration in assessing future damages.

EXAMPLES

Taxing the Patience of the Jury

7. Assume that Hubble's case is tried in a jurisdiction that allows the jury to consider the effect of taxes on future lost earnings. If Hubble will lose $10,000 (in current dollars) in wages for the next five years, how should the jury calculate her lost future income, after taxes, for the five years? Assume that the jury finds that Hubble would have paid an average of 30 percent in taxes during those years, that inflation will run at 4 percent, and that interest rates will be 6 percent. Assume further that

   a. The jurisdiction does not allow inflation adjustments.

   b. Now, assume that the jurisdiction allows adjustments for present value and inflation, using the total offset method.

   c. Instead, assume that the jurisdiction calculates future damages with an inflation adjustment and then reduces them to present value.

   d. Finally, assume that the jurisdiction uses the "real interest rate" method.

Warning: Skip This Example!

8. If you represented Hubble, how would you argue that reducing the future wages to account for taxes only partially accounts for the effect of taxes, and leads to an unfairly low award?

9.   Assume that the court concludes that all three of the issues addressed in this chapter, present value, inflation, and the effect of taxes, should be considered in determining future damages. Can you formulate a workable instruction to inform the jury how it should go about awarding a sum to compensate for future wages, taking each of these factors into account?

Judge Fudd Befuddled

10. Kepler introduces evidence at trial that his injury causes constant, severe pain and suffering, which will continue as long as he lives. At the close of the trial, defense counsel asks Judge Fudd to give the following instruction to the jury:

> If you find that the plaintiff will suffer pain and suffering in the future, you may award him a sum to compensate for that pain and suffering. In the event that your verdict includes an amount for future pain and suffering, that sum should be discounted to present value in the same manner applicable to future wage losses.

How should the Honorable Fudd rule on the motion?

EXPLANATIONS

Back to the Future

1.   Table 16–4 (p. 370) provides the discount rate for calculating the loss. For example, to provide Hubble a dollar at the end of the first year, assuming a 6 percent interest rate, the jury should give her $.94340. To give her 6,000 of them at the end of that year, it should give her (6,000 × $.94340), or $5,660.40. If she puts this out at interest for the year, it will make .06 × $5,660.40, or $339.62. Added to the $5,660.40 award, this equals $6,000.02, with a little splashover for rounding off. Here is how the figures work out when each future year's loss is discounted for the appropriate number of years:

For 2004:	(6,000 × $.94340)	=	$ 5,660.40
For 2005:	(6,000 × $.89000)	=	$ 5,340.00
For 2006:	(6,000 × $.83962)	=	$ 5,037.72
For 2007:	(6,000 × $.79209)	=	$ 4,752.54
For 2008:	(6,000 × $.74726)	=	$ 4,483.56
For 2009:	(6,000 × $.70496)	=	$ 4,229.76
		Total:	$29,503.98

Note several things about this process. First, the present value of the future loss has to be calculated separately for each year's loss, because a different discount rate applies depending on how far in the future the earnings would have been received.

Second, the present value of a $6,000 loss is less for each successive year. This stands to reason: The present value of $6,000 to be received in five years is less than the present value of $6,000 due in one year, because the plaintiff has four extra years to invest the money received before it must replace the future loss.[10]

2.   This example involves future medical costs, not wage loss, but the principle is the same. The jury should determine an amount to award today that a prudent investor may use to yield the needed amount in the year in which the expense will be incurred. Kepler needs $2,000 for next year's therapy, and $2,000 for the following year. The present value of these sums can be calculated using the 10 percent column in Table 16–4 on p. 370.

First year:	$2,000 (.90909)	=	$1,818.18
Second year:	$2,000 (.82645)	=	$1,652.90
		Present value	$3,471.08

If the jury awards Kepler $3,471.08 today, and he puts it out at 10 percent interest, it will grow to a sum that will pay $2,000 at the end of one year, and leave enough to grow to another $2,000 at the end of the second year. Just for fun let's spin out the numbers and make sure that is true.

---

10. Tables are also available to simplify this calculation. These tables give you the present value of an *income stream* for a given number of years. Here's an excerpt from such a table:

Table 16–7: Present Value of $1 Per Year for Specified Number of Years

# of Years	3.00%	4.00%	5.00%	6.00%
1	.97	.96	.95	.94
2	1.91	1.89	1.86	1.83
3	2.83	2.78	2.72	2.67
4	3.72	3.63	3.57	3.47
5	4.58	4.45	4.33	4.21
6	5.42	5.24	5.08	4.92

This table allows the jury to calculate how much to give the plaintiff to provide an income stream of $1 for a period of years at a given interest rate. Instead of calculating each year separately, you can calculate the future income in a single step using a factor from the table. To give Hubble a dollar a year for three years at a 3.00 percent interest rate, give her $2.83 today. To give her a dollar a year for six years assuming a 6.00 percent interest rate, give her $4.92. To give her $6,000 per year for six years at the 6.00 percent rate, give her 6,000 × $4.92, which equals $29,520, very close to the figure I calculated above using my Neanderthal math skills.

> Starts with $3,471.08 jury award, invests at 10 percent
> End of Year 1 has $3,471.08 + $347.11 interest = $3,818.19
> Spends $2,000 on first year's therapy, has $1,818.19 left
> End of Year 2 has $1,818.18 plus $181.82 interest = $2,000
> Pays second year's therapy, has zero left

Very tidy, isn't it?[11]

3.   If you think about it, discounting a sum for a number of years at *different* interest rates is a complicated calculation. The table won't do it for you: You would have to discount the sum at various rates for various periods, to imitate what would actually happen if the award were put out at interest at various rates over various future periods.[12] An economist could doubtless do it, but imagine 12 ordinary citizens from all walks of life trying to do it for a 25 year period with five different interest rates!

Naturally, they will have the good sense not to do that: They will make a rough judgment of the average rate of interest over the entire period and apply the discount table to calculate the approximate future loss. That is all that we can expect them to do, and we'll be lucky if they manage that. Alternatively, they may make a rough estimate based on the figures used by the expert whose interest rate assumptions are closest to their own. Most experts realize this, and it gives them a strong incentive to use realistic assumptions in calculating future losses.

Inflated Expectations

4a.   Under the total offset approach, the jury would determine Hubble's wage loss in current dollars for the five years and add the figures together to reach the award. If they determined that Hubble's wages would not increase due to merit raises or promotions, they would simply award $50,000, five times her current yearly wage.

Even using the offset approach, the figures for the future years may vary. The jury might find that Hubble would receive raises *above* inflation, due to experience, the quality of her work, or productivity increases in

---

11. Even this calculation, of course, is approximate: It assumes that Jones will need $2,000 at the *end* of each period, rather than dispersing it gradually over the year, as is more likely.

12. I guess you would start with the last year's wage loss, discount it back one year at the rate for that year, then discount the discounted sum by the rate for the next-to-the-last year, and so on. Having done that 25 times for the last year's loss, you would start over and do it 24 times for the wages for year 24, and so on.

the industry. And, of course, if she were promoted to a higher paying position, they would award higher sums for the years in the new job. But in either case, they can ignore the confusing inflation and present value adjustments and focus on "real" increases in her compensation.

While the total offset method is simple, its simplicity may be at too great a cost. Since history teaches that interest rates typically outpace inflation, isn't the method automatically inaccurate? Not necessarily; history also teaches that worker productivity tends to rise over time, and that such increases will push up wages over and above inflationary increases. In fact, such productivity increases may well average roughly 2 percent per year. J. Jensen, The Offset Method of Determining Economic Loss, Trial Magazine, Dec. 1983, at 86. If this factor is added to the 4 percent inflation adjustment in the example, it would bring it up to 6, which roughly equals the interest or discount rate. So the total offset method may be accurate enough in most cases.[13]

b. Under this approach, the jury calculates the inflation-adjusted wages for the future years, and then discounts each sum to present value. Table 16–6 (on p. 372) indicates that Hubble's wages for the years 2005-2009 would be $10,400, $10,816, $11,249, $11,699 and $12,167, assuming 4 percent inflation. Each of these figures must be discounted separately, since each will be received at a different time. Here are the calculations, using the 6 percent discount column from Table 16–4:

For 2005:	$10,400 × .94340	=	$9,811.36
For 2006:	$10,816 × .89000	=	$9,626.24
For 2007:	$11,249 × .83962	=	$9,444.89
For 2008:	$11,699 × .79209	=	$9,266.66
For 2009:	$12,167 × .74726	=	$9,091.91
		Total:	$47,241.06

Note that these figures do not account for such factors as merit raises, promotions, or productivity increases within the industry. But there is nothing to prevent the jury from *further* fine-tuning the analysis by adjusting the future wages for these as well so long as plaintiff has offered evidence to support such adjustments. If they do, the predicted future wage, increased for inflation *and* the other factors, would then be discounted to present value.

c. Under the "real interest rate" method, the jury calculates the future wages in terms of current dollars, and uses a discount rate based

---

13. Obviously, however, if the rationale for the method is that productivity increases balance the "real interest rate," the jury should be instructed not to make any separate adjustment for worker productivity increases in determining the plaintiff's future wages.

on the difference between inflation and interest rates. In our case, that difference is 2 percent. The jury would award Hubble's current wage figure, $10,000, for each of the five years (again, assuming they did not find that she would receive promotions, merit raises, or productivity increases). This figure would be discounted using the 2 percent column in the present value table (Table 16–4 on p. 370). Again, this must be done separately for each year:

For 2005:	$10,000 × .98039	=	$9,803.90
For 2006:	$10,000 × .96116	=	$9,611.60
For 2007:	$10,000 × .94232	=	$9,423.20
For 2008:	$10,000 × .92384	=	$9,238.40
For 2009:	$10,000 × .90573	=	$9,057.30
		Total:	$47,134.40

The present value under this approach is quite close to the figure calculated by adjusting up for inflation and then discounting to present value.

The real interest rate approach has more to recommend it than just simplicity. Under this approach, the jury *need not forecast the actual rates of inflation and interest for any future period*: All they have to do is predict the average differential between the two over the period in question. In recent decades, both inflation and interest rates have varied widely, making it hard to predict them accurately. (What jury, for example, at the end of the high interest rate period of the late 1970s, would have predicted the very low rates of the 1990s?) But the *relationship* between inflation and interest rates has remained more stable. Thus, the real interest rate method may provide a shortcut to a fairly reliable inflation adjustment. It will be especially helpful if the parties can agree on a rate before trial, and stipulate that the judge can make the present value calculations using raw figures reached by the jury, thus avoiding the necessity of explaining this whole problem to the jury.

5a. Inflation will affect the actual dollars Kepler will need to pay his future therapy bills, just as it affects the actual dollars Hubble would have received had she continued to work. In a jurisdiction that considers inflation in calculating future wages, it would be hard to justify ignoring it in calculating future medical expenses as well.

b. Kepler's counsel should argue that the general 4 percent inflation rate is not the relevant figure for estimating Kepler's future medical expenses: The jury should consider the rate of inflation for *medical care* instead. It is a matter of common knowledge that those expenses have risen at a far higher rate than expenses in general in recent decades. To fairly compensate Kepler, this more specific inflation rate should be used. See, e.g., *Muenstermann by Muenstermann v. United States*, 787 F. Supp.

499, 524-525 (D. Md. 1992), in which the inflation rate applicable to medical expenses was considered separately.[14]

On the other hand, evidence might show (I really don't know whether it would or not) that much of the inflation increase in the medical area comes from new, expensive equipment and state-of-the-art diagnostic and operative procedures irrelevant to Kepler's treatment. It may be that inflation for *physical therapy* has been much more restrained. If the plaintiff is allowed to produce evidence of rates for medical care, the defendant may justifiably argue for an even more specific focus on the exact type of care Kepler will need. Certainly, this will fine tune the analysis, but it will also increase the complexity of the evidence, the expense to the parties for experts, and the burden on the courts. It is understandable that courts may resist such fine-tuning.

An Interim Question

6. The instruction is virtually always requested by defendants. They reason that, if the jury is not told that the plaintiff gets the full award, the jurors may assume that it will be taxed to the plaintiff when received. If they do, they may calculate the damages and then *increase* the amount to make sure that the plaintiff gets the amount they intended *after taxes*.

For example, if the jury concludes that Hubble has lost $47,000 in future wages, and they anticipate that she will pay about 30 percent of the award to the government, they might increase their award to assure that she will get $47,000 after taxes. Thus, they might award her $67,142 on the theory that, if she receives this much and pays 30 percent of it in taxes, she would actually end up with $47,000. If the jury did this, Hubble would end up with an extra $20,142 (paid, of course, by the defendant) since the award is not taxed as income. To avoid this scenario, the defendant would like the jury to understand during their deliberations that the plaintiff will receive the whole award free of tax.

Taxing the Patience of the jury

7a. If inflation is not considered, the jury would presumably determine the percentage of the plaintiff's future earnings that would go to taxes,

---

14. One economist points out to me, however, that experts have to be cautious in taking this approach. If inflation in any one sector of the economy consistently outstripped that in other areas, it would eventually "gobble up the gross national product." Conversation with Dana C. Hewins, Professor, Regis College. An expert who projected lopsided rates far into the future would thus be open to some powerful impeachment on cross-examination.

and reduce each future year's income by that percentage. If they concluded that Hubble would pay 30 percent in taxes, they would award her $7,000 for each year, and discount each year's projected income using the 6 percent figures in the present value table.[15] Here are the figures:

Wages for 2005	$7,000 × .94340	=	$6,603.80
Wages for 2006	$7,000 × .89000	=	$6,230.00
Wages for 2007	$7,000 × .83962	=	$5,877.34
Wages for 2008	$7,000 × .79209	=	$5,544.63
Wages for 2009	$7,000 × .74726	=	$5,230.82
		Total:	$29,486.59

b. Under the total offset method, the future damages for each year would be reduced to $7,000 to account for taxes, but these numbers would not be adjusted for inflation or discounted to present value. Hubble would receive $35,000 (5 × $7,000) for her future lost wages.

c. Presumably the jury would calculate the future wages for each year, with an upward adjustment for inflation, and then reduce each figure for taxes. The inflation-adjusted wages would be the same as those in Example 4b, but they would be reduced by 30 percent for taxes before discounting at 6 percent:

Tax adjustment:			
For 2005:	$10,400 × .70	=	$7,280.00
For 2006:	$10,816 × .70	=	$7,571.20
For 2007:	$11,249 × .70	=	$7,874.30
For 2008:	$11,699 × .70	=	$8,189.30
For 2009:	$12,167 × .70	=	$8,516.90
Discounting:			
For 2005:	$7,280.00 × .94340	=	$6,867.95
For 2006:	$7,571.20 × .89000	=	$6,738.37
For 2007:	$7,874.30 × .83962	=	$6,611.42
For 2008:	$8,189.30 × .79209	=	$6,486.66
For 2009:	$8,516.90 × .74726	=	$6,364.34
		Total:	$33,068.74

d. It is not clear how the jury should make the calculation under the real interest rate method. They will not actually calculate the future, inflation-adjusted wages, so they cannot make the tax adjustment the way we

---

15. The same result can be reached by calculating present value without considering taxes, and then reducing that figure by 30 percent.

did just above in Example 6c. I suppose they would reduce the *un-adjusted* future wage losses for taxes, as we did in Example 7a, and then discount the reduced wage figures using the 2 percent column in Table 16–4. That approach again yields a figure close to the market interest rate approach:

Wages for 2005	$7,000 × .98039	=	$6,862.73
Wages for 2006	$7,000 × .96116	=	$6,728.12
Wages for 2007	$7,000 × .94232	=	$6,596.24
Wages for 2008	$7,000 × .92384	=	$6,466.88
Wages for 2009	$7,000 × .90573	=	$6,340.11
		Total:	$32,994.08

Not surprisingly, the award under each of these approaches is substantially below the awards in Example 4, which ignored the effect of taxes on the same future lost wages.

Warning: Skip This Example!

8. Don't say I didn't warn you. This example raises an interesting, but complicated, problem. It is called the "reverse tax effect."

Defendants have argued that it is unrealistic to ignore the bite that taxes would have taken on a plaintiff's future income, had it actually been received and taxed in due course. However, if the court accepts this argument, and allows the jury to use post-tax figures in valuing future lost wages, it will have to tiptoe even farther into the actuarial quicksands. There is another wrinkle to the tax problem: When Hubble receives her award, and invests it, and earns interest on that investment, *that interest will be taxed.* Thus, the future growth of that award will not be determined just by the interest rate she earns; it will also have to be adjusted downwards to account for the taxes she pays on that interest.

If you're confused, it's your own fault; I told you to skip this one. But a simple example should illustrate the reverse tax effect. Take a look at Table 16–5, p. 370. That table shows that, to provide Hubble with 10,000 in 2009, the jury should give her $6,805.80 in 2004 (assuming an 8 percent interest rate). Under §104(a)(2) of the Internal Revenue Code, Hubble will not pay any tax on the $6,805.80 when she receives it. However, she *will* pay taxes on the interest she subsequently earns on that sum. Because this is true, her $6,805.80 will not actually grow to $10,000 in 2009; it will be substantially less. Here is a simplified illustration of the point, assuming that Hubble pays 30 percent in taxes on the yearly interest income from her award:

Table 16-8

Jan 2004	Receives $6,805.80		
Jan 2005	Has $6,805.80 + (.70 × $544.46)		
	= $6,805.80 + $381.12	=	$7,186.92
Jan 2006	Has $7,186.92 + (.70 × $574.95)		
	= $7,186.92 + 402.47	=	$7,589.09
Jan 2007	Has $7,589.09 + (.70 × $607.13)		
	= $7,589.09 + 424.99	=	$8,014.08
Jan 2008	Has $8,014.08 + (.70 × $641.13)		
	= $8,014.08 + $448.79	=	$8,462.87
Jan 2009	Has $8,462.87 + (.70 × 677.03)		
	= $8,462.87 + 473.92	=	$8,936.62

As Table 16–8 shows, Hubble would actually have over $1,000 less than the projected $10,000 in 2009. It may be fair enough to disregard this point if taxes on her future earnings are not considered, but once the jury is required to adjust the award *downward* for taxes on the future earnings, they should in fairness be required to adjust the award *upward* as well to compensate for the taxes she will pay on the interest on her award.[16]

Remarkably, in cases of long-term future losses, the taxes on the interest income from the award may actually exceed the taxes that would have been payable on the future wages themselves, so that the plaintiff does *better* if the jury is instructed to consider taxes in assessing the lost wages! S. LaCroix and H. Miller Jr., Lost Earnings Calculations and Tort Law: Reflections on the *Pfeifer* Decision, 8 U. Haw. L. Rev. 31, 44-45 (1986). This will only be true, however, if the jury considers both the taxes that would have been paid on the future wages and the taxes paid on interest income on the award.

Note that for future medical expenses, there is no need to adjust for taxation of the yearly future figures, as there is with wages. However, the *reverse tax effect* still applies, since plaintiff will pay taxes on the interest income she earns on her damage award and that will lower its future growth.

---

16. One method of accounting for taxes on the interest income is to reduce the discount rate by the same percentage as the future wages. See P. Bradford, Measuring Tort Damages for Loss of Earnings Without Deducting Income Taxes: A Wisconsin Rule Which Lost Its Rationale, 70 Marq. L. Rev. 210, 234 n.91 (1987). For example, if the discount rate is 6 percent, and the tax rate used in calculating the future wages is 30 percent, reduce the 6 percent by 30 percent (.06 × .70 = .042 or 4.2 percent). Use the 4.2 percent figure instead of 6 percent in discounting to present value.

9.   Here is an instruction summarizing the necessary calculations that the court quoted with approval in *J.F.P. Offshore, Inc. v. Diamond*, 600 So. 2d 1002, 1005 (Ala. 1992):

> If you should find that the Plaintiff has proved a loss of future earnings, any amount you award for that loss must be reduced to present value. This must be done in order to take into account the fact that the award will be paid now, and the Plaintiff will have the use of that money now and in the near future, even though the total loss will not be sustained until later in the future.
>
> In order to make a reasonable adjustment for the present use of money representing a lump-sum payment of anticipated future loss, you must apply what is called a below-market discount rate.
>
> In making that calculation you should first determine the net, after-tax income the Plaintiff would have received during the remainder of his working life, including any increases he would have received as a result of any factors other than inflation. This future income stream must then be discounted or reduced by applying a below-market discount rate which represents the estimated market interest rate the award could be expected to earn over the period of the loss (adjusted for the effect of any income tax on the interest so earned), and then reduced by the estimated rate of future price inflation.

If you read this instruction carefully, in light of the discussion in the chapter, you will see that it mandates (1) reduction to present value, (2) consideration of taxes which would have been paid on future wages, (3) consideration of the taxes to be paid on interest on the award (the reverse tax effect), and (4) use of the real interest rate approach to present value calculations. While all that is in the instruction, I wouldn't bet the ranch that the instruction is sufficient to *educate* a jury as to how to cope with the complexities addressed in this chapter.

If the jury doesn't really grasp these concepts well enough to perform a true economic projection, what do they do? They probably start with the figure offered by the plaintiff's expert, and make rough adjustments to her estimate of the loss if they view her assumptions on the basic issues, such as inflation and interest rates, as too generous.

Judge Fudd Befuddled

10. The defendant may have a point here. If the jury makes an award for future pain and suffering, that award will be for future damages. Shouldn't those damages be discounted to account for the time value of money, just as damages for future lost wages or medical expenses are?

While the argument has logical appeal, most courts conclude that the jury awards a general figure for the various intangible losses grouped under the rubric of "pain and suffering," rather than calculating discrete amounts for future intangible losses on a year-by-year basis. L. de Jong, Comment,

19 Rutgers L.J. 1119, 1123 (1988). Thus, it would be inappropriate to make actuarial adjustments to it similar to those for economic losses. In effect, most courts acknowledge that the number is so approximate that it would be specious to use that number as the basis for inflation or present value adjustments. Consequently, in assessing pain and suffering, they generally refuse to wade into the quicksands we have explored in this chapter.

17

Compensating Somebody: Wrongful Death and Survival Actions

Introduction

We think of "the olden days" as full of dangers, and thank our stars that we live in a "civilized" era. But no one can emerge from the course in Torts without a sobering sense of how dangerous industrialized society is. A few generations back, the major risks were natural ones: disease, natural disasters, and unruly fellow creatures. Today, these have been surpassed by human contrivances, especially that very mixed blessing, the internal combustion engine.

Too often, the products of human genius cause catastrophic injury and untimely death. This chapter addresses two distinct but related types of claims arising from such deaths. First is the *wrongful death* claim, which is a claim for damages for tortiously causing the death of another. Second is the *survival* claim, which is an action brought by the representative of the estate of a deceased person (called in legal parlance a "decedent") for injuries suffered by the decedent before her death.

Although these actions both arise because of the death of the tort victim, they are quite different. Wrongful death statutes usually allow damages for the losses suffered by surviving relatives, such as the loss of economic support or society of the decedent. The survival action, by

389

contrast, allows the estate of a decedent to enforce a tort claim for damages suffered by the decedent *before* death, which she could have enforced personally had she lived.

Suppose, for example, that Mozart and Haydn are listening to a symphony at the local concert hall when a chandelier, negligently installed by Handel, falls from the ceiling. Mozart is killed instantly. Haydn suffers serious injuries, is hospitalized for seven months, and finally dies of his injuries. At common law, the estates of these decedents would have had no remedies for their injuries, regardless of whether they were negligently inflicted. Under modern tort law, however, Mozart's death would give rise to a claim for wrongful death. Haydn's would support both a survival claim for his predeath losses (such as pain and suffering, medical expenses, and lost wages) and a wrongful death claim, since he ultimately died of his injuries.

The Action for Wrongful Death

Let's first consider the claim arising from Mozart's death. Mozart died instantly; his estate has no claim for predeath pain and suffering, hospital bills, or disability caused by the accident. The sole injury to be recompensed is the death itself. The issue raised is whether Mozart's estate or his surviving relatives have any claim against Handel for negligently causing his death.

Under the English common law, the answer for five or six centuries was "no." Lord Ellenborough put it clearly in *Baker v. Bolton:* "In a civil court, the death of a human being could not be complained of as an injury." 170 Eng. Rep. 1033 (1808). If the rule was clear, the reasons for it were less so. The scholars suggest that it was rooted in the early English "felony-merger doctrine," which barred civil suits to recover damages for acts that constituted a felony. Felonies were punishable by death and forfeiture of the felon's property to the crown. Since causing the death of another, either intentionally or negligently, was a felony, there would be no defendant left to sue for wrongful death, and no property from which to collect a judgment. See *Moragne v. States Marine Lines, Inc.,* 398 U.S. 375, 382 (1970). So there was no point to such a claim.

Other reasons for the common law position were grounded in policy rather than history. Some cases argued that allowing claims for wrongful death would lead to "runaway" damages from sympathetic juries, or that it is somehow immoral to put a price on human life. Last, the cases noted the obvious impossibility of compensating the decedent for the loss of life. S. Speiser, Recovery for Wrongful Death and Injury §1.4 (3d ed. 1992).

Whatever the rationale for the common law rule, the result was that "it was cheaper for the defendant to kill a person than to scratch him." Prosser & Keeton at 942. Prosser's treatise notes the wry suggestion that this rule explains "why passengers in Pullman car berths rode with their heads to the front" and that "the fire axes in railroad coaches were provided to enable the conductor to deal efficiently with those [sic] were merely injured." Prosser & Keeton at 942, n.24. Such speculations make the point well enough: It is manifestly indefensible to allow recovery for personal injury, but bar recovery entirely where the victim suffers the ultimate injury, death.

Although it is easy to criticize the early common law rule, most American courts initially followed it without question. In the American states, as in England, it has been the legislatures, not the courts, which have established the right to recover for wrongful death. England reversed course in 1846, when Lord Campbell's Act authorized a cause of action for wrongful death. Since that time, all American states have enacted statutes (often referred to as "Lord Campbell's Acts") that authorize recovery for wrongful death.

The Statutory Right to Sue

Because actions for wrongful death are based on statutes, they differ from state to state. However, many still track quite closely the language of Lord Campbell's Act. The North Dakota statute, for example, provides:

> Whenever the death of a person shall be caused by a wrongful act, neglect, or default, and the act, neglect, or default is such as would have entitled the party injured, if death had not ensued, to maintain an action and recover damages in respect thereof, then and in every such case the person who, or the corporation . . . or company which, would have been liable if death had not ensued, shall be liable to an action for damages, notwithstanding the death of the person injured . . . although the death shall have been caused under such circumstances as amount in law to felony.

N.D. Cent. Code. §32-21-01.[1] Statutes like this allow recovery for wrongful death if the decedent would have had a cause of action herself had she been injured instead of killed. Thus, an "action for wrongful death" is not a separate tort in itself, it is an action for a recognized tort — such as battery, negligence, or a products liability claim — in which the victim is killed rather than injured. In a wrongful death claim based on negligence, for example, the plaintiff must prove the same elements as in a personal injury negligence claim: duty, breach, causation, and damages. The proof

---

1. The North Dakota statute, in language taken verbatim from Lord Campbell's Act, makes the tortfeasor liable "although the death shall have been caused under such circumstances as amount in law to felony." Although the felony merger doctrine never applied in the American states, this irrelevant clause repudiating the doctrine was copied into many American wrongful death statutes. Therein lies a lesson in the realities — and the shortcomings — of legislative drafting.

of the first three elements will be the same as in an injury case. The major difference between a wrongful death case and other negligence cases involves the last element, damages.

Wrongful Death Damages: Who Gets Compensated?

Damages in personal injury cases compensate the injured person herself for the losses resulting from the accident, such as medical expenses, lost wages, or pain and suffering. Wrongful death statutes, however, do *not* compensate the decedent herself; it is obviously impossible to compensate the decedent for anything. The best the law can do is to compensate survivors who were close to the decedent for the losses *they* suffer as a result of the decedent's death. Thus, wrongful death statutes authorize damages for the economic or emotional losses to the survivors of the decedent, not the loss suffered by the decedent herself.

Assessing the damages to the survivors raises two thorny questions: Which survivors, and for what losses? As to the first question, most wrongful death statutes limit the recovery to the losses suffered by close relatives as a result of the decedent's death. For example, the Virginia statute provided until 1992[2] that the recovery is for the benefit of

> (i) the surviving spouse, children of the deceased and children of any deceased child of the deceased or (ii) if there be none such, then to the parents, brothers and sisters of the deceased . . . or (iii) if the decedent has left both surviving spouse and parent or parents, but no child or grandchild, the award shall be distributed to the surviving spouse and such parent or parents.

Va. Code §8.01-53. South Carolina's statute is a little different:

> Every such action shall be for the benefit of the wife or husband and child or children of the person whose death shall have been so caused, and, if there be no such wife, husband, child or children, then for the benefit of the parent or parents, and if there be none such, then for the benefit of the heirs of the person whose death shall have been so caused. . . .

S.C. Code §15-51-20.

Provisions of this type authorize damages to general classes of relatives likely to be closest to the decedent. If there are none in the closest class, the next group is considered, and so on. Like all efforts to deal generally with human relationships, these legislative classifications may miss the mark in particular cases. Mozart might be survived by a live-in lover to whom he was

---

2. The statute was amended in 1992. This is the pre-1992 version, used for illustration purposes. The current version is discussed in the analysis of Example 3.

very close, and a son who had ignored him for 30 years. Under the Virginia statute, the son's losses would be the measure of damages. Or, Mozart might leave no close relatives. Surely, the gravity of his death is just as profound in such a case, but under the South Carolina statute the only loss to be compensated in such a case would be the losses of remote heirs, who perhaps never saw or cared about Mozart and will consequently be unable to prove substantial damages. However, in most cases the beneficiaries named in the statutes — husbands and wives, children, parents and siblings — are the ones likely to suffer most from the death of the decedent.

Under many wrongful death statutes, the beneficiaries do not bring suit themselves. The executor or administrator of the estate is empowered to bring the action, but the damages are measured by the losses to the statutory beneficiaries and are distributed by the executor or administrator to them. Many statutes provide that the recovery does not become part of the decedent's estate. See, e.g., Ala. Code Tit. 6-5-410(c); R.I. Gen. Law 10-7-10. The major consequence of this is that the recovery does not go to pay the decedent's creditors. Even if the victim dies in debt, the wrongful death damages will go to the survivors the action is meant to compensate, rather than to pay the decedent's debts.

More on Damages: What Losses Are Compensated?

The second thorny question is what losses of the survivors are compensable under wrongful death statutes. The death of a loved one entails many losses. Some are concrete and quantifiable, such as loss of financial support or household services rendered by the decedent. Others are intangible, such as the loss of companionship, sexual consortium, advice, and emotional support, the same types of losses which are compensated as "loss of consortium" when the victim survives. See Chapter 11. In addition to these long-term losses from the death of the decedent, the survivors also suffer tangible immediate losses (funeral and burial expenses) and intangible immediate losses (the grief and mental anguish of learning of the death).

Historically, many wrongful death statutes limited damages to the "pecuniary losses" resulting to the specified survivors, that is, direct financial contributions or services the decedent would have rendered to the survivors. The New Jersey wrongful death statute, for example, provides that the jury may give damages for "the pecuniary injuries resulting from such death, together with the hospital, medical and funeral expenses incurred for the deceased. . . ." N.J. Stats. §2A:31-5. The reason for this limitation is historical: Although Lord Campbell's Act provided that the jury should award the statutory beneficiaries "such damages as they may think proportioned to the injury," the Act was early held to authorize only pecuniary damages. *Blake v. Midland Ry. Co.*, 118 Eng. Rep. 35 (1852). Many of the American statutes either explicitly incorporated the "pecuniary loss" measure of damages (as the New Jersey statute does) or were initially interpreted to authorize only such damages. Under such statutes, damages for intangible losses such as loss of the society, sexual relationship, or advice and counsel of the decedent were not compensable.

Unless the decedent leaves a dependent spouse or children, the "pecuniary loss" standard, strictly construed to include only economic contributions the decedent would have made to the beneficiaries, is highly restrictive. In many cases, actual pecuniary losses in the nature of lost financial contributions from the decedent will be impossible to prove. If Mozart is survived by his parents only, who are financially secure, there would likely be no compensable damages under a strict "pecuniary loss" standard, and hence no recovery other than funeral and burial expenses. The same may be true if he is survived by adult children or siblings who are financially independent.[3] And, of course, the standard — if literally applied — provides no recovery for the primary loss the survivors suffer: the loss of the opportunity to be with, learn from, and receive solace and emotional support from the decedent.

The inadequacy of the pecuniary loss standard is most glaring when the decedent is a young child. In such cases, the emotional loss to the parents is frightful, yet there is seldom evidence or likelihood of actual financial loss to the survivors. Such compelling cases have led many courts to evade the strictures of the pecuniary loss standard by tortured interpretation. In *Green v. Bittner*, 424 A.2d 210 (N.J. 1980), for example, the New Jersey Supreme Court allowed recovery under a "pecuniary loss" standard for the pecuniary value of the companionship and advice a daughter would have provided to her parents as they grew older. See also *Clymer v. Webster*, 596 A.2d 905, 914 (Vt. 1991) (loss of comfort and companionship of adult child "is a real, direct and personal loss that can be measured in pecuniary terms").

Clearly, *Green* and *Clymer* have stretched the concept of pecuniary loss far beyond its ordinary meaning. Such cases have deliberately blurred the distinction between a financial loss and a noneconomic loss that can be compensated — in some sense — by an award of money, in order to allow substantial damages in cases in which the survivors suffer little finan-

---

3. Some states interpret their wrongful death statutes to allow recovery for loss of inheritance. See Minzer, Nates §22.04. This would allow some recovery for pecuniary loss even if the decedent was making no contributions to the statutory beneficiaries before he died. Presumably, the plaintiff would still have to show that the beneficiary would have inherited the decedent's estate, *and* that he or she was in the class of beneficiaries eligible to take under the wrongful death statute.

cial loss but great emotional loss as a result of the death. This parallels the modern trend to allow recovery for loss of consortium in injury cases, at least to the spouse of the direct victim, and sometimes to her children or parents. It hardly makes sense to allow consortium recovery for *impairment* of these relationships when the direct victim is injured, but to deny recovery for similar losses (by strict interpretation of the term "pecuniary loss") when the relationship is completely *destroyed* because the direct victim is killed.

Some legislatures have responded to this incongruity by amending their statutes to provide that the term "pecuniary loss" *includes* such elements as loss of companionship or mental anguish. See, e.g., Ark. Stats. 16-62-102(f)(1) (including spouse's loss of services and companionship as pecuniary loss). Others have simply amended their wrongful death statutes to authorize recovery for intangible damages *as well as* more typical pecuniary losses such as financial contributions and services by the decedent. The Kansas statute, for example, allows the "heirs at law" to recover pecuniary losses, as well as the following:

(1) Mental anguish, suffering or bereavement;
(2) loss of society, companionship, comfort or protection;
(3) loss of marital care, attention, advice or counsel;
(4) loss of filial care or attention;
(5) loss of parental care, training, guidance or education; and
(6) reasonable funeral expenses for the deceased.

Kan. Stat. Ann. §60-1904. This statute clearly allows recovery for many types of intangible emotional losses due to the death of the decedent. It even allows damages for grief itself, which is usually barred in actions for loss of consortium, and is barred under many wrongful death statutes as well. However, a separate section of the Kansas statute tempers the liberality of this damages provision by limiting the nonpecuniary damages to §250,000. Kan. Stat. Ann §60-1903(a). Other statutes, however, authorize unlimited damages for pecuniary and consortium damages alike. The Hawaii statute, for example, provides that:

> such damages may be given as under the circumstances shall be deemed fair and just compensation, with reference to the pecuniary injury and loss of love and affection, including (1) loss of society, companionship, comfort, consortium, or protection, (2) loss of marital care, attention, advice or counsel, (3) loss of care, attention, advice, or counsel of a reciprocal beneficiary as defined in Chapter 572C, (4) loss of filial care or attention, or (5) loss of parental care, training, guidance or education, suffered as a result of the death. . . .

Haw. Rev. Stat. §663-3(b).[4]

---

4. Subsection (4), added in 1997, extends the right to recover for wrongful death to "reciprocal beneficiaries," including same-sex partners.

An Alternative Approach

A few states take a different approach to wrongful death damages, focusing on the loss to the decedent's *estate* from his premature death. See, e.g., N.H. Rev. Stat. Ann. §556:12, which allows the jury to consider (as to damages caused by the death itself) "the reasonable expenses occasioned to the estate by the injury, the probable duration of life but for the injury, and the capacity to earn money during the deceased party's probable working life." Under statutes of this type, damages are frequently measured by calculating the decedent's future earnings, subtracting the amount the decedent would have spent on living expenses, and reducing the net figure to "present value." (See Chapter 16 for a discussion of present value.) The rationale for this measure is that whatever the decedent saved from his income would have gone either to support his family while he was alive or into his estate and been distributed to his heirs or legatees after death.

The loss-to-the-estate rule provides a purely economic measure of damages, and shares some of the problems of the strict pecuniary loss rule. The loss-to-the-estate formula might not support any damages for the death of a retired person who lives on her current income. Similarly, there would be no loss to the estate of even a young person whose earnings did not exceed her living expenses. See F. McChesney, Problems in Calculating and Awarding Compensatory Damages For Wrongful Death Under the Federal Tort Claims Act, 36 Emory L.J. 149, 162-164 (1987) (concluding that persons with incomes below $20,000 in 1980-1981 dollars are unable to save at all). It seems likely that in many cases where strict application of the loss-to-the-estate standard or pecuniary loss standard would lead to no recovery, juries have ignored such instructions on the measure of damages and assessed a reasonable figure according to their own sense of justice.

Damages for Loss of Life Itself

In one sense, Lord Ellenborough's pronouncement that "the death of a human being could not be complained of as an injury" remains true. Although the loss of life itself is perhaps the most grievous loss imaginable, most wrongful death statutes do not authorize damages for the years of living that the decedent would have enjoyed but for the wrongful death. Some of the economic value of these lost years is compensated, under either the loss-to-survivors approach or the loss-to-the-estate approach, since damages are awarded for lost earnings that would have gone to the decedent's survivors. However, the most basic loss of the *experience* of living, the opportunity to enjoy life in all its richness, is not.

As stated earlier, the loss of life itself was viewed as beyond compensation, since the decedent obviously cannot benefit from any compensation awarded; any award for these lost years would simply be a windfall to her survivors. In addition, courts and legislatures have doubtless feared that, if juries were allowed to award damages for the decedent's lost years, verdicts would be too speculative and difficult to control. Thus, wrongful death statutes have focused on the damages to the survivors or the estate as both more certain and more obviously compensatory.

Survival Statutes: Preserving Claims for Pre-Death Damages

So much for the erstwhile Mozart; now let's consider Haydn's case. He also died as a result of Handel's negligent act. Consequently his estate or survivors will have a cause of action for wrongful death. But he suffered other injuries as well from Handel's negligence: He lingered for seven months, suffered pain and suffering, incurred medical expenses, and was out of work and unable to enjoy his usual activities. Had he recovered at the end of those seven months, instead of dying, he would have had a right to sue for these losses. Shouldn't his estate be able to sue for these pre-death damages, even though he died?

The common law took a hard line on these cases as well. Tort cases were classified as "personal" actions, and under the common law personal actions could only be prosecuted by the injured person herself. Speiser, §14.1[5] Haydn could sue for his injuries while alive, but no one else could do it for him. If he died before bringing suit, the estate had no right to pursue the claim. If he brought suit but died before the suit went to a verdict or judgment, most courts held that the action "abated" and could not be prosecuted further. See 1 Am. Jur. 2d Abatement, Survival, and Revival, §61. The principle applied to the defendant as well. A tort action had to be brought against her personally; if she died before suit was brought, the plaintiff could not sue her estate.

This hoary common law principle, like the bar on recovery for wrongful death itself, has been supplanted by statute. Most states now have "survival" statutes, which provide that causes of action "survive" rather than abating at the death of either the tortfeasor or the injured party. Note that it is the *claim itself* that survives, not the plaintiff or defendant: The very point of a survival statute is that the party need not survive for suit to be brought. Typically, where the injured party dies, the statute authorizes the decedent's executor or administrator to bring suit

---

5. Like so many issues, the common law dealt with this one by throwing a little legal Latin at it: "actio personalis moritur cum persona," translated "a personal action dies with the person." Speiser at §14.1, p.2 n.l.

(or continue one already in progress) to recover for the decedent's injuries. While the statutes vary, the Maine survival provision is simple and representative:

> No personal action or cause of action is lost by the death of either party, but the same survives, for and against the personal representative of the deceased. . . .

Me. Rev. Stat. Ann. 18-A §3-817(a). Under a provision such as this, Haydn's estate could still recover for Haydn's predeath injuries, whether or not suit had been brought before Haydn died. If Haydn had not brought suit before his death, the executor or administrator of his estate could file suit. If Haydn had sued but died before the case was decided, his executor or administrator would be substituted as the plaintiff and continue the litigation.

A simple diagram may help to distinguish survival actions from wrongful death actions. Fig. 17-1 is a time line, running from the point of Haydn's injury forward. At common law, Haydn had to sue himself, while alive, to recover for any damages he incurred during Period A, the period after the injury but before his death. If he did not sue, or died before a suit went to judgment, no recovery was allowed for the predeath damages. Under a survival statute, however, Haydn's estate is authorized to bring an action, after Haydn's death, for such damages. These damages will include medical expenses, lost wages, and pain and suffering Haydn sustained from the date of the accident until his death.[6] Since Haydn died from his injuries, the wrongful death statute also authorizes a separate action for damages caused by the death itself, that is, losses incurred by his survivors during Period B, after Haydn's death.

The rationale for allowing causes of action to survive where the tort victim dies is not far to seek. Although a survival action, like a wrongful death action, cannot compensate the decedent, the recovery usually goes into the decedent's estate and passes to her heirs. Though the decedent takes no direct benefit from the action, she may at least take solace before death in the knowledge that *somebody* will be compensated for the tort,

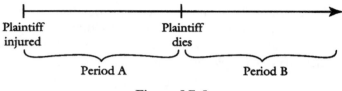

Figure 17-1

---

6. Some survival statutes do not allow recovery by the estate for predeath pain and suffering. See, e.g., Ariz. Rev. Stat., §14.3110.

and that those somebodies will be of her choosing. In addition, there is an obvious anomaly between allowing recovery if a tort suit goes to judgment a day before the victim dies, but not if judgment is entered the day after.

Survival statutes similarly allow recovery in cases where the *tortfeasor* dies. At common law, the plaintiff was out of luck if the tortfeasor died before she sued for her injuries. However, under a survival statute, the plaintiff may bring suit against the decedent's estate for the tort. The plaintiff in such cases is as much in need of compensation whether the defendant lives or dies. If the defendant leaves substantial assets, it seems reasonable that they should go to compensate the victim. In addition, in many cases the decedent's insurer is effectively the defendant, since it will defend the action and pay any damages awarded. It seems inappropriate that the insurer should get a windfall and the injured person go uncompensated if the negligent person fortuitously dies before recovery is awarded.

Although often associated with wrongful death statutes, survival statutes do not apply only in cases where the defendant's negligence causes death. Under a statute like Maine's, Haydn's damage claim survives whether he dies of the injuries suffered in the accident or of unrelated causes. Similarly, his claim would survive if Handel died from the accident or any other cause. Handel's administrator or executor would simply be substituted as the defendant in the action.

Because wrongful death and survival claims are based on statutes, there is a good deal of variation on the approaches discussed above. However, the basic patterns are fairly uniform. The following examples illustrate those patterns. For an example of a complaint that asserts claims under both a survival statute and a wrongful death statute, see Chapter 18, p. 425.

EXAMPLES

A Dandelion from the Bluebook Garden

1.　The following statement sometimes sprouts, weed-like, in my spring bluebooks: "If the plaintiff cannot prove a claim for negligence, she may be able to recover damages for Smith's death under the applicable wrongful death statute." Can you articulate the misconception that underlies this statement?

Laws of Relativity

2.　Purcell is run down and killed instantly. He is survival by his parents, whom he has not seen for 30 years, and a disabled sister, for whom he is the sole source of support.

    a. Who would be entitled to damages under the Virginia statute quoted at p. 392?

    b. Who would be entitled to damages under the South Carolina statute quoted at p. 392?

3.   Assume that Purcell is survived by an adult son, his disabled sister, and his elderly parents, with whom he has a close relationship. Who would be entitled to damages for his death under the version of the Virginia statute quoted at p. 392?

4.   Assume the same facts given in Example 3, but that the case arose under the Hawaii statute, which authorizes damages for both pecuniary and intangible damages "suffered as a result of the death of the person by the surviving spouse, children, father, mother, and by any person wholly or partly dependant upon the deceased person." Haw. Stat. §663-3. Who will recover, and how will the damages for each beneficiary be ascertained?

5.   What will be the result under the South Carolina statute if Purcell dies without leaving any close relatives?

6.   Brahms, a highly successful musician, dies leaving an adult daughter with a large income, a six-year-old son, a wife who does not work outside the home, and an elderly mother whom he frequently helps out financially. What damages could each recover if the Virginia beneficiary provision quoted at p. 392 applied and

    a. the measure of damages was limited to pecuniary loss, strictly construed?

    b. the applicable measure of damage was the same as the Kansas statute quoted at p. 395?

    c. the "loss to the estate" measure of damages applied?

"The Lawsuit Was a Success but the Plaintiff Died"

7.   Verdi and Vivaldi are seriously injured when Strauss drops a tuba from a scaffold above the stage. Verdi survives for a year in constant pain and is unable to work. He then dies of his injuries. Vivaldi suffers a broken arm, is out of work for three months, and suffers permanent reduction of function in the arm.

    a. What causes of action would Verdi and Vivaldi have against Strauss at common law?

    b. If the Maine survival statute quoted at p. 398 applied, what damages could Verdi's estate recover in the survival action?

    c. If Verdi's executor sought damages under the survival statute, could he also sue for wrongful death?

8.   Assume that Verdi suffers a broken hip from the accident and is laid up in bed. Six months later, he dies of an unrelated stroke, without having brought any suit against Strauss for his tuba injury. What actions may his executor or administrator bring against Strauss, if any?

Consorting with Confusion

9. On the facts in Example 8, could Jane Verdi, his widow, bring an action against Strauss for loss of consortium under the survival statute?

10. Assume that Verdi dies instantly when the tuba falls on him, leaving his widow, Jane, who is appointed administratrix of his estate. Six months later, before suit is brought against him, Strauss dies.

  a. What statute is implicated here, the wrongful death statute or the survival statute?

  b. Assume that the applicable wrongful death statute only authorizes recovery for pecuniary loss and is strictly construed to encompass solely economic losses. Jane's complaint includes a count for wrongful death, and a second count for loss of consortium with her husband. What is the problem here?

  c. Assume that Jane, still hoping to recover for consortium losses due to her husband's death, adds a third count in her complaint, asserting a "claim for negligence" and asking for consortium damages on that claim. What is the problem with this count?

Substance and Procedure in the Law of Wrongful Death

11. Mahler, a student from North Dakota studying at the University of Kansas, is killed in an accident on a school trip. The accident takes place in Tennessee. His parents retain you to bring an action to recover for his death. What crucial strategic question will you need to confront at the outset in representing them?

Judge Fudd on an Off Day

12. Assume that Mendelssohn dies immediately from his fall, and his estate sues Brahms for wrongful death. Brahms pleads as a defense that Mendelssohn was contributorily negligent for standing behind Brahms at the edge of the stage during the crescendo. Assume that contributory negligence is a complete defense to a negligence action in the relevant jurisdiction. Assume also that the language of the applicable wrongful death statute is the same as the North Dakota wrongful death provision quoted on p. 391. At trial, the Honorable Fudd instructs the jury as follows:

> If you find by a preponderance of the evidence that the decedent was contributorily negligent, and that his negligence was a proximate cause of the accident which led to his death, then you must find for the defendant.

Is Fudd's instruction proper?

EXPLANATIONS

A Dandelion from the Bluebook Garden

1.   This statement is based on the premise that there is a distinct "cause of action for wrongful death" apart from the traditional torts live plaintiffs can recover for. That isn't so. Wrongful death statutes typically allow recovery if the decedent would have had a right to recover if she had lived. See, e.g., the language in the North Dakota statute, p. 391. If the injured party could have recovered for negligence, had she lived, the personal representative may recover if the negligence caused the decedent death. If the decedent would have had a battery claim had she lived, the representative may recover when the battery causes death. And so on. In other words, there is no separate tort called "wrongful death." Wrongful death statutes create a remedy for existing torts when those torts lead to the death of the victim.

Laws of Relativity

2a.   The Virginia statute allows recovery to siblings and parents if the decedent does not leave a spouse, child, or grandchild. That is true here, so both the sister and the parents are eligible to receive damages for the death. However, it appears unlikely that the parents will be able to prove substantial damages, since they have been cut off from Purcell for many years. Thus, if the damages are assessed to the sister and parents according to their actual losses, she will receive a substantial award and they will receive little or nothing.

b.   Under the South Carolina statute, the action is "for the benefit of the parent or parents" if there is no spouse or child. Thus, it appears that only they would be entitled to damages, while the sister, who suffered compelling losses, would not be entitled to recover.

3.   In this example, Purcell is survived by a number of close relatives, all of whom may have suffered compensable losses, at least if the measure of damages includes consortium losses such as companionship, advice, and comfort. However, the version of the statute quoted on p. 392 limits the recovery to the son. He falls within the class of beneficiaries in clause (i) of the statute, and the statute apparently denies recovery to parents and siblings if there are clause (i) beneficiaries. Cf. *Carroll v. Sneed*, 179 S.E.2d 620, 623 (Va. 1971) (suggesting that presence of a child precludes any recovery to parents under the Virginia statute).

Obviously, specifying classes of beneficiaries in this way can lead to pretty unsatisfactory results. Although it is likely in this case that the heaviest losses, both pecuniary and emotional, were suffered by the elderly parents and dependant sister, they would obtain no compensation, while the lesser losses of the son will be the sole measure of damages. One wonders if courts haven't found some way around such results, despite apparently clear statutory language. See Prosser & Keeton at 947 and accompanying notes (suggesting that some cases have winked at the statutory limits, but others have not).

In 1992, the Virginia legislature amended its wrongful death statute to address this problem. The current version allows recovery for "any other relative who is primarily dependent on the decedent for support or services and is also a member of the same household as the decedent," even if there is a beneficiary in the primary class. Va. Code §8.01-53, as amended by 1992 Va. Acts ch. 74. This provision would only help Purcell's sister, however, if she actually lived with him. Nor would it change the result as to Purcell's parents.

4. The Hawaii statute avoids the problem illustrated in Example 3, because it authorizes damages for close relatives who suffer loss from the decedent's death without setting priorities that exclude other beneficiaries. (A fair number of statutes now take this approach.) Thus, Purcell's son, parents, and sister would be entitled to recover. Presumably, their awards would depend on the actual pecuniary and consortium losses each proves at trial. If, for example, the son is estranged from the decedent, the jury would likely award him minimal damages, while the dependent sister's damages would presumably be very substantial.

This statute obviously provides greater flexibility in assessing the wrongful death damages of various survivors, but it is also quite open ended, leading to greater exposure. If the victim is Bach, who has 14 children, a close relationship to his parents, and several live-in siblings, the defendant may be hit with a very substantial verdict.

5. The last clause of the South Carolina statute provides that, if there are no statutory beneficiaries, the recovery will go to those who inherit the decedent's estate. Thus, if Purcell leaves no close relatives, the wrongful death recovery will go into his estate and be distributed to his heirs, probably collateral relatives such as cousins, nieces and nephews, and aunts and uncles.

However, the damages assessed will still have to be based on actual damages suffered by these collateral relatives. The more distant these survivors are, the more difficult it will be for them to prove substantial damages — either economic or emotional — as a result of Purcell's death.

6a. Under the Virginia beneficiaries provision, the wife and children would recover, but presumably the mother would not, since she is not in the first class of beneficiaries. Under a strict pecuniary loss standard, the wife and children would recover damages for the lost financial contributions and household services Brahms would have rendered to them. As to the adult daughter, this is likely to be small, but it will clearly be substantial as to the wife and son, who were entirely dependent on Brahms for support.

It should include, for example, the cost of maintaining the son for 12 years at home, and quite likely four more years of college. If the evidence supports it, the damages might also include four more years in medical school or seven studying mathematical linguistics in graduate school. There might also be proof that Brahms would have made monetary gifts to his children over the years, for tax reasons or maybe even out of the goodness of his heart. The wife's damages might include the cost of her support for the balance of her life expectancy, and perhaps the loss of the inheritance she would have received had Brahms accumulated a substantial estate and predeceased her. Funeral and burial expenses would also be recoverable under a pecuniary loss standard.

b.   If the Kansas damages provision applied, Brahms's survivors would recover fully for the pecuniary losses discussed above, and up to $250,000 for grief, mental anguish, and consortium losses.[7]

In a jurisdiction that authorized unlimited recovery for consortium losses, the eligible beneficiaries would all be entitled to full recovery for the loss of society, care, counsel, and guidance that they suffered due to Brahms's death, in addition to proven pecuniary loss. However, if a provision like the Virginia statute applied, limiting the eligible beneficiaries, the mother would not recover anything for economic or consortium losses, since she is not within the first tier of beneficiaries.

c.   Under the loss-to-the-estate theory, the damages are often calculated by determining how much the decedent would have earned, subtracting the amount he would have spent on his own maintenance, and then discounting the resulting figure to present value. This figure represents the excess income the decedent could have contributed to his survivors or left to them in his estate.

Obviously, this measure provides nothing for consortium losses, and will not support a substantial award if the decedent had little income. In other cases, however, the loss-to-the-estate measure of damages will yield

---

7. An interesting question is how the $250,000 allowed for consortium damages under the Kansas statute would be allocated, if the intangible damages exceed that amount. Presumably, the options would be proportional to the actual damages, or pro rata (equal shares). Suppose, for example, that the jury came back with $300,000 in consortium losses for the wife, $200,000 for the son, and $100,000 for the daughter. Under a proportional approach to distributing the $250,000 authorized in the statute, the mother would get $125,000 ($300,000/600,000ths), the son $83,333 (200,000/600,000ths), and the daughter $41,667 (100,000/600,000ths). Under a pro rata approach, each would get $83,333.33 (one-third of $250,000).

One problem with statutory damage caps is that legislatures tend to enact them and then forget them. Over time, the authorized damages lose much of their value due to inflation, yet it is difficult to garner the necessary support to convince fiscally conscious legislators to raise them.

a much higher award than the loss-to-survivors approach. Consider a case in which the decedent is survived by his elderly parents. Under the loss-to-survivors approach there will likely be little in the way of provable financial loss to the parents. Even if the relevant statute allows recovery for consortium losses, they will be limited due to the parents' relatively short life expectancy. Thus the award in a loss-to-survivors state is unlikely to approach the loss-to-the-estate measure, which considers the decedent's future income stream over decades.

The analysis of this example must go one step further, however, because the example asks how much *each* beneficiary would receive. In a jurisdiction that uses the loss-to-the-estate measure of damages, the *estate* will recover the decedent's lost income, minus personal consumption. But how will the recovery then be distributed to the actual beneficiaries? Here, for example, it is clear that the minor son has suffered a greater loss than the adult daughter. At least some loss-to-the-estate statutes provide that the proceeds of the wrongful death recovery shall be distributed as general assets of the estate. See, e.g., N.H. Rev. Stat. Ann. §556:14 (damages "shall become a part of the decedent's estate and be distributed in accordance with the applicable provisions of law"). Very likely, the statute of distribution would call for equal distribution to the two children in this case despite the difference in the losses they suffered as a result of the decedent's death.

"The Lawsuit Was a Success but the Plaintiff Died"

7a.   This example illustrates the anomalous effects of the common law abatement rule. Under that rule Vivaldi would recover in full for his injuries, since he lived, and is personally able to bring this "personal" cause of action. At common law, however, Verdi's claim abated at his death unless he obtained judgment against Strauss before he died. His estate had no right to sue for his predeath losses, such as the pain and suffering, lost wages, and disability he experienced during the year before he died. Nor did Verdi's estate have a cause of action for wrongful death, since the common law barred wrongful death claims as well.

b.   In Maine, as in virtually all states today, Verdi's claim would survive his death and could be enforced by the representative of his estate. But remember that the survival action is for Verdi's *predeath* losses from the tort. It is not a claim for wrongful death, it is for the losses Verdi suffered before death that he could have recovered himself had he lived. Thus, his executor or administrator could recover for his predeath pain and suffering, lost wages, medical bills, and other compensable damages suffered during the year that he lingered.

c.   Absolutely. The right to sue under the survival statute for losses suffered by the victim before death does not bar the right to sue for wrongful death. The two actions address distinct injuries, and often benefit different parties. The survival action compensates Verdi's estate for damages he suffered before death that he could have recovered himself if he had lived. The wrongful death action (in most jurisdictions) compensates the survivors (whichever are eligible under the statute) for their losses as a result of the death.

8.   In this case, Verdi had a claim against Strauss for his injuries in the accident, but he died of an unrelated cause before bringing suit to enforce it. Under a survival statute the right survives to his estate, regardless of the cause of his death. The rationale for survival statutes is that the tortfeasor should compensate the victim's estate for the losses he caused to the victim before the victim died, even though the victim dies before suing for those injuries herself. This rationale applies equally, whether the victim dies of injuries inflicted by the tortfeasor or from an unrelated cause. Thus, Verdi's estate may recover under the survival statute for the medical expenses, lost wages, and pain and suffering from the time of the injury until his death, even though the hip injury did not cause his death.

However, Verdi's executor or administrator would not have a wrongful death claim in this example. Verdi died of a stroke, not the broken hip suffered in the accident. Under basic negligence law, Strauss cannot be held liable for damages he didn't cause.

Consorting with Confusion

9.   Verdi's widow has a claim against Strauss for loss of consortium, but the survival statute has nothing to do with it. Survival statutes allow a decedent's estate to bring a claim the decedent could have brought before death. The consortium claim is a claim for Jane's own consortium losses as a result of Verdi's injury, suffered during the period when he was incapacitated. She is still alive and may bring the consortium claim in her own name against Strauss.

Her consortium claim will be limited to the impairment of her relationship with Verdi during the six months he was incapacitated by the accident. The relationship was then cut off entirely by his death from an unrelated cause.

10a.   Both are. First, the survival statute authorizes suit against the estate of Strauss for negligently causing Verdi's death. Unlike Examples 7 and 8, in which the victim died before enforcing his claim, here it is the tortfeasor who escapes the rigors of litigation by dying before suit is brought against him. Under survival statutes death is no escape for either party: The claim survives if the tortfeasor dies or if the victim does. See, e.g., the Maine statute quoted on p. 398. If Verdi had recovered instead of dying, he would have invoked the survival statute to sue Strauss's estate. Since Verdi also died, his estate will do so instead.

The wrongful death statute is also implicated in this example, because it authorizes Jane, as administratrix of Verdi's estate, to recover damages for Verdi's death. The suit will be an action for wrongful death, authorized to be brought against Strauss's estate under the survival statute. It will be entitled *Jane Verdi, Administratrix v. Estate of Strauss.*

b. In this case, the applicable wrongful death statute only authorizes recovery for the actual economic losses Jane suffers as a result of Verdi's death (because the "pecuniary loss" provision is strictly construed). It makes no provision for the consortium losses she sustains as a result of the destruction of her relationship to her husband. So Mrs. V. has simply asserted a separate count in her complaint for loss of consortium as well.

This creative effort to circumvent the limits of the wrongful death statute will fail. Because Verdi died instantly, Jane's loss of consortium claim is for the loss of his company, companionship, advice, support, and society *after* death. It is, in other words, a claim for damages resulting from the death. But these damages are *not* allowed under the applicable wrongful death statute, which has been construed to limit recovery to "pecuniary loss" in the strict sense. Since the right to recover for wrongful death is defined by the statute, the court will confine recovery to that allowed by the statute itself, and dismiss Jane's second claim.[8]

There is certainly a strong policy argument for Jane's position, however. Had Verdi survived, she would have been entitled to recover for the impairment of her relationship with him while he was incapacitated, under a count for "loss of consortium." See Example 8. Why shouldn't she have the same right when the relationship is completely cut off by his death? Does it make sense to retain the pecuniary loss measure of damages for wrongful death where much broader compensation is provided for consortium losses when the direct victim is merely injured?

This argument has led many states to amend their wrongful death statutes to authorize broad consortium damages in wrongful death cases. For example, if the Kansas provision on p. 395 applied, Verdi's widow could recover damages for loss of society, companionship, advice, counsel, and so forth, the same elements compensated under loss of consortium where the direct victim is merely injured.

---

8. At least one court has refused to follow this reasoning, See, *Giuliani v. Guiler*, 951 S.W.2d 318 (Ky. 1997), which **did** recognize a common law loss of consortium claim due to the death of a parent, even though the relevant wrongful death statute did not allow consortium damages. A strong dissent argued for the position in the text above. Compare *Bratcher v. Galusha*, 417 Mass. 28, 30-31 (1994) (rejecting similar claim made by parents of the decedent; court declined to "rewrite or ignore the plain language of the statute"). As Oliver Wendell Holmes once said, "No generalization is worth a damn, including this one."

c.   The problem here is that the claim for negligence is really no different from the claim for wrongful death. A wrongful death claim must be based on a recognized tort that the decedent could have asserted had he survived. Here, that claim would be negligence, for carelessly dropping the tuba on Verdi. The wrongful death action is simply a negligence action in which the damage resulting from the defendant's negligent act is death. To sue separately for negligence is simply to state the same thing another way.

A slightly different route to the same conclusion is based on the fact that there was no right to recover for wrongful death at common law. The right is defined by statute, and recovery is limited to the terms of the statute. Thus, Verdi's wife has a claim under the wrongful death statute, but no separate right to assert a common law negligence claim against Strauss for causing Verdi's death. Thus, her third count does not state a claim for which relief can be granted.

Substance and Procedure in the Law of Wrongful Death

11. This chapter illustrates that the extent of the damages available for wrongful death varies dramatically from state to state. For the most part, tort law is state law, and each state is free to create its own rules, whether by statute or judicial decision, without regard to what the rules are in another state. Some states inevitably will have more generous rules than others.

A corollary of this basic tenet of tort law is that a plaintiff may fare a lot better under one state's tort law than under another state's. In the case on which this example is based,[9] Kansas imposed (at the time) a $100,000 cap on intangible damages, while North Dakota had no cap. Since the case involved the wrongful death of a college student, who was probably not making financial contributions to his parents, the intangible damages were probably the major item of damages. Thus, the case would be "worth" a lot more under North Dakota law than under Kansas law. (No one argued for Tennessee law, another candidate.)

So, as counsel for Mahler's family, you might choose to sue in North Dakota, on the premise that it would be likely to apply its own statute to the wrongful death of a North Dakota domiciliary. But there might not be personal jurisdiction over all of the defendants in North Dakota for a Tennessee accident.

Alternatively, you might sue in Tennessee or Kansas, but argue that the court should *apply North Dakota law to the case.* In every case involving multi-state contacts, the court must decide which state's law to apply

---

9. *MacDonald v. General Motors Corp.*, 110 F.3d 337 (6th Cir. 1997).

to the case. Every state has pesky "choice-of-law" rules about this, and they do not always lead courts to apply their own law. In this instance, the court in Tennessee concluded that the North Dakota statute should apply, since the claim was for the death of a North Dakota domiciliary.

The point is that, given the wide variation in tort rules, and the often broad reach of personal jurisdiction, there is room for creative lawyers to maximize their clients' opportunities by choosing a favorable forum. Even if they can't sue in the state with the most advantageous tort law,[10] they may still be able to convince the court in another state to apply that state's tort law, due to important contacts of the case with that state. So, before bringing suit, you should consider the wrongful death statutes of the states in which suit might be brought, and the choice-of-law rules of those states, in order to maximize the chances of having the case decided under the most favorable wrongful death statute.

Judge Fudd on an Off Day

12. Fudd is only "off" here because he's right on. The North Dakota statute, like many wrongful death acts, authorizes wrongful death recovery for claims that "would have entitled the party injured, if death had not ensued, to maintain an action and recover damages in respect thereof. . . ." If Mendelssohn had lived and brought suit, he would not have been entitled to "recover damages in respect thereof," since his contributory negligence would have been a complete defense (the example assumes). Consequently, the wrongful death suit is barred as well.[11]

An argument can (as always) be made to the contrary. The wrongful death recovery is for the benefit of the survivors. If *they* have not been negligent, arguably their recovery should not be reduced. But most courts have considered themselves bound by statutory language like North Dakota's, or by the obvious fact that the decedent's conduct would have barred recovery if he had survived.

An interesting variant on this issue is the situation where a beneficiary is negligent. Suppose, for example, that the decedent's father was the statutory beneficiary but was driving negligently at the time of the accident and was a cause of the accident that caused the son's death. Most cases under the loss-to-the-survivors type of wrongful death statute bar (or

---

10. Of course, even if all defendants could be sued in the state with the most generous measure of wrongful death damages, that state might choose, under its choice-of-law rules, to apply the law of *another state* to the case. But there is a subtle yet clear tendency of courts to apply forum law where there is a basis to do so.

11. In a comparative negligence jurisdiction, the decedent's negligence will reduce recovery in a wrongful death case, just as it would have if the decedent had survived. Prosser & Keeton at 955.

reduce, under comparative negligence) recovery by the negligent beneficiary. See Speiser, §5.9. However, in jurisdictions that measure damages
by the loss to the estate, the father might recover despite his negligence.
Under that approach, the *estate* is the beneficiary; it is to be compensated
for the decedent's pecuniary losses, and who actually inherits the assets in
the estate may be viewed as an irrelevant fortuity. See *In Re Estate of
Infant Fontaine*, 519 A.2d 227 (N.H. 1986) (concluding that the
mother's negligence was irrelevant in action for wrongful death of her
fetus, even though she was a beneficiary of the child's estate).

PART SIX

*Interlude:
Analyzing
a Personal
Injury Case*

18

Some Legal Anatomy: Thinking Like a Tort Lawyer

Introduction

If you had chosen medical school, your course in human anatomy would probably have been broken down into topics, like the brain, the circulatory system, the digestive system, the skeletal system, and so on. But bodies don't operate that way, they function as a unified system in which all elements interact to form a living organism.

Similarly, while most of the chapters in this book, like the Torts course itself, focus on particular elements or types of tort claims, cases do not arrive in lawyers' offices in such neat categories. Accidents present complex, miscellaneous, unorganized facts that lawyers must reconceptualize in terms of the theoretical framework of tort law. The challenge of a torts practice is to fit these unorganized real world facts into the recognized elements and defenses of a negligence claim. This chapter provides a brief opportunity to look at tort claims the way a practitioner does, to reason from raw data to legally supportable claims for damages.

To begin with, remember that the plaintiff must prove all the basic elements of a negligence claim in order to recover. If Bernhart is injured in a boating accident, the fact that she is seriously injured and needs compensation is not enough to support recovery. She must also prove that the pilot of the other boat was negligent, and that her negligence caused the accident. If Terry sells stock at a serious loss after an inaccurate financial statement is published by the corporation's accountants, she will still not recover if the court concludes that the accountants owed her no duty, or that the drop in value of the stock was not caused by the accountants' negligence. A torts chain is only as strong as its weakest link; you have to examine the whole chain to give a realistic assessment of the chances of recovery.

In addition, while we often speak broadly of a "claim for negligence," many types of negligence claims require more specific analysis. A plaintiff cannot recover for infliction of emotional distress, for example, simply by showing that the defendant's negligent conduct caused her distress. Courts have imposed additional requirements to limit emotional distress claims, such as physical contact, the *Dillon* standards, or presence in the "zone of danger." See generally Chapter 11. Similarly, plaintiffs seeking recovery for loss of consortium must show more than negligence, causation, and damages: Courts generally conclude that a defendant only owes a duty to avoid loss of consortium if a close relationship exists between the plaintiff and the direct victim. See Chapter 11, pp. 244-246. Similarly, in wrongful death cases, only certain parties are allowed to recover. See Chapter 17. Counsel must analyze such cases with a view to these constraints on recovery for negligence.

Third, counsel must consider carefully what damages are recoverable in a negligence case. The fact that a defendant is liable does not necessarily mean that she is liable for every loss the plaintiff has suffered. This may be true because the law limits the types of damages recoverable (as in wrongful death cases), because the defendant did not cause all the plaintiff's damages (as in some multiple tortfeasor situations), or because, as a matter of policy, the law refuses to shift the loss for certain damages, under a proximate cause or duty analysis.

Without further ado, let's explore some of these limitations on negligence recovery based on the facts of this relatively simple accident case:

> Isadora Dunton was a famous opera star. On March 1, 2004, she and her husband Booth were pulling out of their driveway on to Main Street in the town of Elkton, West Dakota. Burton came speeding around a curve and hit their car broadside. Isadora, who was three months pregnant at the time, was severely injured. John, son of Isadora and Booth, was playing basketball in the driveway, about 25 feet from the point of the accident, heard the collision, and ran to the scene immediately. Isadora suffered the loss of sight in one eye and multiple internal injuries, and was hospitalized in serious condition. The baby suffered fetal distress and cardiac arrhythmia from the trauma of the accident, and was stillborn a week later. Four months later, on July 1, Isadora died as a result of her injuries.
>
> Booth suffered minor facial lacerations. John was extremely upset by the accident. He subsequently became withdrawn, suffered a severe decline in his high school grades, and more or less "dropped out." Lydia, a married daughter of Isadora, was also seriously affected

by the accident. She became tense, impatient with her husband, cried a lot, and had difficulty sleeping. She also became difficult to work with and was skipped over for promotion. She also missed her mother.

Garrick was Isadora's costar in many important productions and a close personal friend. He was extremely upset by her injury, suffered a nervous breakdown, and never quite fully recovered. Unable to find a comparable costar, his career was limited thereafter to minor supporting roles.

Burton, the other driver, was also seriously injured. He died a year later of unrelated causes.

The following examples consider the elements, special requirements and limitations on relief for the different types of claims that may be asserted based on the Dunton accident. In analyzing the claims, focus on the claims that the plaintiffs could raise, even if some claims may be vulnerable to legal or factual challenge by the defendant or strategically dubious. Assume that West Dakota has a survival statute, a wrongful death statute that authorizes pecuniary and emotional damages for survivors, and that it recognizes claims for spousal consortium but has not decided whether children can recover for loss of parental consortium.

EXAMPLES

Setting the Stage

1. Assume that Isadora did not initiate suit before her death. Booth, the administrator of her estate, comes to you after her death, to inquire about potential claims for damages as a result of her physical injuries.

    a. What would you advise Booth about the effect of Isadora's death on the right to recover for her injuries?

    b. What would you advise Booth about the effect of Burton's death on Isadora's claims?

Act One

2. Booth retains you to bring an action against Burton for damages for Isadora's injuries. Which of the following elements of damages would you claim in a *survival* action for predeath losses suffered by Isadora?

    a. pain and suffering
    b. lost future earning capacity
    c. loss of enjoyment of life
    d. medical bills
    e. loss of consortium with members of her family
    f. infliction of emotional distress

3.   Assume that Booth also wishes to assert a *wrongful death* claim resulting from Isadora's death. Which of the following elements of damages would you seek in the wrongful death claim?
   a. pain and suffering
   b. lost earning capacity
   c. loss of enjoyment of life
   d. loss of consortium suffered by Isadora
   e. loss of consortium suffered by Booth and other family members due to Isadora's death

Act Two

4.   Booth also inquires as to claims he may assert on behalf of the deceased child Isadora was carrying at the time of the accident. What would you advise him as to the prospects of recovery for the child's death, and the elements of damages?

5.   Booth also inquires as to the claims he may assert on his own behalf as a result of the accident.
   a. What would you advise Booth as to the elements of damages for his own physical injuries?
   b. What would you advise Booth as to his right to assert claims for loss of consortium?
   c. What would you advise Booth concerning other claims he might have?

6.   Booth brings John with him. John is also interested in asserting claims against Burton's estate. What claims may he have, and what problems do you anticipate in recovering on them?

7.   A week after your interview with Booth and John, Lydia comes in to inquire about possible claims against Burton. What claims may she have, and what problems do you anticipate in recovering on them?

Supporting Actors

8.   Next to come in is Garrick, Isadora's costar in the opera. What would you advise him as to his rights against Burton arising from the accident?

Putting the Show on the Road

9.   Draft a complaint seeking relief on behalf of Isadora's estate, Booth, John, and Lydia. Assume that the West Dakota law allows both survival and wrongful death claims and recognizes fetal wrongful death claims, but has not yet addressed claims for loss of consortium on behalf of parents or children. Assume also that it is unclear what the standards are in West Dakota to state an adequate claim for negligent infliction of emotional distress.

EXPLANATIONS

Setting the Stage

1a. The right to recover for Isadora's injuries depends on the applicable survival and wrongful death statutes, which vary from state to state. Thus, you might advise Booth, as lawyers frequently do, that you don't know whether suit can be brought, but will find out. However, if you were an experienced West Dakota practitioner, you would probably be familiar with the local law on these issues.

As Chapter 17 explains, virtually all states have modified the common law doctrine denying recovery for wrongful death. Here, for example, West Dakota has a wrongful death statute, which authorizes recovery of pecuniary and consortium damages suffered by Isadora's survivors as a result of her death and a survival statute which authorizes Booth, as Isadora's executor, to recover for predeath losses Isadora suffered as a result of the accident.

b. The question here is whether Isadora's claims "survive" the death of Burton, the tortfeasor. Most states now provide by statute that tort claims survive the tortfeasor's death and may be brought against the tortfeasor's estate. This is true regardless of the cause of the tortfeasor's death. Thus, it makes no difference here that Burton died of causes unrelated to the accident.

Act One

2a. Most survival statutes allow recovery by the estate of a deceased tort victim for losses suffered by the decedent prior to death. Under these survival statutes, the estate recovers any damages the plaintiff sustained from the date of the accident until her death, and which she could have recovered herself if she had survived.

Had Isadora survived and filed suit herself, she could have recovered for pain and suffering. Thus, the physical pain and emotional anguish she sustained during this four month period as a result of her injuries should be proper elements of damages in the survival action.

Of course, any recovery under the survival claim will not compensate Isadora for having suffered it; she is beyond compensation in any worldly sense. Consequently, a few states view recovery for pain and suffering as a "windfall to the heirs" (see Prosser & Keeton at 943) and bar recovery for pain and suffering in survival actions. See, e.g., Ariz. Rev. Stat. Ann. §14-3110. Most states, however, allow recovery for the decedent's predeath pain and suffering: If these damages are not allowed in the survival action, the *defendant* will get a windfall due to the victim's death. Although these damages cannot benefit her, at least her survivors, through her estate, can receive the benefit of the recovery.

b. Lost future earning capacity refers to the tort victim's loss of the ability to earn money in the future, that is, after the trial. See Chapter 15, p. 344. Under most survival statutes, this is not a proper element of a survival claim, which only encompasses losses suffered prior to death. Minzer, Nates §21.02. Only her *predeath* lost earnings, for the four months from the accident until her death, would be properly sought under the survival claim. Her future earning capacity will be taken into account in assessing the damages for wrongful death. See Example 3b.

Here again, there are statutory variations. In a few states, lost earning capacity *is* allocated to the survival claim. See, e.g., *Wetzel v. McDonnell Douglas Corp.*, 491 F. Supp. 1288 (E.D. Pa 1980). In a state with a statute of this type, the court must be very careful to assure that these same damages are not assessed again under the wrongful death claim.

c. All states recognize that an injured plaintiff's loss of the ability to enjoy normal activities and pleasures of living is a compensable element of damages in tort actions. As Chapter 15 indicates, some states view this as included in pain and suffering, while others treat "loss of enjoyment of life" as a distinct element of damages. Presumably Isadora's estate would recover for loss of her enjoyment of life during the four months she survived, since this is a loss she suffered prior to death, for which she could have recovered herself had she lived. However, as with her earnings, she cannot recover for *future* loss of enjoyment in a survival action.

As noted above, a few states specifically bar claims for pain and suffering in survival actions. If the Dunton case arose in one of these states, counsel for Burton's estate would doubtless argue that the exclusion for pain and suffering damages also bars recovery for the related loss of enjoyment damages.

d. Under most survival statutes, medical expenses incurred prior to death would be included in the survival claim. These are losses suffered by the decedent prior to death as a result of the defendant's negligence. Had she lived, she would have been able to sue for them herself. The estate steps into her shoes for purposes of enforcing this predeath claim.

e. This is a tricky question. Isadora does not have a claim for loss of consortium as a result of her *own* injuries. Consortium claims are claims by family members of an injured person, alleging that the injury has impaired the injured person's ability to interact with those family members. Booth, John, and Lydia may have consortium claims based on the impairment of Isadora's ability to relate to them as a result of her injury, but Isadora will not. Her claim for impairment of her ability to relate to others caused by her injuries is a "loss of enjoyment" claim, which is part of the survival claim for her predeath damages. See Example 2c.

f. Emotional distress is a slippery term that covers a lot of ground. It includes, for example, the anxiety and depression Isadora suffered due to her own injuries, fear of the impending collision, or anguish due to the fear of dying. These damages are part of the "pain and suffering" endured by Isadora prior to death. In states that allow recovery for pain and suffering in survival actions, her estate could recover for these damages, suffered over the four-month period prior to her death.

"Emotional distress" also encompasses the traumatic distress Isadora suffers from witnessing physical injury to *others*, such as Booth. This distress, suffered at the time of the accident, is also a predeath injury; if it is compensable at all, it will be under the survival statute. Whether Isadora will recover for this type of emotional distress depends on the applicable law governing indirect infliction claims. Isadora's estate would state a claim for indirect infliction if West Dakota applied the zone-of-danger rule, since she was in the zone of danger from the defendant's negligence (and in fact suffered injury herself from it). She would also have a claim for the trauma of witnessing injury to Booth if West Dakota follows *Dillon*, since she witnessed the accident and is closely related to Booth.

3a. Neither Isadora's estate nor her survivors would have a claim for future pain and suffering because Isadora, due to her death, will not experience any. Had she lived and sued, she might well have had such a claim, since she would have faced the prospect of continued suffering. (As Example 2a indicates, the claim for her predeath pain and suffering would be part of the survival claim in most states.)

b. Under most wrongful death statutes, the decedent's survivors may recover for pecuniary support they would have received from the decedent. See generally Chapter 17, pp. 393-395. This recovery will not exactly equal Isadora's lost earning capacity; it only includes that part of her future earnings that would have gone to support the survivors. Certainly John would have a substantial claim, since he was still at home and dependent on his parents for support. Booth might also recover such damages under the wrongful death statute. Because Isadora was very successful, her income doubtless contributed substantially to the family's lifestyle. The loss of this income is a pecuniary loss to Booth, even if he is still able to support himself in the food-and-shelter sense of the term without it.

Lydia, however, will have a harder time making out a claim for pecuniary losses due to Isadora's death, since she was financially independent. However, if she could prove that Isadora made gifts to her from time to time (as wealthy, tax-conscious parents are known to do) she might claim that she has also suffered pecuniary losses compensable under the wrongful death statute.

c. If Isadora had lived but been disabled, either temporarily or permanently, she would have had a claim for future loss of enjoyment of life caused by any impairment she sustained as a result of the accident. For example, if she survived the accident but lost an eye, this would interfere with Isadora's enjoyment of life as long as she lived. However, since she died as a result of the accident, there will be no claim for loss of enjoyment of life for any period after her death. Recovery for any damages due to her death is governed by the wrongful death statute, which compensates survivors for their losses due to the decedent's death, not the decedent for hers. See Chapter 17, pp. 392-395. While there is surely no greater loss of enjoyment than the loss of life itself, this is a loss to Isadora, not her survivors.

d. Any claim for loss of consortium suffered by Isadora would be based on injuries to *other* family members that impaired their ability to relate to her. If, for example, Booth had been seriously injured, her estate might have a claim, asserted under the survival statute for her loss of consortium with him for the period prior to her death. However, even if Booth were seriously injured, her estate would have no claim for Isadora's loss of consortium with him for any period after her death.

e. Under many wrongful death statutes, immediate survivors of the decedent are entitled to compensation for consortium-type damages — their loss of the comfort, companionship, advice, society, and counsel of the decedent — for the period after the decedent's death. See, e.g., Kan. Stat. Ann. §60-1904, quoted at Chapter 17, p. 395, supra. Since the West Dakota wrongful death statute authorizes recovery for these emotional damages (the Introduction tells us), Booth and Isadora's children will recover for this loss for the future years they otherwise would have enjoyed their relationship with Isadora.

Act Two

4.   For many years, the courts barred claims for injury or death of a fetus, on the theory that no *duty* was owed to an unborn child. Prosser & Keeton, §55, at 367. More recently, many states have allowed such claims, but others have held that the term "person" in their wrongful death statutes does not apply to a fetus, and passed the buck to the legislature to change the rule. See, e.g., *Witty v. American Gen. Capital Distrib., Inc.,* 727 S.W.2d 503 (Tex. 1987). Thus, whether there is a claim for the unborn child's death will turn on how the court interprets West Dakota's wrongful death statute.

If the wrongful death statute allows recovery for causing the death of a fetus, the damages will depend on the terms of the wrongful death statute. Many such statutes authorize damages for both pecuniary and consortium losses to closely related survivors such as parents and siblings. Naturally, assessing the monetary contributions this child would have made to her parents in the future, or the quality of the relationship that would have developed between the child and her family, is a surreal process. Certainly, the losses could be great, since the relationship is destroyed from the outset and all monetary contributions the child might have made are lost. If this claim is allowed, it will introduce a very emotional and uncertain element into the trial that will doubtless have great settlement value from the plaintiffs' point of view.

Are there any other claims you might assert on behalf of the deceased child? The facts indicate that Isadora miscarried a week after the accident, and that during that period the baby suffered fetal distress and cardiac arrhythmia. This suggests that the baby, though in utero, suffered pain and suffering prior to the miscarriage. Advancing medical knowledge suggests that fetuses have a good deal more awareness than previously thought. As plaintiff's counsel in this case, you might draw on this advancing medical knowledge to argue for a new type of claim for "fetal pain and suffering."

Presumably, such claims would be asserted under a survival statute, as an injury suffered by the child prior to death. It is highly doubtful that a state that rejects fetal wrongful death claims would recognize a claim for its predeath pain and suffering, but the argument might be accepted in a jurisdiction that allows fetal wrongful death claims.

Issues like fetal suffering prior to death are grim to contemplate. As plaintiff's counsel, however, it is your job to contemplate them, and to seek compensation for such losses if they may be allowable. It is through such constant probing of the boundaries by creative plaintiff's counsel that tort law grows.

5a. You would advise Booth that he is entitled to sue for his medical bills, pain and suffering, and lost wages, and for property damage to the car if he owned it. However, you would also advise him that these damages are not likely to be great, since he suffered minor injuries. Clearly, the substantial claims available to Booth are for his intangible damages — his emotional distress and loss of consortium claims arising from the serious injuries sustained by Isadora.

b. Pardon me for being repetitious, but recall again that Booth's loss of consortium claims will be based on the injuries to other family members that impair their ability to relate to Booth. For example, Booth would certainly have a loss of consortium claim resulting from the injury to Isadora, his wife, since her serious injuries impaired her ability to relate to Booth as she had before. However, this consortium claim will be limited to the four-month period prior to her death. The loss of Isadora's consortium suffered by Booth *as a result of* her death is part of the wrongful death claim discussed earlier. Since the West Dakota wrongful death statute authorizes damages for loss of the relationship with the decedent, Booth will recover damages for this post-death loss. But he will do so under the wrongful death statute, and will have no separate "loss of consortium" claim for the post-death period. If he were allowed to sue for post-death "loss of consortium," and for the same losses under the wrongful death statute, he would recover twice for the same loss.

Booth has also lost the ability to relate to his unborn child due to the child's death. However, this claim is also a claim for post-death loss of consortium, and will be compensable, if at all, under the wrongful death statute. See Example 4.

It is also possible that Booth has a claim for loss of consortium with his son John, due to John's injuries. A few jurisdictions allow a parent to recover for loss of consortium with an injured child, though many do not. See Chapter 11, pp. 245-246. The facts suggest that John has suffered emotional injuries from witnessing the accident, and that these emotional injuries have affected his ability to relate to others. However, allowing Booth to assert a consortium claim as a result of this injury to John involves piling one claim for indirect injury (Booth's consortium claim for interference with his relationship to John) onto another indirect injury claim (John's indirect infliction of emotional distress claim due to witnessing injury to Isadora and Booth). The results could be fairly absurd if courts allowed such add-ons to the third and fourth power. This claim is doubtful, and if it was made to a jury, might be viewed by them as overreaching.

c. Booth will likely have a claim for indirect infliction of emotional distress. He witnessed traumatic, serious injury to Isadora and was himself injured in the same accident. If West Dakota followed the zone of danger rule Booth would recover for indirect infliction of emotional distress, since he was within the zone of danger created by Burton's negligence. If the *Dillon* factors applied, he would also recover, since he was present and witnessed injury to his wife.

6.   John suffered no direct impact or physical injury in the accident. However, he did rush to the scene immediately and witness the traumatic impact of the accident on members of his family. Whether he can recover for this depends on West Dakota's law on indirect infliction of emotional distress. Courts following the impact rule would deny recovery. Under the zone-of-danger approach, John's claim would turn on whether John was close enough to the collision to be endangered by it (how about flying debris?). Under the *Dillon* approach, John will state a claim if the court concludes that he "witnessed" injury to close family members by hearing the crash, even though he did not see it. (See Chapter 11, Example 1c for a discussion of this issue.)

Some jurisdictions also require resulting physical symptoms in order to recover for indirect infliction. The facts indicate that John became withdrawn and his grades went down. Although it would be hard to characterize these as physical symptoms, some courts might find such dubious "physical injuries" sufficient. See Chapter 11, Example 4f.

John may also have a claim for loss of consortium with Isadora for the four-month period prior to her death. Clearly her injuries impaired her ability to relate to John. Many jurisdictions do not allow children to sue for loss of consortium with their parents, but some do. The result will turn on how West Dakota decides this issue. However, John's claim for loss of the relationship with Isadora for the period after her death is compensable, if at all, under the wrongful death claim.

7.   Lydia suffered no physical injuries, but apparently did experience a great deal of emotional distress. However, it is highly doubtful that she can recover on an indirect infliction claim. Most jurisdictions limit indirect infliction claims to those who are in the zone of danger or witness the accident or its immediate aftermath.

Lydia might seek recovery for loss of consortium. Like John's claim, the result will depend on whether West Dakota allows children to recover for loss of consortium due to injury to their parents. If such claims are recognized in West Dakota, Lydia's recovery on this claim will be limited to the four months during which Isadora survived. Her claims for loss of consortium with Isadora for the period after her death, like John's, will be governed by the wrongful death statute. Even states that deny loss of consortium claims for an *injured* parent may allow the children to recover for consortium losses under their wrongful death statutes if the parent is killed.

Even if the wrongful death statute allows damages for consortium losses, the court will probably not allow the jury to award consortium losses for such extended consequences as Lydia's missed promotion. Loss of consortium is meant to compensate for the interference with the relationship with the directly injured party, not for collateral economic consequences of that interference. The defense would doubtless argue that such attenuated consequences were not "proximately caused" by Burton's negligence.

Supporting Actors

8.   Garrick has suffered serious injury due to the negligence of Burton, but it is very unlikely that he will recover damages from Burton's estate. Certainly, Garrick has no indirect infliction claim, since he is not related to Isadora, did not witness traumatic injury to anyone, suffered no impact, and was not in the zone of danger. Nor does he have a loss of consortium claim: Such claims are limited to family members, not operatic partners.

But doesn't he have a just plain "negligence" claim? Burton had a duty to drive carefully, he didn't, and his negligence caused injury to Isadora and consequent damages to Garrick. This is true, but most courts would hold that Burton's *duty* to drive with due care was owed to other drivers, perhaps to family members, but not to others who suffer secondary emotional or economic losses as a result of the accident. Other courts might reach the same result by holding that Burton's negligence was not the "legal cause" or "proximate cause" of the consequential injuries suffered by Garrick. Even if Garrick's injuries are foreseeable, the court must draw the line on secondary damages at some point, as a matter of policy. Whether on duty or proximate cause grounds, virtually all courts would reject Garrick's claim.

Putting the Show on the Road

9.   The complaint below is an example of the type of complaint that might be filed in the *Dunton* case. In reading the complaint, consider how the various claims for relief have been drafted to allege the elements necessary to support the claims. After the complaint are some notes on the reasoning underlying it.

STATE OF WEST DAKOTA

SUPERIOR COURT
CHEYENNE COUNTY

CIVIL ACTION NO. 05-1341

BOOTH DUNTON, Individually and as the Administrator of the estates of ISADORA DUNTON and BABY DUNTON, JOHN DUNTON and LYDIA DUNTON

PLAINTIFFS

v.

ELIZABETH BURTON, executrix of the estate of ROBERT BURTON,

DEFENDANT

<u>COMPLAINT AND DEMAND FOR JURY TRIAL</u>

<u>PARTIES</u>

1. Isadora Dunton is an individual, formerly residing at 43 Keane Drive, Elkton, West Dakota, who died on July 1, 2004, of injuries suffered in the motor vehicle accident which is the subject of this action.

2. Baby Dunton is the child of Isadora and Booth Dunton, who died in utero on March 8, 2004 of injuries suffered in the motor vehicle accident which is the subject of this action.

3. The plaintiff Booth Dunton is an individual residing at 43 Keane Drive, Elkton, West Dakota. He is the widower and duly appointed administrator of the estates of Isadora Dunton and Baby Dunton.

4. The plaintiff John Dunton is the minor son of Isadora and Booth Dunton. He resides at 43 Keane Drive, Elkton, West Dakota.

5. The plaintiff Lydia Dunton is the daughter of Isadora and Booth Dunton. She resides at 1138 Lankton Boulevard, Elkton, West Dakota.

6. The decedent Robert J. Burton is an individual, formerly residing at 12 Lake Street, Burns, West Dakota, who died on February 15, 2005.

7. The defendant Elizabeth Burton is the daughter and duly appointed executrix of the estate of Robert J. Burton.

FACTS

8. On March 1, 2004, the decedents Isadora Dunton and Baby Dunton were passengers in a 1998 Toyota Camry station wagon, driven by the plaintiff, Booth Dunton.

9. At approximately 11:05 a.m., Booth Dunton started the car in the family driveway at 43 Keane Drive, Elkton, West Dakota, and began to back out of the driveway onto Keane Drive, in order to proceed in an easterly direction on Keane Drive.

10. As the car backed into Keane Drive, a Ford Taurus, driven by the decedent Robert J. Burton, came around the corner, traveling east at an excessive speed and without keeping a proper lookout, in violation of West Dakota St. Ann. Tit. 32, §§90 and 93.

11. As a result of his negligent driving, the decedent Robert J. Burton was unable to stop his vehicle or avoid colliding with the plaintiffs' vehicle backing out of the driveway at 43 Keane Drive.

12. As a direct and proximate result of the negligence of the decedent, Robert J. Burton, his vehicle collided violently with the Dunton vehicle, demolishing the Dunton vehicle and causing serious personal injuries to Isadora Dunton, Booth Dunton, and Baby Dunton.

13. As a direct and proximate result of the accident, the decedent Isadora Dunton suffered multiple internal traumas and extensive damage to her left eye, causing permanent blindness. She was taken to Elkton General Hospital, where she remained in the intensive care unit until her death on July 1, 2004 from injuries suffered in the accident.

14. As a direct and proximate result of the accident, the decedent Baby Dunton suffered traumatic injuries, resulting in fetal distress and cardiac arrhythmia. On March 8, 2004, Isadora Dunton miscarried, causing the death of Baby Dunton.

15. As a direct and proximate result of the accident, Booth Dunton suffered multiple lacerations requiring medical treatment, experienced pain and suffering, extreme emotional distress and temporary disability, and lost wages in excess of $2,000.

16. At the time of the accident, the plaintiff John Dunton was standing in the driveway at 43 Keane Drive, in the immediate vicinity of the collision. He witnessed the accident, rushed to aid the injured members of his family and observed his mother and father covered in blood and suffering from extreme shock and pain.

17. As a result of the accident and the injuries suffered by her parents, the plaintiff Lydia Dunton has suffered serious emotional distress, inability to sleep, difficulties at work, and other damages.

18. At all times relevant to the events in this action, the plaintiffs and their decedents were in the exercise of due care.

FIRST CLAIM FOR RELIEF:
WRONGFUL DEATH OF ISADORA DUNTON

19. The plaintiff repeats and realleges the allegations in paragraphs 1 to 18 of the complaint.

20. As a result of the collision proximately caused by the decedent Robert Burton's negligence, Isadora Dunton suffered extensive personal injuries which led to her death on July 1, 2004, at the age of forty-three.

21. As a result of the death of Isadora Dunton negligently caused by the decedent Robert Burton, her husband Booth Dunton and her children John and Lydia Dunton have been deprived of both the financial support and the comfort, companionship, advice, society, and counsel they would have received from Isadora Dunton had she lived.

Wherefore, the plaintiff Booth Dunton, in his capacity as administrator of the estate of Isadora Dunton, seeks damages under the West Dakota Wrongful Death Statute, West Dakota St. Ann. Tit. 12 §143, on behalf of Booth Dunton, John Dunton, and Lydia Dunton, for the loss of financial support, comfort, companionship, advice, society, and counsel of the decedent Isadora Dunton, and for funeral and burial expenses, together with interest and costs of suit.

SECOND CLAIM FOR RELIEF:
SURVIVAL CLAIM FOR PREDEATH DAMAGES OF
ISADORA DUNTON

22. The plaintiff repeats and realleges the allegations in paragraphs 1 to 18 of the complaint.

23. As a result of the collision proximately caused by the decedent Robert Burton's negligence, Isadora Dunton suffered extensive personal injuries, emotional distress, pain and suffering for a period of four months prior to her death, suffered loss of the normal pleasures and enjoyment of life over the four month period, lost substantial earnings from her work as a soloist with the West Dakota Civic Opera, and incurred great medical and other expenses for her care, all of which she would have been entitled to recover in an action against the defendant had she survived.

Wherefore, the plaintiff Booth Dunton, in his capacity as administrator of the estate of Isadora Dunton, seeks damages under the West Dakota survival statute, St. Ann. Tit. 12 §147, on behalf of the estate of Isadora Dunton, for her lost earnings, medical expenses, pain and suffering, and loss of enjoyment of life from March 1, 2004 until her death on July 1, 2004, together with interest and costs of suit.

THIRD CLAIM FOR RELIEF:
WRONGFUL DEATH OF BABY DUNTON

24. The plaintiff repeats and realleges the allegations in paragraphs 1 to 18 of the complaint.

25. At the time of the accident, the decedent Isadora Dunton was pregnant with a baby girl, the decedent Baby Dunton.

26. As a result of the collision proximately caused by the decedent Robert Burton's negligence, Isadora Dunton suffered extensive personal injuries which led to the death and miscarriage of her child, Baby Dunton, on March 8, 2004.

27. As a result of the death of Baby Dunton negligently caused by the decedent Robert Burton, the plaintiffs Booth Dunton, Lydia Dunton and John Dunton have been deprived of both the financial support and the comfort, companionship, advice, society, and counsel they would have received from Baby Dunton had she lived.

Wherefore, the plaintiff Booth Dunton, in his capacity as administrator of the estate of Baby Dunton, claims damages under the West Dakota Wrongful Death Statute, West Dakota St. Ann. Tit. 12 §143, on behalf of Booth Dunton, for the loss of financial support, comfort, companionship, advice, society, and counsel of the decedent Baby Dunton, as well as for funeral and burial expenses, together with interest and costs of suit.

FOURTH CLAIM FOR RELIEF:
SURVIVAL CLAIM FOR PREDEATH DAMAGES OF BABY DUNTON

28. The plaintiff repeats and realleges the allegations in paragraphs 1 to 18 of the complaint.

29. As a result of the collision proximately caused by the decedent Robert Burton's negligence, Isadora Dunton suffered extensive personal injuries which caused the child Baby Dunton to suffer cardiac arrhythmia and extreme fetal distress from the date of the accident until her death, injuries for which she could have recovered herself had she lived.

Wherefore, the plaintiff Booth Dunton, in his capacity as administrator of the estate of Baby Dunton, claims damages under the West Dakota survival statute, St. Ann. Tit. 12 §147, on behalf of the estate of Baby Dunton, for the pain and suffering she experienced from March 1, 2004 until her death on March 8, 2004, together with interest and costs of suit.

FIFTH CLAIM FOR RELIEF:
BOOTH DUNTON'S CLAIM FOR PERSONAL INJURIES

30. The plaintiff repeats and realleges the allegations in paragraphs 1 to 18 of the complaint.

31. As a result of the collision proximately caused by the decedent Robert Burton's negligence, Booth Dunton suffered facial lacerations, incurred lost wages and medical bills, experienced pain and suffering, and was temporarily disabled.

Wherefore, the plaintiff Booth Dunton, suing in his individual capacity, seeks damages from the defendant for pain and suffering, medical expenses, lost wages, and loss of the enjoyment of life suffered as a result of his injuries, together with interest and costs of suit.

SIXTH CLAIM FOR RELIEF:
BOOTH DUNTON'S CLAIM FOR LOSS OF CONSORTIUM
WITH ISADORA DUNTON

32. The plaintiff repeats and realleges the allegations in paragraphs 1 to 18 of the complaint.

33. As a result of the collision proximately caused by the decedent Robert Burton's negligence, Isadora Dunton suffered extensive personal injuries which led to her death on July 1, 2004.

34. As a result of the serious personal injuries suffered by Isadora Dunton, the plaintiff Booth Dunton suffered the loss of his wife's comfort, companionship, advice, society, and counsel from the date of the accident until her death on July 1, 2004.

Wherefore, the plaintiff Booth Dunton claims damages from the defendant for loss of consortium with his wife, Isadora Dunton.

SEVENTH CLAIM FOR RELIEF:
JOHN AND LYDIA DUNTON'S CLAIMS FOR
LOSS OF CONSORTIUM WITH ISADORA DUNTON

35. The plaintiffs repeat and reallege the allegations in paragraphs 1 to 18 of the complaint.

36. As a result of the collision proximately caused by the decedent's negligence, Isadora Dunton suffered extensive personal injuries which led to her death on July 1, 2004.

37. As a result of the serious personal injuries suffered by Isadora Dunton, her children Lydia Dunton and John Dunton suffered the loss of their mother's comfort, companionship, advice, society, and counsel from the date of the accident until her death on July 1, 2004.

Wherefore, the plaintiffs Lydia and John Dunton claim damages from the defendant for loss of consortium with their mother, Isadora Dunton.

EIGHTH CLAIM FOR RELIEF: BOOTH DUNTON'S CLAIMS FOR NEGLIGENT INFLICTION OF EMOTIONAL DISTRESS

38. The plaintiff repeats and realleges the allegations in paragraphs 1 to 18 of the complaint.

39. As a result of the collision proximately caused by the decedent's negligence, Isadora Dunton suffered extensive personal injuries which led to her death on July 1, 2004. Booth Dunton was also present and sustained personal injuries in the accident.

40. Immediately after the collision, Booth observed his wife in extreme pain, shock and distress from the injuries suffered in the accident.

41. As a result of the terrifying experience of observing the accident and its aftermath, Booth Dunton suffered immediate emotional trauma and permanent psychic damage, as well as direct physical injury.

Wherefore, the plaintiff Booth Dunton claims damages from the defendant for negligent infliction of emotional distress.

NINTH CLAIM FOR RELIEF: JOHN DUNTON'S CLAIMS FOR NEGLIGENT INFLICTION OF EMOTIONAL DISTRESS

42. The plaintiff repeats and realleges the allegations in paragraphs 1 to 18 of the complaint.

43. As a result of the collision proximately caused by the decedent's negligence, Isadora Dunton suffered extensive personal injuries which led to her death on July 1, 2004.

44. At the time of the accident, John Dunton was standing in the immediate vicinity of the collision, and immediately became aware that his parents had been involved in a serious accident.

45. Immediately after the collision, John Dunton rushed to the scene and observed his mother and father in extreme pain, shock and distress from the injuries suffered in the accident.

46. As a result of the terrifying experience of observing the accident and its aftermath, John Dunton suffered both immediate emotional trauma and long term psychological damage. Since the accident, he has become withdrawn and uncommunicative, has received low grades, lost touch with his friends, and shows other signs of post traumatic stress syndrome.

Wherefore, the plaintiff John Dunton claims damages from the defendant for negligent infliction of emotional distress.

_____

The plaintiffs claim trial by jury on all issues in this action.

Allison Barrymore

Allison Barrymore
Attorney for Plaintiffs
132 Hayes Boulevard
Elkton, West Dakota 11111
(419) 832-1239

Comments on the Dunton Complaint

Barrymore, the Duntons' counsel, has put a lot of thought into drafting this complaint based on the facts of the Dunton accident. Doubtless, there are problems with some of the claims, either because it is not clear that they are legally sufficient, or because of difficulties of proof. Barrymore's job at this stage is to determine which claims may be legally and factually supportable, not to determine which will actually prevail at trial.

The comments below reflect some of the analysis which went into drafting this negligence complaint.

1. Barrymore has broken down the various claims both by parties and by the particular types of claims. As the Introduction suggests, she has taken these miscellaneous facts and reconceptualized them in terms of legally recognized claims for tort damages. For example, the First Claim for Relief seeks damages for wrongful death of Isadora, and the Second for the predeath damages to Isadora. Even though these claims are both based on injuries to the same person and are both asserted by the same plaintiff, it facilitates an understanding of the claims to set them forth separately because negligence law analyzes the claims differently.

2. Barrymore has included some claims in the complaint even though it is unclear whether they are legally sufficient. For example, the Second Claim for Relief seeks damages for Isadora's loss of enjoyment of life for the period from the accident until her death. It may be unclear under West Dakota law whether such damages can be recovered in the survival action. As long as the estate *may* be entitled to such damages, the estate may properly assert them; nothing requires them to confine their claims to those which are absolutely certain to be recognized as legally valid. See Fed. R. Civ. P. 11(b)(2) (authorizing assertion of claims which are supported by existing law or a nonfrivolous argument for extension or changes in existing law).

Similarly, the Seventh Claim for Relief alleges loss of consortium claims on behalf of John and Lydia, though it is unclear whether West Dakota law will recognize claims for loss of parental consortium. Barrymore has also included the frontier theory of a survival claim on behalf of Baby Dunton, though this one is a very long shot indeed. If such claims were clearly not viable, it would be improper to assert them, but where there may be a right to recover on these claims, Barrymore is entitled to present them and let the court decide whether they are legally cognizable.

Although Barrymore may have given considerable thought and research to these various unresolved issues, the complaint holds no hint of the doubts she may entertain about the strength of these claims. Defendant's counsel will have to assess their viability and challenge those which she concludes are legally unsound.

3.   Other parts of the complaint reveal how the Duntons' counsel crafted the allegations to reflect the substantive requirements of each theory of relief. For example, the Ninth Claim for Relief, seeking recovery for negligent infliction of emotional distress upon John, alleges that John immediately arrived on the accident scene and viewed his injured relatives in a sorry state. Paragraph 45. Barrymore may anticipate that West Dakota will adopt the *Dillon* approach to indirect infliction claims, which focuses on the immediacy of the event, the nearness of the bystander to the accident, and the closeness of the relationship of the bystander to the injured victims.

The allegations in Paragraph 44 lay the groundwork for an indirect infliction claim under the zone-of-danger rule as well. Barrymore has alleged that John was in the "immediate vicinity" of the accident. It is not entirely clear that he *was* in the zone of danger: The facts indicate that he was 25 feet from the collision. But it is not clear that this is too far away either, so the allegation leaves the door open to litigate the issue. Similarly, she has alleged symptoms that John suffered as a result of his emotional distress which might suffice to establish "resulting physical injuries" if West Dakota law turns out to require this.

Similarly, in Booth's count for negligent infliction of emotional distress, Barrymore realleges that Booth was a direct victim of the accident. See par. 39. Should West Dakota stick with the requirement of impact to support an emotional distress claim, this allegation will lay the groundwork for an argument that he can sue for *indirect* infliction because he suffered an impact. See Chapter 11, Example 1a.

Barrymore's complaint does not specifically allege that any one of these standards for recovery applies. It is not necessary to allege the exact legal standard in the complaint, but it is important to allege facts that demonstrate that the legal standard — whichever one the court ultimately applies — can be met.

4.   Barrymore has given thought to other problems of proof as well. For example, she has alleged that Burton's driving violated several West Dakota statutes. Presumably, she has included these allegations to lay the groundwork for an instruction to the jury that Burton was "negligent per se" for violating these statutes. See Chapter 5.

5.   The damage allegations in the various claims also reflect Barrymore's analysis of the substantive law. For example, the wrongful death claims seek damages for the financial support and consortium losses of the survivors, presumably echoing the language of the West Dakota wrongful death statute. See the "wherefore" clauses in the First and Third Claims for Relief. (Note that recovery is sought in the First Claim for Relief on behalf of Booth, John, and Lydia, for wrongful death of Isadora. But recovery is only sought on behalf of Booth in the Third Claim for Relief

for wrongful death of Baby Dunton. This presumably reflects the fact that parents and children, but not siblings, are in the "first tier" of beneficiaries under the West Dakota wrongful death statute.) The survival claims, by contrast, seek damages for losses suffered prior to death. Note also that Barrymore has been careful to assert the various claims on behalf of the proper plaintiffs. The survival and wrongful death claims are asserted by Booth as administrator of the estates of Isadora and Baby Dunton, while the other claims are asserted on behalf of the individuals named in each claim.

6.   Some issues considered by counsel have not made their way into the complaint at all. There is no claim at all for Booth's loss of consortium with John due to John's emotional distress claim. (See the discussion of this claim in Example 5b.) Counsel may have concluded that this is too long a shot, and that including it would detract from the overall credibility of the complaint. (A similar conclusion might have been warranted with regard to the Fourth Claim for Relief, the survival claim on behalf of Baby Dunton.)

7.   Naturally, the questionable claims in Barrymore's complaint will not go unnoticed. Burton's counsel will likely challenge the legal sufficiency of some claims, such as the claim for prenatal pain and suffering and the claims for loss of parental consortium.

She will also probe, through discovery, the plaintiffs' ability to prove their allegations. For example, damages for the wrongful death of Baby Dunton will be very difficult to establish, not to mention the creative claim for her pain and suffering prior to death. Indeed, proof problems led the Duntons' counsel to omit one claim entirely, Isadora's claim for indirect infliction of emotional distress for witnessing injury to Booth. Without her testimony it would be very difficult to establish this claim.

Burton's counsel will also challenge the plaintiffs' ability to prove causation on some claims. Even if John is entitled to recover for infliction of emotional distress, for example, he will have to establish that his withdrawal and poor performance in school were caused by witnessing the injury to Isadora, rather than other causes, such as the usual catatonia of the teenage years.

8.   A colleague with a wealth of litigation experience suggests that a very practical consideration would figure heavily in this case: Because of Isadora's success, and the wrongful death claims, the potential damages in this case are great, probably much greater than Burton's estate, even with insurance, will be able to pay. This has several implications. First, it may make sense to leave out some lesser or dubious claims in order to focus the jury on the big ticket issues in the case, since the entire judgment will not likely be paid anyway. Second, since the judgment is not likely to be fully paid, conflicts may arise among the various plaintiffs concerning the

allocation of any payments received. Counsel will have to be very careful to make sure that all plaintiffs are aware of this problem, and to consider the possibility that conflicts among the plaintiffs might call for separate representation.

A third implication is that counsel will surely want to look for other potential defendants, to tap their resources as well. If, for example, poor road design contributed to the accident, counsel should consider a claim against the city or town that maintains the road. Or, if brake problems contributed, a claim against the repair shop or manufacturer could also increase the potential recovery.

PART SEVEN

Liability of Multiple Defendants

19

Joint and Several Liability: The Classic Rules

Introduction

We saw in the chapters on causation that a plaintiff will frequently have claims against more than one tortfeasor, where several have contributed to causing her injury. This chapter, and the next, address the manner in which tort law distributes the damages in such cases. This chapter deals with the traditional common law rules governing the liability of "joint tortfeasors." The next analyzes principles of contribution, the right of a tortfeasor who has paid the plaintiff's claim to seek partial reimbursement from other defendants liable for the same injury.

Joint Tortfeasors Distinguished from Joint Conduct

First, let's distinguish the case of "true" joint tortfeasors from the much more common type of joint and several liability discussed in this chapter. True joint tortfeasors are parties who agree to engage in a course of tortious conduct. Suppose that Kelvin and Curie go looking for Marconi, planning to beat him up. They find him, and Curie breaks his jaw. Because Kelvin and Curie acted in concert to injure Marconi, both are liable to him, even though it was Curie who administered the blow. Even though Kelvin didn't hit Marconi, he encouraged and participated in the common scheme to injure Marconi. Tort law traditionally held — and still holds — actors involved in such joint conduct liable for the acts of either, in much the same way that conspirators are criminally responsible for the acts of other conspirators. See Restatement (Third) of Torts, Apportionment of Liability §15. Similarly, if Ford and Hudson decide to race their cars on the highway, they are both liable if one of their cars hits Lenoir, since they jointly engaged in the negligent conduct that led to Lenoir's injury.

Such "true" joint tortfeasor cases, in which parties agree to engage in tortious conduct, are relatively rare. It is much more common for the independent conduct of two actors to combine to injure the plaintiff. Suppose, for example, that Fermi was a passenger in Joule's car, which collided with a truck driven by Edison due to negligence by both drivers, and that Fermi suffered a broken collar bone. Here, Edison and Joule did not act together, probably did not know each other, may not even have known of the other's presence. However, their independent acts have contributed to cause a single injury. As we saw in the discussion of causation, each is a "but for" cause of the harm, even though they did not act together.

The traditional common law rule was — and still is in many cases today — that each tortfeasor in a case like Fermi's is liable to the plaintiff for her full damages, since his negligence was a "but for" cause of the plaintiff's injury. Courts generally refer to the defendants in such cases as "joint tortfeasors." This is clearly loose language, though universally used. Fermi and Edison did not do anything "jointly," in the sense that Kelvin and Curie did in the battery example, since they acted separately, without agreement. It is the resulting *injury* that is joint, not the actions of the defendants. The phrase "joint tortfeasors" simply means that the defendants both contributed to a single, indivisible injury to the plaintiff and are each fully liable for that injury.

Here is another example to drive home the point. Watt, a worker on a construction site, negligently leaves an excavation unguarded, and Planck, an oblivious jogger, bumps Curie and knocks her into it, breaking her leg. Here again, Curie would have negligence claims against both Watt and Planck for her injuries, since the negligence of each defendant contributed to causing the harm. Watt and Planck are, in the common parlance, joint tortfeasors, each fully liable for Curie's injury.

It is often said that the defendants in cases like the Fermi and Curie examples are "jointly and severally liable" for the injury. This means that each is liable for the full amount of the plaintiff's damages, and may be sued for those damages either singly or along with the other tortfeasors. If the plaintiff prevails in an action against joint tortfeasors, she is entitled to a judgment against each for her full damages. For example, if the jury found both Joule and Edison liable for Fermi's injury, and found Fermi's damages to be $27,000, the court would enter judgment against both Joule and Edison for $27,000. Fermi would obtain a judgment like that in Figure 19–1, on p. 442. Alternatively, had she sued Fermi alone she would have gotten a judgment against him for the full $27,000.

Joint and several liability did not apply, however, if the defendants caused separate damages. Suppose that Farmer Jones and Farmer Smith both decided to burn the stubble off their fields on a windy day, and both fires got away. If Farmer Jones's fire burned two acres on the west side of Doe's property, and Farmer Smith's burned five acres on the east side, it stands to reason that Jones would pay for the two-acre fire but not for the five-acre fire caused by Smith. Jones's negligence caused the two-acre fire, but (assuming that Jones and Smith acted independently) was not a "but for" cause of the five-acre fire, so Jones was not liable for it. The same was true for Smith, who was liable for the five-acre fire but not the two-acre blaze. In such cases, where the damages could rationally be apportioned separately to the tortfeasors, the courts would do so. Restatement (Second) of Torts, §881.

Satisfaction of Judgments

Under the judgment in Figure 19–1 (p. 442), Fermi would be entitled to collect his $27,000 from either Edison or Joule. Of course, he could not get $27,000 from each of them, for a total of $54,000. The plaintiff was entitled to one full "satisfaction" of his damages from joint tortfeasors, but no more. Thus, if Joule paid Fermi $27,000, the judgment was deemed satisfied, and Fermi could not collect any additional amount from Edison. Similarly, if he obtained a judgment against Edison and Edison paid, Fermi could not collect from Joule for the same injuries. D. Dobbs, The Law of Torts 1078.

Suppose, however, that Fermi sued Edison alone and obtained a judgment for $27,000, but Edison was unable to satisfy the judgment. Early cases held that once Fermi obtained a judgment against one tortfeasor, the judgment extinguished his claim against all the tortfeasors, so that he could not sue Joule separately if Edison failed to pay. The theory was that the plaintiff had a single, indivisible claim, which could only be sued upon once. D. Dobbs, The Law of Torts 1083. However, the courts later came around to the position that, as long as Fermi's judgment had not been *satisfied*, he was entitled to sue Joule for the same injury, and try to collect from him instead. Or, if Edison had a $10,000 insurance policy, and paid that much, Fermi could seek a separate judgment against Joule and collect the remaining $17,000 from him.

Suppose that Joule was a close friend of Fermi's (or his boss) and Fermi, understandably reluctant to sue Joule, sued Edison only. At common law if a joint tortfeasor like Edison were found liable and paid the judgment, he had no right to force other tortfeasors to "contribute" to the judgment. Edison was liable for the damages, was justly made to pay them, and had no complaint if Joule got off without paying. The courts refused to adjust the loss as between the wrongdoers, just as it refused

```
                    STATE OF WEST DAKOTA

COOK COUNTY, SS;              CIVIL ACTION NO. 03-1305

ENRICO FERMI,

          Plaintiff

     v.                           JUDGMENT

MAX JOULE
THOMAS EDISON,

          Defendants
```

   This action came on for trial before the Court and a jury, Honorable Constance Pallotta, presiding. The issues having been duly tried and the jury having rendered its verdict, it is Ordered and Adjudged

   That the plaintiff Enrico Fermi recover from the defendants Thomas Edison and Max Joule the sum of $27,000 with interest thereon at the rate of 7% as provided by law, and his costs of action.

   Dated at Cody, West Dakota, this 25th day of May, 2004.

_____   _____
   Justice   Clerk of Court

Figure 19–1

(under the doctrine of contributory negligence) to adjust a loss between a negligent plaintiff and a negligent defendant. This classic no-contribution rule is no longer the law in most states, but it was for many years. See Chapter 20, which analyzes the basic principles of contribution among joint tortfeasors, and Chapter 24, which illustrates some of the current variations.

Settlement and Release of Claims

Other issues arose if Fermi settled his claim against one tortfeasor and then sued the other. Suppose, for example, that Fermi settled with Joule, agreeing to release his tort claim against Joule for $13,000. When the plaintiff settled with a tortfeasor, he would ordinarily give that defendant a "release" in exchange for payment of the settlement amount. The release would waive all of the plaintiff's claims against that defendant arising out of a particular accident or dispute. Figure 19–2 is a simple example of a release.

A Practical Question

1.   If Joule, as a joint tortfeasor, is fully liable for the entire injury to Fermi, and the likely damages are close to $30,000, why would Fermi let him off the hook for $13,000?

_____

At common law, giving one tortfeasor a release was a tricky business, because the early cases held that a release to one tortfeasor released the

---

RELEASE AND SETTLEMENT OF CLAIM

In consideration of thirteen thousand dollars ($13,000), receipt of which is hereby acknowledged, I, Enrico Fermi, of Saginaw, West Dakota, on behalf of myself and my heirs, legal representatives and assigns, hereby release Max Joule of Johnstown, West Dakota, or his heirs or representatives, from all liability, claims, demands, rights or causes of action incident to property damage and personal injury sustained by me in an automobile accident that occurred on May 4, 2002 at Johnstown, West Dakota, involving an automobile driven by Max Joule. This release covers all claims which I had, now have or may have in the future against Max Joule, his heirs or representatives arising out of the May 4, 2002 accident.

By executing this instrument, I do not waive any claim or claims that I may now or hereafter have against any person, firm or corporation other than Max Joule, the releasee named herein. I understand that Max Joule does not, by making the payment set forth above, admit any liability or responsibility for the above-described accident or the consequences thereof.

In witness whereof, I have executed this release at Saginaw, West Dakota, on July 29, 2003.

Signature _Enrico Fermi_

Figure 19–2

plaintiff's claims against *all* joint tortfeasors. If Fermi gave a release to Joule, he was deemed to have released Edison, Watt, and any other possible defendants as well, regardless of the amount Joule paid for the release. Historically, there were several reasons for the rule. First, the plaintiff was considered to have a single cause of action for her injuries, even though each defendant was fully liable on that cause of action. *Cooper v. Robert Hall Clothes, Inc.,* 390 N.E.2d 155, 157 (Ind. 1979); D. Dobbs, The Law of Torts 1083. By giving a release to any tortfeasor, Fermi relinquished the cause of action itself. Thus, he was barred from bringing a subsequent suit on that cause of action against another tortfeasor.

A second, less formalistic rationale for the common law rule that a release barred suit against other tortfeasors was the concern that the plaintiff would settle successively with each tortfeasor and collect more than the value of her claim. Since each tortfeasor was liable for the full amount of the plaintiff's damages, a plaintiff could divide and conquer by extracting substantial settlements from each. Fermi, for example, might settle with Joule for $18,000 and with Edison for $18,000. Both might have the incentive to accept the settlement, since it is $9,000 less than the (assumed) $27,000 value of the claim. If they both settled, Fermi would be overcompensated by $9,000 ($36,000 − $27,000). The rule that a release barred suit against the other tortfeasors prevented this: Once Fermi gave a release to Joule, Edison would have no incentive to settle, since the release barred suit against Edison as well as Joule.

The release rule applied even if the plaintiff tried to limit the release to the settling tortfeasor. Thus, the second paragraph of Fermi's release in Figure 19–2, which states that it does not affect his claims against any other joint tortfeasor, was given no effect. Under the common law view, Fermi was trying to have his cake and eat it too, that is, to continue to prosecute a cause of action that had been surrendered by the release.

Another Practical Question

2.   Did the common law release rule encourage or discourage settlements?

This early rule that a release of one tortfeasor released them all was later abandoned, for several reasons. First, the formalistic view that the claims against Joule and Edison constitute a single, indivisible cause of action is no longer accepted. In recent decades, courts have recognized that, even if Fermi's *damages* are indivisible, he has independent claims for those damages against each tortfeasor. Consequently, it is no longer logical to infer that he abandons claims against one tortfeasor by settling with the other.

Second, the release rule prevented settlements with individual tortfeasors who were willing to pay a part of the plaintiff's damages, but not to pay enough to induce the plaintiff to release her entire claim. This led to creative efforts by lawyers to find a way of settling with one tortfeasor without relinquishing the right to sue others. The most common device for evading the common law release rule was the "covenant not to sue," by which the plaintiff covenanted (agreed) not to sue the defendant on the claim. In theory, she had not surrendered her claim, but merely promised that she would not bring a law suit to enforce it against the settling defendant.[1] This was fighting formalism with formalism. The actual effect of the covenant not to sue was the same as the release: Plaintiff gave up her claim against the defendant in exchange for a money payment. But, since it did not technically "release" the claim, plaintiffs argued that they were still entitled to sue other joint tortfeasors on the claim.

Because the release rule was an obstacle to sensible settlement of tort claims, some courts sanctioned its evasion through the covenant not to sue. In these states, the common law rule that a release barred any further suit against other tortfeasors became a dead letter. Counsel simply styled the settlement agreement as a covenant not to sue instead of a release, thus achieving settlement with one tortfeasor without waiving the right to sue others. Defendants went along with the practice, because they also benefitted from such settlements: They could settle legitimate claims without having to pay more than their fair share of the plaintiff's damages. Thus a kernel of common sense was rescued from a shell of outdated legal doctrine.

Other courts, rather than endorsing evasion of the release rule through the covenant not to sue, have overruled it outright. In these jurisdictions, a release or covenant not to sue given to one tortfeasor does not release other parties, unless the release so stipulates. See Restatement (Second) of Torts §885. Under this approach, the release in Figure 19-2 would preserve Fermi's right to sue Edison, since it not only shows no intent to release Edison, but affirmatively states that it does not. See generally Harper, James & Gray, §10.1, at 32-37.

Through one of these avenues, most states have arrived at the same basic approach to settlements: The plaintiff may settle with one tortfeasor, and go to trial against others. Under the traditional joint and several liability rules, any judgment she obtained against the remaining defendants would be reduced, dollar for dollar, by the amount paid to her by the settling tortfeasor.

These joint and several liability rules have been changed in many states over the past 20 years or so. Some states now apply "several liability," under which individual tortfeasors pay only a part of the plaintiff's damages.

---

1. For example, a covenant not to sue might provide that the plaintiff "covenants with Max Joule, of Saginaw, West Dakota, his heirs, legal representatives and assigns, to never institute any suit or action at law or in equity against Max Joule by reason of any claim I now have or may hereafter acquire relating to an accident that occurred on May 4, 2002, at Johnstown, West Dakota...".

Others apply joint and several liability in some circumstances, but several liability in others. These variations are explored in Chapter 24. However, no matter where you practice, it is important to understand the traditional joint and several liability rules. First, these rules continue to apply to all cases in some states, and to some cases in most states. Second, you have to understand the basic doctrines to grasp the elegant variations state legislatures have recently grafted onto them.

EXAMPLES

Sue and Sue Alike

3.   Bell is driving home late at night when her car dies. She pulls into the breakdown lane, but fails to put on her hazard lights or put out flares. Marconi negligently fails to see her, drifts into the breakdown lane and hits Bell's car, injuring Thatcher, a passenger in Bell's car. Thatcher sues Marconi for damages. If the jury concludes that Bell and Marconi were both negligent, and assesses Thatcher's damages at $60,000, what verdict should it render against Marconi, assuming it has been properly instructed on the principles of joint and several liability (and understood them!)?

4.   Suppose that Thatcher had sued both Bell and Marconi, the jury found both negligent, and assessed the damages at $60,000.

    a. What verdict should the jury render?

    b. How much could she collect from each defendant?

5.   Whiting and Hahn, two employees of an electrical contractor, are working together to install wiring in Pringle's house. They agree that Whiting will stop in the basement to cut off the power to an exposed junction box on the wall, but Whiting forgets to do it. An hour later, Shattuck, a plasterer, negligently swings his ladder into the junction box, causing a short circuit and resulting fire. Pringle's house sustains $50,000 in damages.

    a. Which of the three are liable for the damage?

    b. How much is each liable for?

    c. Assume that Pringle settled with Whiting for $40,000, and gave her a
       release. She then sues Shattuck for her injuries. In a jurisdiction that
       applied the strict common law release rule, what would the court do?

    d. What would the court do if Pringle gave Whiting a covenant not
       to sue, in a jurisdiction that allowed evasion of the common law
       release rule through a covenant not to sue?

6.   In the Edison/Joule example in the Introduction, Edison and Joule caused Fermi $27,000 in damages between them. Without regard to history, one sensible and seemingly fair solution would be to split the damages, that is, to hold Edison liable for $13,500 and Joule for the same.

    a. Why would this solution appear illogical to a traditional common
       law judge?

b. Suppose in a jurisdiction that applies joint and several liability, that a bill came before the legislature to introduce this approach to the liability of multiple tortfeasors. Who would oppose it, plaintiffs or defendants?

Dissatisfaction of Judgments

7. Erg sues Kelvin for negligence in causing a fire and recovers a judgment for $16,000. Kelvin, who is bankrupt, does not pay. Can Erg now sue Volt, whose negligence also caused the fire, to recover for the fire damage?

8. Suppose that Erg settles his claim against Kelvin for damages arising from the fire, for $7,000, the amount of Kelvin's insurance coverage. Now he sues Volt for the same injuries.

a. If the jury finds that Erg's damages are $16,000, and a judgment is entered against him for that amount, how much will Volt have to pay?

b. Suppose that Volt only has $5,000, and pays that. Can Erg sue Planck, another tortfeasor who allegedly caused the fire?

c. Assume that Erg sued Volt, after settling with Kelvin for $7,000, and the jury determined that Erg's damages were $4,500. What would Volt have to pay?

d. Assume that Erg settled with Kelvin for $4,000, and in a subsequent action against Volt the jury determined his damages to be $16,000. How much must Volt pay to Erg? How much must Kelvin pay to Volt?

9. Erg settles with Kelvin for $7,000, and then goes to trial against Volt. At the close of trial, Volt asks the judge to instruct the jury that Erg has already received $7,000 in compensation for his injuries.

a. Should the jury be told this?

b. If they are, what else should they be told as well?

Joint *and* Several Liability

10. Bethune is driving a backhoe during the construction of a storm drain. She negligently backs up without looking or sounding her beeper and hits Maltby, a passing pedestrian, breaking her leg and knocking her over next to the excavation. DeWolfe, a construction worker down in the pit, negligently throws a large stone up out of the excavation without looking. The stone hits Maltby on the head, causing a severe concussion. She sues them both for her injuries.

a. Are they jointly and severally liable to Maltby?

b. Suppose that this case goes to trial against both Bethune and DeWolfe. The jury finds them both negligent, and that Maltby's total damages are $60,000. What judgment should the judge enter against each defendant?

Bewitched, Bewildered, and BeFuddled

11. Assume that Fermi suffered a serious back injury in his accident with Joule and Edison. The undisputed evidence shows that he was out of work for six months, suffered $26,000 in lost wages, paid $21,000 in medical bills, and sustained serious pain and suffering, as well as some permanent disability.

At trial, Judge Fudd instructs the jury as follows:

> If you find that the defendants were both negligent, and that the negligence of each defendant was a cause of the plaintiff's injuries, then you must find the defendants liable for the full amount of damages suffered by the plaintiff.

The jury comes back with the verdict in Figure 19–3. Fermi's attorney is amazed that the jury could have only awarded $50,000 in damages, which

---

STATE OF WEST DAKOTA

COOK COUNTY, SS;   CIVIL ACTION NO. 04-1305

ENRICO FERMI,

      Plaintiff

    v.   VERDICT

MAX JOULE
THOMAS EDISON,

      Defendants

    We the Jury, find for the plaintiff against defendant Joule for $____50,000____. (Strike out if inapplicable)

    We find for the plaintiff against the defendant Edison for $____50,000____. (Strike out if inapplicable)

    ~~We find for the defendants.~~ (Strike out if inapplicable)

                           Benjamin Franklin
                           Jury Foreperson

Figure 19–3

allows a mere $3,000 over the proven economic losses to compensate Fermi for pain and suffering and disability. Something, she suspects, has gone amiss in the jury's deliberations.

    a. What do you think the jury did, and how did Judge Fudd's ambiguous instruction lead them to do it?

    b. How should the plaintiff have avoided the problem?

Joint Sheepfeasors

12. Farmer Jones's prize field of Kentucky blue grass is eaten clean when Herder's and Shepherd's sheep escape from their pens. Investigation reveals that both Shepherd and Herder were negligent and that 30 of Shepherd's sheep got into Jones's field and ten of Herder's got in. Are Shepherd and Herder jointly and severally liable to Jones?

EXPLANATIONS

A Practical Question

1.   There are many reasons why a plaintiff might settle a claim against one tortfeasor for less than the full value of her damages. She might have doubts about her ability to prove that the particular party is liable, and therefore settle for less than the full value of her claim to account for the risk that she would lose entirely at trial. (The reasonable risk-averse client would obviously prefer $13,000 in hand to a 25 percent chance of collecting $27,000.) The plaintiff might know that the party is unable to pay more than the insurance coverage available, so there is little point in obtaining an unenforceable judgment for more. She might not want to try the case against a particular party, due to jury sympathy or an anticipated aggressive defense by that party. It might also cost more to pursue the case against that defendant than she gives up by settling, perhaps due to the need for expensive expert testimony to prove negligence by that defendant.

In addition, tort claims often involve intangible damages such as pain and suffering or disfigurement. In such cases, neither party knows what value the jury will place on the plaintiff's injuries. Thus even a plaintiff who expects to win at trial may settle for less than the apparent full value of the claim, to avoid the risk that a jury will return a meager verdict.

Thus, a settlement against Joule for $13,000 may make good sense for Fermi, even if he believes that a jury would give him a $27,000 verdict. It makes particularly good sense if Fermi *retains his right to sue Edison*, since he may still collect the balance of his damages from him. The $13,000 he collects from Joule would be credited against the later judgment, but he would still be made whole despite his settlement with one of the tortfeasors.

Another Practical Question

2.   The common law release rule discouraged settlements. Because a release barred the plaintiff from suing any other party on the same claim, a plaintiff would only settle with one of several tortfeasors if the amount offered came close to the amount she would likely recover if she tried the case against them all. In other words, the settlement against one had to be good enough to induce the plaintiff to abandon her claims against everyone; she couldn't settle with one tortfeasor for part of her damages with the hope of recovering more from someone else. Since the common law rule forced the plaintiff to set a high price on settlement, individual defendants in a multidefendant case would be less likely to ante up the amount necessary to settle the case.

Sue and Sue Alike

3.   The jury should render a verdict against Marconi for $60,000. His negligent driving was a "but for" cause of the harm. Consequently, he is a tortfeasor. Under joint and several liability he is liable to Thatcher for her full damages.

It is true that Bell is a tortfeasor too, since her negligence was another cause of the accident. Under principles of joint and several liability, Thatcher was free to sue either of the tortfeasors and recover her full damages. She could, of course, have sued them both. But she didn't have to. She could choose ... and it was not uncommon for a plaintiff like Thatcher to choose *not* to sue the driver of the car she was in.

4a.   If Thatcher sued both drivers, and both were found liable, she would get a verdict against each for $60,000.

b.   Thatcher could collect $60,000 from either defendant. Each was jointly and severally liable for the whole damages she suffered, so either could justly be made to pay the entire judgment. Of course, if she collected it from one, she could not seek $60,000 more, or any amount more, from the other. Once her judgment was satisfied, she had no further rights against either tortfeasor.

5a.   In this case, Whiting was negligent in failing to cut off the power, and Shattuck was negligent in swinging the ladder into the junction box. Their independent acts together caused the fire. Thus, they are joint tortfeasors in the sense that their separate negligent acts concurred to cause indivisible harm to Pringle. Both are liable to her.

What of Hahn, who was working with Whiting? The facts do not indicate that she was negligent, since she was not responsible for cutting off the power. Nor is she liable for Whiting's negligence simply because she was working on the same job with her. That would be a tough rule indeed, making employees liable for the torts of any co-worker.

It is true that she and Whiting agreed that Whiting would turn off the power. But agreeing to split up the work in a particular way is quite different from agreeing to engage in tortious conduct. This is not a "joint tort" situation, like the concerted action example in which two drivers engage in a drag race. There, two actors consciously engaged in negligent conduct together, which they knew created unreasonable risks to others. Here, while Hahn and Whiting were both engaged in the construction work, Hahn did not agree to engage in any negligent course of conduct with Whiting. Thus, Hahn is not liable for the negligence of Whiting.[2]

b.   Under traditional causation analysis, both Whiting and Shattuck were causes of the fire, since the negligence of each was a but-for cause leading to it. Thus, each caused the plaintiff's entire loss, and was held liable for that entire loss. As joint tortfeasors, Whiting and Shattuck would each be liable for $50,000.

c.   Under the strict common law release rule, a party who gave a release of her claim to any tortfeasor surrendered her right to sue all possible defendants on that claim. Thus, Pringle would be barred from bringing any further suit on the same claim against Whiting or Shattuck. If this rule applied, Pringle's suit would be dismissed.

d.   In a jurisdiction that held that a covenant not to sue did not waive any rights against other tortfeasors, Pringle would still be entitled to bring suit against Shattuck. However, if she recovered $50,000, the $40,000 already paid by Whiting in settlement of the claim against her would be credited against the judgment. Shattuck would only have to pay $10,000.

6a. Logically, there is no reason why the multiple tortfeasor problem could not be dealt with by dividing the plaintiff's damages in this way. If there were two tortfeasors, each would be liable for half the damages; if there were seven, each would be liable for a seventh, and so on.

However, this pragmatic solution was antithetical to the conceptual approach of the common law, which viewed both Edison and Joule as having caused *all* of Fermi's damages, not half. But for Edison's negligent driving, no accident would have taken place, and Fermi would have suffered no injury. Because of Edison's negligence (helped along, admittedly, by Joule's as well), Fermi suffered $27,000 in damages. The same was true of Joule. Because both defendants had caused the full harm, courts refused to divide the damages in half.[3]

---

2. As another example, suppose they agreed that Whiting would go to the hardware store while Hahn started work, and Whiting had an accident on the way. Clearly, he alone would be liable for the accident.

3. On the other hand, once courts accept the concept of contribution between joint tortfeasors, essentially the same division may ultimately result, if one tortfeasor pays the full judgment and sues the other for contribution.

b.   Plaintiffs would resist this Solomonic solution fiercely. Under the traditional rules of joint and several liability, both Edison and Joule were fully liable. If Edison were insolvent, Joule would still have to pay the full damages under the classic rules. By contrast, if the rule were changed so that each was "severally" liable for half the damages, Fermi would collect $13,500 from Joule and nothing from an insolvent Edison. Thus, Fermi would be the loser if Edison were unable to pay. Under joint and several liability, however, *Joule* takes the risk of Edison's insolvency, and the plaintiff has twice the chance of being fully compensated for his injuries.

Dissatisfaction of Judgments

7.   Under the earlier cases, the answer to this question was "no." A judgment was treated like a release of all tortfeasors; that is, getting a judgment on a tort cause of action was deemed to extinguish the underlying cause of action, leaving the judgment instead. But that rule later gave way to the more recent common law rule stated in the introduction, that a judgment against one tortfeasor did not bar suit against another, unless the first judgment was satisfied. Thus, Erg could still sue Volt and get a second *judgment* for her damages, but could not *collect* more than her actual assessed damages.

8a.   Because no plaintiff was entitled to more than one full satisfaction of his damages, Volt would get a credit against the $16,000 judgment for the $7,000 Erg has received in settlement from Kelvin. Thus, he would have to pay $9,000 to Erg.

b.   At this point, Erg has received $7,000 in settlement from Kelvin and $5,000 from Volt under the judgment. He is still short $4,000. Since he has not yet received full satisfaction of his damages, he can still bring suit against Planck to recover for the remaining $4,000.

c.   In this example, Erg settled with Kelvin for more than the jury ultimately determines Erg's damages to be. Volt would get a credit for the settlement, and that would more than cover the judgment amount. Volt would pay nothing. On the other hand, Kelvin would not get anything back either. A deal is a deal; he bought his peace, and he cannot later claim that he paid too much for it.

d.   Here again, Volt gets a credit for the settlement amount. He will be liable to Erg for $12,000 (the $16,000 judgment minus the $4,000 paid by Kelvin in settlement). He will have paid more than half of the damages, but at common law this did not give him any right of contribution from Kelvin. As stated previously, the common law had no trouble requiring Volt to pay the *full* $16,000 in damages he had caused. Thus, courts were not troubled if, on facts like these, he paid some lesser amount but still more than his "share." Even today, many jurisdictions protect settling tortfeasors like Kelvin from claims for contribution.

9a. Usually, there is no reason to tell the jury that Erg has received some compensation by settling with Kelvin. The jury's job is to determine Erg's damages and to decide whether Volt is liable for them. The mention of a settlement figure is only likely to distract them from that task. They might, for example, infer that $7,000 is the value the plaintiff places on her claim, which may not be the case at all. (See Explanation 1, which suggests a number of reasons why a plaintiff will settle low with one tortfeasor.)

In most cases, the better course is to tell the jury nothing about the settlement, and to let the judge adjust the resulting verdict to give Volt a credit for the settlement. If the jury finds Erg's damages to be $24,000, for example, the judge would apply the dollar-credit rule by entering judgment against Volt for $17,000.[4]

b. If the jury is told of the settlement, they ought to be told what to do about it: They should be told to determine the plaintiff's damages without regard to the settlement, and then to render a verdict by reducing the damages by the settlement amount. It will be less confusing, however, if the judge tells the jury nothing about the settlement and simply reduces the verdict to account for it herself.

Joint *and* Several Liability

10a. In this example, Bethune and DeWolfe are joint tortfeasors as to part of Maltby's injuries, but not as to all of them. The negligence of both Bethune and DeWolfe caused the concussion. Maltby would not have been hit by the stone if Bethune had not knocked her into harm's way, or if DeWolfe had not negligently thrown the stone out of the pit. It is a case of successive negligent acts that together cause the harm. So long as DeWolfe's subsequent negligence is foreseeable, it does not insulate Bethune from liability. As to Maltby's concussion, Bethune and DeWolfe are joint tortfeasors.

However, DeWolfe is not a joint tortfeasor with Bethune in causing Maltby's broken leg. DeWolfe's negligence had no part in causing the broken leg, which happened before DeWolfe entered the picture. Thus, Bethune would be solely liable for this injury, but both would be liable for Maltby's concussion damages.

b. The problem here is that the jury's general verdict does not separate the leg damages from the concussion damages. As to Bethune, it

---

4. There may be some cases, however, when the jury should be informed at least of the *fact* of settlement, if not of the amount. The settling tortfeasor will frequently testify at trial. The fact that she no longer has a direct stake in the matter could affect her incentive to testify favorably to one or another of the parties. If so, the other party may have a good argument for informing the jury that the settlor no longer faces personal liability in the action.

doesn't matter, since she is liable for both. The judge should enter a judgment against her for $60,000. But DeWolfe should only be held liable for the concussion damages, and the jury's verdict doesn't indicate how much they are.

The court should avoid this problem by using a special verdict form that asks the jury to specify the amount of damages the plaintiff has suffered from the leg injury and the amount attributable to the concussion. Then the judge can enter judgment against Bethune for the total damages and against DeWolfe for the separate amount attributed to the concussion.

Bewitched, Bewildered, and BeFuddled

11a. It is very likely that the ambiguity in Judge Fudd's instruction led the jury to render a verdict that does not convey their intended meaning. The jury in this case probably found Fermi's damages to be $100,000 (a more likely figure given the extent of his intangible injuries), and thought it was rendering a verdict that would require *each* defendant to pay $50,000, for a total of $100,000.

Unfortunately, under principles of jointly and several liability, the jury's verdict slip only makes Joule and Edison liable for a *total* of $50,000. Fermi can collect that amount from either, or part from each, but cannot receive more than a total of $50,000. (Compare the judgment in Figure 19–1.) Judge Fudd's instruction was open to this misinterpretation, since it required the jury to find "the defendants" liable for the plaintiff's full damages, not *each* defendant liable for the plaintiff's full damages.

The verdict slip in Figure 19–3 compounded the judge's error. The verdict slip simply indicates which defendants are found liable, and how much each is liable for; it does not clearly state the plaintiff's total damages or that the jury must find each defendant liable for the plaintiff's full damages.

b. The plaintiff could have avoided this problem by pointing out the ambiguity in the judge's instruction before he gave it. Counsel for all parties will be given a chance to review proposed jury instructions before the judge instructs the jury, so that they may object to instructions that wrongly state the applicable law. If plaintiff's counsel had realized the problem, she could have asked Judge Fudd to revise the instruction along the following lines:

> If you find that both defendants were negligent, and that the negligence of each defendant was a cause of the plaintiff's injuries, then you must find each defendant liable for the full damages suffered by the plaintiff.

The distinction between this instruction and Judge Fudd's is not very great, but the difference in the effect of the two is dramatic. If the jury understood the instruction, and it actually intended the plaintiff to recover $100,000, this instruction would clearly require them to return a verdict for $100,000, not $50,000, against each defendant.

A cogent criticism of jury trial is that juries often do not understand the subtleties of their instructions. Their verdict must be based on instructions on complicated principles that they are given once, often orally. To put the matter in perspective, consider whether you, after brief treatment of joint and several liability in your torts class, would feel prepared to go into a jury room and apply these rules accurately to an actual case.

Fermi's lawyer could also have reduced the risk of jury misunderstanding by asking the court to use a special verdict form like that in Figure 19-4, which requires the jury to make specific factual findings on negligence and damages. Under this verdict, the jury does not have to fully understand the governing liability rules. So long as they answer the factual questions accurately, the court can enter an appropriate judgment under joint and several liability principles. If the jury had rendered the verdict in Figure 19-4, the judge would have clearly understood that the jury intended Fermi to recover $100,000, and would have entered judgment against each defendant for that amount.

Joint Sheepfeasors

12. As the Introduction states, defendants are held jointly and severally liable for the plaintiff's damages if the damages cannot rationally be apportioned among them, if they are 'indivisible." Here, it is doubtless impossible to determine which sheep ate which blades of grass, but there is a basis for a rough apportionment of the damages based on the number of sheep of each defendant that joined the repast. Assuming a sheep is a sheep when it comes to appetite, it is a fair inference that Shepherd's sheep ate about three-quarters of the grass, and Herder's ate the other quarter. Most courts would apportion the damages between Shepherd and Herder on that basis, rather than holding them jointly and severally liable. Restatement (Second) of Torts §433A cmt. d.

While courts will endeavor to make such apportionment, even where it requires some approximation, it is worth reiterating that in most cases that is simply not possible. When two negligent acts combine to cause a broken back, a fatal heart attack, or a fire that burns the plaintiff's barn, it is simply not possible to ascribe part of the injury to one defendant's negligence and part to the other's. In this large class of cases, joint and several liability has been the classic rule because apportionment is not a feasible alternative.

STATE OF WEST DAKOTA

COOK COUNTY, SS;   CIVIL ACTION NO. 04-1305

ENRICO FERMI,

      Plaintiff

    v.   VERDICT

MAX JOULE
THOMAS EDISON,

      Defendants

1. Do you find that the defendant Max Joule was negligent?

    Yes __✔__   No_____

2. Do you find that the defendant Thomas Edison was negligent?

    Yes __✔__   No_____

3. If the defendant Max Joule was negligent, was his negligence a proximate cause of the plaintiff's damages?

    Yes __✔__   No_____

4. If the defendant Thomas Edison was negligent, was his negligence a proximate cause of the plaintiff's damages?

    Yes __✔__   No_____

5. If you find that either defendant was negligent, and that his negligence was a proximate cause of the accident, what amount do you find will fairly and reasonably compensate the plaintiff for the injuries caused by the accident?

    $____100,000____

_____
        E. Isaac Newton
        Jury Foreperson

Figure 19–4

20

Honor Among Thieves: Basic Principles of Contribution

Introduction

The last chapter explored the common law rules governing the liability of joint tortfeasors. As that discussion indicates, where joint and several liability applies, each tortfeasor who contributed to an indivisible injury is fully liable for the plaintiff's damages. This reflects the fundamental policy choice underlying joint and several liability, that the plaintiff should be fully compensated as long as at least one of the tortfeasors is able to pay the judgment.

However, the rule of joint and several liability can lead to unfair results. Suppose that Nash negligently left his bicycle in the road, and Benchley, not looking where he was going, drove into it, lost control of the car, and injured Twain. Under the common law, Twain could sue either Nash or Benchley for his injuries. The plaintiff was in control, and could choose to impose the full loss on either of the joint tortfeasors. If Benchley was his brother-in-law, Twain could keep peace in the family by suing Nash instead. If he sued Nash and recovered, Nash would have to pay Twain's full damages, and Benchley would pay nothing, even if he also caused the accident.

Of course, in many cases the plaintiff took the prudent course of suing all possible defendants, since he might only prove that one was negligent, or that the negligence of one had caused the injury. But even if Twain sued both

Nash and Benchley in our example, and recovered judgment against both, he could still choose to *collect* the judgment from either one. So he could still target Nash and let Benchley off the hook entirely if Nash was able to pay.

For many years, the courts held that if Nash did pay, he had no right to force Benchley to "contribute to the judgment," that is, to reimburse him for part of the damages he had paid to Twain. The common law, with its somewhat moralistic view of these matters, had no problem with the fact that Nash ended up paying the entire judgment. Nash was a wrongdoer, had caused Twain's injuries, and could fairly be made to pay. Justice was done between the plaintiff and the defendant, and that was that. Nash would not be heard to complain that Benchley had gotten off scot free, so long as Nash had actually caused the damages he was forced to pay.

Although the common law rule denying contribution from joint tortfeasors was widely applied for many years, it was also widely criticized. Prosser sums up the attack with his usual incisiveness:

> There is an obvious lack of sense and justice in a rule which permits the entire burden of a loss, for which two defendants were equally, unintentionally responsible, to be shouldered onto one alone, according to the accident of a successful levy of execution, the existence of liability insurance, the plaintiff's whim or spite, or the plaintiff's collusion with the other wrongdoer, while the latter goes scot free.

Prosser & Keeton at 337-338. Most critics of the no-contribution rule accepted the basic proposition that each defendant should be fully liable to the *plaintiff*. However, they argued that a defendant who paid the plaintiff's damages should be able to redistribute the loss by making the other tortfeasors contribute to the payment of the common liability.

Most states have responded to such criticism by creating a right to contribution among joint tortfeasors, either by statute or by judicial decision. Many statutes creating the right to contribution were modeled closely on the Uniform Contribution Among Tortfeasors Act, a model contribution statute drawn up in 1955.[1] This chapter introduces the basic principles of contribution, using the Uniform Act as an example. The relevant sections of the Uniform Act are set forth on p. 466 below.

The Right to Contribution

The Uniform Act starts out by creating the right to contribution among joint tortfeasors:

> 1(a) Except as otherwise provided in this Act, where two or more persons become jointly or severally liable in tort for the same injury

---

1. Uniform Contribution Among Tortfeasors Act, 12 U.L.A. 7(1982). An earlier version of the Uniform Contribution Among Tortfeasors Act was promulgated in 1939. It was superseded by the 1955 Act.

to person or property or for the same wrongful death, there is a right of contribution among them even though judgment has not been recovered against all or any of them.

(b) The right of contribution exists only in favor of a tortfeasor who has paid more than his pro rata share of the common liability, and his total recovery is limited to the amount paid by him in excess of his pro rata share. No tortfeasor is compelled to make contribution beyond his pro rata share of the entire liability....

These provisions of the Uniform Act allow a negligent tortfeasor[2] who has paid more than his "pro rata" share of the plaintiff's damages to recover contribution from other tortfeasors who are liable for the same injury. Suppose, for example, that Twain recovered a judgment of $20,000 against Nash for his injuries in the auto accident, and Nash paid the judgment. Section 1(a) of the Uniform Act authorizes Nash to recover contribution from Benchley, if Benchley was "jointly or severally liable in tort for the same injury...." Thus, to establish his right to contribution, Nash would have to show that Benchley was also liable to Twain for his injuries in the accident.

Section 1(b) determines *how much* Nash can seek from Benchley. It authorizes Nash to seek contribution for amounts above his (Nash's) "pro rata" share. In this context, "pro rata" means equal. If there are three tortfeasors, the pro rata share of each is one-third; if there are five, it is one-fifth, and so on. Since there are two tortfeasors in the example, Nash's pro rata share is one-half. Thus, if he paid the $20,000, he could recover one-half the judgment, or $10,000, from Benchley. If there were four tortfeasors, the pro rata shares of each would be $5,000. On those facts, if Nash paid the $20,000 to Twain he would only be entitled to $5,000 from Benchley, since §1(b) limits each tortfeasor's liability for contribution to his pro rata share. Nash would have to go after the other two tortfeasors for their shares to obtain full contribution. If all three paid their shares to Nash, Nash would collect $15,000 in contribution and end up paying $5,000 of the judgment, his own pro rata share.

Enforcing the Right to Contribution

Suppose that Twain had sued Nash alone and recovered his $20,000 judgment. As indicated above, Nash could not simply demand $10,000 from Benchley. Under §1(a), Benchley is only liable for contribution if he is a joint tortfeasor. Thus, before he could recover contribution from Benchley,

---

2. The Uniform Act, like most contribution statutes, bars contribution claims by an intentional tortfeasor. See §1(c), quoted at p. 466. The recent Restatement of Torts: Apportionment of Liability, however, would allow intentional tortfeasors to seek contribution. Restatement (Third) of Torts: Apportionment of Liability, §23 cmt. 1. The discussion in this chapter assumes that all claims are based on negligence.

Nash would have to prove that Benchley was *also liable to Twain* for the damages Nash had already paid.

The simplest way for Nash to do this would be to bring Benchley into the original suit when Twain sued him. Most states allow a defendant in Nash's position to "implead" a joint tortfeasor for contribution, that is, to make him a party to the original suit. See, e.g., Okla. Code of Civ. Proc. tit. 12 §2014 (allowing defendant to implead a person who may be liable to him for all or part of plaintiff's claim against him); Va. Sup. Ct. Rules, Rule 3:10 (same). If Nash impleaded Benchley, the court would determine in a single trial whether Benchley and Nash were liable for Twain's injury. If both were found liable and Nash then paid the judgment (remember, he is still fully liable to *Twain* based on the principle of joint and several liability), he would make a motion in the original suit for contribution from Benchley. Section 3(b) of the Uniform Act expressly authorizes such orders for contribution in the original suit.

Suppose, however, that Twain sued Nash only, and Nash did not (or could not)[3] implead Benchley. If Nash were found liable, and paid the judgment, he could then bring a separate action for contribution against Benchley. This is a new lawsuit. Nash is the plaintiff, Benchley is the defendant, and the claim is for recovery of Benchley's pro rata share of the judgment which Nash has paid. Section 3 of the Uniform Act authorizes such separate suits for contribution, (see §3(a)) and establishes limitations periods for them (§3(c), (d)). Figure 20-1 is a simple example of a complaint for contribution.

Like all pleadings, Nash's complaint is basically commonsensical. Since Benchley was not a defendant in the original action, it has never been determined that he is in fact liable for Twain's injuries. Thus, to obtain contribution Nash must allege and prove that Benchley is liable to Twain for the accident due to his negligence. See par. 8, 9. He also alleges each of the further requirements for contribution established in the statute: That he (Nash) has been sued by the injured plaintiff and held liable for the same injury (par 3-6), that he has paid more than his pro rata share (par. 7, 10), and that he is entitled to pro rata contribution under the statute (par. 10). The relief demanded in the last paragraph of the complaint is, of course, Benchley's pro rata share of the judgment.

Effect of Settlement on the Right to Contribution

It is not unusual for the plaintiff to settle with one tortfeasor and proceed to trial against others.[4] Suppose that Twain settles with Nash for $2,000,

---

3. Nash might not be able to implead Benchley, for example, if the court in which Twain brought suit lacked personal jurisdiction over Benchley.

4. Some of the reasons for doing so are explored in Chapter 19, Example 1.

STATE OF WEST DAKOTA
SUPERIOR COURT

GALLATIN COUNTY, SS: CIVIL ACTION NO. 04-0129

OGDEN NASH,

    Plaintiff

    v.   COMPLAINT FOR CONTRIBU-
                                 TION

ROBERT BENCHLEY,

    Defendant

1. The plaintiff Ogden Nash is an individual residing at 14 Stow Street, Sutter, West Dakota.

2. The defendant Robert Benchley is an individual residing at 2116 Twelfth Street, Bridger, West Dakota.

3. On March 11, 2002, Mark Twain commenced a civil action, captioned *Twain v. Nash*, Civil Action No. 02-219, against Ogden Nash in the Superior Court for Glacier County, West Dakota.

4. The claim in *Twain v. Nash* arose out of an accident which took place on Maple Street in the town of Sutter, West Dakota, on June 7, 2001. Twain was injured in that accident when a collision between a bicycle owned by Ogden Nash and a car driven by Robert Benchley caused the Benchley car to swerve into him.

5. The plaintiff in *Twain v. Nash* alleged that his injuries resulted from the negligence of Nash in leaving his bicycle in the road.

6. On November 7, 2003, the court entered judgment against Ogden Nash in *Twain v. Nash*, in the amount of $20,000 plus interest and costs.

7. On December 15, 2003, Nash, the contribution plaintiff in this action, satisfied the judgment in *Twain v. Nash* by paying $20,279 to the plaintiff in that action, including $63 in post-judgment interest and $216 in costs.

Figure 20–1

8. At the time of the accident which gave rise to the judgment in *Twain v. Nash*, the contribution defendant, Benchley, was also negligent in failing to keep a proper lookout. As a result of his negligence, he drove into the bicycle, swerved and ran into Twain. Such negligence was a proximate cause of the accident.

9. As a result of his negligence, the contribution defendant Benchley is a joint tortfeasor fully liable for the injuries sustained by Twain.

10. Plaintiff in this action has satisfied the judgment in *Twain v. Nash* in full. Thus, he has paid more than his pro rata share of the common liability and is entitled to contribution from Benchley under the provisions of West Dak. Stat. Tit. VII, §1(a) and (b), in the amount of one-half of the judgment.

11. The plaintiff in this action has demanded payment from Benchley of his pro rata share of the judgment, but he has refused to pay.

WHEREFORE, the plaintiff demands judgment against the defendant in this action in the amount of $10,139.50, plus costs of suit.

By his attorney
Angela Wu
42 River Street
Sutter, West Dakota 68534
(123) 335-8895

Figure 20–1 (*continued*)

releasing his claim against Nash only, and then recovers a judgment against Benchley for $20,000. What is the effect of Nash's settlement with Twain on Benchley's right to recover contribution from Nash?

Here are the relevant provisions of the Uniform Act:

4. When a release or convenant not to sue or not to enforce judgment is given in good faith to one of two or more persons liable in tort for the same injury or the same wrongful death:

(a) It does not discharge any of the other tortfeasors from liability for the injury or wrongful death unless its terms so provide, but it reduces the claim against the others to the extent of any amount stipulated by the release or the covenant, or in the amount of the consideration paid for it, whichever is the greater; and,

(b) It discharges the tortfeasor to whom it is given from all liability for contribution to any other tortfeasor.

The first clause of §4(a) reverses the common law rule that releasing one tortfeasor released them all. Under §4(a), Twain may still sue Benchley even though he gave a release to Nash. However, if Benchley is found liable, §4(a) provides that he will get a credit against the judgment for the amount Nash paid in settlement. This basically codifies the equitable principle that the plaintiff is entitled to full satisfaction of her judgment, but no more. In this example, if Twain recovered a $20,000 judgment against Benchley, Benchley would only have to pay $18,000 after the credit for the $2,000 Nash paid in settlement.

However, §4(b) of the Uniform Act *bars Benchley from recovering contribution from Nash*, the settling tortfeasor. Thus, on these facts Benchley will pay $18,000 of Twain's damages, while Nash pays only $2,000. Naturally, this provision has little appeal for Benchley. If Nash had not settled, and both he and Benchley had been found liable, Benchley could still have been forced to pay $20,000 to Twain, but he would have had the right to recover $10,000 in contribution from Nash. Thus, he would only have been out $10,000. Why should he have to pay an extra $8,000 simply because Twain made a deal with Nash? Isn't this provision grossly unfair to the remaining defendant?

There are several arguments in favor of barring contribution from a settling tortfeasor. *First*, the purpose of settling a lawsuit is to buy one's peace, to extinguish the liability, close the file and get on to other things. If Benchley is free to come back against Nash for contribution, Nash has gained little by settling. He is still exposed to $10,000 in liability (his pro rata share), and has simply paid $2,000 of it early. If contribution from the settling tortfeasor is not barred, there is little incentive to settlements, which are generally encouraged as a civilized, less expensive alternative to litigation.

Second, Benchley is free to settle too. Indeed, the risk of paying an outsized share encourages him to do so. Thus, the settling tortfeasor's immunity promotes settlements. In many cases the plaintiff will settle with all tortfeasors rather than risk a loss at trial. In a sense, everyone wins in this scenario.

Third, it may turn out that Nash settled for *more* than his pro rata share. When Nash settles, he does not know how much a jury will award in damages. In our hypo, they awarded Twain $20,000 for his injuries, but damages are very difficult to predict; they might have given $50,000. To avoid that risk, Nash might pay $16,000 to settle the case instead of $2,000. If he did, and the jury later assessed the damages at $20,000 in Twain's suit against Benchley, Benchley would only have to pay Twain $4,000 — the $20,000 judgment minus the $16,000 Nash paid in settlement (Benchley gets a credit for the settlement under the Uniform Act, §4(a), second clause). As you can see, these possibilities make settlement an interesting business for all parties involved.

Fourth, the statute contains a good faith requirement. Uniform Act, §4. If the court is convinced that Twain and Nash colluded by settling for an insufficient amount, it need not bar contribution from Nash.

An alternative way to take account of a settlement with one tortfeasor is to give the remaining tortfeasor a pro rata credit for the settlement instead of a dollar credit. Under this approach, Twain would be viewed as selling half of his cause of action to Nash by settling with him. Thus, he could only recover from Benchley on the other half. Suppose, for example, that Nash settled for $2,000, and Twain later recovered a $20,000 judgment against Benchley. Under the pro rata credit approach, Twain would be viewed as having sold half of his claim for the $2,000. Obviously, if the jury determines later that his damages are $20,000, that half of the claim was worth $10,000, and Twain badly undersold it. Under the pro rata credit approach, he would be entitled to collect only one half of the judgment, or $10,000 from Benchley. He would receive only $12,000 in total. By contrast, under the dollar credit approach he would get $18,000 (the judgment amount minus the amount of the settlement) from Benchley and $20,000 altogether.

Let's do one more example of the pro rata approach to accounting for settlements. Assume that there were three tortfeasors in Twain's case, and that he settled with Nash for $2,000. Under the pro rata approach, Twain would be viewed as selling one-third of his claim for that amount. When he later obtained a judgment against the other two tortfeasors for $20,000, it would be reduced by one-third ($6,666) to account for the settlement. He could then collect $13,334 from either of the remaining defendants. He would thus collect a total of $15,334 ($2,000 from Nash and $13,334 under the judgment).

The pro rata method of accounting for settlements has gained renewed popularity under comparative negligence, with the important modification that the pro rata shares are not equal, but proportional to the percentage of negligence ascribed to the settling tortfeasor at trial.

Under this approach, if Nash settled for $2,000, and he was later found to be 40 percent at fault in causing Twain's damages, the other tortfeasors would get a 40 percent credit against the judgment to account for Nash's settlement. Again, the logic is that Twain has sold that part of the common liability represented by Nash for the settlement amount. We'll explore this approach in more detail in Chapter 24.

A Tactical Question

1.   Accounting for the settlement under this pro rata approach seems more fair. Twain gets what he bargained for from Nash, as well as Benchley's fair share of the damages from him. What is the disadvantage of this variation?

Can a Settling Tortfeasor Seek Contribution?

Now let's look at the other side of the equation. Suppose that Twain settles with Nash for $16,000, and gives Nash a release of his liability. Later, Nash is surprised to learn that the jury in the suit against Benchley assessed his total damages at $20,000. Benchley has lucked out: under §4(a) of the Uniform Act, which provides for a dollar credit, he will only have to pay Twain $4,000. Can Nash, the settling defendant, recover $6,000 in contribution from Benchley? The Uniform Act says no:

> 1(d) A tortfeasor who enters into a settlement with a claimant is not entitled to recover contribution from another tortfeasor whose liability for the injury or wrongful death is not extinguished by the settlement. . . .

Under §1(d) Nash has no right to seek contribution from Benchley, since Twain only released Nash, not both defendants. Since Nash made an unfavorable settlement (at least, unfavorable in retrospect), he ends up paying more than he would have if he had lost at trial and paid half the judgment. Even here, however, he may still "win" in some sense. He has saved the expense of trying the case, and he has avoided the risk—always difficult to assess—that the jury would award much higher damages, say, $100,000. If Nash had not settled, and the jury had done that, he would have paid at least $50,000, and perhaps $100,000 if Benchley were insolvent.

Since the adoption of comparative negligence, many states have modified the basic contribution principles of the Uniform Act. Some of the current permutations are explored in Chapter 24. However, it is important to master the basic principles of contribution, both because they remain applicable in many cases and because it is impossible to understand varying approaches to contribution without appreciating the basic concepts from which they have evolved. In analyzing the following examples, assume that the Uniform Act applies unless otherwise stated. The relevant provisions of the Act are as follows:

Uniform Contribution Among Tortfeasors Act

(1)(a) Except as otherwise provided in this Act, where two or more persons become jointly or severally liable in tort for the same injury to person or property or for the same wrongful death, there is a right of contribution among them even though judgment has not been recovered against all or any of them.

(b) The right of contribution exists only in favor of a tortfeasor who has paid more than his pro rata share of the common liability, and his total recovery is limited to the amount paid by him in excess of his pro rata share. No tortfeasor is compelled to make contribution beyond his pro rata share of the entire liability....

(c) There is no right of contribution in favor of any tortfeasor who has intentionally ... caused or contributed to the injury or wrongful death.

(d) A tortfeasor who enters into a settlement with a claimant is not entitled to recover contribution from another tortfeasor whose liability for the injury or wrongful death is not extinguished by the settlement....

(2) In determining the pro rata shares of tortfeasors in the entire liability (a) their relative degrees of fault shall not be considered; (b) if equity requires the collective liability of some as a group shall constitute a single share; and (c) principles of equity applicable to contribution generally shall apply.

(3)(a) Whether or not judgment has been entered in an action against two or more tortfeasors for the same injury or wrongful death, contribution may be enforced by separate action.

(b) Where judgment has been entered in an action against two or more tortfeasors for the same injury or wrongful death, contribution may be enforced in that action by judgment in favor of one against other judgment defendants by motion upon notice to all parties to the action.

(c) If there is a judgment for the injury or wrongful death against the tortfeasor seeking contribution, any separate action by him to enforce contribution must be commenced within one year after the judgment has become final by lapse of time for appeal or after appellate review.

(d) If there is no judgment for the injury or wrongful death against the tortfeasor seeking contribution, his right of contribution is barred unless he has either (1) discharged by payment the common liability within the statute of limitations period applicable to claimant's right of action against him and has commenced his action for contribution within one year after payment, or (2) agreed while action is pending against him to discharge the common liability and has within one year after the agreement paid the liability and commenced his action for contribution.

(e) The recovery of a judgment for an injury or wrongful death against one tortfeasor does not of itself discharge the other tortfeasors from liability for the injury or wrongful death unless the judgment is satisfied....

(4) When a release or covenant not to sue or not to enforce judgment is given in good faith to one of two or more persons liable in tort for the same injury or the same wrongful death:

(a) It does not discharge any of the other tortfeasors from liability for the injury or wrongful death unless its terms so provide; but it reduces the claim against the others to the extent of any amount stipulated by the release or the covenant, or in the amount of the consideration paid for it, whichever is the greater; and,

(b) It discharges the tortfeasor to whom it is given from all liability for contribution to any other tortfeasor.

In analyzing the examples below, assume that joint and several liability and the Uniform Contribution Act apply.

EXAMPLES

Burning Issues

2. Rogers, owner of a small business, gives a Fourth of July barbecue for his employees behind the building. Impatient for the barbecued chicken, Dunne throws gasoline on the coals, and Thurber throws a lighted match into the grill. The resulting fire causes extensive damage to the building. Rogers brings a negligence suit against Dunne for the damage, and gets judgment for $42,000.
   a. Could Dunne obtain contribution from Thurber at common law? If so, how much?
   b. Could Dunne obtain contribution from Thurber under the Uniform Act? If so, how much?

3. Dunne is held liable for $42,000. He pays Rogers $21,000, and refuses to pay any more, arguing that Thurber is responsible for the other $21,000. Will the court order Dunne to pay him any more?

4. Rogers gets a judgment against Dunne for $42,000, but Dunne does not pay. Could Rogers sue Thurber for the damage if the Uniform Act applied?

Fudd Fudges the Figures

5. Rogers sues Dunne and Thurber, and gets a judgment against them both for $42,000. Dunne pays Rogers $34,000, all he is able to. He then makes a motion for contribution from Thurber and Judge Fudd orders Thurber to pay Dunne $17,000. What is wrong with Fudd's order?

Permutations

6. Assume that Rogers sued both Dunne and Thurber, and the jury found Thurber liable, but not Dunne. After paying Rogers the $42,000 judgment, Thurber seeks contribution from Dunne. May he recover contribution, and, if so, how much?

7. Assume that Rogers sued both Dunne and Thurber, and the jury found them both liable. After paying Rogers $42,000, Thurber seeks $21,000 contribution from Dunne. Dunne, however, argues that White, another guest at the picnic, was *also* negligent in starting the fire, because he placed the grill much too close to the building and left the trash sitting next to it. How much must Dunne pay in contribution?

8. Rogers sues Dunne, Thurber, and White for their negligence in starting the fire. He recovers a judgment against all three for $42,000 and tries to collect it from White. Unfortunately, White has no money and pays nothing, so Rogers demands payment from Dunne, who pays the entire judgment. Dunne then seeks contribution from Thurber. How much will he get?

Some Unsettling Cases

9. Rogers sues Dunne and Thurber for the fire damage. Dunne offers to settle with Rogers for $12,000. Rogers accepts, and releases Dunne from liability in exchange for payment of that amount. Rogers then recovers a judgment for $42,000 against Thurber. (In analyzing this example, assume that Dunne and Thurber are the only tortfeasors.)
   a. How much will Rogers collect from Thurber if the Uniform Act applies?
   b. After paying Rogers, Thurber seeks contribution from Dunne. How much will he recover if the Uniform Act applies?
   c. How much would Rogers collect from Thurber if the relevant contribution statute gave Thurber a pro rata credit for Dunne's settlement?

10. Assume that Rogers settled with Dunne for $35,000 and gave Dunne a release of his liability only. Subsequently, Rogers sues Thurber. The jury finds Thurber liable for the fire and assesses $42,000 in damages.
   a. Assuming that the Uniform Act applies, how much must Thurber pay Rogers?
   b. After the judgment is entered and Thurber satisfies it, Dunne sues Thurber for contribution. How much would he receive under the Uniform Act?
   c. Assume that this settlement took place in a jurisdiction that gives the remaining defendant a pro rata credit for settlements by other tortfeasors. How much would Rogers collect altogether?

Confusion Worse Confounded

11. Assume that Rogers sues four tortfeasors, Dunne, Thurber, Mauldin and Burgess. Dunne settles for $15,000. Rogers recovers judgment against the others for $100,000.

   a. Assume that the Uniform Act applies. How much can Rogers collect from Thurber?

   b. How much can Thurber recover in contribution from Mauldin?

12. Porter, driving a Reliable Furniture Company truck, collides with Simon's car. The car is thrown onto the sidewalk, injuring Allen. Allen sues Porter, Simon, and Reliable Furniture Company (on the ground that it is liable for Porter's torts in the scope of employment). The jury finds that the negligence of both drivers caused the accident, and awards Allen $60,000 in damages. Simon pays the judgment. How much can he obtain in contribution from Porter? From Reliable?

Unlucky Number 13

13. Assume, after the accident described in Example 12, that the parties exchange papers at the scene, fill out accident reports, and go their separate ways. Simon, a patent lawyer and a worrywart, looks up the statute of limitations and discovers that it is two years. He worries daily for two years, waiting for the process server to serve him with papers in a lawsuit by Allen. She never shows; the magic date passes without incident. Simon breathes a deep sigh of relief.

   Not so fast, Simon. Why should he continue to worry?

A Sense of Proportion

14. Assume that Allen, on the facts of Example 12, sued Simon and Porter in a jurisdiction that applies comparative negligence. At trial, the jury finds that Simon was 20 percent at fault in causing the accident, and Porter was 80 percent at fault. It determines that Allen's damages are $100,000.

   a. If Porter pays the judgment, what could he get in contribution from Simon under the Uniform Act?

   b. What might be a more logical way to redistribute the judgment between the two tortfeasors?

EXPLANATIONS

A Tactical Question

1. Under the pro rata credit approach, plaintiffs have less incentive to settle than under the dollar credit approach. In a state that applies the dollar credit approach, Twain can still recover his full damages, even if he settles with Nash for less than Nash's full share: Benchley is still liable for the entire judgment, and will only get a credit for the amount Nash actually paid. For example, if Twain's damages are $20,000, he can settle with Nash for $5,000 and recover $15,000 from Benchley.

However, under the pro rata credit approach, Twain gives up 50 percent of his claim when he settles with Nash. If he settles for $5,000, and the jury assesses his damages at $20,000, he will end up with only $15,000, five from Nash and ten from Benchley (the $20,000 judgment minus Nash's pro rata share). Here is a comparison of the results under the two approaches:

	Settlement w/Nash	Jury Award at trial	Benchley pays	Plaintiff receives
Dollar credit approach:	$5,000	$20,000	$15,000	$20,000
Pro rata credit approach:	$5,000	$20,000	$10,000	$15,000

Thus, under the pro rata credit approach, a plaintiff is unlikely to sell half of his claim for much less than half its value.

Burning Issues

2a.   As the introduction indicates, there was no right at common law to demand contribution from a joint tortfeasor. If Dunne paid the judgment, he had no recourse against Thurber and was stuck with the entire liability, simply because Rogers chose to sue him instead of Thurber.

b.   Dunne has no right to contribution under the Uniform Act. Surprised? Well, this answer is a little bit cute. The facts do not indicate that Dunne has paid anything to Rogers. The right to contribution arises in favor of a tortfeasor who has *paid* more than his pro rata share, not one who has been found liable. Uniform Act, §1(b). The difference between incurring a judgment for $42,000 and paying over $42,000 is dramatic; it is the difference between a bird in the hand and a bird in the bush.

Assuming that Dunne paid the $42,000 to Rogers, he would have a right to pro rata contribution from Thurber under the Uniform Act. He would be entitled to recover $21,000 from Thurber, *if* he proved that Thurber was also liable to Rogers for negligently causing the fire. Since Rogers only sued Dunne, Thurber has never been adjudged liable for the fire. Thus, Dunne would have to bring a contribution action against Thurber and prove Thurber's negligence in that suit before he could recover contribution.

3.   Assuming that joint and several liability applies, the court will order Dunne to pay the entire judgment. The Uniform Act, like many contribution statutes, does not alter the fundamental premise that each tortfeasor is *fully liable* to the plaintiff. The plaintiff may still sue whichever tortfeasor he chooses, and collect the damages from whichever he chooses.

Contribution only deals with adjusting the payment of the damages among the defendants, after one has paid more than his share of the judgment. Dunne may pay Rogers $42,000 and seek $21,000 from

Thurber, but he cannot pay $21,000 and force Rogers to chase Dunne for the balance. That, in essence, would make the two tortfeasors "severally" liable for their pro rata shares, rather than "jointly and severally" liable for the plaintiff's full damages.[5] The very purpose of joint and several liability is to assure the plaintiff's right to collect fully from any one of the tortfeasors.

4. At early common law, a judgment against one tortfeasor barred suit against others who might also be liable. The rationale was that a tort claim was a "single cause of action." Once sued upon, it was extinguished and replaced by the judgment. See Chapter 19, pp. 441-442. The courts later abandoned that approach, however, replacing it with the rule that a plaintiff could bring a second action against another party responsible for his injuries, so long as the prior judgment had not been fully satisfied. Section 3(e) of the Uniform Act codifies this later approach, which allows a plaintiff who has obtained a judgment against one tortfeasor to sue other tortfeasors until his claim is fully satisfied. Under §3(e), Roger's judgment against Dunne does not bar him from suing Thurber, since the judgment has not been paid.

Fudd Fudges the Figures

5. The Uniform Act allows a tortfeasor who has paid "more than his pro rata share" of the liability to recover contribution. Section 1(b). Dunne's pro rata share would be $21,000, one-half of the judgment. Since he has paid more than that, and Thurber has been held liable for the injury as well, Dunne is entitled to contribution. Fudd was right in awarding him contribution. His error was in determining the amount.

You can see the logic for Fudd's order; it makes Thurber absorb half of Dunne's payment. The Uniform Act, however, provides otherwise. Under §1(b), Dunne can recover "the amount paid by him in excess of his pro rata share." Dunne's pro rata share is $21,000, Since he has paid $34,000, he can recover $13,000 from Thurber.

The logic of the Uniform Act provision is illustrated by considering what would happen if Fudd's order were upheld. Thurber would pay $17,000, but he would still be liable to Rogers for $8,000, the part of Rogers's judgment that he has not yet collected. If he paid $17,000 to Dunne and Rogers then demanded $8,000 more from him, he would end up paying $25,000, $4,000 more than his pro rata share, while Dunne paid $17,000, $4,000 less than his.[6]

---

5. Many states have now switched from joint and several liability to several liability, at least in limited classes of cases. Some examples are given in Chapter 24, pp. 556-557.

6. I suppose he could then demand contribution from Dunne, but that seems like a circuitous means of redistributing the loss.

The Second Restatement of Torts takes the position that a tortfeasor cannot seek contribution at all until the plaintiff has been fully paid. See §886A(2) & cmt. f. Presumably, the logic for this position is that, if Thurber only has limited funds, Rogers should get first crack at them: Thurber should not pay contribution to Dunne and be left unable to satisfy the remainder of Rogers's judgment. However, §1(b) of the Uniform Act does not include a similar requirement.

Permutations

6.   Since Dunne is not liable to Rogers, he is not liable to Thurber for contribution. A tortfeasor may only recover contribution from someone who is liable to the plaintiff. See Uniform Act, §1(a) (authorizing contribution "where two or more persons become jointly or severally liable in tort"). He can hardly be liable for contribution as a joint tortfeasor if he isn't a tortfeasor at all, and that's what the jury decided in this case. See Uniform Act. §3(f) (providing that the findings as to the liability of the various defendants in the plaintiff's suit are binding in a subsequent contribution action).

7.   Under the Uniform Act, any person who "becomes jointly liable in tort for the same injury" is liable to contribute to the damages. Although White was not sued in the original action, he may still be a joint tortfeasor. Rogers might have decided not to sue him for myriad reasons; that decision does not necessarily mean that he is not "liable" for the injury. If his negligence contributed to the accident, he should be counted in calculating the pro rata shares of each tortfeasor. Thus, when Thurber seeks contribution, the court will have to determine whether White was also negligent in order to calculate Dunne's pro rata share. If it determines that White was also a tortfeasor, it will order Dunne to pay one-third of the judgment to Thurber ($14,000) instead of one-half.

8.   Clearly, Dunne is entitled to contribution from Thurber. If White were solvent, he could recover $14,000 from Thurber and $14,000 from White. Since White cannot pay, shouldn't Thurber pay $21,000?

Section 1(b) of the Uniform Act suggests that Dunne would only recover $14,000, since it provides that "[n]o tortfeasor is compelled to make contribution beyond his pro rata share of the entire liability." Thurber's pro rata share is one-third, or $14,000; under §1(b), he can only be required to pay that to Dunne. If this is the answer, Dunne, having paid $42,000, will end up $28,000 out of pocket, because he cannot collect contribution from White. The burden of White's insolvency would fall on him.

Most courts view contribution as an equitable doctrine; on facts like these they would likely require Thurber to pay $21,000. See Restatement (Second) of Torts §886A, cmt. c (when one tortfeasor is insolvent, court may "do what is fair and equitable under the circumstances" in ordering contribution). This flexibility to account for the circumstances is preserved in §2(c) of the Uniform Act, which provides that, in determining the pro rata shares, "principles of equity applicable to contribution generally shall apply." Under this provision, the court would likely require Thurber to pay $21,000 in contribution to Dunne, despite the language of §1(b).

Some Unsettling Cases

9a. Thurber is still liable for the full judgment, but he receives a dollar credit for the amount of the settlement with Dunne. Uniform Act, §4(a). Thus, he will have to pay Rogers $30,000. As this example illustrates, once Dunne has settled, Thurber risks paying more than half of the damages unless he settles as well.

b. As the introduction indicates, §4(b) of the Uniform Act bars contribution from a settling tortfeasor. Thurber will not be able to force Dunne to pay anything above the $12,000 he paid to settle with Rogers. This gives defendants a strong incentive to settle cases. If Dunne can induce the plaintiff to settle for less than half of the likely damage amount, he will avoid paying his full "share" of the liability.

Thurber might argue that the settlement is so low that it is not "in good faith," that Rogers and Dunne have conspired to force Thurber to bear the brunt of the damages by settling for an unreasonably low amount. However, many factors affect the parties' judgment about how much a claim is worth, and many of these factors are quite subjective, such as the risk that the settling defendant's negligence cannot be proved at trial, or the adverse effect of having a sympathetic defendant before the court. Due to such factors, it is doubtful that the court will find that the settlement was in bad faith simply because Dunne paid less than his pro rata share of the plaintiff's damages.

c. Under a pro rata credit approach, Rogers effectively sells half of his claim to Dunne by settling with him. He would then be entitled to collect one-half of the damages verdict from Thurber. If the total damages found by the jury are $42,000, Rogers would collect $21,000 from Thurber, and $12,000 from Dunne, for a total of $33,000. Naturally, this approach makes plaintiffs cautious about settling with the first tortfeasor.

10a. Under joint and several liability, Thurber is liable for the full amount of Rogers's damages, but gets a dollar for dollar credit for the amount paid in settlement. He must pay Rogers $7,000 ($42,000–$35,000).

b. Dunne is barred from seeking contribution from Thurber by §1(d), which provides that a settling tortfeasor cannot obtain contribution unless he has obtained a release of the other tortfeasor's liability as well. The example indicates that Dunne received a release of *his* liability, but not Thurber's; thus, he cannot ask Thurber to contribute. Dunne cannot undo his bargain by seeking contribution if his settlement turns out to be higher than his share of the damages awarded. If Dunne had settled for *less* than half the damages assessed, he would not have had to pay contribution to Thurber. See Example 9b. Under the Uniform Act it works both ways, or, more accurately, neither way. If Dunne makes a good deal, he shifts more than half of the damages to Thurber, If he makes a bad deal, as he did here, he ends up paying more than half himself.

c. In a pro rata jurisdiction, Rogers is viewed as having sold half of his claim to Dunne by settling with him. Thus, he may collect only the other half of the $42,000 judgment from Thurber, or $21,000. This amount, together with the $35,000 he obtained in settlement from Dunne, comes to $56,000 for a case in which the jury has determined the damages to be $42,000. Under the pro rata credit approach, the *plaintiff* gets the advantage of a favorable settlement; she collects more than the jury's damage award. Compare Example 10a, which illustrates that the *nonsettling defendant* gets the benefit from a high settlement in a dollar credit jurisdiction.

Confusion Worse Confounded

11a. Dunne can recover $85,000 from Thurber. The Uniform Act gives Thurber a dollar credit for Dunne's settlement, (§4(a)) but he remains jointly and severally liable for the remaining damages.

b. Under §1(b) of the Uniform Act, each tortfeasor may only be made to pay up to its pro rata share of the damages. The problem here is determining Mauldin's share: Are there three shares (the three defendants who lost at trial) or four (those three plus Dunne, the settling tortfeasor)?

Dunne is certainly a party who could be held "jointly or severally liable in tort for the same injury . . . ," so it seems that he ought to be included. If so, there are four tortfeasors, and Mauldin must contribute $25,000. However, if this is true, Thurber could only recover $25,000 from Burgess, too. He'd get $50,000 back and end up paying $35,000 himself.

Despite the argument for this result based on the language of the Act, it makes more sense to divide the $85,000 liability that is common to *the remaining tortfeasors* equally. Under this approach Thurber would recover $28,333 from Mauldin, the same amount from Burgess, and end up paying that amount himself. It seems likely that a court would reach this result, under §2(c) of the Uniform Act and basic principles of equity.

12. At first glance, it seems that there are three tortfeasors, so that Simon should get $20,000 from Porter, another $20,000 from Reliable, and end up paying $20,000 himself. However, there really aren't three tortfeasors in this example, only two. Simon was negligent and Porter was negligent. Reliable is not a tortfeasor itself; rather it is a party responsible for the negligence of Porter.

Under the doctrine of respondeat superior, Reliable can be made to pay for Porter's tort. For example, Allen could demand $60,000 from Reliable under this judgment, since Porter is liable for the full damages under joint and several liability and consequently, Reliable is liable for the same amount under respondeat superior. By the same logic, Reliable could be made to pay any contribution amount that Porter must pay. Since there are two tortfeasors, there are two pro rata shares; if Simon pays the judgment, Porter would be liable to contribute $30,000 to Simon. Under respondeat superior, Reliable could be made to pay that share, but the fact that it is liable for Porter's share does not make it a third tortfeasor. See §2(b) of the Uniform Act, which provides that, where equity so requires, "the collective liability of some as a group shall constitute a single share."

Unlucky Number 13

13. If Simon were a tort lawyer, he would realize that he isn't off the hook. Maybe Allen didn't sue him, but maybe she *did* sue Porter. If she did, and if she wins, and if Porter pays, he can then come after Simon for contribution *within one year after he loses to Porter*. In other words, a losing defendant can seek contribution against another tortfeasor long after the original plaintiff is barred from suing that tortfeasor directly. This provision is necessary: Otherwise, Allen could defeat Simon's right to contribution by suing Simon alone, just before the limitations period ran.

Figure 20–2 illustrates how Porter could come knocking on Simon's door some four-and-a-half years after the statute of limitations had run on a direct claim against Simon.[7]

---

7. As a practical matter, if Allen sues Porter, Simon is likely to find out. One of the parties will doubtless want to depose him in the action, and he will likely be called to testify at trial as well.

Simon's Surprise

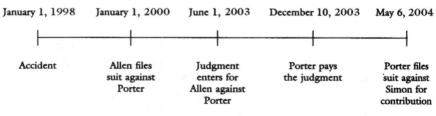

Figure 20–2

A Sense of Proportion

14a.   Under the Uniform Act, Porter would receive one-half, or $50,000 in contribution from Simon.

b.   Wouldn't it make more sense to redistribute the judgment in proportion to the fault of the parties? Under this approach, since Porter was 80 percent at fault and Simon 20 percent, Simon would pay Porter $20,000 in contribution. Had Simon paid the judgment, he would have obtained $80,000 in contribution from Porter. This proportional approach to contribution has rapidly gained popularity in comparative negligence jurisdictions. It is analyzed in more detail in Chapter 24.

21

Please Pass the Liability: Respondeat Superior and Nondelegable Duties

Introduction

The last two chapters have considered the allocation of liability in cases involving "joint tortfeasors." As those chapters indicate, when more than one party's negligence contributes to an injury, each negligent party is liable, but may be able to seek contribution from other tortfeasors. This chapter addresses the related situation in which one defendant incurs liability, not due to his own negligence, but due to the negligence of another. We focus on two common examples of such "vicarious liability": liability of an employer for the torts of its employees, and liability of one who employs an independent contractor for torts committed by the independent contractor.

Rationales for Imposing Vicarious Liability on Employers

The common law has long accepted the premise that employers should be liable for the torts of their employees in the scope of employment. The premise is sufficiently entrenched to merit its own legal Latin, "respondeat superior," which is loosely translated, "let the master respond." While virtually all jurisdictions impose liability on employers for the torts of their employees, the rationales for the respondeat superior doctrine have varied.

It is sometimes said that the employer should pay because she can select and control her employees, and thereby prevent injuries due to negligence. It is doubtless true, as a general matter, that employers can reduce accidents by requiring their employees to exercise care, and that making employers liable for employees' torts gives them an incentive to enforce careful conduct. However, employers frequently have no realistic chance of preventing a particular negligent act by an employee, as when an employee drives alone to pick up a package or goes out alone to repair an elevator. Employers cannot hover over their employees from minute to minute, and, as an actuarial matter, even employees who are carefully selected and supervised will be negligent on occasion, despite the employer's most rigorous efforts to promote safety.[1] When they are, the employer is liable even if it took stringent measures to prevent accidents. This liability, in other words, is truly vicarious; it flows automatically from the employee's tort, regardless of the care the employer exercised in selecting or supervising him.

More skeptical observers have suggested that respondeat superior liability is simply a device to provide a "deep pocket" defendant able to pay the plaintiff's damages. Prosser & Keeton at 500. Certainly it serves this purpose in many cases, since employers are more likely to have the resources to pay judgments than their employees. Yet, if vicarious liability is imposed solely to assure a deep pocket, it might equally well be imposed on *any* party with substantial resources: We could make millionaires vicariously liable for torts, or any insurance company with a headquarters building over 25 stories, or—what the heck—how about the government? Clearly, while assuring compensation is a factor, respondeat superior is intended to assure that such compensation comes from a party that is fairly made to pay it.

Another rationale increasingly cited for the doctrine is that employers are in a position to spread the costs of accidents by purchasing liability insurance and raising the price of their products to reflect the inherent accident costs of the enterprise. This argument, like economic analysis of tort law in general, looks at the issue not as a matter of individual fairness or blame, but rather as a question of the overall societal impact of placing the cost of accidents in one place or another. Respondeat superior encourages employers to insure; the cost of insurance gets incorporated into the price of the product, which consequently reflects more accurately the actual costs of producing it, including the accident costs. This argument makes sense,

---

1. Vicarious liability may even *increase* the risk of negligence in many cases, since the employee, knowing that the employer will be liable, will have less incentive to exercise due care. Note, An Efficiency Analysis of Vicarious Liability Under the Law of Agency, 91 Yale L.J. 168, 172-173 (1981).

but, like the deep pocket argument, courts would probably not accept it if they did not view respondeat superior as inherently fair as well.

Perhaps the most basic rationale for the doctrine is that the employee acts for the master in the performance of the master's work. In the course of that work, he creates risks to further the master's goals, including the risk of injuries due to negligence. Where such risks are created for the master's benefit, it seems intuitively fair to ascribe the conduct to the party for whose benefit it was undertaken. As stated in an early English case, "the reason that I am liable is this, that by employing [an employee] I set the whole thing in motion; and what he does, being done for my benefit and under my direction, I am responsible for the consequences of doing it." *Duncan v. Findlater*, 7 Eng. Rep. 934, 940 (H.L. 1839). On the simplest level, if the master did not have the work done by another, he would have to do it himself, and would be liable for any torts committed in doing so. Under respondeat superior, the acts done at the master's bidding are treated, for liability purposes, as though he had performed them himself.

The Meaning of "Employee"

An employer is only liable for the torts of a worker if the worker is its employee and acts in the scope of his employment. In many cases it is unclear whether a party who acts for another is an employee or instead acts as an independent contractor. Suppose, for example, that Bogart hires Bacall to maintain his yard. Bacall could be an employee or an independent contractor, depending on the particular facts of the relationship. If Bogart provides all the tools, pays Bacall by the hour, determines when she will work and exactly what she will do, Bacall would likely be characterized as an employee. On the other hand, if Bacall works with her own truck and tools, comes whenever she chooses, is paid by the season, provides her own insurance, and decides for herself what needs to be done to make the yard sparkle, she would likely be characterized as an independent contractor.

It is often stated that a person is an employee (or, in common law parlance, a "servant") if the employer has the right of control over the person in the performance of the work.

> A servant is a person employed to perform services in the affairs of another and who with respect to the physical conduct in the perfor- mance of the services is subject to the other's control or right to control.

Restatement (Second) of Agency §220(1); accord, Restatement (Third) of Agency (Tentative Draft No. 5) §7.07(3). However, this control test does not clearly resolve close cases, since even independent contractors are subject to some degree of control. Doubtless Bogart would have the authority to tell Bacall not to use chemical fertilizer, or to trim the rose bushes in the fall rather than the spring, even if Bacall's business was independent in most respects. Thus, courts have elaborated a number of factors that they consider in determining whether an actor is an employee. Section 220 of the Second Restatement of Agency, for example, lists the following factors:

- **The extent of control which the master is authorized to exercise over the details of the work.** Clearly, the more supervisory authority the employer has to specify how the work will proceed, the more likely it is that the worker will be viewed as an employee.
- **Whether the actor is engaged in a distinct occupation or business.** If Bogart employs a handy person to work around the house, she will more likely be viewed as an employee than if he calls in a computer repair person or an electrician.
- **Whether the type of work is customarily performed under the employer's supervision or by a specialist without supervision, and the extent of the skill required.** If the work involves a skilled task typically hired out to a specialized contractor, it will more likely be viewed as a contract situation. If Bogart hires Greenstreet to move his house, Greenstreet is more likely to be viewed as an independent contractor than if he is hired to wash it.
- **Who supplies the tools, other equipment and place of work.** If Bacall goes to Bogart's place of business every day to sew shirts and uses Bogart's sewing machines and material, she will probably be viewed as an employee. On the other hand, if she does piecework at home on her own machine, she may be an independent contractor.
- **The length of time for which the person is employed.** Frequently, persons hired for a single purpose and a brief period look more like independent contractors, since there is less of a relationship and a greater likelihood that she was called in to perform a specific task in her own manner. However, like the other factors, this one does not always help. If Bogart hires Bacall for a fall afternoon to rake leaves, she will likely be viewed as an employee. If he hires her for a season to maintain the grounds, she may well be a landscaping contractor.
- **Whether the person is paid on a time basis or by the job.** Workers hired by the hour or the week tend to be viewed as employees, since they are at the employer's "beck and call" on a regular basis. By contrast, contractors are typically hired to accomplish a given end result—such as building a house, or repairing a bridge—without detailed supervision during the process, and paid a flat sum to accomplish that result.
- **Whether the employer is in business, and whether the work is part of the employer's regular business.** If Bogart is a jeweler, and hires Bacall to cut diamonds, a court is likely to infer that she is an employee. On the other hand, if he hires her to renovate his jewelry

store, the more likely inference is that she is an independent contractor hired on a one-time basis to accomplish a particular task.

- **The parties' belief as to the nature of the relation.** It is relevant,
though not dispositive, that the parties view the relation as an
employment relation, or otherwise. This belief may be reflected in
various arrangements. For example, an employer is likely to pay
employment and worker's compensation taxes, to provide insurance,
and to comply with various other regulatory requirements regarding
employees. The fact that the employer has treated the worker as an
employee is suggestive that the master/servant relation actually exists.

This multi-factor test for determining employment status is widely
accepted, not only in the context of tort liability, but in others as well.
See, e.g., Rev. Rul. 87-41 (stating that common law test governs in determining employment status under the Internal Revenue Code, and listing
factors similar to those discussed above). Like so many legal standards
these days, this test is hardly cut and dried, and will often pose questions
of fact for the jury. On the other hand, while ambiguous cases arise, in
most cases it is pretty clear whether the individual is an employee or an
independent contractor.

Acting in the Scope of Employment

Even if the court concludes that Bacall was Bogart's employee at the time
that she negligently injured the plaintiff, Bogart will only be liable for her
negligence if she acted in the scope of her employment. Bogart obviously
is not liable for private acts of Bacall, but only those properly attributable
to her employment.

Isn't the law tiresome in the way it finds interpretive problems around
every corner? Perhaps so, but these interpretive problems arise from the
necessary process of determining the outer limits of a principle. Unless we
are to hold Bogart liable for everything Bacall does, we must define the
limit of his responsibility. He should not be liable if Bacall gets in a motor
vehicle accident over the weekend, because her driving is unrelated to her
work for Bogart. Even if she gets in the accident on her lunch hour,
Bogart should probably not be liable. This trip is for her own purposes,
outside of Bogart's premises and control. On the other hand, Bogart
clearly would be vicariously liable if Bacall hit a passing pedestrian with a
ladder while working as a house painter for Bogart's painting company.
Since this act took place in the course of and for the furtherance of the
employer's work, it seems fair that it should pay.

The Restatement (Second) of Agency offers the following definition
of "scope of employment":

(1) Conduct of a servant is within the scope of employment if, but only if:
    (a) it is of the kind he is employed to perform;
    (b) it occurs substantially within the authorized time and space limits;
    (c) it is actuated, at least in part, by a purpose to serve the master, and
    (d) if force is intentionally used by the servant against another, the use of force is not unexpectable by the master

Restatement (Second) of Agency §228. This definition works well enough in the easy cases, but is less helpful in the close ones, such as acts that are incidental to the work experience but do not directly further the work. Suppose, for example, that Bacall starts a fire while smoking on the job or bumps into a visitor while on the way to the bathroom. These acts do not directly further the master's enterprise, but they are normal incidents of the work experience.

Although early cases limited "scope of employment" to acts intended to directly further the employer's business, the tendency in more recent cases is to hold incidental acts in the course of the work (such as lunch or smoking breaks) within the scope of employment. They take place at the employer's place of business, during working hours, and are related in a general way to the accomplishment of the work. If the rationale for vicarious liability is that the risks engendered by an enterprise should be absorbed and distributed by that enterprise, it seems supportable to hold the employer liable for such incidental risks. *George v. Bekins Van & Storage Co.*, 205 P.2d 1037, 1043 (Cal. 1949); see Restatement (Third) of Agency (Tentative Draft No. 5) 131 (personal acts during the work day within scope of employment as "incidental to the employee's performance of assigned work").

Vicarious Liability for Intentional Torts

Another difficult problem is determining when employers will be held vicariously liable for intentional torts by employees. Intentional torts require, by definition, a deliberate decision by the actor to invade another's rights. In almost all cases, such deliberate invasions are unwanted, discouraged, and probably forbidden by the employer. There is some force, therefore, to the employer's argument that he should not be held liable for such acts in clear contravention of his wishes.

Despite these arguments courts do hold employers liable for at least some intentional torts. For example, courts have fairly consistently held employers liable where an employee commits an intentional tort in order to serve (however misguidedly) the employer's purposes. Prosser & Keeton at 505. An employee of a repossession company who assaults an owner while repossessing his car is clearly trying to do her job. Similarly, a bouncer who uses excessive force in evicting a patron from a bar is motivated to serve his employer, albeit overzealously. He is probably not doing it the way the employer wants him to, but neither is an employee who is negligent. Once again, if the basis for respondeat superior is that the employer's business has created the risk, these cases appear to be good candidates for application of the doctrine.

A second category of cases involves brawls that arise in the course of the work. For example, Bacall, while delivering pizzas for Bogart, might get into a dispute with another driver at a traffic light and punch him, or two assembly line workers might argue about the proper way to do the job, causing one to hit the other with a wrench.

The "motivation to serve" test would not support recovery in many of these cases: The worker does not assault another to accomplish the work, but from frustration stemming from its performance. The cases tend to impose vicarious liability in this scenario, on the theory that the tort is incidental to the work, in the same sense that a smoking break or a trip to the bathroom is. See R. Brill, The Liability of an Employer for the Wilful Torts of his Servants, 45 Chi.-Kent L. Rev. 1, 11-14 (1968). One court suggests that vicarious liability applies in this class of cases if the assault arises "in response to the plaintiff's conduct which was presently interfering with the employee's ability to successfully perform his duties." *Miller v. Federated Department Stores, Inc.*, 304 N.E.2d 573, 580 (Mass. 1973).

A third common scenario involves sexual contacts in the course of medical care or pyschotherapy. See, e.g., *Lisa M. v. Henry Mayo Newhall Memorial Hospital*, 907 P.2d 358 (Cal. 1995) (sexual assault by ultrasound technician during examination); *Birkner v. Salt Lake County*, 771 P.2d 1053 (Utah 1989) (social worker engaged in sexual activity with patient during counseling). The acts in these cases clearly do not serve the master's purposes, but they are a peculiar risk of certain kinds of work. Few courts would have held an employer liable for these torts 50 years ago; today, the cases are mixed. Some courts, taking a broad view of the costs an enterprise should absorb, will impose liability. See, e.g., *Fahrendorff v. North Homes, Inc.*, 597 N.W.2d 905 (Minn. 1999); *Plummer v. Center Psychiatrists, Ltd.*, 476 S.E.2d 172 (Va. 1996). Others, emphasizing the personal motivation of the tortfeasor, deny recovery. See, e.g., *Birkner*, 771 P.2d at 1058.

The new Restatement of Agency would resolve intentional tort cases based on the distinction between serving the employer's purposes and "an independent course of conduct not intended by the employee to serve any purpose of the employer." Restatement (Third) of Agency (Tentative Draft No. 5) §7.07(2). This test appears to narrow the ambit of liability somewhat. For example, under this test, a fight after a traffic accident would likely not be held in the scope of employment. Although the employment provides the occasion for the employee's assault, the assault hardly serves a purpose of the employer. See id. illus. 7, 8, 9.

A related issue arises when an employee's official position facilitates commission of an intentional tort. In *White v. County of Orange*, 212 Cal. Rptr. 493, 495-496 (Cal. Ct. App. 1985), for example, a deputy sheriff stopped a motorist and threatended to rape and murder her. In *Lo v. Superior Court*, 79 Cal Rptr. 2d 561 (Cal. Ct. App. 2d Dist. 1998), a judge threatened a defendant with adverse treatment in sentencing if she did not engage in sexual acts with him. Even courts that would generally deny recovery for such assaults may find the employer liable in these cases, based on the special authority vested in the tortfeasor that created a unique risk of abuse. See Restatement (Second) of Agency, §219(2)(d) (employer liability when agent is aided by the agency relationship in committing tort); see also *Doe v. Forrest*, 853 A.2d 48 (Vt. 2004) (sheriff's department could be liable under §219(2)(d) for acts of police officer who used his authority to force store clerk to perform sexual acts).

In another common scenario, the employee's tort has no relation to accomplishing the master's purpose, but the employment simply furnishes the opportunity for a completely unrelated tort. For example, a waiter might steal money from a customer's purse. In this scenario, the intentional tort is *related* to the employment, in the "but for" sense that the job creates the opportunity for the tort, but the tort is not motivated by the work or by any work-related purpose. See, e.g., *Effort Enterprises, Inc. v. Crosta*, 391 S.E.2d 477 (Ga. Ct. App. 1990) (employer not liable where employees stole jewelry while moving other items into plaintiff's house). Virtually all courts deny recovery against the employer in these cases.

Courts that take a broad approach to vicarious liability may formulate broader tests than the traditional "motivation to serve" approach. Some courts have held that the employee's act must be foreseeable in the sense that it is "not . . . so unusual or startling that it would be unfair to include the loss caused by the injury among the costs of the employer's business." *Leafgreen v. American Family Mut. Ins. Co.*, 393 N.W.2d 275, 280 (S.D. 1986). Others have simply required the conduct to be foreseeable or incidental to the work. *Martinez v. Hagopian*, 227 Cal. Rptr. 763, 766 (Cal. Ct. App. 1986). Such tests, while broader than the serving-the-employer's-purpose test, are too malleable to help much with the hard intentional tort cases.

Ultimately, the disparate results in the intentional tort cases "represent differing judgments about the desirability of holding an employer liable for his subordinates' wayward behavior." *Faragher v. City of Boca Raton*, 118 S. Ct. 2275, 2287 (1998). In other words, the outcome is a policy choice upon which courts differ. Such opposite outcomes in similar cases tend to frustrate students — and professors — who would like to see all the cases cleanly resolved by a single rule. Unfortunately no such universal rule exists, or will so long as we have 50 different states entitled to make their own tort law.

The Consequences of Independence

While employers are generally liable for the torts of their employees in the scope of employment, they generally are *not* liable for torts of an independent contractor, even though they arise from the contractor's work for the employer. Restatement (Second) of Torts, §409. (For the sake of clarity, I will call the party who hires an independent contractor the "owner," rather than the "employer" throughout this chapter.) This "rule of insulation" from tort liability (C. Morris and C. Morris Jr., Morris on Torts 256 (2d ed. 1980)) will obviously influence the way parties structure their business relationships. Owners may choose to hire independent contractors to perform work rather than using their own employees, simply to insulate themselves from tort liability. Of course, where the owner knows he is avoiding a potential liability, the contractor knows that he is assuming it. Consequently, the cost of insuring against tort liability will be considered in setting the price of the work.

Exceptions to the Rule: Nondelegable Duties

While hiring an independent contractor usually insulates an owner from liability for torts in the course of the work, it will not always do so. In some situations, courts have refused to allow owners to insulate themselves from liability, *even if* they use a contractor to do the work. In such situations, it is often said that the owner's duty of care is "nondelegable," so that the owner remains liable for tortious injury from the performance of the work, even though the tort was committed by an independent contractor.

The phrase *nondelegable duty* is something of a misnomer. The owner *has* delegated the work to an independent contractor in these cases; what the courts mean is that the owner may delegate the *work* but cannot delegate away the *liability* for tortious acts in the course of the work. Like the employer under respondeat superior, the owner is liable in these cases *vicariously* for the torts of the independent contractor.

Several widely accepted categories of nondelegable duties illustrate the typical rationales for imposing vicarious liability for the acts of independent contractors. For example, courts often hold a duty nondelegable because the work involves inherent danger or requires special precautions. See Restatement (Second) of Torts §416 (owner liable for contractor's negligence if the work is "likely to create during its progress a peculiar risk of physical harm to others unless special precautions are taken"). The Restatement gives the example of an owner who hires a contractor to tear down a town house, knowing that special precautions must be taken to avoid injury to the party wall of the next building. Restatement (Second) of Torts §416, illus. 2. If the contractor's employees fail to take these precautions, and injury results from this "peculiar risk," the owner will be liable for that injury. The evident rationale for this exception is that, where the owner is aware that special precautions are needed to avoid injury, it should assure that they are taken or incur the liability if they are not. For an example applying this exception, see *McMillan v. United States,* 112 F.3d 1040 (9th Cir. 1997) (clear cutting of large trees held nondelegable because inherently dangerous).

For similar reasons, §427 of the Second Restatement provides that the owner will be liable for the contractor's negligence in the performance of work "involving a special danger to others which the employer knows or has reason to know to be inherent in or normal to the work." This might apply, for example, to the repair of windows on a tall building in a city, which poses a risk that objects will fall on pedestrians. If an employee of the contractor fails to put up a sidewalk scaffold, and a pedestrian is injured by falling debris, the owner of the building will be liable vicariously for this negligent act.

Owners may also be held vicariously liable for their contractors' negligence in construction or repair of instrumentalities used in highly dangerous activities, such as transmission of high voltage electricity (see Restatement (Second) of Torts §423) and in the conduct of abnormally dangerous activities, such as blasting. See Restatement (Second) of Torts §427A. Here again, the unusual danger inherent in the work, which necessarily imposes a risk of injury and is done for the owner's benefit, supports holding the owner liable for the contractor's torts in the course of such activities.

Courts have also held owners vicariously liable for negligence of their contractors in the course of work done in a public place. Restatement (Second) of Torts §417. Under this exception an electric company would be liable, for example, if it hired an independent tree surgeon to trim trees along its power lines over the sidewalks, and the tree surgeon caused an accident by cutting a branch down in the path of the plaintiff's car. Similarly, owners are vicariously liable for torts of their independent contractors in maintaining highways and other public property (Restatement (Second) of Torts §418) and in maintaining premises open to the public for business purposes. Restatement (Second) of Torts §425. Vicarious liability in these cases is presumably based on the wide risk created by work done in public places, and the obvious need for particular care to protect the public from injury.

It has been said repeatedly that "the rule [insulating the owner from liability] is now primarily important as a preamble to the catalog of its exceptions." *Pacific Fire Ins. Co. v. Kenny Boiler & Mfg. Co.,* 277 N.W. 226, 228 (Minn. 1937). However, this catchy phrase is a bit of an overstatement. In many garden variety cases independent contractors are solely liable for their torts. If Bogart hires Bacall to resurface his driveway, and she backs into the street causing an accident, most likely she alone will bear the liability. If he hires an electrical contractor to rewire his office, most likely the contractor alone will be liable if she negligently starts a fire in the course of the work.

It is not possible to catalog here all situations in which courts have applied the nondelegable duty doctrine. The central point of this discussion is to illustrate that the contractor's independence does not always absolve the owner of responsibility, since courts often refuse, for policy reasons, to allow owners to wash their hands of the matter by hiring out the work.

Liability for the Owner's Own Negligence

The nondelegable duty theory will frequently allow a plaintiff injured by a contractor's negligence to recover from the owner who hired the contractor, even though the owner has exercised due care. However, it is important to remember that owners can be negligent too; frequently, a plaintiff will have a claim against the owner based on his *own* negligence in connection with the contract work.

An owner may be negligent in various ways even though the work is delegated to an independent contractor. He may hire a contractor who is clearly incompetent to perform the type of work required. He may fail to properly supervise the contractor. He may fail to require the contractor to take necessary precautions, or specify that the work be done in an inappropriate manner. He may fail to inspect the work after it is done, or negligently perform work over which he retains control. See generally Restatement (Second) of Torts, §§410-415 (detailing bases of liability for owner's negligence in connection with contract work). In such cases, the owner is liable for his *own* negligence, not vicariously liable for negligence of the contractor.

Frequently, a plaintiff will assert claims against the owner based on both the owner's own negligence and on vicarious liability theories, but it is important to distinguish these two bases for holding the owner liable: Even if there is no basis for holding the owner vicariously liable, he must still answer for his own conduct in connection with the work.

The examples below illustrate the nature and the limits of vicarious liability, both for the acts of employees and of independent contractors.

EXAMPLES

Respondeat Inferior

1. Grant, an employee of Metro Studios, is sued by Bergman, a passerby, for injuries arising from an accident in the course of making a movie.

Grant answers the complaint, denying liability on the ground that he was acting in the scope of his employment for Metro at the time of the accident. Bergman moves to strike the defense as insufficient. Should the motion be granted?

2.   Based on the accident, Bergman sues Grant and Metro (on a respondeat superior theory) for her injuries. Both are held liable for $50,000.

    a.   Grant pays the judgment and seeks contribution from Metro. What result?

    b.   Assume that Metro pays the judgment. How much should it be entitled to collect from Grant?

3.   Assume, on the facts of Example 1, that the movie was a Western. Grant, while waiting for a scene to begin, was sitting on his horse, Trigger, who bolted when a tourist unexpectedly exploded a firecracker. Bergman, another tourist watching from the sidelines, was knocked down by Trigger. Would Metro be liable to Bergman under respondeat superior?

Expert Employment

4.   Kildare, a physician with a general practice, is hired to conduct physical exams for Apex, a large manufacturing company. Apex specifies which employees will be examined, what the examinations will entail, what lab tests will be required, and how long Kildare has to submit his reports. The parties agree that Kildare will examine the patients at his office, will conduct a minimum of 20 exams per month, and that he will be paid a set amount for each exam. Kildare negligently injures Garbo during a physical, and she sues Apex. Is Apex liable on the basis of respondeat superior?

5.   Freud, a psychiatrist, is hired by Columbia Hospital, a mental health facility, to conduct psychotherapy with in-patients at the hospital. Freud agrees to spend ten hours per week at the hospital, to treat patients designated by Columbia, and to accept one-fourth of a full time salary and associated benefits for her work. The parties agree that Freud shall have sole authority over the method of treatment of the patients she sees; however, she is subject to the general administrative regulations of the hospital concerning such matters as treatment notes, guidelines for medicating patients, informed consent, and others. Jones, one of Freud's patients, commits suicide, and his estate sues Columbia for alleged negligence of Freud in failing to take steps to prevent the suicide. Should Freud be found to be an employee of Columbia for respondeat superior purposes?

Forewarned and Forearmed

6.   Rogers is a sales clerk for the Wild West Gun Shop, which sells firearms and ammunition. Evans, his boss, repeatedly reminds him that he is

not to sell to minors. Garner, a 15-year-old, comes into the shop, and Rogers (who is aware of Garner's age) sells him a box of cartridges. Garner is injured using the cartridges and sues Wild West. Would respondeat superior apply?

The Master's Business?

7. Larry, a house painter for Beta Construction Company, is painting an office with an electric paint sprayer when Curley, a fellow employee, happens by. Larry, in a spirit of horseplay, chases Curley around the room, aiming the sprayer at him and threatening to paint him blue. Unfortunately, he pulls the spray hose too far, knocking over the spray pump and spilling paint on the floor. The paint seeps through the ceiling and ruins office equipment in Moe's office below. Is Beta liable for the damage?

8. Grimsley, a pitcher for the Baltimore Orioles, is harassed by fans while warming up in the bullpen. Thoroughly annoyed, he finally heaves the ball at the fans, injuring Flynn. Flynn sues the Baltimore Orioles Baseball Club. If you represented him, which of the tests discussed in the introduction concerning respondeat superior liability for intentional torts would you prefer to see the court apply?

9. Hyde, a child care worker at Child Haven Day Care Center, secretly abuses three children who are cared for at the center. The children sue Child Haven for damages. Which of the various tests for holding the employer liable for an intentional tort would be most favorable to the plaintiffs?

10. Jones, a teacher in a program for severely mentally disabled children, beats one of the children with a ruler for urinating in his pants. The school rules specifically forbid corporal punishment. Can the school district be liable under respondeat superior?

Respondeat Judge Fudd

11. Charles Electronics tries to make employees feel appreciated. Often, on Friday afternoon, Loy, the assembly supervisor, would buy beer for the crew, and they would all tip a few before heading home for the weekend. One Friday, Nick, one of the assembly workers, had five beers before leaving, and then headed downtown to meet his wife for dinner. On the way, he injured Nora in an accident. She sues Charles Electronics for her injuries.

At trial, Judge Fudd indicates that he will give the following instruction:

If you find that, at the time of the accident, Nick was not in the course of his work for the defendant, was not on the premises of the defendant, and was not acting to further the purposes of the defendant, then you must find for the defendant.

What objection should Nora raise to the proposed instruction?

12. Colbert, an employee of Alpha Highway Construction Company, is ordered to keep watch over a large air compressor that powers several jack hammers used in making road cuts. At mid-morning, she slips off to place a bet with a bookie. While she is gone, the machine malfunctions, and the hose whips across the street injuring Gable. He sues Alpha for his injuries. Is Alpha liable for Colbert's conduct under respondeat superior?

Deja Vu

13. Tracy hires Hepburn Construction Company to rebuild the fire escapes on its apartment building, which immediately abuts Main Street. In the course of the work, a Hepburn employee negligently attaches a load of iron railings to a crane cable, and they fall, injuring Stewart, a passerby. Stewart sues Hepburn, the contractor, which denies liability on the ground that the duty of care was nondelegable because it involves a risk of injury unless special precautions are taken. Is this a good defense?

14. Stewart sues both Hepburn and Tracy, and both are found liable for Hepburn's negligence. Hepburn pays and seeks contribution from Tracy. What result?

Nondelegable Nonnegligence

15. Assume, on the facts of the Hepburn example, that the load of iron railings was not negligently attached, but fell when the crane's hoisting cable snapped. Although the cable was new, subsequent metallurgical analysis revealed that it had an undetectable defect, which caused it to snap under a normal load. Is Tracy liable for Stewart's injury?

Delegable Duties

16. Tracy hires Hepburn Construction Company to build a garage for him. In the course of the work, Cagney, a Hepburn employee, is required to cut two-by-fours on a table saw. He fails to use the blade guard, and the force of the blade throws a piece of wood into the air, injuring Stewart's eye as he passes by on the street. Is Tracy liable?

17. Assume that Tracy hires Hepburn Construction to rebuild the fire escapes on its high rise. A Hepburn employee leaves a metal railing on the ground, protruding onto the sidewalk. Colbert trips over it and is injured. Is Tracy, the owner, liable for her injury?

EXPLANATIONS

Respondeat Inferior

1. The judge should grant the motion. Grant is evidently under the impression (as many of my students are initially) that an employee is not personally liable for his torts in the scope of employment, since the employer is liable under respondeat superior. On the contrary, while respondeat superior provides *another*, potentially more solvent target for the plaintiff, the doctrine does not bar suit against an employee for his own tortious conduct. Both may be sued, and frequently both will be.

2a. Contribution statutes allow a tortfeasor who has paid a judgment to recover part of the judgment from other tortfeasors. It does not apply between Grant and Metro, however, because they are not joint tortfeasors. Metro is not a tortfeasor at all, but rather is vicariously liable for the tort of someone else. Although Metro is liable to Bergman under respondeat superior, it need not reimburse Grant, who caused the injury, if he pays the judgment. Respondeat superior exists to assure that the *plaintiff* can collect from Metro; it is not intended to insulate the actual tortfeasor from incurring the loss. If Grant pays, he will not recover any reimbursement from Metro.

   b. Most courts hold that an employer who pays the damages caused by his employee is entitled to indemnity — full reimbursement — from the employee, since the employee's negligence actually caused the injury and gave rise to the liability. Indemnity, unlike contribution, involves situations in which one party is liable with another, yet is able to seek reimbursement for the *entire* damages from the other. (Another common example of indemnity is a retail seller who is held liable without fault for selling a defective product, but has a right of indemnity from the manufacturer who actually produced the product. See Restatement (Second) of Torts §886B.)

   Although employers held liable under respondeat superior have a right of indemnity from the negligent employee, it is seldom exercised. An action for indemnity would frequently be futile, since the employee is unable to pay. In addition, such losses are often paid by an insurance policy covering both the employer and employee. And, of course, such actions do not make for positive employee relations.

3. Respondeat superior makes the employer liable for torts committed by its employees in the scope of employment. This question does not suggest that Grant did anything negligent. If he did not, he is not a tortfeasor. Since he would not be liable to Bergman, neither would Metro.

   Put another way, respondeat superior liability is not strict liability; it does not make employers liable for all *injuries* caused by their employees in the scope of employment. It makes them liable for *torts* committed by employees in the scope of employment. If Bergman's injury is a pure accident, caused by the unforeseeable act of the tourist, Grant is not liable and neither is Metro.

Trigger, by the way, is not an employee or a tortfeasor. Animals can't commit torts, though they can cause injuries. An employee may be liable for those injuries if her negligence somehow leads to that injury. If Grant had failed to protect the tourists from the horses in some appropriate manner, Grant (and therefore Metro) would be liable for the injury caused by Trigger. But this would be due to the negligence of Grant, not Trigger.

Expert Employment

4.   Although Apex exercises some control over Dr. Kildare's work, the court will very likely conclude that he has acted as an independent contractor. Kildare is a practicing physician, a professional whose business is entirely distinct from that of Apex. He is hired to perform a task it requires, but that is not a normal part of its business. He works at his own office, using his own tools and equipment and is paid on a per capita basis. He doubtless schedules the exams according to his own availability and continues to see other patients as well.

It is true that Apex has specified in detail what it wants Kildare to do, but this is true in many contract situations. On a complex road construction job, for example, there will be hundreds of pages of specifications, yet it is clear that a contractor is being hired to perform the entire job for a fixed price. While Apex has specified particular aspects of the exams, it will clearly not hover over Kildare to control his detailed performance of the exams. Apex has contracted for a specified result; it has not hired Kildare to work for it on a day-to-day basis subject to detailed supervision.

5.   Although Freud, like Kildare, is a physician, she will likely be held an employee of Columbia on these facts. Freud comes to Columbia to deliver services that are part of the hospital's basic function. She is paid as a salaried employee. True, she only works part time, but nothing in the test for employment suggests that part-time workers cannot be employees. Columbia assigns Freud her patients, provides her work space, and treats her like an employee for benefits purposes. She is also subject to Columbia's general administrative supervision while working there.

On the other hand, if the fundamental test for employment is the right to control the details of the work, Freud has an argument that she cannot be an employee: As a doctor, she is bound by the ethical code of the medical profession to exercise independent medical judgment in the treatment of patients. If Columbia cannot control her in the performance of her central task, the treatment of patients, how can she be an employee?

If this argument were accepted, virtually any professional or skilled worker would have to be viewed as independent. Accountants, lawyers, clergy, and psychologists, for example, frequently work for institutions, and look in virtually all other respects like employees, yet are bound by codes of conduct. Similarly, architects and engineers, as well as pilots, plumbers, electricians, and myriad other skilled workers are subject to statutory codes that prevent their employers from exercising complete control over their work. Yet their employers do exercise broad control over the administrative aspects of their work life: when they work, where they work, how they are paid, their general conduct, their benefits, and many others. In such cases, courts have held professionals employees if the employer exercises control over these other aspects of their work. See Restatement (Second) of Agency §223 cmt. a (lawyers and physicians can be employees if such factors suggest an employment relationship).

Forewarned and Forearmed

6.   The issue here is whether Rogers's act is in the scope of employment where Wild West expressly prohibited it, but Rogers sold to a minor anyway. Since one of the rationales for vicarious liability is that the employer can control negligence of its employees, you might think that where the employer exercised that control but the employee was negligent anyway, the employer would avoid respondeat superior liability.

The cases generally hold otherwise: The employer is liable despite its exercise of care to prevent negligence by its employees. See Restatement (Second) of Agency §230 & cmt. b. This result actually makes a good deal of sense. *First,* while it may seem unfair in the particular case, across-the-board liability will provide an incentive for Wild West to continue to work to prevent injuries. Perhaps it will discipline Rogers or increase employee education efforts. *Second,* as a practical matter, allowing the employer to avoid liability by offering evidence of its care to prevent accidents would introduce a broad new issue — the employer's general quality control measures — into the suit. *Third,* inducing employers to minimize injuries is only one of the rationales for respondeat superior. Others, such as encouraging loss spreading, internalizing the costs of an enterprise, and placing the loss on the party for whose benefit the risk was created, still support application of the doctrine in this case.

The Master's Business?

7.   Although horseplay of this sort is common in the course of many jobs, it obviously does not further the purposes of the employer; Beta hardly pays Larry to chase other workers with the spray gun. On the other hand, smoking does not further the employer's purposes either. Like smoking, a certain

amount of joking among co-workers is a foreseeable part of the ordinary course of the work experience, takes place in the workplace and during the course of the work, and serves to relieve the tedium of repetitive work.

Acts of horseplay have been held "in the course of employment" in worker's compensation cases, on the following rationale:

> Men do not discard their personal qualities when they go to work. Into the job they carry their intelligence, skill, habits of care and rectitude. Just as inevitably they take along also their tendencies to carelessness and camaraderie, as well as their emotional make-up. In bringing men together, work brings these qualities together, causes frictions between them, creates occasions for lapses into carelessness, and for fun-making and emotional flare-up ... [t]hese expressions of human nature are incidents inseparable from working together.

Hartford Accident & Indem. Co. v. Cardillo, 112 F.2d 11, 15 (D.C. Cir. 1940). For a recent example, see *Varela v. Fisher Roofing Co. Inc.,* 572 N.W.2d 780 (Neb. 1998) (worker who fell from roof while arm wrestling with co-worker in scope of employment). However, this rationale has not been generally accepted in respondeat superior cases involving horseplay, which frequently deny recovery against the employer on the ground that horseplay does not further the work in any way. See, e.g., *Bryant v. CSX Transp., Inc.,* 577 So. 2d 613, 615-616 (Fla. Dist. Ct. App. 1991); *Thomas v. Poole,* 262 S.E.2d 854, 857 (N.C. Ct. App. 1980).

Liability would likely be imposed for horseplay under broader scope-of-employment tests. It is certainly a "foreseeable risk" of the employment, clearly "incidental" to the work, and would satisfy a test that imposes liability for acts that are "an outgrowth" of the performance of the work. The test suggested in the current Restatement of Agency, however, denies recovery for "an independent course of conduct not intended ... to serve any purpose of the employer," Restatement (Third) of Agency, (Tentative Draft No. 5) §7.07(2). This formula would likely deny recovery in most horseplay situations, though the result seems dubious.

8.   Flynn would likely lose under a more traditional test, such as whether the act was motivated in part by a desire to serve the employer. Grimsley's act is motivated by annoyance, not any effort to prepare to enter the game. Nor would Grimsley be viewed as having a position of authority that facilitated this intentional tort. On the other hand, his act certainly does appear motivated by "present interference" with the ability to serve the master's purposes, since the heckling interfered with his concentration while warming up.[2] A fuzzy foreseeability test would also probably get Flynn to the jury, since this kind of harassment and retaliation is increasingly common in

---

2. In the case upon which this example is based, the court held that the Orioles could be liable under this test. See *Manning v. Grimsley,* 643 F.2d 20, 24-25 (1st Cir. 1981).

an age of declining manners. The proposed test of the Third Restatement of Agency would likely bar recovery, since heaving baseballs at fans is hardly intended to serve any purpose of the employer.

9.   Most of the tests for imposing respondeat superior liability for intentional torts would not support liability on these facts. Surely it does not further the employer's purposes or stem from present interference with the accomplishment of the work. The best argument would be that Child Haven has placed Hyde in a position of authority over the children that creates a unique risk of the intentional tort. The opportunity to commit the tort in this case arises from Hyde's work with children, and his position of authority over them assists him in doing so.

If respondeat superior is meant to assure that enterprises internalize the costs of risks they create, liability on these facts may be warranted. Although child abuse is the last thing any day care center wants, its activity does create the risk of such abuse. However, many courts, swayed by the repugnant nature of the conduct, the purely personal motivation of the employee, and the obvious damage the conduct does to the employer's interests, would deny recovery. See, e.g., *Worcester Ins. Co. v. Fells Acres Day Sch., Inc.,* 558 N.E.2d 958, 967 (Mass. 1990).

10.   This example is based on *Tall v. School Commissioners,* 706 A.2d 659 (Md. Ct. App. 1998). The *Tall* court held that the teacher's intentional tort fell outside the scope of employment, relying heavily on the fact that corporal punishment was forbidden by the district's rules.

The decision reflects a very narrow view of respondeat superior. First, as Example 6 indicates, it is well established that an act is not necessarily outside the scope of employment because it violates an employer's rules. Second, there are some strong arguments for respondeat superior liability in this case. Jones may have been acting in the scope of employment even under the most traditional test: His act may have been meant to serve the district's purpose by disciplining a student for disruptive behavior. Alternatively, the beating may have arisen from the employee's frustration created by the work, like the traffic argument cases discussed in the introduction. Many cases support respondeat superior liability in such situations. Although Jones's conduct was unauthorized, even reprehensible, its connection to the employment activity is still strong, much stronger, for example, than the child abuse in Example 9.

Respondeat Judge Fudd

11. Judge Fudd's mistake here is to focus on Nick's driving as the sole basis for imposing respondeat superior liability on Charles. Nora's counsel should hasten to point out to him that the negligent act of another employee — Loy — may also subject Charles to liability.

Even if Charles is not vicariously liable for Nick's driving, since the work day was over and Nick was on his way to dinner, it very likely *is* liable for the negligence of Loy in furnishing alcohol to Nick. Many courts would find that this act was in the scope of Loy's employment. Doubtless, such efforts to maintain employee morale, while peripheral to the physical production of the company's products, are intended to further the work of the employer in a general way, as do company picnics, the firm dinner dance, and similar happy occasions. Thus, if Loy was negligent in providing alcohol to Nick this will provide a separate basis for holding the employer liable. Nora should explain to Judge Fudd that his instruction is insufficient, because her claim against Charles is based not only on Nick's negligence, but also on Loy's.

12. If you really thought about this one, it shouldn't have given you much of a problem. Certainly, placing bets is not in the scope of Colbert's employment, but Gable's claim is not based on Colbert's act of placing a bet; it is based on her negligent supervision of the compressor. There is no question that this is part of Colbert's assigned duties, that she has negligently performed that duty, and that Gable's claim arises out of this negligence. Even though the claim arises from an omission to act as the work required, rather than a negligent act, Alpha will be liable for it.

Deja Vu

13. It is entirely likely that the duty here is nondelegable, since lifting heavy objects with a crane above the sidewalk poses an obvious risk to the perambulating public unless special precautions are taken. Restatement (Second) of Torts §416. However, finding the duty nondelegable would not relieve Hepburn, the independent contractor, of liability. Just as respondeat superior does not bar suit against a negligent employee, the fact that an owner is vicariously liable in nondelegable duty situations does not bar the plaintiff from suing the contractor for its negligence. It simply means that the owner is liable for it as well. Thus, the fact that the duty is nondelegable is not a proper defense for Hepburn.

14. Here again, as in the analogous circumstances of Example 2, Tracy is not liable to the contractor for contribution. He is not a joint tortfeasor, or any other kind of tortfeasor; he is vicariously liable for damages caused by Hepburn's tort. Because his liability arises from Hepburn's negligence, he is entitled to indemnity from Hepburn, but it has no right to contribution or indemnity from him.

Indemnity is much more likely to be sought in this context than in the employer/employee situation, since the contractor is more likely to have adequate resources and insurance to cover the loss. Indeed, Tracy's lawyer should be careful to include a clause in the contract requiring evidence that

Hepburn is fully insured, so that this right of indemnity would protect his client from absorbing losses caused by Hepburn's negligence.

Nondelegable Nonnegligence

15. This accident did not result from negligence by Hepburn's employees, since the defect was undetectable. If its employees were not negligent, Hepburn would not be liable for Stewart's injury. If so, Tracy would not be liable either. Declaring a duty "nondelegable" does not mean that the owner is strictly liable for *any* accident that occurs in the course of the work. It only means that he is vicariously liable for his contractor's *tortious* conduct. Tracy, as the owner, would be liable if Hepburn was negligent in failing to take necessary precautions, but if Stewart was injured without negligence, he has no claim against Hepburn, and therefore none against Tracy either.

Although Hepburn's employees were not negligent in causing the cable to snap, Stewart's counsel should consider whether they may have failed to take other appropriate precautions. It may be, for example, that if the worksite was properly cordoned off, Stewart would not have been within range of the railings. If such special precautions were necessary, and Hepburn failed to take them, Tracy could be held vicariously liable for that negligence.

Delegable Duties

16. Sawing two-by-fours may well be dangerous if the special precaution of putting the safety guard down is not taken. On the other hand, virtually *any* activity other than bookkeeping or watch repair involves some risk of injury if it is not done cautiously. If a duty is nondelegable whenever some appropriate precaution is omitted, the owner would be liable under the special precautions exception whenever its contractor is negligent. The exception would swallow the general rule that the contractor, not the owner, is liable for his torts.

Clearly, the special precautions exception is meant to apply to a narrower class of cases involving unusual risks.

> The situation is one in which a risk is created which is not a normal, routine matter of customary human activity, such as driving an automobile, but is rather a special danger to those in the vicinity, arising out of the particular situation created, and calling for special precautions.

Restatement (Second) of Torts §413 cmt. b. The examples offered by the Restatement, demolishing a building or digging an excavation (see §413 cmt. c), clearly involve unusual dangers not encountered in sawing boards to build a garage.

17. As the Introduction notes, courts often hold that activities involving peculiar risk give rise to "nondelegable duties." This means that, while an owner can hire an independent contractor to conduct the work, the owner remains liable for tortious injuries that result from the unusual risks the work poses. For example, a buildng owner can't hire a contractor to take down a skyscraper, and avoid liability if, due to the contractor's negligence, falling debris injures a passerby. This is dangerous work, done for the owner's benefit. Declaring the duty of care in the course of such work "nondelegable" means that, even though the owner contracts out the work, it can be sued for injuries negligently caused by the contractor, much as if it had done the work with its own employees.

However, the owner's vicarious liability in these nondelegable duty cases only applies to the particular risks that led the court to impose vicarious liability, not for any negligent act that takes place in the course of the job. Suppose, for example, in the skyscraper case, that the contractor sent an employee to the hardware store, and she had an accident on the way. The contractor would be liable for that, but the owner of the building would not. While a building demolition contract may require driving, demolition gives rise to a "nondelegable" duty because of the risk of damage from falling debris, not from driving, an ordinary activity that may take place in any kind of work.

Similarly, in this example, the risk that makes the work nondelegable is the risk of falling objects if special precautions are not taken, not the risk that an obstruction would be left on the sidewalk. This is "collateral negligence" that could take place in any kind of construction. Hepburn will be liable for Colbert's injury, but not Tracy. See Restatement (Second) of Torts, §426.

PART EIGHT

The Effect of Plaintiff's Conduct

22

The Once and Future Defense: Assumption of the Risk

Introduction

The late nineteenth century was the formative era of the common law of negligence. It was a time of rugged individualism, which emphasized freedom of action, personal initiative and the right of self-determination. The ideal was the Horatio Alger type, the self-made man who grasped the myriad possibilities of an expanding nation through strong character and hard work. Doubtless, the reality of most people's lives had little to do with this ideal, but it still conditioned the thinking of the time, including legal thinking.

It is not surprising that judges steeped in such ideas should accept the principle that the individual is master of his own fate, with the right to choose a course of action and the responsibility to accept the consequences of the choice. The concept of contributory negligence, that a plaintiff whose careless acts contributed to his injuries should bear the consequences, is an example. Another example, also with roots in the nineteenth century, is the doctrine of assumption of the risk.

The basic premise of assumption of the risk is that a person who is aware of a risk, and knowingly decides to encounter it, accepts responsibility for the consequences of that decision, and may not hold a defendant who created the risk liable for resulting injury. The premise was articulated in nineteenth century terms by Professor Bohlen:

> The maxim *volenti non fit injuria* [that to which a person assents is not deemed in law an injury] is a terse expression of the individualistic

501

tendency of the common law, which, proceeding from the people and asserting their liberties, naturally regards the freedom of individual action as the keystone of the whole structure. Each individual is left free to work out his own destinies; he must not be interfered with from without, but in the absence of such interference he is held competent to protect himself ... the common law does not assume to protect him from the effects of his own personality and from the consequences of his voluntary actions or of his careless misconduct.

Bohlen, Voluntary Assumption of the Risk, 20 Harv. L. Rev. 14 (1906). Based on this individualistic premise, assumption of the risk became an established shield to negligence liability, just as the analogous privilege of consent avoids liability for intentional torts.

Many of the early cases applying assumption of the risk arose in the context of injuries to workers on the job. A worker might accept employment in a factory with unguarded vats of molten metal, or requiring work on high scaffolds without railings. If he fell into the vat or off of the scaffold, the employer would argue that, by taking the job with knowledge of the working conditions, he had assumed the risk of injury from the known conditions of employment, and could not complain of the consequences of that choice.[1] Other cases arose in the context of injuries on land of another, where a guest or other licensee suffered injury due to an openly dangerous condition, such as an unfenced quarry or icy steps. As in the employee cases, the owner would argue that the plaintiff who chose to enter the premises with knowledge of open and obvious dangers accepted responsibility for possible injuries from those known risks.

In these and other contexts, courts accepted the argument that the plaintiff's knowing choice to encounter danger relieved the defendant of responsibility for resulting injury, even if the defendant *negligently created the risk* that caused it. Assumption of the risk became a companion defense along with contributory negligence. It differed, of course, in that assumption of the risk required a showing that the plaintiff actually knew of a danger and chose to proceed. If the plaintiff should have known of a risk, but did not, contributory negligence would apply but assumption of the risk would not.

An example may help to illustrate the relationship between assumption of risk and contributory negligence. Suppose that Newman lent his car to Knieval, and told him that the brakes didn't work. If Knieval

---

1. "Assumption of risk ... developed in response to the general impulse of common law courts at the beginning of this period [the industrial revolution] to insulate the employer as much as possible from bearing the 'human overhead' which is an inevitable part of the cost — to someone — of the doing of industrialized business. The general purpose behind this development in the common law seems to have been to give maximum freedom to expanding industry." *Tiller v. Atl. Coast Line R.R.*, 318 U.S. 54, 58-59 (1943) (footnotes omitted).

shrugged and said he would go slow and use the emergency brake, he assumed the risk of injury from the defective brakes. He might well be negligent in making such a conscious choice; if so, he both assumed the risk and was contributorily negligent. On the other hand, if Newman did not tell Knieval about the brakes, but Knieval noticed that the pedal felt loose before he started the car and didn't investigate before driving, he was probably contributorily negligent but did not assume the risk of the defective brakes. He was negligent because he should have checked the brakes when he noticed a problem. But he did not assume the risk of defective brakes, because he did not make a deliberate choice to drive without brakes with full knowledge of the risk.

The assumption of risk principle is confusing in practice because it has been applied in a variety of situations. Some of these overlap negligence analysis, while others are confusingly similar to contributory negligence. In addition, courts have not been consistent in the way they classify assumption of risk cases. See Gaetanos, Essay—Assumption of Risk: Casuistry in the Law of Negligence, 83 W. Va. L. Rev. 471, 473 (1981) (noting five different classification schemes adopted by various torts scholars). Despite this confusion, it is important to come to grips with assumption of the risk, because, unlike contributory negligence, assumption of the risk is clearly *not* a wave of the past. In at least some of its incarnations, the doctrine is recognized today and will continue to be in the future.

This chapter is intended to give you an understanding of the basic situations in which courts have applied the concept of assumption of the risk, and of the areas in which it remains a "once and future defense."

Express Assumption of the Risk

Perhaps the clearest assumption of the risk cases are those in which the plaintiff expressly agrees that she will not hold the defendant liable for injury she suffers from a risk created by the defendant. Suppose, for example, that Knieval decides to try skydiving, and hires Newman to teach him the sport. Newman may agree only if Knieval consents in writing not to hold Newman liable for any resulting injuries. Or, Newman might agree to let Knieval use his land for motorcycle jumping practice, conditioned on a similar promise not to sue for any resulting injuries.

As a general matter, such express agreements to assume a risk, even a negligently created risk, are enforced by the courts. Restatement (Third) of Torts: Apportionment of Liability §2; Restatement of Contracts (Second) §195(2) & cmt. a. The 19th century belief in individual initiative and freedom of choice persists, including the right to make silly choices, or even dangerous ones, and accept the consequences. Some people prefer that life should be interesting rather than safe, and such venturous souls may claim substantial accomplishments, such as discovering America and going to the moon. To a great extent, our culture continues to support such choices, even where there is little social value gained by accepting the risk.[2] Allowing participants to agree in advance to accept the risk of injury from high risk activities (that is, to agree *not* to sue if such injuries occur) promotes the availability of exciting and varied opportunities, by insulating providers from the high cost of injuries resulting from the activity.

While the principle of express assumption is generally accepted, it has been hedged around with some qualifications. *First*, it is essential that the consent to accept the risk is freely given: A consent extracted from a party with little bargaining power is inconsistent with the free choice principle underlying the doctrine, and will not be honored by the courts. For example, courts have struck down contractual "consents" to unsanitary living conditions in public housing or negligent treatment in local hospitals, on the theory that the plaintiff has no meaningful alternative, and therefore has not really consented at all. Similarly, courts have held that providers of quasi monopolistic public services, such as rail or electric service, cannot condition service on the passenger's acceptance of the risk of injury. Here again, the lack of choice makes the consumer's "consent" illusory. Interestingly, although assumption of the risk doctrine developed in the employment context, it is now generally held that the inequality of bargaining power inherent in the employment relationship bars express assumption of the risk by employees. Restatement (Second) of Torts §496B, cmt. f; Prosser & Keeton at 482.

A second qualification, which also follows from the rationale of assumption of the risk, is that the plaintiff must clearly consent to accept the particular risk that led to the injury. For example, some courts have held that a provision releasing the defendant from "all claims for personal injury" does not waive recovery for injury due to *negligence* of the defendant, since it does not sufficiently bring home to the plaintiff the extent of the risks she is accepting. See Harper, James & Gray, §21.6, at 251; but see *Boyce v. West*, 862 P.2d 592, 598 (Wash. Ct. App. 1993) (release held to encompass negligence though it did not specifically refer to negligence). Generally, contractual clauses assuming risk (also called waiver of liability or exculpatory clauses) are drafted by the party providing the risky activity — the skydiving school, the quarry owner that allows rock climbing for a fee, the horseback riding ranch. Such releases are construed against the drafter, and must be quite clear in stating the risks allocated to the participant.

Contractual assumptions of risk are also limited by general contractual principles concerning the understanding of the parties. Thus, an agreement

---

2. Witness the widespread resistance to mandatory seatbelt or helmet laws. For an interesting defense of the socially constructive role of risk-taking in self-actualization, see D. Judges, Of Rocks and Hard Places: The Value of Risk Choice, 42 Emory L.J. 1, 11-26 (1993).

to assume the risk of injuries will not extend to collateral risks beyond their contemplation. For example, if Ruth signs a general waiver of liability for injuries from playing in a baseball game, he would realize that he was assuming usual risks of playing baseball, such as being hit by the ball or another player. But he would not have in mind the risk of a sink hole in the base paths. If he fell into one, he would not be barred by express assumption of the risk, since the parties did not have this risk in mind at the time of contracting.[3]

Implied Assumption: Inherent Risk Cases

A plaintiff may also accept risks simply by engaging in an activity with knowledge that it entails certain risks. Many activities involve a risk of injury even if conducted with due care. In such cases participants assume the risks of injuries from the inherent dangers of the activity. Here are a few examples:

- The plaintiff, after watching patrons at a fair try to maintain their balance on an inclined, moving belt called "The Flopper," buys a ticket, steps on the belt, and is thrown off, fracturing his knee cap.
- The plaintiff decides to take wilderness survival training in Minnesota in mid-winter. The plaintiff gets lost in a snowstorm and suffers serious frostbite.
- The plaintiff goes skating at the defendant's skating rink, is hit by a poor skater who loses control, and is injured when she hits the wall of the rink.
- The plaintiff takes rock climbing instruction and is injured when a seemingly solid rock is dislodged by a climber and falls on her.

In each of these cases, the defendant has offered an activity to the plaintiff, which he is under no duty to offer, and which the plaintiff is under no duty to attempt. That activity cannot be conducted without certain unavoidable risks of injury, even if conducted with due care, and the plaintiff has chosen to engage in the activity. As in the express assumption cases, the plaintiff considers the trade-off worthwhile, and accepts the possibility of injury because she enjoys the activity.

---

3. Express assumption may also be barred in situations where it would undermine legislative intent. For example, if a statute mandated certain safety standards for public stadiums (such as number of exits or a maximum number of patrons), a court would likely refuse to enforce a release on the plaintiff's ticket accepting risks of injury due to negligence covered by the statute. Stadium operators should not be allowed to avoid the statutory purpose by requiring the protected class to waive its protection in order to see the game. See generally A. Cava & D. Wiesner, Rationalizing a Decade of Judicial Responses to Exculpatory Clauses, 28 Santa Clara L. Rev. 611, 630-638 (1988).

As in the express assumption cases, courts have honored the choice to encounter risk in implied assumption cases too. Plaintiffs who choose to engage in unavoidably risky activities assume the inherent risks of the activity, and have no claim for injuries resulting from those risks. Although this is often described as assumption of the risk of injury, the defendant has actually not breached the duty of due care in such cases. It is not negligent to organize a flag football league, to run a horseback riding ranch, or to offer hang gliding instruction, even though these activities involve some risk of injury. The plaintiff who knowingly engages in such sports impliedly accepts the inherent risks they entail, and cannot sue the defendant who offered it to her simply because those inherent risks lead to injury.

Because primary asumption of the risk is based on the fact that certain risks are inherent in the activity and unavoidable at a reasonable cost, primary assumption only applies where that is in fact the case. If Henne goes ice skating, she accepts the risk that she may be hit by other skaters. This is an obvious danger inherent in the sport. It does not result from negligence of the operator, and it cannot be eliminated at a reasonable cost. However, Henne would not assume the risk of a dangerous condition in the ice or a broken handrail along the edge. These risks are not inherent in the activity itself; they are dangers created by negligent operation of the rink. The plaintiff does not impliedly accept these risks by merely deciding to go skating.

Harper, James & Gray argue that the term "assumption of risk" should not apply to inherent risk situations at all; they are simply situations in which the defendant acted reasonably and the plaintiff suffered injury from a reasonable risk of the activity. Harper, James & Gray, §21.0. This makes good sense; the plaintiff in these cases cannot prove her prima facie case of negligence, because the defendant has not breached the duty of due care. It would be clearer to ask in these cases whether the defendant violated the duty of care than to use assumption of the risk terminology. However, courts frequently analyze these as "primary assumption of the risk" or "primary implied assumption of the risk" cases. As a result, these situations (in which there is no negligence because the risk the defendant created was reasonable) are frequently confused with other cases (discussed immediately below) in which assumption of risk is properly viewed as a defense.

Secondary Implied Assumption: The Negligent Defendant and the Venturous Plaintiff

In the situations discussed immediately above, the defendant created reasonable risks that plaintiffs chose to encounter. However, a plaintiff may also encounter risks created by a defendant's *unreasonable* conduct. Here are some examples:

- The defendant lends plaintiff his car. She notices that the car swerves sharply to the left while braking, but proceeds anyway, and is injured when she brakes for a light and swerves into an opposing car.
- The defendant is setting off fireworks in the public street. Plaintiff, anxious to see the show, stands next to him and is injured when a firecracker explodes.
- The defendant waxes part of the floor of his store while open for business. The plaintiff sees the wet floor, but anxious to get a box of Wheetabix for breakfast, walks on the wet floor and falls.
- The defendant riding stable provides the plaintiff an unruly horse. The plaintiff, after watching the horse start and buck, decides to try to ride it anyway.

In each of these cases, unlike the limited duty cases discussed above, the defendant breached the standard of due care by creating an unreasonable risk. If that negligence injured the plaintiff before she became aware of the risk, the defendant would be liable. For example, if the plaintiff who borrowed the car was injured the first time she applied the brake, she could sue, because it is negligent to lend someone a car without informing the person of known defects that may cause injury. Similarly, if the plaintiff in the fireworks example was an unsuspecting passerby, she could recover for her injury in the explosion, since it is negligent to explode firecrackers in the immediate vicinity of others.

However, in these cases the plaintiff, after becoming aware of the unreasonable risk created by the defendant, chooses to encounter it, and suffers injury as a result. This type of case is often called "secondary assumption of the risk" or "secondary implied assumption," presumably because the plaintiff's choice is secondary to (comes after) the negligence of the defendant. In secondary assumption situations the plaintiff has been injured due to the defendant's negligence, but the defendant argues that the plaintiff's free choice to encounter the negligently created risk should bar her recovery.

Arguably, the defendant should still be liable in these cases: He has created a risk through his negligence that injured the plaintiff. On the other hand, the plaintiff has freely chosen to encounter it for her own purposes, be it enjoyment of the fireworks display, immediate access to Wheetabix, or available but unsafe transportation. Just as the plaintiff's acceptance of deliberate invasions of her person prevents liability for an intentional tort (under the consent privilege), plaintiff's choice to encounter a negligently created risk should arguably avoid liability as well.

True to its individualistic assumptions, the common law held that the plaintiff, by knowingly encountering a danger created by the defendant's negligence, "assumed the risk" of resulting injury, and was barred from suing for that injury. Restatement (Second) of Torts §496C. Under secondary assumption of risk, the courts honored the plaintiff's willingness to confront negligently created risk, just as they honored her willingness to encounter inherent risk under the related doctrine of primary assumption of the risk. However, in secondary assumption cases, the doctrine really was an affirmative defense, since it barred the plaintiff from recovering even though she could establish a prima facie case of negligence by the defendant.

Reasonable and Unreasonable Assumption

In secondary assumption cases, the plaintiff's decision to encounter the risk may be either reasonable or unreasonable. The decision to stand next to an adolescent playing with fireworks will virtually always be unreasonable. It might be reasonable to drive a car with bad brakes to get a heart attack victim to the hospital, but not to get to a poker game on time. A rescuer's decision to rescue a child from a fire is eminently reasonable, though it knowingly subjects the rescuer to a risk of injury.

Where the plaintiff's decision to encounter the risk was unreasonable, assumption of the risk overlapped with contributory negligence: By definition, the reasonable person does not voluntarily encounter unreasonable risks. At common law, both defenses could be pleaded. If the plaintiff's choice to encounter the risk was an unreasonable one, that choice would constitute both contributory negligence and assumption of the risk. Either defense sufficed to bar the plaintiff's recovery.

Where the plaintiff *reasonably* assumed a risk, contributory negligence would not bar recovery. *However*, assumption of the risk still did. The basis for the defense was individual choice, not fault. Even if the plaintiff chose to encounter the risk for good reason, the courts still "honored" the choice by denying recovery.

Nine Lives: Assumption of Risk in the Comparative Negligence Era

The advent of comparative negligence has sparked some controversy about the continued role of secondary implied assumption of the risk. Under comparative negligence, the plaintiff's negligence reduces her recovery, but does not usually bar it. Suppose, however, that the plaintiff's negligence consists of unreasonable but knowing assumption of the risk (secondary implied assumption); should it bar or reduce recovery? For example, assume that the defendant owns a warehouse without a fire alarm or sprinkler system. Gallo knows this, but decides to store her goods there because it is cheaper. This decision may well be negligent. It is also, however, a deliberate, knowing acceptance of the risk.

At common law, this case posed no problem: *Either* contributory negligence or assumption of the risk barred recovery entirely. In a comparative negligence state, however, if Gallo's conduct were treated as negligence, it would reduce her recovery rather than bar it entirely. On the other hand, if unreasonable assumption of the risk persists as a separate defense, *she would still be fully barred.* There is an argument for the latter result, since assumption of the risk is based on consent to encounter a risk, not on fault. If Gallo has accepted the risk with full knowledge, arguably the long standing assumption of risk rule denying recovery should continue to apply.

Despite this argument, most comparative negligence jurisdictions conclude that secondary *unreasonable* assumption of the risk should be treated as a form of negligence. Under this approach, the jury assigns a percentage of negligence to Gallo's unreasonable choice to accept the risk, and her recovery is reduced by that percentage. Some comparative negligence statutes specifically require this result.[4] In other states, this same sensible result has been reached by judicial interpretation. See *Blackburn v. Dorta*, 348 So. 2d 287 (Fla. 1977); see generally Schwartz, Comparative Negligence, §9.4(B).

It is fairly easy to conclude that comparative negligence displaces unreasonable secondary assumption of risk, because unreasonable assumption is by definition a form of negligence. It is more difficult to decide how *reasonable* secondary assumption should be meshed with comparative negligence. Suppose, for example, that the warehouse without a sprinkler was the only place within 75 miles of Gallo's home, and she was required to go away on business for three months. The decision to take the small risk of a fire loss might well be reasonable on such facts. If so, how should the decision affect her recovery under a comparative negligence statute?

Arguably her knowing choice to take the risk should not affect her recovery at all, since it was (by definition) a reasonable choice and recovery is only to be reduced for negligence. Some cases have taken this position. See *Rini v. Oaklawn Jockey Club*, 861 F.2d 502 (8th Cir. 1988) (a well reasoned case applying Arkansas law), see also Restatement (Third) of Torts: Apportionment of Liability, §3 and cmt. c. However, a few have argued that reasonable secondary assumption should completely bar recovery. Comparative negligence statutes only address the effect of the plaintiff's *fault*, the rationale for assumption of risk as a defense is knowing *consent* to take a risk, not fault. Arguably, the passage of a comparative

---

4. The Washington comparative negligence statute, for example, defines "fault" to include "unreasonable assumption of risk." Wash. Rev. Code Ann. §4.22.015. The evident purpose of such a provision is to treat unreasonable assumption as a damage-reducing factor rather than a complete bar to recovery.

negligence statute, which modifies the effect of plaintiff's *negligence*, should not affect the defense of reasonable assumption of risk. See, e.g., *Siglow v. Smart*, 539 N.E.2d 636 (Ohio Ct. App. 1987). Restatement (Second) of Torts, §496A, cmt. (c)(3).

The 1980s, the era of Ronald Reagan and the collapse of communism, witnessed a renewed emphasis on the nineteenth-century values of individual responsibility and freedom of choice. This megatrend has even found expression in obscure corners of tort law like assumption of risk. While it appeared that secondary assumption of the risk would fade away with the advent of comparative negligence, some cases and articles have argued for retaining reasonable secondary assumption as a complete defense. See, e.g., *Ford v. Gouin*, 266 Cal. Rptr. 870 (Cal. Ct. App. 1st Dist. 1990), *aff'd by a divided court*, 834 P.2d 724 (Cal. 1992); Rosenlund & Killion, Once a Wicked Sister: The Continuing Role of Assumption of Risk Under Comparative Fault in California, 20 U.S.F.L. Rev. 225, 278-283 (1986); Spell, Stemming the Tide of Expanding Liability: The Coexistence of Comparative Negligence and Assumption of Risk, 8 Miss. C. L. Rev. 159 (1988).[5]

The major anomaly of this approach, of course, is that it totally bars recovery by a plaintiff who made a *reasonable* choice to assume a risk, while unreasonable assumption only reduces recovery under comparative negligence. Those who advocate a separate defense of reasonable assumption of risk argue that this is not inconsistent, since the defense is based on consent, not on fault. However, if plaintiff's "consent" to encounter the risk bars recovery where her decision is reasonable, it seems logical that it should *also* bar recovery where it is unreasonable. Yet, under most comparative negligence regimes, unreasonable assumption of the risk is treated as a form of plaintiff's negligence, which reduces a plaintiff's recovery rather than barring it. Since that is true, it seems consistent to treat a plaintiff's reasonable choice to encounter a risk negligently created by the defendant as nonnegligent conduct, which should not reduce or bar her recovery from the defendant.

---

5. The following passage from the Spell article, for example, is reminiscent of the nineteenth century arguments for assumption of the risk:

> Notions of choice do not go so far as to afford the plaintiff, who once stood at the threshold of action armed with both knowledge of the risks ahead and the opportunity to avoid those risks, the ability to cast back upon the defendant the cost of his choice. The more equitable approach is to enforce the "fundamental principle" of assumption of risk that "where the plaintiff has voluntarily and intelligently consented to relieve the defendant of liability for certain known risks, the plaintiff's choice should be enforced."

8 Miss. C. L. Rev. at 171 (quoting from the Rosenlund and Killion article at 255).

An Attempted Summary

All of this is a bit confusing. This is mostly because the courts are inconsistent in the way they analyze the various assumption of risk situations. In some cases, it is clear that the judges themselves did not fully grasp the distinctions, or could not agree with their colleagues about the proper approach to choose. Here is an attempt to describe the current state of the law on assumption of the risk:

- Express assumption of the risk, that is, the waiver by advance agreement of the right to sue the defendant for her negligence, remains a viable defense. Such waivers will not be enforced in certain contexts involving essential services, and they may be construed narrowly, but usually they will be honored by the courts.

- Implied primary assumption of the risk, properly construed, reflects the idea that an activity may entail risks of injury even when carefully conducted by the operator. If a participant is injured due to those inherent risks, she will lose an action against the operator because she will not prove negligence. A skier hit by another skier, or a spectator hit by a foul ball at a baseball game, will likely lose because it was not negligent to offer the activity, even though such injuries occasionally happen. Courts still declare in such cases that the "plaintiff assumed the risk" of injury, but the real basis for rejecting the claim is that the operator was not negligent.

- Cases of secondary assumption of risk arise when the defendant *was* negligent, and that negligence created a dangerous situation. The plaintiff became aware of the negligently created risk, encountered it, and suffered injury.
    - If the plaintiff's choice to encounter the risk was an unreasonable one, this is negligent conduct. Most courts that apply comparative negligence treat this form of assumption of risk as a type of plaintiff's fault. Thus, the jury will be instructed to assign a percentage of fault to the plaintiff if they find that she negligently chose to encounter the risk. In this type of jurisdiction, there is no separate defense of secondary assumption of the risk, so the jury will be told nothing about it.
    - A few jurisdictions continue to treat secondary assumption of the risk as a separate defense.[6] In these jurisdictions, the defendant's choice to encounter the risk will bar her recovery, rather than being treated as a form of comparative negligence.

- If a plaintiff makes a knowing choice to encounter the risk negligently created by the defendant, and that choice is a reasonable one, courts

---

6. See, e.g., *Kennedy v. Providence Hockey Club*, 376 A.2d 329 (R.I. 1977); see generally V. Schwartz, Comparative Negligence, §9.03.

take different positions. Most courts today that apply comparative negligence would allow the plaintiff to recover fully, since her conduct was not faulty and should not reduce recovery.[7] A few, however, may still analyze this as a matter of choice rather than fault, and bar such plaintiffs from recovery entirely.

Hopefully, the following examples will help you to understand the basic situations in which the assumption of risk issue arises, and the different ways each may be resolved.

EXAMPLES

False Assumptions

1.   Killey decides to ski the Big Mountain Ski Bowl. He arrives at the ski area, buys a small lift ticket that attaches to the lapel of his ski jacket, and starts to ski. While riding in the chair lift up to the expert trails, he is injured when the chair separates from the drive cable and falls to the ground. When he threatens to sue Big Mountain, its lawyer points out the following language printed on the back of the lift ticket: "The purchaser assumes all risks of injury from any source whatever, arising in the course of the activities authorized by this ticket, whether due to the negligence of the ski operator or third persons, or any other cause." Is Killey barred by express assumption of the risk?

2.   Assume the same facts, except that before he began skiing, Killey was required to read and sign a form containing the following language: "The undersigned acknowledges that skiing is a hazardous sport; that bare spots, ice, changing snow, bumps, stumps, stones, trees, and other hazards exist in any ski area. By purchasing this ticket, the purchaser recognizes such dangers, whether marked or unmarked, accepts the hazards of the sport and the fact that injury may result therefrom, and agrees to assume all risk of such injuries." Is Killcy barred from recovering for his injuries by express assumption?

3.   Gavin decides to go skydiving and signs up for lessons with Freeflight Skydiving Inc. Freeflight requires him to sign the following release:

> I understand and acknowledge that skydiving is a dangerous sport involving a serious risk of injury. By engaging in the sport, I recognize the risk of injury from skydiving, assume all risk of injury from doing so, and agree not to sue Freeflight Skydiving Inc. for any injury that may result from my participation in it.

On his first dive, Gavin suffers a punctured ear drum as a result of the rapidly changing air pressure. Although he had realized that he might

---

7. See, e.g., *Rini v. Oaklawn Jockey Club*, 861 F.2d 502, 508-510 (8th Cir. 1988) (applying Arkansas law).

suffer broken bones, or even death from a failed parachute, Gavin never understood that there was a risk of injuries to his ears from skydiving. He sues for damages and Freeflight raises the release as a defense. Has Gavin assumed the risk?

Negative Implications

4. On the facts of Killey's ski lift accident, is he barred from suing Big Mountain by primary implied assumption of the risk?

5. Killey skis the expert slopes at Big Mountain. While coming down a particularly steep slope he is hit by another skier who had negligently failed to notice a turn in the trail and lost control. Killey's leg is broken. Is he barred from suing Big Mountain by primary implied assumption of the risk?

6. Rogers, a novice at horseback riding, goes to the Circle-R Ranch to ride. While out on the trail a rattlesnake glides across the trail, startling Rogers's horse. The horse rears, throwing Rogers to the ground and injuring him. Rogers sues the Ranch for his injuries, and the Ranch pleads assumption of the risk as a defense. Rogers claims that the defense does not apply because he did not know that snakes would cause a horse to rear and throw a rider.

   a. What form of assumption of the risk, if any, is implicated in this case?

   b. Assuming that Rogers really did not know of this risk, is he barred from recovery?

   c. In what way has Circle R "pleaded wrong" in raising its defense?

Taking Negligence to Newcastle

7. Hermit, who lives on a little-traveled rural road, hitches a ride to town for supplies with a passing driver. It is apparent to Hermit that Driver has been drinking heavily. However, Hermit climbs aboard, and is injured when Driver swerves into a ditch.

   a. What type of assumption of risk, if any, applies here?

   b. What would be the effect of Hermit's conduct in a jurisdiction that applies common law contributory negligence and assumption of risk doctrine?

   c. How would his conduct affect his right to recover in a comparative negligence jurisdiction?

8. Farmer, who also lives on a little-traveled rural road, suffers a serious leg injury while harvesting wheat. He hails a passing car and beseeches the driver, Hillary, to take him to the hospital. Hillary says, "Look, my brakes are acting up, but if you're willing to chance it, I'll take you." Farmer agrees and is injured when the brakes lock at a traffic light and the car is

hit from behind. Which type of assumption of risk, if any, applies in this case?

9.   Assume that Hillary said nothing about the brakes. However, Farmer watched Hillary apply the brakes several times during the ride, and observed that they locked abruptly as soon as applied. Anxious to get medical help, Farmer stays aboard.

    a. What type of assumption of the risk, if any, would this entail?

    b. Assume that, after Farmer realizes that the brakes are bad, they lock at the light and Farmer is injured. Would Farmer be barred from recovery in a jurisdiction that applies the common law contributory negligence and assumption of risk doctrines?

    c. On the same facts, would assumption of the risk bar recovery in a comparative negligence jurisdiction?

Judge Fudd Assumes the Risk

10. Dewey, a teacher in a West Dakota high school, agrees to participate in a "donkey basketball" game for the school scholarship fund. The game is what it says it is; the players play basketball while riding donkeys provided by the Buckeye Donkey Basketball Company. It is really very funny and a lot of students would gladly pay to see their teachers make such asses of themselves. Before the game, an employee of Buckeye explains to the teachers that the donkeys sometimes stop short and lower their heads, and there is a small risk of falling off. In the middle of the game, Dewey's donkey executes such a maneuver, and Dewey is thrown, suffering a dislocated shoulder. He sues Buckeye for his injuries.

West Dakota has adopted a comparative negligence statute that provides for reducing plaintiff's damages to account for his fault. The statute also provides that "the defense of assumption of the risk is abolished." At trial, Buckeye's lawyer asks Judge Fudd to instruct the jury that they should find for the defendant if they conclude that Dewey assumed the risk of being thrown. Judge Fudd responds, "Counsel, I don't see how I can grant that instruction. It says right in the statute that assumption of the risk is abolished." Is Fudd right in rejecting the assumption of the risk argument?

A Little Knowledge of a Dangerous Thing

11. Pearson is driving down a little used country road behind Moses, a poky Sunday driver. Frustrated and hurried, he decides to pass. There is a curve in the road and Pearson can't see whether a car is coming the other way. Pearson attempts to pass but hits Henderson, who is driving in the opposite lane and speeding. Pearson sues for his injuries. Would he be barred by assumption of the risk if the jurisdiction applies the traditional assumption-of-risk doctrine?

Legal Shape-Sorting

12. Try to fit the following examples into the categories discussed in the Introduction.

   a. Mansfield rents a rustic cabin two hundred miles away, sight unseen, for his family's summer vacation in the North Woods. When they arrive, they discover that the cabin is not quite finished, and there is no railing on the stairs to the second floor. On the fifth day of their stay, Mansfield stumbles on the stairs and falls off due to the lack of a railing.

   b. Bohlen borrows a table saw from Wade to use in putting a porch on his house. The saw had a kill switch on the side which, when engaged, would cause the blade to stop if the wood going through the saw was pushed too hard. This prevents the wood from kicking back and injuring the user. Wade had disabled the kill switch, however, by "hotwiring" around it, because it slowed down the work when the kill switch engaged. Bohlen is not very familiar with table saws, does not realize the switch has been disabled, and is injured when a piece of wood is thrown back at him by the blade.

   c. James, an experienced mason, is working on a scaffold three stories above the street, putting the brick facade on a new building. When he goes to break for lunch, he remembers that another worker borrowed the ladder that he had used to climb the scaffold, but has not returned it. Impatient to get to lunch, he starts to climb down the angled supports of the scaffolding, and is injured when he slips off.

   d. Dobbs sees a small child playing obliviously in the path of a driver backing out of a driveway without looking. He rushes to rescue the child and is hit by the car.

Risk Twist

13. Story and Holmes attend a football game together. They have a few beers. Well, they have *quite* a few beers. After the game they get in Story's car, and Story drives off. Ten minutes later they have an accident, when Cardozo pulls out of a side street without looking and broadsides Story's car. Holmes sues Cardozo.

   a. What brand of assumption of risk is implicated by Holmes's conduct?
   b. What effect should his conduct have on his right to recover from Cardozo?

EXPLANATIONS

False Assumptions

1. As the Introduction states, parties can assume risks, including the risk of another's negligence, by an express agreement to do so. And the

language in this release clause is certainly broad enough to cover the accident Killey suffered, since it specifically refers to injury "from any source whatever" and includes negligence of the operator. If Killey has accepted the release clause, he would be barred.

However, the gravamen of assumption of risk is the plaintiff's choice to assume the risks. Courts are wary of applying the doctrine of express assumption unless the party clearly chose to accept the risks that were being allocated to her. Killey will argue that he did not assume the risk of injury because he never knowingly agreed to the terms of the release. Since the terms were placed in fine print on the back of the lift ticket, where most people would not even read them, the court is likely to agree. See Restatement (Second) of Torts §496B cmt. c: "it must appear that the terms were in fact brought home to him and understood by him, before it can be found that he has accepted them." See also Restatement (Third) of Torts: Apportionment of Liability §2, cmt. d (size of print a factor in determining whether release is enforceable).

2.   Clearly not. While he has assumed many of the risks of skiing itself by signing this form, it contains no language assuming the risk of negligent maintenance of the facility. The purchaser would not contemplate such negligence as one of the inherent hazards of skiing. In fact, by enumerating various natural risks, the form tends to confirm that other risks, such as negligent maintenance of the equipment, were not within the contemplation of the clause. Consequently, because the language does not clearly include this risk, Killey has not assumed it.

3.   This is an interesting problem. On the one hand, Gavin has expressly agreed to assume responsibility for injuries resulting from skydiving, and Freeflight provided the service with an understanding that this allocation of the risks would protect it from liability. On the other hand, if assumption of the risk turns on knowing acceptance of the risk, Gavin did not assume this risk, since he did not realize (whether he should have or not) that ear problems might result.

This case would likely turn on the basic contracts concept of the intent of the parties. If it is clear from the language of the release and the circumstances that Gavin understood that he was assuming the risk of *any* injury, anticipated or not, the release would probably be enforced. Express assumption usually honors the parties' choice in allocating the risk. If the parties clearly allocated this one to Gavin, he is likely to be barred by his express assumption of it, even though he did not know what the risk was. See Restatement (Second) of Torts §496D cmt. a (plaintiff may expressly assume unknown risk if agreement so intends); Prosser & Keeton at 489 (plaintiff may "consent to take his chances as to unknown conditions").

Perhaps, as a matter of good lawyering, Freeflight's counsel should draft the release to reveal as many potential risks as possible. A release that specifically refers to the risk of ear damage clearly demonstrates that this risk was within the parties' contemplation at the time of contracting. (A release that described in detail all the risks involved might, of course, have a depressing effect on business.) The release should also specify that the plaintiff assumes the risks of the activity, even if he is not aware of them. This strengthens the argument that the plaintiff has chosen to accept all the risks, not just the ones she expected to encounter.

Negative Implications

4.   Primary assumption applies where the defendant has not breached a duty of due care, since the risk that injures the plaintiff is inseparable from the activity itself. The defendant is not liable in such cases, because it is not negligent, even though the activity it offered involves some risk. Primary assumption would bar Killey from suing if he were injured from the inherent risks of skiing, such as patches of icy snow, sharp drops in expert trails, trees along the side of the trail, bare spots, and others. But he does not assume the risk that the chair lift will fall off the cable. That is not an inherent risk of the sport if it is conducted with due care.

5.   The issue here is whether negligent acts of other skiers are an inherent risk of skiing that skiers assume by engaging in the sport. I would think so. Just as a quarterback can expect some overzealous hits, and a jockey some aggressive jockeying for position on the track, a skier should expect that there will be a few overconfident hot dogs on the expert slopes who will fail to keep a proper lookout or attempt maneuvers beyond their skills. It appears likely that, by choosing to ski the expert slopes, Killey assumes the risk of this accident. Stated another (and, I think, clearer) way, it is likely that Big Mountain is not negligent in conducting a ski operation, even though it entails this risk.

6a.   The question here is whether primary implied assumption of the risk applies, that is, was Circle-R negligent for offering horseback riding even though it entails a risk that a snake might cause a horse to start and throw a rider? If such events are rare, and generally do not result in riders being thrown, it may be reasonable to offer horseback riding to the public despite this risk. Thus, the basic issue is the traditional Hand-formula question as to whether, in light of the magnitude of the risk and the extent of injury to be anticipated from snake-starting, Circle-R was reasonable to offer the activity (or to offer it without some special precaution, such as a snake eradication program along its trails).

     Although I don't know much about horseback riding — or snakes — I'll guess that Rogers's accident is a pretty rare occurrence, so that Circle-R would not be deemed negligent for subjecting its patrons to this risk. If so, many courts would say that Rogers "assumes the risk" of snakes, and deny him recovery for his injury. But it would be analytically clearer to reach the same result on the simple ground that Circle-R was not negligent.

b.   If Rogers didn't know about the snake-starting risk, how can he assume it? If the premise underlying assumption of the risk is *subjective acceptance* of the risk, the doctrine shouldn't apply to Rogers, and he ought to recover.

However, in primary implied assumption cases, the real premise for denying recovery is lack of negligence, not the plaintiff's choice. Plaintiffs like Rogers lose because Circle-R's conduct was reasonable, not because they consciously accepted the risk of snakes. Similarly, a first-time skier hit by another would doubtless be denied recovery, even if she did not understand the risk of a collision.

Although this makes sense, the case law often obscures the point by using assumption-of-the-risk language, which seems to require that the plaintiff actually perceives and appreciates the risk. Rogers will rely on such language to argue that he isn't barred if he didn't actually know the risk. The confusion in this area is such that he might even win on this argument. But, analytically, he shouldn't.

c.   If the issue here is whether Circle-R acted reasonably in offering horseback riding, it can raise the issue in its answer simply by denying negligence; there is no need to plead an "affirmative defense" of assumption of the risk in this type of case. Indeed, pleading "no negligence" has an important advantage to Circle-R, since, if the issue is negligence, *Rogers* will bear the burden of proof on it; whereas, if the issue is an affirmative defense, Circle-R will.

However, careful counsel, knowing of the confusion in this area, will doubtless throw in assumption of the risk as a defense, out of concern that—if the judge thinks of it as a defense—they will have waived the issue. Thus, the confusion gets perpetuated.

Taking Negligence to Newcastle

7a.   Hermit has not expressly agreed in advance to assume the risk here. Nor is this implied primary assumption: Drunk driving is not an inherent risk of accepting a ride in a car. This is an example of secondary implied assumption of the risk. Hermit becomes aware of negligent conduct of Driver which poses a risk of injury to him, yet, fully appreciating the risk, chooses to encounter it. More specifically, this is *unreasonable* secondary assumption since Hermit need not get to town immediately and should have waited for a more suitable chauffeur.

b.   At common law, assumption of a risk barred recovery entirely, even if the risk was negligently created by the defendant. The gist of the action, as reiterated before, was consent and free choice, and here Hermit made a misguided but informed choice to proceed despite the risk. The common law "honored" Hermit's right to choose by barring him from recovering from Driver.

Since Hermit's choice was unreasonable, it would constitute contributory negligence as well. At common law Hermit would have been barred from recovery by either defense.

c.   Under most comparative negligence regimes, Hermit's unreasonable decision would be treated as negligent conduct, and would be compared to the negligence of the defendant in assessing liability. If, for example, the jury concluded that Hermit was 33 percent responsible for his injuries for riding with a drunk driver, they would reduce his damages by 33 percent. Thus, unreasonable secondary assumption reduces damages under most comparative negligence statutes, but no longer acts as a complete bar. But, as the Introduction indicates, a few states continue to treat it as a full defense analogous to consent.

8.   Hillary clearly is negligent for driving with defective brakes; he would, for example, be liable to the driver of the other car in this case. But Farmer has *expressly* assumed the risk in this case. Hillary has no duty to take Farmer into town, but has offered to do so if Farmer is willing to accept the risk of injury due to the defective condition of the brakes. The principle of free choice says parties can make such arrangements to assume the risk. Farmer has agreed in advance not to hold Hillary liable for the risks to which he is exposed. While express assumption is usually by contract, it need not be, and consideration is not essential to make the assumption binding. See Restatement (Second) of Torts §496B cmt. a.

It is true that this case looks a good deal like reasonable implied secondary assumption as well. Hillary is negligent for driving with defective brakes, and Farmer decides, for a compelling reason, to take the risk. However, since Farmer agrees in advance to relieve Hillary of a duty of care, it is best classified as express assumption. Note that the characterization makes a big difference in the outcome of the case: If it is express assumption, Farmer will be barred; if it is secondary implied assumption, he probably would not be. See Example 9c.

9a.   This is probably an example of reasonable implied secondary assumption of the risk. Secondary assumption arises when the defendant negligently subjects the plaintiff to a risk, and the plaintiff becomes aware of the risk yet chooses to encounter it anyway. Leaving aside any applicable guest statute, Hillary owes Farmer a duty of due care, and violates that duty by giving him a ride in a car with faulty brakes. However, when Farmer becomes aware of the risk posed by Hillary's negligence, he stays aboard because of the exigency caused by his injury. Although he signals no agreement to Hillary, he accepts the risk for his own sufficient reasons.

b.   Assuming that Farmer's decision was reasonable under the circumstances, contributory negligence would not bar his recovery. However, in a jurisdiction that applied common law principles, he would still be barred by assumption of the risk, since he understood the risk and chose to encounter it. The basis for the defense was individual choice, whether reasonable or unreasonable. So long as the choice was made with full understanding of the risk, the defense applied. Note the symmetry under the common law approach between express assumption and reasonable secondary implied assumption. Whether the plaintiff agreed in advance to take on the risk, as in Example 8, or impliedly agreed by staying on board, as here, the result was to bar recovery despite the defendant's negligence.

The best argument for avoiding assumption of the risk in a case like this would be that Farmer did not fully comprehend the nature of the risk posed by the brakes. Because secondary assumption turns on appreciation of the specific risk that causes injury, the defense only applies if the risk is fully understood. Many courts have rescued plaintiffs from the assumption of risk defense by holding that they did not appreciate the *exact* risk that led to the injury. See, e.g., *Gault v. May,* 79 Cal. Rptr. 858 (Cal. Ct. App. 1969) (although plaintiff was aware that roller skate pulled to left, she did not know of defective wheel, which caused injury). Here, Farmer might argue that, though he realized there was *something* wrong with the brakes, he did not realize that they would lock completely, and therefore did not assume the risk.

c.   The result in a comparative negligence jurisdiction depends on the way the jurisdiction treats reasonable secondary assumption. As the Introduction indicates, most states conclude that reasonable secondary assumption of the risk should not reduce or bar the plaintiff's claim. In these states, Farmer would recover fully, despite his understanding of the risk posed by the brakes. In some states, however, secondary assumption — whether reasonable or unreasonable — remains a complete defense. In these states, Farmer would lose, because he chose to encounter the risk, even if that was a reasonable choice.

A court in a comparative negligence state might even hold that Farmer is barred by reasonable assumption of the risk, even though Hermit would not be barred in Example 7. The logic would be that the comparative negligence statute specifies that unreasonable assumption of risk be treated as a form of plaintiff's fault, which reduces but does not bar her recovery. But reasonable assumption is not negligence, and therefore is not addressed by the comparative negligence statute. Hence, the court is still free to analyze it as a form of voluntary acceptance of the risk, a separate defense based on choice.

This last approach seems particularly dubious. It seems anomalous that Hermit should recover substantial (albeit reduced) damages while Farmer takes nothing. In addition, if reasonable assumption of risk is a bar, Farmer's lawyer is placed in the bizarre position of trying to prove that Farmer was negligent, but only a little: Since unreasonable assumption of risk is treated as damage-reducing conduct under the comparative negligence statute, a minimally negligent plaintiff will recover most of her damages. But if plaintiff argues that her conduct was completely reasonable, and the jury agrees, she recovers nothing!

Judge Fudd Assumes the Risk

10. Although the comparative negligence statute here appears to broadly eliminate assumption of risk, it must be read in light of the purposes of the comparative negligence statute and the various meanings of assumption of risk. This provision almost certainly was intended to make the plaintiff's choice to encounter a negligently created risk a damage-reducing factor rather than a complete bar to recovery. In other words, it calls for treating the *defense* of secondary implied assumption like negligence by the plaintiff.

However, Buckeye's argument is not really based on the *defense* of assumption of the risk. Buckeye is arguing that it was not negligent to offer donkey basketball, even though it entails a small risk of injury. In other words, its argument is based on *primary* implied assumption of the risk, or, more clearly, the simple argument that Buckeye was not negligent. This is not a "defense" at all, but challenges the plaintiff's ability to establish an element of her prima facie case — breach of the duty of due care.

A number of comparative negligence statutes include language abolishing the "defense" of assumption of the risk. See, e.g., Mass. Gen. Laws ch. 231, §85. Only by fully understanding the different ways in which the phrase "assumption of the risk" has been used can you clearly evaluate the effect — and the limits — of a provision such as this. Here, if Buckeye's counsel had phrased his argument in terms of due care, he could have avoided confusing Judge Fudd with assumption of the risk concepts entirely, and sidestepped any implication that his argument was based on a "defense" that had been abolished.

A Little Knowledge of a Dangerous Thing

11. In a sense, Pearson assumes a risk by passing on the curve. He knows a car could be coming, and that if so a collision may result. But the risk here is general. If recognizing that an act is unreasonably risky constitutes assumption of the risk, virtually any conscious negligent act would qualify. A carpenter who works too close to a bulldozer would assume the risk of being hit. A window washer who leans too far out would assume the risk of a fall. A driver who feels tired would assume the risk of an accident from falling asleep.

The cases suggest that the plaintiff must be aware of a more specific risk in order to assume it. Certainly, Pearson would assume the risk of a collision if he saw Henderson coming and could see that he was speeding. He probably would assume it even if he saw Henderson but didn't know that he was speeding. In either case, he perceives a very specific danger and decides to chance it. This is qualitatively different from realizing that the potential for danger exists and that it would be wiser to avoid it by being more cautious.

Of course, in a comparative negligence jurisdiction that treats secondary implied assumption of the risk as a form of negligence by the plaintiff, it won't be necessary to decide whether the risk here is specific enough to be assumed. Even if it is, Pearson's choice is treated as negligence, which reduces but does not bar his recovery. Since the effect is the same whether dubbed assumption of the risk or negligence, the court can avoid the difficult task of characterizing it as one or the other.

Legal Shape-Sorting

12a.   The owner is negligent to rent out a cabin with dangerous stairs, so Mansfield can probably make a prima facie case for liability. However, the owner will assert as a defense that Mansfield assumed the risk by using the stairs anyway.

The reasonable person would probably not turn around and go home just because the stair lacked a railing; likely she would just be a bit more careful negotiating the stairs. Thus, this is probably reasonable secondary assumption by Mansfield. Whether Mansfield's decision bars recovery will depend on how the jurisdiction treats reasonable assumption of risk.

b.   This is not assumption of risk at all. Bohlen did not knowingly decide to take the risk of operating the saw without the switch; he never knew it existed or appreciated the risk of using the saw without it. He may be contributorily negligent for failing to learn more about a dangerous power tool before using it, but he has not deliberately chosen to encounter the risk that caused his injury.

c.   This is unreasonable secondary assumption of the risk. The other worker was negligent in failing to return the ladder, but James has deliberately encountered the resulting unreasonable risk. As an experienced mason, James is aware that it is dangerous to climb on these supports, but he decides to do so anyway rather than wait for someone to return with the ladder. This was an unreasonable choice, a negligent choice, but it was also knowing assumption of the risk. In most comparative negligence jurisdictions, it would be treated as a damage-reducing factor like other negligence by the plaintiff.

d.   You may have already come across the "rescue doctrine" in Torts class. The doctrine holds that injury to a rescuer is foreseeable, and therefore the negligence of the person who made the rescue necessary is a proximate cause of resulting injury to the rescuer. See, e.g., *Wagner v. Intl. Ry. Co.*, 133 N.E. 437 (N.Y. 1921). But why aren't these cases resolved under assumption of risk doctrine instead? They appear to be the very paradigm of reasonable implied secondary assumption of the risk: The plaintiff becomes aware of a risk negligently created by the defendant, and makes an eminently reasonable choice to encounter it.

A few courts *have* barred recovery to a rescuer on the ground of assumption of the risk. See, e.g., *Siglow v. Smart*, 539 N.E.2d 636 (Ohio Ct. App. 1987). See also *Eckert v. Long Island R.R. Co.*, 43 N.Y. 502 (1871) (Allen, J., dissenting) (arguing that rescuer should be barred by assumption of the risk). The Second Restatement avoids this harsh result, however, by concluding that rescue is not "voluntary":

> The plaintiff's acceptance of a risk is not voluntary if the defendant's tortious conduct has left him no reasonable alternative course of conduct in order to ... avert harm to himself or another.

Restatement (Second) of Torts §496E(2)(a). This is a laudable result, but it raises a fundamental question about the meaning of secondary assumption of the risk. If Dobbs's choice here is not voluntary, is a plaintiff's choice to confront a negligently created risk ever voluntary? In most cases, the plaintiff does not *prefer* to be confronted with the risk negligently created by the defendant: She would rather that the defendant had not been negligent in the first place. Here Dobbs would prefer not to have confronted the risk created by the driver's negligence. Similarly, in the vacation home example, the vacationer would have preferred that the stairs have a railing.

The plaintiff in these cases reluctantly goes forward to meet the danger, but in a sense her decision is not "voluntary," since she would prefer not to have been put to an unpalatable choice of alternatives in the first place. See K. Simons, Assumption of Risk and Consent in the Law of Torts: A Theory of Full Preference, 67 B.U. L. Rev. 213, 218-224 (1987), which argues that the doctrine should only apply where the plaintiff "fully prefers" to encounter the risk created by the defendant, rather than being placed in a position of having to choose between several unpalatable alternatives.

Risk Twist

13a. Holmes deliberately chose to drive with Story, even though he knew he had been drinking heavily. As in Example 7, this would be secondary implied assumption of the risk. That is, after recognizing Story's negligent conduct, Holmes has elected—by getting into the car with him—to take the risk created by it.

b.   In most comparative negligence jurisdictions, a plaintiff's conscious, unreasonable choice to encounter a risk like this would be treated as a form of negligence, which would reduce the plaintiff's recovery. However, Holmes's conduct should have no effect on his recovery in this case. Holmes unreasonably chose to accept the risk of negligence by Story in driving while intoxicated. But Holmes was not injured by that risk—as far as the example indicates, Story's driving was fine. Holmes was injured by negligent driving *by Cardozo*. Thus, whether we call Holmes's conduct negligence in riding with Story or voluntary acceptance of that risk, that conduct was not the proximate cause of his injury. It isn't negligent to drive with a drunk driver because *some other driver* might drive carelessly and cause a collision. Consequently, Holmes's choice should not affect his recovery from Cardozo at all.

23

Casting the Second Stone: Comparative Negligence

Introduction

Somewhere in the Bible lies the telling maxim: "Let he who is without sin cast the first stone." A rich understanding of human experience lies behind this phrase; for few of us are so pure that we can forswear responsibility for life's vicissitudes or piously condemn others without considering our own failings.

For many years, the common law refused to account for this basic truth in tort cases. The contributory negligence doctrine reflected the absolutist moral view that the plaintiff who was blameless was entitled to full vindication in a court of law, but that one who shared the taint of sin in any degree must be sent forth to languish in the wilderness. Today we are less pious and more pragmatic about accident causation. This more "modern" view is reflected in the widespread adoption of comparative negligence, which replaces the all-or-nothing approach of contributory negligence with a system that reduces a party's damages to account for her fault.

I hesitate to call this a "modern" view, because there is nothing new about it, really. Comparative negligence was apparently known to those most practical of lawmakers, the Romans, and has prevailed widely in civil law countries since the nineteenth century.[1] American admiralty practice also adopted a rough form of comparative negligence: Under the "equal

---

1. See E. Turk, Comparative Negligence on the March, 28 Chi.-Kent L. Rev. 189, 239-244 (1950).

division rule," if two ships were at fault in a collision, the court divided the damages equally, regardless of their relative degrees of fault. Suppose, for example, that the Queen Mary collided with the Queen Elizabeth, and sustained $200,000 in damage. If both ships were partly at fault in causing the collision, the owners of the Queen Mary would recover $100,000. This was true even if the Queen Mary's skipper was 1 percent at fault and the Queen Elizabeth's was 99 percent to blame. This may seem like a crude system, but it was a substantial retreat from contributory negligence: Under contributory negligence, the Queen Mary's owners would have recovered nothing at all.

Dissatisfaction with the all-or-nothing feature of contributory negligence also led several states to experiment with a *slight/gross* comparative negligence system. Under an early Nebraska statute, for example, a plaintiff whose negligence was "slight" compared to that of the defendant was allowed to recover, but her recovery was reduced "in proportion to the amount of contributory negligence attributable to the plaintiff." Neb. Rev. Stat. §25-21,185. This provision changed the result in those cases in which contributory negligence operated most harshly: where the plaintiff was only minimally negligent. However, even under the slight/gross system, if the jury found that plaintiff's negligence was more than "slight," the traditional contributory negligence rule applied, and plaintiff lost entirely.[2]

Such early systems showed that the contributory negligence rule was not immutable, but it was not until about 1965 that this trickle of reform turned into a flood. Since that date, most states have replaced contributory negligence with one form or another of comparative negligence. In some states the change has come from the courts—since contributory negligence is a judicial doctrine, some courts have been willing to abandon it by judicial decision. In many, however, comparative negligence has been introduced by statute. At this writing, only four states retain the contributory negligence doctrine.

Pure Comparative Negligence

Most states have adopted either *pure comparative negligence* or several common variations (called "modified comparative negligence"), which are described below. Under pure comparative negligence, advocated by most scholars, an injured party may recover, regardless of her degree of fault, but her recovery is reduced by her percentage of fault. For example, the Washington (state) statute provides in part:

> In an action based on fault seeking to recover damages for injury or
> death to person or harm to property, any contributory fault chargeable

---

2. This Nebraska statute was replaced by a modified comparative negligence statute for cases arising after February 8, 1992. See Nebraska Laws 1992, L.B. 262, §12.

to the claimant diminishes proportionately the amount awarded as compensatory damages for an injury attributable to the claimant's contributory fault, but does not bar recovery.

Wash. Rev. Code Ann §4.22.005. Assume that the Queen Mary's skipper was 40 percent at fault in causing the collision. Under a pure comparative negligence statute like Washington's, the owners of the Queen Mary would recover, but their damages would be reduced by 40 percent to reflect the Queen Mary's contribution to the accident. Thus, they would recover 60 percent of their damages, or $120,000. If the Queen Mary was only 1 percent at fault, they would recover 99 percent of their damages. If the Queen Mary was 99 percent at fault and suffered a million dollars in damages, its owners would recover $10,000 (1 percent of $1,000,000).

While there is a pleasing symmetry about pure comparative negligence, it has had its critics too. It may not seem "fair" to pay damages to one who is the overwhelming cause of his own misfortune. If the Queen Mary's skipper was 99 percent at fault, the Queen Elizabeth's owners may be understandably reluctant to pay its owners a penny, much less $10,000, which is one million pennies.

Modified Comparative Negligence

Many states have compromised between the extremes of contributory negligence on the one hand and pure comparative negligence on the other. The slight/gross system was an early example, but it proved hard to apply, due to the difficulty in defining "slight" negligence and controlling jury verdicts based on such an amorphous standard. A more popular approach, particularly in states that have switched to comparative negligence by statute rather than judicial decision, has been *modified* comparative negligence. Modified comparative negligence systems, like the slight/gross system, bar the claimant from any recovery if her negligence reaches a certain level, but they set the level at the point where the plaintiff's negligence either equals or exceeds that of the defendant.

The Kansas comparative negligence statute, for example, provides that a party's negligence will not bar her recovery

> if such party's negligence was less than the causal negligence of the party or parties against whom claim for recovery is made, but the award of damages to any party in such action shall be diminished in proportion to the amount of negligence attributed to such party.

Kan. Stat. Ann. §60-258a(a). This statute is typical of the *not-as-great-as* form of modified comparative negligence. Under this approach, the plaintiff recovers her damages, reduced by her percentage of fault, so long as her fault was not as great as that of the defendant or defendants. A plaintiff who was 45 percent at fault would recover 55 percent of her damages under this type of statute, but a plaintiff who was 70 percent negligent would recover nothing. In the frequent scenario in which the jury concludes that the parties were equally at fault, the plaintiff loses, since her fault is as great as that of the defendant.

The other common system of modified comparative negligence allows the plaintiff to recover reduced damages so long as her negligence was *not greater than* that of the defendant:

> Contributory negligence shall not bar recovery in an action by any person or his legal representative to recover damages for negligence resulting in death or injury to person or property, if such negligence was not greater than the negligence of the person against whom recovery is sought or was not greater than the combined negligence of the persons against whom recovery is sought. Any damages sustained shall be diminished by the percentage sustained of negligence attributable to the person recovering.

N.J. Stat. Ann. §2A:15-5.1. This approach is the same as the not-as-great-as system in every case except where the plaintiff's and defendant's negligence is equal. While the plaintiff loses in the 50/50 case in a not-as-great-as state, she recovers 50 percent of her damages in a not-greater-than state like New Jersey. Since juries frequently conclude that the parties are equally at fault, this can change the result in quite a few cases.

Modified comparative negligence is perhaps less logically defensible than pure comparative negligence. Suppose that Hobbes is 51 percent at fault in causing an accident and suffers $100,000 in damages. Suppose also that Mill, the other driver, is 49 percent at fault, suffers $100,000 in damages and counterclaims for his injuries. In a modified comparative negligence jurisdiction, Hobbes recovers nothing; he will absorb all of his own loss, and pay Mill $51,000 as well (since Mill is only 49 percent at fault and thus entitled to recover his damages reduced by 49 percent). This disparity in recovery hardly seems justified on the basis of a 2 percent difference in the negligence of the parties. By contrast, under pure comparative negligence, Hobbes would recover $49,000 from Mill, and Mill would recover $51,000 from Hobbes.[3]

Despite examples like this, most states that have adopted comparative negligence by statute have chosen one of the modified forms. Perhaps the best explanation, other than pure political compromise between contributory and comparative negligence, is that of a sponsor of the New Hampshire statute, whose "sandlot instinct" rebelled against allowing recovery to a party who is primarily to blame for her own injury.[4]

---

3. See R. Keeton, Comment on *Maki v. Frelk*, 21 Vand. L. Rev. 906, 911 (1968).

4. Nixon, The Actual "Legislative Intent" Behind New Hampshire's Comparative Negligence Statute, 12 N.H.B.J. 17, 24-25 (1969).

Under both pure and modified systems, the seeming precision of the calculations is obviously illusory. It is people — usually 12 ordinary people — who apply the comparative negligence rules to actual cases. Affixing exact percentages of negligence in complex accidents at a trial four or five years after the fact is a dubious business. However, as Dean Prosser persuasively notes, any system of assigning damages in negligence cases is inherently imprecise:

> [A] division of the plaintiff's damages [on the basis of comparative fault] is at least more accurate than one based on the arbitrary conclusion that 100 percent of the responsibility rests with the plaintiff and none whatever with the defendant, or, if the last clear chance is applicable, 100 percent with the defendant and none with the plaintiff — both of which are demonstrably wrong. Nor is such an estimate in itself any more foolish, or more difficult, than the one which assigns $2,000 as fair value and compensation for the pain of a broken leg, or the humiliation of a disfigured nose, to say nothing of estimates based on a prognosis of speed of recovery, future earnings or permanent disability.

W. Prosser, Comparative Negligence, 51 Mich. L. Rev. 465, 475 (1953).

Who Is Compared?

Some practical problems arise in applying comparative negligence to specific cases, especially under modified comparative negligence. A basic question is who gets compared to whom. For example, assume that Rousseau's car collides with Locke's and Rousseau suffers $100,000 in damages. He sues Locke for negligent driving and the city for leaving a pothole in the road, which contributed to causing the accident. At trial, the jury concludes that Rousseau was 45 percent at fault, Locke 15 percent, and the city 40 percent. In a modified comparative negligence jurisdiction (of either type) Rousseau will lose if his fault is compared to that of each defendant *individually*, since his is greater than either of theirs. However, if his fault is compared to the *total negligence* of the defendants together, he can still recover 55 percent of his damages, since 45 percent is less than their combined total of 55 percent.

Some states take the harder line on this issue, comparing the plaintiff's negligence to that of each defendant individually. These states bar the plaintiff from recovering from any defendant who is less negligent, though he may recover from others who are more negligent. Most modified comparative negligence states, however, compare the plaintiff's negligence to the combined negligence of the defendants. See V. Schwartz, Comparative Negligence, §3.05[c][i] (4th ed. 2002).

There are cogent arguments for both approaches. Comparing Rousseau's negligence to all defendants combined seems unfair since Locke will be held liable to Rousseau for $55,000 (55 percent of $100,000), even though he was only 15 percent to blame and Rousseau's fault was three times greater. That result looks like pure comparative negligence, since a party more at fault recovers from one less at fault. On the other hand, comparing the plaintiff's negligence to each defendant's individually places a plaintiff at a disadvantage if there are multiple parties: She may lose even if her negligence is substantially less than 50 percent. It also leaves defendants who are found more negligent than the plaintiff holding the bag for others who contributed to the accident but were less negligent than the plaintiff. For example, if Rousseau were 35 percent at fault, the city 40 percent, and Locke 25 percent, the city would be liable for 65 percent of Rousseau's damages (since it is more negligent than him), while Locke would not be liable at all.

What Is Compared?

Another basic issue in applying comparative negligence is what is compared among the parties: is it the *negligence* of each party, or the degree to which each party's negligence *caused* the plaintiff's injury? This problem is conceptually difficult: How do you distinguish causation from the extent of negligence? It is hard to think about degrees of causation: Either the negligence contributed to the accident or it didn't. Suppose, for example, that Montesquieu makes a left turn without putting on his turn indicator, and is hit head on by Milton, who is doing 75 m.p.h. in a 35 m.p.h. zone. Most jurors would find Milton more to blame, but that both acts equally "caused" the harm. If the goal of comparative negligence is to place the greater burden on the more culpable party, it seems that Milton should be found substantially more responsible than Montesquieu.

Changing the example a bit, assume that Montesquieu was driving while severely intoxicated and made the same left turn without looking, leading to the same accident with the speeding Milton. On these facts, as in the first example, both parties contributed to causing the accident, but the relative culpability of the parties is much more nearly equal, and most juries would ascribe a higher percentage of fault to Montesquieu than in the first example.

Dean Prosser is emphatically of the view that it is the degrees of negligence of the parties that is compared. See W. Prosser, Comparative Negligence, 51 Mich. L. Rev. 465, 481-482 (1953). Many statutes appear to take this position, since they require the jury to consider the comparative "fault" or "negligence" of the parties. However, the Uniform Comparative Fault Act explicitly requires the jury to consider both:

> In determining the percentages of fault, the trier of fact shall consider both the nature of the conduct of each party at fault and the

extent of the causal relation between the conduct and the damages claimed.[5]

As a practical matter, it probably doesn't matter in most cases which approach is taken. Assessing fault is not a scientific process; the jury makes an instinctive judgment about the culpability of each party without focusing on the technical distinction between negligence and causation. However, one thing can be said with certainty: If the plaintiff's negligence was not an actual cause of the injury the jury should not consider it. If the plaintiff is hit from behind while stopped at a light, irrelevant negligence in failing to get her brakes checked should not reduce her recovery.

Caveat: A Fundamental Fundamental of Comparative Negligence

A final, fundamental point should be made here, and it is one that is easily missed. Comparative negligence regimes allow a plaintiff who is partly at fault to recover reduced damages, and provide a formula for calculating those reduced damages. But the adoption of comparative negligence, by itself, does *not* change the basic rule of joint and several liability, under which each defendant is liable for the entire judgment awarded to the plaintiff. Nor does adoption of comparative negligence, of itself, change the basic contribution rules governing the redistribution of damages among the defendants.

For example, if Rousseau recovers from Locke and the city in the example given earlier, he will be entitled to 55 percent of his damages, or $55,000. If traditional joint and several liability principles are still followed in the relevant jurisdiction, both Locke and the city would be liable to Rousseau for $55,000. Put another way, the adoption of comparative negligence does *not* mean that the plaintiff's judgment will be apportioned to the defendants in proportion to their negligence. In the Rousseau case, the city will not be ordered to pay $40,000 of the judgment, and Locke only $15,000. Judgment will enter against each for $55,000, because, under joint and several liability, each defendant who is liable to the plaintiff is liable for the entire judgment. Rousseau will be entitled to collect $55,000 from either Locke or the city. If Locke pays he can seek contribution from the city, or vice versa, under applicable principles of contribution. See Chapter 20.

---

5. Uniform Comparative Fault Act, §2(b), 12 U.L.A. 45 (Supp. 1994). The Uniform Comparative Fault Act is a model act, written by the National Conference of Commissioners on Uniform State Laws, an organization devoted to encouraging uniform state legislation on issues of general applicability. See also Restatement (Third) of Torts: Apportionment of Liability §8 (also noting relevance of causation in assessing percentages of fault).

Since the adoption of comparative negligence, many states have also changed the traditional principles of joint and several liability and contribution. Chapter 24 explores some of the changes to contribution principles and joint and several liability that have been prompted by the adoption of comparative negligence. But it is important to understand that the adoption of comparative negligence *does not in itself change these principles,* and some states that have adopted comparative negligence still apply traditional approaches to both contribution and joint and several liability.

The following examples illustrate the application of the various types of comparative negligence to actual cases. Assume in analyzing them that joint and several liability applies. After the examples and explanations, there is a short discussion of special verdicts, with several examples to illustrate how comparative negligence issues are usually submitted to the jury.

EXAMPLES

Comparing Comparative Negligence

1.   Paine is injured when his hand is caught in a printing press operated by Burke. He sues Burke for negligence. The jury finds that Paine has suffered $60,000 in damages, and that each party was 50 percent at fault.
    a. How much would Paine recover in a jurisdiction that applies a not-as-great-as form of comparative negligence?
    b. How much would Paine recover in a not-greater-than jurisdiction?
    c. How much would Paine recover under a pure comparative negligence approach?
    d. How much would Paine recover in a jurisdiction that retains contributory negligence?

2.   Assume that Paine sued both Burke and Calkins, who had recently repaired the press. The jury finds that Paine was 65 percent negligent in causing his own injuries, that Burke was 15 percent negligent and that Calkins was 20 percent negligent. Paine's damages are again $60,000.
    a. Would Burke or Calkins be liable to Paine if the suit were brought under pure comparative negligence?
    b. How much would Burke or Calkins be liable for, if anything?
    c. Assume that the accident takes place in a state that applies the not-as-great-as approach. Who would be liable to Paine?
    d. Who would be liable under the not-greater-than approach?

3.   Assume that the jury found Paine $33^{1}/_{3}$ percent negligent, Calkins $33^{1}/_{3}$ percent negligent, and Burke $33^{1}/_{3}$ percent negligent. Paine's damages are again $60,000.
    a. How much would Paine recover from each defendant under pure comparative negligence?

  b. How much would he recover under the not-as-great-as version of modified comparative negligence?

  c. How much would he recover under the not-greater-than approach?

Judgments, More or Less

4.   Descartes sues Mill, Calkins, and Newton for injuries arising from a boating accident. The jury concludes that Descartes was 25 percent at fault, Mill was 10 percent at fault, Calkins was 25 percent at fault, and Newton was 40 percent at fault. They assess Descartes's damages at $100,000. Assume that the suit is brought in a not-as-great-as jurisdiction which compares the negligence of the plaintiff to that of each defendant individually.

  a. Who may Descartes recover from?

  b. Will Descartes recover $75,000, $61,538, or $40,000?

  c. Assume that the applicable comparative negligence statute allows recovery if the plaintiff's negligence was not as great as that of the defendant or defendants, and that the plaintiff's negligence is compared to the defendants as a group. Assume further that Newton is insolvent. How much could Descartes recover from Mill?

5.   Suppose, on the same facts, that Descartes had only sued Mill. How much, if anything, would he recover from her?

Judge Fudd Redux

6.   Pascal sues Hume for negligently dropping a board on him from a ladder. Hume claims that Pascal was also negligent, for philosophizing under the ladder during construction. The case is tried before the indomitable Fudd, who instructs the jury as follows:

> If you find that the plaintiff was negligent, then you must reduce the damages awarded in the proportion that the plaintiff's negligence bears to the defendant's.

The jury finds that Pascal suffered $60,000 in damages, that he was 20 percent at fault and that Hume was 80 percent at fault.

  a. How much should the jury award to Pascal under Judge Fudd's instruction?

  b. What is wrong with the instruction and how much did the error cost Pascal?

  c. What should the instruction be?

7.   Assume, on the facts of Example 6, that Pascal claims that Hume had the last clear chance to avoid the injury by warning him that the board was falling. In a contributory negligence jurisdiction, this, if proved, would require the jury to disregard Pascal's negligence. See generally Prosser & Keeton, 462-468. Should the judge instruct the jury to disregard

Pascal's negligence if they find that Hume had the last clear chance to avoid the accident?

8.   Assume that Hume was also injured in the foregoing fiasco, when Pascal jumped back, knocking over the ladder. He counterclaims against Pascal in the suit, and the jury assesses his damages at $200,000. They assign the same percentages of negligence to Pascal (20 percent) and to Hume (80 percent).

   a. What judgments would result in a contributory negligence jurisdiction?
   b. What judgments would result in a pure comparative negligence jurisdiction?

Comparing Apples and Outrages

9.   Hamilton, a tenant in the Philosophers' Corner condominium complex, was assaulted in his unit when Sly, a burglar, broke in through the front door. (Unfortunately, the lock was loose but Hamilton had not had it repaired.) Hamilton sues Spencer Security Co., the company that provided security for the complex, claiming that they failed to adequately patrol the premises.

   a. Assume that the case takes place in a jurisdiction that requires the jury to consider the fault of all tortfeasors, not just the parties before the court. What will Spencer Security argue should be done in apportioning fault?
   b. What is the best argument that the jury should be told to ignore Sly in apportioning fault?
   c. What is the best argument that the jury should be told to include Sly in apportioning fault?
   d. Why would Spencer care whether Sly is included in apportioning fault?

EXPLANATIONS

Comparing Comparative Negligence

1a.   Paine will not recover at all in a not-as-great-as jurisdiction, since his negligence was as great as that of Burke. This form of comparative negligence bars a plaintiff from recovery if her fault equals (or exceeds) the defendant's.

   b.   In a not-greater-than jurisdiction, Paine would recover $30,000. He is not barred from recovery, because his fault was not greater than Burke's. However, his damages will be reduced by his percentage of negligence (.50 × $60,000).

   c.   The result in a pure comparative negligence jurisdiction is the same as in the last example. Paine may recover but his fault reduces his recovery proportionally, to $30,000.

d.   Obviously, Paine would recover nothing in a contributory negligence jurisdiction, since his negligence contributed in part to causing the accident.

2a.   Both Burke and Calkins are liable to Paine under pure comparative negligence, since both were negligent. The fact that Paine was *more* negligent than either of them does not bar him from recovering under a pure comparative negligence statute. It will, however, reduce the amount he recovers proportionally.

b.   In a pure comparative negligence jurisdiction, Paine's judgment will be reduced by 65 percent to reflect his negligence. He will therefore recover $21,000 ($60,000 − (.65 × 60,000)). As the Introduction indicates, in many jurisdictions Burke and Calkins will both be liable to Paine for this amount, since they are jointly and severally liable for the damages their negligence contributed to causing. Even though each was considerably less at fault than Paine, each is liable to Paine for $21,000.

c.   Neither defendant is liable to Paine under the not-as-great-as form of comparative negligence, since Paine's negligence was greater than that of the defendants. This case, in which the plaintiff is primarily at fault, demonstrates the most marked difference between pure and modified comparative negligence systems. Under pure comparative negligence, plaintiff recovers, with a reduction for her percentage of negligence. Under modified comparative negligence, she loses entirely.

d.   Paine loses under the not-greater-than approach too, since her negligence was greater than that of the defendants. Both forms of modified comparative negligence bar the plaintiff from recovery if she is more than 50 percent at fault.

3a.   In a pure comparative negligence jurisdiction, Paine would recover his full damages, $60,000, reduced by his own percentage of fault, or $40,000 ($60,000 − (.333 × 60,000)). Each defendant would be liable for the $40,000 judgment, assuming that joint and several liability applies.[6]

b.   The answer here depends on whether the jurisdiction compares Paine's negligence to that of Burke and Calkins individually, or to the total negligence of all defendants. Most comparative negligence statutes provide for comparison to the combined negligence of all defendants. Under this approach, Paine's negligence would be compared to the combined negligence of Burke and Calkins. Paine would recover, since his negligence ($33\frac{1}{3}$ percent) is less than that of Burke and Calkins combined ($66\frac{2}{3}$ percent). His recovery would be reduced by $33\frac{1}{3}$ percent, to $40,000, to account for his negligence.

If the traditional rules of joint and several liability apply, Paine will get a judgment for $40,000 against each defendant. Note again, as in Example 1,

---

6. Of course, Paine could only collect a total of $40,000, as explained in Chapter 19, p. 441.

that pure and modified comparative negligence systems reduce Paine's damages in the same manner. The difference is that under modified comparative negligence, Paine loses entirely if his fault reaches a certain percentage.

If this case were tried in a state which applies the not-as-great-as approach, but compares the plaintiff's negligence to *each defendant individually*, Paine would lose entirely, since his fault is as great as that of each of the other defendants.

c.   Under the not-greater-than approach Paine would recover even if his negligence were compared to Locke's and Calkins's individually. Because his negligence is not greater than that of either defendant, he would recover a judgment for $40,000 against each defendant, assuming joint and several liability applies.

Judgments, More or Less

4a.   Since the case arises in a state that compares the plaintiff's negligence to each of the defendants individually, Descartes may recover against Newton, because his negligence was not as great as Newton's. But he cannot recover from Calkins, since his negligence equals Calkins's. And, *a fortiori,* he cannot recover from Mill, who was less at fault.

b.   Descartes will recover $75,000 from Newton, his total damages reduced by his own percentage of negligence. This may seem unfair to Newton, since it makes Newton bear the damages (adjusted for Descartes's negligence), even though two other parties who contributed to it are not liable at all. Wouldn't it be fairer to ignore the negligence of the other defendants, and compare Descartes's negligence (25 percent) to the combined total of his and Newton's (25 percent + 40 percent, or 65 percent), the only liable defendant? That's how I got the $61,538 figure, which reduces Descartes's damages by 25/65ths of $100,000. Alternatively, it may seem appropriate to make the one liable defendant pay only his percentage of negligence. This approach would yield the $40,000 figure.

Maybe that would be fairer, but many comparative negligence statutes do not change the basic principle that those defendants who are liable are liable for the plaintiff's damages, reduced only by her percentage of fault. They do *not* limit a defendant's liability to her own percentage of negligence. If the rule seems unfair, remember that under the common law approach, every defendant who was found negligent at all was *fully* liable to the plaintiff, even if other tortfeasors also contributed to the injury. In this case, Newton at least has his liability reduced to account for Descartes's contribution to the accident. But if Mill and Calkins are not liable (because they are less negligent than the plaintiff, and they are each compared to the plaintiff individually), Newton will end up holding the bag. He will have to pay the $75,000 judgment without getting any contribution from them (since they are not liable at all), even though their negligence also contributed to the accident.

c.   If we compare Descartes's negligence to that of the defendants combined, his is less than theirs (25 percent versus 75 percent). So he is entitled to a judgment for his damages, reduced by his percentage of negligence, against all three defendants. Descartes would get a judgment for $75,000 against each defendant.

Newton, the example assumes, can't pay. However, if joint and several liability applies, Descartes could collect $75,000 from Mill (or Calkins). After paying, Mill may be able to get some of the judgment back from Calkins, under contribution principles, but won't get any back from Newton. Thus, the example illustrates that a fairly minor player in the accident can end up bearing substantial liability, if the jurisdiction compares the plaintiff's negligence to that of the defendants as a group.

Under this version of modified comparative negligence, more plaintiffs will recover, since their negligence is less likely to exceed that of all defendants together. More defendants will end up splitting the damages, since they will be liable even if they were less negligent than the plaintiff. The judgment will likely then be spread among them through contribution.

5.   This example introduces a perplexing problem. In assessing percentages of negligence, should the jury only consider the parties to the lawsuit, or should they consider all persons who may have contributed to causing the accident? Here, if only Descartes and Mill are considered, and the jury must make their causal negligence add up to 100 percent, they might well assign Descartes more than 50 percent of the negligence. If they do, Descartes loses, even though, if all the actors involved in the accident were assigned percentages, his would drop below 50 percent.

Clearly, this gives Descartes an incentive to sue all potential defendants. By divvying up the liability among more parties, he will probably drive his percentage of fault down, which means his judgment will be bigger. And, if we assume the jurisdiction compares his negligence to that of the defendants as a group, by suing more defendants he increases the chance that their collective fault will exceed his. On the other hand, it is not always possible to sue all tortfeasors. Some may be bankrupt, or never identified (as in the case of a hit-and-run driver), or not subject to personal jurisdiction.

Approaches to this problem vary. Some courts have held that the plaintiff's negligence should only be compared to that of the parties before the court. See, e.g., *Shantigar Foundation v. Bear Mountain Builders*, 441 Mass. 131 (2004). This seems somewhat artificial — Calkins and Newton were involved in the accident, may have been the major causes of it, but the jury is supposed to act as though only Mill and Descartes caused it. This may also make Descartes's recovery turn in part on procedural factors, such as whether some tortfeasors have filed for bankruptcy or can't be sued in a particular state.

Other jurisdictions require the jury to consider all actors who may have contributed to the accident in assigning negligence percentages. See, e.g., *Allied Signal Inc. v. Fox,* 623 So. 2d 1180, 1182 (Fla. 1993). In these states, the parties before the court will litigate the negligence of other tortfeasors who are not. Although this can be awkward, it allows a more realistic assessment of the percentages of fault of the parties, since all contributors to the accident are considered. In other states, some absentees, but not others (such as immune tortfeasors) are considered. See generally V. Schwartz, Comparative Negligence, §15.05.[7]

Judge Fudd Redux

6a.   Under Judge Fudd's instruction, the jury should reduce Pascal's award by 20/80, or 25 percent, "the proportion that his negligence bears to the defendant's." He would recover $45,000.

b.   The judge's error has cost Pascal $3,000. The problem with the instruction is that it asks the jury to relate the plaintiff's negligence to the defendant's, rather than to the total negligence of all parties. The proper method would be to reduce Pascal's award by 20/100, to $48,000.

c.   Jury instructions frequently require the jury to "reduce the total amount of plaintiff's damages by the proportion or percentage of negligence attributable solely to the plaintiff." Illinois Pattern Jury Instructions, A45.05. It would be even clearer to instruct as follows:

> If you find that the plaintiff was negligent, then you must reduce the damages awarded to the plaintiff by the proportion which her negligence bears to the total negligence of all parties.

This instruction makes it clear to the jury that the plaintiff's negligence is to be compared to that of all parties, not just to that of the defendant.

7.   The issue posed here is whether the last clear chance doctrine applies in a jurisdiction that has changed over to comparative negligence. The last clear chance doctrine provided a means of avoiding the harshest applications of contributory negligence. The court would find for the plaintiff, despite her negligence, if the defendant had the last chance to avoid the

---

7. An interesting related issue is how to compare the parties' negligence in a multi-*plaintiff* case. Is the negligence of each plaintiff compared to the negligence of the defendants, or is the negligence of all the parties, plaintiffs and defendants, calculated to add up to 100 percent? In *Churchill v. F/V Fjord,* 892 F.2d 763, 772 (9th Cir. 1989), for example, the following percentages of negligence were assigned at trial: P1, 20 percent; P2, 20 percent; D1, 35 percent; D2, 25 percent; D3, zero percent. The appellate court reversed, holding that the negligence of each plaintiff must be compared *separately* against the negligence of the defendants. Thus, in calculating each plaintiff's negligence, the jury must ignore the negligence of the other plaintiff, just as they ignore the negligence of absent tortfeasors in a state that considers only the negligence of parties before the court.

accident (and hence was at least arguably the more negligent party). Here, Pascal argues that, since Hume had the last clear chance to avoid the accident, his (Pascal's) negligence should be ignored entirely, as it was before the adoption of comparative negligence.

Once comparative negligence is adopted there is no need for a doctrine that ignores the plaintiff's negligence simply because the defendant was (arguably) more negligent. If the defendant is more negligent, she can be assigned a higher percentage of negligence, but the plaintiff's negligence can still be taken into account. On this rationale, most courts have concluded that the last clear chance doctrine does not apply under comparative negligence. See Schwartz §7.02 (discussing both positions); see also Restatement (Third) of Torts: Apportionment of Liability, §3b (advocating abrogation of last clear chance under comparative fault). If the court adopts the majority position, Pascal would still be assigned a percentage of negligence, which would reduce his damages, even though Hume had the last chance to avoid the accident.

As Chapter 22 explains (see pp. 508-510), many jurisdictions have similarly concluded that secondary unreasonable implied assumption of the risk should not be a complete bar to recovery once comparative negligence is adopted. Instead, the plaintiff's unreasonable decision to encounter a risk should be considered a form of "fault" that the jury uses in assessing her percentage of negligence.

8a.   In a contributory negligence state, neither party would recover, since each was partially at fault. The court would enter a judgment dismissing each party's claim against the other.

b.   There is nothing to prevent an injured defendant from recovering from a plaintiff under comparative negligence. After all, if Hume had gone to court first, he would have been the plaintiff; he shouldn't be prejudiced by merely losing the race to the courthouse. Thus, if both parties are injured, and both are negligent, each may be entitled to some recovery in a pure comparative negligence jurisdiction. Here, Pascal would recover $48,000 from Hume ($60,000 reduced by 20 percent) and Hume would recover $40,000 from Pascal ($200,000 reduced by 80 percent).

Comparing Apples and Outrages

9a.   Spencer will argue that the jury should apportion the fault among Hamilton, Spencer, and Sly, the burglar. If the jury is so instructed, they will presumably assign a large percentage of fault to Sly, the intentional tortfeasor, and a lesser percentage to Spencer, which merely failed to prevent the criminal act.

b.   The title of this chapter is "comparative negligence." The doctrine arose as a substitute for the earlier doctrine of contributory negligence, which applied where both the plaintiff and the defendant were negligent. Traditionally, contributory negligence was *not* a defense to an intentional tort. So there is a strong argument that legislatures that enacted "comparative negligence" statutes never intended that intentional conduct should be compared to negligence, as Spencer will argue here.

c.   In a state that generally requires the jury to consider the fault of all tortfeasors (including absent tortfeasors), ignoring Sly (the party with the lion's share of the fault) seems totally artificial. If an absent party whose conduct was merely negligent will be considered, it is hard to see why a more faulty party — the intentional tortfeasor — should be ignored.

Cases like this may arise in many contexts. A school district might be sued for negligently hiring a bus driver who sexually abuses a child. A psychiatrist might be sued for failing to warn of a dangerous patient who assaults a family member. A hotel might be sued for negligent security after a guest is assaulted in the parking garage. In such cases, the liability of the negligent defendant may depend on how the intentional tortfeasor is treated in allocating fault.

Some of the cases on the point have turned on the wording of the state's comparative negligence statute. In *Welch v. Southland Corp.*, 952 P.2d 162 (Wash. 1998), for example, the court looked at the definition of "fault" in the Washington comparative fault statute, and concluded that the legislature had not intended comparison of negligent and intentional conduct. Other courts, however, have held that intentional tortfeasors should be compared, noting the artificiality of making the comparison in these cases without including them. "To penalize the negligent tortfeasor in such circumstances not only frustrates the purposes of the [comparative fault] statute, but violates the commonsense notion that a more culpable party should bear the financial burden caused by its intentional act." *Weidenfeller v. Star*, 2 Cal. Rptr. 2d 14, 16 (1991). The Restatement (Third) of Torts: Apportionment of Liability would allow apportionment to intentional tortfeasors. See §1, cmt. b, c. However, it is hard to view this as a "restatement" of the law, since the cases are sharply divided on the issue. See *Whitehead v. Food Max of Mississippi, Inc.*, 163 F.3d 265, 281-282 (5th Cir. 1998) (citing numerous cases taking both positions).

d.   Maybe Spencer wouldn't care. If joint and several liability applies, assigning a percentage of fault to Sly will not reduce Spencer's liability: It will be liable for the plaintiff's damages, reduced only by the plaintiff's percentage of fault. In fact, including Sly in the apportionment might have the effect of driving down the plaintiff's percentage of fault. For example, if the jury only considers the fault of Hamilton and Spencer, they might find Hamilton 25 percent at fault, for failing to repair the lock, and Spencer 75 percent at fault, for failing to patrol. If they consider Sly as well, however, they might assign Hamilton 10 percent of the fault, Spencer 20 percent, and Sly 70 percent. On these assumptions, and the further assumption that joint and several liability applies, Spencer pays more — 90 percent of Hamilton's damages instead of 75 percent — if Sly is considered.

On the other hand, if the jurisdiction has moved to *several liability,* under which each defendant only pays in proportion to its fault, including Sly makes a dramatic difference in the outcome. Spencer now pays 20 percent of Hamilton's damages if fault is apportioned to Sly, but 75 percent if Sly is ignored. Since Sly probably can't pay his part of the judgment, Hamilton loses big time if Sly's fault is considered. Naturally, it has been plaintiffs who argue vehemently against including intentional tortfeasors in the apportionment of fault.

Special Verdicts: Guiding the Jury in Applying Comparative Negligence

While comparative negligence may be fairer than the all-or-nothing contributory negligence rule, it is more complicated for a jury to apply. Under contributory negligence, the jury's role was clear. If it found that the plaintiff was negligent, it rendered a verdict for the defendant, since any negligence barred the plaintiff from recovery. If it found that the plaintiff was not negligent, but that the defendant was, it decided how much the plaintiff should be awarded in damages to compensate her for her injuries, and came back with a verdict for the plaintiff for that amount.

Under comparative negligence, by contrast, the jury must decide the percentage of negligence of each party, including the plaintiff, and perhaps of absent tortfeasors as well. It must then determine the value of the plaintiff's damages, and apply the comparative negligence statute to reduce those damages and render a verdict for the reduced damages against the appropriate defendants. Since the jurors presumably know little about comparative negligence, they must be fully instructed as to how to compare the negligence of the parties, the effect of the plaintiff's negligence, and how the damages are to be reduced.

These instructions will be complicated. If the jury simply renders a general verdict ("verdict for plaintiff for $50,000" or "verdict for the defendant"), it will be impossible to know whether they understood and followed the instructions. Many states address this problem by authorizing or requiring the use of special verdicts, which ask the jury to make factual determinations about the negligence of each party and damages, and leave it to the court to apply the comparative negligence statute to fashion a proper judgment. For example, if the Rousseau case (see p. 529) were tried in a pure comparative negligence jurisdiction, the court might use a special verdict form like that in Figure 23-1 (see p. 542).

STATE OF WEST DAKOTA

SUTTER COUNTY   SUPERIOR COURT
                                NO. 04-3217

JOHN J. ROUSSEAU,

    Plaintiff,

    v.   SPECIAL VERDICT

JOHN LOCKE,
CITY OF PARIS

    Defendants
- - - - - - - - - - - - - - - - - -

   We, the jury in the above entitled case, find the
following special verdict on the issues submitted
to us:

    Issue #1: Were the defendants, or either of
              them, negligent? (Answer ''yes'' or
              ''no'')

       Answer: Defendant John Locke   **YES**
                                         _____

               Defendant City of Paris   **NO**
                                         _____

               [If you answered ''yes'' as to ei-
               ther defendant, then answer the next
               issue]

    Issue #2: Was the negligence of the defendant,
              or either of them, a proximate cause
              of the injury to the plaintiff?
              (Answer ''yes'' or ''no'')

       Answer: Defendant John Locke   **YES**
                                         _____

               Defendant City of Paris _____

               [If you answered ''yes'' to Issue #2
               as to either defendant, please answer
               Issue #3]

Figure 23–1

Issue #3: Was the plaintiff negligent? (Answer ''yes'' or ''no'')

Answer: ___**YES**___

[If you answered ''yes'' to Issue #3, then answer the next issue]

Issue #4: Was the plaintiff's negligence a proximate cause of his injury? (Answer ''yes'' or ''no'')

Answer: ___**YES**___

[If you answered ''yes'' to both Issue #1 and Issue #2, then answer the next issue]

Issue #5: Without taking into consideration the question of reduction of damages due to the negligence of the plaintiff, if any, what is the total amount of damages suffered by the plaintiff?

Answer: ___**$40,000**___

[If you have answered Issues #1, 2, 3 and 4 ''yes,'' then answer the following issue]

Issue #6: Assuming that 100 percent represents the combined negligence of the plaintiff and of the defendant[s] whose negligence contributed as a proximate cause to plaintiff's injury, what proportion of such combined negligence is attributable to the plaintiff and what proportion is attributable to each defendant?

Answer: To plaintiff: ___**55**___ %

To defendant Locke ___**45**___ %

To defendant City of Paris ___**0**___ %

Total: 100%

J. Stuart Mill
Jury Foreperson

Figure 23–1 (*continued*)

A special verdict form like Figure 23-1 allows the court to ensure that the more complex comparative negligence rules are properly applied. The jury is simply instructed to make the necessary factual findings concerning the negligence of each party and the plaintiff's resulting damages. The jury fills in these findings on the special verdict form. After the jury renders the special verdict, the judge applies the comparative negligence statute to its findings by reducing the plaintiff's damages to account for her negligence and entering judgment against the defendants who are liable under the statute, or if the statute requires, entering a judgment for the defendant. The special verdict procedure simplifies the jury instructions, since the judge does not have to explain to the jury how to compare the negligence of the various parties in fashioning a final judgment.

For example, if the Rousseau case were tried under pure comparative negligence doctrine, and the jury rendered the special verdict in Figure 23-1, the judge would enter judgment for Rousseau against Locke for $18,000 (45 percent of $40,000), but dismiss the claim against the city, since the jury did not find it negligent. If the case had been tried in a modified comparative negligence state, the judge would enter judgment for both defendants, since the plaintiff was more than 50 percent negligent.

EXAMPLES

Verdicts and Judgments

10. Assume that the jury returned the special verdict shown in Figure 23-2 (see p. 545), in a not-greater-than state that compares the plaintiff's negligence to the aggregate negligence of the defendants.

   a. What judgment should the judge render?
   b. What if the jurisdiction compared plaintiff's negligence to each defendant individually?

11. One of the advantages of the special verdict is that the jury need not be given complicated instructions on the effect of their factual findings. For example, they do not need to know that the plaintiff will lose if she is more negligent than the defendant in a modified comparative negligence state. All they need do is find the actual percentages, since the judge fashions the verdict based on their findings. However, some states require the judge to inform the jury of the effect of finding the plaintiff more negligent than the defendant, even though logically it is unnecessary — or perhaps even an impediment to rational decision making — for them to know. See, e.g., Iowa Code Ann. §668.3(5). Under such a statute, the judge would give an instruction like this in a state which applies the 50 percent bar rule:

STATE OF WEST DAKOTA

SUTTER COUNTY   SUPERIOR COURT
                                NO. 04-3217

JOHN J. ROUSSEAU,

    Plaintiff,

    v.   SPECIAL VERDICT

JOHN LOCKE,
CITY OF PARIS

    Defendants

We, the jury in the above entitled case, find the
following special verdict on the issues submitted
to us:

Issue #1: Were the defendants, or either of them,
         negligent? (Answer ''yes'' or ''no'')

    Answer: Defendant John Locke   **YES**

             Defendant City of Paris **YES**

         [If you answered ''yes'' as to either
         defendant, then answer the next issue]

Issue #2: Was the negligence of the defendants,
         or either of them, a proximate cause of
         the injury to the plaintiff?
         (Answer ''yes'' or ''no'')

    Answer: Defendant John Locke   . **YES**

             Defendant City of Paris **YES**

         [If you answered ''yes'' to Issue #2 as
         to either defendant, please answer Issue
         #3]

Figure 23-2

Issue #3: Was the plaintiff negligent? (Answer ''yes'' or ''no'')

Answer: __YES__

[If you answered ''yes'' to Issue #3, then answer the next issue]

Issue #4: Was the plaintiff's negligence a proximate cause of his injury? (Answer ''yes'' or ''no'')

Answer: __YES__

[If you answered ''yes'' to both Issue #1 and Issue #2, then answer the next issue]

Issue #5: Without taking into consideration the question of reduction of damages due to the negligence of the plaintiff, if any, what is the total amount of damages suffered by the plaintiff?

Answer: __$100,000__

[If you have answered Issues #1, 2, 3 and 4 ''yes,'' then answer the following issue]

Issue #6: Assuming that 100 percent represents the combined negligence of the plaintiff and of the defendant[s] whose negligence contributed as a proximate cause to plaintiff's injury, what proportion of such combined negligence is attributable to the plaintiff and what proportion is attributable to each defendant?

Answer: To plaintiff: __45__ %

To defendant Locke __50__ %

To defendant City of Paris __5__ %

Total: 100%

J. Stewart Mill
Jury Foreperson

Figure 23–2 (*continued*)

> If the plaintiff's negligence is as great as or greater than the negligence of the defendant, she may not recover. If the plaintiff's negligence is less than that of the defendant, she may recover her damages, reduced in proportion to her negligence in causing the accident.

Who wants the jury to be given this instruction, the defendant or the plaintiff?

12. Assume that the state applies pure comparative negligence. The jury fills out the form as shown in Figure 23–3 below at p. 548. What should the judge do?

EXPLANATIONS

Verdicts and Judgments

10a.   The judge should enter judgment for Rousseau for $55,000 against both Locke and the city. Rousseau is entitled to recover since his negligence is not greater than that of all defendants combined but his $100,000 in damages will be reduced by 45 percent. If joint and several liability applies, both defendants are liable for the resulting judgment of $55,000, despite the disparity in their degrees of negligence.

   b.   If the jurisdiction compared the plaintiff's negligence to each defendant's individually, the judge would enter a judgment for Rousseau against Locke for $55,000, and a judgment dismissing Rousseau's claim against the city, since Rousseau's negligence is greater than the city's negligence.

11.   Naturally, the plaintiff will seek this instruction, since it alerts the jury to the fact that, if they find the plaintiff as faulty as the defendant (or more at fault), she will lose entirely. Realistically, this is likely to influence a jury in a close case to find the plaintiff 49 percent negligent instead of 50 percent (or 55 percent, or 60 percent for that matter). Statutes that require an instruction like this recognize the practical reality that juries often structure their findings to divide the damages in close cases, and that in a practical torts world there is nothing particularly shocking about that.

12.   The special verdict here indicates that the jury has failed to follow its instructions. If the city's negligence was not a proximate cause of the accident, as the answer to the second question indicates, the jury should not have considered it in assigning the percentages of negligence at the end. The jury may have concluded that, as long as *some* defendant's negligence caused the accident, both could be liable. Or, perhaps the jurors misunderstood proximate cause (now really, how could they?) to mean the most important cause, and they answered "no," since it found Locke much more negligent. For whatever reason, the jury's factual findings are inconsistent; it has assigned negligence percentages to all parties despite its finding that the city's negligence was not a proximate cause of Rousseau's injuries.

```
                    STATE OF WEST DAKOTA


SUTTER COUNTY                SUPERIOR COURT
                             NO. 04-3217


JOHN J. ROUSSEAU,
                             │
    Plaintiff,               │
                             │
    v.                       │
                             │   SPECIAL VERDICT
                             │
JOHN LOCKE,                  │
CITY OF PARIS                │
                             │
    Defendants               │
                             │
─────────────────────────────┘
```

   We, the jury in the above entitled case, find the
following special verdict on the issues submitted
to us:

   Issue #1: Were the defendants, or either of them,
            negligent? (Answer ''yes'' or ''no'')

      Answer: Defendant John Locke   _**YES**_

              Defendant City of Paris _**YES**_

         [If you answered ''yes'' as to either
         defendant, then answer the next issue]

   Issue #2: Was the negligence of the defendant, or
            either of them, a proximate cause of
            the injury to the plaintiff?
            (Answer ''yes'' or ''no'')

      Answer: Defendant John Locke   _**YES**_

              Defendant City of Paris _**NO**_

         [If you answered ''yes'' to Issue #2 as to
         either defendant, please answer Issue #3]

Figure 23-3

Issue #3: Was the plaintiff negligent? (Answer ''yes'' or ''no'')

Answer: __YES__

[If you answered ''yes'' to Issue #3, then answer the next issue]

Issue #4: Was the plaintiff's negligence a proximate cause of his injury? (Answer ''yes'' or ''no'')

Answer: __YES__

[If you answered ''yes'' to both Issue #1 and Issue #2, then answer the next issue]

Issue #5: Without taking into consideration the question of reduction of damages due to the negligence of the plaintiff, if any, what is the total amount of damages suffered by the plaintiff?

Answer: __$100,000__

[If you have answered Issues #1, 2, 3 and 4 ''yes,'' then answer the following issue]

Issue #6: Assuming that 100% represents the combined negligence of the plaintiff and of the defendant[s] whose negligence contributed as a proximate cause to plaintiff's injury, what proportion of such combined negligence is attributable to the plaintiff and what proportion is attributable to each defendant?

Answer: To plaintiff: __10__ %

To defendant Locke __75__ %

To defendant City of Paris __15__ %

Total: 100%

J. Stuart Mill
Jury Foreperson

Figure 23–3 (*continued*)

If the jury comes back with this verdict, the judge can reinstruct it on proximate cause and send it back to deliberate further and clarify its verdict. This may well "save the trial" if the jury comes back with a consistent verdict after the supplemental instruction.

Consider what would have happened if the jury had simply been asked to render a general verdict in this case. If it mistakenly considered the city's negligence, even though it did not cause the injuries, it probably would have come back with a verdict against each defendant for $90,000 (Rousseau's damages reduced by his 10 percent negligence). This would look on the surface like a perfectly permissible verdict, even though in fact it was based on a misunderstanding of the law. The general verdict often hides such mistakes. That is its virtue or its vice, depending on how you look at it.

Interestingly, although the special verdict appears to make so much sense in comparative negligence cases, not all states favor them. Some require the court to use a special verdict; others permit them, and one or two, remarkably, *bar* them entirely, despite their obvious utility in revealing the jury's reasoning process. See, e.g., Vt. Stat. Ann. tit. 12 §1036 (requiring use of general verdict).

24

The Fracturing of the Common Law: Loss Allocation in the Comparative Negligence Era

Introduction

Until recently, negligence doctrine developed largely through the evolutionary process of case law. Successive court opinions refined basic principles such as duty, breach, and causation, and affirmative defenses such as assumption of the risk and contributory negligence. Throughout this formative era, there was never any doubt that legislatures had the power to change such common law principles. Indeed, dramatic changes were made by statute in certain areas, such as workers' compensation and wrongful death. But these were exceptions; for the most part, negligence law was common law.

In the last few decades, however, legislatures have gotten heavily into the business of restructuring the common law of torts. The prime example, of course, is comparative negligence, which has been adopted by statute in many jurisdictions. Many states have also enacted statutes placing caps on noneconomic damages, creating screening panels for medical malpractice cases and limiting the scope of the collateral source rule.

Legislatures have been especially tempted to tinker with two traditional doctrines governing the allocation of negligence damages: joint and several liability and contribution. Recent statutes have fractured these fairly straightforward doctrines into a profusion of idiosyncratic approaches, many applicable only in a single state. These legislative changes to the principles allocating damages among tortfeasors illustrate a movement, found in many areas of the law, from general principles that work well in the broad run of cases but may operate unfairly in some, to more precise, detailed rules that may be more "fair" but also introduce administrative complexities.

This chapter illustrates some of the changes legislatures have made to basic doctrines governing liability of multiple tortfeasors. It is not intended to make you an expert in the details of any state's doctrine, but rather as a case study of the extent to which legislatures have fractured previously monolithic common law principles in the search for greater equity.

Comparative Negligence: The Catalyst for Change

As earlier chapters explain, before comparative negligence the defendants' responsibility for damages was determined by principles of joint and several liability and contribution. Each tortfeasor was fully liable for the plaintiff's damages. A tortfeasor who paid the plaintiff was entitled to collect "pro rata" contribution from the other tortfeasors. That is, the tortfeasors shared the damages equally; if there were two tortfeasors, the one who paid would recover half in contribution from the other, if there were six, each paid a sixth, and so forth.

In most states, these principles were well established before the advent of comparative negligence. While the adoption of comparative negligence did not automatically change them, it provided new information about the relative fault of the parties which suggested that the classic principles were too blunt.

Suppose, for example, that Nell sued Fagan and Twist for negligence, and the jury found Nell 20 percent at fault, Fagan 70 percent at fault and Twist a mere 10 percent at fault. If Nell's damages were $100,000, she would be entitled to recover $80,000, her full damages reduced by her percentage of negligence. Under joint and several liability, Fagan and Twist would each be liable for the $80,000, the plaintiff's damages adjusted to account for her negligence.[1] Under traditional contribution doctrine, whichever defendant

---

1. This assumes that Nell's negligence is compared to the defendants' combined negligence, as it is in most modified comparative negligence jurisdictions. See generally pp. 529-530.

paid that amount would recover a pro rata share, or $40,000, from the other (assuming the contributing tortfeasor was able to pay).

However, in light of the parties' percentages of negligence, these results appear inequitable. Twist, who was found only 10 percent at fault, will argue that he should not be liable to Nell (who was twice as faulty) for $80,000, as he would be under joint and several liability. Similarly, he will argue that if Fagan pays the judgment, Fagan should get much less than half of it (which he would get under pro rata contribution) back from Twist, since Twist was only one-seventh as faulty as Fagan.

Logical Implications: Proportional Contribution

Perhaps the most obvious implication of comparative negligence is that contribution among tortfeasors should be in proportion to their degrees of fault. Under this approach Fagan would contribute seven-eighths of the judgment ($70,000) and Twist would contribute one-eighth ($10,000). Because the defendant's relative degrees of fault are determined in comparative negligence cases, this appears both simple and fair: The proportions can be calculated from the jury's verdict, and tortfeasors who are more "faulty" will pay more than those who are less so. If each defendant is able to pay, each will end up contributing to the judgment in proportion to the fault assigned by the jury.[2]

Some tinker-prone legislatures have adopted such "proportional" or "comparative" contribution. The Rhode Island contribution statute, for example, provides:

> The right of contribution exists among joint tortfeasors; provided however, that when there is a disproportion of fault among joint tortfeasors, the relative degree of fault of the joint tortfeasors shall be considered in determining their pro rata shares.

R.I. Gen. Laws §10-6-3. Under a statute like this, after the plaintiff has been paid, the judgment will be redistributed among the defendants through contribution, in proportion to the tortfeasors' percentages of fault, rather than equally or "pro rata."

While proportional contribution distributes the loss in proportion to the fault of the parties, calculating the defendants' shares is more complex under proportional contribution than it is under pro rata contribution. Instead of simply dividing by the number of tortfeasors, judges and juries have to deal with fractions. In the example, Twist should bear 10/80ths of the judgment ($10,000) and Fagan 70/80ths ($70,000). (The proportions

---

2. In fact, so does the plaintiff, in a sense, since 20 percent of her damages is deducted from her recovery to account for her negligence.

can be calculated by adding the defendants' percentages of negligence together to form the denominator of the fraction; each individual tortfeasor's percentage will form the numerator for that tortfeasor.) If Fagan paid Nell her $80,000 (remember that he is liable for the whole judgment under joint and several liability), he would receive 10/80ths ($10,000) from Twist, and absorb 70/80ths ($70,000) of the judgment himself.

These fractions don't seem so bad; this amount of increased complexity is clearly worth it for the gain in fairness. As the following examples illustrate, however, applying proportional contribution not only requires judges to dust off their math skills, but also raises administrative problems. In considering these examples, don't get bogged down in the math; the concept of proportional contribution, and the complexities it can raise, are the main point. (The explanations begin on p. 561.)

EXAMPLES

Out of Proportion

1. Flite sues Micawber, Heap, and Murdstone for negligence. The jury finds Flite 20 percent at fault, Micawber 50 percent, Heap 20 percent, and Murdstone 10 percent. They find Flite's damages to be $60,000.
    a. Assume that the case takes place in a modified comparative negligence jurisdiction which compares the plaintiff's negligence to that of all defendants combined. Assume further that joint and several liability and the Rhode Island proportional contribution statute apply. How much would Flite be entitled to collect from Heap?
    b. If Heap paid the judgment, how much would he recover in contribution from Murdstone?
    c. Assume that the case takes place in a modified comparative negligence jurisdiction that compares the plaintiff's negligence to that of each defendant individually, and allows her to recover from any defendant as long as she was not more negligent than that defendant. If Heap paid the judgment, and proportional contribution applied, how much would he recover from Micawber in contribution?

2. Suppose that Heap pays the judgment and seeks contribution from Turveydrop, who allegedly was *also* negligent in causing the accident, but wasn't sued by Flite. How should Turveydrop's liability for contribution be determined?

More Logical Implications: Proportional Credit for Settlements

Once comparative percentages of fault are established, another logical implication is to give a proportional or comparative credit for a settlement with one tortfeasor, instead of the traditional dollar credit provided in the Uniform Contribution Among Joint Tortfeasors Act (see §4(a) p. 463). Suppose, for example, that Nell sued Fagan and Twist, and settled with Fagan for $25,000. She then tries her case against Twist, in a jurisdiction that requires the jury to assign percentages of negligence to all tortfeasors (including Fagan, in this case). The jury comes back with a finding that Nell was 20 percent at fault, Fagan 70 percent and Twist 10 percent. It finds Nell's damages to be $100,000.

In a jurisdiction that retains joint and several liability, Twist would be liable to Nell for $80,000, her damages reduced by 20 percent to account for her negligence. If the jurisdiction applied the Uniform Act's dollar credit for settlements, Twist would pay $55,000, after her dollar credit for Fagan's settlement payment.

Now, let's consider what Twist would owe in a jurisdiction that gives him a proportional credit for Fagan's settlement. Under this approach, (advocated in the Restatement (Third) of Torts: Apportionment of Liability, §16), Fagan is viewed as selling his proportion of the ultimate judgment to Nell for the agreed settlement amount. Thus, Twist would get a credit against the judgment for Fagan's proportion of their combined fault, or 70/80ths of the $80,000 judgment. Twist would end up paying $10,000 to Nell under this approach, instead of $55,000 under the dollar credit approach.[3]

Another example may help. Assume that Nell had settled for $3,000 with Twist, and the jury returned the same verdict when Nell went to trial against Fagan. Fagan would get a 10/80ths credit against the $80,000 judgment. He would end up paying $70,000 to Nell.

EXAMPLE

Credit Transactions

3.   Take the facts of Example 1, in which the jury found Flite (the plaintiff) 20 percent at fault, Micawber 50 percent, Heap 20 percent and Murdstone 10 percent. They find Flite's damages to be $60,000. Assume that Flite settles with Heap for $22,000 before trial. Assume that the jurisdiction applies joint and several liability, compares plaintiff's fault to the combined fault of the defendants, and gives a proportional credit for settlements.

    a. How much is Murdstone liable for, before considering any credit for Heap's settlement?

    b. How much will Murdstone actually have to pay, after adjusting the judgment to account for Heap's settlement?

    c. How much will Flite collect altogether?

---

3. Of course, when they settled, the parties did not know what percentages of negligence the jury would assign to them. So Twist may do better if Fagan settles, but also may do worse.

Ultimate Implications: Several Liability

The adoption of proportional contribution does not change the principle of joint and several liability. It only changes the rules for *reallocating* the loss once one of the tortfeasors has paid the judgment amount to the plaintiff. Thus, proportional contribution still requires a two-step process: a suit by the plaintiff that establishes her right to recover damages, followed by a second action for contribution by the tortfeasor who pays those damages (or a motion for contribution in the original action). Similarly, giving a proportional credit for settlements requires the entry of a judgment, followed by a proportional adjustment for the settlement.

Logically, wouldn't it be simpler to make the defendants separately liable to the plaintiff for their *respective shares of the judgment?* In Nell's action, for example, Fagan would be liable to Nell for 70/80ths of her adjusted damages ($70,000) and Twist would be liable for 10/80ths ($10,000). Nell would recover $80,000 (her raw damages reduced by her percentage of negligence) just as she did under joint and several liability, but each defendant would only be "severally" liable for her own portion of the damages.

Obviously, one great advantage of this approach is that it eliminates the need for contribution entirely: None of the defendants need seek contribution, since none pays in excess of his "share" of the damages. However, several liability has a great *disadvantage* from the plaintiff's point of view: It casts the burden of the insolvent tortfeasor on her. If Fagan cannot pay, Nell will only recover $10,000 under several liability, because Twist is not liable for Fagan's share. Under joint and several liability, by contrast, both tortfeasors would be liable to Nell for the entire judgment. If Fagan were insolvent, Nell could collect his share from Twist. Of course, this advantage of joint and several liability to the plaintiff carries a corresponding *disadvantage* to defendants: Under joint and several liability, Twist could end up paying the entire judgment if Fagan is insolvent, even though he was only 10 percent at fault.[4]

An increasing number of states have adopted several liability, either for all cases or for some situations. Utah's comparative negligence statute, for example, provides

> No defendant is liable to any person seeking recovery for any amount in excess of the proportion of fault attributable to that defendant under Section 78-27-39.

---

4. This assumes that Nell's fault is compared to the *combined* negligence of the defendants.

Utah Code Ann. §78-27-38(3). Similarly, Vermont's statute provides that

> [E]ach defendant shall be liable for that proportion of the total dol-
> lar amount awarded as damages in the ratio of the amount of his
> causal negligence to the amount of causal negligence attributed to
> all defendants against whom recovery is allowed.

Vt. Stat. Ann. tit. 12, §1036.

The following examples illustrate how Flite's case might come out
under several liability. Assume in each example that the jurisdiction applies
comparative negligence of the "not greater than" variety, compares the
plaintiff's fault to the combined fault of all defendants, and has switched
to several liability. Again, the examples illustrate that the attempt to make
the rules more equitable carries its own problems of administration.

Several Examples

4.   Assume the same facts as in Example 1: Flite sues Micawber, Heap,
and Murdstone for negligence. The jury finds Flite 20 percent at fault,
Micawber 50 percent, Heap 20 percent, and Murdstone 10 percent. They
find Flite's damages to be $60,000.

    a. If all defendants are solvent, how much will Flite recover from
       each defendant under several liability?

    b. If Micawber pays the judgment against him, how much can he get
       in contribution from Murdstone?

5.   Assume that Flite's case was litigated in a state that requires the jury to
assign percentages to all tortfeasors, including tortfeasors who are not
before the court at trial. Assume that Flite settled with Micawber for
$9,000 before trial. The jury assigns 20 percent to Flite, 50 percent to
Micawber, 20 percent to Heap, and 10 percent to Murdstone. The damages
are again assessed at $60,000 How much should Heap and Murdstone pay
to Flite?

One Among Several

6.   Suppose that Flite sued Micawber only, that under the applicable statute the negligence is apportioned only to the parties at trial, and the jury
determined that Flite was 25 percent at fault and Micawber was 75 percent at fault.

    a. Assuming again that the damages are $60,000, how much would
       Micawber be liable for?

    b. Could Micawber implead Heap and Murdstone in the action, to
       assure that their negligence is considered in allocating percen-
       tages?

7.   Suppose that Flite sued Micawber and Murdstone only, that under
applicable law only the negligence of parties before the court at trial is

considered, and that the jury apportions the negligence 25 percent to Flite, 45 percent to Micawber, and 30 percent to Murdstone.

    a. Assuming again that the damages are $60,000, how much would Micawber and Murdstone be liable for?

    b. Suppose that, after getting the judgment against Micawber and Murdstone and collecting from Micawber, Flite learns that Murdstone is insolvent. Since he has not been fully compensated, he sues Heap, another tortfeasor he left out of his first action. How should Heap's liability be determined?

8. It is sometimes said that several liability makes more sense, because it allocates the loss according to the amount of damage caused by each tortfeasor. What would a classic old common law judge like Judge Fudd think about this reasoning?

9. Assuming that it appears that Murdstone's negligence was a relatively minor factor in causing the accident, how would you expect the switch to several liability to affect the dynamics of settlement negotiations between him and Flite?

More Legislative Tinkering: Reallocating the Uncollectible Share

Once tempted to tinker, states have become even more finicky about fine-tuning loss allocation principles among tortfeasors. An example is the enactment of statutes that redistribute the shares of insolvent tortfeasors.

Consider the example of Nell, who was found 20 percent at fault, versus Fagan (70 percent) and Twist (10 percent). If Fagan was unable to pay, Twist, as a joint tortfeasor, had to pay the full judgment, with no hope of contribution. The common law had little sympathy for a defendant who ended up paying the entire judgment because other tortfeasors were insolvent. A tortfeasor was a tortfeasor, and was expected to take his medicine without complaint.

This result is arguably unfair, since the risk of Fagan's insolvency falls entirely on Twist. If, on the other hand, the jurisdiction switches to several liability, *it falls entirely on Nell instead*, who would collect nothing from Fagan and could not collect Fagan's share from Twist.

Some states have fine-tuned their allocation schemes to address this apparent unfairness — but again only at the expense of increased complexity. Under Minnesota law, for example, tortfeasors are severally liable to the plaintiff but uncollectible shares are reallocated among the plaintiff and defendants:

> Upon motion made not later than one year after judgment is entered, the court shall determine whether all or part of a party's equitable share of the obligation is uncollectible from that party and

shall reallocate any uncollectible amount among the other parties, including a claimant at fault, according to their respective percentages of fault....

Minn. Stat. Ann. §604.02(2). Under this statute, Fagan's share, which is $70,000 (70/80ths of $80,000) would be redistributed between Twist and Nell. They would absorb it in proportion to their fault. Nell would absorb 20/30ths[5] of Fagan's share ($46,666.66)—that is, she would be barred from recovering this amount as her "share" of Fagan's liability. Twist is severally liable to Nell for his share ($10,000) plus 10/30th of Fagan's share ($23,333.33). Thus, Nell could collect $33,333.33 from Twist.

Under the Minnesota version, a negligent plaintiff absorbs a part of the uncollectible share. Some states reallocate the uncollectible share among the other tortfeasors only. See, e.g., Ariz. Rev. Stat. Ann. §12-2508.

To get a general understanding of such reallocation provisions, consider the following example.

Spreading the Risk

10. Assume again that the jury finds Flite 20 percent at fault, Micawber 50 percent, Heap 20 percent and Murdstone 10 percent, in a jurisdiction that applies several liability. They find Flite's damages to be $60,000. Assume that Heap is insolvent.
    a. If the case took place in Minnesota, how much could Flite collect from Micawber, including adjustment for Heap's uncollectible share?
    b. How much would Micawber owe Flite if several liability applied, and the governing statute called for reallocating Heap's uncollectible share proportionally among the other tortfeasors only?

Potpourri: A Sampling of Comparative Apportionment Statutes

All of this fine tuning makes the classic liability rules look like pretty blunt instruments, though perhaps blissfully so. Yet recent statutes illustrate even more idiosyncratic variations on the basic allocation rules. Here are three statutes that illustrate the breadth of statutory approaches to apportioning damages under comparative negligence.

Let's start with a fairly straightforward several liability statute. The Indiana comparative fault statute provides:

---

5. Once again, the denominator is determined by adding the percentages of the parties who absorb the uncollectible share. Here that is Nell (20 percent) and Twist (10 percent), so the denominator is 30.

(1) The jury shall determine the percentage of fault of the claimant, of the defendant, and of any person who is a nonparty ... The percentage of fault of parties to the action may total less than one-hundred percent (100%) if the jury finds that fault contributing to cause the claimant's loss has also come from a nonparty or nonparties. (2) If the percentage of fault of the claimant is greater than fifty percent (50%) of the total fault involved in the incident which caused the claimant's death, injury or property damage, the jury shall return a verdict for the defendants and no further deliberation of the jury is required. (3) If the percentage of fault of the claimant is not greater than fifty percent (50%) of the total fault, the jury then shall determine the total amount of damages the claimant would be entitled to recover if contributory fault were disregarded. (4) The jury next shall multiply the percentage of fault of each defendant by the amount of damages determined under subdivision (3) and shall enter a verdict for the claimant in the amount of the product of that multiplication.

Ind. Code §34-51-2-7(b).

The Iowa comparative fault statute retains joint and several liability only for defendants found at least 50 percent at fault. Even for them, joint and several liability only applies to economic damages, not to intangible or "noneconomic" damages:

In actions brought under this chapter, the rule of joint and several liability shall not apply to defendants who are found to bear less than fifty percent of the total fault assigned to all parties. However, a defendant found to bear fifty percent or more of fault shall only be jointly and severally liable for economic damages and not for any noneconomic damage awards.

Iowa. Code Ann. §668.4.

Last, here's one that Oregon tried for a while, but has since abandoned in favor of a simpler several liability statute.

(2) In any civil action arising out of bodily injury, death or property damage, including claims for emotional injury or distress, loss of care, comfort, companionship and society, and loss of consortium, the liability of each defendant for noneconomic damages awarded to plaintiff shall be several only and shall not be joint. (3) The liability of a defendant who is found to be less than 15 percent at fault for the economic damages awarded the plaintiff shall be several only. (4) The liability of a defendant who is found to be at least 15 percent at fault for the economic damages awarded the plaintiff shall be joint and several, except that a defendant whose percentage of fault is less than that allocated to the plaintiff is liable to the plaintiff only for that percentage of the recoverable economic damages.

Or. Rev. Stat. §18.485 (superseded under 1995 Or. Laws c. 696).

These statutes illustrate that the monolithic common law approach to allocating liability has yielded to a good many experiments in the "laboratory" of the states.[6] While these statutes fine-tune the liability rules in an effort to make the punishment fit the crime, they are obviously more complex for courts and parties to apply. Consider how the following case would come out under these fractured approaches to allocating liability.

Compound Fractures

11. Jingle sues Weller and Snubbin for negligence. After trial, the jury finds Jingle 20 percent at fault, Weller 60 percent and Snubbin 20 percent. The jury further finds, by special verdict, that Jingle's economic damages are $20,000, and his noneconomic damages are $60,000.

    a. How much would Jingle recover from Weller under each statute?

    b. How much would he recover from Snubbin under each statute?

EXPLANATIONS

Out of Proportion

1a.   Because Flite's negligence is less than the total negligence attributed to the defendants, she would recover a judgment of $48,000, her raw damages reduced by 20 percent. Under joint and several liability, each defendant, including Heap, would be liable for that amount. Proportional contribution does *not* change the principle of joint and several liability to the plaintiff; it simply changes the rules for reallocating the judgment after one of the tortfeasors pays it.

    b.   To determine Murdstone's liability for contribution, it is necessary to calculate his proportion of the judgment. As the introduction indicates, Murdstone's proportion can be calculated by taking the total of the negligence percentages of all defendants as the denominator (here 80) and Murdstone's percentage (10) as the numerator. Multiply that fraction times the judgment amount, which is $48,000. If Heap paid $48,000 to Flite, he should recover 10/80ths of it from Murdstone, or $6,000. He'll get 50/80ths ($30,000) from Micawber, and absorb 20/80ths ($12,000) himself.

    c.   The problem here is in determining the proportional shares. Since the jurisdiction compares the negligence of the plaintiff to that of each defendant individually, Flite cannot recover from Murdstone, who was less negligent. She can recover from Micawber, and from Heap, whose negligence was equal to hers. If joint and several liability applies, Heap and Micawber are still liable to Flite for $48,000, 80 percent of her

---

6. *New State Ice Co. p. Liebmann,* 285 U.S. 262, 311 (1932) (Brandeis, J., dissenting).

damages. Heap pays the $48,000, and now seeks proportional contribution from Micawber.

Since Murdstone is not liable to Flite, he is also presumably not required to contribute to the judgment: It doesn't seem logical that a defendant should recover contribution from Murdstone when the plaintiff can't recover anything from him. Contribution statutes typically provide for contribution among parties "jointly liable in tort," or "liable for the same injury." Since Murdstone is not liable, he presumably cannot be forced to contribute.[7]

So, Heap and Micawber should contribute proportionally to the $48,000 judgment. Between them, they account for 70 percent of the fault. Presumably Heap should pay 20/70ths and Micawber should pay 50/70ths. Thus, Heap will recover 50/70ths of 48,000 ($34,286) in contribution from Micawber. He ends up paying $13,714, which is 20/70ths of $48,000.

2.   Our theme is simplicity versus fairness. It is probably more equitable to make contribution proportional, but this example illustrates the price that must be paid in terms of increased complexity of administration. If all tortfeasors are parties to the first action, proportional contribution is fairly simple to administer: The jury's findings can be applied to redistribute the judgment according to the defendants' percentages of negligence. But the plaintiff need not sue every tortfeasor. Here, for example, Flite did not sue Turveydrop, and no negligence percentage was assigned to him. Heap, who paid the judgment, should be entitled to contribution from Turveydrop, but it is not clear how to calculate the proportion of the judgment Turveydrop should pay.

Some courts require the jury in comparative negligence actions to assess percentages of negligence for *all* tortfeasors, even if the plaintiff has not made a claim against them and they are not before the court. (Others restrict the jury to assessing percentages for the parties before the court at trial.) However, even if Turveydrop were assigned a percentage in Flite's initial suit, it would not bind him, since he has not had the opportunity to litigate his proportion of negligence. See J. Glannon, Civil Procedure: Examples and Explanations 510, 512 (4th ed. 2001), Example 1 (explaining leniency of surly myrmidons toward parties who have not litigated issue in prior action). Alternatively, some comparative negligence statutes require the defendant to implead other tortfeasors in the original suit to obtain contribution from them. However, this has problems too, since there may not be personal jurisdiction over all tortfeasors in the plaintiff's initial action.

---

7. Most cases have so held. See, e.g., *Horton by Horton v. Orbeth, Inc.,* 342 N.W.2d 112 (Minn. 1984) (refusing contribution on similar facts since there was no "common liability"); but see *Otis Elevator Co. v. F.W. Cunningham & Sons,* 454 A.2d 335 (Me. 1983) (despite plaintiff's inability to recover, considerations of fairness support contribution from the less negligent tortfeasor).

Since Turveydrop was not a party to the first action, it appears that the court in the contribution action would have to make a new finding of the relative percentages of negligence of all the parties, including Turveydrop. Turveydrop would be liable for the percentage allocated to him in the contribution action, but presumably the other tortfeasors would pay according to the percentages assessed against them in the original action. This is awkward — somehow, the accounting is not going to work out right — and imposes an additional burden on the court in the contribution action.

Credit Transactions

3a. Under joint and several liability, Murdstone is liable for Flite's damages, $60,000, reduced by her 20 percent of fault, or $48,000.

b. Murdstone is entitled to a proportional credit for Heap's settlement. The credit should be 20/80ths or 1/4 of the $48,000. (It is calculated by putting Heap's percentage over that of all defendants as a group, and then taking the credit against the judgment amount — not the raw damages.)[8] So Murdstone pays $36,000 to Flite.

c. Flite collects $58,000, the $36,000 he gets from Murdstone plus the $22,000 Heap paid in settlement. This is $10,000 more than the jury decided she should get, since Flite made a good deal with Heap, who paid well in excess of his "share" of the fault. The Restatement (Third) of Torts: Apportionment of Liability approves this result. "Since the plaintiff bears the risk of an inadequate settlement (in which case the plaintiff will recover less than the damages determined by the factfinder), the plaintiff should also obtain the benefit of a favorable settlement." §16, cmt. e.

Of course, when Heap paid his $22,000 he didn't know what the jury would ultimately do, so he may have made a reasonable decision (even leaving legal fees and costs of going to trial aside). And remember, so long as joint and several liability applies, he could have ended up paying the whole $48,000, if he didn't settle and the other defendants were insolvent.

Although Flite made out well in this example, she could also end up collecting less than $48,000 if the court uses the proportional credit approach. If Heap had settled for $5,000, Flite would have collected a total of $41,000 ($36,000 from Murdstone or Micawber and $5,000 from Heap). These possibilities make settlement an interesting exercise for all parties.

Several Examples

4a. Flite should recover a total of $48,000 if all defendants pay their several shares. Micawber is liable for 50/80ths of the damages after adjustment

---

8. Yes, you can reach the same result by taking a 20 percent credit against the raw damages. But I find it clearer to think of Heap having sold his portion of the judgment, and therefore using the judgment as the figure against which to take the credit.

for Flite's negligence, or $30,000. Heap pays 20/80ths of the adjusted judgment, or $12,000. And Murdstone owes 10/80ths of $48,000, or $6,000. Their three several shares together total $48,000.

Thus, Flite recovers the same amount as she would under joint and several liability, as long as everyone is solvent. The difference is that each defendant pays according to his proportion of negligence, instead of being liable for the full judgment. And, of course, Flite must *do the collecting* from each defendant; she cannot collect the full judgment from one and leave him to seek contribution from the other defendants. Since collecting judgments can be an arduous and expensive process in itself, this is a significant shift in the burden on the parties.

b.   Micawber recovers nothing in contribution from Murdstone. The judgment against Micawber will be for his share ($30,000) but no more, since he is only liable to Flite for his share. Thus, he has no right of contribution from any other tortfeasor. Nor does anyone have a right of contribution from him. This is an obvious advantage of several liability.

5.   Under several liability, a tortfeasor who settles simply extinguishes liability for his share. There is no need to give anyone else a credit for the payment, because they are only separately liable for their own shares. If Micawber had not settled, his share would have been $30,000, but Flite settled this share for $9,000. The remaining tortfeasors are only liable for their shares. Heap would pay 20/80ths of $48,000, or $12,000, and Murdstone would pay 10/80ths, or $6,000.

Thus, Flite would recover $27,000 altogether ($9,000 from Micawber, $12,000 from Heap and $6,000 from Murdstone). She would collect less than her full judgment because she sold Micawber's share ("worth" $30,000 (50/80ths of $48,000)) for $9,000. Of course, when she settled with Micawber, she did not know how the jury would allocate fault, so her choice was at best a guess.

One Among Several

6a.   Here is another example that illustrates that several liability, while arguably more equitable, is also more complicated than it first appears. While several liability is meant to confine each defendant's liability to his share, the plaintiff has a good deal of control over what that share will be, since a tortfeasor's share depends on whose fault is considered. Here, since Micawber is the only defendant, and absent tortfeasors' negligence is not considered in this jurisdiction, he will be liable for 75 percent of the damages, or $45,000. Yet, in a several liability jurisdiction he will have no right to contribution, since he is only paying his share. Had Flite sued Heap and Murdstone as well, Micawber's percentage would presumably have been considerably smaller, since they were also partially at fault.

It would seem that the logical way to address this problem would be to require the jury to assign shares to all tortfeasors, whether or not they are made parties to the action. Under this approach, Micawber could reduce his share by proving that Heap and Murdstone were also negligent, even though they are not defendants. However, there are jurisdictions that have moved to several liability, yet only allow apportionment among the parties present at trial. See, e.g., Vt. Stat. tit. 12 §1036; *McCormack v. State*, 553 A.2d 566 (Vt. 1988).

b. Since the jurisdiction only allows the jury to consider the negligence of the parties to the suit, Micawber would clearly like to bring the other tortfeasors in as third-party defendants so that their negligence would also be considered. However, many impleader rules only allow a defendant to bring in other parties who may be liable to *him*, that is, to the defendant, not to the plaintiff. See, e.g., Fed. R. Civ. P. 14(a). Typically, other tortfeasors are brought in for contribution, but in a jurisdiction that applies several liability, there is no contribution. See Example 4b.

Some comparative negligence statutes authorize a defendant to prove that other tortfeasors were also partly at fault in causing the plaintiff's injury, even though they are not made parties. This approach can be awkward, however, since the non-parties' negligence is being assessed, but they are not there litigating the issue before the jury. Any percentage of fault attributed to such an absent tortfeasor could not bind her if the plaintiff later sued her separately.

Other statutes deal with this problem, that a defendant sued alone risks disproportionate liability, by allowing that defendant to join other tortfeasors as additional defendants in the action, even though those tortfeasors would only be liable to the plaintiff, not to the original defendant for contribution (since there is no contribution under several liability). See, e.g., Conn. Gen. Stat. Ann. §52-102b (allowing defendant to join in the action non-party who is or may be liable for a proportionate share of the plaintiff's damages). One problem with this approach, however, is that it may not be possible to join the absent tortfeasor, because she was never identified, has settled, or is not subject to personal jurisdiction in the action.

7a. Flite's damages should be reduced by 25 percent to account for her negligence. This brings them down to $45,000. Under several liability, Murdstone would be liable for 30/75ths, or $18,000. Micawber would be liable for 45/75ths, or $27,000.

b. This is another imponderable. Percentages have already been assigned to Micawber and Murdstone, but no room has been left to add Heap! If Flite now sues Heap, presumably percentages would only be assigned to Flite and him in the second trial. Thus Heap (like Micawber in Example 6) may be assigned a fairly high percentage of fault because he is the only tortfeasor before the court. If he were found 60 percent at fault and Flite 40 percent, and the damages are $60,000, what would he pay? Is his "several share" $36,000 (60 percent of $60,000)? If so, Flite collects $63,000 ($27,000 plus $36,000), which is much too high.

I don't know the answer to this problem, but it does illustrate that while several liability appears to be a simple means of distributing the damages, it entails some thorny administrative problems. Had all these been anticipated, some states might have resisted the urge to tinker, and stuck with the rough and ready older rules instead.

8.   Judge Fudd would think this was arrant nonsense. Under traditional causation analysis any person whose act is a but-for cause of the harm has caused *all* the harm, not a part of it. That is still true under comparative negligence: the jury still must find that each defendant's negligence caused indivisible harm to the plaintiff before that defendant is liable. (If they caused divisible harm, they would be separately liable for that harm only. See Chapter 19, Example 12.)

Thus, the jury does not assign a party a 15 percent share of the negligence because she only caused 15 percent of the plaintiff's damages. When juries assign percentages of negligence, they are making findings as to how *faulty* each defendant was in causing the single, indivisible harm the plaintiff suffered. In finding one defendant 15 percent at fault and another 85 percent, they are saying that the one was considerably less negligent than the other, even though each was a but-for cause of *all* of the plaintiff's resulting damages.

9.   Under several liability, Murdstone's potential damage exposure is much less than it is under joint and several liability, because he is only liable for his percentage share of the total damages. He will therefore take a harder line in settlement negotiations than he could under joint and several liability, which exposes him to liability for the plaintiff's full damages. Under joint and several liability, plaintiff could argue, "Look, as long as the jury finds you negligent at all—even one percent—you are liable to me for the entire judgment." This is a forceful argument in many cases because, even though a plaintiff like Murdstone has a theoretical right of contribution from more negligent tortfeasors, they are often unable to pay.

Under several liability, this sword of Damocles is removed; Murdstone is only at risk for the share of fault that the jury assesses to him. If this is likely to be small, defendants like Murdstone are likely to be a good deal more stingy in considering settlement.

Spreading the Risk

10a.   Under the Minnesota statute, Heap's uncollectible share, $12,000, would be reallocated among Flite, Micawber, and Murdstone. Flite should absorb 20/80ths of it ($3,000); Micawber 50/80ths ($7,500), and Murdstone 10/80ths ($1,500).[9] Thus, Micawber owes his own share ($30,000) plus his reallocated portion of Heap's share ($7,500). Flite collects $37,500 from Micawber.

b. Under this type of reallocation statute, Heap's $12,000 share should be reallocated between Micawber and Murdstone in proportion to their degrees of fault. Micawber should absorb 50/60ths of Heap's $12,000 ($10,000). Micawber should pay Flite his own share ($30,000) plus the $10,000 reallocated to him, for a total of $40,000. (Murdstone would pay his share ($6,000) plus $2,000 (10/60ths of Heap's share) or $8,000.) Thus, Flite recovers her entire $48,000 judgment, since, under this type of reallocation statute, she does not absorb part of the uncollectible share.

Compound Fractures

11a. *Indiana:* Indiana's modified comparative negligence statute allows the plaintiff to recover as long as her negligence is 50 percent or less. Section 2. If this is true (as it is in Jingle's case), each defendant is severally liable in proportion to his percentage of fault. Jingle gets a judgment against Weller for 60 percent of his total damages, or $48,000.

Iowa: Under Iowa's statute, a defendant who is more than 50 percent at fault is jointly and severally liable for the economic damages only. This distinction is sometimes found in comparative negligence regimes. Retaining joint and several liability for the "hard" losses like medical expenses and lost earnings makes it likely that these out-of-pocket losses will be paid. At the same time, imposing several liability for intangible damages, such as pain and suffering and loss of consortium, limits the exposure of defendants. The distinction may suggest that there is something less real about the intangible consequences of a serious injury. Or, it may reflect simple doubt that these intangible consequences can actually be recompensed by a money award.

Under the Iowa statute, Weller is liable for $16,000 for Jingle's economic damages. You take the $20,000 and reduce it for Jingle's fault, to $16,000, but Weller is liable for all of this under the statute, since his fault is more than 50 percent. Weller is also severally liable for 60 percent of Jingle's noneconomic damages, or $36,000. So Jingle could collect a total of $52,000 from Weller.

Oregon: Under Oregon's (now superseded) statute, defendants are severally liable for noneconomic damages. But a defendant more than 15 percent at fault is jointly and severally liable for the economic damages (after reduction for the plaintiff's fault), if his percentage of fault is greater

---

9. Note again that the fractions are constructed by adding the negligence percentages of the parties involved (Flite, Micawber, and Murdstone) and using that as the denominator. The numerators are the negligence percentages of each party.

than the plaintiff's. Since Weller is more than 15 percent at fault, and more negligent than Jingle, he is liable for $16,000 for Jingle's economic damages (again, these still get reduced to account for Jingle's share of fault). He is severally liable for 60 percent of Jingle's noneconomic damages, so again his total liability is $52,000.

b. *Indiana*: Under the Indiana several liability statute, Snubbin is liable for 20 percent of the total damages, or $16,000.

Iowa: Since Snubbin is less than 50 percent at fault, his liability is several. He would owe Jingle $16,000.

Oregon: Under §4 of the Oregon statute, Snubbin's liability for economic damages would be joint and several. His percentage of fault is at least 15, and he is not less faulty than Jingle. His liability for noneconomic damages is several, under §2. So he owes $16,000 for the economic damages and $12,000 (20 percent of $60,000) for the intangible damages, for a total of $28,000.

Now, was that fun, or what?

PART NINE

Taking a Torts Essay Exam

25

The Pot at the End of the Rainbow: Analyzing Torts Issues on an Essay Exam

Most of this book has dealt with the substance of tort law, analyzing the liability standards courts apply to claims for personal injury. This Part has a different goal: to introduce you to the type of analysis you will be expected to perform in answering an essay question on your Torts exam.

A major goal—in fact, *the* major goal—of the first year curriculum is to develop students' analytic skills, to teach you to "think like lawyers." And the primary way in which we determine whether students have absorbed that skill is through essay exams. Most students have never encountered essay exams quite like the typical law school exam. It seems appropriate to give you some explanation of the logic behind these exams, together with examples of the type of analysis we expect you to produce.

This Part includes three chapters on the nature of the legal analysis expected on a Torts exam. This chapter discusses the basic analytic approach required on a Torts essay, by pulling single issues out of an essay and illustrating how to address them. The next chapter comes at the problem from the other direction. It provides examples of the typical mistakes students make in answering essay questions. These can be kind of fun, and my explanations should help you to avoid these pitfalls and highlight the proper approach. The last chapter includes several essay questions, with sample answers and some suggestions, from the professor's point of view, about how to approach the questions.

I should offer a disclaimer here. While I believe the approach in these chapters would be endorsed by a large majority of your professors, some may draft their exams differently. Your Torts professor may have taken a heavily philosophical approach to the course, engaging in extended discussion of economic analysis, critical legal studies perspectives, or feminist legal analysis. If so, she may write an exam that emphasizes high altitude policy perspectives more than effective application of doctrine to facts, as I do. On the other hand, even a professor who luxuriated all semester in philosophical speculations may surprise you with an exam that looks much like mine, since analytical skills are fundamental and are easier to test than more freewheeling policy analysis.

The Basics: Applying Law to Fact

On the most basic level, what your professor wants to see you do on a Torts essay is to apply the law, as insightfully as possible, to the facts of the question she has set before you. She wants you to recognize a legal problem, grasp the relevant rule of law that a court will use to resolve it, explain how the court will resolve that issue given the peculiarities of the facts in the question, and most important, explain *why* the court will reach the conclusion you predict. Call it IRAC (Issue/Rule/Application/Conclusion) if you like, or whatever; the important thing is that you *do it*, that you explain why, on the facts presented, the court will reach a particular outcome.

Enough generalities; let's get down to cases. Consider this short snippet from one of my exams:

> Jackson, a trucker, picked up a load of construction debris to be hauled to a landfill. She took off, without securing the tarpaulin over the load, as required by statute for all debris hauling.
>
> Later, Jackson stopped for coffee at a rest area on the turnpike. Since there were no parking spaces she started to back into an area behind the restaurant, marked No Parking—Tow Zone. Behind a fence was a large tank. Jackson backed into the space. Somehow, the truck hit the tank, which exploded and threw a large plank out of the back of Jackson's truck. The plank flew 200 feet and hit Polk, knocking him face down on the ground. Cleveland, a stranger, ran over and rolled Polk over to check his breathing. Because Polk had suffered several broken ribs, this caused internal bleeding.
>
> Jackson was shaken up by the blast, but managed to get out of her truck. She saw Polk on the ground. Although she was trained as an emergency medical technician, she did not immediately go to help Polk.

Let's focus on a single issue raised by these facts. When you saw that phrase "as required by statute," it should have set off a small alarm bell in the torts corner of your brain. "Aha! He's setting up a violation-of-statute-as-negligence issue." Indeed I was. So let's pull this small issue out and take a look at it.

As Chapter 5 illustrates, a court will sometimes find a party negligent for violating a safety statute. Sometimes, but not always: The court will only "borrow" the statute if it was enacted to protect persons like the plaintiff from the type of harm that the plaintiff suffered. That is all you need to know to respond to the statutory issue here:

> Polk may argue that Jackson can be found negligent for violating the statute requiring a tarpaulin over the load of debris. However, a court will only find negligence due to the violation if the statute was meant to avoid the type of harm Polk suffered. Here, the tarpaulin statute was probably enacted to prevent debris from blowing out of the truck on the highway and hitting or obstructing other vehicles. It is farfetched indeed to argue that legislators, when they enacted this statute, had in mind protecting pedestrians from debris thrown out of trucks by an explosion. Thus, the court will not find Jackson negligent per se for violating the tarpaulin statute.

This is simple and straightforward, almost a no-brainer. But the writer has shown her ability to see an issue ("whether Jackson will be negligent per se for violating a statute"), state the applicable rule ("a court will only hold a party negligent per se for a statutory violation if the statute was intended to protect against the type of harm suffered by the plaintiff"), apply the law to the facts ("this statute was aimed at debris blowing out during travel, not explosions throwing planks out of trucks"), and explain the result the court will reach ("the court will not find Jackson negligent for violating the statute"). In IRAC terms, issue, rule, application and conclusion.

A couple of points about this. First, law students talk a lot about "issue spotting," but if you content yourself with spotting the issues on your exams you should resign yourself to getting low Cs at best. It isn't very hard to spot issues, and, more important, it doesn't demonstrate the skill we are trying to test: your ability to analyze and predict the outcome of cases. Consider this response to the Jackson negligence per se issue:

> There is an issue here as to whether Jackson will be held
> negligent per se for violating the tarpaulin statute. If the court,
> applies the negligence per se doctrine, Jackson will be found
> negligent, because she did not put on the tarpaulin.

As my seven-year-old daughter used to say "*Pah-leeese!*" All this writer says is that there's an issue about negligence per se, and that if the doctrine applies it applies. Sure, the student has "spotted the issue," but she has not done the real work of the exercise: to explain the governing rule and apply it insightfully to the facts. You've got to do more than parrot back the issues I wrote into the exam. You have to analyze how the court will resolve them and tell me why it will resolve them that way.

Just to nail down the point, imagine that you were a practicing lawyer, and that Jackson came to you for advice on her liability to Polk. Imagine that you advised her as follows:

> Well, Jackson, there's an issue here as to whether the court will find you negligent per se for violating the tarpaulin statute. If the court applies the negligence per se doctrine, you will be found negligent, because you did not put on the tarpaulin.

What would Jackson say to you after hearing this pithy oration? She would have good sense to ask, "Well, *will* the court apply the negligence per se doctrine or not?" She came to you for solutions, or at least educated judgments, not for a restatement of the problem. To show your ability to advise Jackson, you must go beyond spotting the issues.

Second, even if you go beyond the issue to state the relevant rule of law, you still haven't tackled the real job your professor expects of you. Consider this response to the negligence per se issue:

> There is an issue here as to whether Jackson will be held
> negligent per se for violating the tarpaulin statute. Courts will find
> a party negligent per se for violating a statute if the plaintiff is in
> the class of persons the statute was enacted to protect, and if the
> statute was intended to protect against the type of harm the
> plaintiff suffered. If the court finds the tarpaulin statute was
> enacted to protect against the type of injury Polk suffered,
> Jackson will be negligent per se.

This writer has gone beyond spotting the negligence per se issue: She has stated the legal principle the court will use to resolve it. Good! ... You can't *apply* a legal principle effectively if you don't know what it is. But the real goal of the exam is *not* to test your memory of legal principles. This is not high school; we are not primarily trying to teach you rules, and we are not content to see that you remember what the rules are. We want to teach you — and, therefore, to test you on — *legal judgment*, the ability to make sophisticated predictions about how a court is likely to apply a principle to a new case. Consequently, about 80 percent of the IRAC job is in the "A", applying the principle to the facts. Can you see that the writer of this excerpt has contented herself with the "I" and the "R," but avoided shouldering the main burden these elements lead up to?

Somehow this doesn't seem fair. You spend all that time learning principles of tort law, like the negligence per se rules, and it doesn't get you anywhere! But it does get you somewhere: Stating the rule puts you in the position to analyze the facts and apply the rule to them. And, without doubt, the more sophisticated your understanding of the rules is, the better job you will do in applying them to the new facts in the question. But no, we are not testing you primarily on your knowledge of the rules, and simply regurgitating the rules will not serve you well in the merry month of May.

On the other hand, it's a dirty little secret that you really don't have to know an awful lot of law to do well on a first year exam. Sure, you need to study the material and have a good grasp of the basic doctrines you studied. But most of the issues — even those much more difficult than the Jackson issue — involve sophisticated application of *basic doctrine* rather than encyclopedic knowledge of the farthest reaches of the torts landscape. Most students spend inordinate amounts of time learning more and more rules, and very little time practicing the skill of applying the fundamental rules to new facts. You would be wiser to spend less time memorizing rules and more time applying them. That's why Chapter 27 offers example essays to work with (and also why there are examples in every chapter in this book).

Another Snippet — and Another Rule

Let's illustrate the basic point again, with another snippet from a different exam:

> Phelps bought a used bike and started riding home on the sidewalk (a practice forbidden by statute). As he passed Jill's house, Jill was on her lawn with her dog Woof. They had just come back from a walk, during which Jill had kept Woof on his leash, as required by the town leash ordinance. However, as she reached her lawn, Jill took off the leash and started throwing a ball for Woof to retrieve. Woof, a frisky adolescent, took off and ran right at the front wheel

of Phelps's bike. Woof hit the wheel, knocking the bike over and sending Phelps flying over the handlebars into the street.

Phelps landed hard, and scraped his leg on a parking meter stub as he landed, tearing his pants and suffering a serious laceration. Phelps was knocked out by the impact, and lay bleeding from his wound. Jill saw the accident, but did nothing to help Phelps.

This short passage raises a number of issues (including several negligence per se issues). But let's focus for the moment on the issue raised by the fact that Jill did nothing to help Phelps after the accident.

Clearly, there is a duty issue here, and, on the facts given, it is not a very hard one. Although there is some ambiguity as to whether Jill was negligent, you should recognize that she has a duty to assist Phelps whether she was negligent or not. Courts impose a duty on an actor whose act causes bodily injury to another to go to the victim's assistance, even if the actor caused the injury without negligence. Restatement (Second) of Torts, §322. Here's a response that analyzes Jill's liability appropriately:

> Jill may be liable to Phelps for failing to aid him after Woof knocked him off the bike and injured him. Where a party causes injury to another, even without negligence, she has a duty to go to the injured party's aid. Thus, <u>whether or not</u> Jill was negligent (for violating the ordinance or under general reasonable care analysis), she had a duty to help Phelps, since her act of releasing Woof caused the injury. If Phelps suffered any additional injury from Jill's failure to assist him, Jill may be liable for the additional injury.

Again, this is a very basic example; seeing that Jill has a duty on these facts is not rocket science. Other issues will be more complex. But the basic process is much the same, even for more sophisticated issues: explaining your educated judgment about how an issue will be resolved on a given set of facts.

More Layers of the Onion

Individual issues like the ones illustrated above are the basic building blocks of a law school essay question. Your exam will have plenty of them, probably more than you can fully address in the time allotted. Some will be straightforward, like those above. Professors put some relatively easy issues on their exams to make sure students can do basic legal analysis — the few students who flub these are headed for the door. The students who handle these competently — but only these — will barely scrape by.

Other issues in the exam will be considerably more complex, and will require consideration of multiple principles to resolve effectively. Professors put these more complex issues in the exam in order to make distinctions among the stronger students, to decide who gets the *A*s and who gets the *B*s. The more sophisticated the problem, the more clearly the bluebooks break down into categories. I like to think of it in terms of layers of an onion. The mediocre student will only see the outer layer; a better student will peel off another layer of the problem, but the student who has really mastered the analytic technique will keep going, peeling more and more layers, showing that she understands the true elegance of the problem.

Let's try another negligence per se example, which shows how an effective analysis of the issue becomes more complex as you consider more issues. This example is not a killer, but involves a few more layers of the onion.

> Holmes went to a football game with his friend, Cardozo. As they were driving home, somewhat tipsy from the beers they had had at the game, Holmes noticed that Cardozo was driving about ten miles over the speed limit. He said nothing. Suddenly the right front tire blew out, sending the car spinning across the opposite lane of traffic, toward the far side of the road.
>
> Brennan was driving a flatbed truck coming the other way. The truck was loaded with steel reinforcing rod — in fact, it was overloaded. Although a statute limited truck loads to 40,000 pounds, Brennan had 46,000 pounds on his. (Almost all truckers in the state *did* violate the weight limits — it was pretty widely known that the police wouldn't give you a hard time unless loads were about 25 percent above the limit.) Brennan jammed on his brakes as he saw Cardozo's car swerve across his path. Cardozo, seeing the truck barreling toward him, jerked the steering wheel to the left, away from the truck, just as the car skidded into a phone pole on the side of the road. Holmes was thrown against the windshield and injured. Brennan's truck barely missed hitting Cardozo's car.

Once again, there's a statute in the fact pattern. Doubtless, it's in there for a reason — you've probably heard that every word in the law school essay question is there for a reason. This may not be literally true, but it's a fair working assumption that most of the facts in the question are pertinent to some issue to be addressed. And, again, the obvious issue is negligence per se. The statute establishes a weight limit, and Brennan violated it. Will he be found negligent for doing so?

This one is a little more subtle than the first. Some students argued that the weight limit is irrelevant to Holmes's injury:

> Although Brennan violated the statutory weight limit, this will not make him negligent per se, because the statute was not meant to protect plaintiffs like Holmes from the type of injury he suffered. Weight limits are meant to protect against excessive wear on the roads, not traffic accidents.

But others recognized that a weight limit may have more than one purpose, and that one may be to protect plaintiffs like Holmes:

> Holmes faces several problems in asserting a claim against Brennan for his injuries. First, if he tries to establish that Brennan was negligent per se for violating the weight statute, he will have to show that the statute was enacted to protect against traffic accidents such as his. If the statute was intended solely to protect against excessive wear on the roads, Holmes would not be able to establish negligence per se based on the violation. However, it seems likely that the legislature <u>also</u> had in mind the fact that overweight trucks are more difficult to control and to stop. Holmes has a strong argument that Brennan's violation of the weight limit is relevant, since the legislature meant to assure adequate ability to control trucks, and Brennan's excess weight likely affected his ability to do so.

Wouldn't you agree that the second answer has peeled more layers off of the onion? This student went beyond the first level answer to a more comprehensive analysis of the issue. Imagine that you represented Holmes, who wanted advice on whether to sue Brennan. "No, Holmes, don't bother to make a negligence per se claim against him; the statute's irrelevant." This would not be effective representation, would it? The situation is more complicated than that, and your advice should recognize that there is more to it. On the exam, we want you to show us that you can go beyond the superficial to a more sophisticated application of law to facts.

Let's take this example a bit further, because another aspect of onion peeling is to recognize the interrelatedness of various issues in the course. Suppose that the statute *was* intended to protect against accidents, so that Brennan may be found negligent per se for violating it. A good onion peeler should recognize that Holmes faces several further hurdles to establish that Brennan is liable for violating it. First, courts allow a violator to offer evidence of excuse, so the student will have to consider any indication of an excuse in the fact pattern.

Assuming that the statute was intended to protect against traffic accidents, Brennan might raise the excuse that truckers customarily violated the statute, and that the police did not generally enforce it. This is a weak argument. It is the <u>legislature</u> that sets the policy, not the public or even the police. As a matter of policy, the courts ought not authorize either truckers or the police to overrule the statute by ignoring it. (Distinguish the role of custom where there is no statute; it is relevant evidence of due care in that context, but courts would very likely reject it where it <u>contradicts</u> the statute.) The court will likely hold, as a matter of law, that this is not an adequate excuse.

This is a nice little issue. I had never discussed the relationship between negligence per se and custom in class, so the student was not given "the answer" to this before seeing the issue on the exam. Does this seem unfair? I don't think so; legal analysis is about extrapolating what you *do* know to new situations. This twist requires the student to think about the relation between two doctrines, negligence per se and custom. If she really understands the rationales of the two rules, the answer should be fairly clear. Admittedly, the exercise is more sophisticated than basic IRAC. The better students will do it better, some won't do it at all. So, the issue helps me to separate the books.

Let's keep going with some more layers of the onion. Even if no acceptable excuse is available, Brennan might still escape liability for his negligence:

Even if Brennan is negligent for violating the statute, he will only be liable if his negligence <u>caused</u> Holmes's injury. Although Brennan's truck never hit Cardozo's car, his violation of the weight limit might still be found a cause of the accident. Had the truck been lighter, he could have stopped sooner, and Cardozo might not have turned the wheel to avoid Brennan. However, the facts indicate that Cardozo saw Brennan and swerved as he was about to hit the pole. If he was that close, he presumably would have hit the pole whether he swerved or not. If this is true, Brennan's negligence did not cause the harm.

How's that for onion peeling? This student has recognized that proving Brennan's negligence only establishes breach of the duty of due care, that there are three other elements to the claim, and that the facts suggest a serious problem in proving causation. If I were Brennan, I would want to be represented by this student. She's going down each branch of the decision tree, to predict the issues that will arise in the case and the various defenses to be asserted on my behalf. That's good lawyering; showing that you can do it is good exam writing.[1]

Let's reconsider the first answer, from the student who concluded that the statute was irrelevant. She certainly gets some credit for her answer: She has recognized the problem and applied the appropriate rule, though in a conclusory manner. This isn't a flunker, but if all issues were addressed on this level she would end up pretty low in the pack. *More importantly,* by failing to recognize that the statute may be relevant, she has failed to peel the other layers of the onion, to spin out the implications of a claim against Brennan.[2] Compare the two analyses of Brennan's liability:

Student #1:

> Although Brennan violated the statutory weight limit, this will not make him negligent per se, because the statute was not meant to protect plaintiffs like Holmes from the type of injury he suffered. Weight limits are meant to protect against excessive wear on the roads, not traffic accidents.

---

1. We still haven't peeled the last layer of this simple little scenario. For example, Holmes knew that Cardozo had been drinking, but drove with him anyway. Could Brennan assert an assumption of risk defense if sued by Holmes? Presumably not; Holmes may have assumed the risk of injury due to Cardozo's intoxication, but he did not assume the risk of *Brennan's* negligent driving.

2. This student might still address those issues if she recognizes that negligence per se is *only one way of proving a defendant negligent.* Brennan may be negligent under common law reasonable care analysis for overloading his truck. If the student realized this, she should still discuss the causation and assumption of the risk issues.

Student #2:

> Holmes faces several problems in asserting a claim against Brennan for his injuries. First, if he tries to establish that Brennan was negligent per se for violating the weight statute, he will have to show that the statute was enacted to protect against traffic accidents such as his. If the statute were solely to protect against excessive wear on the roads, Holmes would not be able to establish negligence per se based on the violation. However, it seems likely that the legislature <u>also</u> had in mind the fact that overweight trucks are more difficult to control and to stop. Holmes has a strong argument that Brennan's violation of the weight limit is relevant, since the legislature meant to assure adequate ability to control trucks, and Brennan's excess weight likely affected his ability to do so.
>
> Assuming that the statute was intended to protect against traffic accidents, Brennan might raise the excuse that truckers customarily violated the statute, and that the police did not generally enforce it. This is a weak argument. It is the <u>legislature</u> that sets the policy, not the public or even the police. As a matter of policy, the courts ought not authorize either truckers or the police to overrule the statute by ignoring it. (Distinguish the role of custom where there is no statute; it is relevant evidence of due care in that context, but courts would very likely reject it where it <u>contradicts</u> the statute.) The court will likely hold, as a matter of law, that this is not an adequate excuse.
>
> Even if Brennan is found negligent, he will only be liable if his negligence caused Holmes's injury. Although Brennan's truck never hit Cardozo's car, his violation of the weight limit might still be found a cause of the accident. Had the truck been lighter, he could have stopped sooner, and Cardozo might not have turned the wheel to avoid Brennan. However, the facts indicate that Cardozo swerved as he was about to hit the pole. If he was that close, he presumably would have hit the pole whether he swerved or not. If this is true, Brennan's negligence did not cause the harm.

Looking at the two side-by-side, it isn't hard to see which answer will receive the better grade.

Let's Do It Again

Peeling the onion is important enough that I want to illustrate it again, using the duty issue from the Jackson exam on p. 572. The first step, of course, is to recognize that there is an issue as to whether Jackson owes a duty of care to Polk. If you don't see the issue, you can't show your onion peeling prowess. On the other hand, when I grade an essay I do not knock students down for missing a few issues. There are always too many to discuss fully, so I don't assign grades by tallying up points for issues seen or missed. If the student sees the important issues and discusses them effectively, she can do very well even though she has not seen some others. Some professors may take a more mechanical issue-counting approach. But even issue counters will give credit for the quality of analysis as well as the number of issues seen, so peeling the onion remains important in taking their exams as well.

Let's look first at several responses to this issue that fail at the most basic level—understanding the legal rules themselves.

> Although Jackson did not go to Polk's aid, she will not be liable for failing to do so. Under §314 of Restatement, a bystander has no duty to give aid to another simply because the other is in need of assistance. Even though Jackson is an EMT, she owes no duty to Polk.

This response falters on the R in IRAC. The student doesn't know the basis rule that Jackson has a duty to assist Polk based on the fact that her conduct led to Polk's injury. See Chapter 10, pp. 218-219. The student's failure to see this hurts in two ways: First, it makes me think the student doesn't know the basic doctrine. Second, it means that she will not go on to consider whether Jackson fulfilled her duty toward Polk.

Here's another answer that reveals problems at the *R* level:

> Jackson will be liable for failing to aid Polk after the injury. Jackson is an EMT, with special training in providing emergency care to injured persons. Thus, she has a duty to assist as a reasonable EMT would under the circumstances.

This response shows basic substantive confusion, since the more fact that a person possesses special training that would make her a good rescuer does not impose a legal duty to assist. See Chapter 10, Example 7. Both of these students are headed for trouble because they simply don't know the rules. If all their responses looked like this they would obviously fail.

Most students *do* know the rules, however, and state them adequately on the exam. They survive the *R* and falter at the *A* stage, by failing to apply the principle effectively to the facts. Here's a student who knows the rule, but still provides an unpeeled answer to the duty issue:

> Jackson has a duty to assist the injured Polk, because she caused injury to him. (This is true whether Jackson was negligent in causing the explosion or not.) Therefore, since she did not go to Polk's aid, she is liable to Polk.

As I already reiterated, the name of the game is not just knowing the rule, but applying it intelligently to the facts. This student states the basic rule, but her application to the facts is totally conclusory. If *you* represented Jackson, would you give up this easily? If so, you aren't representing her effectively, because Polk faces several serious problems in holding Jackson liable for failing to aid. This student's analysis places her exam in the low *C* range.

Here's a student who takes the analysis of Polk's liability a step further:

> Because Jackson's driving caused the injury to Polk, she has a duty to go to his assistance (whether she negligently or innocently caused the explosion). However, Jackson's duty is to exercise <u>reasonable care</u> to aid Polk. Here, Jackson was shaken up, and stumbled out of her truck. A reasonable person in those circumstances would probably not be able to rush over and render aid. Thus, while Jackson owed a duty to Polk, she may not have breached it.

That's true, isn't it? When negligence law imposes a duty, it's a duty of reasonable care, not an absolute duty no matter what the circumstances. If Jackson did as well as the reasonable person would have under similar circumstances, Polk will fail to establish element #2, negligence. By peeling off the breach issue as well, this student shows that she recognizes that duty is the beginning of the analysis, not the end of it. This answer is moving into the *B* range, depending on the quality of the discussion.

Of course, there's more. Even if Jackson owed a duty and was negligent, he may yet escape liability:

> Should the court find that Jackson owed a duty to aid Polk, and that a reasonable person in her circumstances would have rushed to Polk's aid, Jackson may still not be liable. A person who owes a duty to aid is liable for the <u>additional</u> injury suffered as a result of the failure to aid, so Polk will have to show that Jackson's failure to aid caused him further injury. The facts indicate that Polk was 200 feet away from the truck. It is extremely unlikely that the most diligent rescuer in Jackson's position would have reached Polk before Cleveland rolled him over. Thus, even if Jackson had a duty to aid and breached it, we cannot say that but for her failure to aid Polk, Polk would not have suffered the internal bleeding.

This student is on an onion peeling roll. I said above that we want to watch you *think like a lawyer,* and this student is really thinking in a comprehensive way about the problems in establishing Jackson's liability. She's in the high-*B*/low-*A* range if she keeps this up. Maybe a straight *A,* depending on the quality of her explanation.

This Jackson issue works well for testing onion peeling. There are even a couple more layers to peel. For example, even if Jackson had a duty, *and* breached, *and* could have reached Polk before Cleveland, she might have rolled him over, just as Cleveland did, since Jackson probably would not have known that Polk had broken ribs. And, even if Jackson could tell that Polk had broken ribs, breathing is important stuff; it might be perfectly reasonable to roll Polk over anyway to clear the airway. Last, you could round out the discussion nicely by pointing out that, if Jackson was negligent in causing the explosion that knocked Polk down (and if the flying plank was foreseeable), the whole duty-to-aid issue is moot: She would be liable for all of Polk's injuries anyway, including those from Cleveland's foreseeable rescue effort, as the initial tortfeasor!

Summing Up

If all this seems too much to ask, remember that your professors don't expect you to belabor every issue in the fact pattern, and to spot every permutation. They expect you to do the best you can in the time allotted. You will be graded relative to what a good first-year law student can do. The more you see the ramifications of the facts, and the more insightfully you explore them, the better you will do.

If you get the hang of this basic analytical technique, it will serve you well over your entire law school career (and after). The following examples should help to drive the point home. The explanation begin on p. 588.

EXAMPLES

Stretched on the IRAC

1.   Consider the following short essay question:

> While King was driving north on a two-lane rural road, his tire blew out, causing the car to pull sharply to the right. King turned the wheel back to the left to avoid going off the road; the car then swerved into the southbound lane. Phil, traveling south, ran into it. King's car rolled off the road and down an incline. Debris from the crash was scattered in the southbound lane, including the tailpipe and muffler from Phil's car.
>
> Phil ran to King's assistance. Queen was traveling north behind King, on her way to an important meeting. She stopped and picked up some of the debris, but not the tailpipe, which was quite hot. Then she left to make her meeting. Deuce, an off-duty emergency medical technician, passed the accident, saw the debris in the road, and drove on. Trip, King's partner in a house painting business, was driving behind King in their truck; they were going to start a job that morning. Trip did not stop.
>
> Ace came around the curve, going south at 40 m.p.h. in a 30 m.p.h. zone, and saw the tailpipe in the road. He decided to drive over it rather than swerve to avoid it. When he did, the truck went out of control. Ace suffered serious injuries.
>
> Discuss the claims Ace may assert based on these facts, and the major issues he will face in establishing liability of the possible defendants. *Explain fully how you expect the issues to be resolved and why.*

a.   What claims should you *definitely not* discuss in writing this essay?
b.   What major issues do you see in the fact pattern?
c.   Which issue gets your vote for the easiest issue in the question?
d.   Which issue do you think is the most complex?

2.   Consider the following three responses on the duty of Trip to stop and assist at the accident scene. In IRAC terms, what is missing from each?

a.
> There is an issue here as to whether Trip will be liable to Ace for failing to stop and clear the debris from the roadway after the initial accident. Here, because Trip did fail to stop, and Ace ran into the tailpipe, Trip has breached his duty to aid, and will be liable to Ace for his injuries.

b.

> Trip may be liable to Ace if he owed a duty to stop and assist at the scene of the accident. Ordinarily a person does not owe a duty to stop and assist, simply because a dangerous situation exists. However, a duty may be imposed if the person either created the risk that threatens injury (in this case the debris in the road) or has a special relationship that imposes a duty to assist. Here, since Trip did not stop and assist, he will be liable to Ace for his injuries

c.

> Trip may be held liable to Ace if he had a duty to stop and help but failed to do so. Here Trip owed a duty, since he was King's partner in the painting business. Thus, he will be liable to Ace for his injury.

3.   Draft a more effective analysis of Trip's liability.

Onion Rings

4.   Assume that you conclude that Trip did owe a duty to assist after the initial accident. What further layers would you peel off the onion in assessing his liability to Ace?

5.   Let's round out the discussion by peeling the layers off a rather subtle issue. Consider this excerpt from one of my past exams, which raises an intentional tort issue.

> Alou, a pedestrian, was hit on the head by a flower pot that fell from an apartment building. As he lay groaning in the street (a pedestrian way closed to all but emergency traffic), Sanchez rushed up. Alou, who was having trouble breathing, cried, "Don't touch me!" However, Sanchez could see a fire truck rushing down the street, and thought it might hit Alou unless he was moved. Thus, he grabbed Alou by the arm and dragged him toward the curb. At this point, the fire truck pulled up in front of them and two fire fighters jumped out; they were responding to a call from a neighbor informing them of Alou's accident.
>
> The fire fighters rushed Alou to the hospital, where he was diagnosed with a concussion and a broken rib, which had somehow punctured a lung.

The following three analyses address the question whether Sanchez battered Alou by dragging him from the street. Please grade them, on a scale from D to A. Assume that the authors had all read *Clayton v. New Dreamland*

Skating Rink, Inc., 82 A.2d 458 (N.J. 1951), in which a woman broke her arm while skating, and the attendant set the arm over her protests to leave her alone. The court held that the attendant committed a battery by doing so.

Student #1:

> Sanchez may have committed battery when he grabbed Alou and pulled him out of the street, since Alou told him not to touch him. A contact can be tortious even if it is well intended—a virtuous motive won't protect Sanchez if he intentionally made a harmful or offensive contact with Alou. (See skating rink case.)
>
> Here, however, Sanchez was acting to protect Alou from the danger of the oncoming fire truck. A reasonable person would do the same thing, even if Alou said not to. The privilege of necessity applies where a person inflicts an unwanted contact in order to prevent a greater harm. That is exactly what Sanchez did here, so he will not be liable to Alou, even if he caused additional injury to Alou by pulling him.

Student #2:

> The facts here raise a question as to whether Sanchez battered Alou when he grabbed him and dragged him by the arm. Even though Alou said not to touch him, Sanchez pulled him out of the road anyway. A person commits a battery when he intentionally makes an unconsented contact that the reasonable person would find harmful or offensive. This protects people's autonomy and prevents unwanted contacts. The law of battery is meant to protect people from contacts that they don't want, even if they are not harmful. The contact must be intentional, that is, it must be done with a purpose to cause the contact or with knowledge to a substantial certainty that it will cause one.
>
> Here, Sanchez knew that Alou did not want to be touched, because Alou said so. Thus, he made a tortious contact when he pulled Alou out of the street after Alou told him not to. This was a deliberate, offensive contact with Alou. When he acted he knew that Alou did not want him to touch him. Therefore Sanchez is liable for battery, since he went ahead and did it anyway.

Student #3:

> Sanchez will probably not be liable to Alou for battery. Sanchez committed a prima facie battery when he grabbed Alou after Alou said not to touch him, since he knew Alou did not want to be touched. This contact would be battery, even if he did it to help. Compare the case where the attendant set the woman's arm against her protest.
>
> However, Sanchez may have a privilege to act despite Alou's refusal. If both Sanchez and Alou possessed all the facts, Sanchez would not have a privilege, even if he thought the touching was necessary. Sanchez would have the right to refuse the contact even if the reasonable person would accept it. But here Alou may not be aware of the fire truck coming at him. If this is true, his refusal is given without all the relevant facts. Just as a <u>consent</u> without all the relevant facts may not be valid (e.g., consent to sex with a partner who does not reveal a sexually transmitted disease), a court would likely allow Sanchez to ignore Alou's refusal if he were ignorant of a fact crucial to his decision (the fire truck).
>
> This is not inconsistent with the skating rink case. There, both parties had the same information, and the attendant simply ignored the patron's wishes. Here, Sanchez can reasonably infer that Alou would consent if he knew about the truck, and act accordingly. (The more accurate analogy to the skating rink case would be if the Zamboni were bearing down on the patron and she didn't know it.)
>
> As it turned out, Sanchez was wrong; the truck would not have hit Alou since it was coming to rescue him. However, the court would doubtless accord him a privilege anyway if his mistake was reasonable under the circumstances.

EXPLANATIONS

Stretched on the IRAC

1a. Please, in writing a law school essay, answer the question that is asked. You'd be amazed how often students ignore this maxim! One reason students complain about insufficient time to write their essays is that they discuss all sorts of issues they don't have to. Here, the closing paragraph is explicit: discuss *Ace's* claims. If you spend half your time on claims King or Phil might assert, you have wasted half your writing time. I can't give you credit for this. It would be unfair to the other students who followed my directions to grade you on this irrelevant discussion.

b.   Needless to say, this small vignette is replete with interesting torts issues. Let's pull out the major ones, in order of their occurrence in the facts.

1. Breach: Can we establish negligence of King based on the fact that his tire blew out, using res ipsa loquitur?
2. Breach: Was King negligent in swerving back across the road after the tire blew out?
3. Duty: Did Phil (or King) have a duty to clear the debris out of the roadway?
4. Breach: If Phil did have a duty to clear the debris, was he negligent in performing the duty? (He went to help King instead.)
5. Duty: Did Queen owe a duty to Ace to stop and clear the road. If not, did she assume one by stopping and doing part of the job? If she had a duty, did she breach it?
6. Duty: Did Deuce, the E.M.T., owe a duty to assist at the accident scene. If he did, did the duty extend to clearing the debris?
7. Duty: Did Trip, King's partner, owe a duty to stop and assist?
8. Actual Causation: If Trip owed a duty and breached by failing to stop, did that breach cause the accident that injured Ace?
9. Proximate cause: Was injury to Ace from running into the debris foreseeable? If so, was it foreseeable to Queen, to Phil, or to everyone?
10. Breach: Was Ace negligent in driving over the tailpipe instead of swerving? Was he negligent in driving over the speed limit?
11. Negligence per se/Proximate cause: Assuming that Ace was negligent per se for speeding, was the speed limit aimed at preventing the kind of accident he suffered when he ran over the tailpipe?

Students often ask me how they should structure their essay answers. Most students address the issues sequentially as they arise in the fact pattern. I have no problem with that, or with any other clear organizational principle for that matter. Dealing with the issues as they appear in the question helps you to make sure you address them all, and is generally fairly easy for the reader to follow.

c.   I vote for the duty of Deuce as the easiest issue. The law is clear that Deuce has no duty to aid. As a stranger to the events that caused the accident, the somewhat callous no-duty-to-aid rule allows him to drive by with impunity. See Chapter 10, pp. 214-216. The fact that he has some medical training, which would make him a competent rescuer, does not impose a duty to aid. Even if it did, any claim by *Ace* would be based on the failure to stop and clear the road, not the failure to stop and render medical assistance. Deuce's medical training is doubly irrelevant to that claim.

d.   Perhaps you picked proximate cause as the most complex issue, since proximate cause tends to be puzzling. However, there is little doubt that a person who leaves debris in the road can anticipate that it will cause an accident to another driver who comes along. It is also foreseeable that a driver will speed, so Ace's speed may make him comparatively negligent, but does not make injury to him unforeseeable.

A much more subtle and interesting issue is the duty of Trip to stop and assist. Trip is King's partner, and they are engaged in a joint enterprise at the time — or at least, they are *on their way to* a joint enterprise, the paint job. Does this impose a duty on Trip to stop and assist? If so, does he owe that duty to Ace? At least one court has imposed duties on persons engaged in a joint venture to assist *each other*, based on their relationship. See *Farwell v. Keaton*, 240 N.W.2d 217 (Mich. 1976). That rationale would support a duty for Trip to assist King, though perhaps not a duty to act to avoid injury to Ace.

Most courts would hold that King, since he caused the accident that created the risk, owes a duty to do what he can to mitigate that risk, whether he was negligent or not. Restatement (Second) §321. Isn't there an argument to be made here that Trip, who engaged in risk-creating conduct with King by driving to the job, owes a duty to act to mitigate the danger caused by their joint activity?

I don't know the "answer" to this issue, if there is one. But the student who sees this issue and analyzes it effectively, based on analogous principles studied in the course, shows me that she can get to the heart of the onion, to mix a few metaphors.

2a. In IRAC terms, this excerpt states the issue, and gives a conclusion, but leaves the reader guessing as to what legal principle the writer has applied, and why that principle leads her to the conclusion she has reached.

Issue	There is an issue here as to whether Trip will be liable to Ace for failing to stop and clear the debris from the roadway after the initial accident.
Conclusion	Here, because Trip did fail to stop, and Ace ran into the tailpipe, Trip has breached his duty to aid, and will be liable to Ace.

From the grader's point of view, the "I" and the "C" are the least important parts of the exercise, bookends for the much meatier matter in between: The explanation of the applicable legal principle and the analysis of how it will apply to the facts. Stating the issue simply sets up the "R" and the "A." If you state the applicable principle and apply it effectively, it will be abundantly clear what the issue is. And, if you discuss insightfully how a court is likely to apply a principle to the facts, the conclusion will also be perfectly clear. So the "C" is a mere coda; you could skip it entirely and lose little.

b.   This student is batting three for four, but she left out the most important part of the job. The excerpt states the issue and describes applicable duty principles, then jumps to the conclusion without explaining her reasoning. Again, let's break it into components:

Issue	Trip may be liable to Ace if he owed a duty to stop and assist at the scene of the accident.
Rule	Ordinarily a person does not owe a duty to stop and assist, simply because a dangerous situation exists. However, a duty may be imposed if the person either created the risk that threatens injury (in this case the debris in the road) or has a special relationship that imposes a duty to assist.
Conclusion	Here, since Trip did not stop and assist, he will be liable to Ace for his injuries.

The writer leaves us wondering whether she reached her conclusion through guesswork or inexorable reasoning. In my grading process you get little credit for reaching the "right" conclusion . . . on the juicy issues, I usually don't know what the "right" conclusion is. It is the quality of your reasoning I want to assess, and if you *do it in your head only,* as this student has, I can't give you points for it.

Often, students come in to go over an exam and are able to explain to me why they put a certain conclusion in their answer. ("Professor Glannon, that's exactly what I meant," they say.) But I can only grade you on what you explain on the exam, not the private ruminations that led you to a conclusion. If you decline to share your reasoning (the "A" in IRAC) with me in the bluebook, I can't give you any credit for it.

c.   This answer states the issue, and makes a passing effort at analysis. However, it is impossible to follow the student's reasoning.

Issue	Trip may be held liable to Ace if he had a duty to stop and help but failed to do so.
Analysis	Here Trip owed a duty, since he was King's partner in the painting business.
Conclusion	Thus, he will be liable to Ace for his injury.

In this excerpt, not only is the "A" much too brief, but the student's failure to state what principle of tort law she is applying — the "R" in IRAC — makes it impossible to evaluate the reasoning. Are partners always liable for their partners' torts? Are they vicariously liable? What is the nature of the duty Trip owed? Why is it breached on these facts? Remember that I want to *watch you think*, not just compare your conclusions to mine. This answer gives me very little on which to evaluate the writer's reasoning.

3.   Here are two responses that grapple effectively with the duty issue.

Answer #1:

> If Ace asserts a claim against Trip, King's partner, for failing to stop and clear the roadway after the accident, Ace will have a major problem establishing that Trip owed him a duty to assist. Usually courts impose a duty to aid where the defendant created the risk that threatens injury, or where the defendant has a special relationship to the injured person. Trip has no relationship to Ace, so the only potential source of duty would be creating the risk. It might be argued that Trip jointly created the risk with King, because they were partners driving to the same job site. However, the two were not actually working together, they were simply driving to the job. It seems unlikely, on these facts, that the court would impose a duty on Trip to respond to an accident caused independently by King.

Answer #2:

> If Ace sues Trip for failing to stop and clear the debris, he will have to show that Trip owed him a duty to do so. Ordinarily, there is no duty to assist a stranger, but this case may be distinguishable. Trip was engaged in a joint venture with King, who created (either innocently or negligently) the danger from the debris in the road. Courts have held that even innocent risk creators have a duty to assist to avert a danger they have created. And, at least one case (the one involving the two teenagers who went cruising and got in a fight) imposed a duty on one actor engaged in a joint venture to aid the other. It would be a small step to regard King and Trip's driving to the job as joint risk creation, and impose a duty on Trip to help avert the risk created by King. The joint venture argument would be stronger if they were driving from one job site to another, rather than if they were independently commuting from home.

Note several things about these answers. First, although they reach oppo-site conclusions, both students have gone to the heart of the matter. They have seen the duty problem, and focused on the risk-creation argument as the one likely to resolve it. They have explained why, based on the appli-cable legal principle, they conclude that the court would or would not impose a duty. Both are good answers.

Now, I naturally have my own views about what the court would do. I would be disingenuous to suggest that those views have *no* effect on the grading process. But I can say with conviction that well-reasoned analysis that focuses on the relevant issue and gives detailed reasons for the writ-er's prediction of the outcome always fares well, even if the writer doesn't reach the same conclusion I would.

Second, these answers are a little longer than the inadequate answers given in Example 2. True, good answers tend to be longer, because it takes more words to go into one's reasons for a conclusion. But that does not mean that longer is always better. Some students manage to go on at length without providing meaningful analysis. Others manage to get to the heart of the matter in relatively few words. Believe me, when facing 70 or 80 bluebooks, I value such economy!

Third, a quick note about the way the second student has used a case in her answer. The second answer notes that the duty issue here is some-what like that in a case she had read,[3] and then explains how finding a duty here would extend the principle in that case. It is always helpful to draw analogies in analyzing an issue: Analogical reasoning is one of the primary tools of a legal system based on precedent. Often, cases read for class furnish useful analogies, so it is appropriate to use them to explain your reasoning. But don't worry about the case names. It's the limits of the principles we want to test, not the names of the cases that exemplify them. Identifying the case as the cruising teenagers case is fine with me.

Onion Rings

4.   Even if Trip owed a duty to stop and clear the debris left by the initial accident, there are other problems in establishing his liability for Ace's injury. First, there is a subtle factual issue that might absolve Trip. The facts indicate that King's car was thrown down an incline, so that

---

3. The case referred to is *Farwell v. Keaton,* 240 N.W.2d 217 (Mich. 1976). In *Farwell,* the decedent and the defendant were out drinking together, talked to some girls, and then were chased by the girls' friends. The decedent was badly beaten. The defendant put him in his car, put ice on his head, drove around for a few hours, then left the decedent in the back of the car at his grandparents' house. The boy died of his injuries, and the defendant was sued for failing to obtain further medical assistance for him.

Trip may not have seen it. Would Trip have a duty to avert the hazard if King, his joint venturer, had created it but Trip *did not know that he had?* It is hard to imagine that a court would find Trip liable for failing to stop and assist unless he realized (or, perhaps, should have realized) that his partner was involved in the accident. This issue is very subtle. If a student even *saw* this issue I'd be impressed. I'd be bowled over if she offered a reasoned judgment about how it should be resolved.

Second, Trip might get off for lack of actual causation. If he had a duty to clear the debris, it was a duty to exercise reasonable care, not an absolute duty regardless of the circumstances. If Ace came barreling along before Trip would have been able to reach the tailpipe, then his failure to stop would not be an actual cause of Ace's accident.

There are some other issues too. Trip might argue that, had he stopped, he reasonably would have gone to King's assistance before dealing with the debris. If his joint venture gave rise to a duty to respond to King's accident, it probably also gave rise to a duty to aid his joint venturer. If this is so, he could make another argument that his failure to stop was not a "but for" cause of Ace's injury: If he had stopped, he would have reasonably helped King first instead of clearing the debris. (There is, of course, a counter argument: Phil was already helping King, so arguably the reasonable person in Trip's position would have dealt with the debris instead.)

There is also a proximate cause issue, though this one seems like a slam dunk: Surely Trip can foresee Ace's accident if he is negligent in failing to deal with the tailpipe.[4]

5.   Let's talk first about Student #2's response. This is the weakest, because the student talks on about the meaning of battery, but never gets to the hard issue in the case. Basically all she says is that Sanchez is liable because he touched Alou without his consent, and an unconsented touching is a battery. However, while Sanchez committed a prima facie battery by ignoring Alou's words, the more complex question is whether Sanchez may have a privilege defense to the battery. This answer stops with the easy issue, beats it over the head, and misses the opportunity to grapple with the tough one. This can't get better than a *C*.

Student #1's response is better. The student went beyond the first layer to recognize that Sanchez will raise a privilege defense, based on the risk of greater harm to Alou. The student suggests a reason why the court would accept the defense: As in the necessity cases, the court accepts a lesser harm caused by the actor in order to avert a greater one. This is a

---

4. Trip might also argue that, even if he owed a duty, he did not breach, since the tailpipe was hot. Queen declined to touch it, but she may have been negligent for failing to do so; you can always kick the thing out of the road. In addition, the pipe may have cooled by the time Trip got there.

solid response — I'd give it a *B–* or a *B* — but it fails to really knock heads with the underlying dilemma: would the court allow Sanchez, by comparing the two harms, to *displace Alou's expressed choice* with his own judgment about what is "good for him." The law is pretty clearly to the contrary: For example, it is established that a rational patient may refuse a blood transfusion, even at risk of death. How do we reconcile this autonomy principle with our gut feeling that Sanchez ought not to be held liable?

The third student's response really peels the problem to the core: The crux of the matter here is the apparent difference in what Sanchez and Alou understand about the facts. Sanchez may well believe that Alou has refused without understanding his danger, and that his choice would be different if he understood the facts as Sanchez does. Yet there is no time to debate the matter; Sanchez has to act before the truck arrives. It seems likely that the court would allow Sanchez to view Alou's refusal as ineffective in these circumstances, and act instead on his reasonable perception (even if wrong, as it was here).

To emphasize the point, change (or, rather, clarify) the facts a little. Suppose Alou was looking down the street, saw the fire truck, believed it was coming to help, and also could tell that he had an internal injury that could be aggravated by movement. If he communicated all *that* to Sanchez, it seems clear that Sanchez would no longer have a privilege based on his own perception of the greater or lesser harm. The crux of the matter is not Sanchez's right to displace Alou's choice, but to make one for him where Alou has not really made a knowing decision based on all the facts.

This is a very subtle issue, more subtle than most. Class provided no "answer" to it; the student must extrapolate from various battery principles we *did* study to predict the outcome of a case with a new twist. When you practice law, many of your cases will have new twists. Your ability to predict how those twists will be resolved by a court is your stock in trade. We have a right to test this ability. The more insightfully you rise to the challenge, the better you will do. This student gets an *A*.

26

Dandelions in the Bluebook Garden: Six Classic Exam Writing Mistakes

The last chapter explored the type of analysis most law professors want to see on first-year law essay exams. It is a skill you can learn, once you recognize what we want. Once you grasp the basic approach, you can continue to improve at it through practice.

This chapter comes at the topic from the other direction: the classic mistakes students make, year after year, in answering essay questions. These mistakes reflect basic misconceptions students have about the nature of legal analysis and the exam process. If you learn to recognize these misconceptions before taking your finals, you will be able to avoid these dandelions, and to focus on the type of analysis we *do* want, as illustrated in the previous chapter.

Here's a question from one of my old exams, which I will use to illustrate the various dandelions to be rooted out of your exam-taking strategy.

> The football season at Grumbling State was the high point of the year. In recent years, Grumbling had become a football power, and games had almost always been sold out. Officials made every effort to cram as many paying spectators as possible into the 50-year-old stadium, to fund those lavish athletic scholarships.

This year, before the season began, Allen, the athletic director, noticed some weakness in section C of the stadium stands. He wondered if the supporting structure was sound, and decided to hire a contractor to look it over. He called in Munoz Construction Company to inspect the section and perform any necessary repairs.

Upon examination, Brian, a Munoz supervisor, determined that several of the vertical wooden beams supporting section C had deteriorated. He ordered Griffin, an employee, to replace them with metal "I" beams. Although "I" beams would have been stronger, Griffin replaced the beams with new wooden beams he had on hand, identical to the ones he removed. Other Munoz employees then bolted the new beams in place to the horizontal girders.

The tenth game of the season, against Texas Agricultural, a traditional rival, was a thriller. The fans were on their feet, doing the "wave" and cheering wildly. All of a sudden section C collapsed completely, sending the fans down into the bowels of the stadium. The entire section was reduced to splinters. Jane Aragna, sister of the Grumbling quarterback, was injured. The Grumbling mascot, Sticky (an absurd looking porcelain porcupine which had cost the athletic department $25,000) was smashed to smithereens. Hal Aragna, the Grumbling quarterback, heard the noise, froze, and looked for his sister, who had disappeared when the stands collapsed. At that moment, a Texas player tackled him from behind, injuring his throwing hand and ending a promising football career. (Aragna had been seriously scouted by the L.A. Raiders of the National Football League.)

Upon investigation, it was discovered that Allen had failed to get a permit to hold the game, which was required by the state entertainment licensing statute.

Please discuss the claims that Jane, Hal and Grumbling University might assert against the possible defendants. What problems do you see with the plaintiffs' claims and how do you think the court is likely to rule on them? What defenses will the defendants raise, and how are they likely to be resolved? *Explain your reasoning fully; this is more important than your "bottom line" conclusions on the various issues.*

This chapter does not include an "answer" to the Grumbling problem, since the goal here is to provide examples of typical ways in which students go astray in responding to questions like this. However, in some cases I have rewritten the examples to illustrate a better approach.

So, let's proceed to some dandelions.

Dandelion #1: The Abstract Expressionist

Let's begin with one of the most common mistakes students make. Consider the following excerpt from the Expressionist's bluebook:

This fact pattern raises issues of negligence liability. Tort law provides that parties can be held liable for their negligence under certain conditions. However, defendants are not always held liable simply because they cause injury. Sometimes they are not liable even if they negligently cause injury. In order to recover, the plaintiff must establish that the defendant owed her a duty of care, breached that duty of care, that is, was negligent, and that the defendant's negligence caused resulting injury to her. If all these elements are satisfied, the plaintiff may recover in tort from the defendant.

Negligence is determined by comparing the defendant's conduct to that of the reasonable person under the same circumstances. If the defendant acted in an emergency, for example, his conduct will be compared to that of the reasonable person acting in a similar emergency. Or, if the defendant was acting as a professional, such as a doctor, her conduct will be compared to the conduct of the reasonable doctor under the circumstances, or even of the reasonable doctor in the same specialty as the defendant. There are special standards for persons acting under disability, such as those with physical disabilities—someone who is blind or deaf, for example—and for children, who are held to the standard of a reasonable child of like age, intelligence, and experience under the same circumstances.

However, most jurisdictions do not apply a special standard to persons with mental disabilities. And no special allowance is made for the person who has poor judgment. In <u>Vaughan v. Menlove</u>, for example, the defendant argued that he should only be held to the standard of having acted in good faith to the best of his judgment, even if his judgment wasn't very good. The court rejected the argument and applied the usual reasonable-person-under-the-circumstances test.

Even if a person is negligent, he will not be held liable if he did not owe a <u>duty</u> to the plaintiff. Duties may be imposed on parties who create a risk that injures the plaintiff. In other cases, a court may hold that the defendant owed a duty to the plaintiff because he had a special relationship to the plaintiff, such as an innkeeper, or a jailer, or even a psychiatrist who treated a patient. Other special relationships courts have recognized include...

This one really is a classic. Any law professor will recognize it as a common weed in the bluebook garden. If you read it through, however, it doesn't sound bad. In fact, there is nothing "wrong" with the Expressionist's description of the relevant law. The problem is that she has *not answered the question*. Instead, having stuffed a great deal of tort doctrine into her head, the Expressionist is determined to show me that she did, so she launches into an abstract dissertation on tort rules.

This would be a fair answer if the question were different. Here's the question the Expressionist evidently thinks that I wrote:

> Describe the principles of tort law, including the elements of a claim for negligence and the various defenses available to an action for negligence.

This unimaginative question asks the student to regurgitate general information to see if she did her homework. *This isn't going to happen on your law school exams.* We aren't testing your memory of the rules: We want to watch you *apply* those rules to the facts in the question. This student hasn't done that; she has already written several pages and hasn't even mentioned the question! Where are Hal and Jane? Where are Sticky, Grumbling, and Munoz Construction? Isn't it obvious that the student could have written this answer without ever reading the question?

One of the goals of a good exam question is to determine whether the student can separate relevant tort rules — those a court would use in resolving the issues raised — from the irrelevant. The Expressionist's answer refuses to take the gambit. It includes all kinds of general doctrine of no relevance to the question. There's no child in the Grumbling question. There's no doctor. No one acted in an emergency. No one has argued that she should be judged by the *Menlove* subjective standard.

Usually, students who indulge in abstract expressionism (about 20 percent of my students do) eventually go on to tackle the issues in the question. Five or six pages in, I get to a sentence that starts, "In Hal and Jane's case..." That's where I start to pay attention. The long wind-up I skim with annoyance. By the time the Expressionist gets down to the real business at hand she has wasted valuable time on an exercise that gets little, if any, credit. Students always claim they don't have enough time on exams, but frequently this is because they waste time disgorging general information before they go for the jugular: analyzing the facts of the case.

Don't get me wrong. I don't mean to suggest that you should never state principles of law in writing a law school essay. You should, but you should state the principle in the course of applying it to specific issues in the question. For example, in addressing the liability of Griffin, you will want to state basic negligence principles in order to discuss Griffin's liability:

> Griffin acted as a risk creator by repairing the stands.
> Consequently he has a duty to act with reasonable care and will
> be liable if he failed to act like a reasonable person when he used
> the wooden beams instead of the metal "I" beams. In this case,
> Griffin was probably not negligent under the reasonable person
> standard, even though he ignored his supervisor's instructions.
> The wooden beams he used were identical to those that had held
> up the stadium for 50 years...

This opening shows that the writer recognizes the source of a duty owed by Griffin, and that he will only be liable if he failed to use reasonable care under the circumstances. Then, the writer proceeds to the crucial step: measuring his conduct against this standard. The writer shows that she knows the law by stating the particular legal principle that applies to the issue she is addressing. She doesn't shoot with buckshot, as the Abstract Expressionist does, but aims right at the target.

The cure for abstract expressionism is to read the instruction paragraph of the question (usually the closing paragraph), read it again, and then make sure that you *do what the professor has asked you to do.* Usually, that last paragraph will resemble the one in the Grumbling question. "Please evaluate the claims the plaintiffs may assert, and the various defenses the defendants are likely to raise," or some such language. Your answer should focus right in on that task. A good first sentence in answering the Grumbling question might be. "The first claim Jane might raise would be a negligence claim against..." Skip the generalities and get down to cases, or more particularly, the Grumbling case.

Dandelion #2: The Antiphonalist

The "antiphonal" answer is another way students avoid doing the real work of an essay exam. The name of this dandelion comes from early music. In the medieval churches there were often two choirs; one would sing, then the other would answer, back and forth.

> In this case, Jane will argue that Allen was negligent for failing to
> inspect the stands after the repairs were completed. Allen will
> argue, however, that he had no duty to inspect the stands, and
> that, even if he had, he would not have discovered the defect that
> caused the collapse.
>
> Jane will argue that Griffin was negligent, because he replaced the
> wooden beams with new wooden beams instead of with the metal

"I" beams. Griffin will argue, however, that he was not negligent, because the beams were the same as the ones that had been used before. Jane will also argue that he was negligent in disregarding his instructions from Brian, but Griffin will argue that he is not liable, even though he did disregard his instructions, if he used a reasonable method of supporting the stands.

Jane will argue that she can prove negligence of Griffin by invoking res ipsa loquitur, since stadium seats do not ordinarily collapse unless someone was negligent in constructing or repairing them. Griffin will argue that he was not the only one who worked on the stands, and they could have collapsed from another problem, so that the negligence was not necessarily his.

Hal will argue that he can sue Griffin for negligent infliction of emotional distress, since he witnessed the incident and was very upset. Griffin, however, will argue . . .

It is important to recognize the fallacy involved in the antiphonal response. Students often repeat the shibboleth that you should "argue both sides" on law exams, and think that what the student did above is what is wanted. It is not. The Antiphonalist has not argued *either* side. She has set up the pieces on the chess board, but refused to make any moves. All she has done is to state that the plaintiff will argue for one result, and the defendant for the opposite. She has nicely avoided the real work of the exam — *evaluating* the strength of the arguments. Oliver Wendell Holmes once said that "the science of law is the prediction of what a judge will do." The Antiphonalist has nicely avoided making and explaining her predictions about the Grumbling case.

Suppose that you represented Jane, and she came to you for advice on whether to sue Griffin. Could you really send Jane a bill for telling her that she will argue that Griffin was negligent in replacing the beams, and that he will argue that he wasn't? Of course not, that's just restating the problem, not offering a judgment about the outcome.

Consider this rewrite of one issue touched on in the antiphonal response:

Jane may sue Griffin for using the wooden beams instead of "I" beams, arguing that he was negligent for disregarding his boss's instructions. However, the court will probably not be persuaded by this argument. Griffin's conduct will be tested under the reasonable person standard: whether the reasonable construction worker under the circumstances would have used wooden beams, not whether Griffin did as he was told. (If Griffin had been told to use inadequate beams, and had done so, I doubt that the court would treat his boss's orders as a defense!)

There is a strong argument that Griffin was not negligent under the reasonable person standard. He used new beams of a type that had sufficed for 50 years, and continued to hold the rest of the stadium. The evidence might very well show that this was reasonable care. At any rate, the court will focus on that issue, not whether he was instructed otherwise or whether. "I" beams would have been stronger.

Jane might argue that those beams were not adequate because more people are being allowed to occupy the stands these days. However, it is not clear that more people do come to the games than used to. Even if they do, only section C collapsed, although all sections had the same beams. This suggests that the problem may not have been the beams at all. For example, the other employees may have failed to bolt the beams in. . . .

This student does a lot more than indicate what the parties will argue. Unlike the Antiphonalist, she grasps the opportunity to show that she can think like a lawyer. She states the relevant rule, uses the facts effectively, and explains her reasons, based on those facts, for predicting that the court will accept one argument over the other.

Dandelion #3: The Reiterator

Here's another problem that is more common than you would think.

In this case, Allen, the athletic director, noted problems with section C and hired Munoz Construction to inspect and repair the section. When Brian found weakened beams in section C he ordered Griffin to replace the beams with metal "I" beams, but Griffin used wooden beams like the old ones instead. Later, that section of the stands collapsed, and Jane Aragna was injured in the collapse. Her brother Hal, the captain of the football team, was also injured when a player tackled him from behind. Sticky, an unusual team mascot worth $25,000, was also broken when the stands collapsed. . . .

This one hardly requires explanation. The writer has simply restated the facts. This drives me nuts. I *wrote* the facts. Why does the Reiterator insist on telling me what they are? More important, how can I possibly give her any credit for it? I'm not testing the ability to read a paragraph and restate it; I'm testing the ability to explain how the facts will influence the outcome of the case. Facts are indeed important, but you need to tell me *why* they are important, not just what the facts are.

For example, the fact that Sticky cost $25,000 is an important fact; clearly I stuck that in there (excuse the pun) for a reason. Restating the fact that Sticky is expensive gets you no credit, but recognizing why that fact is (or is not) relevant gets you lots. Consider this excerpt, which *analyzes* the relevance of Sticky's value, rather than simply reiterating it.

> In this case, Sticky is a highly unusual and valuable piece of personal property. The defendants may argue that they are not liable for the loss of Sticky, because it is unforeseeable that a $25,000 porcelain porcupine would be in the stands. However, where a defendant negligently causes injury to property, she need not foresee the exact nature of the property in order to be held liable. As long as she can foresee damage of the general nature that took place, she will be liable for whatever damage actually occurs. The defendants in this case could foresee injury to objects in the stands if they collapsed. And it hardly seems surprising that the team mascot would be in the stands at a football game. Thus, the no-proximate-cause argument is likely to fail here.

Like Abstract Expressionists, Reiterators usually get on eventually to actually answering the question. However, before they do they lose valuable time telling me what I wrote. As a result, they often don't finish answering the question. When I see "Out of Time" written at the end of these answers, I have little sympathy.

Dandelion #4: The Tantalizer

Tantalus, a mythological king, was doomed to stand in water that receded when he tried to drink, and beneath ripe, hanging fruit he could not reach. When I read answers like the example below I share a little of his frustration.

> Jane might try to prove that Munoz Construction was negligent using the doctrine of res ipsa loquitur. If Jane can prove that the accident

> that happened to her was the type of accident that does not ordinarily happen without negligence, and that, if someone was negligent, it was probably Munoz Construction, then she can recover on a res ipsa theory
>
> Jane might also try to recover from Allen, the athletic director, for failing to inspect section C after the work was done. If Allen owed a duty to inspect the stadium after completion of the repairs, he could be held liable for her injury.
>
> Hal may sue Munoz Construction for negligent infliction of emotional distress. If Hal can show that he satisfies the Dillon standards for a negligent infliction claim, or whichever standard applies in the relevant jurisdiction, he will recover. . . .

Can you see why I call this writer the Tantalizer? There hangs a nice juicy legal issue, just waiting to be plucked. The Tantalizer notes the issue, states a relevant principle of law, but never sinks her teeth into the analysis. It is true that Jane can use res ipsa if she can prove that the accident would probably not have happened without negligence, and that the negligence was likely Munoz's. But *can she prove those things?* Does res ipsa apply on these facts, and if so, why? Similarly, it is true that Allen may be liable for failing to inspect if he owes a duty to inspect, but *does he owe such a duty, and why?* Please don't hide your light under a bushel; share with me your views on these matters, and your reasons. These are what I will grade you on.

Basically, the Tantalizer suffers from "A"-aversion, unwillingness to apply the law to the facts. We discussed the importance of the IRAC "A" in the last chapter, but I repeat it here because failure to apply the law to the facts in a meaningful manner is the most common failing in student answers. Explaining why res ipsa does or does not apply to Jane's case is where you can really show your stuff. Don't miss your chance — as the Tantalizer has — by giving me the wind-up (issue and rule, if you like) but failing to deliver the pitch.

Consider this rewrite of part of the Tantalizer's answer:

> Since the stands were badly damaged, Jane will have a problem proving what caused them to collapse. However, she may well be able to invoke res ipsa loquitur against Munoz Construction Company. First, this is the type of accident that does not ordinarily happen without negligence: Stands in a stadium do not fall in if properly built and maintained, especially stands recently examined

and repaired. (Note that no section other than C collapsed, though all were presumably crowded.) Second, the facts fairly clearly point to negligence of Munoz. They had recently repaired section C. The fact that that section collapsed suggests that they made some mistake in repairing the stands. We don't know exactly what it was—or which Munoz employee did it—but it is a fair inference that negligence during the repair caused the problem. As long as the evidence permits a reasonable inference that some Munoz employee negligently caused the collapse, Munoz can be held liable under res ispa and respondant superior.

A problem for Jane will be that the stands collapsed ten weeks after Munoz repaired them. Munoz was not "in control" of the stands at that point. But the control test is too restrictive: The real question is whether the general facts about the accident point to negligence of Munoz. Here, a jury could reasonably conclude that they do.

This analysis states the basic res ipsa requirements, but it goes well beyond that, to explain how the writer predicts that they would be applied by a court, and why.

Dandelion #5: The Fly-Swatter

Here's an excerpt from an answer that sounds pretty good, but has serious problems in terms of exam-taking strategy.

Jane may decide to sue Munoz Construction Company for negligence in repairing the stands. However, courts do not always hold negligent actors liable in tort. The defendant must also owe a duty to the plaintiff. Munoz will only be liable if it owed a duty to Jane to exercise care in doing the inspection and repairs. Generally parties owe a duty of care to others who might foreseeably be injured from conduct that creates a risk of injury to others. For example, in driving a car we create the risk of an accident to those around us; thus, we owe them a duty to drive with reasonable care.

A second source of duty arises from special relationships between the victim and the defendant. In many situations actors assume a duty of care, as by taking a patient or a client, or by taking charge of a person in need of assistance.

> In this case, Munoz engaged in risk-creating conduct by undertaking to repair the stands. By working on the stands, it created risks of injury if the repairs were faulty. They could foresee injury to patrons at the game if they negligently supported the stands or otherwise failed to exercise due care. It isn't surprising that, if the beams aren't strong enough, or the bolts are left out, they will collapse, and that with all that weight in the stands someone might be injured. Having all those people in the stands creates a risk of injury if the stands aren't sufficiently strong. Munoz should know this. Thus, a court would very likely hold that Munoz owed a duty of care to patrons at the game, including Jane.

Everything said in this excerpt is true. The problem, however, is that the writer has used a sledgehammer to swat a fly. She has belabored the obvious, spent a lot of valuable time arguing at great length a proposition that is quite clear. Everyone should know that Munoz has a duty to exercise due care in doing the repairs. I can't give you a lot of credit for recognizing that fact.

In the heat of an exam, it is a relief to see an issue you know you can handle. "Great," says the Fly-swatter, "I've got this one nailed down. The answer to some of those other issues is really unclear, so I'll spend my time on the issue I know I can answer. Watch my dust."

This is bad strategy. Even thought it is disconcerting to deal with issues to which you don't know "the answer," it is just those issues, the tough, ambiguous issues, where the answer is anything but obvious and creative reasoning is needed, that gives you the chance to shine. In answering the exam, you have to learn to recognize which issues are clear, and to dispose of them quickly so you can concentrate on the tough ones. Consider this rewrite:

> Munoz owes a duty to exercise reasonable care in repairing the stands, since it created a foreseeable risk of injury if it negligently repaired the stands. The real problem will be proving that Munoz, or someone who worked for it, was negligent. Jane may be able to establish negligence by...

The writer disposes quickly of the easy question, and turns immediately to the more difficult negligence question. In the process, she saves all that time the Fly-swatter spent going into unnecessary detail on the duty question.

Very frequently, it is the first issue in the exam that evokes fly swatting. Instead of assessing which issues to spend the most time on before starting to write, the student launches in, beats the first issue to death, and then discovers as she goes along that she doesn't have time to adequately address more sophisticated ones. I'm not a great fan of outlining exam answers, but you should at least make a list of major issues to make sure you spend the most time on the issues that have the most substance.

The trick, of course, is learning to recognize which issues are meaty and which are straightforward. I don't have a magic formula that will help you do that: In part, developing such judgment is what the first year of law school is about. However, practice will help a lot. The next chapter offers a chance to do just that. It provides several sample questions, offers you the chance to practice spotting the harder and easier issues in those questions, and gives some illustrative answers with comments.

Dandelion #6: The Editor

I include this one mostly for fun, but I do find that it crops up fairly frequently in my bluebooks. Here's a short sample from the Editor's answer:

Jane may try to sue Munoz Construction for her injuries. If Munoz's employees had replaced the beams with smaller beams which were too weak to do the job, they would be found negligent and could be held liable for her injuries.

Grumbling may try to recover the value of Sticky from Munoz. If Munoz had been told that Sticky was kept in section C, and that he was worth $25,000, they would foresee injury to Sticky from negligent repair and could be liable for it.

Hal may sue Munoz and Griffin for negligent infliction of emotional distress. He would be entitled to recover for such distress under the <u>Dillon</u> standards if he had been sitting with Jane in the stands and had actually seen her fall.

Do you see what the Editor has done? Perhaps in doubt that she can answer the tough issues posed by the question, she has rewritten it to make the issues easy, and then answered her own question! Of course Munoz would be negligent if it used beams too small for the job. Of course Munoz would be liable if they knew they were building the stands to hold Sticky. Of course the *Dillon* standards would apply if Hal sat next to Jane and saw her fall.

I purposely designed the facts to make the issues tougher, so that I can watch you do more sophisticated analysis. The Editor has missed her chance to shine, by ignoring the tough issues. Not only that, in the process she has made me mad. You should know by now that law professors are very egotistical: When we write an exam, we want you to answer *our* question, not rewrite it to suit yourself.

Another syndrome similar to the Editor's is to address a bunch of issues raised by the facts that the question does not ask you to address. Often, the instruction paragraph in the question will ask you to discuss a subset of the possible claims. For example, my closing paragraph in the Grumbling question asks you to evaluate the claims of Jane, Hal, and Grumbling. Please, don't go off on a discussion of Brian's contribution claims against Griffin, or other claims not called for in the question. When you become a law professor, you can write your own question; for now, remember that the professor sets the agenda.

Where students do address issues I didn't ask for, I will do my best to ignore the discussion of those issues. I owe it to my students to evaluate each on the same material. It wouldn't be fair to let one student essentially analyze a different — perhaps easier — question while the rest of the class labors away on the Sysiphean task I asked them to undertake. Consequently, the time students spend addressing claims I didn't raise are a waste of that most valuable resource on an exam — time.

The dandelions reviewed above appear not because students lack the ability to answer law exams, but from basic misconceptions about what is expected. It is worth your time to learn to recognize these misconceptions now, and train yourself to avoid them in your own exam writing. For some practice, try the next chapter.

27

Practice Makes Perfect: Examples and Explanations

Introduction

This may sound like heresy, but the plain fact of the matter is that most students spend entirely too much time studying for their first-year exams.

Let me clarify what I mean. Most students study for their finals by reviewing their notes, rereading material from the casebook, writing outlines, and memorizing the legal doctrines studied in the course. All this is very well, and should be done, but learning every minute rule in the Torts course is not the best way to assure a strong performance. The best way to prepare for your law exams, once you have mastered the basic legal rules, is to *take some law exams*. There's a big difference between reading about chess and playing the game. If you were going to a chess tournament, you would prepare by playing a lot of chess. Similarly, there's a big difference between learning legal rules and using them effectively to answer an essay question. If you want to develop a facility for clearly applying the law you have studied to new facts, the best way to do it is to practice at it.

This chapter is meant to facilitate that process, which should help you on all your first-year exams. If you're going to practice, you need some sample questions to practice on. So this chapter presents two Torts essay questions covering basic concepts taught by most Torts professors. Once you have outlined, read and studied, you should sit down and take the first exam, in the allotted time, *without looking at my suggested answer.*

Then, you should read my comments about the question, and my suggested answer.

Then, *do it again*, using my second question. Practice really does make perfect. Again, be honest; don't peek. Much of the learning takes place from trying your own hand at the question, and *then* comparing your analysis to mine. If you just passively read the question and my answer, you will lose the benefit of working through the process yourself. Then, you'll have to do it for the first time in the exam room. You wouldn't want to play your first game of chess at the chess finals, would you?

You needn't wait until you have finished studying for the Torts final to do this, but you should do a basic review of your outline before sitting down to answer the first question. One of the virtues of writing practice answers is that the process will highlight the issues you need to study further. If you get to a duty issue, for example, and are unsure how to address it, you will realize that you need to spend more time studying the duty material. Then, when you go back to do so, you'll go back with a purpose, so your further study will be much more effective.

After you read the question, jot down the issues that you see before you start to write. Make a tentative choice about the order in which you will discuss the issues. Any sensible approach that works for you will probably be acceptable to your professor. Some students take the facts line by line and discuss the issues as they arise. Another reasonable approach to organizing your answer is to first discuss the elements of the torts that might be claimed, and then discuss defenses, vicarious liability, and other peripheral issues. Often, the question will dictate the organization. If the question asks you to analyze the claims of Mary Smith and the defenses to those claims, do just that. *Always* focus ruthlessly on the instructions in the question to make sure you answer the question the professor has posed.

EXAMPLES

McGee's Bad Day

1. Read the first practice question, on the next page. Write out quickly the issues you see. Put an asterisk next to the ones you think are important or complicated, to make sure you leave the time necessary to address them adequately.

2. Now, start the clock and give yourself 90 minutes to write out an answer. If you aren't able to spend 90 minutes on it, spend 45 on half the issues. Remember that you are not only trying to learn how to answer a question like this; you are trying to learn how to do so under exam conditions. So writing out the question at your leisure would be useful, but not nearly as useful as taking it under time constraints.

If you are tempted just to read the question and then read the sample answer, resist the temptation. Painful as the process of taking the exam may be, spending the time to do this *will easily be worth more than three or four hours of regular study time.*

McGee's Bad Day (90 minutes)

The ventilating system at Elston General Hospital was giving out. Elston retained Climatrol Corporation, an established company with a AAA safety rating, to rebuild the system. The plan was to replace the large blowers on the roof first, and then to empty one ward at a time to rebuild the duct work in the individual rooms.

The first blower arrived at about 10:00 A.M. on a gusty Monday morning, weighing in at about 7,000 pounds. Archer, an employee of Climatrol, began rigging a cable from a crane to the blower to hoist it up to the roof. McGee, a mechanical engineer on his way to the hospital to visit his wife, stopped to watch. He stood about 30 feet back from the crane, even though the crane had signs on it saying "Warning! Danger! Stay 100 feet back!" McGee was surprised to see Archer rig the blower with single-braided cable, since he knew that triple-braided cable was usually used on such jobs. Archer's boss had suggested using triple-braided cable, but the crane was equipped with single-braided cable, which was rated for 14,000 pounds anyway, so Archer rigged the blower with that. He then got into the cab and started to hoist the blower up to the roof.

He got the blower up to the level of the roof, but as it rose above the roof a sudden gust of high wind started the blower swinging back and forth. Archer, fearing that the blower would smash against the building, quickly swung the crane away from the building. Unfortunately, as it swung out, the blower hit the edge of the roof, tipped, snapped one of the cables and tumbled to the pavement below.

To make matters worse, a ChemHaul Company truck was delivering a large cylinder of potentially explosive acid to the hospital at the time. The acid should have been delivered the night before — state law required all hazardous chemicals to be transported outside of "normal working hours." The truck had just finished depositing the cylinder in the acid storage area, and hooked it up for service, when the blower landed. The concussion from the blower hitting the pavement caused the cylinder, some 70 feet away, to explode. The force of the explosion threw McGee to the ground, puncturing his eardrum and causing a concussion.

Alas, McGee's wife, who was recovering from serious heart surgery, was watching out the window and witnessed the accident. Several minutes later, she suffered heart failure and died, without moving or uttering a word. Her sister Marla was in the room at the time and thought she had fallen asleep. A few minutes later she went to wake her, realized she was dead, and suffered extreme emotional distress.

Please evaluate the personal injury claims that might be brought based on this unfortunate chain of events, and the defenses you would expect to be asserted. Discuss the problems you see in establishing the various claims and defenses. Explain your reasoning fully; this is more important than your "bottom line" conclusions as to who will win or lose on particular issues.

Sir Galahad Gretsky

3.   After taking the McGee practice question, go off and do other things. Then, a few days later perhaps, try your hand again at this process, focusing on the Gretsky question below. It tests much the same material as the McGee question, so you should be able to focus on the process itself. Once again, start by reading the question and taking a few minutes to list the issues you see, noting the ones that you think will require more time to discuss.

4.   After doing your quick-issues list, answer the exam question in the time allotted. I know, its bad enough to take exams once, without doing it multiple times. All I can say is that this exercise will help you more than anything else you can do to prepare for the Big Day.

Sir Galahad Gretsky (90 minutes)

It all started when Suffield University decided to build a building on Ridgewood Lane. The site was small and the excavation had to be deep.

Lawrence Construction Company, the general contractor, excavated the site to a depth of 30 feet. To shore up the sides of the excavation, it placed heavy planks against the sides of the excavation, and braced them with vertical beams pounded into the bottom of the pit.

While all this was going on, Rivera, a driver for Riley's Refuse Company, arrived carrying a large dumpster for use in disposing of construction debris. There was no room in the excavation for it, so Roberts, Lawrence's foreperson, ordered Rivera to leave it at the side of Ridgewood Lane, a few feet from the edge of the excavation. Rivera didn't want to leave it there, because a city ordinance barred obstructing a public way with a dumpster. There was not quite enough room to put the dumpster down without extending into the lane; his company could get a ticket. However, Roberts ordered him to do so, so Rivera complied. He made his feelings about the order known, however, by letting the dumpster drop down off the truck unusually hard next to Roberts, making him start.

Brontas, an engineering professor at Suffield, was watching the work from the sidewalk. She saw the dumpster drop, and the ground shake, but didn't say anything to anyone about it.

An hour later, Gretsky arrived to deliver a rented backhoe to be used in the construction. As he drove it down into the excavation, he noticed that the shoring along the side of the excavation near the dumpster was bulging out. He thought it might be giving way, so he drove the backhoe toward the wall. He placed the bucket of the backhoe against the bulging planks, to prevent a collapse until something could be done. However, as he moved the bucket against the wall, it caught on one of the buckled planks. He jostled the bucket to get it loose, but it made the buckling worse. Suddenly, the wall collapsed. The dumpster, which was on wheels, rolled into the excavation; Rivera, in his irritated state, had failed to secure the brakes.

Gretsky was thrown from the backhoe, half buried in the collapsing planks and earth, and severely injured. To make matters worse, as the earth continued to slide, water came pouring out of the side of the excavation, and began to fill the pit. A large water main, unmarked on any available engineering drawings, ran under Ridgewood Lane, and burst when the earth around it collapsed into the excavation.

The story gets worse. While frantically trying to extricate Gretsky by digging away the earth, Yee, a construction worker, undermined the dumpster, and it settled on Gretsky, making it harder to extricate him. They finally managed to get Gretsky out, soaking wet and chilled, and rushed him to the hospital. He had sustained multiple serious injuries, and later contracted pneumonia as well. He died three weeks after the accident.

Discuss the problems Gretsky's estate will face in determining who is liable for the accident, and for what damages. Consider both the problems of establishing liability and the possible defenses. Please explain how you think each of the issues is likely to be resolved. *Explain your reasoning fully.*

EXPLANATIONS

McGee's Bad Day

1.   The McGee question raises lots of issues, more issues than you can fully explore in the time allotted. Here's my own list of issues in the McGee question:

1.   Vicarious liability of Elston (non-delegable) and Climatrol for negligence of Archer
*2.   Negligence in using single-braided cable (relevance of custom to use triple braided)
3.   Causation — did single-braided cable cause the harm?
4.   Proximate cause — high wind as unforeseeable
5.   Emergency doctrine — Archer's reaction to swaying of blower
6.   Duty — McGee's failure to say anything about use of lighter cable
*7.   Negligence of McGee in standing nearby
*8.   Assumption of the risk by McGee in standing nearby
*9.   Causation — did McGee's negligence in standing too near cause the harm?

*10. Superseding cause — explosion of acid tank
   11. Negligence per se — violation of statute by delivering acid during the day
   12. Negligence of Elston — working while hospital open
*13. Negligent infliction of emotional distress on Mrs. McGee (causation, thin skull problem)
   14. Negligent infliction on Marla
*15. Strict liability for dangerous activity

These may not be all the issues in the question, but they are the main ones. If you hit these, or most of them, you will do fine. In jotting down the issues, it is worth using some quick system — like my asterisks — to flag the issues that you think are more complex, so you can plan to spend more time on them. Remember, as discussed in Chapter 25, that the more complex the issue is, the better you can show your ability to perform effective legal analysis. So don't shy away from these!

2.   Despite my preaching about the value of practice questions, I must confess that I have seldom given out sample essay answers to my students. One reason for this is that my answer might be wrong, and the students might expose me as a fraud. (Most law professors harbor this fear, no matter how much they may deny it.)

But there is a more respectable reason as well. In giving out a model answer, I have two choices. First, I could hand out an answer typical of what a good student can produce in the time allotted. However, no student can produce a perfect and complete analysis of a problem like McGee's in 90 minutes, so this type of model answer will doubtless miss some issues, and analyze some others ineffectively. So this sample answer could be misleading.

Alternatively, I could hand out an answer I deem "right" — whatever that means — in its analysis of all the issues. Doubtless, I would slave for about a week to write *that* answer, to avoid the fraud-exposure risk mentioned above. Obviously, this type of model won't give students a realistic sense of what I expect from them either.

The answer below is a bit of a compromise between the two extremes. It is meant to illustrate a basically sound analysis of the issues, but at a level of sophistication that a good student could produce in an exam setting. Thus, it is representative of good student analysis, but probably more consistently so than I would see, even from a strong student, on a timed exam.[1] Over all, it should give you a good sense of the type of analysis your professor is looking for.

---

1. I showed this answer to a colleague and asked him if it was a fair example. His response was that a very good student should discuss most or all of the issues discussed in this answer, but probably wouldn't do it as clearly as this answer does.

Sample Answer: McGee's Bad Day

Let's start with whether Archer was negligent. If he wasn't, the McGees may have no claim at all. McGee may argue that Archer was negligent in rigging the crane with single-strand cable. The issue will be whether Archer acted as the reasonable crane operator would in rigging up the blower. McGee's surprise (as an engineer with relevant experience) that he used single-strand cable, and Archer's boss's suggestion to use triple, suggest that most riggers use triple. Usual practice is certainly admissible on the question of Archer's reasonableness, but not dispositive. The cable was "rated for 14,000 pounds," so it may have been reasonable to use it, even if triple would have been stronger. Archer doesn't have to use the strongest cable, or even the usual cable, so long as he made a reasonable choice.

It may be that single-strand would hold 14,000 pounds if it just had to hold the weight, but not if it was going to be raised and swung, which puts more stress on the cable. This depends on facts we don't have about what it means to 'rate' the cable for that amount of weight.

Archer's decision to swing the blower away from the building due to the wind may have been reasonable. The sudden gust suggests an unanticipated emergency—if so, Archer's decision will be evaluated in light of the need to make a quick decision. However, since the day was "gusty," Archer should have anticipated this risk. If so, he may not be negligent for his reaction to the wind, but may be for creating the emergency by doing the job on a windy day, or without more precautions. In addition, even if he responded reasonably to the emergency, he could still be liable based on the initial negligent act of using inadequate cable. Maybe triple-strand would have held if subjected to the jolt of hitting the building.

Depending on how gusty it was, Archer might argue that, even if he was negligent in using single-strand cable, the sudden wind is an unforeseeable event, so that his negligence is not a proximate cause of the fall. However, even on a quiet day, crane operators should probably anticipate winds, including sudden winds, when they raise objects high in the air. This argument will likely fail.

Archer might also argue that even if his use of single-strand cable was negligent, it was not the actual cause of the accident. If even triple-braided cable would have broken when the blower jolted against the building, his use of weaker cable would not be a "but for" cause of the harm. We don't have enough information to evaluate this argument.

Doubtless, expert testimony would be useful on the point.

Archer will argue that the explosion of the acid cylinder is a superseding cause that avoids liability to McGee. McGee was injured due to the blast, not due to the landing of the blower; thus the explosion was a concurrent cause of his injury. The fact that there were two causes of the accident does not protect Archer, but if he could not have anticipated the explosion, he may avoid liability on proximate cause grounds. However, the facts indicate that there was an acid storage area nearby, and that a truck had just delivered a cylinder of acid there. Archer probably should have been aware of the risk of dangerous chemicals in the area. He may not have <u>known</u> that they were explosive, but he probably should have anticipated that they <u>might</u> be, and that is all that is required. However, even if this is true, he may still have not reasonably anticipated that the concussion from dropping the blower would cause the tank to explode. The blower did not drop on the tank and cause the explosion; the concussion is a different, unusual mechanism of harm that Archer can at least argue he had no reason to anticipate.

Archer will likely argue that McGee was negligent for standing too close to the crane. The crane company can't define reasonableness by telling people how far back to stand, but McGee may still have been too close for safety. However, even if he was, this negligent act is not the actual cause of his harm: The blower didn't fall on him; it triggered the explosion that knocked him down. It may well be that McGee, had he obeyed the 100 foot warning, would have been closer to the tank and injured more! Thus, depending on the facts, McGee's negligence, if any, in standing too close to the crane is probably not an actual cause of his injury.

Archer might argue that McGee should have said something about the cable. However, McGee, as a bystander, owes no duty to intervene in Archer's work, even if he has some relevant knowledge about engineering.

Archer will also argue that McGee 'assumed the risk' of the injury by standing too close. However, it probably doesn't apply, even if the jurisdiction still recognizes the traditional assumption of the risk defense. To assume a risk created by the defendant's negligence, McGee would have to be fully aware of the specific risk. The standard is not what McGee should have known, but what he actually, subjectively knew. McGee may have assumed the risk of the blower falling on his head, but it hardly seems that he was fully aware of the risk that the blower would trigger an explosion. In addition, most jurisdictions now treat a plaintiff's negligent choice to encounter a risk (secondary implied assumption) as comparative negligence, so if the defense applies, it would only reduce recovery.

McGee might sue ChemHaul for violating the statute requiring deliveries outside of working hours. The statute was probably aimed at preventing deliveries during busy periods when accidents would be more likely to happen, so it may establish a relevant standard of care. However, the violation was not a "but for" cause of the accident. The facts state that ChemHaul was done and the tank all hooked up when the accident happened. Presumably the accident would have happened the same way if the tank had been delivered during the night instead of ten minutes before. Thus, McGee cannot show that, but for ChemHaul's violation of the statute, his injury would not have happened.

If Archer is liable to McGee, Climatrol will be as well, as Archer's employer. Under respondeat superior, the employer is liable if Archer's act was in the scope of employment. Raising the blower here clearly was, even if Archer ignored his instructions about the cable.

A more interesting issue is whether Elston General would be liable (absent some charitable immunity) for negligence of Climatrol. Perhaps it can be argued that Elston was negligent toward McGee (an invitee) for doing the work while the hospital was operating, but this is doubtful; such work is probably commonly done on buildings in use. The better argument would be based on non-delegable duty, that the work of moving heavy objects around the construction area by crane, while the premises remain open to the public, is a dangerous activity requiring special precautions. This is a strong argument. If the duty is non-delegable, it is no defense that Elston hired a company with an excellent safety rating: The liability isn't based on negligent selection, but on the nature of the work.

McGee might argue that Climatrol would be strictly liable for the crane work under the Second Restatement as "abnormally dangerous" activity. However, crane work is very common in built-up areas, and can generally be done without serious risks. The argument should fail. A tougher question is whether ChemHaul could be strictly liable for the explosion, based on the activity of selling an explosive chemical. Even if this activity satisfies the standards of the Restatement (Second) §520, however, ChemHaul had finished its "activity" of <u>selling</u> the chemical. It isn't clear to me that ChemHaul's exposure to strict liability should continue after it has sold the chemical: Such liability would be endless — it would essentially be a form of product liability, not based on the <u>activity</u> of selling it. The hospital might be liable for the activity of <u>storing</u> an explosive chemical, depending on further facts about the Restatement factors.

Last are the emotional distress claims. Mrs. McGee's claim would be brought by her estate under the local wrongful death statute, since the distress allegedly led to her death. Recovery for Mrs. McGee's distress at witnessing the accident will depend on the jurisdiction's standard for indirect infliction claims. She was probably not in the zone of danger (though if the explosion was big enough perhaps she could argue this) but might well satisfy the Dillon standards. She's a close relative and saw the accident. True, she was not that physically close, but seeing the accident would probably suffice, since actually seeing the injury makes a traumatic emotional reaction likely. (If the court holds otherwise, the Dillon test would collapse into the zone of danger test.) The heart attack would satisfy a "resulting physical injury" requirement, if it was caused by the emotional distress. In addition, of course, the estate could only recover if the defendant <u>was negligent</u>: the Dillon standards go to the issue of duty, but the other elements of a negligence claim must still be proved.

Mrs. McGee's estate will have a difficult causation problem. Since she was recovering from "serious heart surgery," she may have died from her cardiac illness, not from the shock of witnessing the accident. Her estate will have to establish that the trauma of seeing her husband injured caused the death, not the underlying heart condition. If the estate proves this, it could recover under the "thin skull" rule even if a normal person would not have suffered substantial injury.

Marla will not recover for indirect infliction. Although she may have been watching when her sister died, she did not witness a traumatic event at all. She didn't know at the time that Mrs. McGee had died. Her distress is from learning later that her sister had died. Even if Archer's negligence caused Mrs. McGee's death, indirect infliction claims are based on witnessing a shocking, traumatic injury to the direct victim, not general distress at another's injury.

Some Comments on the McGee Answer

Note that there is very little abstract statement of legal principles in the McGee answer. Instead, concepts like proximate cause and negligence, assumption of the risk and indirect infliction are discussed *as they apply* to the facts of the question. The answer is not an abstract exposition of tort law; it is more like a memorandum to a partner detailing the likely outcomes of issues that both the writer and the reader basically understand. It isn't meant to tell an uninitiated reader general principles about the law of torts; it's meant to explain to another lawyer how torts concepts you both understand would likely be applied to a new set of facts, and why.

If you go over this answer, and list the torts concepts you need to understand to write it, you'll see that the question tests the basic, central issues that most professors focus on in the course. Some professors may test more fringe stuff than I do, but most will zero in on the core issues emphasized in class — issues like intent, the negligence test, statutory duty, actual cause, proximate cause, comparative negligence, and assumption of the risk. Since this is true, skill at applying such central concepts will serve you better than an encyclopedic knowledge of more esoteric rules touched on in the course.

Note, too, that the analysis in the answer does not mechanically tick off each element of each tort discussed. It focuses on the problems the writer expects in proving each claim. For example, the answer doesn't discuss McGee's damages. It is clear that he suffered damages — the concussion — and that if Archer is liable McGee would collect for it.[2] Similarly, it's clear that Archer owed McGee a duty of care in lifting the blower. The problems in proving McGee's claim lie in the causation and negligence elements, so the answer focuses on these.

One of the subtlest issues in the exam is whether ChemHaul is strictly liable for the ultrahazardous activity of selling the acid, even though the sale is complete when it explodes. I really don't know the answer to this, and I certainly didn't expect my students to know it. (See, for some discussion on the point, *Indiana Harbor Belt R. Co. v. American Cyanamid Co.*, 916 F.2d 1174, 1181 (7th Cir. 1990) (noting that strict liability applies to activities, not to substances).) Here, the student recognized the issue and noted the implications of holding the supplier liable for *future* explosions just because it supplied a hazardous substance. This is a great answer, though it doesn't resolve the issue. For some issues in the exam, like this one, the process is as much about seeing problems and implications as it is about offering firm solutions.

---

2. Compare the answer to the Gretsky question, in which the facts about Gretsky's injuries raise issues about what damages each defendant caused that should be analyzed.

Out of curiosity, I did a word count on this sample answer: It contains about 1,700 words. This is fairly realistic for a 90 minute question: I actually checked a number of old bluebooks and found that the average number of words for a 90-minute answer was 1,580. So you do have time to write a full answer: The important thing is to avoid spending your time writing the wrong stuff.

Sir Galahad Gretsky

3.   Here's my list of issues in the Gretsky question, with asterisks just to flag the issues that require more discussion:
  1. Negligence of Lawrence (shoring; location of dumpster)
  *2. Negligence of Rivera (location, dropping hard, not setting wheels)
  3. Violation of statute by placing dumpster
  4. Assault by Rivera
  5. Negligence of Gretsky (emergency doctrine)
  6. Assumption of risk — Gretsky
  *7. Actual causation of collapse
  *8. Lawrence's negligence as proximate cause of Gretsky's harm
  9. Rescue as foreseeable
  10. Duty — Brontas
  *11. Yee's liability — aggravation of harm
  12. Vicarious liability of Suffield as landowner
  13. Liability of Suffield (vicarious for contractor)
  *14. Indivisible damages — cause of Gretsky's death
  *15. Water main collapse — proximate cause
  16. Survival/wrongful death

4.   Below is a suggested answer to the Gretsky question. Again, it's more comprehensive than most students would produce in the time allotted, but it is fairly representative of good analysis.

Sample Answer: Sir Galahad Gretsky

Let's begin with Gretsky's claims against Lawrence Construction. It could be liable for constructing the wall of the excavation inadequately. However, it isn't clear that it was negligent: The shoring may have bulged due to the "unusual" blow from the Dumpster. But the walls should probably be built strong enough to withstand hard drops from Dumpsters. It is foreseeable that heavy loads will be dropped along the edge of construction sites. Thus, Lawrence may be negligent for not building a wall strong enough to withstand such a blow.

Gretsky might argue that Roberts was negligent for telling Rivera to leave the Dumpster near the edge of the excavation. However, the site was small; there may have been no other options. Presumably, if the excavation is properly done, it would support heavy objects along the side, so it would not be negligent to place them there.

Rivera's dropping the Dumpster hard was an intentional act, perhaps an assault on Roberts—he apparently meant to place Roberts in fear that the Dumpster would fall on him. It is a tougher question whether this intentional act is a superseding cause that will exonerate Lawrence even if its workers negligently built the wall. Frankly, I don't know. Lawrence could anticipate a very similar occurrence by negligence, or even non-negligent delivery of Dumpsters, which are common (as are other heavy loads) at construction sites. So one might argue that Lawrence should have foreseen hard Dumpster drops, and that Rivera's intentional act was simply a similar risk that happened in a slightly unusual manner, as opposed to an unforeseeable act. Rivera's act does not seem so antisocial, or so unusual in the context, that it should relieve Lawrence from liability for what otherwise seems like a very foreseeable risk.

Gretsky will not be able to establish negligence based on violation of the highway ordinance. Even if ordinances were given "per se" effect, this one was clearly aimed at avoiding obstruction of streets, not collapse of excavations.

It may be that the shoring would have held if Gretsky hadn't messed with it. Thus, Gretsky may be a cause of the harm along with inadequate shoring. However, even if he was a cause of his own injury, Lawrence would still be liable if its employees were a concurrent negligent cause of it. Gretsky's negligence would simply reduce his recovery under comparative negligence. In determining Gretsky's negligence, his conduct would be assessed in light of the need for quick action. Even though he caught the plank, he may still have acted reasonably in light of the emergency, or even in a _perceived_ but not actual emergency if his perception was reasonable.

Lawrence might argue that Gretsky knowingly assumed the risk of the collapse by going to the rescue. If Lawrence was negligent in building the wall, this would be secondary assumption—but it may well be _reasonable_ assumption, since Gretsky acted to prevent a dangerous collapse. If so, most jurisdictions would not treat his conscious choice as a defense to negligence liability. In addition, some courts would hold that a rescuer does not have a "real" choice, so that assumption of risk does not apply.

Rivera may be liable for Gretsky's injuries. Dropping a heavy Dumpster hard on the edge of a deep excavation poses a foreseeable risk of causing the wall to collapse, so he was clearly negligent with regard to this risk. And we know that rescuers are foreseeable ("Danger invites rescue . . ."). The difficult issue will be actual causation: It isn't clear that the planking bulged because of the Dumpster drop. Maybe the stuff even bulges a bit when it's perfectly safe. It may be that Gretsky's rescue effort caused the whole problem, or Lawrence's negligence. This will be a difficult proof problem. Rivera would obviously try to find evidence that the wall bulged out <u>before</u> his delivery.

Gretsky was not injured at first by the Dumpster itself. However, if the drop contributed to the <u>collapse</u>, Rivera would be liable for the entire chain of events that followed, including the immediate injuries from the shoring, the extra injury from the Dumpster settling on Gretsky, and the chills from immersion in water.

If Rivera was negligent—and maybe even if he committed an assault—Riley Refuse would likely be liable under respondeat superior. Riley might argue that Rivera's act was outside the scope of employment, but dropping the Dumpster is part of his work. He simply did it aggressively out of pique, but it is part of accomplishing the master's work. An employer would be liable for an employee who drove aggressively, or a bar bouncer who used a bit too much force in throwing out a patron. Most courts would hold Rivera's overreaction to be within the scope of employment.

Yee, if negligent, could be liable for any aggravation of Gretsky's injury due to the settling of the Dumpster. By undertaking to rescue Gretsky, he assumes a duty to exercise care in assisting him. Since he acted in an obvious emergency, the reasonableness of his conduct will also be measured in light of the need to act fast to extricate Gretsky. As a practical matter, however, it may be impossible to separate the damages from Gretsky's initial injury and the settling of the Dumpster. If this cannot be done, Yee could be held liable for the entire injury. If Gretsky died from pneumonia, Yee could argue that he was already soaked before he acted, so that he was not an actual cause of the death. However, he may have died of pneumonia because he was so weakened from other injuries. If so, Yee could still be a cause of the death if he contributed to injuries that made him susceptible to pneumonia.

Rivera was negligent for failing to secure the brakes on the Dumpster. This did not contribute to the initial collapse. However, it <u>may</u> have caused the Dumpster to fall into the pit when the wall fell. If so, Rivera would be liable for any aggravation of damages from the falling Dumpster. As with Yee, if it is impossible to separate the damages, he would be fully liable for wrongful death. And, of course, if his dropping of the Dumpster caused the initial collapse, (and was negligent), he is fully liable for Gretsky's death on that basis.

The fact that no one knew about the water main under the street is irrelevant, at least as to Rivera's liability. He never saw the plans, so he had no idea what was under there. But he certainly could foresee that utilities like water lines would run under the street, so he can't argue lack of proximate cause because he did not know that it was there. (The bursting water main may not have caused Gretsky's death anyway; it could have been his other injuries.)

The issue is more complicated as to Lawrence: Since the main was not on the plans, it may have reasonably thought there was none. However, Lawrence's workers knew that, if they did not adequately shore the wall, the whole area could collapse. It is doubtful that they shored the wall any differently in reliance on the lack of a water main. If they were negligent, the presence of an unmarked utility is probably foreseeable.

Gretsky will not have a claim against Brontas. As a bystander, Brontas has no duty to intervene or warn about a risk of collapse even if she was aware of that risk. Although she works for Suffield, she's a professor, not a construction supervisor. It is very doubtful that a court would impose a duty on her, even though she might realize the danger because of her expertise. It would be extremely awkward for a bystander like Brontas to go around telling construction contractors about risks in circumstances like these. It could even create more risks if they had to enter the construction area. (It also isn't clear that Brontas was negligent: The facts don't say she saw the planks bulge, only that she saw the Dumpster drop, probably not that unusual an event at a construction site.)

Suffield, as the landowner here, would owe Gretsky a duty of due care if he were an invitee. I'm not sure if a worker doing construction on an owner's property is an invitee. If so, it doesn't appear that Suffield has beached the duty. It's duty would be to act with reasonable care for Gretsky's safety. Here, the university did not create the risk or find out about it before the accident. Even if Brontas realized the danger, it is doubtful that this knowledge would be imputed to Suffield just because an employee with unrelated responsibilities was aware of it.

> However, Suffield may be liable for negligence of Lawrence on a non-delegable duty theory. Digging and shoring a deep excavation is work that involves a serious risk and requires special precautions. Thus, <u>if Lawrence was negligent</u>, many jurisdictions would hold Suffield vicariously liable for that negligence, absent charitable immunity of some sort.
>
> Last, because Gretsky died of his injury, the measure of damages for Gretsky's death, and the beneficiaries entitled to receive them, will depend on the state's wrongful death statue. His claims for injuries prior to death, such as pain and suffering and medical bills, will be governed by the state survival statute. (Some survival statutes bar recovery for pain and suffering.)

Some Comments on the Gretsky Answer

Just a few comments about this second answer. Note that the writer does not discuss claims that might be brought by other parties, such as Riley for the value of the Dumpster, or Lawrence for the construction delay and costs caused by the collapse. There's a really interesting issue in the facts about whether Rivera committed an assault on Roberts, but the writer only discusses it as it affects liability to Gretsky, not to Roberts. The question asks about Gretsky's claims, and the writer rightly sticks to those.

At several points, the writer frankly admits to not knowing some legal rules. For example she doesn't know whether a worker like Gretsky on Suffield's property is an invitee. Maybe this narrow point of law was covered in class, or maybe it wasn't. Either way, the really important point is that Suffield's duty to Gretsky may differ depending on how he is classified. The writer recognizes this, *and* has peeled a further layer of the onion, by recognizing that, even if Gretsky is owed a duty of due care, Suffield probably hasn't breached it. Don't be shy about admitting ignorance at times; in practice you can always look up the answer if you ask the right question. Show the examiner that you see the issue, why the issue is relevant, and how the outcome will be affected by the decision of that issue.

For those compulsives who really want to get the most out of this exercise, I'll offer one more suggestion. After writing out answers to these questions, and reading the sample answers, try taking one of them again. Writing one out with some foreknowledge of the analysis will allow you to concentrate on the process of organizing and expressing your analysis, and further your understanding of how to write an effective answer.

OK, that's that. Hope it helps.

Index